FAR FROM THE MADDING CROWD

AN AUTHORITATIVE TEXT
BACKGROUNDS
CRITICISM

Bathsheba and Liddy attempting Bible-and-key divination as portrayed in Helen Paterson's illustration in the *Cornhill Magazine* edition of *Far from the Madding Crowd*.

≫ A NORTON CRITICAL EDITION ≪

THOMAS HARDY

FAR FROM THE MADDING CROWD

AN AUTHORITATIVE TEXT
BACKGROUNDS
CRITICISM

≫ ≪

Edited by

ROBERT C. SCHWEIK

STATE UNIVERSITY OF NEW YORK

COLLEGE AT FREDONIA

W. W. NORTON & COMPANY
NEW YORK • LONDON

Howard Babb: Howard Babb, "Setting and Theme in *Far From the Madding Crowd*" in *English Literary History* (1963). Reprinted by permission of Johns Hopkins University Press.

Peter J. Casagrande: Peter J. Casagrande, "A View of Bathsheba Everdene" from *Critical Approaches to the Fiction of Thomas Hardy*, edited by Dale Kramer. Reprinted with permission of Macmillan, London and Basingstoke, and of Barnes & Noble Books, Totowa, NJ.

Alan Friedman: From Alan Friedman, *The Turn of the Novel*. Copyright © 1966. Reprinted by permission of the publishers, Oxford University Press, and Alan Friedman.

S. J. Gatrell: From S. J. Gatrell, "Hardy the Creation: *Far From the Madding Crowd* in *Critical Approaches to the Fiction of Thomas Hardy*, edited by Dale Kramer. Copyright © 1979. Reprinted by permission of S. J. Gatrell.

Ian Gregor: From "Reading a Story: Sequence, Pace, and Recollection" in *Reading the Victorian Novel*, edited by Ian Gregor. Permission granted by Barnes and Noble Books, Totowa, NJ.

F. E. Hardy: From *The Life of Thomas Hardy, 1840–1928*. Copyright © 1962. Reprinted by permission of Macmillan, London and Basingstoke.

Thomas Hardy's "study" copy of the Wessex Edition of *Far From the Madding Crowd*: Reprinted by permission of The Estate of the late Miss E. A. Dugdale and the Trustees of the Thomas Hardy Memorial Collection in the Dorset County Museum, Dorchester, Dorset.

Thomas Hardy: From Chapter XLIII of the manuscript of *Far From the Madding Crowd*. Reprinted by permission of E. Thorne.

Thomas Hardy's Letters: From Volume I of *The Collected Letters of Thomas Hardy*, edited by Richard Little Purdy and Michael Millgate (1978). Reprinted by permission of Oxford University Press.

J. Hillis Miller: Reprinted by permission of the publishers from *Thomas Hardy: Distance and Desire* by J. Hillis Miller, Cambridge, Mass.: The Belknap Press of Harvard University Press, Copyright © 1970 by the President and Fellows of Harvard College.

Michael Millgate: From *Thomas Hardy* by Michael Millgate. Copyright © 1971 by Michael Millgate. Reprinted by permission of Random House, Inc. and A. D. Peters & Co. Ltd.

Roy Morell: From Roy Morell, *Thomas Hardy: The Will and the Way*. Copyright © 1965 by the University of Malaya Press, Kuala Lumpur. Reprinted by permission.

Michael Piret and Robert Schweik: From Michael Piret and Robert Schweik, "Editing Hardy" in *Browning Institute Studies: An Annual of Victorian Literary and Cultural History* (1981). Reprinted by permission of the Editor of *Browning Institute Studies*.

Richard Little Purdy: From *Thomas Hardy: A Biographical Study* by Richard Little Purdy (1954). Reprinted by permission of Oxford University Press.

Penelope Vigar: From Penelope Vigar, *The Novels of Thomas Hardy: Illusion and Reality*. Copyright © 1974. Reprinted by permission of The Athlone Press, London.

Library of Congress Cataloging-in-Publication Data
Hardy, Thomas, 1840-1928.
  Far from the madding crowd.
  Bibliography: p.
  1. Hardy, Thomas, 1840-1928. Far from the madding crowd.   I. Schweik, Robert C.   II. Title.
PR4745.A2S38   1986   823'.8   85-21784
ISBN 0-393-95408-0

W. W. Norton & Company, Inc., 500 Fifth Avenue, New York, N. Y. 10110
W. W. Norton & Company Ltd., 37 Great Russell Street, London WC1B 3NU

1 2 3 4 5 6 7 8 9 0

For Jo, Sue, and Char

A Note on the Frontispiece

The frontispiece is one of Helen Paterson Allingham's woodcut illustrations of *Far from the Madding Crowd* in the *Cornhill Magazine*. A former student of John Everett Millais and Frederick Leighton, her work was praised by both Carlyle and Ruskin. Mrs. Allingham's marriage took place in the same year as Hardy's to Emma Gifford, and, looking back on that time in a letter to Edmund Gosse in 1906, Hardy made these comments about her and her work:

The illustrator of *Far from the Madding Crowd* began as a charming young lady, Miss Helen Paterson, and ended as a married woman—charms unknown—wife of Allingham the poet. I have never set eyes on her since she was the former and I met her and corresponded with her about the pictures of the story. She was the best illustrator I ever had. She and I were married about the same time . . . but not to each other, which I fear rather spoils the information. Though I have never thought of her for the last 20 years . . . you might hunt her up and tell me what she looks like as an elderly woman. If you do, please give her my kind regards, but you must not add that those two almost simultaneous weddings would have been one but for a stupid blunder of God Almighty.

Contents

Criticism

Foreword

Thomas Hardy began the composition of *Far from the Madding Crowd* in 1873. It was the culmination of a five-year apprenticeship in the writing of fiction that was certainly remarkable for its diversity if not always for high achievement. Hardy began his career as a novelist by writing a clumsy, satirical attack on the upper classes; that first novel, titled *The Poor Man and the Lady*, was completed in 1868, but it was so flawed that, on the advice of a publisher's reader, he set it aside and turned his hand to produce a second novel, full of melodramatic mystery and sensational turns of plot, for which, under the title *Desperate Remedies*, he finally found a publisher in 1871. *Desperate Remedies* received mixed reviews, but one particularly savage attack no doubt helped to turn Hardy in the new direction he took in his next novel, *Under the Greenwood Tree* (1872), whose delicate rural charm and slight story of almost-innocent rustic courtship were about as far removed from the tone and manner of *Desperate Remedies* as they could possibly be. The favorable reception of *Under the Greenwood Tree* led, in turn, to an invitation to write a novel for serial publication, and the result was a departure in still another direction—a novel titled *A Pair of Blue Eyes* (1873), which combined wit-battles between the sexes with sharply drawn dramatic scenes to create a bittersweet romance with a highly ironic ending.

A *Pair of Blue Eyes* was set in Cornwall, where Hardy had been making visits to court his future wife, Emma Lavinia Gifford. Those visits had grown out of Hardy's work as an architect's assistant, but, in 1874, having completed his next novel, *Far from the Madding Crowd*, Hardy abandoned architecture to devote himself to his writing. *Far from the Madding Crowd* was the beginning of a sequence of novels that was to include *The Return of the Native* (1878), *The Mayor of Casterbridge* (1886), *The Woodlanders* (1887), *Tess of the d'Urbervilles* (1891), and *Jude the Obscure* (1895). During the time that he wrote these, Hardy produced other novels of often much lower quality, but the six major novels that began with *Far from the Madding Crowd* surely constitute a most extraordinary achievement in the history of English fiction, and one that was distinctively his.

Yet no single novel of Hardy's can be said to typify that achievement fully, for his is a complex art, and each of the major works has its own peculiar richness which gives it a special quality of its own. Even the features that go to make up the distinctive character of *Far from the Madding Crowd* are themselves remarkably varied. There is, first of all, Hardy's lavish treatment of the pastoral setting: many of his novels have a rural backdrop, but never again would he allow himself such lovingly detailed accounts of rural activities, and, although rustic characters are another of the staple features of Hardy's fiction, in *Far from the Madding Crowd* they rise to heights of such extraordinarily rich comedy that, of their kind, they have scarcely been equaled in the history of English literature. This is not, of course, to suggest that *Far from the Madding Crowd* is a flawless work of art. In rushing to finish it before his impending marriage, Hardy slipped briefly into the melodramatic mode of *Desperate Remedies*; but, far more frequently, he used sensational elements in a way that subordinated them to more serious artistic purposes. Hence, it is perhaps worth emphasizing that, in spite of its comic elements, *Far from the Madding Crowd* is a serious novel, and although its plot involves a rural romance that begins on a note of almost lighthearted comedy, it turns gradually to a more stark tale of rash thoughtlessness, unhappy marriage, abandonment, death, and derangement; even the relative happiness of its ending is muted by a sober awareness of past pain and a tempering of hope that the grim unpredictability of life has imposed upon the survivors. With *Far from the Madding Crowd*, Hardy began placing an increased emphasis on the stern inexorability with which apparently trivial actions and small chance events bring about consequences of disproportionate severity—an emphasis that would in various and highly distinctive ways be embodied in every one of the major novels he would subsequently write.

It was in *Far from the Madding Crowd*, also, that for the first time Hardy adopted the term "Wessex" to designate the geographical area in the south of England that was to serve as the locale for so many of his later works in prose and poetry. What Hardy created in "Wessex" is a remarkable compound of the partly real and partly fictional, but, of course, even the "realities" that Hardy imports into his fictional world are treated freely, creatively, and, above all, selectively, with an eye to such details as contribute to the total effect of the work of art. Hence, although this edition provides maps of Hardy's "Wessex" that reveal the many ways it conforms to the real geography of southwest England (Hardy himself began the practice of supplying such maps for his readers), it is important to keep in mind that Hardy's allusions to features of the southwestern countryside are only one element in the wide range of materials that he orchestrated to evoke his fictional world.

Those materials comprise an unusual mix—of minutely particular descriptions, often with rich symbolic overtones, alternating with broad, direct, and relatively abstract authorial generalizations; of much distinctive local detail, but often so freely adapted and modified as to render it scarcely recognizable; of occasionally stiff and ponderously formal character descriptions interspersed amid a wealth of shrewdly phrased and perceptive observations on the human condition; of allusions to the Bible, to Greek and Roman myth, and to works of art, often made with remarkable point and aptness, though they sometimes seem awkward and artificial; and of narrative modes sometimes loose and occasionally slack, but joined with more leisurely developed passages that are finely detailed and can rise to an extraordinary lyric intensity. In short, Hardy's *Far from the Madding Crowd* is a compound of such highly diverse materials and narrative modes that it would be surprising if there were not occasionally passages a reader might feel flat or awkward. But for those, such as they are, there are more than ample compensations: for again and again in *Far from the Madding Crowd*, Hardy manages to convey a vision of human life so honest and so deeply rich and circumstantial that it resonates with a dense and subtle suggestiveness that all too easily slips through the crude nets of critics' formulations but remains for readers one major source of its greatness.

That remarkable suggestiveness and dramatic power that Hardy so often achieved in *Far from the Madding Crowd* is certainly no accident; it is clearly the result of Hardy's unremitting concern for the details of his text—a concern amply attested by the history of his repeated and extensive revisions of *Far from the Madding Crowd* from its earliest manuscript drafts to the last printings over which he had any control. In this Norton Critical Edition, I have attempted to take that process of revision into account and to provide a critical text that represents in every respect Hardy's final deliberate intention. The procedures followed in preparing this edition are described in notes that follow the text of the novel itself; there, editorial principles are briefly set forth; the texts collated are listed; the copy-text adopted is specified; and emendations of that copy-text are recorded. In addition, certain variant readings that were not adopted for this edition, but that I judge to have a special interest in their own right, are discussed in the essay *Textual Notes*; these include readings both from the manuscript and from later texts.

In preparing this edition, I have incurred many indebtednesses I am happy to acknowledge here. I wish to thank the Trustees of the Hardy Estate for permission to make quotations from unpublished materials. To E. Thorne I am especially grateful for permission to examine the manuscript of *Far from the Madding Crowd* and to quote from it. Mr. G. H. Ballantyne of the Signet Library, Edinburgh, and Mr. Roger Peers, Curator of the Dorset County Museum, have graciously provided access to special materials held in their collections. Many of the problems of locating and obtaining materials were smoothed by the fine cooperation of John Saulitis, the Director of Library Services at Fredonia State University College, and by the faculty of Reed Library, particularly Gary Barber, Margaret Pabst, and Yvonne Wilensky. Of the many colleagues who provided help with special questions and/or with the reading of proof, I wish particularly to thank Ronald Ambrosetti, Tristram Barnard, Robert Boenig, Patrick Courts, Walter S. Hartley, James Huffman, David Lunde, Malcolm Nelson, William Neville, John Ramsey, Henry Salerno, George Sebouhian, James Shokoff, Peter Steese, Theodore Steinberg, John Stinson, and Jacqueline Trace. I am especially grateful to my colleague Albert Dunn, whose expertise in Victorian literature I have repeatedly drawn upon. Scholars and friends from elsewhere, to whose special assistance and knowledgeable advice I am indebted, include Professor Lennart Björk of Stockholm University, Dr. Simon Gatrell of the New University of Ulster, the late Professor Helmut Gerber of Arizona State University, Dr. Desmond Hawkins, Professor Dale Kramer of the University of Illinois, Professor Michael Millgate of the University of Toronto, Professor Dieter Riesner of the University of Trier, and Professor Vincent Tollers of the State University of New York, College at Brockport.

Charlotte R. Morse of the State University of New York, College at Fredonia, gave special assistance with graphics. The Department of English, in cooperation with the office of the Vice President for Academic Affairs of the State University of New York, College at Fredonia, provided support that enabled me to have the valuable assistance of John Beebe in preparing some portions of this edition. I wish particularly to thank John Benedict and Marian Johnson of W. W. Norton and Company for their exceptionally careful editing and valuable suggestions.

It is a particular pleasure to acknowledge the indispensable help provided by Michael Piret of the University of Michigan and Susan M. Schweik of Yale University, both of whom not only gave generously of their time to assist me in collating texts but also suggested resolutions to many of the problems that arose in that process.

My most important debt, however, is to Joanne L. Schweik, from whose sharp intelligence, wise counsel, and steady support I have benefited more than any acknowledgment could express.

ROBERT C. SCHWEIK

The Text of
Far from the
Madding Crowd

Contents

Preface

In reprinting this story for a new edition I am reminded that it was in the chapters of "Far from the Madding Crowd,"[1] as they appeared month by month in a popular magazine,[2] that I first ventured to adopt the word "Wessex"[3] from the pages of early English history, and give it a fictitious significance as the existing name of the district once included in that extinct kingdom. The series of novels I projected being mainly of the kind called local, they seemed to require a territorial definition of some sort to lend unity to their scene. Finding that the area of a single county did not afford a canvas large enough for this purpose, and that there were objections to an invented name, I disinterred the old one. The region designated was known but vaguely, and I was often asked even by educated people where it lay. However, the press and the public were kind enough to welcome the fanciful plan, and willingly joined me in the anachronism of imagining a Wessex population living under Queen Victoria;—a modern Wessex of railways, the penny post,[4] mowing and reaping machines, union workhouses,[5] lucifer matches,[6] labourers who could read and write, and National school children.[7] But I believe I am correct in stating that, until the existence of this contemporaneous Wessex in place of the usual counties who announced in the present story, in 1874, it had never been heard of in fiction and current research, if at all, and that the expression, "a Wessex peasant," or "a Wessex custom," would theretofore have been taken to refer to nothing later in date than the Norman Conquest.

I did not anticipate that this application of the word to modern story would extend outside the chapters of these particular chronicles. But it was soon taken up elsewhere, the first to adopt it being the now defunct *Examiner*, which, in the impression bearing date July 15, 1876, entitled one of its articles "The Wessex Labourer," the article turning out to be no dissertation on farming during the Heptarchy, but on the modern peasant of the south-west counties.

Since then the appellation which I had thought to reserve to the horizons and landscapes of a partly real, partly dream-country, has

---

1. Hardy's title alludes to the following lines from Thomas Gray's "Elegy Written in a Country Churchyard":

Far from the madding crowd's ignoble strife, / Their sober wishes never learned to stray; / Along the cool sequestered vale of life / They kept the noiseless tenor of their way.

2. The *Cornhill Magazine*, where *Far from the Madding Crowd* was serialized monthly from January to December of 1874.

3. The name Hardy gave in his fiction to an area of southwest England whose central county is Dorset; see the maps of Hardy's "Wessex" and the locales of *Far from the Madding Crowd*

included in this edition, pp 325–326.

4. The "penny post"—whose innovations included postage stamps and uniform postal rates based on weight—began in 1840.

5. Brought into being by the Poor Law of 1834, which obliged adjacent parishes to unite in constructing and supporting workhouses to which paupers were required to go for relief.

6. The first practical friction matches, invented by John Walter in 1826.

7. Children attending units of an Anglican elementary school system originated by Andrew Bell in 1811. By 1851 some 3,400 National Schools were in existence.

become more and more popular as a practical provincial definition; and the dream-country has, by degrees, solidified into a utilitarian region which people can go to, take a house in, and write to the papers from. But I ask all good and idealistic readers to forget this, and to refuse steadfastly to believe that there are any inhabitants of a Victorian Wessex outside these volumes in which their lives and conversations are detailed.

Moreover, the village called Weatherbury,[8] wherein the scenes of the present story of the series are for the most part laid, would perhaps be hardly discernible by the explorer, without help, in any existing place nowadays; though at the time, comparatively recent, at which the tale was written, a sufficient reality to meet the descriptions, both of backgrounds and personages, might have been traced easily enough. The church remains, by great good fortune, unrestored and intact[9] and a few of the old houses; but the ancient malt-house, which was formerly so characteristic of the parish, has been pulled down these twenty years; also most of the thatched and dormered cottages that were once lifeholds. The heroine's fine old Jacobean house[1] would be found in the story to have taken a witch's ride of a mile or more from its actual position; though with that difference its features are described as they still show themselves to the sun and moonlight. The game of prisoner's-base, which not so long ago seemed to enjoy a perennial vitality in front of the worn-out stocks, may, so far as I can say, be entirely unknown to the rising generation of schoolboys there. The practice of divination by Bible and key,[2] the regarding of valentines as things of serious import, the shearing-supper, the long smock-frocks,[3] and the harvest-home, have, too, nearly disappeared in the wake of the old houses; and with them has gone, it is said, much of that love of fuddling[4] to which the village at one time was notoriously prone. The change at the root of this has been the recent supplanting of the class of stationary cottagers, who carried on the local traditions and humours, by a population of more or less migratory labourers, which has led to a break of continuity in local history, more fatal than any other thing to the preservation of legend, folk-lore, close inter-social relations, and eccentric individualities. For these the indispensable conditions of existence are attachment to the soil of one particular spot by generation after generation.

1895–1902.   T. H.

8. "Weatherbury" is one of the many places cited in *Far from the Madding Crowd* that were based, more or less closely, on real locales in and around Dorset, the center of Hardy's fictional "Wessex." For identifications of the real locales upon which Hardy's fictional locales are based, see the maps provided in this edition, pp. 325–326.

9. This is no longer the case (1912) [*Hardy's note*].

1. Probably based in part on Waterston House near Puddleton, the hamlet that served as the model for Hardy's "Weatherbury."

2. In chapter 13, Bathsheba and Liddy use a Bible and key to attempt to foretell whom Bathsheba will marry.

3. A long, loose-fitting garment formerly worn by rural workers—so called because it was traditionally decorated with the kind of needlework called "smocking."

4. Getting drunk (dialect).

I

Description of Farmer Oak—An Incident

When Farmer Oak smiled, the corners of his mouth spread till they were within an unimportant distance of his ears, his eyes were reduced to chinks, and diverging wrinkles appeared round them, extending upon his countenance like the rays in a rudimentary sketch of the rising sun.

His Christian name was Gabriel, and on working days he was a young man of sound judgment, easy motions, proper dress, and general good character. On Sundays he was a man of misty views, rather given to postponing, and hampered by his best clothes and umbrella: upon the whole, one who felt himself to occupy morally that vast middle space of Laodicean[1] neutrality which lay between the Communion people[2] of the parish and the drunken section,—that is, he went to church, but yawned privately by the time the congregation reached the Nicene creed,[3] and thought of what there would be for dinner when he meant to be listening to the sermon. Or, to state his character as it stood in the scale of public opinion, when his friends and critics were in tantrums, he was considered rather a bad man; when they were pleased, he was rather a good man; when they were neither, he was a man whose moral colour was a kind of pepper-and-salt mixture.

Since he lived six times as many working-days as Sundays, Oak's appearance in his old clothes was most peculiarly his own—the mental picture formed by his neighbours in imagining him being always dressed in that way. He wore a low-crowned felt hat, spread out at the base by tight jamming upon the head for security in high winds, and a coat like Dr. Johnson's;[4] his lower extremities being encased in ordinary leather leggings and boots emphatically large, affording to each foot a roomy apartment so constructed that any wearer might stand in a river all day long and know nothing of damp—their maker being a conscientious man who endeavoured to compensate for any weakness in his cut by unstinted dimension and solidity.

Mr. Oak carried about him, by way of watch, what may be called a small silver clock; in other words, it was a watch as to shape and intention, and a small clock as to size. This instrument being several years older than Oak's grandfather, had the peculiarity of going either too fast or not at all. The smaller of its hands, too, occasionally slipped

---

1. An allusion to Revelation 3:14–16 in which St. John rebukes the Laodiceans for being "neither cold nor hot."
2. Anglicans who regularly took part in the Communion Service, as opposed to those who, like Oak, went to church without regularly taking the sacrament.
3. A statement of Christian beliefs adopted by the Council of Nicea in A.D. 325 and recited as part of the Anglican Communion Service.
4. In Boswell's *Journal of a Tour to the Hebrides*, Dr. Johnson is described as wearing "a very wide brown cloth great-coat with pockets which might have almost held the two volumnes of his folio dictionary."

round on the pivot, and thus, though the minutes were told with precision, nobody could be quite certain of the hour they belonged to. The stopping peculiarity of his watch Oak remedied by thumps and shakes, and he escaped any evil consequences from the other two defects by constant comparisons with and observations of the sun and stars, and by pressing his face close to the glass of his neighbours' windows, till he could discern the hour marked by the green-faced time-keepers within. It may be mentioned that Oak's fob[5] being difficult of access, by reason of its somewhat high situation in the waistband of his trousers (which also lay at a remote height under his waistcoat), the watch was as a necessity pulled out by throwing the body to one side, compressing the mouth and face to a mere mass of ruddy flesh on account of the exertion, and drawing up the watch by its chain, like a bucket from a well.

But some thoughtful persons, who had seen him walking across one of his fields on a certain December morning—sunny and exceedingly mild—might have regarded Gabriel Oak in other aspects than these. In his face one might notice that many of the hues and curves of youth had tarried on to manhood: there even remained in his remoter crannies some relics of the boy. His height and breadth would have been sufficient to make his presence imposing, had they been exhib-ited with due consideration. But there is a way some men have, rural and urban alike, for which the mind is more responsible than flesh and sinew: it is a way of curtailing their dimensions by their manner of showing them. And from a quiet modesty that would have become a vestal,[6] which seemed continually to impress upon him that he had no great claim on the world's room, Oak walked unassumingly, and with a faintly perceptible bend, yet distinct from a bowing of the shoulders. This may be said to be a defect in an individual if he depends for his valuation more upon his appearance than upon his capacity to wear well, which Oak did not.

He had just reached the time of life at which 'young' is ceasing to be the prefix of 'man' in speaking of one. He was at the brightest period of masculine growth, for his intellect and his emotions were clearly separated: he had passed the time during which the influence of youth indiscriminately mingles them in the character of impulse, and he had not yet arrived at the stage wherein they become united again, in the character of prejudice, by the influence of a wife and family. In short, he was twenty-eight, and a bachelor.

The field he was in this morning sloped to a ridge called Norcombe Hill. Through a spur of this hill ran the highway between Emminster and Chalk-Newton.[7] Casually glancing over the hedge, Oak saw

---

5. A watch pocket just below the waistband of the trousers.
6. A chaste woman.
7. Emminster and Chalk-Newton are Hardy's fictional names for Beaminster and Maiden Newton. At the beginning of chapter 2, we learn that Norcombe Hill is "not far from lonely Toller-Down." For locations of these and other places mentioned in the novel, see the maps provided on pp. 325–326.

coming down the incline before him an ornamental spring waggon,[8] painted yellow and gaily marked, drawn by two horses, a waggoner walking alongside bearing a whip perpendicularly. The waggon was laden with household goods and window plants, and on the apex of the whole sat a woman, young and attractive. Gabriel had not beheld the sight for more than half a minute, when the vehicle was brought to a standstill just beneath his eyes.

'The tailboard of the waggon is gone, Miss,' said the waggoner.

'Then I heard it fall,' said the girl, in a soft, though not particularly low voice. 'I heard a noise I could not account for when we were coming up the hill.'

'I'll run back.'

'Do,' she answered.

The sensible horses stood perfectly still, and the waggoner's steps sank fainter and fainter in the distance.

The girl on the summit of the load sat motionless, surrounded by tables and chairs with their legs upwards, backed by an oak settle, and ornamented in front by pots of geraniums, myrtles, and cactuses, together with a caged canary—all probably from the windows of the house just vacated. There was also a cat in a willow basket, from the partly-opened lid of which she gazed with half-closed eyes, and affectionately surveyed the small birds around.

The handsome girl waited for some time idly in her place, and the only sound heard in the stillness was the hopping of the canary up and down the perches of its prison. Then she looked attentively downwards. It was not at the bird, nor at the cat; it was at an oblong package tied in paper, and lying between them. She turned her head to learn if the waggoner were coming. He was not yet in sight; and her eyes crept back to the package, her thoughts seeming to run upon what was inside it. At length she drew the article into her lap, and untied the paper covering; a small swing looking-glass was disclosed, in which she proceeded to survey herself attentively. She parted her lips and smiled.

It was a fine morning, and the sun lighted up to a scarlet glow the crimson jacket she wore, and painted a soft lustre upon her bright face and dark hair. The myrtles, geraniums, and cactuses packed around her were fresh and green, and at such a leafless season they invested the whole concern of horses, waggon, furniture, and girl with a peculiar vernal charm. What possessed her to indulge in such a performance in the sight of the sparrows, blackbirds, and unperceived farmer who were alone its spectators,—whether the smile began as a factitious one, to test her capacity in that art,—nobody knows; it ended certainly in a real smile. She blushed at herself, and seeing her reflection blush, blushed the more.

The change from the customary spot and necessary occasion of

8. A wagon mounted on springs to cushion the ride.

such an act—from the dressing hour in a bedroom to a time of travelling out of doors—lent to the idle deed a novelty it did not intrinsically possess. The picture was a delicate one. Woman's prescriptive infirmity has stalked into the sunlight, which had clothed it in the freshness of an originality. A cynical inference was irresistible by Gabriel Oak as he regarded the scene, generous though he fain would have been. There was no necessity whatever for her looking in the glass. She did not adjust her hat, or pat her hair, or press a dimple into shape, or do one thing to signify that any such intention had been her motive in taking up the glass. She simply observed herself as a fair product of Nature in the feminine kind, her thoughts seeming to glide into far-off though likely dramas in which men would play a part— vistas of probable triumphs—the smiles being of a phase suggesting that hearts were imagined as lost and won. Still, this was but conjecture, and the whole series of actions was so idly put forth as to make it rash to assert that intention had any part in them at all.

The waggoner's steps were heard returning. She put the glass in the paper, and the whole again into its place.

When the waggon had passed on, Gabriel withdrew from his point of espial, and descending into the road, followed the vehicle to the turnpike-gate some way beyond the bottom of the hill, where the object of his contemplation now halted for the payment of toll.[9] About twenty steps still remained between him and the gate, when he heard a dispute. It was a difference concerning twopence between the persons with the waggon and the man at the toll-bar.

"Mis'ess's niece is upon the top of the things, and she says that's enough that I've offered ye, you great miser, and she won't pay any more.' These were the waggoner's words.

'Very well; then mis'ess's niece can't pass,' said the turnpike-keeper, closing the gate.

Oak looked from one to the other of the disputants, and fell into a reverie. There was something in the tone of twopence remarkably insignificant. Threepence had a definite value as money—it was an appreciable infringement on a day's wages, and, as such, a higgling[1] matter; but twopence——'Here,' he said, stepping forward and handing twopence to the gatekeeper; 'let the young woman pass.' He looked up at her then; she heard his words, and looked down.

Gabriel's features adhered throughout their form so exactly to the middle line between the beauty of St. John and the ugliness of Judas Iscariot, as represented in a window of the church he attended, that not a single lineament could be selected and called worthy either of distinction or notoriety. The red-jacketed and dark-haired maiden

---

9. In nineteenth-century England, the upkeep of main highways called *turnpikes* was paid from tolls collected at toll-gates—usually small houses in which a toll-keeper stayed and tended a "pike," or bar, that stretched across the road and could be turned aside to allow travelers to pass upon payment of the appropriate toll.

1. Bargaining.

seemed to think so too, for she carelessly glanced over him, and told her man to drive on. She might have looked her thanks to Gabriel on a minute scale, but she did not speak them; more probably she felt none, for in gaining her a passage he had lost her her point, and we know how women take a favour of that kind.

The gatekeeper surveyed the retreating vehicle. 'That's a handsome maid," he said to Oak.

'But she has her faults,' said Gabriel.

'True, farmer.'

'And the greatest of them is—well, what it is always.'

'Beating people down? ay, 'tis so.'

'O no.'

'What, then?'

Gabriel, perhaps a little piqued by the comely traveller's indifference, glanced back to where he had witnessed her performance over the hedge, and said, 'Vanity.'

II

Night—The Flock—An Interior—Another Interior

It was nearly midnight on the eve of St. Thomas's,[1] the shortest day in the year. A desolating wind wandered from the north over the hill whereon Oak had watched the yellow waggon and its occupant in the sunshine of a few days earlier.

Norcombe Hill—not far from lonely Toller-Down—was one of the spots which suggest to a passer-by that he is in the presence of a shape approaching the indestructible as nearly as any to be found on earth. It was a featureless convexity of chalk and soil—an ordinary specimen of those smoothly-outlined protuberances of the globe which may remain undisturbed on some great day of confusion, when far grander heights and dizzy granite precipices topple down.

The hill was covered on its northern side by an ancient and decaying plantation of beeches, whose upper verge formed a line over the crest, fringing its arched curve against the sky, like a mane. To-night these trees sheltered the southern slope from the keenest blasts, which smote the wood and floundered through it with a sound as of grumbling, or gushed over its crowning boughs in a weakened moan. The dry leaves in the ditch simmered and boiled in the same breezes, a tongue of air occasionally ferreting out a few, and sending them spinning across the grass. A group or two of the latest in date amongst the dead multitude had remained till this very mid-winter time on the twigs which bore them, and in falling rattled against the trunks with smart taps.

1. December 21.

Between this half-wooded half-naked hill, and the vague still horizon that its summit indistinctly commanded, was a mysterious sheet of fathomless shade—the sounds from which suggested that what it concealed bore some reduced resemblance to features here. The thin grasses, more or less coating the hill, were touched by the wind in breezes of differing powers, and almost of differing natures—one rubbing the blades heavily, another raking them piercingly, another brushing them like a soft broom. The instinctive act of humankind was to stand and listen, and learn how the trees on the right and the trees on the left wailed or chaunted to each other in the regular antiphonies of a cathedral choir; how hedges and other shapes to leeward then caught the note, lowering it to the tenderest sob; and how the hurrying gust then plunged into the south, to be heard no more.

The sky was clear—remarkably clear—and the twinkling of all the stars seemed to be but throbs of one body, timed by a common pulse. The North Star was directly in the wind's eye, and since evening the Bear[2] had swung round it outwardly to the east, till he was now at a right angle with the meridian. A difference of colour in the stars—oftener read of than seen in England—was really perceptible here. The sovereign brilliancy of Sirius pierced the eye with a steely glitter, the star called Capella was yellow, Aldebaran and Betelgueux shone with a fiery red.

To persons standing alone on a hill during a clear midnight such as this, the roll of the world eastward is almost a palpable movement. The sensation may be caused by the panoramic glide of the stars past earthly objects, which is perceptible in a few minutes of stillness, or by the better outlook upon space that a hill affords, or by the wind, or by the solitude; but whatever be its origin the impression of riding along is vivid and abiding. The poetry of motion is a phrase much in use, and to enjoy the epic form of that gratification it is necessary to stand on a hill at a small hour of the night, and, having first expanded with a sense of difference from the mass of civilized mankind, who are dreamwrapt and disregardful of all such proceedings at this time, long and quietly watch your stately progress through the stars. After such a nocturnal reconnoitre it is hard to get back to earth, and to believe that the consciousness of such majestic speeding is derived from a tiny human frame.

Suddenly an unexpected series of sounds began to be heard in this place up against the sky. They had a clearness which was to be found nowhere in the wind, and a sequence which was to be found nowhere in nature. They were the notes of Farmer Oak's flute.

The tune was not floating unhindered into the open air: it seemed

---

2. The constellation Ursa Major, otherwise called Charles's Wain, the Big Dipper, or the Plough; Sirius is the biggest star in the heavens; Capella is the brightest star in the constellation Auriga; the brightest star in the constellation Taurus is Aldebaran; Betelgueux is the brightest in the constellation Orion.

muffled in some way, and was altogether too curtailed in power to spread high or wide. It came from the direction of a small dark object under the plantation hedge—a shepherds's hut—now presenting an outline to which an uninitiated person might have been puzzled to attach either meaning or use.

The image as a whole was that of a small Noah's Ark on a small Ararat,[3] allowing the traditionary outlines and general form of the Ark which are followed by toy-makers—and by these means are established in men's imaginations among their firmest, because earliest impressions—to pass as an approximate pattern. The hut stood on little wheels, which raised its floor about a foot from the ground. Such shepherds' huts are dragged into the fields when the lambing season comes on, to shelter the shepherd in his enforced nightly attendance.

It was only latterly that people had begun to call Gabriel 'Farmer' Oak. During the twelvemonth preceding this time he had been enabled by sustained efforts of industry and chronic good spirits to lease the small sheep-farm of which Norcombe Hill was a portion, and stock it with two hundred sheep. Previously he had been a bailiff for a short time, and earlier still a shepherd only, having from his childhood assisted his father in tending the flocks of large proprietors, till old Gabriel sank to rest.

This venture, unaided and alone, into the paths of farming as master and not as man, with an advance of sheep not yet paid for, was a critical juncture with Gabriel Oak, and he recognized his position clearly. The first movement in his new progress was the lambing of his ewes, and sheep having been his speciality from his youth, he wisely refrained from deputing the task of tending them at this season to a hireling or a novice.

The wind continued to beat about the corners of the hut, but the flute-playing ceased. A rectangular space of light appeared in the side of the hut, and in the opening the outline of Farmer Oak's figure. He carried a lantern in his hand, and closing the door behind him came forward and busied himself about this nook of the field for nearly twenty minutes, the lantern light appearing and disappearing here and there, and brightening him or darkening him as he stood before or behind it.

Oak's motions, though they had a quiet energy, were slow, and their deliberateness accorded well with his occupation. Fitness being the basis of beauty, nobody could have denied that his steady swings and turns in and about the flock had elements of grace. Yet, although if occasion demanded he could do or think a thing with as mercurial a dash as can the men of towns who are more to the manner born, his special power, morally, physically, and mentally, was static, owing little or nothing to momentum as a rule.

---

3. Cf. Genesis 8:4: "And the ark rested . . . upon the mountains of Ararat."

A close examination of the ground here about, even by the wan starlight only, revealed how a portion of what would have been casually called a wild slope had been appropriated by Farmer Oak for his great purpose this winter. Detached hurdles thatched with straw were stuck into the ground at various scattered points, amid and under which the whitish forms of his meek ewes moved and rustled. The ring of the sheep-bell, which had been silent during his absence, recommenced, in tones that had more mellowness than clearness, owing to an increasing growth of surrounding wool. This continued till Oak withdrew again from the flock. He returned to the hut, bringing in his arms a new-born lamb, consisting of four legs large enough for a full-grown sheep, united by a seemingly inconsiderable membrane about half the substance of the legs collectively, which constituted the animal's entire body just at present.

The little speck of life he placed on a wisp of hay before the small stove, where a can of milk was simmering. Oak extinguished the lantern by blowing into it and then pinching the snuff, the cot being lighted by a candle suspended by a twisted wire. A rather hard couch, formed of a few corn sacks thrown carelessly down, covered half the floor of this little habitation, and here the young man stretched himself along, loosened his woollen cravat, and closed his eyes. In about the time a person unaccustomed to bodily labour would have decided upon which side to lie, Farmer Oak was asleep.

The inside of the hut, as it now presented itself, was cosy and alluring, and the scarlet handful of fire in addition to the candle, reflecting its own genial colour upon whatever it could reach, flung associations of enjoyment even over utensils and tools. In the corner stood the sheep-crook, and along a shelf at one side were ranged bottles and canisters of the simple preparations pertaining to ovine[4] surgery and physic; spirits of wine, turpentine, tar, magnesia, ginger, and castor-oil being the chief. On a triangular shelf across the corner stood bread, bacon, cheese, and a cup for ale or cider, which was supplied from a flagon beneath. Beside the provisions lay the flute, whose notes had lately been called forth by the lonely watcher to beguile a tedious hour. The house was ventilated by two round holes, like the lights of a ship's cabin, with wood slides.

The lamb, revived by the warmth, began to bleat, and the sound entered Gabriel's ears and brain with an instant meaning, as expected sounds will. Passing from the profoundest sleep to the most alert wakefulness with the same ease that had accompanied the reverse operation, he looked at his watch, found that the hour-hand had shifted again, put on his hat, took the lamb in his arms, and carried it into the darkness. After placing the little creature with its mother he stood and carefully examined the sky, to ascertain the time of night from the altitudes of the stars.

4. Pertaining to sheep.

The Dog-star[5] and Aldebaran, pointing to the restless Pleiades, were half-way up the Southern sky, and between them hung Orion, which gorgeous constellation never burnt more vividly than now, as it soared forth above the rim of the landscape. Castor and Pollux with their quiet shine were almost on the meridian: the barren and gloomy Square of Pegasus was creeping round to the north-west; far away through the plantation Vega sparkled like a lamp suspended amid the leafless trees, and Cassiopeia's chair stood daintily poised on the uppermost boughs.

'One o'clock,' said Gabriel.

Being a man not without a frequent consciousness that there was some charm in this life he led, he stood still after looking at the sky as a useful instrument, and regarded it in an appreciative spirit, as a work of art superlatively beautiful. For a moment he seemed impressed with the speaking loneliness of the scene, or rather with the complete abstraction from all its compass of the sights and sounds of man. Human shapes, interferences, troubles, and joys were all as if they were not, and there seemed to be on the shaded hemisphere of the globe no sentient being save himself; he could fancy them all gone round to the sunny side.

Occupied thus, with eyes stretched afar, Oak gradually perceived that what he had previously taken to be a star low down behind the outskirts of the plantation was in reality no such thing. It was an artificial light, almost close at hand.

To find themselves utterly alone at night where company is desirable and expected makes some people fearful; but a case more trying by far to the nerves is to discover some mysterious companionship when intuition, sensation, memory, analogy, testimony, probability, induction—every kind of evidence in the logician's list—have united to persuade consciousness that it is quite in isolation.

Farmer Oak went towards the plantation and pushed through its lower boughs to the windy side. A dim mass under the slope reminded him that a shed occupied a place here, the site being a cutting into the slope of the hill, so that at its back part the roof was almost level with the ground. In front it was formed of boards nailed to posts and covered with tar as a preservative. Through crevices in the roof and side spread streaks and dots of light, a combination of which made the radiance that had attracted him. Oak stepped up behind, where, leaning down upon the roof and putting his eye close to a hole, he could see into the

5. A common name for the star Sirius. "Pleiades": in classical mythology, the seven daughters of Atlas, who were transformed into stars after their deaths and form a cluster of stars in the constellation Taurus; these stars appear to twinkle—hence Hardy's word *restless*. Orion is a constellation near Gemini and Taurus containing the stars Betelgeuse and Rigel. Castor and Pollux are the two brightest stars in the constellation Gemini. Pegasus is a constellation in which four stars form a great square; presumably the size of the square and the relatively few stars visible within it account for Hardy's adjectives *barren* and *gloomy*. Vega is the brightest star in the constellation Lyra. The five brightest stars in the constellation Cassiopeia form a roughly chairlike shape.

interior clearly.

The place contained two women and two cows. By the side of the latter a steaming bran-mash stood in a bucket. One of the women was past middle age. Her companion was apparently young and graceful; he could form no decided opinion upon her looks, her position being almost beneath his eye, so that he saw her in a bird's-eye view, as Milton's Satan first saw Paradise.[6] She wore no bonnet or hat, but had enveloped herself in a large cloak, which was carelessly flung over her head as a covering.

'There, now we'll go home,' said the elder of the two, resting her knuckles upon her hips, and looking at their goings-on as a whole. 'I do hope Daisy will fetch round again now. I have never been more frightened in my life, but I don't mind breaking my rest if she recovers.'

The young woman, whose eyelids were apparently inclined to fall together on the smallest provocation of silence, yawned without parting her lips to any incovenient extent, whereupon Gabriel caught the infection and slightly yawned in sympathy.

'I wish we were rich enough to pay a man to do these things,' she said.

'As we are not, we must do them ourselves,' said the other; 'for you must help me if you stay.'

'Well, my hat is gone, however,' continued the younger. 'It went over the hedge, I think. The idea of such a slight wind catching it.'

The cow standing erect was of the Devon breed,[7] and was encased in a tight warm hide of rich Indian red,[8] as absolutely uniform from eyes to tail as if the animal had been dipped in a dye of that colour, her long back being mathematically level. The other was spotted, grey and white. Beside her Oak now noticed a little calf about a day old, looking idiotically at the two women, which showed that it had not long been accustomed to the phenomenon of eyesight, and often turning to the lantern, which it apparently mistook for the moon, inherited instinct having as yet had little time for correction by experience. Between the sheep and the cows Lucina[9] had been busy on Norcombe Hill lately.

'I think we had better send for some oatmeal,' said the elder woman; 'there's no more bran.'

'Yes, aunt; and I'll ride over for it as soon as it is light.'

'But there's no side-saddle.'[1]

'I can ride on the other: trust me.'

Oak, upon hearing these remarks, became more curious to observe her features, but this prospect being denied him by the hooding effect

---

6. In book 4, lines 181–207, of Milton's *Paradise Lost*, Satan is described as sitting "like a Cormorant" in the Tree of Life while viewing all of Paradise below him.

7. A breed of reddish beef cattle developed in Devonshire, England.

8. A deep red pigment made from iron oxide.

9. The Roman goddess of childbirth.

1. A saddle that enables a woman to sit with both legs on one side of the horse. In the mid-nineteenth century, it would be deemed unproper for a well-bred woman to ride astride.

of the cloak, and by his aërial position, he felt himself drawing upon his fancy for their details. In making even horizontal and clear inspections we colour and mould according to the wants within us whatever our eyes bring in. Had Gabriel been able from the first to get a distinct view of her countenance, his estimate of it as very handsome or slightly so would have been as his soul required a divinity at the moment or was ready supplied with one. Having for some time known the want of a satisfactory form to fill an increasing void within him, his position moreover affording the widest scope for his fancy, he painted her a beauty.

By one of those whimsical coincidences in which Nature, like a busy mother, seems to spare a moment from her unremitting labours to turn and make her children smile, the girl now dropped the cloak, and forth tumbled ropes of black hair over a red jacket. Oak knew her instantly as the heroine of the yellow waggon, myrtles, and looking-glass: prosily, as the woman who owed him twopence.

They placed the calf beside its mother again, took up the lantern, and went out, the light sinking down the hill till it was no more than a nebula. Gabriel Oak returned to his flock.

III

A Girl on Horseback—Conversation

The sluggish day began to break. Even its position terrestrially is one of the elements of a new interest, and for no particular reason save that the incident of the night had occurred there Oak went again into the plantation. Lingering and musing here he heard the steps of a horse at the foot of the hill, and soon there appeared in view an auburn pony with a girl on its back, ascending by the path leading past the cattleshed. She was the young woman of the night before. Gabriel instantly thought of the hat she had mentioned as having lost in the wind; possibly she had come to look for it. He hastily scanned the ditch, and after walking about ten yards along it found the hat among the leaves. Gabriel took it in his hand and returned to his hut. Here he ensconced himself, and peeped through the loophole in the direction of the rider's approach.

She came up and looked around—then on the other side of the hedge. Gabriel was about to advance and restore the missing article, when an unexpected performance induced him to suspend the action for the present. The path, after passing the cowshed, bisected the plantation. It was not a bridle-path—merely a pedestrian's track, and the boughs spread horizontally at a height not greater than seven feet above the ground, which made it impossible to ride erect beneath them. The girl, who wore no riding-habit, looked around for a moment, as if to assure herself that all humanity was out of view, then dexterously dropped backwards flat upon the pony's back, her head over its tail, her feet against its shoulders, and her eyes to the sky. The rapidity of her glide into this position was that of a kingfisher—its noiselessness that of a hawk. Gabriel's eyes had scarcely been able to follow her. The tall lank pony seemed used to such doings, and ambled along unconcerned. Thus she passed under the level boughs.

The performer seemed quite at home anywhere between a horse's head and its tail, and the necessity for this abnormal attitude having ceased with the passage of the plantation, she began to adopt another, even more obviously convenient than the first. She had no side-saddle, and it was very apparent that a firm seat upon the smooth leather beneath her was unattainable sideways. Springing to her accustomed perpendicular like a bowed sapling, and satisfying herself that nobody was in sight, she seated herself in the manner demanded by the saddle, though hardly expected of the woman, and trotted off in the direction of Tewnell Mill.

Oak was amused, perhaps a little astonished, and hanging up the hat in his hut went again among his ewes. An hour passed, the girl returned, properly seated now, with a bag of bran in front of her. On nearing the cattle-shed she was met by a boy bringing a milking-pail, who held the reins of the pony whilst she slid off. The boy led away the horse, leaving the pail with the young woman.

Soon soft spirts alternating with loud spirts came in regular succession from within the shed, the obvious sounds of a person milking a cow. Gabriel took the lost hat in his hand, and waited beside the path she would follow in leaving the hill.

She came, the pail in one hand, hanging against her knee. The left arm was extended as a balance, enough of it being shown bare to make Oak wish that the event had happened in the summer, when the whole would have been revealed. There was a bright air and manner about her now, by which she seemed to imply that the desirability of her existence could not be questioned; and this rather saucy assumption failed in being offensive because a beholder felt it to be, upon the whole, true. Like exceptional emphasis in the tone of a genius, that which would have made mediocrity ridiculous was an addition to recognized power. It was with some surprise that she saw Gabriel's face rising like the moon behind the hedge.

The adjustment of the farmer's hazy conceptions of her charms to the portrait of herself she now presented him with was less a diminution than a difference. The starting-point selected by the judgment was her height. She seemed tall, but the pail was a small one, and the hedge diminutive; hence, making allowance for error by comparison with these, she could have been not above the height to be chosen by women as best. All features of consequence were severe and regular. It may have been observed by persons who go about the shires with eyes for beauty that in Englishwomen a classically-formed face is seldom found to be united with a figure of the same pattern, the highly-finished features being generally too large for the remainder of the frame; that a graceful and proportionate figure of eight heads[1] usually goes off into random facial curves. Without throwing a Nymphean tissue over a milkmaid,[2] let it be said that here criticism checked itself as out of place, and looked at her proportions with a long consciousness of pleasure. From the contours of her figure in its upper part she must have had a beautiful neck and shoulders; but since her infancy nobody had even seen them. Had she been put into a low dress she would have run and thrust her head into a bush. Yet she was not a shy girl by any means; it was merely her instinct to draw the line dividing the seen from the unseen higher than they do it in towns.

That the girl's thoughts hovered about her face and form as soon as she caught Oak's eyes conning the same page was natural, and almost certain. The self-consciousness shown would have been vanity if a little more pronounced, dignity if a little less. Rays of male vision seem to have a tickling effect upon virgin faces in rural districts; she brushed hers with her hand, as if Gabriel had been irritating its pink surface by actual touch, and the free air of her previous movements was reduced at the same time to a chastened phase of itself. Yet it was the man who blushed, the maid not at all.

'I found a hat,' said Oak.

'It is mine,' said she, and, from a sense of proportion, kept down to a small smile an inclination to laugh distinctly: 'it flew away last night.'

'One o'clock this morning?'

'Well—it was.' She was surprised. 'How did you know?' she said.

'I was here.'

'You are Farmer Oak, are you not?'

'That or thereabouts. I'm lately come to this place.'

'A large farm?' she inquired, casting her eyes round, and swinging back her hair, which was black in the shaded hollows of its mass; but it being now an hour past sunrise the rays touched its prominent curves with a colour of their own.

'No ; not large. About a hundred.' (In speaking of farms the word 'acres' is omitted by the natives, by analogy to such old expressions as 'a stag of ten.')

'I wanted my hat this morning,' she went on. 'I had to ride to Tewnell Mill.'

'Yes, you had.'

'How do you know?'

'I saw you.'

'Where?' she inquired, a misgiving bringing every muscle of her lineaments and frame to a standstill.

1. The classical ideal for the well-proportioned human body was a height eight times the length of the head.

2. Without attempting to suggest that a milkmaid had the legendary beauty of a nymph.

'Here—going through the plantation, and all down the hill,' said Farmer Oak, with an aspect excessively knowing with regard to some matter in his mind, as he gazed at a remote point in the direction named, and then turned back to meet his colloquist's eyes.

A perception caused him to withdraw his own eyes from hers as suddenly as if he had been caught in a theft. Recollection of the strange antics she had indulged in when passing through the trees was succeeded in the girl by a nettled palpitation, and that by a hot face. It was a time to see a woman redden who was not given to reddening as a rule; not a point in the milkmaid but was of the deepest rose-colour. From the Maiden's Blush, through all varieties of the Provence down to the Crimson Tuscany[3] the countenance of Oak's acquaintance quickly graduated; whereupon he, in considerateness, turned away his head.

The sympathetic man still looked the other way, and wondered when she would recover coolness sufficient to justify him in facing her again. He heard what seemed to be the flitting of a dead leaf upon the breeze, and looked. She had gone away.

With an air between that of Tragedy and Comedy Gabriel returned to his work.

Five mornings and evenings passed. The young woman came regularly to milk the healthy cow or to attend to the sick one, but never allowed her vision to stray in the direction of Oak's person. His want of tact had deeply offended her—not by seeing what he could not help, but by letting her know that he had seen it. For, as without law there is no sin, without eyes there is no indecorum; and she appeared to feel that Gabriel's espial had made her an indecorous woman without her own connivance. It was food for great regret with him; it was also a *contretemps*[4] which touched into life a latent heat he had experienced in that direction.

The acquaintanceship might, however, have ended in a slow forgetting but for an incident which occurred at the end of the same week. One afternoon it began to freeze, and the frost increased with evening, which drew on like a stealthy tightening of bonds. It was a time when in cottages the breath of the sleepers freezes to the sheets; when round the drawing-room fire of a thick-walled mansion the sitters' backs are cold, even whilst their faces are all aglow. Many a small bird went to bed supperless that night among the bare boughs.

As the milking-hour drew near Oak kept his usual watch upon the cowshed. At last he felt cold, and shaking an extra quantity of bedding round the yeaning ewes[5] he entered the hut and heaped more fuel upon the stove. The wind came in at the bottom of the door, and to prevent it Oak laid a sack there and wheeled the cot round a little more

---

3. Names of roses ranging in color from pink to deep red.

4. French for "mischance."

5. Female sheep giving birth.

to the south. Then the wind spouted in at a ventilating hole—of which there was one on each side of the hut.

Gabriel had always known that when the fire was lighted and the door closed one of these must be kept open—that chosen being always on the side away from the wind. Closing the slide to windward he turned to open the other; on second thoughts the farmer considered that he would first sit down, leaving both closed for a minute or two, till the temperature of the hut was a little raised. He sat down.

His head began to ache in an unwonted manner and, fancying himself weary by reason of the broken rests of the preceding nights, Oak decided to get up, open the slide, and then allow himself to fall asleep. He fell asleep, however, without having performed the necessary preliminary.

How long he remained unconscious Gabriel never knew. During the first stages of his return to perception peculiar deeds seemed to be in course of enactment. His dog was howling, his head was aching fearfully—somebody was pulling him about, hands were loosening his neckerchief.

On opening his eyes he found that evening had sunk to dusk in a strange manner of unexpectedness. The young girl with the remarkably pleasant lips and white teeth was beside him. More than this—astonishingly more—his head was upon her lap, his face and neck were disagreeably wet, and her fingers were unbuttoning his collar.

'Whatever is the matter?' said Oak vacantly.

She seemed to experience mirth, but of too insignificant a kind to start enjoyment.

'Nothing now,' she answered, 'since you are not dead. It is a wonder you were not suffocated in this hut of yours.'

'Ah, the hut!' murmured Gabriel. 'I gave ten pounds for that hut. But I'll sell it, and sit under thatched hurdles as they did in old times, and curl up to sleep in a lock of straw! It played me nearly the same trick the other day!' Gabriel, by way of emphasis, brought down his fist upon the floor.

'It was not exactly the fault of the hut,' she observed in a tone which showed her to be that novelty among women—one who finished a thought before beginning the sentence which was to convey it. 'You should, I think, have considered, and not have been so foolish as to leave the slides closed.'

'Yes, I suppose I should,' said Oak absently. He was endeavouring to catch and appreciate the sensation of being thus with her, his head upon her dress, before the event passed on into the heap of bygone things. He wished she knew his impressions; but he would as soon have thought of carrying an odour in a net as of attempting to convey the intangibilities of his feeling in the coarse meshes of language. So he remained silent.

She made him sit up, and then Oak began wiping his face and shaking himself like a Samson.[6] 'How can I thank'ee?' he said at last gratefully, some of the natural rusty red having returned to his face.

'Oh, never mind that,' said the girl, smiling, and allowing her smile to hold good for Gabriel's next remark, whatever that might prove to be.

'How did you find me?'

'I heard your dog howling and scratching at the door of the hut when I came to the milking (it was so lucky, Daisy's milking is almost over for the season, and I shall not come here after this week or the next). The dog saw me, and jumped over to me, and laid hold of my skirt. I came across and looked round the hut the very first thing to see if the slides were closed. My uncle has a hut like this one, and I have heard him tell his shepherd not to go to sleep without leaving a slide open. I opened the door, and there you were like dead. I threw the milk over you, as there was no water, forgetting it was warm, and no use.'

'I wonder if I should have died?' Gabriel said in a low voice, which was rather meant to travel back to himself than to her.

'O no!' the girl replied. She seemed to prefer a less tragic probability; to have saved a man from death involved talk that should harmonize with the dignity of such a deed—and she shunned it.

'I believe you saved my life, Miss——I don't know your name. I know your aunt's, but not yours.'

'I would just as soon not tell it—rather not. There is no reason either why I should, as you probably will never have much to do with me.'

'Still I should like to know.'

'You can inquire at my aunt's—she will tell you.'

'My name is Gabriel Oak.'

'And mine isn't. You seem fond of yours in speaking it so decisively, Gabriel Oak.'

'You see, it is the only one I shall ever have, and I must make the most of it.'

'I always think mine sounds odd and disagreeable.'

'I should think you might soon get a new one.'

'Mercy!—how many opinions you keep about you concerning other people, Gabriel Oak.'

'Well, Miss—excuse the words—I thought you would like them. But I can't match you, I know, in mapping out my mind upon tongue. I never was very clever in my inside. But I thank you. Come, give me your hand!'

She hesitated, somewhat disconcerted at Oak's old-fashioned earnest conclusion to a dialogue lightly carried on. 'Very well,' she said,

6. In Judges 16:20 Samson is described as awakening from sleep and saying, "I will go out as at other times before, and shake myself."

and gave him her hand, compressing her lips to a demure impassivity. He held it but an instant, and in his fear of being too demonstrative, swerved to the opposite extreme, touching her fingers with the lightness of a small-hearted person.

'I am sorry,' he said the instant after.

'What for?'

'Letting your hand go so quick.'

'You may have it again if you like; there it is.' She gave him her hand again.

Oak held it longer this time—indeed, curiously long. 'How soft it is—being winter time, too—not chapped or rough, or anything!' he said.

'There—that's long enough,' said she, though without pulling it away. 'But I suppose you are thinking you would like to kiss it? You may if you want to.'

'I wasn't thinking of any such thing,' said Gabriel simply; 'but I will——'

'That you won't!' She snatched back her hand.

Gabriel felt himself guilty of another want of tact.

'Now find out my name,' she said teasingly; and withdrew.

IV

Gabriel's Resolve—The Visit—The Mistake

The only superiority in women that is tolerable to the rival sex is, as a rule, that of the unconscious kind; but a superiority which recognizes itself may sometimes please by suggesting possibilities of capture to the subordinated man.

This well-favoured and comely girl soon made appreciable inroads upon the emotional constitution of young Farmer Oak.

Love being an extremely exacting usurer (a sense of exorbitant profit, spiritually, by an exchange of hearts, being at the bottom of pure passions, as that of exorbitant profit, bodily or materially, is at the bottom of those of lower atmosphere), every morning Oak's feelings were as sensitive as the money-market in calculations upon his chances. His dog waited for his meals in a way so like that in which Oak waited for the girl's presence that the farmer was quite struck with the resemblance, felt it lowering, and would not look at the dog. However, he continued to watch through the hedge for her regular coming, and thus his sentiments towards her were deepened without any corresponding effect being produced upon herself. Oak had nothing finished and ready to say as yet, and not being able to frame love phrases which end where they begin; passionate tales—

—Full of sound and fury
—Signifying nothing—[1]

he said no word at all.

By making inquiries he found that the girl's name was Bathsheba Everdene, and that the cow would go dry in about seven days. He dreaded the eighth day.

At last the eighth day came. The cow had ceased to give milk for that year, and Bathsheba Everdene came up the hill no more. Gabriel had reached a pitch of existence he never could have anticipated a short time before. He liked saying 'Bathsheba' as a private enjoyment instead of whistling; turned over his taste to black hair, though he had sworn by brown ever since he was a boy, isolated himself till the space he filled in the public eye was contemptibly small. Love is a possible strength in an actual weakness. Marriage transforms a distraction into a support, the power of which should be, and happily often is, in direct proportion to the degree of imbecility it supplants. Oak began now to see light in this direction, and said to himself, 'I'll make her my wife, or upon my soul I shall be good for nothing!'

All this while he was perplexing himself about an errand on which he might consistently visit the cottage of Bathsheba's aunt.

He found his opportunity in the death of a ewe, mother of a living lamb. On a day which had a summer face and a winter constitution—a fine January morning, when there was just enough blue sky visible to make cheerfully-disposed people wish for more, and an occasional gleam of silvery sunshine, Oak put the lamb into a respectable Sunday basket, and stalked across the fields to the house of Mrs. Hurst, the aunt—George, the dog, walking behind, with a countenance of great concern at the serious turn pastoral affairs seemed to be taking.

Gabriel had watched the blue wood-smoke curling from the chimney with strange meditation. At evening he had fancifully traced it down the flue to the spot of its origin—seen the hearth and Bathsheba beside it—beside it in her out-door dress; for the clothes she had worn on the hill were by association equally with her person included in the compass of his affection; they seemed at this early time of his love a necessary ingredient of the sweet mixture called Bathsheba Everdene.

He had made a toilet of a nicely-adjusted kind—of a nature between the carefully neat and the carelessly ornate—of a degree between fine-market-day and wet-Sunday selection. He thoroughly cleaned his silver watch-chain with whiting, put new lacing straps to his boots, looked to the brass eyelet-holes, went to the inmost heart of the plantation for a new walking-stick, and trimmed it vigorously on his way back; took a new handkerchief from the bottom of his clothes-box,

1. Quoted from Shakespeare's *Macbeth*, act 5, scene 5, in which Macbeth reacts to the news of his wife's death by describing life as "a tale / Told by an idiot, full of sound and fury, / Signifying nothing."

put on the light waistcoat patterned all over with sprigs of an elegant flower uniting the beauties of both rose and lily without the defects of either, and used all the hair-oil he possessed upon his usually dry, sandy, and inextricably curly hair, till he had deepened it to a splendidly novel colour, between that of guano and Roman cement,[2] making it stick to his head like mace round a nutmeg,[3] or wet seaweed round a boulder after the ebb.

Nothing disturbed the stillness of the cottage save the chatter of a knot of sparrows on the eaves; one might fancy scandal and rumour to be no less the staple topic of these little coteries on roofs than of those under them. It seemed that the omen was an unpropitious one, for, as the rather untoward commencement of Oak's overtures, just as he arrived by the garden gate he saw a cat inside, going into various arched shapes and fiendish convulsions at the sight of his dog George. The dog took no notice, for he had arrived at an age at which all superfluous barking was cynically avoided as a waste of breath—in fact, he never barked even at the sheep except to order, when it was done with an absolutely neutral countenance, as a sort of Commination-service[4] which, though offensive, had to be gone through once now and then to frighten the flock for their own good.

A voice came from behind some laurel-bushes into which the cat had run:

'Poor dear! Did a nasty brute of a dog want to kill it;—did he, poor dear!'

'I beg yer pardon,' said Oak to the voice, 'but George was walking on behind me with a temper as mild as milk.'

Almost before he had ceased speaking Oak was seized with a misgiving as to whose ear was the recipient of his answer. Nobody appeared, and he heard the person retreat among the bushes.

Gabriel meditated, and so deeply that he brought small furrows into his forehead by sheer force of reverie. Where the issue of an interview is as likely to be a vast change for the worse as for the better, any initial difference from expectation causes nipping sensations of failure. Oak went up to the door a little abashed: his mental rehearsal and the reality had had no common grounds of opening.

Bathsheba's aunt was indoors. 'Will you tell Miss Everdene that somebody would be glad to speak to her?' said Mr. Oak. (Calling one's self merely Somebody, without giving a name, is not to be taken as an example of the ill-breeding of the rural world: it springs from a refined modesty of which townspeople, with their cards and announcements, have no notion whatever.)

2. Guano is a whitish fertilizer composed mostly of the excrement of birds and bats; Roman cement is composed of chalk or clay, sand, lime, and water.

3. Like the dried covering that tightly clings to the seed of the nutmeg tree.

4. A service prescribed to be held as part of Morning Prayer in Anglican churches on Ash Wednesday; it includes a recital of divine curses against sinners, intended to make them "walk more warily in these dangerous days."

Bathsheba was out. The voice had evidently been hers.

'Will you come in, Mr. Oak?'

'Oh, thank 'ee,' said Gabriel, following her to the fireplace. 'I've brought a lamb for Miss Everdene. I thought she might like one to rear; girls do.'

'She might,' said Mrs. Hurst musingly; 'though she's only a visitor here. If you will wait a minute Bathsheba will be in.'

'Yes, I will wait,' said Gabriel, sitting down. 'The lamb isn't really the business I came about, Mrs. Hurst. In short, I was going to ask her if she'd like to be married.'

'And were you indeed?'

'Yes. Because if she would I should be very glad to marry her. D'ye know if she's got any other young man hanging about her at all?'

'Let me think,' said Mrs. Hurst, poking the fire superfluously. . . . 'Yes—bless you, ever so many young men. You see, Farmer Oak, she's so good-looking, and an excellent scholar besides—she was going to be a governess once, you know, only she was too wild. Not that her young men ever come here—but, Lord, in the nature of women, she must have a dozen!'

'That's unfortunate,' said Farmer Oak, contemplating a crack in the stone floor with sorrow. 'I'm only an every-day sort of man, and my only chance was in being the first comer. . . . Well, there's no use in my waiting, for that was all I came about: so I'll take myself off home-along, Mrs. Hurst.'

When Gabriel had gone about two hundred yards along the down, he heard a 'hoi-hoi!' uttered behind him, in a piping note of more treble quality than that in which the exclamation usually embodies itself when shouted across a field. He looked round, and saw a girl racing after him, waving a white handkerchief.

Oak stood still—and the runner drew nearer. It was Bathsheba Everdene. Gabriel's colour deepened: hers was already deep, not, as it appeared, from emotion, but from running.

'Farmer Oak—I——' she said, pausing for want of breath, pulling up in front of him with a slanted face, and putting her hand to her side.

'I have just called to see you,' said Gabriel pending her further speech.

'Yes—I know that,' she said, panting like a robin, her face red and moist from her exertions, like a peony petal before the sun dries off the dew. 'I didn't know you had come to ask to have me, or I should have come in from the garden instantly. I ran after you to say—that my aunt made a mistake in sending you away from courting me.'

Gabriel expanded. 'I'm sorry to have made you run so fast, my dear,' he said, with a grateful sense of favours to come. 'Wait a bit till you've found your breath.'

'—It was quite a mistake—aunt's telling you I had a young man already,' Bathsheba went on. 'I haven't a sweetheart at all—and I never had one, and I thought that, as times go with women, it was *such* a pity to send you away thinking that I had several.'

'Really and truly I am glad to hear that!' said Farmer Oak, smiling one of his long special smiles, and blushing with gladness. He held out his hand to take hers, which, when she had eased her side by pressing it there, was prettily extended upon her bosom to still her loud-beating heart. Directly he seized it she put it behind her, so that it slipped through his fingers like an eel.

'I have a nice snug little farm,' said Gabriel, with half a degree less assurance than when he had seized her hand.

'Yes; you have.'

'A man has advanced me money to begin with, but still, it will soon be paid off, and though I am only an every-day sort of man I have got on a little since I was a boy.' Gabriel uttered 'a little' in a tone to show her that it was the complacent form of 'a great deal.' He continued: 'When we be married, I am quite sure I can work twice as hard as I do now.'

He went forward and stretched out his arm again. Bathsheba had overtaken him at a point beside which stood a low stunted holly bush, now laden with red berries. Seeing his advance take the form of an attitude threatening a possible enclosure, if not compression, of her person, she edged off round the bush.

'Why, Farmer Oak,' she said over the top, looking at him with rounded eyes, 'I never said I was going to marry you.'

'Well—that *is* a tale!' said Oak with dismay. 'To run after anybody like this, and then say you don't want him!'

'What I meant to tell you was only this,' she said eagerly, and yet half conscious of the absurdity of the position she had made for herself—'that nobody has got me yet as a sweetheart, instead of my having a dozen, as my aunt said; I *hate* to be thought men's property in that way, though possibly I shall be had some day. Why, if I'd wanted you I shouldn't have run after you like this; 'twould have been the *forwardest* thing! But there was no harm in hurrying to correct a piece of false news that had been told you.'

'Oh, no—no harm at all.' But there is such a thing as being too generous in expressing a judgment impulsively, and Oak added with a more appreciative sense of all the circumstances—'Well, I am not quite certain it was no harm.'

'Indeed, I hadn't time to think before starting whether I wanted to marry or not, for you'd have been gone over the hill.'

'Come,' said Gabriel, freshening again; 'think a minute or two. I'll wait a while, Miss Everdene. Will you marry me? Do, Bathsheba. I love you far more than common!'

'I'll try to think,' she observed rather more timorously; 'if I can think out of doors; my mind spreads away so.'

'But you can give a guess.'

'Then give me time.' Bathsheba looked thoughtfully into the distance, away from the direction in which Gabriel stood.

'I can make you happy,' said he to the back of her head, across the bush. 'You shall have a piano in a year or two—farmers' wives are getting to have pianos now—and I'll practise up the flute right well to play with you in the evenings.'

'Yes; I should like that.'

'And have one of those little ten-pound gigs[5] for market—and nice flowers, and birds—cocks and hens I mean, because they be useful,' continued Gabriel, feeling balanced between poetry and practicality.

'I should like it very much.'

'And a frame for cucumbers—like a gentleman and lady.'

'Yes.'

'And when the wedding was over, we'd have it put in the newspaper list of marriages.'

'Dearly I should like that!'

'And the babies in the births—every man jack of 'em! And at home by the fire, whenever you look up, there I shall be—and whenever I look up, there will be you.'

'Wait, wait, and don't be improper!'

Her countenance fell, and she was silent awhile. He regarded the red berries between them over and over again, to such an extent that holly seemed in his after life to be a cypher signifying a proposal of marriage. Bathsheba decisively turned to him.

'No; 'tis no use,' she said. 'I don't want to marry you.'

'Try.'

'I've tried hard all the time I've been thinking; for a marriage would be very nice in one sense. People would talk about me and think I had won my battle, and I should feel triumphant, and all that. But a husband——'

'Well!'

'Why, he'd always be there, as you say; whenever I looked up, there he'd be.'

'Of course he would—I, that is.'

'Well, what I mean is that I shouldn't mind being a bride at a wedding, if I could be one without having a husband. But since a woman can't show off in that way by herself, I shan't marry—at least yet.'

'That's a terrible wooden story!'

At this criticism of her statement Bathsheba made an addition to her dignity by a slight sweep away from him.

'Upon my heart and soul I don't know what a maid can say stupider than that,' said Oak. 'But dearest,' he continued in a palliative voice, 'don't be like it!' Oak sighed a deep honest sigh—none the less so in

---

5. A small two-wheeled horse cart then valued at about ten English pounds.

that, being like the sigh of a pine plantation, it was rather noticeable as a disturbance of the atmosphere. 'Why won't you have me?' he appealed, creeping round the holly to reach her side.

'I cannot,' she said, retreating.

'But why?' he persisted, standing still at last in despair of ever reaching her, and facing over the bush.

'Because I don't love you.'

'Yes, but——'

She contracted a yawn to an inoffensive smallness, so that it was hardly ill-mannered at all. 'I don't love you,' she said.

'But I love you—and, as for myself, I am content to be liked.'

'O Mr. Oak—that's very fine! You'd get to despise me.'

'Never,' said Mr. Oak, so earnestly that he seemed to be coming, by the force of his words, straight through the bush and into her arms. 'I shall do one thing in this life—one thing certain—that is, love you, and long for you, and *keep wanting you* till I die.' His voice had a genuine pathos now, and his large brown hands perceptibly trembled.

'It seems dreadfully wrong not to have you when you feel so much!' she said with a little distress, and looking hopelessly around for some means of escape from her moral dilemma. 'How I wish I hadn't run after you!' However, she seemed to have a short cut for getting back to cheerfulness and set her face to signify archness. 'It wouldn't do, Mr. Oak. I want somebody to tame me; I am too independent; and you would never be able to, I know.'

Oak cast his eyes down the field in a way implying that it was useless to attempt argument.

'Mr. Oak,' she said, with luminous distinctness and common sense, 'you are better off than I. I have hardly a penny in the world—I am staying with my aunt for my bare sustenance. I am better educated than you—and I don't love you a bit: that's my side of the case. Now yours: you are a farmer just beginning, and you ought in common prudence, if you marry at all (which you should certainly not think of doing at present) to marry a woman with money, who would stock a larger farm for you than you have now.'

Gabriel looked at her with a little surprise and much admiration. 'That's the very thing I had been thinking myself!' he naïvely said.

Farmer Oak had one-and-a-half Christian characteristics too many to succeed with Bathsheba: his humility, and a superfluous moiety of honesty. Bathsheba was decidedly disconcerted.

'Well, then, why did you come and disturb me?' she said, almost angrily, if not quite, an enlarging red spot rising in each cheek.

'I can't do what I think would be—would be——'

'Right?'

'No: wise.'

'You have made an admission *now*, Mr. Oak,' she exclaimed with even more hauteur, and rocking her head disdainfully. 'After that, do you think I could marry you? Not if I know it.'

He broke in passionately: 'But don't mistake me like that! Because I am open enough to own what every man in my shoes would have thought of, you make your colours come up your face and get crabbed with me. That about you not being good enough for me is nonsense. You speak like a lady—all the parish notice it, and your uncle at Weatherbury is, I've heerd, a large farmer—much larger than ever I shall be. May I call in the evening, or will you walk along with me o' Sundays? I don't want you to make up your mind at once, if you'd rather not.'

'No—no—I cannot. Don't press me any more—don't. I don't love you—so 'twould be ridiculous,' she said, with a laugh.

No man likes to see his emotions the sport of a merry-go-round of skittishness. 'Very well,' said Oak firmly, with the bearing of one who was going to give his days and nights to Ecclesiastes[6] for ever. 'Then I'll ask you no more.'

V

Departure of Bathsheba—A Pastoral Tragedy

The news which one day reached Gabriel that Bathsheba Everdene had left the neighbourhood, had an influence upon him which might have surprised any who never suspected that the more emphatic the renunciation the less absolute its character.

It may have been observed that there is no regular path for getting out of love as there is for getting in. Some people look upon marriage as a short cut that way, but it has been known to fail. Separation, which was the means that chance offered to Gabriel Oak by Bathsheba's disappearance, though effectual with people of certain humours, is apt to idealize the removed object with others—notably those whose affection, placid and regular as it may be, flows deep and long. Oak belonged to the even-tempered order of humanity, and felt the secret fusion of himself in Bathsheba to be burning with a finer flame now that she was gone—that was all.

His incipient friendship with her aunt had been nipped by the failure of his suit, and all that Oak learnt of Bathsheba's movements was done indirectly. It appeared that she had gone to a place called Weatherbury,[1] nearly twenty miles off, but in what capacity—whether as a visitor or permanently, he could not discover.

Gabriel had two dogs. George, the elder, exhibited an ebony-tipped nose, surrounded by a narrow margin of pink flesh, and a coat marked in random splotches approximating in colour to white and slaty grey;

6. A book of the Old Testament whose themes include the vanity of human desires and the inevitability of adversity in life.

1. Hardy's fictional Weatherbury corresponds to Puddletown, about five miles northeast of Dorchester; see the map on p. 326.

but the grey, after years of sun and rain, had been scorched and washed out of the more prominent locks, leaving them of a reddish-brown, as if the blue component of the grey had faded, like the indigo[2] from the same kind of colour in Turner's[3] pictures. In substance it had originally been hair, but long contact with sheep seemed to be turning it by degrees into wool of a poor quality and staple.[4]

This dog had originally belonged to a shepherd of inferior morals and dreadful temper, and the result was that George knew the exact degrees of condemnation signified by cursing and swearing of all descriptions better than the wickedest old man in the neighbourhood. Long experience had so precisely taught the animal the difference between such exclamations as 'Come in!' and 'D——ye, come in!' that he knew to a hair's breadth the rate of trotting back from the ewes' tails that each call involved, if a staggerer with the sheep-crook was to be escaped. Though old, he was clever and trustworthy still.

The young dog, George's son, might possibly have been the image of his mother, for there was not much resemblance between him and George. He was learning the sheep-keeping business, so as to follow on at the flock when the other should die, but had got no further than the rudiments as yet—still finding an insuperable difficulty in distinguishing between doing a thing well enough and doing it too well. So earnest and yet so wrong-headed was this young dog (he had no name in particular, and answered with perfect readiness to any pleasant interjection) that if sent behind the flock to help them on he did it so thoroughly that he would have chased them across the whole county with the greatest pleasure if not called off, or reminded when to stop by the example of old George.

Thus much for the dogs. On the further side of Norcombe Hill was a chalk-pit, from which chalk had been drawn for generations, and spread over adjacent farms. Two hedges converged upon it in the form of a V, but without quite meeting. The narrow opening left, which was immediately over the brow of the pit, was protected by a rough railing.

One night, when Farmer Oak had returned to his house, believing there would be no further necessity for his attendance on the down,[5] he called as usual to the dogs, previously to shutting them up in the outhouse till next morning. Only one responded—old George; the other could not be found, either in the house, lane, or garden. Gabriel then remembered that he had left the two dogs on the hill eating a dead lamb (a kind of meat he usually kept from them, except when other food ran short), and concluding that the young one had not finished his meal he went indoors to the luxury of a bed, which latterly he had only enjoyed on Sundays.

2. A deep blue but unstable pigment that tends to fade when used in paintings.
3. J. M. W. Turner (1775–1851), an English painter noted for the brilliant color of his works.
4. Wool fiber graded for length.
5. A down is a grassy hill used for grazing.

It was a still, moist night. Just before dawn he was assisted in waking by the abnormal reverberation of familiar music. To the shepherd, the note of the sheep-bell, like the ticking of the clock to other people, is a chronic sound that only makes itself noticed by ceasing or altering in some unusual manner from the well-known idle tinkle which signifies to the accustomed ear, however distant, that all is well in the fold. In the solemn calm of the awakening morn that note was heard by Gabriel, beating with unusual violence and rapidity. This exceptional ringing may be caused in two ways—by the rapid feeding of the sheep bearing the bell, as when the flock breaks into new pasture, which gives it an intermittent rapidity, or by the sheep starting off in a run, when the sound has a regular palpitation. The experienced ear of Oak knew the sound he now heard to be caused by the running of the flock with great velocity.

He jumped out of bed, dressed, tore down the lane through a foggy dawn, and ascended the hill. The forward ewes were kept apart from those among which the fall of lambs would be later, there being two hundred of the latter class in Gabriel's flock. These two hundred seemed to have absolutely vanished from the hill. There were the fifty with their lambs, enclosed at the other end as he had left them, but the rest, forming the bulk of the flock, were nowhere. Gabriel called at the top of his voice the shepherd's call:

'Ovey, ovey, ovey!'[6]

Not a single bleat. He went to the hedge; a gap had been broken through it, and in the gap were the footprints of the sheep. Rather surprised to find them break fence at this season, yet putting it down instantly to their great fondness for ivy in wintertime, of which a great deal grew in the plantation, he followed through the hedge. They were not in the plantation. He called again: the valleys and furthest hills resounded as when the sailors invoked the lost Hylas on the Mysian shore;[7] but no sheep. He passed through the trees and along the ridge of the hill. On the extreme summit, where the ends of the two converging hedges of which we have spoken were stopped short by meeting the brow of the chalk-pit, he saw the younger dog standing against the sky—dark and motionless as Napoleon at St. Helena.[8]

A horrible conviction darted through Oak. With a sensation of bodily faintness he advanced: at one point the rails were broken through, and there he saw the footprints of his ewes. The dog came

6. It is somewhat singular—possibly a survival from the Roman occupation of Britain—that the shepherds of this region should call their sheep in Latin [*Hardy's note*]. The Latin word for sheep is *ovis* [*Editor's note*].

7. When Hercules and the Argonauts landed on the coast of Mysia, Hylas, a favorite of Hercules, was attracted by nymphs in a spring where he had gone to get water. Hercules and his sailors called for him in vain; the nymphs had carried Hylas off with them. The fable is recorded in the thirteenth idyll of Theocritus.

8. Hardy probably had in mind one of a number of pictures of Napoleon brooding silhouetted against the sky during his exile on the island of St. Helena.

up, licked his hand, and made signs implying that he expected some great reward for signal services rendered. Oak looked over the precipice. The ewes lay dead and dying at its foot—a heap of two hundred mangled carcases, representing in their condition just now at least two hundred more.

Oak was an intensely humane man: indeed, his humanity often tore in pieces any politic intentions of his which bordered on strategy, and carried him on as by gravitation. A shadow in his life had always been that his flock ended in mutton—that a day came and found every shepherd an arrant traitor to his defenceless sheep. His first feeling now was one of pity for the untimely fate of these gentle ewes and their unborn lambs.

It was a second to remember another phase of the matter. The sheep were not insured. All the savings of a frugal life had been dispersed at a blow; his hopes of being an independent farmer were laid low— possibly for ever. Gabriel's energies, patience, and industry had been so severely taxed during the years of his life between eighteen and eight-and-twenty, to reach his present stage of progress, that no more seemed to be left in him. He leant down upon a rail, and covered his face with his hands.

Stupors, however, do not last for ever, and Farmer Oak recovered from his. It was as remarkable as it was characteristic that the one sentence he uttered was in thankfulness:—

'Thank God I am not married: what would *she* have done in the poverty now coming upon me!'

Oak raised his head, and wondering what he could do, listlessly surveyed the scene. By the outer margin of the pit was an oval pond, and over it hung the attenuated skeleton of a chrome-yellow moon, which had only a few days to last—the morning star dogging her on the left hand. The pool glittered like a dead man's eye, and as the world awoke a breeze blew, shaking and elongating the reflection of the moon without breaking it, and turning the image of the star to a phosphoric streak upon the water. All this Oak saw and remembered.

As far as could be learnt it appeared that the poor young dog, still under the impression that since he was kept for running after sheep, the more he ran after them the better, had at the end of his meal off the dead lamb, which may have given him additional energy and spirits, collected all the ewes into a corner, driven the timid creatures through the hedge, across the upper field, and by main force of worrying had given them momentum enough to break down a portion of the rotten railing, and so hurled them over the edge.

George's son had done his work so thoroughly that he was considered too good a workman to live, and was, in fact, taken and tragically shot at twelve o'clock that same day—another instance of the untoward fate which so often attends dogs and other philosophers who follow out a train of reasoning to its logical conclusion, and attempt perfectly consistent conduct in a world made up so largely of compromise.

Gabriel's farm had been stocked by a dealer—on the strength of Oak's promising look and character—who was receiving a percentage from the farmer till such time as the advance should be cleared off. Oak found that the value of stock, plant, and implements which were really his own would be about sufficient to pay his debts, leaving himself a free man with the clothes he stood up in, and nothing more.

VI

The Fair—The Journey—The Fire

Two months passed away. We are brought on to a day in February, on which was held the yearly statute or hiring fair[1] in the county-town of Casterbridge.

At one end of the street stood from two to three hundred blithe and hearty labourers waiting upon Chance—all men of the stamp to whom labour suggests nothing worse than a wrestle with gravitation, and pleasure nothing better than a renunciation of the same. Among these, carters and waggoners were distinguished by having a piece of whip-cord twisted round their hats; thatchers wore a fragment of woven straw; shepherds held their sheep-crooks in their hands; and thus the situation required was known to the hirers at a glance.

In the crowd was an athletic young fellow of somewhat superior appearance to the rest—in fact, his superiority was marked enough to lead several ruddy peasants standing by to speak to him inquiringly, as to a farmer, and to use 'Sir' as a finishing word. His answer always was,—

'I am looking for a place myself—a bailiff's.[2] Do ye know of anybody who wants one?'

Gabriel was paler now. His eyes were more meditative, and his expression was more sad. He had passed through an ordeal of wretchedness which had given him more than it had taken away. He had sunk from his modest elevation as pastoral king into the very slime-pits of Siddim;[3] but there was left to him a dignified calm he had never before known, and that indifference to fate which, though it often makes a villain of a man, is the basis of his sublimity when it does not. And thus the abasement had been exaltation, and the loss gain.

In the morning a regiment of cavalry had left the town, and a

---

1. An annual event in many nineteenth-century rural towns; on a day set aside by statute, workers seeking employment stood along the streets waiting to be hired for the coming year.
2. A general overseer or manager of a farm or estate.
3. In Genesis 14:3–10, the vale of Siddim, on the shores of the Dead Sea, is described as "full of slime pits."

sergeant and his party had been beating up for recruits through the four streets. As the end of the day drew on, and he found himself not hired, Gabriel almost wished that he had joined them, and gone off to serve his country. Weary of standing in the marketplace, and not much minding the kind of work he turned his hand to, he decided to offer himself in some other capacity than that of bailiff.

All the farmers seemed to be wanting shepherds. Sheep-tending was Gabriel's specialty. Turning down an obscure street and entering an obscurer lane, he went up to a smith's shop.

'How long would it take you to make a shepherd's crook?'

'Twenty minutes.'

'How much?'

'Two shillings.'

He sat on a bench and the crook was made, a stem being given him into the bargain.

He then went to a ready-made clothes shop, the owner of which had a large rural connection. As the crook had absorbed most of Gabriel's money, he attempted, and carried out, an exchange of his overcoat for a shepherd's regulation smock-frock.[4]

This transaction having been completed he again hurried off to the centre of the town, and stood on the kerb of the pavement, as a shepherd, crook in hand.

Now that Oak had turned himself into a shepherd it seemed that bailiffs were most in demand. However, two or three farmers noticed him and drew near. Dialogues followed, more or less in the subjoined form:—

'Where do you come from?'

'Norcombe.'

'That's a long way.'

'Fifteen miles.'

'Whose farm were you upon last?'

'My own.'

This reply invariably operated like a rumour of cholera. The inquiring farmer would edge away and shake his head dubiously. Gabriel, like his dog, was too good to be trustworthy, and he never made advance beyond this point.

It is safer to accept any chance that offers itself, and extemporize a procedure to fit it, than to get a good plan matured, and wait for a chance of using it. Gabriel wished he had not nailed up his colours as a shepherd, but had laid himself out for anything in the whole cycle of labour that was required in the fair. It grew dusk. Some merry men were whistling and singing by the corn-exchange. Gabriel's hand, which had lain for some time idle in his smock-frock pocket, touched his flute, which he carried there. Here was an opportunity for putting

---

4. A long, loose-fitting garment formerly worn by rural workers—so called because it was traditionally decorated with the kind of needlework called "smocking."

his dearly bought wisdom into practice.

He drew out his flute and began to play 'Jockey to the Fair'[5] in the style of a man who had never known a moment's sorrow. Oak could pipe with Arcadian[6] sweetness, and the sound of the well-known notes cheered his own heart as well as those of the loungers. He played on with spirit, and in half an hour had earned in pence what was a small fortune to a destitute man.

By making inquiries he learnt that there was another fair at Shottsford the next day.

'How far is Shottsford?'[7]

'Ten miles t'other side of Weatherbury.'

Weatherbury! It was where Bathsheba had gone two months before. This information was like coming from night into noon.

'How far is it to Weatherbury?'

'Five or six miles.'

Bathsheba had probably left Weatherbury long before this time, but the place had enough interest attaching to it to lead Oak to choose Shottsford fair as his next field of inquiry, because it lay in the Weatherbury quarter. Moreover, the Weatherbury folk were by no means uninteresting intrinsically. If report spoke truly they were as hardy, merry, thriving, wicked a set as any in the whole county. Oak resolved to sleep at Weatherbury that night on his way to Shottsford, and struck out at once into the high road which had been recommended as the direct route to the village in question.

The road stretched through water-meadows traversed by little brooks, whose quivering surfaces were braided along their centres, and folded into creases at the sides; or, where the flow was more rapid, the stream was pied with spots of white froth, which rode on in undisturbed serenity. On the higher levels the dead and dry carcases of leaves tapped the ground as they bowled along helter-skelter upon the shoulders of the wind, and little birds in the hedges were rustling their feathers and tucking themselves in comfortably for the night, retaining their places if Oak kept moving, but flying away if he stopped to look at them. He passed by Yalbury Wood[8] where the game-birds were rising to their roosts, and heard the crack-voiced cock-pheasants' 'cu-uck, cuck,' and the wheezy whistle of the hens.

By the time he had walked three or four miles every shape in the landscape had assumed a uniform hue of blackness. He descended Yalbury Hill and could just discern ahead of him a waggon, drawn up

5. An eighteenth-century song that, with a simplified tune, was popular in the nineteenth century; its lyrics concern Jockey and Jenny, who run away together to a fair. This and other songs mentioned in *Far from the Madding Crowd* are contained in manuscript music books that belonged to the Hardy family and are now in the Dorset County Museum.

6. Of a region of Greece—Arcadia—which is the legendary habitat of the god Pan, whose piping entranced his listeners with its beauty.
7. Hardy's fictional name for Blandford Forum; see the map on p. 326.
8. Hardy's fictional name for Yellowham Wood; see the map on p. 326.

under a great over-hanging tree by the roadside.

On coming close, he found there were no horses attached to it, the spot being apparently quite deserted. The waggon, from its position, seemed to have been left there for the night, for beyond about half a truss of hay which was heaped in the bottom, it was quite empty. Gabriel sat down on the shafts of the vehicle and considered his position. He calculated that he had walked a very fair proportion of the journey; and having been on foot since daybreak, he felt tempted to lie down upon the hay in the waggon instead of pushing on to the village of Weatherbury, and having to pay for a lodging.

Eating his last slices of bread and ham, and drinking from the bottle of cider he had taken the precaution to bring with him, he got into the lonely waggon. Here he spread half of the hay as a bed, and, as well as he could in the darkness, pulled the other half over him by way of bed-clothes, covering himself entirely, and feeling, physically, as comfortable as ever he had been in his life. Inward melancholy it was impossible for a man like Oak, introspective far beyond his neighbours, to banish quite, whilst conning the present untoward page of his history. So, thinking of his misfortunes, amorous and pastoral, he fell asleep, shepherds enjoying, in common with sailors, the privilege of being able to summon the god instead of having to wait for him.

On somewhat suddenly awaking, after a sleep of whose length he had no idea, Oak found that the waggon was in motion. He was being carried along the road at a rate rather considerable for a vehicle without springs, and under circumstances of physical uneasiness, his head being dandled up and down on the bed of the waggon like a kettledrum-stick. He then distinguished voices in conversation, coming from the forepart of the waggon. His concern at this dilemma (which would have been alarm, had he been a thriving man; but misfortune is a fine opiate to personal terror) led him to peer cautiously from the hay, and the first sight he beheld was the stars above him. Charles's Wain[9] was getting towards a right angle with the Pole star, and Gabriel concluded that it must be about nine o'clock—in other words, that he had slept two hours. This small astronomical calculation was made without any positive effort, and whilst he was stealthily turning to discover, if possible, into whose hands he had fallen.

Two figures were dimly visible in front, sitting with their legs outside the waggon, one of whom was driving. Gabriel soon found that this was the waggoner, and it appeared they had come from Casterbridge fair, like himself.

A conversation was in progress, which continued thus:—

'Be as 'twill, she's a fine handsome body as far's looks be concerned. But that's only the skin of the woman, and these dandy cattle[1] be as

---

9. The constellation Ursa Major; the Pole star   1. Good-looking people (dialect).
is Polaris, the North Star.

proud as a lucifer in their insides.'

'Ay—so 'a do seem, Billy Smallbury—so 'a do seem.' This utterance was very shaky by nature, and more so by circumstance, the jolting of the waggon not being without its effect upon the speaker's larynx. It came from the man who held the reins.

'She's a very vain feymell—so 'tis said here and there.'

'Ah, now. If so be 'tis like that, I can't look her in the face. Lord, no: not I—heh-heh-heh! Such a shy man as I be!'

'Yes—she's very vain. 'Tis said that every night at going to bed she looks in the glass to put on her nightcap properly.'

'And not a married woman. Oh, the world!'

'And 'a can play the peanner, so 'tis said. Can play so clever that 'a can make a psalm tune sound as well as the merriest loose song a man can wish for.'

'D'ye tell o't! A happy time for us, and I feel quite a new man! And how do she pay?'

'That I don't know, Master Poorgrass.'

On hearing these and other similar remarks, a wild thought flashed into Gabriel's mind that they might be speaking of Bathsheba. There were, however, no grounds for retaining such a supposition, for the waggon, though going in the direction of Weatherbury, might be going beyond it, and the woman alluded to seemed to be the mistress of some estate. They were now apparently close upon Weatherbury, and not to alarm the speakers unnecessarily Gabriel slipped out of the waggon unseen.

He turned to an opening in the hedge, which he found to be a gate, and mounting thereon he sat meditating whether to seek a cheap lodging in the village, or to ensure a cheaper one by lying under some hay or corn stack. The crunching jangle of the waggon died upon his ear. He was about to walk on, when he noticed on his left hand an unusual light—appearing about half a mile distant. Oak watched it, and the glow increased. Something was on fire.

Gabriel again mounted the gate, and, leaping down on the other side upon what he found to be ploughed soil, made across the field in the exact direction of the fire. The blaze, enlarging in a double ratio by his approach and its own increase, showed him as he drew nearer the outlines of ricks[2] beside it, lighted up to great distinctness. A rick-yard was the source of the fire. His weary face now began to be painted over with a rich orange glow, and the whole front of his smock-frock and gaiters was covered with a dancing shadow pattern of thorn-twigs—the light reaching him through a leafless intervening hedge—and the metallic curve of his sheep-crook shone silver-bright in the same abounding rays. He came up to the boundary fence, and stood to regain breath. It seemed as if the spot was unoccupied by a living soul.

---

2. Stacks of straw or of wheat, barley, or other grain.

The fire was issuing from a long straw-stack, which was so far gone as to preclude a possibility of saving it. A rick burns differently from a house. As the wind blows the fire inwards, the portion in flames completely disappears like melting sugar, and the outline is lost to the eye. However, a hay or a wheat rick, well put together, will resist combustion for a length of time if it begins on the outside.

This before Gabriel's eyes was a rick of straw, loosely put together, and the flames darted into it with lightning swiftness. It glowed on the windward side, rising and falling in intensity like the coal of a cigar. Then a superincumbent bundle rolled down with a whisking noise; flames elongated, and bent themselves about with a quiet roar, but no crackle. Banks of smoke went off horizontally at the back like passing clouds, and behind these burned hidden pyres, illuminating the semi-transparent sheet of smoke to a lustrous yellow uniformity. Individual straws in the foreground were consumed in a creeping movement of ruddy heat, as if they were knots of red worms, and above shone imaginary fiery faces, tongues hanging from lips, glaring eyes, and other impish forms, from which at intervals sparks flew in clusters like birds from a nest.

Oak suddenly ceased from being a mere spectator by discovering the case to be more serious than he had at first imagined. A scroll of smoke blew aside and revealed to him a wheat-rick in startling juxtaposition with the decaying one, and behind this a series of others, composing the main corn produce of the farm; so that instead of the straw-stack standing, as he had imagined, comparatively isolated, there was a regular connection between it and the remaining stacks of the group.

Gabriel leapt over the hedge, and saw that he was not alone. The first man he came to was running about in a great hurry, as if his thoughts were several yards in advance of his body, which they could never drag on fast enough.

'O, man—fire, fire! A good master and a bad servant is fire, fire!—I mane a bad servant and a good master. O Mark Clark—come! And you, Billy Smallbury—and you, Maryann Money—and you, Jan Coggan, and Matthew there!' Other figures now appeared behind this shouting man and among the smoke, and Gabriel found that, far from being alone, he was in a great company—whose shadows danced merrily up and down, timed by the jigging of the flames, and not at all by their owners' movements. The assemblage—belonging to that class of society which casts its thoughts into the form of feeling, and its feelings into the form of commotion—set to work with a remarkable confusion of purpose.

'Stop the draught under the wheat-rick!' cried Gabriel to those nearest to him. The corn stood on stone staddles,[3] and between these, tongues of yellow hue from the burning straw licked and darted

---

3. Pillars supporting platforms upon which ricks stand.

playfully. If the fire once got *under* this stack, all would be lost.

'Get a tarpaulin—quick!' said Gabriel.

A rick-cloth was brought, and they hung it like a curtain across the channel. The flames immediately ceased to go under the bottom of the corn-stack, and stood up vertical.

'Stand here with a bucket of water and keep the cloth wet,' said Gabriel again.

The flames, now driven upwards, began to attack the angles of the huge roof covering the wheat-stack.

'A ladder,' cried Gabriel.

'The ladder was against the straw-rick and is burnt to a cinder,' said a spectre-like form in the smoke.

Oak seized the cut ends of the sheaves, as if he were going to engage in the operation of 'reed-drawing,'[4] and digging in his feet, and occasionally sticking in the stem of his sheep-crook, he clambered up the beetling face. He at once sat astride the very apex, and began with his crook to beat off the fiery fragments which had lodged thereon, shouting to the others to get him a bough and a ladder, and some water.

Billy Smallbury—one of the men who had been on the waggon—by this time had found a ladder, which Mark Clark ascended, holding on beside Oak upon the thatch. The smoke at this corner was stifling, and Clark, a nimble fellow, having been handed a bucket of water, bathed Oak's face and sprinkled him generally, whilst Gabriel, now with a long beech-bough in one hand, in addition to his crook in the other, kept sweeping the stack and dislodging all fiery particles.

On the ground the groups of villagers were still occupied in doing all they could to keep down the conflagration, which was not much. They were all tinged orange, and backed up by shadows of varying pattern. Round the corner of the largest stack, out of the direct rays of the fire, stood a pony, bearing a young woman on its back. By her side was another woman, on foot. These two seemed to keep at a distance from the fire, that the horse might not become restive.

'He's a shepherd,' said the woman on foot. 'Yes—he is. See how his crook shines as he beats the rick with it. And his smock-frock is burnt in two holes, I declare! A fine young shepherd he is too, ma'am.'

'Whose shepherd is he?' said the equestrian in a clear voice.

'Don't know, ma'am.'

'Don't any of the others know?'

'Nobody at all—I've asked 'em. Quite a stranger, they say.'

The young woman on the pony rode out from the shade and looked anxiously around.

'Do you think the barn is safe?' she said.

'D'ye think the barn is safe, Jan Coggan?' said the second woman,

4. A process of preparing straw to be used in thatching by combing it through a frame designed for that purpose.

passing on the question to the nearest man in that direction.

'Safe now—leastwise I think so. If this rick had gone the barn would have followed. 'Tis that bold shepherd up there that have done the most good—he sitting on the top o' rick, whizzing his great long arms about like a windmill.'

'He does work hard,' said the young woman on horseback, looking up at Gabriel through her thick woollen veil. 'I wish he was shepherd here. Don't any of you know his name?'

'Never heard the man's name in my life, or seed his form afore.'

The fire began to get worsted, and Gabriel's elevated position being no longer required of him, he made as if to descend.

'Maryann,' said the girl on horseback, 'go to him as he comes down and say that the farmer wishes to thank him for the great service he has done.'

Maryann stalked off towards the rick and met Oak at the foot of the ladder. She delivered her message.

'Where is your master the farmer?' asked Gabriel, kindling with the idea of getting employment that seemed to strike him now.

''Tisn't a master; 'tis a mistress, shepherd.'

'A woman farmer?'

'Ay, 'a b'lieve, and a rich one too!' said a bystander. 'Lately 'a came here from a distance. Took on her uncle's farm, who died suddenly. Used to measure his money in half-pint cups. They say now that she've business in every bank in Casterbridge, and thinks no more of playing pitch-and-toss sovereign than you and I do pitch-halfpenny[5]—not a bit in the world, shepherd.'

'That's she, back there upon the pony,' said Maryann; 'wi' her face a-covered up in that black cloth with holes in it.'

Oak, his features smudged, grimy, and undiscoverable from the smoke and heat, his smock-frock burnt into holes and dripping with water, the ash stem of his sheep-crook charred six inches shorter, advanced with the humility stern adversity had thrust upon him up to the slight female form in the saddle. He lifted his hat with respect, and not without gallantry: stepping close to her hanging feet he said in a hesitating voice,—

'Do you happen to want a shepherd, ma'am?'

She lifted the wool veil tied round her face, and looked all astonishment. Gabriel and his cold-hearted darling, Bathsheba Everdene, were face to face.

Bathsheba did not speak, and he mechanically repeated in an abashed and sad voice,—

'Do you want a shepherd, ma'am?'

---

5. Pitch-and-toss is a game in which players throw coins at a line, the winner being the player whose coin falls nearest the line; playing with sovereigns would be playing with gold coins four hundred and eighty times more valuable than a halfpenny.

VII

Recognition—A Timid Girl

Bathsheba withdrew into the shade. She scarcely knew whether most to be amused at the singularity of the meeting, or to be concerned at it its awkwardness. There was room for a little pity, also for a very little exultation: the former at his position, the latter at her own. Embarrassed she was not, and she remembered Gabriel's declaration of love to her at Norcombe only to think she had nearly forgotten it.

'Yes,' she murmured, putting on an air of dignity, and turning again to him with a little warmth of cheek; 'I do want a shepherd. But——'

'He's the very man, ma'am,' said one of the villagers, quietly.

Conviction breeds conviction. 'Ay, that 'a is,' said a second, decisively.

'The man, truly!' said a third, with heartiness.

'He's all there!' said number four, fervidly.

'Then will you tell him to speak to the bailiff?' said Bathsheba.

All was practical again now. A summer eve and loneliness would have been necessary to give the meeting its proper fulness of romance.

The bailiff was pointed out to Gabriel, who, checking the palpitation within his breast at discovering that this Ashtoreth of strange report was only a modification of Venus[1] the well-known and admired, retired with him to talk over the necessary preliminaries of hiring.

The fire before them wasted away. 'Men,' said Bathsheba, 'you shall take a little refreshment after this extra work. Will you come to the house?'

'We could knock in a bit and a drop[2] a good deal freer, Miss, if so be ye'd send it to Warren's Malthouse,' replied the spokesman.

Bathsheba then rode off into the darkness, and the men straggled on to the village in twos and threes—Oak and the bailiff being left by the rick alone.

'And now,' said the bailiff, finally, 'all is settled, I think, about your coming, and I am going home-along. Good-night to ye, shepherd.'

'Can you get me a lodging?' inquired Gabriel.

'That I can't, indeed,' he said, moving past Oak as a Christian edges past an offertory-plate when he does not mean to contribute. 'If you follow on the road till you come to Warren's Malthouse, where they are all gone to have their snap of victuals,[3] I daresay some of 'em will tell you of a place. Good-night to ye, shepherd.'

The bailiff who showed this nervous dread of loving his neighbour

---

1. In I Kings 11:1–5, Solomon is described as loving "many strange women," including Astoreth, the goddess of the Sidonians; Venus is the Roman goddess of love.

2. Consume a little food and drink (dialect).

3. A quick snack (dialect).

as himself, went up the hill, and Oak walked on to the village, still astonished at the rencounter with Bathsheba, glad of his nearness to her, and perplexed at the rapidity with which the unpractised girl of Norcombe had developed into the supervising and cool woman here. But some women only require an emergency to make them fit for one.

Obliged to some extent to forego dreaming in order to find the way, he reached the churchyard, and passed round it under the wall where several ancient trees grew. There was a wide margin of grass along here, and Gabriel's footsteps were deadened by its softness, even at this indurating period of the year. When abreast of a trunk which appeared to be the oldest of the old, he became aware that a figure was standing behind it. Gabriel did not pause in his walk, and in another moment he accidentally kicked a loose stone. The noise was enough to disturb the motionless stranger, who started and assumed a careless position.

It was a slim girl, rather thinly clad.

'Good-night to you,' said Gabriel heartily.

'Good-night,' said the girl to Gabriel.

The voice was unexpectedly attractrive; it was the low and dulcet note suggestive of romance; common in descriptions, rare in experience.

'I'll thank you to tell me if I'm in the way for Warren's Malthouse?' Gabriel resumed, primarily to gain the information, indirectly to get more of the music.

'Quite right. It's at the bottom of the hill. And do you know——' The girl hesitated and then went on again. 'Do you know how late they keep open the Buck's Head Inn?'[4] She seemed to be won by Gabriel's heartiness, as Gabriel had been won by her modulations.

'I don't know where the Buck's Head is, or anything about it. Do you think of going there to-night?'

'Yes——' The woman again paused. There was no necessity for any continuance of speech, and the fact that she did add more seemed to proceed from an unconscious desire to show unconcern by making a remark, which is noticeable in the ingenuous when they are acting by stealth. 'You are not a Weatherbury man?' she said timorously.

'I am not. I am the new shepherd—just arrived.'

'Only a shepherd—and you seem almost a farmer by your ways.'

'Only a shepherd,' Gabriel repeated, in a dull cadence of finality. His thoughts were directed to the past, his eyes to the feet of the girl; and for the first time he saw lying there a bundle of some sort. She may have perceived the direction of his face, for she said coaxingly,—

'You won't say anything in the parish about having seen me here, will you—at least, not for a day or two?'

'I won't if you wish me not to,' said Oak.

'Thank you, indeed,' the other replied. 'I am rather poor, and I

4. A real inn of this name stood on the road from Puddletown to Dorchester in the nineteenth century.

don't want people to know anything about me.' Then she was silent and shivered.

'You ought to have a cloak on such a cold night,' Gabriel observed. 'I would advise 'ee to get indoors.'

'O no! Would you mind going on and leaving me? I thank you much for what you have told me.'

'I will go on,' he said; adding hesitatingly,—'Since you are not very well off, perhaps you would accept this trifle from me. It is only a shilling, but it is all I have to spare.'

'Yes, I will take it,' said the stranger gratefully.

She extended her hand; Gabriel his. In feeling for each other's palm in the gloom before the money could be passed, a minute incident occurred which told much. Gabriel's fingers alighted on the young woman's wrist. It was beating with a throb of tragic intensity. He had frequently felt the same quick, hard beat in the femoral artery of his lambs when overdriven. It suggested a consumption too great of a vitality which, to judge from her figure and stature, was already too little.

'What is the matter?'

'Nothing.'

'But there is?'

'No, no, no! Let your having seen me be a secret!'

'Very well; I will. Good-night, again.'

'Good-night.'

The young girl remained motionless by the tree, and Gabriel descended into the village of Weatherbury, or Lower Longpuddle as it was sometimes called. He fancied that he had felt himself in the penumbra of a very deep sadness when touching that slight and fragile creature. But wisdom lies in moderating mere impressions, and Gabriel endeavoured to think little of this.

VIII

The Malthouse—The Chat—News

Warren's Malthouse[1] was enclosed by an old wall inwrapped with ivy, and though not much of the exterior was visible at this hour, the character and purposes of the building were clearly enough shown by its outline upon the sky. From the walls an overhanging thatched roof sloped up to a point in the centre, upon which rose a small wooden

1. In an early nineteenth-century malthouse, dampened grain, usually barley or wheat, would be spread on the floor and periodically turned with a shovel until, in from four to nine days, it was nearly ready to sprout; at this point, the maltster would roast the grain in a large fire-heated oven called a "kiln." The malt that resulted from this process could then be ground and used for such purposes as brewing beer or ale.

lantern, fitted with louvre-boards[2] on all the four sides, and from these openings a mist was dimly perceived to be escaping into the night air. There was no window in front; but a square hole in the door was glazed with a single pane, through which red, comfortable rays now stretched out upon the ivied wall in front. Voices were to be heard inside.

Oak's hand skimmed the surface of the door with fingers extended to an Elymas-the-Sorcerer pattern,[3] till he found a leathern strap, which he pulled. This lifted a wooden latch, and the door swung open.

The room inside was lighted only by the ruddy glow from the kiln mouth, which shone over the floor with the streaming horizontality of the setting sun, and threw upwards the shadows of all facial irregularities in those assembled around. The stone-flag floor was worn into a path from the doorway to the kiln, and into undulations everywhere. A curved settle of unplaned oak stretched along one side, and in a remote corner was a small bed and bedstead, the owner and frequent occupier of which was the maltster.

This aged man was now sitting opposite the fire, his frosty white hair and beard overgrowing his gnarled figure like the grey moss and lichen upon a leafless apple-tree. He wore breeches and the laced-up shoes called ankle-jacks; he kept his eyes fixed upon the fire.

Gabriel's nose was greeted by an atmosphere laden with the sweet smell of new malt. The conversation (which seemed to have been concerning the origin of the fire) immediately ceased, and every one ocularly criticized him to the degree expressed by contracting the flesh of their foreheads and looking at him with narrowed eyelids, as if he had been a light too strong for their sight. Several exclaimed meditatively, after this operation had been completed:—

'Oh, 'tis the new shepherd, 'a b'lieve.'

'We thought we heard a hand pawing about the door for the bobbin,[4] but weren't sure 'twere not a dead leaf blowed across,' said another. 'Come in, shepherd; sure ye be welcome, though we don't know yer name.'

'Gabriel Oak, that's my name, neighbours.'

The ancient maltster sitting in the midst turned at this—his turning being as the turning of a rusty crane.

'That's never Gable Oak's grandson over at Norcombe—never!' he said, as a formula expressive of surprise, which nobody was supposed to take literally.

'My father and my grandfather were old men of the name of Gabriel,' said the shepherd placidly.

2. An arrangment of sloping boards, overlapping so as to exclude rain but with spaces between so as to allow for circulation of air and for the escape of vapors from the drying malt.
3. In a groping way. In Acts 13:4–11, Elymas was stricken blind and "went about seeking someone to lead him by the hand."
4. A rounded piece of wood attached to the leathern strap that Oak pulled to lift the latch of the malthouse door.

'Thought I knowed the man's face as I seed him on the rick!—thought I did! And where be ye trading o't to now, shepherd?'

'I'm thinking of biding here,' said Mr. Oak.

'Knowed yer grandfather for years and years!' continued the maltster, the words coming forth of their own accord as if the momentum previously imparted had been sufficient.

'Ah—and did you!'

'Knowed yer grandmother.'

'And her too!'

'Likewise knowed yer father when he was a child. Why, my boy Jacob there and your father were sworn brothers—that they were sure—weren't ye, Jacob?'

'Ay, sure,' said his son, a young man about sixty-five, with a semi-bald head and one tooth in the left centre of his upper jaw, which made much of itself by standing prominent, like a milestone in a bank.[5] 'But 'twas Joe had most to do with him. However, my son William must have knowed the very man afore us—didn't ye, Billy, afore ye left Norcombe?'

'No, 'twas Andrew,' said Jacob's son Billy, a child of forty, or thereabouts, who manifested the peculiarity of possessing a cheerful soul in a gloomy body, and whose whiskers were assuming a chinchilla[6] shade here and there.

'I can mind Andrew,' said Oak, 'as being a man in the place when I was quite a child.'

'Ay—the other day I and my youngest daughter, Liddy, were over at my grandson's christening,' continued Billy. 'We were talking about this very family, and 'twas only last Purification Day[7] in this very world, when the use-money[8] is gied away to the second-best poor folk, you know, shepherd, and I can mind the day because they all had to traypse up to the vestry—yes, this very man's family.'

'Come, shepherd, and drink. 'Tis gape and swaller[9] with us—a drap of sommit,[1] but not of much account,' said the maltster, removing from the fire his eyes, which were vermillion-red and bleared by gazing into it for so many years. 'Take up the God-forgive-me, Jacob. See if 'tis warm, Jacob.'

Jacob stooped to the God-forgive-me, which was a two-handled tall mug standing in the ashes, cracked and charred with heat: it was rather furred with extraneous matter about the outside, especially in the

---

5. A stone set by the side of a road and carved to indicate the number of miles from a town; one set on an embankment would stand out prominently.

6. Chinchillas have pearly gray fur.

7. February 2, the feast of the Purification of the Virgin Mary, a feast day in the calendar of the Church of England commemorating the events described in Luke 2:22–35.

8. The money annually derived from the in-terest on invested funds donated to endow charities—in this case for a class of paupers described by Billy Smallbury as "second-best poor folk."

9. Open one's mouth wide and swallow (dialect).

1. A drop of something (dialect)—a phrasing used by the maltster in a deprecating way to refer to the cider in the "God-forgive-me."

crevices of the handles, the innermost curves of which may not have seen daylight for several years by reason of this encrustation thereon —formed of ashes accidentally wetted with cider and baked hard; but to the mind of any sensible drinker the cup was no worse for that, being incontestably clean on the inside and about the rim. It may be observed that such a class of mug is called a God-forgive-me in Weatherbury and its vicinity for uncertain reasons; probably because its size makes any given toper feel ashamed of himself when he sees its bottom in drinking it empty.

Jacob, on receiving the order to see if the liquor was warm enough, placidly dipped his forefinger into it by way of thermometer, and having pronounced it nearly of the proper degree, raised the cup and very civilly attempted to dust some of the ashes from the bottom with the skirt of his smock-frock, because Shepherd Oak was a stranger.

'A clane cup for the shepherd,' said the maltster commandingly.

'No—not at all,' said Gabriel, in a reproving tone of considerateness. 'I never fuss about dirt in its pure state, and when I know what sort it is.' Taking the mug he drank an inch or more from the depth of its contents, and duly passed it to the next man. 'I wouldn't think of giving such trouble to neighbours in washing up when there's so much work to be done in the world already,' continued Oak in a moister tone, after recovering from the stoppage of breath which is occasioned by pulls at large mugs.

'A right sensible man,' said Jacob.

'True, true; it can't be gainsaid!' observed a brisk young man—Mark Clark by name, a genial and pleasant gentleman, whom to meet anywhere in your travels was to know, to know was to drink with, and to drink with was, unfortunately, to pay for.

'And here's a mouthful of bread and bacon that mis'ess have sent, shepherd. The cider will go down better with a bit of victuals. Don't ye chaw quite close, shepherd, for I let the bacon fall in the road outside as I was bringing it along, and may be 'tis rather gritty. There, 'tis clane dirt; and we all know what that is, as you say, and you bain't a particular man we see, shepherd.'

'True, true—not at all,' said the friendly Oak.

'Don't let your teeth quite meet, and you won't feel the sandiness at all. Ah! 'tis wonderful what can be done by contrivance!'

'My own mind exactly, neighbour.'

'Ah, he's his grandfer's own grandson!—his grandfer were just such a nice unparticular man!' said the maltster.

'Drink, Henry Fray—drink,' magnanimously said Jan Coggan, a person who held Saint-Simonian notions[2] of share and share alike where liquor was concerned, as the vessel showed signs of approaching him in its gradual revolution among them.

2. Ideas about communal sharing of property such as were held by the French socialist Claude Henri, Comte de Saint-Simon (1760–1825).

Having at this moment reached the end of a wistful gaze into mid-air, Henry did not refuse. He was a man of more than middle age, with eyebrows high up in his forehead, who laid it down that the law of the world was bad, with a long-suffering look through his listeners at the world alluded to, as it presented itself to his imagination. He always signed his name 'Henery'—strenuously insisting upon that spelling, and if any passing schoolmaster ventured to remark that the second 'e' was superfluous and old-fashioned, he received the reply that 'H-e-n-e-r-y' was the name he was christened and the name he would stick to—in the tone of one to whom orthographical differences were matters which had a great deal to do with personal character.

Mr. Jan Coggan, who had passed the cup to Henery, was a crimson man with a spacious countenance and private glimmer in his eye, whose name had appeared on the marriage register of Weatherbury and neighbouring parishes as best man and chief witness in countless unions of the previous twenty years; he also very frequently filled the post of head godfather in baptisms of the subtly-jovial kind.

'Come, Mark Clark—come. Ther's plenty more in the barrel,' said Jan.

'Ay—that I will; 'tis my only doctor,' replied Mr. Clark, who, twenty years younger than Jan Coggan, revolved in the same orbit. He secreted mirth on all occasions for special discharge at popular parties.

'Why, Joseph Poorgrass, ye han't had a drop!' said Mr. Coggan to a self-conscious man in the background, thrusting the cup towards him.

'Such a modest man as he is!' said Jacob Smallbury. 'Why, ye've hardly had strength of eye enough to look in our young mis'ess's face, so I hear, Joseph?'

All looked at Joseph Poorgrass with pitying reproach.

'No—I've hardly looked at her at all,' simpered Joseph, reducing his body smaller whilst talking, apparently from a meek sense of undue prominence. 'And when I seed her, 'twas nothing but blushes with me!'

'Poor feller,' said Mr. Clark.

' 'Tis a curious nature for a man,' said Jan Coggan.

'Yes,' continued Joseph Poorgrass—his shyness, which was so painful as a defect, filling him with a mild complacency now that it was regarded as an interesting study. ' 'Twere blush, blush, blush with me every minute of the time, when she was speaking to me.'

'I believe ye, Joseph Poorgrass, for we all know ye to be a very bashful man.'

' 'Tis a' awkward gift for a man, poor soul,' said the maltster. 'And ye have suffered from it a long time, we know.'

'Ay, ever since I was a boy. Yes—mother was concerned to her heart about it—yes. But 'twas all for nought.'

'Did ye ever go into the world to try and stop it, Joseph Poorgrass?'

'Oh ay, tried all sorts o' company. They took me to Greenhill[3] Fair, and into a great gay jerry-go-nimble show,[4] where there were women-folk riding round—standing upon horses, with hardly anything on but their smocks; but it didn't cure me a morsel. And then I was put errand-man at the Women's Skittle Alley[5] at the back of the Tailor's Arms[6] in Casterbridge. 'Twas a horrible sinful situation, and a very curious place for a good man. I had to stand and look ba'dy[7] people in the face from morning till night; but 'twas no use—I was just as bad as ever after all. Blushes hev been in the family for generations. There, 'tis a happy providence that be no worse.'

'True,' said Jacob Smallbury, deepening his mind to a profounder view of the subject.' 'Tis a thought to look at, that ye might have been worse; but even as you be, 'tis a very bad afflication for 'ee, Joseph. For ye see, shepherd, though 'tis very well for a woman, dang it all, 'tis awkward for a man like him, poor feller?'

' 'Tis—'tis,' said Gabriel, recovering from a meditation. 'Yes, very awkward for the man.'

'Ay, and he's very timid, too,' observed Jan Coggan. 'Once he had been working late at Yalbury Bottom, and had had a drap of drink, and lost his way as he was coming home-along through Yalbury Wood,[8] didn't ye, Master Poorgrass?'

'No, no, no; not that story!' expostulated the modest man, forcing a laugh to bury his concern.

'——And so 'a lost himself quite,' continued Mr. Coggan, with an impassive face, implying that a true narrative, like time and tide, must run its course and would respect no man. 'And as he was coming along in the middle of the night, much afeared, and not able to find his way out of the trees nohow, 'a cried out, "Man-a-lost! man-a-lost!" A owl in a tree happened to be crying "Whoo-whoo-whoo!" as owls do, you know, shepherd' (Gabriel nodded), 'and Joseph, all in a tremble, said, "Joseph Poorgrass, of Weatherbury, sir!" '

'No, no, now—that's too much!' said the timid man, becoming a man of brazen courage all of a sudden. 'I didn't say *sir*. I'll take my oath I didn't say "Joseph Poorgrass o' Weatherbury, sir." No, no; what's right is right, and I never said sir to the bird, knowing very well that no man of a gentleman's rank would be hollering there at that time o' night. "Joseph Poorgrass of Weatherbury,"—that's every word I said, and I shouldn't ha' said that if 't hadn't been for Keeper Day's metheg-

---

3. Hardy's name for Woodbury Hill; in the nineteenth century an annual fair was held there each September.
4. A circus.
5. Skittles is a game of ninepins, similar to bowling, in which a wooden disk or ball is thrown to knock down pins set in a frame at the end of an "alley"; in the nineteenth century,

special alleys were reserved for women, and these gained a reputation for attracting disreputable customers.
6. The name of a hotel.
7. Bawdy (dialect).
8. Hardy's names for Yellowham Wood and a nearby low-lying area, or "bottom."

lin[9]. . . . There, 'twas a merciful thing it ended where it did.'

The question of which was right being tacitly waived by the company, Jan went on meditatively:—

'And he's the fearfullest man, bain't ye, Joseph? Ay, another time ye were lost by Lambing-Down Gate, weren't ye, Joseph?'

'I was,' replied Poorgrass, as if there were some conditions too serious even for modesty to remember itself under, this being one.

'Yes; that were the middle of the night, too. The gate would not open, try how he would, and knowing there was the Devil's hand in it, he kneeled down.'

'Ay,' said Joseph, acquiring confidence from the warmth of the fire, the cider, and a perception of the narrative capabilities of the experience alluded to. 'My heart died within me, that time; but I kneeled down and said the Lord's Prayer, and then the Belief[1] right through, and then the Ten Commandments, in earnest supplication. But no, the gate wouldn't open; and then I went on with Dearly Beloved Brethren, and, thinks I, this makes four, and 'tis all I know out of book, and if this don't do it nothing will, and I'm a lost man. Well, when I got to Saying After Me,[2] I rose from my knees and found the gate would open—yes, neighbours, the gate opened the same as ever.'

A meditation on the obvious inference was indulged in by all, and during its continuance each directed his vision into the ashpit, which glowed like a desert under a vertical sun, shaping their eyes long and liny, partly because of the light, partly from the depth of the subject discussed.

Gabriel broke the silence. 'What sort of a place is this to live at, and what sort of a mis'ess is she to work under?' Gabriel's bosom thrilled gently as he thus slipped under the notice of the assembly the innermost subject of his heart.

'We d' know little of her—nothing. She only showed herself a few days ago. Her uncle was took bad, and the doctor was called with his world-wide skill; but he couldn't save the man. As I take it, she's going to keep on the farm.'

'That's about the shape o't, 'a b'lieve,' said Jan Coggan. 'Ay, 'tis a very good family. I'd as soon be under 'em as under one here and there. Her uncle was a very fair sort of man. Did ye know en, shepherd—a bachelor-man?'

'Not at all.'

'I used to go to his house a-courting my first wife, Charlotte, who was his dairymaid. Well, a very good-hearted man were Farmer

9. Metheglin is a kind of mead, a liquor made from fermented honey and spices; Geoffrey Day, the keeper of Yalbury Wood, appears as a character in Hardy's novel *Under the Greenwood Tree*.

1. The Apostles' Creed.

2. "Dearly Beloved Brethren" and "Saying After Me" are the opening and closing words of the exhortation to general confession of sin that is read to the congregation as part of the Morning and Evening Prayer in the Anglican Church.

Everdene,[3] and I being a respectable young fellow was allowed to call and see her and drink as much ale as I liked, but not to carry away any—outside my skin I mane, of course.'

'Ay, ay, Jan Coggan; we know yer maning.'

'And so you see 'twas beautiful ale, and I wished to value his kindness as much as I could, and not to be so ill-mannered as to drink only a thimbleful, which would have been insulting the man's generosity——'

'True, Master Coggan, 'twould so,' corroborated Mark Clark.

'——And so I used to eat a lot of salt fish afore going, and then by the time I got there I were as dry as a lime-basket—so thorough dry that that ale would slip down—ah, 'twould slip down sweet! Happy times! heavenly times! Such lovely drunks as I used to have at that house! You can mind, Jacob? You used to go wi' me sometimes.'

'I can—I can,' said Jacob. 'That one, too, that we had at Buck's Head on a White Monday[4] was a pretty tipple.'[5]

''Twas. But for a wet[6] of the better class, that brought you no nearer to the horned man than you were afore you begun, there was none like those in Farmer Everdene's kitchen. Not a single damn allowed; no, not a bare poor one, even at the most cheerful moment when all were blindest, though the good old word of sin thrown in here and there at such times is a great relief to a merry soul.'

'True,' said the maltster. 'Nater requires her swearing at the regular times, or she's not herself; and unholy exclamations is a necessity of life.'

'But Charlotte,' continued Coggan—'not a word of the sort would Charlotte allow, nor the smallest item of taking in vain. . . . Ay, poor Charlotte, I wonder if she had the good fortune to get into Heaven when 'a died! But 'a was never much in luck's way and perhaps 'a went downwards after all, poor soul.'

'And did any of you know Miss Everdene's father and mother?' inquired the shepherd, who found some difficulty in keeping the conversation in the desired channel.

'I knew them a little,' said Jacob Smallbury; 'but they were townsfolk, and didn't live here. They've been dead for years. Father, what sort of people were mis'ess' father and mother?'

'Well,' said the maltster, 'he wasn't much to look at; but she was a lovely woman. He was fond enough of her as his sweetheart.'

'Used to kiss her scores and long-hundreds[7] o' times, so 'twas said,' observed Coggan.

---

3. The character Farmer Everdene is also briefly mentioned in chapters 17 and 31 of Hardy's *The Mayor of Casterbridge*.
4. "White Monday" is usually called Whitmonday, the Monday in the Anglican ecclesiastical year following Whitsunday, the second Sunday after Ascension Day.
5. A nice drunk (dialect).
6. Drink (dialect).
7. One hundred and twenty; six score.

'He was very proud of her, too, when they were married, as I've been told,' said the maltster.

'Ay,' said Coggan. 'He admired her so much that he used to light the candle three times a night to look at her.'

'Boundless love; I shouldn't have supposed it in the universe!' murmured Joseph Poorgrass, who habitually spoke on a large scale in his moral reflections.

'Well, to be sure,' said Gabriel.

'Oh, 'tis true enough. I knowed the man and woman both well. Levi Everdene—that was the man's name, sure. "Man," saith I in my hurry, but he were of a higher circle of life than that—'a was a gentleman-tailor really, worth scores of pounds. And he became a very celebrated bankrupt two or three times.'

'Oh, I thought he was quite a common man!' said Joseph.

'O no, no! That man failed for heaps of money; hundreds in gold and silver.'

The maltster being rather short of breath, Mr. Coggan, after absently scrutinizing a coal which had fallen among the ashes, took up the narrative, with a private twirl of his eye:—

'Well, now, you'd hardly believe it, but that man—our Miss Everdene's father—was one of the ficklest husbands alive, after a while. Understand, 'a didn't want to be fickle, but he couldn't help it. The poor feller were faithful and true enough to her in his wish, but his heart would rove, do what he would. He spoke to me in real tribulation about it once. "Coggan," he said, "I could never wish for a handsomer woman than I've got, but feeling she's ticketed as my lawful wife, I can't help my wicked heart wandering, do what I will." But at last I believe he cured it by making her take off her wedding-ring and calling her by her maiden name as they sat together after the shop was shut, and so 'a would get to fancy she was only his sweetheart, and not married to him at all. And as soon as he could thoroughly fancy he was doing wrong and committing the seventh,[8] 'a got to like her as well as ever, and they lived on a perfect picture of mutel love.'

'Well, 'twas a most ungodly remedy,' murmured Joseph Poorgrass; 'but we ought to feel deep cheerfulness that a happy Providence kept it from being any worse. You see, he might have gone the bad road and given his eyes to unlawfulness entirely—yes, gross unlawfulness, so to say it.'

'You see,' said Billy Smallbury, 'the man's will was to do right, sure enough, but his heart didn't chime in.'

'He got so much better that he was quite godly in his later years, wasn't he, Jan?' said Joseph Poorgrass. 'He got himself confirmed over again in a more serious way, and took to saying "Amen" almost as loud as the clerk, and he liked to copy comforting verses from the

---

8. Breaking the seventh commandment, "Thou shalt not commit adultery."

tombstones. He used, too, to hold the money-plate at Let Your Light so Shine,[9] and stand godfather to poor little come-by-chance[1] children; and he kept a missionary box upon his table to nab folks unawares when they called; yes, and he would box the charity-boys' ears, if they laughed in church, till they could hardly stand upright, and do other deeds of piety natural to the saintly inclined.'

'Ay, at that time he thought of nothing but high things,' added Billy Smallbury. 'One day Parson Thirdly[2] met him and said, "Good-morning, Mister Everdene; 'tis a fine day!" "Amen," said Everdene, quite absent-like, thinking only of religion when he seed a parson. Yes, he was a very Christian man.'

'Their daughter was not at all a pretty chiel[3] at that time,' said Henery Fray. 'Never should have thought she'd have growed up such a handsome body as she is.'

"Tis to be hoped her temper is as good as her face.'

'Well, yes; but the baily will have most to do with the business and ourselves. Ah!' Henery gazed into the ashpit, and smiled volumes of ironical knowledge.

'A queer Christian, like the Devil's head in a cowl,[4] as the saying is,' volunteered Mark Clark.

'He is,' said Henery, implying that irony must cease at a certain point. 'Between we two, man and man, I believe that man would as soon tell a lie Sundays as working-days—that I do so.'

'Good faith, you do talk!' said Gabriel.

'True enough,' said the man of bitter moods, looking round upon the company with the antithetic laughter that comes from a keener appreciation of the miseries of life than ordinary men are capable of. 'Ah, there's people of one sort, and people of another, but that man—bless your souls!'

Gabriel thought fit to change the subject. 'You must be a very aged man, malter, to have sons growed up so old and ancient,' he remarked.

'Father's so old that 'a can't mind his age, can ye, father?' interposed Jacob. 'And he's growed terrible crooked, too, lately,' Jacob continued, surveying his father's figure, which was rather more bowed than his own. 'Really, one may say that father there is three-double.'[5]

'Crooked folk will last a long while,' said the maltster, grimly, and not in the best humour.

'Shepherd would like to hear the pedigree of yer life, father— wouldn't ye, shepherd?'

---

9. "Let Your Light so Shine" is a quotation from Matthew 5:16, which an Anglican priest recites at the beginning of the Offertory of the Communion Service, during which the "money plate" is passed for donations.
1. Illegitimate.
2. Parson Thirdly also appears as a character in Hardy's poem "Channel Firing."
3. Child (dialect).
4. This phrase is a conjectural emendation of the unintelligible expression, "as the Devil said to the Owl," used by the natives [*Hardy's note*].
5. Bent or doubled over in three parts.

'Ay, that I should,' said Gabriel, with the heartiness of a man who had longed to hear it for several months. 'What may your age be, malter?'

The maltster cleared his throat in an exaggerated form for emphasis, and elongating his gaze to the remotest point of the ashpit, said, in the slow speech justifiable when the importance of a subject is so generally felt that any mannerism must be tolerated in getting at it, 'Well, I don't mind the year I were born in, but perhaps I can reckon up the places I've lived at, and so get it that way. I bode at Upper Longpuddle[6] across there' (nodding to the north) 'till I were eleven. I bode seven at Kingsbere' (nodding to the east) 'where I took to malting. I went therefrom to Norcombe, and malted there two-and-twenty years, and two-and-twenty years I was there turnip-hoeing and harvesting. Ah, I knowed that old place, Norcombe, years afore you were thought of, Master Oak' (Oak smiled sincere belief in the fact). Then I malted at Durnover four year, and four year turnip-hoeing; and I was fourteen times eleven months at Millpond St. Jude's' (nodding north-west-by-north). 'Old Twills wouldn't hire me for more than eleven months at a time, to keep me from being chargeable to the parish if so be I was disabled. Then I was three year at Mellstock, and I've been here one-and-thirty year come Candlemas. How much is that?'

'Hundred and seventeen,' chuckled another old gentleman, given to mental arithmetic and little conversation, who had hitherto sat unobserved in a corner.

'Well, then, that's my age,' said the maltster emphatically.

'O no, father!' said Jacob. 'Your turnip-hoeing were in the summer and your malting in the winter of the same years, and ye don't ought to count both halves, father.'

'Chok' it all! I lived through the summers, didn't I? That's my question. I suppose ye'll say next I be no age at all to speak of?'

'Sure we shan't,' said Gabriel soothingly.

'Ye be a very old aged person, malter,' attested Jan Coggan, also soothingly. 'We all know that, and ye must have a wonderful talented constitution to be able to live so long, mustn't he, neighbours?'

'True, true; ye must, malter, wonderful;' said the meeting unanimously.

The maltster, being now pacified, was even generous enough to voluntarily disparage in a slight degree the virtue of having lived a great many years, by mentioning that the cup they were drinking out of was three years older than he.

While the cup was being examined, the end of Gabriel Oak's flute became visible over his smock-frock pocket, and Henery Fray exclaimed, 'Surely, shepherd, I seed you blowing into a great flute by now at Casterbridge?'

---

6. Hardy's name for a town slightly north of Puddletown—possibly Piddletrenthide.

'You did,' said Gabriel, blushing faintly. 'I've been in great trouble, neighbours, and was driven to it. I used not to be so poor as I be now.'

'Never mind, heart!' said Mark Clark. 'You should take it careless-like, shepherd, and your time will come. But we could thank ye for a tune, if ye bain't too tired?'

'Neither drum nor trumpet have I heard since Christmas,' said Jan Coggan. 'Come, raise a tune, Master Oak!'

'That I will,' said Gabriel, pulling out his flute and putting it together. 'A poor tool, neighbours; but such as I can do ye shall have and welcome.'

Oak then struck up 'Jockey to the Fair,' and played that sparkling melody three times through, accenting the notes in the third round in a most artistic and lively manner by bending his body in small jerks and tapping with his foot to beat time.

'He can blow the flute very well—that 'a can,' said a young married man, who having no individuality worth mentioning was known as 'Susan Tall's husband.' He continued, 'I'd as lief as not[7] be able to blow into a flute as well as that.'

'He's a clever man, and 'tis a true comfort for us to have such a shepherd,' murmured Joseph Poorgrass, in a soft cadence. 'We ought to feel full o' thanksgiving that he's not a player of ba'dy songs instead of these merry tunes; for 'twould have been just as easy for God to have made the shepherd a loose low man—a man of iniquity, so to speak it—as what he is. Yes, for our wives' and daughters' sakes we should feel real thanksgiving.'

'True, true,—real thanksgiving!' dashed in Mark Clark conclusively, not feeling it to be of any consequence to his opinion that he had only heard about a word and three-quarters of what Joseph had said.

'Yes,' added Joseph, beginning to feel like a man in the Bible; 'for evil do thrive so in these times that ye may be as much deceived in the clanest shaved and whitest shirted man as in the raggedest tramp upon the turnpike, if I may term it so.'

'Ay, I can mind yer face now, shepherd,' said Henery Fray, criticizing Gabriel with misty eyes as he entered upon his second tune. 'Yes—now I see 'ee blowing into the flute I know 'ee to be the same man I see play at Casterbridge, for yer mouth were scrimped up and yer eyes a-staring out like a strangled man's—just as they be now.'

' 'Tis a pity that playing the flute should make a man look such a scarecrow,' observed Mr. Mark Clark, with additional criticism of Gabriel's countenance, the latter person jerking out, with the ghastly grimace required by the instrument, the chorus of 'Dame Durden':—[8]

'Twas Moll' and Bet', and Doll' and Kate',
And Dor'-othy Drag'-gle Tail'.

---

7. An archaic phrase that has about the sense of modern English "I'd rather."

8. A folk song about a woman who had five serving men and five maids.

'I hope you don't mind that young man's bad manners in naming your features?' whispered Joseph to Gabriel.

'Not at all,' said Mr. Oak.

'For by nature ye be a very handsome man, shepherd,' continued Joseph Poorgrass with winning suavity.

'Ay, that ye be, shepherd,' said the company.

'Thank you very much,' said Oak, in the modest tone good manners demanded, thinking, however, that he would never let Bathsheba see him playing the flute; in this resolve showing a discretion equal to that related of its sagacious inventress, the devine Minerva[9] herself.

'Ah, when I and my wife were married at Norcombe Church,' said the old maltster, not pleased at finding himself left out of the subject, 'we were called the handsomest couple in the neighbourhood— everybody said so.'

'Danged if ye bain't altered now, malter,' said a voice with the vigour natural to the enunciation of a remarkably evident truism. It came from the old man in the background, whose offensiveness and spiteful ways were barely atoned for by the occasional chuckle he contributed to general laughs.

'O no, no,' said Gabriel.

'Don't ye play no more, shepherd,' said Susan Tall's husband, the young married man who had spoken once before. 'I must be moving, and when there's tunes going on I seem as if hung in wires. If I thought after I'd left that music was still playing, and I not there, I should be quite melancholy-like.'

'What's yer hurry then. Laban?' inquired Coggan. 'You used to bide as late as the latest.'

'Well, ye see, neighbours, I was lately married to a woman, and she's my vocation now, and so ye see——' The young man halted lamely.

'New lords new laws, as the saying is, I suppose,' remarked Coggan.

'Ay, 'a b'lieve—ha, ha!' said Susan Tall's husband, in a tone intended to imply his habitual reception of jokes without minding them at all. The young man then wished them good-night and withdrew.

Henery Fray was the first to follow. Then Gabriel arose and went off with Jan Coggan, who had offered him a lodging. A few minutes later, when the remaining ones were on their legs and about to depart, Fray came back again in a hurry. Flourishing his finger ominously he threw a gaze teeming with tidings just where his eye alighted by accident, which happened to be in Joseph Poorgrass's face.

'O—what's the matter, what's the matter, Henery?' said Joseph, starting back.

9. In classical mythology, Minerva, the goddess of wisdom and of the arts, was said to have invented the flute but then threw it away because blowing it contorted her features.

'What's a-brewing, Henery?' asked Jacob and Mark Clark.

'Baily Pennyways—Baily Pennyways—I said so; yes, I said so!'

'What, found out stealing anything?'

'Stealing it is. The news is, that after Miss Everdene got home she went out again to see all was safe, as she usually do, and coming in found Baily Pennyways creeping down the granary steps with half a bushel of barley. She fleed[1] at him like a cat—never such a tomboy as she is—of course I speak with closed doors?'[2]

'You do—you do, Henery.'

'She fleed at him, and, to cut a long story short, he owned to having carried off five sack altogether, upon her promising not to persecute him. Well, he's turned out neck and crop,[3] and my question is, who's going to be baily now?'

The question was such a profound one that Henery was obliged to drink there and then from the large cup till the bottom was distinctly visible inside. Before he had replaced it on the table, in came the young man, Susan Tall's husband, in a still greater hurry.

'Have ye heard the news that's all over parish?'

'About Baily Pennyways?'

'But besides that?'

'No—not a morsel of it!' they replied, looking into the very midst of Laban Tall as if to meet his words half-way down his throat.

'What a night of horrors!' murmured Joseph Poorgrass, waving his hands spasmodically. 'I've had the news-bell[4] ringing in my left ear quite bad enough for a murder, and I've seen a magpie all alone!'[5]

'Fanny Robin—Miss Everdene's youngest servant—can't be found. They've been wanting to lock up the door these two hours, but she isn't come in. And they don't know what to do about going to bed for fear of locking her out. They wouldn't be so concerned if she hadn't been noticed in such low spirits these last few days, and Maryann d' think the beginning of a crowner's[6] inquest has happened to the poor girl.'

'O—'tis burned—'tis burned!' came from Joseph Poorgrass's dry lips.

'No—'tis drowned!' said Tall.

'Or 'tis her father's razor!' suggested Billy Smallbury with a vivid sense of detail.

'Well—Miss Everdene wants to speak to one or two of us before we go to bed. What with this trouble about the baily, and now about the girl, mis'ess is almost wild.'

They all hastened up the lane to the farmhouse, excepting the old maltster, whom neither news, fire, rain, nor thunder could draw from

---

1. Flew (dialect).
2. Speak confidentially.
3. Altogether, bodily (dialect).
4. A ringing in the ears superstitiously interpreted to foreshadow the coming of bad news

(dialect).
5. In folk tradition, to see a single magpie is a portent of coming sorrow.
6. Coroner's (dialect).

his hole. There, as the others' footsteps died away, he sat down again, and continued gazing as usual into the furnace with his red, bleared eyes.

From the bedroom window above their heads Bathsheba's head and shoulders, robed in mystic white, were dimly seen extended into the air.

'Are any of my men among you?' she said anxiously.

'Yes, ma'am, several,' said Susan Tall's husband.

'To-morrow morning I wish two or three of you to make inquiries in the villages round if they have seen such a person as Fanny Robin. Do it quietly; there is no reason for alarm as yet. She must have left whilst we were all at the fire.'

'I beg yer pardon, but had she any young man courting her in the parish, ma'am?' asked Jacob Smallbury.

'I don't know,' said Bathsheba.

'I've never heard of any such thing, ma'am,' said two or three.

'It is hardly likely, either,' continued Bathsheba. 'For any lover of hers might have come to the house if he had been a respectable lad. The most mysterious matter connected with her absence—indeed, the only thing which gives me serious alarm—is that she was seen to go out of the house by Maryann with only her indoor working gown on—not even a bonnet.'

'And you mean, ma'am, excusing my words, that a young woman would hardly go to see her young man without dressing up,' said Jacob, turning his mental vision upon past experiences. 'That's true—she would not, ma'am.'

'She had, I think, a bundle, though I couldn't see very well,' said a female voice from another window, which seemed that of Maryann. 'But she had no young man about here. Hers lives in Casterbridge, and I believe he's a soldier.'

'Do you know his name?' Bathsheba said.

'No, mistress; she was very close about it.'

'Perhaps I might be able to find out if I went to Casterbridge barracks,' said William Smallbury.

'Very well; if she doesn't return to-morrow, mind you go there and try to discover which man it is, and see him. I feel more responsible than I should if she had had any friends or relations alive. I do hope she has come to no harm through a man of that kind. . . . And then there's this disgraceful affair of the bailiff—but I can't speak of him now.'

Bathsheba had so many reasons for uneasiness that it seemed she did not think it worth while to dwell upon any particular one. 'Do as I told you, then,' she said in conclusion, closing the casement.

'Ay, ay, mistress; we will,' they replied, and moved away.

That night at Coggan's Gabriel Oak, beneath the screen of closed eyelids, was busy with fancies, and full of movement, like a river flowing rapidly under its ice. Night had always been the time at which he saw Bathsheba most vividly, and through the slow hours of shadow he tenderly regarded her image now. It is rarely that the pleasures of the imagination will compensate for the pain of sleeplessness, but they possibly did with Oak to-night, for the delight of merely seeing her effaced for the time his perception of the great difference between seeing and possessing.

He also thought of plans for fetching his few utensils and books from Norcombe. *The Young Man's Best Companion, The Farrier's Sure Guide, The Veterinary Surgeon, Paradise Lost, The Pilgrim's Progress, Robinson Crusoe*, Ash's *Dictionary*, and Walkingame's *Arithmetic*, constituted his library;[7] and though a limited series, it was one from which he had acquired more sound information by diligent perusal than many a man of opportunities has done from a furlong of laden shelves.

IX

The Homestead—A Visitor—Half-Confidences

By daylight, the bower of Oak's new-found mistress, Bathsheba Everdene, presented itself as a hoary building, of the early stage of Classic Renaissance[1] as regards its architecture, and of a proportion which told at a glance that, as is so frequently the case, it had once been the manorial hall upon a small estate around it, now altogether effaced as a distinct property, and merged in the vast tract of a non-resident landlord, which comprised several such modest demesnes.

Fluted pilasters,[2] worked from the solid stone, decorated its front, and above the roof the chimneys were panelled or columnar, some coped gables with finials[3] and like features still retaining traces of their Gothic extraction. Soft brown mosses, like faded velveteen, formed cushions upon the stone tiling, and tufts of the houseleek or sengreen[4] sprouted from the eaves of the low surrounding buildings. A gravel walk leading from the door to the road in front was encrusted at the sides with more moss—here it was a silver-green variety, the nut-brown of the gravel being visible to the width of only a foot or two in the centre. This circumstance, and the generally sleepy air of the whole prospect here, together with the animated and contrasting state

7. Oak's library not only includes older literary classics like Milton's *Paradise Lost* (1667), but also relatively more up-to-date books on animal care as John Hinds's *The Veterinary Surgeon* (1827).

1. An architectural style characteristic of the late sixteenth century, combining features of Gothic with those of the Classical Revival style.

2. Shallow rectangular projections from a wall, ornamented with vertical grooves and characteristic of Classical Revival architecture.

3. Gables with protective stone cappings, ornamented with small vertical projections, characteristic of Gothic architecture.

4. An herb with pink flowers often found growing on roofs and walls of houses.

of the reverse façade, suggested to the imagination that on the adaptation of the building for farming purposes the vital principle of the house had turned round inside its body to face the other way. Reversals of this kind, strange deformities, tremendous paralyses, are often seen to be inflicted by trade upon edifices—either individual or in the aggregate as streets and towns—which were originally planned for pleasure alone.

Lively voices were heard this morning in the upper rooms, the main staircase to which was of hard oak, the balusters, heavy as bed-posts, being turned and moulded in the quaint fashion of their century, the handrail as stout as a parapet-top, and the stairs themselves continually twisting round like a person trying to look over his shoulder. Going up, the floors above were found to have a very irregular surface, rising to ridges, sinking into valleys; and being just then uncarpeted, the face of the boards was seen to be eaten into innumerable vermiculations.[5] Every window replied by a clang to the opening and shutting of every door, a tremble followed every bustling movement, and a creak accompanied a walker about the house, like a spirit, wherever he went.

In the room from which the conversation proceeded Bathsheba and her servant-companion, Liddy Smallbury, were to be discovered sitting upon the floor, and sorting a complication of papers, books, bottles, and rubbish spread out thereon—remnants from the household stores of the late occupier. Liddy, the maltster's great-granddaughter, was about Bathsheba's equal in age, and her face was a prominent advertisement of the light-hearted English country girl. The beauty her features might have lacked in form was amply made up for by perfection of hue, which at this winter-time was the softened ruddiness on a surface of high rotundity that we meet with in a Terburg or a Gerard Douw;[6] and, like the presentations of those great colourists, it was a face which kept well back from the boundary between comeliness and the ideal. Though elastic in nature she was less daring than Bathsheba, and occasionally showed some earnestness, which consisted half of genuine feeling, and half of mannerliness superadded by way of duty.

Through a partly-opened door the noise of a scrubbing-brush led up to the charwoman, Maryann Money, a person who for a face had a circular disc, furrowed less by age than by long gazes of perplexity at distant objects. To think of her was to get good-humoured; to speak of her was to raise the image of a dried Normandy pippin.[7]

'Stop your scrubbing a moment,' said Bathsheba through the door to her. 'I hear something.'

Maryann suspended the brush.

5. Wormlike grooves and ridges.
6. Gerard Terburg (1617–81) and Gerard Douw (1613–75), Dutch painters noted for their handling of color.
7. A dull yellow apple.

The tramp of a horse was apparent, approaching the front of the building. The paces slackened, turned in at the wicket, and, what was most unusual, came up the mossy path close to the door. The door was tapped with the end of a crop or stick.

'What impertinence!' said Liddy, in a low voice. 'To ride up the footpath like that! Why didn't he stop at the gate? Lord! 'tis a gentleman! I see the top of his hat.'

'Be quiet!' said Bathsheba.

The further expression of Liddy's concern was continued by aspect instead of narrative.

'Why doesn't Mrs. Coggan go to the door?" Bathsheba continued.

Rat-tat-tat-tat resounded more decisively from Bathsheba's oak.

'Maryann, you go!' said she, fluttering under the onset of a crowd of romantic possibilities.

'O ma'am—see, here's a mess!'

The argument was unanswerable after a glance at Maryann.

'Liddy—you must,' said Bathsheba.

Liddy held up her hands and arms, coated with dust from the rubbish they were sorting, and looked imploringly at her mistress.

'There—Mrs. Coggan is going!' said Bathsheba, exhaling her relief in the form of a long breath which had lain in her bosom a minute or more.

The door opened, and a deep voice said—

'Is Miss Everdene at home?'

'I'll see, sir,' said Mrs. Coggan, and in a minute appeared in the room.

'Dear, what a thirtover[8] place this world is!' continued Mrs. Coggan (a wholesome-looking lady who had a voice for each class of remark according to the emotion involved; who could toss a pancake or twirl a mop with the accuracy of pure mathematics, and who at this moment showed hands shaggy with fragments of dough and arms encrusted with flour). 'I am never up to my elbows, Miss, in making a pudding but one of two things do happen—either my nose must needs begin tickling, and I can't live without scratching it, or somebody knocks at the door. Here's Mr. Boldwood[9] wanting to see you, Miss Everdene.'

A woman's dress being a part of her countenance, and any disorder in the one being of the same nature with a malformation or wound in the other, Bathsheba said at once—

'I can't see him in this state. Whatever shall I do?'

Not-at-homes were hardly naturalized in Weatherbury farmhouses, so Liddy suggested—'Say you're a fright with dust, and can't come down.'

'Yes—that sounds very well,' said Mrs. Coggan critically.

'Say I can't see him—that will do.'

---

8. Contrary, unruly.
9. Farmer Boldwood is a character also briefly

mentioned in chapter 31 of Hardy's *The Mayor of Casterbridge.*

Mrs. Coggan went downstairs, and returned the answer as requested, adding, however, on her own responsibility, 'Miss is dusting bottles, sir, and is quite a object—that's why 'tis.'

'Oh, very well,' said the deep voice indifferently. 'All I wanted to ask was, if anything had been heard of Fanny Robin?'

'Nothing, sir—but we may know to-night. William Smallbury is gone to Casterbridge, where her young man lives, as is supposed, and the other men be inquiring about everywhere.'

The horse's tramp then recommenced and retreated, and the door closed.

'Who is Mr. Boldwood?' said Bathsheba.

'A gentleman-farmer at Little Weatherbury.'[1]

'Married?'

'No, miss.'

'How old is he?'

'Forty, I should say—very handsome—rather stern-looking—and rich.'

'What a bother this dusting is! I am always in some unfortunate plight or other,' Bathsheba said complainingly. 'Why should he inquire about Fanny?'

'Oh, because, as she had no friends in her childhood, he took her and put her to school, and got her her place here under your uncle. He's a very kind man that way, but Lord—there!'

'What?'

'Never was such a hopeless man for a woman! He's been courted by sixes and sevens—all the girls, gentle and simple, for miles round, have tried him. Jane Perkins worked at him for two months like a slave, and the two Miss Taylors spent a year upon him, and he cost Farmer Ives's daughter nights of tears and twenty pounds' worth of new clothes; but Lord—the money might as well have been thrown out of the window.'

A little boy came up at this moment and looked in upon them. This child was one of the Coggans, who, with the Smallburys, were as common among the families of this district as the Avons and Derwents among our rivers. He always had a loosened tooth or a cut finger to show to particular friends, which he did with an air of being thereby elevated above the common herd of afflictionless humanity—to which exhibition people were expected to say 'Poor child!' with a dash of congratulation as well as pity.

'I've got a pen-nee!' said Master Coggan in a scanning measure.[2]

'Well—who gave it you, Teddy?' said Liddy.

'Mis-terr Bold-wood! He gave it to me for opening the gate.'

'What did he say?'

'He said, "Where are you going, my little man?" and I said, "To

1. Hardy's name for Druce Farm near   2. With exaggerated stress on the syllables.
Puddletown.

Miss Everdene's, please"; and he said, "She is a staid woman, isn't
she, my little man?" and I said, "Yes." '

'You naughty child! What did you say that for?'

' 'Cause he gave me the penny!'

'What a pucker[3] everything is in!' said Bathsheba discontentedly,
when the child had gone. 'Get away, Maryann, or go on with your
scrubbing, or do something! You ought to be married by this time, and
not here troubling me!'

'Ay, mistress—so I did. But what between the poor men I won't
have, and the rich men who won't have me, I stand as a pelican in the
wilderness!'[4]

'Did anybody ever want to marry you, miss?' Liddy ventured to ask
when they were again alone. 'Lots of 'em, I daresay?'

Bathsheba paused, as if about to refuse a reply, but the temptation to
say yes, since it really was in her power, was irresistible by aspiring
virginity, in spite of her spleen at having been published as old.

'A man wanted to once,' she said, in a highly experienced tone, and
the image of Gabriel Oak, as the farmer, rose before her.

'How nice it must seem!' said Liddy, with the fixed features of
mental realization. 'And you wouldn't have him?'

'He wasn't quite good enough for me.'

'How sweet to be able to disdain, when most of us are glad to say,
"Thank you!" I seem I hear it.[5] "No, sir—I'm your better," or "Kiss
my foot, sir; my face is for mouths of consequence." And did you love
him, miss?'

'Oh, no. But I rather liked him.'

'Do you now?'

'Of course not—what footsteps are those I hear?'

Liddy looked from a back window into the courtyard behind, which
was not getting low-toned and dim with the earliest films of night. A
crooked file of men was approaching the back door. The whole string
of trailing individuals advanced in the completest balance of intention, like the remarkable creatures known as Chain Salpae,[6] which,
distinctly organized in other respects, have one will common to a
whole family. Some were, as usual, in snow-white smock-frocks of
Russia duck,[7] and some in whitey-brown ones of drabbet[8]—marked
on the wrists, breasts, backs, and sleeves with honeycomb-work. Two
or three women in pattens[9] brought up the rear.

---

3. A state of confusion (archaic).

4. An allusion to Psalms 102:6: "I am like a
pelican in the wilderness."

5. Liddy's odd phrasing was probably intended
as rustic dialect for "I seem to hear it," but
Hardy usually does not have Liddy speak in
dialect, and the sentence may have resulted
from a confusion of syntax on Hardy's part.

6. Marine animals whose embryos form groups
linked to one another in chainlike formations.

7. A plain-woven heavy cotton fabric used to
make tents, sails, and work clothing.

8. A coarse linen fabric used to make smock-
frocks and similar work garments.

9. Devices usually consisting of an oval ring
supported by metal rods projecting from a
wooden sole that could be strapped to the
wearer's shoes to raise them above mud or water.

'The Philistines[1] be upon us,' said Liddy, making her nose white against the glass.

'Oh, very well. Maryann, go down and keep them in the kitchen till I am dressed, and then show them in to me in the hall.'

X

Mistress and Men

Half-an-hour later Bathsheba, in finished dress, and followed by Liddy, entered the upper end of the old hall to find that her men had all deposited themselves on a long form and a settle at the lower extremity. She sat down at a table and opened the time-book, pen in her hand, with a canvas money-bag beside her. From this she poured a small heap of coin. Liddy chose a position at her elbow and began to sew, sometimes pausing and looking round, or, with the air of a privileged person, taking up one of the half-sovereigns lying before her, and surveying it merely as a work of art, while strictly preventing her countenance from expressing any wish to possess it as money.

'Now, before I begin, men,' said Bathsheba, 'I have two matters to speak of. The first is that the bailiff is dismissed for thieving, and that I have formed a resolution to have no bailiff at all, but to manage everything with my own head and hands.'

The men breathed an audible breath of amazement.

'The next matter is, have you heard anything of Fanny?'

'Nothing, ma'am.'

'Have you done anything?'

'I met Farmer Boldwood,' said Jacob Smallbury, 'and I went with him and two of his men, and dragged Newmill Pond, but we found nothing.'

'And the new shepherd have been to Buck's Head, by Yalbury, thinking she had gone there, but nobody had seed her,' said Laban Tall.

'Hasn't William Smallbury been to Casterbridge?'

'Yes, ma'am, but he's not yet come home. He promised to be back by six.'

'It wants a quarter to six at present,' said Bathsheba, looking at her watch. 'I daresay he'll be in directly. Well, now then'—she looked into the book—'Joseph Poorgrass, are you there?'

'Yes, sir—ma'am I mane,' said the person addressed. 'I be the personal name of Poorgrass.'

'And what are you?'

---

1. The biblical tribe that repeatedly harassed the people of Israel; Liddy's phrase echoes Judges 16:9.

'Nothing in my own eye. In the eye of other people—well, I don't say it; though public thought will out.'

'What do you do on the farm?'

'I do do carting things all the year, and in seed time I shoots the rooks and sparrows, and helps at pig-killing, sir.'

'How much to you?'

'Please nine and ninepence and a good halfpenny where 'twas a bad one, sir—ma'am I mane.'

'Quite correct. Now here are ten shillings in addition as a small present, as I am a new comer.'

Bathsheba blushed slightly at the sense of being generous in public, and Henery Fray, who had drawn up towards her chair, lifted his eyebrows and fingers to express amazement on a small scale.

'How much do I owe you—that man in the corner—what's your name?' continued Bathsheba.

'Matthew Moon, ma'am,' said a singular framework of clothes with nothing of any consequence inside them, which advanced with the toes in no definite direction forwards, but turned in or out as they chanced to swing.

'Matthew Mark, did you say?—speak out—I shall not hurt you,' inquired the young farmer kindly.

'Matthew Moon, mem,' said Henery Fray, correctly, from behind her chair, to which point he had edged himself.

'Matthew Moon,' murmured Bathsheba, turning her bright eyes to the book. 'Ten and twopence halfpenny is the sum put down to you, I see?'

'Yes mis'ess,' said Matthew, as the rustle of wind among dead leaves.

'Here it is, and ten shillings. Now the next—Andrew Randle, you are a new man, I hear. How came you to leave your last farm?'

'P-p-p-p-p-pl-pl-pl-pl-l-l-l-l-l-ease ma'am, p-p-p-p-pl-pl-pl-pl-please, ma'am-please'm-please'm——'

' 'A's a stammering man, mem,' said Henery Fray in an undertone, 'and they turned him away because the only time he ever did speak plain he said his soul was his own, and other iniquities, to the squire. 'A can cuss, mem, as well as you or I, but 'a can't speak a common speech to save his life.'

'Andrew Randle, here's yours—finish thanking me in a day or two. Temperance Miller—oh, here's another, Soberness—both women, I suppose?'

'Yes'm. Here we be, 'a b'lieve,' was echoed in shrill unison.

'What have you been doing?'

'Tending thrashing-machine, and wimbling haybonds,[1] and saying "Hoosh!" to the cocks and hens when they go upon your seeds, and

---

1. Twisting hay into cords with an augerlike device called a wimble.

planting Early Flourballs and Thompson's Wonderfuls[2] with a dibble.'[3]

'Yes—I see. Are they satisfactory women?' she inquired softly of Henery Fray.

'O mem—don't ask me! Yielding women—as scarlet a pair as ever was!' groaned Henery under his breath.

'Sit down.'

'Who, mem?'

'Sit down.'

Joseph Poorgrass, in the background, twitched and his lips became dry with fear of some terrible consequences, as he saw Bathsheba summarily speaking, and Henery slinking off to a corner.

'Now the next. Laban Tall, you'll stay on working for me?'

'For you or anybody that pays me well, ma'am,' replied the young married man.

'True—the man must live!' said a woman in the back quarter, who had just entered with clicking pattens.

'What woman is that?' Bathsheba asked.

'I be his lawful wife!' continued the voice with greater prominence of manner and tone. This lady called herself five-and-twenty, looked thirty, passed as thirty-five, and was forty. She was a woman who never, like some newly married, showed conjugal tenderness in public, perhaps because she had none to show.

'Oh, you are,' said Bathsheba. 'Well, Laban, will you stay on?'

'Yes, he'll stay, ma'am!' said again the shrill tongue of Laban's lawful wife.

'Well, he can speak for himself, I suppose.'

'O Lord, not he, ma'am! A simple tool. Well enough, but a poor gawkhammer[4] mortal,' the wife replied.

'Heh-heh-heh!' laughed the married man, with a hideous effort of appreciation, for he was as irrepressibly good-humoured under ghastly snubs as a parliamentary candidate on the hustings.[5]

The names remaining were called in the same manner.

'Now I think I have done with you,' said Bathsheba, closing the book and shaking back a stray twine of hair. 'Has William Smallbury returned?'

'No, ma'am.'

'The new shepherd will want a man under him,' suggested Henery Fray, trying to make himself official again by a sideway approach towards her chair.

'Oh—he will. Who can he have?'

'Young Cain Ball is a very good lad,' Henery said, and Shepherd

2. Potato varieties.
3. A pointed stick used to make holes for planting.
4. Brainless or empty-headed (dialect).

5. A temporary platform upon which candidates for Parliament or other public office stood to address their constituents.

Oak don't mind his youth?' he added, turning with an apologetic smile to the shepherd, who had just appeared on the scene, and was now leaning against the doorpost with his arms folded.

'No, I don't mind that,' said Gabriel.

'How did Cain come by such a name?' asked Bathsheba.

'Oh you see, mem, his pore mother, not being a Scripture-read woman, made a mistake at his christening, thinking 'twas Abel killed Cain, and called en Cain, meaning Abel all the time. The parson put it right, but 'twas too late, for the name could never be got rid of in the parish. 'Tis very unfortunate for the boy.'

'It is rather unfortunate.'

'Yes. However, we soften it down as much as we can, and call him Cainy. Ah, pore widow-woman! She cried her heart out about it almost. She was brought up by a very heathen father and mother, who never sent her to church or school, and it shows how the sins of the parents are visited upon the children, mem.'

Mr. Fray here drew up his features to the mild degree of melancholy required when the persons involved in the given misfortune do not belong to your own family.

'Very well then, Cainy Ball to be under-shepherd. And you quite understand your duties?—you I mean, Gabriel Oak?'

'Quite well, I thank you, Miss Everdene,' said Shepherd Oak from the doorpost. 'If I don't, I'll inquire.' Gabriel was rather staggered by the remarkable coolness of her manner. Certainly nobody without previous information would have dreamt that Oak and the handsome woman before whom he stood had ever been other than strangers. But perhaps her air was the inevitable result of the social rise which had advanced her from a cottage to a large house and fields. The case is not unexampled in high places. When, in the writings of the later poets, Jove and his family are found to have moved from their cramped quarters on the peak of Olympus into the wide sky above it, their words show a proportionate increase of arrogance and reserve.[6]

Footsteps were heard in the passage, combining in their character the qualities both of weight and measure, rather at the expense of velocity.

(All.) 'Here's Billy Smallbury come from Casterbridge.'

'And what's the news?' said Bathsheba, as William, after marching to the middle of the hall, took a handkerchief from his hat and wiped his forehead from its centre to its remoter boundaries.

'I should have been sooner, miss,' he said, 'if it hadn't been for the weather.' He then stamped with each foot severely, and on looking down his boots were perceived to be clogged with snow.

---

6. In much classical Greek poetry—e.g., that of Homer or Euripides—the gods inhabit Mount Olympus, the highest mountain in Greece; but by the third century B.C. and after, poets no longer took such myths seriously and tended to image divinities as inhabiting the heavens.

· 'Come at last, is it?' said Henery.

'Well, what about Fanny?' said Bathsheba.

'Well, ma'am, in round numbers, she's run away with the soldiers,' said William.

'No; not a steady girl like Fanny!'

'I'll tell ye all particulars. When I got to Casterbridge Barracks, they said, "The Eleventh Dragoon Guards be gone away, and new troops have come." The Eleventh left last week for Melchester and onwards. The Route[7] came from Government like a thief in the night,[8] as is his nature to, and afore the Eleventh knew it almost, they were on the march. They passed near here.'

Gabriel had listened with interest. 'I saw them go,' he said.

'Yes,' continued William, 'they pranced down the street playing "The Girl I Left Behind Me," so 'tis said, in glorious notes of triumph. Every looker-on's inside shook with the blows of the great drum to his deepest vitals, and there was not a dry eye throughout the town among the public-house people and the nameless women!'

'But they're not gone to any war?'

'No, ma'am; but they be gone to take the places of them who may, which is very close connected. And so I said to myself, Fanny's young man was one of the regiment, and she's gone after him. There, ma'am, that's it in black and white.'

'Did you find out his name?'

'No; nobody knew it. I believe he was higher in rank than a private.'

Gabriel remained musing and said nothing, for he was in doubt.

'Well, we are not likely to know more to-night, at any rate,' said Bathsheba. 'But one of you had better run across to Farmer Boldwood's and tell him that much.'

She then rose; but before retiring, addressed a few words to them with a pretty dignity, to which her mourning dress added a soberness that was hardly to be found in the words themselves:

'Now mind, you have a mistress instead of a master. I don't yet know my powers or my talents in farming; but I shall do my best, and if you serve me well, so shall I serve you. Don't any unfair ones among you (if there are any such, but I hope not) suppose that because I'm a woman I don't understand the difference between bad goings-on and good.'

(All.) 'No'm!'

(Liddy.) 'Excellent well said.'

'I shall be up before you are awake; I shall be afield before you are up; and I shall have breakfasted before you are afield. In short, I shall astonish you all.'

7. A military order to march to a particular destination by a specified route.

8. An allusion to 1 Thessalonians 5:2 ("For yourselves know perfectly that the day of the Lord so cometh as a thief in the night"), by which Billy Smallbury compares the British Government to Jesus with unconscious comic effect.

(All.) 'Yes'm!'
'And so good-night.'
(All.) 'Good-night, ma'am.'

Then this small thesmothete[9] stepped from the table, and surged out of the hall, her black silk dress licking up a few straws and dragging them along with a scratching noise upon the floor. Liddy, elevating her feelings to the occasion from a sense of grandeur, floated off behind Bathsheba with a milder dignity not entirely free from travesty, and the door was closed.

XI

Outside the Barracks—Snow—A Meeting

For dreariness nothing could surpass a prospect in the outskirts of a certain town and military station, many miles north of Weatherbury, at a later hour on this same snowy evening—if that may be called a prospect of which the chief constituent was darkness.

It was a night when sorrow may come to the brightest without causing any great sense of incongruity: when, with impressible persons, love becomes solicitousness, hope sinks to misgiving, and faith to hope: when the exercise of memory does not stir feelings of regret at opportunities for ambition that have been passed by, and anticipation does not prompt to enterprise.

The scene was a public path, bordered on the left hand by a river, behind which rose a high wall. On the right was a tract of land, partly meadow and partly moor, reaching, at its remote verge, to a wide undulating upland.

The changes of the seasons are less obtrusive on spots of this kind than amid woodland scenery. Still, to a close observer, they are just as perceptible; the difference is that their media of manifestation are less trite and familiar than such well-known ones as the bursting of the buds or the fall of the leaf. Many are not so stealthy and gradual as we may be apt to imagine in considering the general torpidity of a moor or waste. Winter, in coming to the country hereabout, advanced in well-marked stages, wherein might have been successively observed the retreat of the snakes, the transformation of the ferns, the filling of the pools, a rising of fogs, the embrowning by frost, the collapse of the fungi, and an obliteration by snow.

This climax of the series had been reached to-night on the aforesaid moor, and for the first time in the season its irregularities were forms without features; suggestive of anything, proclaiming nothing, and without more character than that of being the limit of something else—the lowest layer of a firmament of snow. From this chaotic

---

9. The name given to certain judges in ancient Athens.

skyful of crowding flakes the mead and moor momentarily received additional clothing, only to appear momentarily more naked thereby. The vast arch of cloud above was strangely low, and formed as it were the roof of a large dark cavern, gradually sinking in upon its floor; for the instinctive thought was that the snow lining the heavens and that encrusting the earth would soon unite into one mass without any intervening stratum of air at all.

We turn our attention to the left-hand characteristics; which were flatness in respect of the river, verticality in respect of the wall behind it, and darkness as to both. These features made up the mass. If anything could be darker than the sky, it was the wall, and if anything could be gloomier than the wall it was the river beneath. The indistinct summit of the façade was notched and pronged by chimneys here and there, and upon its face were faintly signified the oblong shapes of windows, though only in the upper part. Below, down to the water's edge, the flat was unbroken by hole or projection.

An indescribable succession of dull blows, perplexing in their regularity, sent their sound with difficulty through the fluffy atmosphere. It was a neighbouring clock striking ten. The bell was in the open air, and being overlaid with several inches of muffling snow, had lost its voice for the time.

About this hour the snow abated: ten flakes fell where twenty had fallen, then one had the room of ten. Not long after a form moved by the brink of the river.

By its outline upon the colourless background a close observer might have seen that it was small. This was all that was positively discoverable, though it seemed human.

The shape went slowly along, but without much exertion, for the snow, though sudden, was not as yet more than two inches deep. At this time some words were spoken aloud:—

'One. Two. Three. Four. Five.'

Between each utterance the little shape advanced about half-a-dozen yards. It was evident now that the windows high in the wall were being counted. The word 'Five' represented the fifth window from the end of the wall.

Here the spot stopped, and dwindled smaller. The figure was stooping. Then a morsel of snow flew across the river towards the fifth window. It smacked against the wall at a point several yards from its mark. The throw was the idea of a man conjoined with the execution of a woman. No man who had ever seen bird, rabbit, or squirrel in his childhood, could possibly have thrown with such utter imbecility as was shown here.

Another attempt, and another; till by degrees the wall must have become pimpled with the adhering lumps of snow. At last one fragment struck the fifth window.

The river would have been seen by day to be of that deep smooth sort which races middle and sides with the same gliding precision, any irregularities of speed being immediately corrected by a small whirlpool. Nothing was heard in reply to the signal but the gurgle and cluck of one of these invisible wheels—together with a few small sounds which a sad man would have called moans, and a happy man laughter—caused by the flapping of the waters against trifling objects in other parts of the stream.

The window was struck again in the same manner.

Then a noise was heard, apparently produced by the opening of the window. This was followed by a voice from the same quarter:

'Who's there?'

The tones were masculine, and not those of surprise. The high wall being that of a barrack, and marriage being looked upon with disfavour in the army, assignations and communications had probably been made across the river before to-night.

'Is it Sergeant Troy?' said the blurred spot in the snow, tremulously.

This person was so much like a mere shade upon the earth, and the other speaker so much a part of the building, that one would have said the wall was holding a conversation with the snow.

'Yes,' came suspiciously from the shadow. 'What girl are you?'

'O, Frank—don't you know me?' said the spot. 'Your wife, Fanny Robin.'

'Fanny!' said the wall, in utter astonishment.

'Yes,' said the girl, with a half-suppressed gasp of emotion.

There was something in the woman's tone which is not that of the wife, and there was a manner in the man which is rarely a husband's. The dialogue went on:

'How did you come here?'

'I asked which was your window. Forgive me!'

'I did not expect you to-night. Indeed, I did not think you would come at all. It was a wonder you found me here. I am orderly to-morrow.'

'You said I was to come.'

'Well—I said that you might.'

'Yes, I mean that I might. You are glad to see me, Frank?'

'O yes—of course.'

'Can you—come to me?'

'My dear Fan, no! The bugle has sounded, the barrack gates are closed, and I have no leave. We are all of us as good as in the county gaol till to-morrow morning.'

'Then I shan't see you till then!' The words were in a faltering tone of disappointment.

'How did you get here from Weatherbury?'

'I walked—some part of the way—the rest by the carriers.'

'I am surprised.'

'Yes—so am I. And Frank, when will it be?'

'What?'

'That you promised.'

'I don't quite recollect.'

'O you do! Don't speak like that. It weighs me to the earth. It makes me say what ought to be said first by you.'

'Never mind—say it.'

'O, must I?—it is, when shall we be married, Frank?'

'Oh, I see. Well—you have to get proper clothes.'

'I have money. Will it be by banns or license?'[1]

'Banns, I should think.'

'And we live in two parishes.'

'Do we? What then?'

'My lodgings are in St. Mary's, and this is not. So they will have to be published in both.'

'Is that the law?'

'Yes. O Frank—you think me forward, I am afraid! Don't, dear Frank—will you—for I love you so. And you said lots of times you would marry me, and—and—I—I—I——'

'Don't cry, now! It is foolish. If I said so, of course I will.'

'And shall I put up the banns in my parish, and will you in yours?'

'Yes.'

'To-morrow?'

'Not to-morrow. We'll settle in a few days.'

'You have the permission of the officers?'

'No—not yet.'

'O—how is it? You said you almost had before you left Caster-bridge.'

'The fact is, I forgot to ask. Your coming like this is so sudden and unexpected.'

'Yes—yes—it is. It was wrong of me to worry you. I'll go away now. Will you come and see me to-morrow, at Mrs. Twills's, in North Street? I don't like to come to the Barracks. There are bad women about, and they think me one.'

'Quite so. I'll come to you, my dear. Good-night.'

'Good-night, Frank—good-night!'

And the noise was again heard of a window closing. The little spot moved away. When she passed the corner a subdued exclamation was heard inside the wall.

'Ho—ho—Sergeant—ho—ho!' An expostulation followed, but it was indistinct; and it became lost amid a low peal of laughter, which was hardly distinguishable from the gurgle of the tiny whirlpools outside.

---

1. Anglican church regulations required that "banns"—notices of intended marriages—be read on three successive Sundays in the parish churches of both parties; an exception to this rule might be had by obtaining a "license" from the bishop of the diocese or his designate.

XII

Farmers—A Rule—An Exception

The first public evidence of Bathsheba's decision to be a farmer in her own person and by proxy no more was her appearance the following market-day in the cornmarket at Casterbridge.

The low though extensive hall, supported by beams and pillars, and latterly dignified by the name of Corn Exchange, was thronged with hot men who talked among each other in twos and threes, the speaker of the minute looking sideways into his auditor's face and concentrating his argument by a contraction of one eyelid during delivery. The greater number carried in their hands ground-ash saplings, using them partly as walking-sticks and partly for poking up pigs, sheep, neighbours with their backs turned, and restful things in general which seemed to require such treatment in the course of their peregrinations. During conversations each subjected his sapling to great varieties of usage—bending it round his back, forming an arch of it between his two hands, overweighting it on the ground till it reached nearly a semicircle; or perhaps it was hastily tucked under the arm whilst the sample-bag was pulled forth and a handful of corn poured into the palm, which, after criticism, was flung upon the floor, an issue of events perfectly well known to half-a-dozen acute town-bred fowls which had as usual crept into the building unobserved, and waited the fulfilment of their anticipations with a high-stretched neck and oblique eye.

Among these heavy yeomen a feminine figure glided, the single one of her sex that the room contained. She was prettily and even daintily dressed. She moved between them as a chaise between carts, was heard after them as a romance after sermons, was felt among them like a breeze among furnaces. It had required a little determination—far more than she had at first imagined—to take up a position here, for at her first entry the lumbering dialogues had ceased, nearly every face had been turned towards her, and those that were already turned rigidly fixed there.

Two or three only of the farmers were personally known to Bathsheba, and to these she had made her way. But if she was to be the practical woman she had intended to show herself, business must be carried on, introductions or none, and she ultimately acquired confidence enough to speak and reply boldly to men merely known to her by hearsay. Bathsheba too had her sample-bags, and by degrees adopted the professional pour into the hand—holding up the grains in her narrow palm for inspection, in perfect Casterbridge manner.

Something in the exact arch of her upper unbroken row of teeth, and in the keenly pointed corners of her red mouth when, with parted lips, she somewhat defiantly turned up her face to argue a point with a tall man, suggested that there was potentiality enough in that lithe slip of humanity for alarming exploits of sex, and daring enough to carry them out. But her eyes had a softness—invariably a softness—which, had they not been dark, would have seemed mistiness; as they were, it lowered an expression that might have been piercing to simple clearness.

Strange to say of a woman in full bloom and vigour, she always allowed her interlocutors to finish their statements before rejoining with hers. In arguing on prices she held to her own firmly, as was natural in a dealer, and reduced theirs persistently, as was inevitable in a woman. But there was an elasticity in her firmness which removed it from obstinacy, as there was a *naïveté* in her cheapening which saved it from meanness.

Those of the farmers with whom she had no dealings (by far the greater part) were continually asking each other, 'Who is she?' The reply would be—

'Farmer Everdene's niece; took on Weatherbury Upper Farm; turned away the baily, and swears she'll do everything herself.'

The other man would then shake his head.

'Yes, 'tis a pity she's so headstrong,' the first would say. 'But we ought to be proud of her here—she lightens up the old place. 'Tis such a shapely maid, however, that she'll soon get picked up.'

It would be ungallant to suggest that the novelty of her engagement in such an occupation had almost as much to do with the magnetism as had the beauty of her face and movements. However, the interest was general, and this Saturday's *début* in the forum, whatever it may have been to Bathsheba as the buying and selling farmer, was unquestionably a triumph to her as the maiden. Indeed, the sensation was so pronounced that her instinct on two or three occasions was merely to walk as a queen among these gods of the fallow, like a little sister of a little Jove, and to neglect closing prices altogether.

The numerous evidences of her power to attract were only thrown into greater relief by a marked exception. Women seem to have eyes in their ribbons for such matters as these. Bathsheba, without looking within a right angle of him, was conscious of a black sheep among the flock.

It perplexed her first. If there had been a respectable minority on either side, the case would have been most natural. If nobody had regarded her, she would have taken the matter indifferently—such cases had occurred. If everybody, this man included, she would have taken it as a matter of course—people had done so before. But the smallness of the exception made the mystery.

She soon knew thus much of the recusant's appearance. He was a gentlemanly man, with full and distinctly outlined Roman features, the prominences of which glowed in the sun with a bronze-like richness of tone. He was erect in attitude, and quiet in demeanour. One characteristic pre-eminently marked him—dignity.

Apparently he had some time ago reached that entrance to middle age at which a man's aspect naturally ceases to alter for the term of a dozen years or so; and, artificially, a woman's does likewise. Thirty-five and fifty were his limits of variation—he might have been either, or anywhere between the two.

It may be said that married men of forty are usually ready and generous enough to fling passing glances at any specimen of moderate beauty they may discern by the way. Probably, as with persons playing whist for love, the consciousness of a certain immunity under any circumstances from that worst possible ultimate, the having to pay, makes them unduly speculative. Bathsheba was convinced that this unmoved person was not a married man.

When marketing was over, she rushed off to Liddy, who was waiting for her beside the yellow gig in which they had driven to town. The horse was put in, and on they trotted—Bathsheba's sugar, tea, and drapery parcels being packed behind, and expressing in some indescribable manner, by their colour, shape, and general lineaments, that they were that young lady-farmer's property, and the grocer's and draper's no more.

'I've been through it, Liddy, and it is over. I shan't mind it again, for they will all have grown accustomed to seeing me there; but this morning it was as bad as being married—eyes everywhere!'

'I knowed it would be,' Liddy said. 'Men be such a terrible class of society to look at a body.'

'But there was one man who had more sense than to waste his time upon me.' The information was put in this form that Liddy might not for a moment suppose her mistress was at all piqued. 'A very good-looking man,' she continued, 'upright; about forty, I should think. Do you know at all who he could be?'

Liddy couldn't think.

'Can't you guess at all?' said Bathsheba with some disappointment.

'I haven't a notion; besides, 'tis no difference, since he took less notice of you than any of the rest. Now, if he'd taken more, it would have mattered a great deal.'

Bathsheba was suffering from the reverse feeling just then, and they bowled along in silence. A low carriage, bowling along still more rapidly behind a horse of unimpeachable breed, overtook and passed them.

'Why, there he is!' she said.

Liddy looked. 'That! That's Farmer Boldwood—of course 'tis—the man you couldn't see the other day when he called.'

'Oh, Farmer Boldwood,' murmured Bathsheba, and looked at him as he outstripped them. The farmer had never turned his head once, but with eyes fixed on the most advanced point along the road, passed as unconsciously and abstractedly as if Bathsheba and her charms were thin air.

'He's an interesting man—don't you think so?' she remarked.

'O yes, very. Everybody owns it,' replied Liddy.

'I wonder why he is so wrapt up and indifferent, and seemingly so far away from all he sees around him.'

'It is said—but not known for certain—that he met with some bitter disappointment when he was a young man and merry. A woman jilted him, they say.'

'People always say that—and we know very well women scarcely ever jilt men; 'tis the men who jilt us. I expect it is simply his nature to be so reserved.'

'Simply his nature—I expect so, miss—nothing else in the world.'

'Still, 'tis more romantic to think he has been served cruelly, poor thing! Perhaps, after all, he has.'

'Depend upon it he has. O yes, miss, he has! I feel he must have.'

'However, we are very apt to think extremes of people. I shouldn't wonder after all if it wasn't a little of both—just between the two— rather cruelly used and rather reserved.'

'O dear no, miss—I can't think it between the two!'

'That's most likely.'

'Well, yes, so it is. I am convinced it is most likely. You may take my word, miss, that that's what's the matter with him.'

XIII

Sortes Sanctorum[1]—The Valentine

It was Sunday afternoon in the farmhouse, on the thirteenth of February. Dinner being over Bathsheba, for want of a better companion, had asked Liddy to come and sit with her. The mouldy pile was dreary in winter-time before the candles were lighted and the shutters closed; the atmosphere of the place seemed as old as the walls; every nook behind the furniture had a temperature of its own, for the fire was not kindled in this part of the house early in the day; and Bathsheba's new piano, which was an old one in other annals, looked particularly sloping and out of level on the warped floor before night threw a shade over its less prominent angles and hid the unpleasantness. Liddy, like a little brook, though shallow, was always rippling; her presence had not so much weight as to task thought, and yet enough to exercise it.

On the table lay an old quarto Bible, bound in leather. Liddy looking at it said,—

Did you ever find out, miss, who you are going to marry by means of

1. Latin for "the oracles of the holy writings."

the Bible and key?'[2]

'Don't be so foolish, Liddy. As if such things could be.'

'Well, there's a good deal in it, all the same.'

'Nonsense, child.'

'And it makes your heart beat fearful. Some believe in it; some don't; I do.'

'Very well, let's try it,' said Bathsheba, bounding from her seat with that total disregard of consistency which can be indulged in towards a dependent, and entering into the spirit of divination at once. 'Go and get the front door key.'

Liddy fetched it. 'I wish it wasn't Sunday,' she said, on returning. 'Perhaps 'tis wrong.'

'What's right week days is right Sundays,' replied her mistress in a tone which was a proof in itself.

The book was opened—the leaves, drab with age, being quite worn away at much-read verses by the forefingers of unpractised readers in former days, where they were moved along under the line as an aid to the vision. The special verse in the Book of Ruth was sought out by Bathsheba, and the sublime words met her eye. They slightly thrilled and abashed her. It was Wisdom in the abstract facing Folly in the concrete. Folly in the concrete blushed, persisted in her intention, and placed the key on the book. A rusty patch immediately upon the verse, caused by previous pressure of an iron substance thereon, told that this was not the first time the old volume had been used for the purpose.

'Now keep steady, and be silent,' said Bathsheba.

The verse was repeated; the book turned round; Bathsheba blushed guiltily.

'Who did you try?' said Liddy curiously.

'I shall not tell you.'

'Did you notice Mr. Boldwood's doings in church this morning, miss?' Liddy continued, adumbrating by the remark the track her thoughts had taken.

'No, indeed,' said Bathsheba, with serene indifference.

'His pew is exactly opposite yours, miss.'

'I know it.'

'And you did not see his goings on!'

'Certainly I did not, I tell you.'

Liddy assumed a smaller physiognomy, and shut her lips decisively.

2. The account of this means of foretelling the future that follows was amplified by an illustration that appeared in the first book edition of the novel and is reproduced here on p. ii. It appears that the method of divination by Bible and key was this: the key was inserted in the Bible at Ruth 1:16–17, and the Bible tied shut with the handle of the key protruding so that the book could be supported by resting the rounded ends of the key handle on one fingertip of Bathsheba and one of Liddy. Bathsheba would then think of possible marriage partners, and if the Bible turned, the man she was thinking of at the time would be her future husband.

This move was unexpected, and proportionately disconcerting. 'What did he do?' Bathsheba said perforce.

'Didn't turn his head to look at you once all the service.'

'Why should he?' again demanded her mistress, wearing a nettled look. 'I didn't ask him to.'

'Oh, no. But everybody else was noticing you; and it was odd he didn't. There, 'tis like him. Rich and gentlemanly, what does he care?'

Bathsheba dropped into a silence intended to express that she had opinions on the matter too abstruse for Liddy's comprehension, rather than that she had nothing to say.

'Dear me—I had nearly forgotten the valentine I bought yesterday,' she exclaimed at length.

'Valentine! who for, miss?' said Liddy. 'Farmer Boldwood?'

It was the single name among all possible wrong ones that just at this moment seemed to Bathsheba more pertinent than the right.

'Well, no. It is only for little Teddy Coggan. I have promised him something, and this will be a pretty surprise for him. Liddy, you may as well bring me my desk and I'll direct it at once.'

Bathsheba took from her desk a gorgeously illuminated and embossed design in post-octavo, which had been bought on the previous market-day at the chief stationer's in Casterbridge. In the centre was a small oval enclosure; this was left blank, that the sender might insert tender words more appropriate to the special occasion than any generalities by a printer could possibly be.

'Here's a place for writing,' said Bathsheba. 'What shall I put?'

'Something of this sort, I should think,' returned Liddy promptly:—

> 'The rose is red,
> The violet blue,
> Carnation's sweet,
> And so are you.'

'Yes, that shall be it. It just suits itself to a chubby-faced child like him,' said Bathsheba. She inserted the words in a small though legible handwriting; enclosed the sheet in an envelope, and dipped her pen for the direction.

'What fun it would be to send it to the stupid old Boldwood, and how he would wonder!' said the irrepressible Liddy, lifting her eyebrows, and indulging in an awful mirth on the verge of fear as she thought of the moral and social magnitude of the man contemplated.

Bathsheba paused to regard the idea at full length. Boldwood's had begun to be a troublesome image—a species of Daniel in her kingdom who persisted in kneeling eastward[3] when reason and common sense said that he might just as well follow suit with the rest, and afford her

---

3. An allusion to Daniel 6:10–16, where Daniel, a captive in Babylon, defies the king's prohibition against praying while facing Jerusalem. Hardy mistakenly has Daniel face east, when, in fact, Jerusalem would be west of Babylon.

the official glance of admiration which cost nothing at all. She was far from being seriously concerned about his nonconformity. Still, it was faintly depressing that the most dignified and valuable man in the parish should withhold his eyes, and that a girl like Liddy should talk about it. So Liddy's idea was at first rather harassing than piquant.

'No, I won't do that. He wouldn't see any humour in it.'

'He'd worry to death,' said the persistent Liddy.

'Really, I don't care particularly to send it to Teddy,' remarked her mistress. 'He's rather a naughty child sometimes.'

'Yes—that he is.'

'Let's toss, as men do,' said Bathsheba idly. 'Now then, head, Boldwood; tail, Teddy. No, we won't toss money on a Sunday, that would be tempting the devil indeed.'

'Toss this hymn-book; there can't be no sinfulness in that, miss.'

'Very well. Open, Boldwood—shut, Teddy. No; it's more likely to fall open. Open, Teddy—shut, Boldwood.'

The book went fluttering in the air and came down shut.

Bathsheba, a small yawn upon her mouth, took the pen, and with off-hand serenity directed the missive to Boldwood.

'Now light a candle, Liddy. Which seal shall we use? Here's a unicorn's head—there's nothing in that. What's this?—two doves—no. It ought to be something extraordinary, ought it not, Lidd? Here's one with a motto—I remember it is some funny one, but I can't read it. We'll try this, and if it doesn't do we'll have another.'

A large red seal was duly affixed. Bathsheba looked closely at the hot wax to discover the words.

'Capital!' she exclaimed, throwing down the letter frolicsomely. ''Twould upset the solemnity of a parson and clerk too.'

Liddy looked at the words of the seal, and read—

'MARRY ME.'

The same evening the letter was sent, and was duly sorted in Caster-bridge post-office that night, to be returned to Weatherbury again in the morning.

So very idly and unreflectingly was this deed done. Of love as a spectacle Bathsheba had a fair knowledge; but of love subjectively she knew nothing.

XIV

Effect of the Letter—Sunrise

At dusk on the evening of St. Valentine's Day Boldwood sat down to supper as usual, by a beaming fire of aged logs. Upon the mantel-shelf before him was a time-piece, surmounted by a spread eagle, and upon the eagle's wings was the letter Bathsheba had sent. Here the bachelor's gaze was continually fastening itself, till the large red seal became as a blot of blood on the retina of his eye; and as he ate and drank he still read in fancy the words thereon, although they were too remote for his sight—

'MARRY ME.'

The pert injunction was like those crystal substances, which, colourless themselves, assume the tone of objects about them. Here, in the quiet of Boldwood's parlour, where everything that was not grave was extraneous, and where the atmosphere was that of a Puritan Sunday[1] lasting all the week, the letter and its dictum changed their tenor from the thoughtlessness of their origin to a deep solemnity, imbibed from their accessories now.

Since the receipt of the missive in the morning, Boldwood had felt the symmetry of his existence to be slowly getting distorted in the direction of an ideal passion. The disturbance was as the first floating weed to Columbus[2]—the contemptibly little suggesting possibilities of the infinitely great.

The letter must have had an origin and a motive. That the latter was of the smallest magnitude compatible with its existence at all, Boldwood, of course, did not know. And such an explanation did not strike him as a possibility even. It is foreign to a mystified condition of mind to realize of the mystifier that the processes of approving a course suggested by circumstance, and of striking out a course from inner impulse, would look the same in the result. The vast difference between starting a train of events, and directing into a particular groove a series already started, is rarely apparent to the person confounded by the issue.

When Boldwood went to bed he placed the valentine in the corner of the looking-glass. He was conscious of its presence, even when his back was turned upon it. It was the first time in Boldwood's life that such an event had occurred. The same fascination that caused him to think it an act which had a deliberate motive prevented him from regarding it as an impertinence. He looked again at the direction. The mysterious influences of night invested the writing with the presence of the unknown writer. Somebody's—some *woman's*—hand had travelled softly over the paper bearing his name; her unrevealed eyes had watched every curve as she formed it; her brain had seen him in imagination the while. Why should she have imagined him? Her mouth—were the lips red or pale, plump or creased?—had curved itself to a certain expression as the pen went on—the corners had

---

1. A Sunday observed with strict seriousness, reflecting the serious and intense nature of Boldwood.

2. During Columbus's voyage in 1492, the sighting of strands of fresh seawood was taken as a sign that land was not far ahead.

moved with all their natural tremulousness: what had been the expression?

The vision of the woman writing, as a supplement to the words written, had no individuality. She was a misty shape, and well she might be, considering that her original was at that moment sound asleep and oblivious of all love and letter-writing under the sky. Whenever Boldwood dozed she took a form, and comparatively ceased to be a vision: when he awoke there was the letter justifying the dream.

The moon shone to-night, and its light was not of a customary kind. His window admitted only a reflection of its rays, and the pale sheen had that reversed direction which snow gives, coming upward and lighting up his ceiling in an unnatural way, casting shadows in strange places, and putting lights where shadows had used to be.

The substance of the epistle had occupied him but little in comparison with the fact of its arrival. He suddenly wondered if anything more might be found in the envelope than what he had withdrawn. He jumped out of bed in the weird light, took the letter, pulled out the flimsy sheet, shook the envelope—searched it. Nothing more was there. Boldwood looked, as he had a hundred times the preceding day, at the insistent red seal: 'Marry me,' he said aloud.

The solemn and reserved yeoman again closed the letter, and stuck it in the frame of the glass. In doing so he caught sight of his reflected features, wan in expression, and insubstantial in form. He saw how closely compressed was his mouth, and that his eyes were wide-spread and vacant. Feeling uneasy and dissatisfied with himself for this nervous excitability, he returned to bed.

Then the dawn drew on. The full power of the clear heaven was not equal to that of a cloudy sky at noon, when Boldwood arose and dressed himself. He descended the stairs and went out towards the gate of a field to the east, leaning over which he paused and looked around.

It was one of the usual slow sunrises of this time of the year, and the sky, pure violet in the zenith, was leaden to the northward, and murky to the east, where, over the snowy down or ewe-lease[3] on Weatherbury Upper Farm, and apparently resting upon the ridge, the only half of the sun yet visible burnt rayless, like a red and flameless fire shining over a white hearthstone. The whole effect resembled a sunset as childhood resembles age.

In other directions the fields and sky were so much of one colour by the snow that it was difficult in a hasty glance to tell whereabouts the horizon occurred; and in general there was here, too, that before-mentioned preternatural inversion of light and shade which attends the prospect when the garish brightness commonly in the sky is found on the earth, and the shades of earth are in the sky. Over the west hung

3. A tract of land set aside for grazing sheep.

the wasting moon, now dull and greenish-yellow, like tarnished brass.

Boldwood was listlessly noting how the frost had hardened and glazed the surface of the snow, till it shone in the red eastern light with the polish of marble; how, in some portions of the slope, withered grass-bents, encased in icicles, bristled through the smooth wan coverlet in the twisted and curved shapes of old Venetian glass; and how the footprints of a few birds, which had hopped over the snow whilst it lay in the state of a soft fleece, were now frozen to a short permanency. A half-muffled noise of light wheels interrupted him. Boldwood turned back into the road. It was the mail-cart—a crazy two-wheeled vehicle, hardly heavy enough to resist a puff of wind. The driver held out a letter. Boldwood seized it and opened it, expecting another anonymous one—so greatly are people's ideas of probability a mere sense that precedent will repeat itself.

'I don't think it is for you, sir,' said the man, when he saw Boldwood's action. 'Though there is no name, I think it is for your shepherd.'

Boldwood looked then at the address—

> To the New Shepherd,
>   Weatherbury Farm,
>   Near Casterbridge.

'Oh—what a mistake!—it is not mine. Nor is it for my shepherd. It is for Miss Everdene's. You had better take it on to him—Gabriel Oak—and say I opened it in mistake.'

At this moment on the ridge, up against the blazing sky, a figure was visible, like the black snuff in the midst of a candle-flame. Then it moved and began to bustle about vigorously from place to place, carrying square skeleton masses, which were riddled by the same rays. A small figure on all fours followed behind. The tall form was that of Gabriel Oak; the small one that of George; the articles in course of transit were hurdles.

'Wait,' said Boldwood. 'That's the man on the hill. I'll take the letter to him myself.'

To Boldwood it was now no longer merely a letter to another man. It was an opportunity. Exhibiting a face pregnant with intention, he entered the snowy field.

Gabriel, at that minute, descended the hill towards the right. The glow stretched down in this direction now, and touched the distant roof of Warren's Malthouse—whither the shepherd was apparently bent. Boldwood followed at a distance.

XV

A Morning Meeting—The Letter Again

The scarlet and orange light outside the malthouse did not penetrate to its interior, which was, as usual, lighted by a rival glow of similar hue, radiating from the hearth.

The maltster, after having lain down in his clothes for a few hours, was now sitting beside a three-legged table, breakfasting off bread and bacon. This was eaten on the plateless system, which is performed by placing a slice of bread upon the table, the meat flat upon the bread, a mustard plaster upon the meat, and a pinch of salt upon the whole, then cutting them vertically downwards with a large pocket-knife till wood is reached, when the severed lump is impaled on the knife, elevated, and sent the proper way of food.

The maltster's lack of teeth appeared not to sensibly diminish his powers as a mill. He had been without them for so many years that toothlessness was felt less to be a defect than hard gums an acquisition. Indeed, he seemed to approach the grave as a hyperbolic curve approaches a straight line—less directly as he got nearer, till it was doubtful if he would ever reach it at all.

In the ashpit was a heap of potatoes roasting, and a boiling pipkin[1] of charred bread, called 'coffee,' for the benefit of whomsoever should call, for Warren's was a sort of clubhouse, used as an alternative to the inn.

'I say, says I, we get a fine day, and then down comes a snapper[2] at night,' was a remark now suddenly heard spreading into the malthouse from the door, which had been opened the previous moment. The form of Henery Fray advanced to the fire, stamping the snow from his boots when about half-way there. The speech and entry had not seemed to be at all an abrupt beginning to the maltster, introductory matter being often omitted in this neighbourhood, both from word and deed, and the maltster having the same latitude allowed him, did not hurry to reply. He picked up a fragment of cheese by pecking upon it with his knife, as a butcher picks up skewers.

Henery appeared in a drab kerseymere great-coat,[3] buttoned over his smock-frock, the white skirts of the latter being visible to the distance of about a foot below the coat-tails, which, when you got used to the style of dress, looked natural enough, and even ornamental—it certainly was comfortable.

Matthew Moon, Joseph Poorgrass, and other carters and waggoners followed at his heels, with great lanterns dangling from their hands, which showed that they had just come from the cart-horse stables, where they had been busily engaged since four o'clock that morning.

1. A small earthenware pot.　　　　3. A heavy woolen overcoat.
2. A sudden change to bad weather.

'And how is she getting on without a baily?' the maltster inquired.

Henery shook his head, and smiled one of the bitter smiles, dragging all the flesh of his forehead into a corrugated heap in the centre.

'She'll rue it—surely, surely!' he said. 'Benjy Pennyways were not a true man or an honest baily—as big a betrayer as Joey Iscariot[4] himself. But to think she can carr'[5] on alone!' He allowed his head to swing laterally three or four times in silence. 'Never in all my creeping up[6]—never!'

This was recognized by all as the conclusion of some gloomy speech which had been expressed in thought alone during the shake of the head; Henery meanwhile retained several marks of despair upon his face, to imply that they would be required for use again directly he should go on speaking.

'All will be ruined, and ourselves too, or there's no meat in gentlemen's houses!' said Mark Clark.

'A headstrong maid, that's what she is—and won't listen to no advice at all. Pride and vanity have ruined many a cobbler's dog. Dear, dear, when I think o' it, I sorrows like a man in travel!'[7]

'True, Henery, you do, I've heard ye,' said Joseph Poorgrass, in a voice of thorough attestation, and with a wire-drawn smile of misery.

''Twould do a martel man no harm to have what's under her bonnet,' said Billy Smallbury, who had just entered, bearing his one tooth before him. 'She can spaik real language, and must have some sense somewhere. Do ye foller me?'

'I do; but no baily—I deserved that place,' wailed Henery, signifying wasted genius by gazing blankly at visions of a high destiny apparently visible to him on Billy Smallbury's smock-frock. 'There, 'twas to be, I suppose. Your lot is your lot, and Scripture is nothing; for if you do good you don't get rewarded according to your works, but be cheated in some mean way out of your recompense.'

'No, no; I don't agree with'ee there,' said Mark Clark. 'God's a perfect gentleman in that respect.'

'Good works good pay, so to speak it,' attested Joseph Poorgrass.

A short pause ensued, and as a sort of *Entr' acte*[8] Henery turned and blew out the lanterns, which the increase of daylight rendered no longer necessary even in the malthouse, with its one pane of glass.

'I wonder what a farmer-woman can want with a harpsichord, dulcimer, pianner,[9] or whatever 'tis they d'call it?' said the maltster. 'Liddy saith she've a new one.'

'Got a pianner?'

'Ay. Seems her old uncle's things were not good enough for her.

4. Henery's name for Judas Iscariot, who betrayed Christ.
5. Carry (dialect).
6. Growing up; life.
7. Travail; giving birth. An allusion to John 16:21.
8. French for "an interval between the acts of a play."
9. Piano (dialect).

She've bought all but everything new. There's heavy chairs for the stout, weak and wiry ones for the slender; great watches, getting on to the size of clocks, to stand upon the chimbley-piece.'

'Pictures, for the most part wonderful frames.'

'And long horse-hair settles for the drunk, with horse-hair pillows at each end,' said Mr. Clark. 'Likewise looking-glasses for the pretty, and lying books for the wicked.'

A firm loud tread was now heard stamping outside; the door was opened about six inches, and somebody on the other side exclaimed—

'Neighbours, have ye got room for a few new-born lambs?'

'Ay, sure, shepherd,' said the conclave.

The door was flung back till it kicked the wall and trembled from top to bottom with the blow. Mr. Oak appeared in the entry with a steaming face, haybands wound about his ankles to keep out the snow, a leather strap round his waist outside the smock-frock, and looking altogether an epitome of the world's health and vigour. Four lambs hung in various embarrassing attitudes over his shoulders, and the dog George, whom Gabriel had contrived to fetch from Norcombe, stalked solemnly behind.

'Well, Shepherd Oak, and how's lambing this year, if I mid say it?' inquired Joseph Poorgrass.

'Terrible trying,' said Oak. 'I've been wet through twice a-day, either in snow or rain, this last fortnight. Cainy and I haven't tined[1] our eyes tonight.'

'A good few twins, too, I hear?'

'Too many by half. Yes; 'tis a very queer lambing this year. We shan't have done by Lady Day.'[2]

'And last year 'twer all over by Sexajessamine Sunday,'[3] Joseph remarked.

'Bring on the rest, Cain,' said Gabriel, 'and then run back to the ewes. I'll follow you soon.'

Cainy Ball—a cheery-faced young lad, with a small circular orifice by way of mouth, advanced and deposited two others, and retired as he was bidden. Oak lowered the lambs from their unnatural elevation, wrapped them in hay, and placed them round the fire.

'We've no lambing-hut here, as I used to have at Norcombe,' said Gabriel, 'and 'tis such a plague to bring the weakly ones to a house. If 'twasn't for your place here, malter, I don't know what I should do, this keen weather. And how is it with you to-day, malter?'

'Oh, neither sick nor sorry, shepherd; but no younger.'

'Ay—I understand.'

'Sit down, Shepherd Oak,' continued the ancient man of malt.

---

1. Shut (dialect).
2. March 25, the Feast of the Annunciation; a day when quarterly rents were due and farm laborers' annual contracts were made and renewed.
3. Joseph's name for Sexagesima Sunday, the second Sunday before Lent.

'And how was the old place at Norcombe, when ye went for your dog? I should like to see the old familiar spot; but faith, I shouldn't know a soul there now.'

'I suppose you wouldn't. 'Tis altered very much.'

'Is it true that Dicky Hill's wooden cider-house is pulled down?'

'O yes—years ago, and Dicky's cottage just above it.'

'Well, to be sure!'

'Yes; and Tompkins's old apple-tree is rooted[4] that used to bear two hogsheads of cider, and no help from other trees.'

'Rooted?—you don't say it! Ah! stirring times we live in—stirring times.'

'And you can mind the old well that used to be in the middle of the place? That's turned into a solid iron pump with a large stone trough, and all complete.'

'Dear, dear—how the face of nations alter, and what we live to see nowadays! Yes—and 'tis the same here. They've been talking but now of the mis'ess's strange doings.'

'What have you been saying about her?' inquired Oak, sharply turning to the rest, and getting very warm.

'These middle-aged men have been pulling her over the coals for pride and vanity,' said Mark Clark; 'but I say, let her have rope enough. Bless her pretty face—shouldn't I like to do so—upon her cherry lips!' The gallant Mark Clark here made a peculiar and well-known sound with his own.

'Mark,' said Gabriel sternly, 'now you mind this: none of that dalliance-talk—that smack-and-coddle[5] style of yours—about Miss Everdene. I don't allow it. Do you hear?'

'With all my heart, as I've got no chance,' replied Mr. Clark cordially.

'I suppose you've been speaking against her?' said Oak, turning to Joseph Poorgrass with a very grim look.

'No, no—not a word I—'tis a real joyful thing that she's no worse, that's what I say,' said Joseph, trembling and blushing with terror. 'Matthew just said——'

'Matthew Moon, what have you been saying?' asked Oak.

'I? Why ye know I wouldn't harm a worm—no, not one under-ground worm?' said Matthew Moon, looking very uneasy.

'Well, somebody has—and look here, neighbours.' Gabriel, though one of the quietest and most gentle men on earth, rose to the occasion, with marital promptness and vigour. 'That's my fist.' Here he placed his fist, rather smaller in size than a common loaf, in the mathematical centre of the maltster's little table, and with it gave a bump or two thereon, as if to ensure that their eyes all thoroughly took in the idea of fistiness before he went further. 'Now—the first man in

---

4. Uprooted (dialect). 5. Kiss-and-embrace (dialect).

the parish that I hear prophesying bad of our mistress, why' (here the fist was raised and let fall, as Thor might have done with his hammer[6] in assaying it)—'he'll smell and taste that—or I'm a Dutchman.'

All earnestly expressed by their features that their minds did not wander to Holland for a moment on account of this statement, but were deploring the difference which gave rise to the figure; and Mark Clark cried 'Hear, hear; just what I should ha' said.' The dog George looked up at the same time after the shepherd's menace, and, though he understood English but imperfectly, began to growl.

'Now, don't ye take on so, shepherd, and sit down!' said Henery, with a deprecating peacefulness equal to anything of the kind in Christianity.

'We hear that ye be a extraordinary good and clever man, shepherd,' said Joseph Poorgrass with considerable anxiety from behind the maltster's bedstead, whither he had retired for safety. ' 'Tis a great thing to be clever, I'm sure,' he added, making movements associated with states of mind rather than body; 'we wish we were, don't we, neighbours?'

'Ay, that we do, sure,' said Matthew Moon, with a small anxious laugh towards Oak, to show how very friendly disposed he was likewise.

'Who's been telling you I'm clever?' said Oak.

' 'Tis blowed about from pillar to post quite common,' said Matthew. 'We hear that ye can tell the time as well by the stars as we can by the sun and moon, shepherd.'

'Yes, I can do a little that way,' said Gabriel, as a man of medium sentiments on the subject.

'And that ye can make sun-dials, and prent folks' names upon their waggons almost like copper-plate, with beautiful flourishes, and great long tails. A excellent fine thing for ye to be such a clever man, shepherd. Joseph Poorgrass used to prent to Farmer James Everdene's waggons before you came, and 'a could never mind which way to turn the J's and E's—could ye, Joseph?' Joseph shook his head to express how absolute was the fact that he couldn't. 'And so you used to do 'em the wrong way, like this, didn't ye, Joseph?' Matthew marked on the dusty floor with his whip-handle

ᒐ A M Ǝ S

'And how Farmer James would cuss, and call thee a fool, wouldn't he, Joseph, when 'a seed his name looking so inside-out-like?' continued Matthew Moon, with feeling.

'Ay—'a would,' said Joseph meekly. 'But, you see, I wasn't so much to blame, for them J's and E's be such trying sons o' witches for the

---

6. In Norse mythology, the fall of the god Thor's hammer produced thunder.

memory to mind whether they face backward or forward; and I always had such a forgetful memory, too.'

' 'Tis a bad affliction for ye, being such a man of calamities in other ways.'

'Well, 'tis; but a happy Providence ordered that it should be no worse, and I feel my thanks. As to shepherd, there, I'm sure mis'ess ought to have made ye her baily—such a fitting man for't as you be.'

'I don't mind owning that I expected it,' said Oak frankly. 'Indeed, I hoped for the place. At the same time, Miss Everdene has a right to be her own baily if she choose—and to keep me down to be a common shepherd only.' Oak drew a slow breath, looked sadly into the bright ashpit, and seemed lost in thoughts not of the most hopeful hue.

The genial warmth of the fire now began to stimulate the nearly lifeless lambs to bleat and move their limbs briskly upon the hay, and to recognize for the first time the fact that they were born. Their noise increased to a chorus of baas, upon which Oak pulled the milk-can from before the fire, and taking a small tea-pot from the pocket of his smock-frock, filled it with milk, and taught those of the helpless creatures which were not to be restored to their dams how to drink from the spout—a trick they acquired with astonishing aptitude.

'And she don't even let ye have the skins of the dead lambs, I hear?' resumed Joseph Poorgrass, his eyes lingering on the operations of Oak with the necessary melancholy.

'I don't have them,' said Gabriel.

'Ye be very badly used, shepherd,' hazarded Joseph again, in the hope of getting Oak as an ally in lamentation after all. 'I think she's took against ye—that I do.'

'O no—not at all,' replied Gabriel hastily, and a sigh escaped him, which the deprivation of lamb skins could hardly have caused.

Before any further remark had been added a shade darkened the door, and Boldwood entered the malthouse, bestowing upon each a nod of a quality between friendliness and condescension.

'Ah! Oak, I thought you were here,' he said. 'I met the mail-cart ten minutes ago, and a letter was put into my hand, which I opened without reading the address. I believe it is yours. You must excuse the accident, please.'

'O yes—not a bit of difference, Mr. Boldwood—not a bit,' said Gabriel readily. He had not a correspondent on earth, nor was there a possible letter coming to him whose contents the whole parish would not have been welcome to peruse.

Oak stepped aside, and read the following in an unknown hand:—

'DEAR FRIEND—I do not know your name, but I think these few lines will reach you, which I write to thank you for your kindness to me the night I left Weatherbury in a reckless way. I also return the money I owe you, which you will excuse my not keeping as a gift. All has ended well, and I am happy to say I am going to be married to the young man

who has courted me for some time—Sergeant Troy, of the 11th
Dragoon Guards, now quartereed in this town. He would, I know,
object to my having received anything except as a loan, being a man of
great respectability and high honour—indeed, a nobleman by blood.

'I should be much obliged to you if you would keep the contents of
this letter a secret for the present, dear friend. We mean to surprise
Weatherbury by coming there soon as husband and wife, though I
blush to state it tq one nearly a stranger. The sergeant grew up in
Weatherbury. Thanking you again for your kindness,

> I am, your sincere well-wisher,
>
> FANNY ROBIN.'

'Have you read it, Mr. Boldwood?' said Gabriel; 'if not, you had
better do so. I know you are interested in Fanny Robin.'

Boldwood read the letter and looked grieved.

'Fanny—poor Fanny! the end she is so confident of has not yet
come, she should remember—and may never come. I see she gives no
address.'

'What sort of a man is this Sergeant Troy?' said Gabriel.

'H'm—I'm afraid not one to build much hope upon in such a case
as this,' the farmer murmured, 'though he's a clever fellow, and up to
everything. A slight romance attaches to him, too. His mother was a
French governess, and it seems that a secret attachment existed between her and the late Lord Severn. She was married to a poor medical
man, and soon after an infant was born; and while money was
forthcoming all went on well. Unfortunately for her boy, his best
friends died; and he got then a situation as second clerk at a lawyer's in
Casterbridge. He stayed there for some time, and might have worked
himself into a dignified position of some sort had he not indulged in
the wild freak of enlisting. I have much doubt if ever little Fanny will
surprise us in the way she mentions—very much doubt. A silly
girl—silly girl!'

The door was hurriedly burst open again, and in came running
Cainy Ball out of breath, his mouth red and open, like the bell of a
penny trumpet, from which he coughed with noisy vigour and great
distension of face.

'Now, Cain Ball,' said Oak sternly, 'why will you run so fast and lose
your breath so? I'm always telling you of it.'

'Oh—I—a puff of mee breath—went—the wrong way, please,
Mister Oak, and made me cough—hok—hok!'

'Well—what have you come for?'

'I've run to tell ye,' said the junior shepherd, supporting his
exhausted youthful frame against the doorpost, 'that you must come
directly. Two more ewes have twinned—that's what's the matter,
Shepherd Oak.'

'Oh, that's it,' said Oak, jumping up, and dismissing for the present
his thoughts on poor Fanny. 'You are a good boy to run and tell me,

Cain, and you shall smell a large plum pudding some day as a treat. But, before we go, Cainy, bring the tarpot, and we'll mark this lot and have done with 'em.'

Oak took from his illimitable pockets a marking iron, dipped it into the pot, and imprinted on the buttocks of the infant sheep the initials of her he delighted to muse on—'B. E.,' which signified to all the region round that henceforth the lambs belonged to Farmer Bathsheba Everdene, and to no one else.

'Now, Cainy, shoulder your two, and off. Good morning, Mr. Boldwood.' The shepherd lifted the sixteen large legs and four small bodies he had himself brought, and vanished with them in the direction of the lambing field hard by—their frames being now in a sleek and hopeful state, pleasantly contrasting with their death's-door plight of half an hour before.

Boldwood followed him a little way up the field, hesitated, and turned back. He followed him again with a last resolve, annihilating return. On approaching the nook in which the fold was constructed, the farmer drew out his pocket-book, unfastened it, and allowed it to lie open on his hand. A letter was revealed—Bathsheba's.

'I was going to ask you, Oak,' he said, with unreal carelessness, 'if you know whose writing this is?'

Oak glanced into the book, and replied instantly, with a flushed face, 'Miss Everdene's.'

Oak had coloured simply at the consciousness of sounding her name. He now felt a strangely distressing qualm from a new thought. The letter could of course be no other than anonymous, or the inquiry would not have been necessary.

Boldwood mistook his confusion: sensitive persons are always ready with their 'Is it I?' in preference to objective reasoning.

'The question was perfectly fair,' he returned—and there was something incongruous in the serious earnestness with which he applied himself to an argument on a valentine. 'You know it is always expected that privy inquiries will be made: that's where the—fun lies.' If the word 'fun' had been 'torture,' it could not have been uttered with a more constrained and restless countenance than was Boldwood's then.

Soon parting from Gabriel, the lonely and reserved man returned to his house to breakfast—feeling twinges of shame and regret at having so far exposed his mood by those fevered questions to a stranger. He again placed the letter on the mantelpiece, and sat down to think of the circumstances attending it by the light of Gabriel's information.

XVI

All Saints' and All Souls'

On a week-day morning a small congregation, consisting mainly of women and girls, rose from its knees in the mouldy nave of a church called All Saints', in the distant barrack-town before-mentioned, at the end of a service without a sermon. They were about to disperse, when a smart footstep, entering the porch and coming up the central passage, arrested their attention. The step echoed with a ring unusual in a church; it was the clink of spurs. Everybody looked. A young cavalry soldier in a red uniform, with the three chevrons of a sergeant upon his sleeve, strode up the aisle, with an embarrassment which was only the more marked by the intense vigour of his step, and by the determination upon his face to show none. A slight flush had mounted his cheek by the time he had run the gauntlet between these women; but, passing on through the chancel arch, he never paused till he came close to the altar railing. Here for a moment he stood alone.

The officiating curate, who had not yet doffed his surplice, perceived the new-comer, and followed him to the communion-space.[1] He whispered to the soldier, and then beckoned to the clerk, who in his turn whispered to an elderly woman, apparently his wife, and they also went up the chancel steps.

' 'Tis a wedding!' murmured some of the women, brightening. 'Let's wait!'

The majority again sat down.

There was a creaking of machinery behind, and some of the young ones turned their heads. From the interior face of the west wall of the tower projected a little canopy with a quarter-jack[2] and small bell beneath it, the automaton being driven by the same clock machinery that struck the large bell in the tower. Between the tower and the church was a close screen, the door of which was kept shut during services, hiding this grotesque clockwork from slight. At present, however, the door was open, and the egress of the jack, the blows on the bell, and the mannikin's retreat into the nook again, were visible to many, and audible throughout the church.

The jack had struck half-past eleven.

'Where's the woman?' whispered some of the spectators.

The young sergeant stood still with the abnormal rigidity of the old pillars around. He faced the south-east, and was as silent as he was still.

The silence grew to be a noticeable thing as the minutes went on, and nobody else appeared, and not a soul moved. The rattle of the

1. The space at the front of the church between the first row of pews and the communion rail.
2. A mechanical figure shaped like a man with a hammer, which is actuated by the clock mechanism to strike a bell at quarter-hour intervals.

quarter-jack again from its niche, its blows for three-quarters, its fussy retreat, were almost painfully abrupt, and caused many of the congregation to start palpably.

'I wonder where the woman is!' a voice whispered again.

There began now that slight shifting of feet, that artificial coughing among several, which betrays a nervous suspense. At length there was a titter. But the soldier never moved. There he stood, his face to the south-east, upright as a column, his cap in his hand.

The clock ticked on. The women threw off their nervousness, and titters and giggling became more frequent. Then came a dead silence. Every one was waiting for the end. Some persons may have noticed how extraordinarily the striking of quarters seems to quicken the flight of time. It was hardly credible that the jack had not got wrong with the minutes when the rattle began again, the puppet emerged, and the four quarters were struck fitfully as before. One could almost be positive that there was a malicious leer upon the hideous creature's face, and a mischievous delight in its twitchings. Then followed the dull and remote resonance of the twelve heavy strokes in the tower above. The women were impressed, and there was no giggle this time.

The clergyman glided into the vestry, and the clerk vanished. The sergeant had not yet turned; every woman in the church was waiting to see his face, and he appeared to know it. At last he did turn, and stalked resolutely down the nave, braving them all, with a compressed lip. Two bowed and toothless old almsmen then looked at each other and chuckled, innocently enough; but the sound had a strange weird effect in that place.

Opposite to the church was a paved square, around which several overhanging wood buildings of old time cast a picturesque shade. The young man on leaving the door went to cross the square, when, in the middle, he met a little woman. The expression of her face, which had been one of intense anxiety, sank at the sight of his nearly to terror.

'Well?' he said, in a suppressed passion, fixedly looking at her.

'O Frank—I made a mistake!—I thought that church with the spire was All Saints', and I was at the door at half-past eleven to a minute as you said. I waited till a quarter to twelve, and found then that I was in All Souls'. But I wasn't much frightened, for I thought it could be to-morrow as well.'

'You fool, for so fooling me! But say no more.'

'Shall it be to-morrow, Frank?' she asked blankly.

'To-morrow!' and he gave vent to a hoarse laugh. 'I don't go through that experience again for some time, I warrant you!'

'But after all,' she expostulated in a trembling voice, 'the mistake was not such a terrible thing! Now, dear Frank, when shall it be?'

'Ah, when? God knows!' he said, with a light irony, and turning from her walked rapidly away.

XVII

In the Market-Place

On Saturday Boldwood was in Casterbridge market-house as usual, when the disturber of his dreams entered, and became visible to him. Adam had awakened from his deep sleep, and behold! there was Eve. The farmer took courage, and for the first time really looked at her.

Material causes and emotional effects are not to be arranged in regular equation. The result from capital employed in the production of any movement of a mental nature is sometimes as tremendous as the cause itself is absurdly minute. When women are in a freakish mood their usual intuition, either from carelessness or inherent defect, seemingly fails to teach them this, and hence it was that Bathsheba was fated to be astonished to-day.

Boldwood looked at her—not slily, critically, or understandingly, but blankly at gaze, in the way a reaper looks up at a passing train—as something foreign to his element, and but dimly understood. To Boldwood women had been remote phenomena rather than necessary complements—comets of such uncertain aspect, movement, and permanence, that whether their orbits were as geometrical, unchangeable, and as subject to laws as his own, or as absolutely erratic as they superficially appeared, he had not deemed it his duty to consider.

He saw her black hair, her correct facial curves and profile, and the roundness of her chin and throat. He saw then the side of her eyelids, eyes, and lashes, and the shape of her ear. Next he noticed her figure, her skirt, and the very soles of her shoes.

Boldwood thought her beautiful, but wondered whether he was right in his thought, for it seemed impossible that this romance in the flesh, if so sweet as he imagined, could have been going on long without creating a commotion of delight among men, and provoking more inquiry than Bathsheba had done, even though that was not a little. To the best of his judgment neither nature nor art could improve this perfect one of an imperfect many. His heart began to move within him. Boldwood, it must be remembered, though forty years of age, had never before inspected a woman with the very centre and force of his glance; they had struck upon all his senses at wide angles.

Was she really beautiful? He could not assure himself that his opinion was true even now. He furtively said to a neighbour, 'Is Miss Everdene considered handsome?'

'O yes; she was a good deal noticed the first time she came, if you remember. A very handsome girl indeed.'

A man is never more credulous than in receiving favourable opinions on the beauty of a woman he is half, or quite, in love with; a mere child's word on the point has the weight of an R.A.'s.[1] Boldwood was satisfied now.

And this charming woman had in effect said to him, 'Marry me.' Why should she have done that strange thing? Boldwood's blindness to the difference between approving of what circumstances suggest, and originating what they do not suggest, was well matched by Bathsheba's insensibility to the possibly great issues of little beginnings.

She was at this moment coolly dealing with a dashing young farmer, adding up accounts with him as indifferently as if his face had been the pages of a ledger. It was evident that such a nature as his had no attraction for a woman of Bathsheba's taste. But Boldwood grew hot down to his hands with an incipient jealousy; he trod for the first time the threshold of 'the injured lover's hell.'[2] His first impulse was to go and thrust himself between them. This could be done, but only in one way—by asking to see a sample of her corn. Boldwood renounced the idea. He could not make the request; it was debasing loveliness to ask it to buy and sell, and jarred with his conceptions of her.

All this time Bathsheba was conscious of having broken into that dignified stronghold at last. His eyes, she knew, were following her everywhere. This was a triumph; and had it come naturally, such a triumph would have been the sweeter to her for this piquing delay. But it had been brought about by misdirected ingenuity, and she valued it only as she valued an artificial flower or a wax fruit.

Being a woman with some good sense in reasoning on subjects wherein her heart was not involved, Bathsheba genuinely repented that a freak which had owed its existence as much to Liddy as to herself, should ever have been undertaken, to disturb the placidity of a man she respected too highly to deliberately tease.

She that day nearly formed the intention of begging his pardon on the very next occasion of their meeting. The worst features of this arrangement were that, if he thought she ridiculed him, an apology would increase the offence by being disbelieved; and if he thought she wanted him to woo her, it would read like additional evidence of her forwardness.

XVIII

Boldwood in Meditation—Regret

Boldwood was tenant of what was called Little Weatherbury Farm, and his person was the nearest approach to aristocracy that this

1. A member of the British Royal Academy of Arts, who presumably would be an authority in judging beauty.
2. An allusion to Milton's *Paradise Lost*, Book 5, lines 449–50: "Love unlibidinous reigned, nor jealousy / Was understood, the injured lover's hell."

remoter quarter of the parish could boast of. Genteel strangers, whose god was their town, who might happen to be compelled to linger about this nook for a day, heard the sound of light wheels, and prayed to see good society, to the degree of a solitary lord, or squire at the very least, but it was only Mr. Boldwood going out for the day. They heard the sound of wheels yet once more, and were re-animated to expectancy: it was only Mr. Boldwood coming home again.

His house stood recessed from the road, and the stables, which are to a farm what a fireplace is to a room, were behind, their lower portions being lost amid bushes of laurel. Inside the blue door, open half-way down, were to be seen at this time the backs and tails of half-a-dozen warm and contented horses standing in their stalls; and as thus viewed, they presented alternations of roan and bay, in shapes like a Moorish arch,[1] the tail being a streak down the midst of each. Over these, and lost to the eye gazing in from the outer light, the mouths of the same animals could be heard busily sustaining the above-named warmth and plumpness by quantities of oats and hay. The restless and shadowy figure of a colt wandered about a loose-box at the end, whilst the steady grind of all the eaters was occasionally diversified by the rattle of a rope or the stamp of a foot.

Pacing up and down at the heels of the animals was Farmer Boldwood himself. This place was his almonry and cloister[2] in one: here, after looking to the feeding of his four-footed dependents, the celibate would walk and meditate of an evening till the moon's rays streamed in through the cobwebbed windows, or total darkness enveloped the scene.

His square-framed perpendicularity showed more fully now than in the crowd and bustle of the market-house. In this meditative walk his foot met the floor with heel and toe simultaneously, and his fine reddish-fleshed face was bent downwards just enough to render obscure the still mouth and the well-rounded though rather prominent and broad chin. A few clear and thread-like horizontal lines were the only interruption to the otherwise smooth surface of his large forehead.

The phases of Boldwood's life were ordinary enough, but his was not an ordinary nature. That stillness, which struck casual observers more than anything else in his character and habit and seemed so precisely like the rest of inanition,[3] may have been the perfect balance of enormous antagonistic forces—positives and negatives in fine adjustment. His equilibrium disturbed, he was in extremity at once. If an emotion possessed him at all, it ruled him; a feeling not mastering him was entirely latent. Stagnant or rapid, it was never slow. He was always hit mortally, or he was missed.

---

1. An arch that narrows at the bottom and hence has a horseshoelike shape.
2. Charities are distributed at an almonry, and cloisters are used for meditation; at Boldwood's stables, his charities would take the form of feeding his horses, after which he meditates.
3. Lack of vigor.

He had no light and careless touches in his constitution, either for good or for evil. Stern in the outlines of action, mild in the details, he was serious throughout all. He saw no absurd sides to the follies of life, and thus, though not quite companionable in the eyes of merry men and scoffers, and those to whom all things show life as a jest, he was not intolerable to the earnest and those acquainted with grief. Being a man who read all the dramas of life seriously, if he failed to please when they were comedies, there was no frivolous treatment to reproach him for when they chanced to end tragically.

Bathsheba was far from dreaming that the dark and silent shape upon which she had so carelessly thrown a seed was a hotbed of tropic intensity. Had she known Boldwood's moods her blame would have been fearful, and the stain upon her heart ineradicable. Moreover, had she known her present power for good or evil over this man, she would have trembled at her responsibility. Luckily for her present, unluckily for her future tranquillity, her understanding had not yet told her what Boldwood was. Nobody knew entirely; for though it was possible to form guesses concerning his wild capabilities from old floodmarks faintly visible, he had never been seen at the high tides which caused them.

Farmer Boldwood came to the stable-door and looked forth across the level fields. Beyond the first enclosure was a hedge, and on the other side of this a meadow belonging to Bathsheba's farm.

It was now early spring—the time of going to grass with the sheep, when they have the first feed of the meadows, before these are laid up for mowing. The wind, which had been blowing east for several weeks, had veered to the southward, and the middle of spring had come abruptly—almost without a beginning. It was that period in the vernal quarter when we may suppose the Dryads[4] to be waking for the season. The vegetable world begins to move and swell and the saps to rise, till in the completest silence of lone gardens and trackless plantations, where everything seems helpless and still after the bond and slavery of frost, there are bustlings, strainings, united thrusts, and pulls-all-together, in comparison with which the powerful tugs of cranes and pulleys in a noisy city are but pigmy efforts.

Boldwood, looking into the distant meadows, saw there three figures. They were those of Miss Everdene, Shepherd Oak, and Cainy Ball.

When Bathsheba's figure shone upon the farmer's eyes it lighted him up as the moon lights up a great tower. A man's body is as the shell, or the tablet, of his soul, as he is reserved or ingenuous, overflowing or self-contained. There was a change in Boldwood's exterior from its former impassibleness; and his face showed that he

4. In Greek mythology, dryads were minor gods presiding over trees and forests.

was now living outside his defences for the first time, and with a fearful sense of exposure. It is the usual experience of strong natures when they love.

At last he arrived at a conclusion. It was to go across and inquire boldly of her.

The insulation of his heart by reserve during these many years, without a channel of any kind for disposable emotion, had worked its effect. It has been observed more than once that the causes of love are chiefly subjective, and Boldwood was a living testimony to the truth of the proposition. No mother existed to absorb his devotion, no sister for his tenderness, no idle ties for sense. He became surcharged with the compound, which was genuine lover's love.

He approached the gate of the meadow. Beyond it the ground was melodious with ripples, and the sky with larks; the low bleating of the flock mingling with both. Mistress and man were engaged in the operation of making a lamb 'take,' which is performed whenever an ewe has lost her own offspring, one of the twins of another ewe being given her as a substitute. Gabriel had skinned the dead lamb, and was tying the skin over the body of the live lamb in the customary manner, whilst Bathsheba was holding open a little pen of four hurdles, into which the mother and foisted lamb were driven, where they would remain till the old sheep conceived an affection for the young one.

Bathsheba looked up at the completion of the manœuvre and saw the farmer by the gate, where he was overhung by a willow tree in full bloom. Gabriel, to whom her face was as the uncertain glory of an April day,[5] was ever regardful of its faintest changes, and instantly discerned thereon the mark of some influence from without, in the form of a keenly self-conscious reddening. He also turned and beheld Boldwood.

At once connecting these signs with the letter Boldwood had shown him, Gabriel suspected her of some coquettish procedure begun by that means, and carried on since, he knew not how.

Farmer Boldwood had read the pantomime denoting that they were aware of his presence, and the perception was as too much light turned upon his new sensibility. He was still in the road, and by moving on he hoped that neither would recognize that he had originally intended to enter the field. He passed by with an utter and overwhelming sensation of ignorance, shyness, and doubt. Perhaps in her manner there were signs that she wished to see him—perhaps not—he could not read a woman. The cabala[6] of this erotic philosophy seemed to consist of the subtlest meanings expressed in misleading ways. Every turn,

5. An allusion to lines from Shakespeare's *Two Gentlemen of Verona*, act 1, scene 3: "Oh! how this spring of love resembleth / The uncertain glory of an April day."

6. A traditional mystical interpretation of scriptures in Judaism; hence, a doctrine having secret or hidden meanings.

look, word, and accent contained a mystery quite distinct from its obvious import, and not one had ever been pondered by him until now.

As for Bathsheba, she was not deceived into the belief that Farmer Boldwood had walked by on business or in idleness. She collected the probabilities of the case, and concluded that she was herself responsible for Boldwood's appearance there. It troubled her much to see what a great flame a little wildfire was likely to kindle. Bathsheba was no schemer for marriage, nor was she deliberately a trifler with the affections of men, and a censor's experience on seeing an actual flirt after observing her would have been a feeling of surprise that Bathsheba could be so different from such a one, and yet so like what a flirt is supposed to be.

She resolved never again, by look or by sign, to interrupt the steady flow of this man's life. But a resolution to avoid an evil is seldom framed till the evil is so far advanced as to make avoidance impossible.

XIX

The Sheep-Washing—The Offer

Boldwood did eventually call upon her. She was not at home. 'Of course not,' he murmured. In contemplating Bathsheba as a woman, he had forgotten the accidents of her position as an agriculturist—that being as much of a farmer, and as extensive a farmer, as himself, her probable whereabouts was out-of-doors at this time of the year. This, and the other oversights Boldwood was guilty of, were natural to the mood, and still more natural to the circumstances. The great aids to idealization in love were present here: occasional observation of her from a distance, and the absence of social intercourse with her—visual familiarity, oral strangeness. The smaller human elements were kept out of sight; the pettinesses that enter so largely into all earthly living and doing were disguised by the accident of lover and loved-one not being on visiting terms; and there was hardly awakened a thought in Boldwood that sorry household realities appertained to her, or that she, like all others, had moments of commonplace, when to be least plainly seen was to be most prettily remembered. Thus a mild sort of apotheosis took place in his fancy, whilst she still lived and breathed within his own horizon, a troubled creature like himself.

It was the end of May when the farmer determined to be no longer repulsed by trivialities or distracted by suspense. He had by this time grown used to being in love; the passion now startled him less even when it tortured him more, and he felt himself adequate to the situation. On inquiring for her at her house they had told him she was at the sheep-washing, and he went off to seek her there.

The sheep-washing pool was a perfectly circular basin of brickwork in the meadows, full of the clearest water. To birds on the wing its glassy surface, reflecting the light sky, must have been visible for miles around as a glistening Cyclops' eye[1] in a green face. The grass about the margin at this season was a sight to remember long—in a minor sort of way. Its activity in sucking the moisture from the rich damp sod was almost a process observable by the eye. The outskirts of this level water-meadow were diversified by rounded and hollow pastures, where just now every flower that was not a buttercup was a daisy. The river slid along noiselessly as a shade, the swelling reeds and sedge forming a flexible palisade upon its moist brink. To the north of the mead were trees, the leaves of which were new, soft, and moist, not yet having stiffened and darkened under summer sun and drought, their colour being yellow beside a green—green beside a yellow. From the recesses of this knot of foliage the loud notes of three cuckoos were resounding through the still air.

Boldwood went meditating down the slopes with his eyes on his boots, which the yellow pollen from the buttercups had bronzed in artistic gradations. A tributary of the main stream flowed through the basin of the pool by an inlet and outlet at opposite points of its diameter. Shepherd Oak, Jan Coggan, Moon, Poorgrass, Cain Ball, and several others were assembled here, all dripping wet to the very roots of their hair, and Bathsheba was standing by in a new riding-habit—the most elegant she had even worn—the reins of her horse being looped over her arm. Flagons of cider were rolling about upon the green. The meek sheep were pushed into the pool by Coggan and Matthew Moon, who stood by the lower hatch, immersed to their waists; then Gabriel, who stood on the brink, thrust them under as they swam along, with an instrument like a crutch, formed for the purpose, and also for assisting the exhausted animals when the wool became saturated and they began to sink. They were let out against the stream, and through the upper opening, all impurities flowing away below. Cainy Ball and Joseph, who performed this latter operation, were if possible wetter than the rest; they resembled dolphins under a fountain, every protuberance and angle of their clothes dribbling forth a small rill.

Boldwood came close and bade her good morning with such constraint that she could not but think he had stepped across to the washing for its own sake, hoping not to find her there; more, she fancied his brow severe and his eye slighting. Bathsheba immediately contrived to withdraw, and glided along by the river till she was a stone's throw off. She heard footsteps brushing the grass, and had a consciousness that love was encircling her like a perfume. Instead of

1. In Greek mythology, the Cyclopes were giant cannibals with only one eye, which was placed in the center of the forehead.

turning or waiting, Bathsheba went further among the high sedges, but Boldwood seemed determined, and pressed on till they were completely past the bend of the river. Here, without being seen, they could hear the splashing and shouts of the washers above.

'Miss Everdene!' said the farmer.

She trembled, turned, and said 'Good morning.' His tone was so utterly removed from all she had expected as a beginning. It was lowness and quiet accentuated: an emphasis of deep meanings, their form, at the same time, being scarcely expressed. Silence has sometimes a remarkable power of showing itself as the disembodied soul of feeling wandering without its carcase, and it is then more impressive than speech. In the same way, to say a little is often to tell more than to say a great deal. Boldwood told everything in that word.

As the consciousness expands on learning that what was fancied to be the rumble of wheels is the reverberation of thunder, so did Bathsheba's at her intuitive conviction.

'I feel—almost too much—to think,' he said, with a solemn simplicity. 'I have come to speak to you without preface. My life is not my own since I have beheld you clearly, Miss Everdene—I come to make you an offer of marriage.'

Bathsheba tried to preserve an absolutely neutral countenance, and all the motion she made was that of closing lips which had previously been a little parted.

'I am now forty-one years old,' he went on. 'I may have been called a confirmed bachelor, and I was a confirmed bachelor. I had never any views of myself as a husband in my earlier days, nor have I made any calculation on the subject since I have been older. But we all change, and my change, in this matter, came with seeing you. I have felt lately, more and more, that my present way of living is bad in every respect. Beyond all things, I want you as my wife.'

'I feel, Mr. Boldwood, that though I respect you much, I do not feel—what would justify me to—in accepting your offer,' she stammered.

This giving back of dignity for dignity seemed to open the sluices of feeling that Boldwood had as yet kept closed.

'My life is a burden without you,' he exclaimed, in a low voice. 'I want you—I want you to let me say I love you again and again!'

Bathsheba answered nothing, and the mare upon her arm seemed so impressed that instead of cropping the herbage she looked up.

'I think and hope you care enough for me to listen to what I have to tell!'

Bathsheba's momentary impulse at hearing this was to ask why he thought that, till she remembered that, far from being a conceited assumption on Boldwood's part, it was but the natural conclusion of serious reflection based on deceptive premises of her own offering.

'I wish I could say courteous flatteries to you,' the farmer continued in an easier tone, 'and put my rugged feeling into a graceful shape: but I have neither power nor patience to learn such things. I want you for my wife—so wildly that no other feeling can abide in me; but I should not have spoken out had I not been led to hope.'

'The valentine again! O that valentine!' she said to herself, but not a word to him.

'If you can love me say so, Miss Everdene. If not—don't say no!'

'Mr. Boldwood, it is painful to have to say I am surprised, so that I don't know how to answer you with propriety and respect—but am only just able to speak out my feeling—I mean my meaning; that I am afraid I can't marry you, much as I respect you. You are too dignified for me to suit you, sir.'

'But, Miss Everdene!'

'I—I didn't—I know I ought never to have dreamt of sending that valentine—forgive me, sir—it was a wanton thing which no woman with any self-respect should have done. If you will only pardon my thoughtlessness, I promise never to——'

'No, no, no. Don't say thoughtlessness! Make me think it was something more—that it was a sort of prophetic instinct—the beginning of a feeling that you would like me. You torture me to say it was done in thoughtlessness—I never thought of it in that light, and I can't endure it. Ah! I wish I knew how to win you! but that I can't do—I can only ask if I have already got you. If I have not, and it is not true that you have come unwittingly to me as I have to you, I can say no more.'

'I have not fallen in love with you, Mr. Boldwood—certainly I must say that.' She allowed a very small smile to creep for the first time over her serious face in saying this, and the white row of upper teeth, and keenly-cut lips already noticed, suggested an idea of heartlessness, which was immediately contradicted by the pleasant eyes.

'But you will just think—in kindness and condescension think—if you cannot bear with me as a husband! I fear I am too old for you, but believe me I will take more care of you than would many a man of your own age. I will protect and cherish you with all my strength—I will indeed! You shall have no cares—be worried by no household affairs, and live quite at ease, Miss Everdene. The dairy superintendence shall be done by a man—I can afford it well—you shall never have so much as to look out of doors at haymaking time, or to think of weather in the harvest. I rather cling to the chaise,[2] because it is the same my poor father and mother drove, but if you don't like it I will sell it, and you shall have a pony-carriage[3] of your own. I cannot say how far above every other idea and object on earth you seem to me—nobody knows—God only knows—how much you are to me!'

Bathsheba's heart was young, and it swelled with sympathy for the deep-natured man who spoke so simply.

2. A carriage with chair-backed seats.
3. A carriage with an underslung axle and lengthwise seats.

'Don't say it: don't! I cannot bear you to feel so much, and me to feel nothing. And I am afraid they will notice us, Mr. Boldwood. Will you let the matter rest now? I cannot think collectedly. I did not know you were going to say this to me. O, I am wicked to have made you suffer so!' She was frightened as well as agitated at his vehemence.

'Say then, that you don't absolutely refuse. Do not quite refuse?'

'I can do nothing. I cannot answer.'

'I may speak to you again on the subject?'

'Yes.'

'I may think of you?'

'Yes, I suppose you may think of me.'

'And hope to obtain you?'

'No—do not hope! Let us go on.'

'I will call upon you again to-morrow.'

'No—please not. Give me time.'

'Yes—I will give you any time,' he said earnestly and gratefully. 'I am happier now.'

'No—I beg you! Don't be happier if happiness only comes from my agreeing. Be neutral, Mr. Boldwood! I must think.'

'I will wait,' he said.

And then she turned away. Boldwood dropped his gaze to the ground, and stood long like a man who did not know where he was. Realities then returned upon him like the pain of a wound received in an excitement which eclipses it, and he, too, then went on.

XX

Perplexity—Grinding the Shears—A Quarrel

'He is so disinterested and kind to offer me all that I can desire,' Bathsheba mused.

Yet Farmer Boldwood, whether by nature kind or the reverse to kind, did not exercise kindness here. The rarest offerings of the purest loves are but a self-indulgence, and no genorosity at all.

Bathsheba, not being the least in love with him, was eventually able to look calmly at his offer. It was one which many women of her own station in the neighbourhood, and not a few of higher rank, would have been wild to accept and proud to publish. In every point of view, ranging from politic to passionate, it was desirable that she, a lonely girl, should marry, and marry this earnest, well-to-do, and respected man. He was close to her doors: his standing was sufficient: his qualities were even supererogatory. Had she felt, which she did not, any wish whatever for the married state in the abstract, she could not reasonably have rejected him, being a woman who frequently appealed to her understanding for deliverance from her whims.

Boldwood as a means to marriage was unexceptionable: she esteemed and liked him, yet she did not want him. It appears that ordinary men take wives because possession is not possible without marriage, and that ordinary women accept husbands because marriage is not possible without possession; with totally differing aims the method is the same on both sides. But the understood incentive on the woman's part was wanting here. Besides, Bathsheba's position as absolute mistress of a farm and house was a novel one, and the novelty had not yet begun to wear off.

But a disquiet filled her which was somewhat to her credit, for it would have affected few. Beyond the mentioned reasons with which she combated her objections, she had a strong feeling that, having been the one who began the game, she ought in honesty to accept the consequences. Still the reluctance remained. She said in the same breath that it would be ungenerous not to marry Boldwood, and that she couldn't do it to save her life.

Bathsheba's was an impulsive nature under a deliberative aspect. An Elizabeth in brain and a Mary Stuart in spirit,[1] she often performed actions of the greatest temerity with a manner of extreme discretion. Many of her thoughts were perfect syllogisms; unluckily they always remained thoughts. Only a few were irrational assumptions; but, unfortunately, they were the ones which most frequently grew into deeds.

The next day to that of the declaration she found Gabriel Oak at the bottom of her garden, grinding his shears for the sheep-shearing. All the surrounding cottages were more or less scenes of the same operation; the scurr of whetting spread into the sky from all parts of the village as from an armoury previous to a campaign. Peace and war kiss each other at their hours of preparation—sickles, scythes, shears, and pruning-hooks ranking with swords, bayonets, and lances, in their common necessity for point and edge.

Cainy Ball turned the handle of Gabriel's grindstone, his head performing a melancholy see-saw up and down with each turn of the wheel. Oak stood somewhat as Eros[2] is represented when in the act of sharpening his arrows: his figure slightly bent, the weight of his body thrown over on the shears, and his head balanced sideways, with a critical compression of the lips and contraction of the eyelids to crown the attitude.

His mistress came up and looked upon them in silence for a minute or two; then she said—

'Cain, go to the lower mead and catch the bay mare. I'll turn the

1. Queen Elizabeth I (1533–1603) was regarded as shrewd and calculating; Mary Stuart (1516–1558), as impulsive and rash.
2. In classical mythology, Eros, also called Cupid, was the god of love, often represented as a boy with a bow and arrows; Hardy may have had in mind the painting titled "Cupid Sharpening His Arrows" by Rafael Mengs (1728–79).

winch of the grindstone. I want to speak to you, Gabriel.'

Cain departed, and Bathsheba took the handle. Gabriel had glanced up in intense surprise, quelled its expression, and looked down again. Bathsheba turned the winch, and Gabriel applied the shears.

The peculiar motion involved in turning a wheel has a wonderful tendency to benumb the mind. It is a sort of attenuated variety of Ixion's punishment,[3] and contributes a dismal chapter to the history of gaols. The brain gets muddled, the head grows heavy, and the body's centre of gravity seems to settle by degrees in a leaden lump somewhere between the eyebrows and the crown. Bathsheba felt the unpleasant symptoms after two three dozen turns.

'Will you turn, Gabriel, and let me hold the shears?' she said. 'My head is in a whirl, and I can't talk.'

Gabriel turned. Bathsheba then began, with some awkwardness, allowing her thoughts to stray occasionally from her story to attend to the shears, which required a little nicety in sharpening.

'I wanted to ask you if the men made any observation on my going behind the sedge with Mr. Boldwood yesterday?'

'Yes, they did,' said Gabriel. 'You don't hold the shears right, miss—I knew you wouldn't know the way—hold like this.'

He relinquished the winch, and enclosing her two hands completely in his own (taking each as we sometimes clasp a child's hand in teaching him to write), grasped the shears with her. 'Incline the edge so,' he said.

Hands and shears were inclined to suit the words, and held thus for a peculiarly long time by the instructor as he spoke.

'That will do,' exclaimed Bathsheba. 'Loose my hands. I won't have them held! Turn the winch.'

Gabriel freed her hands quietly, retired to his handle, and the grinding went on.

'Did the men think it odd?' she said again.

'Odd was not the idea, miss.'

'What did they say?'

'That Farmer Boldwood's name and your own were likely to be flung over pulpit together before the year was out.'

'I thought so by the look of them! Why, there's nothing in it. A more foolish remark was never made, and I want you to contradict it: that's what I came for.'

Gabriel looked incredulous and sad, but between his moments of incredulity, relieved.

'They must have heard our conversation,' she continued.

'Well, then, Bathsheba!' said Oak, stopping the handle, and gazing into her face with astonishment.

---

3. In Greek legend, Ixion was punished by being bound to a perpetually revolving wheel of fire.

'Miss Everdene, you mean,' she said, with dignity.

'I mean this, that if Mr. Boldwood really spoke of marriage, I bain't going to tell a story and say he didn't to please you. I have already tried to please you too much for my own good!'

Bathsheba regarded him with round-eyed perplexity. She did not know whether to pity him for disappointed love of her, or to be angry with him for having got over it—his tone being ambiguous.

'I said I wanted you just to mention that it was not true I was going to be married to him,' she murmured, with a slight decline in her assurance.

'I can say that to them if you wish, Miss Everdene. And I could likewise give an opinion to 'ee on what you have done.'

'I daresay. But I don't want your opinion.'

'I suppose not,' said Gabriel bitterly, and going on with his turning; his words rising and falling in a regular swell and cadence as he stooped or rose with the winch, which directed them, according to his position, perpendicularly into the earth, or horizontally along the garden, his eyes being fixed on a leaf upon the ground.

With Bathsheba a hastened act was a rash act; but, as does not always happen, time gained was prudence ensured. It must be added, however, that time was very seldom gained. At this period the single opinion in the parish on herself and her doings that she valued as sounder than her own was Gabriel Oak's. And the outspoken honesty of his character was such that on any subject, even that of her love for, or marriage with, another man, the same disinterestedness of opinion might be calculated on, and be had for the asking. Thoroughly convinced of the impossibility of his own suit, a high resolve constrained him not to injure that of another. This is a lover's most stoical virtue, as the lack of it is a lover's most venial sin. Knowing he would reply truly she asked the question, painful as she must have known the subject would be. Such is the selfishness of some charming women. Perhaps it was some excuse for her thus torturing honesty to her own advantage, that she had absolutely no other sound judgment within easy reach.

'Well, what is your opinion of my conduct,' she said quietly.

'That it is unworthy of any thoughtful, and meek, and comely woman.'

In an instant Bathsheba's face coloured with the angry crimson of a Danby sunset.[4] But she forbore to utter this feeling, and the reticence of her tongue only made the loquacity of her face the more noticeable.

The next thing Gabriel did was to make a mistake.

'Perhaps you don't like the rudeness of my reprimanding you, for I know it is rudeness; but I thought it would do good.'

She instantly replied sarcastically—

---

4. A reference to the English landscape painter James Frances Danby (1816–75), who was especially known for the brilliant colors of his sunsets.

'On the contrary, my opinion of you is so low, that I see in your abuse the praise of discerning people!'

'I am glad you don't mind it, for I said it honestly and with every serious meaning.'

'I see. But, unfortunately, when you try not to speak in jest you are amusing—just as when you wish to avoid seriousness you sometimes say a sensible word.'

It was a hard hit, but Bathsheba had unmistakably lost her temper, and on that account Gabriel had never in his life kept his own better. He said nothing. She then broke out—

'I may ask, I suppose, where in particular my unworthiness lies? In my not marrying you, perhaps!'

'Not by any means,' said Gabriel quietly. 'I have long given up thinking of that matter.'

'Or wishing it, I suppose,' she said; and it was apparent that she expected an unhesitating denial of this supposition.

Whatever Gabriel felt, he coolly echoed her words—

'Or wishing it either.'

A woman may be treated with a bitterness which is sweet to her, and with a rudeness which is not offensive. Bathsheba would have submitted to an indignant chastisement for her levity had Gabriel protested that he was loving her at the same time; the impetuosity of passion unrequited is bearable, even if it stings and anathematizes—there is a triumph in the humiliation, and a tenderness in the strife. This was what she had been expecting, and what she had not got. To be lectured because the lecturer saw her in the cold morning light of open-shuttered disillusion was exasperating. He had not finished, either. He continued in a more agitated voice:—

'My opinion is (since you ask it) that you are greatly to blame for playing pranks upon a man like Mr. Boldwood, merely as a pastime. Leading on a man you don't care for is not a praiseworthy action. And even, Miss Everdene, if you seriously inclined towards him, you might have let him find it out in some way of true loving-kindness, and not by sending him a valentine's letter.'

Bathsheba laid down the shears.

'I cannot allow any man to—to criticize my private conduct!' she exclaimed. 'Nor will I for a minute. So you'll please leave the farm at the end of the week!'

It may have been a peculiarity—at any rate it was a fact—that when Bathsheba was swayed by an emotion of an earthly sort her lower lip trembled: when by a refined emotion, her upper or heavenward one. Her nether lip quivered now.

'Very well, so I will,' said Gabriel calmly. He had been held to her by a beautiful thread which it pained him to spoil by breaking, rather than by a chain he could not break. 'I should be even better pleased to go at once,' he added.

'Go at once then, in Heaven's name!' said she, her eyes flashing at his, though never meeting them. 'Don't let me see your face any more.'

'Very well, Miss Everdene—so it shall be.'

And he took his shears and went away from her in placid dignity, as Moses left the presence of Pharaoh.[5]

XXI

Troubles in the Fold—A Message

Gabriel Oak had ceased to feed the Weatherbury flock for about four-and-twenty hours, when on Sunday afternoon the elderly gentlemen Joseph Poorgrass, Matthew Moon, Fray, and half-a-dozen others, came running up to the house of the mistress of the Upper Farm.

'Whatever *is* the matter, men?' she said, meeting them at the door just as she was coming out on her way to church, and ceasing in a moment from the close compression of her two red lips, with which she had accompanied the exertion of pulling on a tight glove.

'Sixty!' said Joseph Poorgrass.

'Seventy!' said Moon.

'Fifty-nine!' said Susan Tall's husband.

'—Sheep have broke fence,' said Fray.

'—And got into a field of young clover,' said Tall.

'—Young clover!' said Moon.

'—Clover!' said Joseph Poorgrass.

'And they be getting blasted,'[1] said Henery Fray.

'That they be,' said Joseph.

'And will all die as dead as nits, if they bain't got out and cured!' said Tall.

Joseph's countenance was drawn into lines and puckers by his concern. Fray's forehead was wrinkled both perpendicularly and crosswise, after the pattern of a portcullis, expressive of a double despair. Laban Tall's lips were thin, and his face was rigid. Matthew's jaws sank, and his eyes turned whichever way the strongest muscle happened to pull them.

'Yes,' said Joseph, 'and I was sitting at home looking for Ephesians, and says I to myself, " 'Tis nothing but Corinthians and Thessalonians in this danged Testament,"[2] when who should come in but Henery

---

5. An allusion to Exodus 10:28–29. Pharaoh's words, "Get thee from me . . . see my face no more," are echoed by Bathsheba's "Don't let me see your face any more," and Gabriel Oak's immediate assent parallels Moses' reply, "Thou hast spoken well, I will see thy face again no more."

1. Exceedingly bloated with gas; a condition that afflicts sheep that have eaten too much clover or other green forage.

2. Ephesians is one of three very short books between 2 Corinthians and 1 Thessalonians, hence easily overlooked when thumbing through the New Testament.

there: "Joseph," he said, "the sheep have blasted theirselves——" '

With Bathsheba it was a moment when thought was speech and speech exclamation. Moreover, she had hardly recovered her equanimity since the disturbance which she had suffered from Oak's remarks.

'That's enough—that's enough!—O you fools!' she cried, throwing the parasol and Prayer-book into the passage, and running out of doors in the direction signified. 'To come to me, and not go and get them out directly! O, the stupid numskulls!'

Her eyes were at their darkest and brightest now. Bathsheba's beauty belonging rather to the demonian than to the angelic school, she never looked so well as when she was angry—and particularly when the effect was heightened by a rather dashing velvet dress, carefully put on before a glass.

All the ancient men ran in a jumbled throng after her to the clover-field, Joseph sinking down in the midst when about half-way, like an individual withering in a world which was more and more insupportable. Having once received the stimulus that her presence always gave them they went round among the sheep with a will. The majority of the afflicted animals were lying down, and could not be stirred. These were bodily lifted out, and the others driven into the adjoining field. Here, after the lapse of a few minutes, several more fell down, and lay helpless and livid as the rest.

Bathsheba, with a sad, bursting heart, looked at these primest specimens of her prime flock as they rolled there—

> Swoln with wind and the rank mist they drew.[3]

Many of them foamed at the mouth, their breathing being quick and short, whilst the bodies of all were fearfully distended.

'O, what can I do, what can I do!' said Bathsheba, helplessly. 'Sheep are such unfortunate animals!—there's always something happening to them! I never knew a flock pass a year without getting into some scrape or other.'

'There's only one way of saving them,' said Tall.

'What way? Tell me quick!'

'They must be pierced in the side with a thing made on purpose.'

'Can you do it? Can I?'

'No, ma'am. We can't, nor you neither. It must be done in a particular spot. If ye go to the right or left but an inch you stab the ewe and kill her. Not even a shepherd can do it, as a rule.'

'Then they must die,' she said, in a resigned tone.

'Only one man in the neighbourhood knows the way,' said Joseph, now just come up. 'He could cure 'em all if he were here.'

'Who is he? Let's get him!'

'Shepherd Oak,' said Matthew. 'Ah, he's a clever man in talents!'

---

3. A quotation from Milton's *Lycidas*, line 126.

'Ah, that he is so!' said Joseph Poorgrass.

'True—he's the man,' said Laban Tall.

'How dare you name that man in my presence!' she said excitedly. 'I told you never to allude to him, nor shall you if you stay with me. Ah!' she added, brightening, 'Farmer Boldwood knows!'

'O no, ma'am,' said Matthew. 'Two of his store ewes got into some vetches[4] t'other day, and were just like these. He sent a man on horseback here posthaste for Gable, and Gable went and saved 'em. Farmer Boldwood hev got the thing they do it with. 'Tis a holler pipe, with a sharp pricker inside. Isn't it, Joseph?'

'Ay—a holler pipe,' echoed Joseph. 'That's what 'tis.'

'Ay, sure—that's the machine,' chimed in Henery Fray reflectively, with an Oriental indifference to the flight of time.

'Well,' burst out Bathsheba, 'don't stand there with your "ayes" and your "sures," talking at me! Get somebody to cure the sheep instantly!'

All then stalked off in consternation, to get somebody as directed, without any idea of who it was to be. In a minute they had vanished through the gate, and she stood alone with the dying flock.

'Never will I send for him—never!' she said firmly.

One of the ewes here contracted its muscles horribly, extended itself, and jumped high into the air. The leap was an astonishing one. The ewe fell heavily, and lay still.

Bathsheba went up to it. The sheep was dead.

'O, what shall I do—what shall I do!' she again exclaimed, wringing her hands. 'I won't send for him. No, I won't!'

The most vigorous expression of a resolution does not always coincide with the greatest vigour of the resolution itself. It is often flung out as a sort of prop to support a decaying conviction which, whilst strong, required no enunciation to prove it so. The 'No, I won't' of Bathsheba meant virtually, 'I think I must.'

She followed her assistants through the gate, and lifted her hand to one of them. Laban answered to her signal.

'Where is Oak staying?'

'Across the valley at Nest Cottage.'

'Jump on the bay mare, and ride across, and say he must return instantly—that I say so.'

Tall scrambled off to the field, and in two minutes was on Poll, the bay, bare-backed, and with only a halter by way of rein. He diminished down the hill.

Bathsheba watched. So did all the rest. Tall cantered along the bridle-path through Sixteen Acres, Sheeplands, Middle Field, The Flats, Cappel's Piece, shrank almost to a point, crossed the bridge, and ascended from the valley through Springmead and Whitepits on the other side. The cottage to which Gabriel had retired before taking his final departure from the locality was visible as a white spot on the

4. A variety of climbing herbs cultivated for animal forage and soil improvement.

opposite hill, backed by blue firs. Bathsheba walked up and down. The men entered the field and endeavoured to ease the anguish of the dumb creatures by rubbing them. Nothing availed.

Bathsheba continued walking. The horse was seen descending the hill, and the wearisome series had to be repeated in reverse order: Whitepits, Springmead, Cappel's Piece, The Flats, Middle Field, Sheeplands, Sixteen Acres. She hoped Tall had had presence of mind enough to give the mare up to Gabriel, and return himself on foot. The rider neared them. It was Tall.

'O what folly!' said Bathsheba.

Gabriel was not visible anywhere.

'Perhaps he is already gone!' she said.

Tall came into the inclosure, and leapt off, his face tragic as Morton's after the battle of Shrewsbury.[5]

'Well?' said Bathsheba, unwilling to believe that her verbal *lettre-de-cachet*[6] could possibly have miscarried.

'He says *beggars mustn't be choosers,*' replied Laban.

'What!' said the young farmer, opening her eyes and drawing in her breath for an outburst. Joseph Poorgrass retired a few steps behind a hurdle.

'He says he shall not come onless you request en to come civilly and in a proper manner, as becomes any 'ooman begging a favour.'

'Oh, oh, that's his answer! Where does he get his airs? Who am I, then, to be treated like that? Shall I beg to a man who has begged to me?'

Another of the flock sprang into the air, and fell dead.

The men looked grave, as if they suppressed opinion.

Bathsheba turned aside, her eyes full of tears. The strait she was in through pride and shrewishness could not be disguised longer: she burst out crying bitterly; they all saw it; and she attempted no further concealment.

'I wouldn't cry about it, miss,' said William Smallbury compassionately. 'Why not ask him softer like? I'm sure he'd come then. Gable is a true man in that way.'

Bathsheba checked her grief and wiped her eyes. 'O, it is a wicked cruelty to me—it is—it is!' she murmured. 'And he drives me to do what I wouldn't; yes, he does!—Tall, come indoors.'

After this collapse, not very dignified for the head of an establishment, she went into the house, Tall at her heels. Here she sat down and hastily scribbled a note between the small convulsive sobs of convalescence which follow a fit of crying as a ground-swell follows a storm. The note was none the less polite for being written in a hurry.

5. An allusion to Shakespeare's Henry IV, part 2, act 1, scene 1, in which Morton sadly announces the death of Hotspur.

6. Literally, French for "a letter with a seal"; used to designate a letter from the king of France containing an arbitrary warrant for imprisonment.

She held it at a distance, was about to fold it, then added these words at the bottom:—

'Do not desert me, Gabriel!'

She looked a little redder in refolding it, and closed her lips, as if thereby to suspend till too late the action of conscience in examining whether such strategy were justifiable. The note was despatched as the message had been, and Bathsheba waited indoors for the result.

It was an anxious quarter of an hour that intervened between the messenger's departure and the sound of the horse's tramp again outside. She could not watch this time, but, leaning over the old bureau at which she had written the letter, closed her eyes, as if to keep out both hope and fear.

The case, however, was a promising one. Gabriel was not angry: he was simply neutral, although her first command had been so haughty. Such imperiousness would have damned a little less beauty; and on the other hand, such beauty would have redeemed a little less imperiousness.

She went out when the horse was heard, and looked up. A mounted figure passed between her and the sky, and drew on towards the field of sheep, the rider turning his face in receding. Gabriel looked at her. It was a moment when a woman's eyes and tongue tell distinctly opposite tales. Bathsheba looked full of gratitude, and she said:—

'O, Gabriel, how could you serve me so unkindly!'

Such a tenderly-shaped reproach for his previous delay was the one speech in the language that he could pardon for not being commendation of his readiness now.

Gabriel murmured a confused reply, and hastened on. She knew from the look which sentence in her note had brought him. Bathsheba followed to the field.

Gabriel was already among the turgid, prostrate forms. He had flung off his coat, rolled up his shirt-sleeves, and taken from his pocket the instrument of salvation. It was a small tube or trochar,[7] with a lance passing down the inside; and Gabriel began to use it with a dexterity that would have graced a hospital-surgeon. Passing his hand over the sheep's left flank, and selecting the proper point, he punctured the skin and rumen[8] with the lance as it stood in the tube; then he suddenly withdrew the lance, retaining the tube in its place. A current of air rushed up the tube, forcible enough to have extinguished a candle held at the orifice.

It has been said[9] that mere ease after torment is delight for a time; and the countenances of these poor creatures expressed it now. Forty-nine operations were successfully performed. Owing to the

7. A sharply pointed lance that projects from within a hollow tube.
8. The first of four stomach compartments of the sheep.
9. By Edmund Burke, whose definition of *delight* Hardy paraphrases.

great hurry necessitated by the far-gone state of some of the flock, Gabriel missed his aim in one case, and in one only—striking wide of the mark, and inflicting a mortal blow at once upon the suffering ewe. Four had died; three recovered without an operation. The total number of sheep which had thus strayed and injured themselves so dangerously was fifty-seven.

When the love-led man had ceased from his labours Bathsheba came and looked him in the face.

'Gabriel, will you stay on with me?' she said, smiling winningly, and not troubling to bring her lips quite together again at the end, because there was going to be another smile soon.

'I will,' said Gabriel.

And she smiled on him again.

XXII

The Great Barn and the Sheep-Shearers

Men thin away to insignificance and oblivion quite as often by not making the most of good spirits when they have them as by lacking good spirits when they are indispensable. Gabriel lately, for the first time since his prostration by misfortune, had been independent in thought and vigorous in action to a marked extent—conditions which, powerless without an opportunity as an opportunity without them is barren, would have given him a sure lift upwards when the favourable conjunction should have occurred. But this incurable loitering beside Bathsheba Everdene stole his time ruinously. The spring tides were going by without floating him off, and the neap[1] might soon come which could not.

It was the first day of June, and the sheep-shearing season culminated, the landscape, even to the leanest pasture, being all health and colour. Every green was young, every pore was open, and every stalk was swollen with racing currents of juice. God was palpably present in the country, and the devil had gone with the world to town. Flossy catkins of the later kinds, fern-sprouts like bishops' croziers, the square-headed moschatel, the odd cuckoo-pint,—like an apoplectic saint in a niche of malachite,—snow-white ladies'-smocks, the toothwort, approximating to human flesh, the enchanter's night-shade, and the black-petaled doleful-bells,[2] were among the quainter objects

---

1. Spring tides are the highest; neap tides the lowest.

2. "Flossy catkins": small, fluffy, drooping scalelike flower clusters growing on willow trees, birches, etc.; "bishop's croziers": the pastoral staffs of bishops are coiled at the top; "moschatel": a small, shade-loving plant with light green flowers and a musky smell; "cuckoo-pint": a plant with a spiky flower cluster partly enclosed by a specialized green leaf called a bract; "malachite": a green mineral; "ladies'-smocks": some varieties of this plant have brilliantly white flowers; "toothwort": a fleshy, parasitic plant with cream-colored stems and flesh-colored flowers; "night-shade": any of a variety of plants of the genus *Solanum*, many of them poisonous and traditionally associated with witchcraft; "doleful-bells": a plant with drooping, dark-colored flowers.

of the vegetable world in and about Weatherbury at this teeming time; and of the animal, the metamorphosed figures of Mr. Jan Coggan, the master-shearer; the second and third shearers, who travelled in the exercise of their calling, and do not require definition by name; Henery Fray the fourth shearer, Susan Tall's husband the fifth, Joseph Poorgrass the sixth, young Cain Ball as assistant-shearer, and Gabriel Oak as general supervisor. None of these were clothed to any extent worth mentioning, each appearing to have hit in the matter of raiment the decent mean between a high and low caste Hindoo. An angularity of lineament, and a fixity of facial machinery in general, proclaimed that serious work was the order of the day.

They sheared in the great barn, called for the nonce the Shearing-barn, which on ground-plan resembled a church with transepts.[3] It not only emulated the form of the neighbouring church of the parish, but vied with it in antiquity. Whether the barn had ever formed one of a group of conventual[4] buildings nobody seemed to be aware; no trace of such surroundings remained. The vast porches at the sides, lofty enough to admit a waggon laden to its highest with corn in the sheaf, were spanned by heavy-pointed arches of stone, broadly and boldly cut, whose very simplicity was the origin of a grandeur not apparent in erections where more ornament has been attempted. The dusky, filmed, chestnut roof, braced and tied in by huge collars,[5] curves, and diagonals, was far nobler in design, because more wealthy in material, than nine-tenths of those in our modern churches. Along each side wall was a range of striding buttresses,[6] throwing deep shadows on the spaces between them, which were perforated by lancet openings,[7] combining in their proportions the precise requirements both of beauty and ventilation.

One could say about this barn, what could hardly be said of either the church or the castle, akin to it in age and style, that the purpose which had dictated its original erection was the same with that to which it was still applied. Unlike and superior to either of those two typical remnants of mediævalism, the old barn embodied practices which had suffered no mutilation at the hands of time. Here at least the spirit of the ancient builders was at one with the spirit of the modern beholder. Standing before this abraded[8] pile, the eye regarded its present usage, the mind dwelt upon its past history, with a satisfied sense of functional continuity throughout—a feeling almost of grati-tude, and quite of pride, at the permanence of the idea which had heaped it up. The fact that four centuries had neither proved it to be founded on a mistake, inspired any hatred of its purpose, nor given rise to any reaction that had battered it down, invested this simple grey effort of old minds with a repose, if not a grandeur, which a too curious

3. Trancepts: the lateral arms of a cruciform church.
4. Belonging to a convent or monastery.
5. Horizontal beams tying rafters together.
6. Flying buttresses—arches sprung against the outside wall of a church to help carry the thrust of the roof-vaulting.
7. Very narrow windows with sharply pointed arches.
8. Eroded by time.

reflection was apt to disturb in its ecclesiastical military compeers. For once mediævalism and modernism had a common standpoint. The lancelote windows, the time-eaten arch-stones and chamfers, the orientation of the axis, the misty chestnut work of the rafters,[9] referred to no exploded fortifying art or worn-out religious creed. The defence and salvation of the body by daily bread is still a study, a religion, and a desire.

To-day the large side doors were thrown open towards the sun to admit a bountiful light to the immediate spot of the shearers' operations, which was the wood threshing-floor in the centre, formed of thick oak, black with age and polished by the beating of flails for many generations, till it had grown as slippery and as rich in hue as the state-room floors of an Elizabethan mansion. Here the shearers knelt, the sun slanting in upon their bleached shirts, tanned arms, and the polished shears they flourished, causing these to bristle with a thousand rays strong enough to blind a weak-eyed man. Beneath them a captive sheep lay panting, quickening its pants as misgiving merged in terror, till it quivered like the hot landscape outside.

This picture of to-day in its frame of four hundred years ago did not produce that marked contrast between ancient and modern which is implied by the contrast of date. In comparison with cities, Weatherbury was immutable. The citizen's *Then* is the rustic's *Now*. In London, twenty or thirty years ago are old times; in Paris ten years, or five; in Weatherbury three or four score years were included in the mere present, and nothing less than a century set a mark on its face or tone. Five decades hardly modified the cut of a gaiter, the embroidery of a smock-frock, by the breadth of a hair. Ten generations failed to alter the turn of a single phrase. In these Wessex nooks the busy outsider's ancient times are only old; his old times are still new; his present is futurity.

So the barn was natural to the shearers, and the shearers were in harmony with the barn.

The spacious ends of the building, answering ecclesiastically to nave and chancel[1] extremities, were fenced off with hurdles,[2] the sheep being all collected in a crowd within these two enclosures; and in one angle a catching-pen was formed, in which three or four sheep were continuously kept ready for the shearers to seize without loss of time. In the background, mellowed by tawny shade, were the three women, Maryann Money, and Temperance and Soberness Miller,

9. "Lanceolate": with narrow, pointed arches; "arch-stones": stones cut in wedge shapes to form an arch; "chamfers": beveled corners; "orientation of the axis": the compass direction in which a building is aligned; "misty chestnut work": the pattern of the chestnut wood rafters, perceived as "misty" because they are high up and in dim light.

1. In a cruciform church, the "nave" is the main part of the structure, from the entrance to the transept (see note 3 above); the "chancel" is the part of the structure beyond the transept where the altar is located.

2. Portable barriers usually made of woven wooden saplings and held erect by being fastened to stakes pounded into the ground; they are used for many kinds of temporary fencing on a farm.

gathering up the fleeces and twisting ropes of wool with a wimble for tying them round. They were indifferently well assisted by the old maltster, who, when the malting season from October to April had passed, made himself useful upon any of the bordering farmsteads.

Behind all was Bathsheba, carefully watching the men to see that there was no cutting or wounding through carelessness, and that the animals were shorn close. Gabriel, who flitted and hovered under her bright eyes like a moth, did not shear continuously, half his time being spent in attending to the others and selecting the sheep for them. At the present moment he was engaged in handing round a mug of mild liquor, supplied from a barrel in the corner, and cut pieces of bread and cheese.

Bathsheba, after throwing a glance here, a caution there, and lecturing one of the younger operators who had allowed his last finished sheep to go off among the flock without re-stamping it with her initials, came again to Gabriel, as he put down the luncheon to drag a frightened ewe to his shear-station, flinging it over upon its back with a dexterous twist of the arm. He lopped off the tresses about its head, and opened up the neck and collar, his mistress quietly looking on.

'She blushes at the insult,' murmured Bathsheba, watching the pink flush which arose and overspread the neck and shoulders of the ewe where they were left bare by the clicking shears—a flush which was enviable, for its delicacy, by many queens of coteries, and would have been creditable, for its promptness, to any woman in the world.

Poor Gabriel's soul was fed with a luxury of content by having her over him, her eyes critically regarding his skilful shears, which apparently were going to gather up a piece of the flesh at every close, and yet never did so. Like Guildenstern, Oak was happy in that he was not over happy.[3] He had no wish to converse with her: that his bright lady and himself formed one group, exclusively their own, and containing no others in the world, was enough.

So the chatter was all on her side. There is a loquacity that tells nothing, which was Bathsheba's; and there is a silence which says much: that was Gabriel's. Full of this dim and temperate bliss he went on to fling the ewe over upon her other side, covering her head with his knee, gradually running the shears line after line round her dewlap, thence about her flank and back, and finishing over the tail.

'Well done, and done quickly!' said Bathsheba, looking at her watch as the last snip resounded.

'How long, miss?' said Gabriel, wiping his brow.

'Three-and-twenty minutes and a half since you took the first lock from its forehead. It is the first time that I have ever seen one done in less than half an hour.'

The clean, sleek creature arose from its fleece—how perfectly like

3. An allusion to Guildenstern's words in *Hamlet*, act 2, scene 2.

Aphrodite rising from the foam[4] should have been seen to be realized—looking startled and shy at the loss of its garment, which lay on the floor in one soft cloud, united throughout, the portion visible being the inner surface only, which, never before exposed, was white as snow, and without flaw or blemish of the minutest kind.

'Cain Ball!'

'Yes, Mister Oak; here I be!'

Cainy now runs forward with the tar-pot. 'B. E.' is newly stamped upon the shorn skin, and away the simple dam leaps, panting, over the board into the shirtless flock outside. Then up comes Maryann; throws the loose locks into the middle of the fleece, rolls it up, and carries it into the background as three-and-a-half pounds of unadulterated warmth for the winter enjoyment of persons unknown and far away, who will, however, never experience the superlative comfort derivable from the wool as it here exists, new and pure—before the unctuousness of its nature whilst in a living state has dried, stiffened, and been washed out—rendering it just now as superior to anything *woollen* as cream is superior to milk-and-water.

But heartless circumstance could not leave entire Gabriel's happiness of this morning. The rams, old ewes, and two-shear ewes[5] had duly undergone their stripping, and the men were proceeding with the shearlings and hogs,[6] when Oak's belief that she was going to stand pleasantly by and time him through another performance was painfully interrupted by Farmer Boldwood's appearance in the extremest corner of the barn. Nobody seemed to have perceived his entry, but there he certainly was. Boldwood always carried with him a social atmosphere of his own, which everybody felt who came near him; and the talk, which Bathsheba's presence had somewhat suppressed, was now totally suspended.

He crossed over towards Bathsheba, who turned to greet him with a carriage of perfect ease. He spoke to her in low tones, and she instinctively modulated her own to the same pitch, and her voice ultimately even caught the inflection of his. She was far from having a wish to appear mysteriously connected with him; but woman at the impressionable age gravitates to the larger body not only in her choice of words, which is apparent every day, but even in her shades of tone and humour when the influence is great.

What they conversed about was not audible to Gabriel, who was too independent to get near, though too concerned to disregard. The issue of their dialogue was the taking of her hand by the courteous farmer to help her over the spreading-board[7] into the bright June sunlight outside. Standing beside the sheep already shorn, they went on talking

---

4. In Greek mythology, Aphrodite sprang from the sea foam near the island of Cytherea.
5. Sheep that have been shorn twice.
6. A "shearling" is a sheep that has been shorn once; a "hog" is a sheep that has never been shorn.
7. A board upon which sheep are laid while being sheared.

again. Concerning the flock? Apparently not. Gabriel theorized, not without truth, that in quiet discussion of any matter within reach of the speakers' eyes, these are usually fixed upon it. Bathsheba demurely regarded a contemptible straw lying upon the ground, in a way which suggested less ovine criticism[8] than womanly embarrassment. She became more or less red in the cheek, the blood wavering in uncertain flux and reflux over the sensitive space between ebb and flood. Gabriel sheared on, constrained and sad.

She left Boldwood's side, and he walked up and down alone for nearly a quarter of an hour. Then she reappeared in her new riding-habit of myrtle-green, which fitted her to the waist as a rind fits its fruit; and young Bob Coggan led on her mare, Boldwood fetching his own horse from the tree under which it had been tied.

Oak's eyes could not forsake them; and in endeavouring to continue his shearing at the same time that he watched Boldwood's manner, he snipped the sheep in the groin. The animal plunged; Bathsheba instantly gazed towards it, and saw the blood.

'O Gabriel!' she exclaimed, with severe remonstrance, 'you who are so strict with the other men—see what you are doing yourself!'

To an outsider there was not much to complain of in this remark; but to Oak, who knew Bathsheba to be well aware that she herself was the cause of the poor ewe's wound, because she had wounded the ewe's shearer in a still more vital part, it had a sting which the abiding sense of his inferiority to both herself and Boldwood was not calculated to heal. But a manly resolve to recognize boldly that he had no longer a lover's interest in her, helped him occasionally to conceal a feeling.

'Bottle!' he shouted, in an unmoved voice of routine. Cainy Ball ran up, the wound was anointed, and the shearing continued.

Boldwood gently tossed Bathsheba into the saddle, and before they turned away she again spoke out to Oak with the same dominative and tantalizing graciousness.

'I am going now to see Mr. Boldwood's Leicesters.[9] Take my place in the barn, Gabriel, and keep the men carefully to their work.'

The horses' heads were put about, and they trotted away.

Boldwood's deep attachment was a matter of great interest among all around him; but, after having been pointed out for so many years as the perfect exemplar of thriving bachelorship, his lapse was an anti-climax somewhat resembling that of St. John Long's death by consumption in the midst of his proofs that it was not a fatal disease.[1]

'That means matrimony,' said Temperance Miller, following them out of sight with her eyes.

'I reckon that's the size o't,' said Coggan, working along without

---

8. Critical discussion of sheep.
9. A long-wooled, hornless breed of English sheep developed in Leicestershire.
1. St. John Long (1789–1834) was a quack doc-

tor in London who claimed to be able to cure tuberculosis (consumption) by rubbing his patients with liniments; he himself died of the disease.

looking up.

'Well, better wed over the mixen than over the moor,'[2] said Laban Tall, turning his sheep.

Henery Fray spoke, exhibiting miserable eyes at the same time: 'I don't see why a maid should take a husband when she's bold enough to fight her own battles, and don't want a home; for 'tis keeping another woman out. But let it be, for 'tis a pity he and she should trouble two houses.'

As usual with decided characters, Bathsheba invariably provoked the criticism of individuals like Henery Fray. Her emblazoned fault was to be too pronounced in her objections, and not sufficiently overt in her likings. We learn that it is not the rays which bodies absorb, but those which they reject, that give them the colours they are known by; and in the same way people are specialized by their dislikes and antagonisms, whilst their goodwill is looked upon as no attribute at all.

Henery continued in a more complaisant mood: 'I once hinted my mind to her on a few things, as nearly as a battered frame dared to do so to such a froward piece. You all know, neighbours, what a man I be, and how I come down with my powerful words when my pride is boiling wi' scarn?'[3]

'We do, we do, Henery.'

'So I said, "Mistress Everdene, there's places empty, and there's gifted men willing; but the spite"—no, not the spite—I didn't say spite—"but the villainy of the contrarikind," I said (meaning woman-kind), "keeps 'em out." That wasn't too strong for her, say?'

'Passably well put.'

'Yes; and I would have said it, had death and salvation overtook me for it. Such is my spirit when I have a mind.'

'A true man, and proud as a lucifer.'

'You see the artfulness? Why, 'twas about being baily really; but I didn't put it so plain that she could understand my meaning, so I could lay it on all the stronger. That was my depth! . . . However, let her marry an she will. Perhaps 'tis high time. I believe Farmer Boldwood kissed her behind the spear-bed[4] at the sheep-washing t'other day— that I do.'

'What a lie!' said Gabriel.

'Ah, neighbour Oak—how'st know?' said Henery mildly.

'Because she told me all that passed,' said Oak, with a pharisaical sense that he has not as other shearers in this matter.[5]

'Ye have a right to believe it,' said Henery, with dudgeon; 'a very true right. But I mid[6] see a little distance into things! To be long-

2. A "mixen" is a dunghill, and a "moor" a tract of open, peaty wasteland. The saying is a folk expression meaning that it is better to marry a neighbor you know that a stranger from a distance.

3. Scorn (dialect).

4. A place where reeds are growing.

5. An echo of Luke 18:11: "The Pharisee stood and prayed thus with himself, 'God, I thank thee, that I am not as other men are. . . ' "

6. Might (dialect).

headed enough for a baily's place is a poor mere trifle—yet a trifle more than nothing. However, I look round upon life quite cool. Do you heed me, neighbours? My words, though made as simple as I can, mid be rather deep for some heads.'

'O yes, Henery, we quite heed ye.'

'A strange old piece, goodmen—whirled about from here to yonder, as if I were nothing! A little warped, too. But I have my depths; ha, and even my great depths! I might gird[7] at a certain shepherd, brain to brain. But no—O no!'

'A strange old piece, ye say!' interposed the maltster, in a querulous voice. 'At the same time ye be no old man worth naming—no old man at all. Yer teeth bain't half gone yet; and what's a old man's standing if so be his teeth bain't gone? Weren't I stale in wedlock afore ye were out of arms? 'Tis a poor thing to be sixty, when there's people far past four-score—a boast weak as water.'

It was the unvarying custom in Weatherbury to sink minor differences when the maltster had to be pacified.

'Weak as water! yes,' said Jan Coggan. 'Malter, we feel ye to be a wonderful veteran man, and nobody can gainsay it.'

'Nobody,' said Joseph Poorgrass. 'Ye be a very rare old spectacle, malter, and we all admire ye for that gift.'

'Ay, and as a young man, when my senses were in prosperity, I was likewise liked by a good-few who knowed me,' said the maltster.

' 'Ithout doubt you was— 'ithout doubt.'

The bent and hoary man was satisfied, and so apparently was Henery Fray. That matters should continue pleasant Maryann spoke, who, what with her brown complexion, and the working wrapper of rusty linsey, had at present the mellow hue of an old sketch in oils—notably some of Nicholas Poussin's.[8]—

'Do anybody know of a crooked man, or a lame, or any second-hand fellow at all that would do for poor me?' said Maryann. 'A perfect one I don't expect to get at my time of life. If I could hear of such a thing 'twould do me more good than toast and ale.'

Coggan furnished a suitable reply. Oak went on with his shearing, and said not another word. Pestilent moods had come, and teased away his quiet. Bathsheba had shown indications of anointing him above his fellows by installing him as the bailiff that the farm imperatively required. He did not covet the post relatively to the farm: in relation to herself, as beloved by him and unmarried to another, he had coveted it. His readings of her seemed now to be vapoury and indistinct. His lecture to her was, he thought, one of the absurdest mistakes. Far from coquetting with Boldwood, she had trifled with himself in thus feigning that she had trifled with another. He was

---

7. Scoff or gibe (dialect).
8. Nicolas Poussin (1594–1665), French painter whom Hardy recorded in a notebook as one of the "inventors of the Grand Historial Landscape."

inwardly convinced that, in accordance with the anticipations of his easy-going and worse-educated comrades, that day would see Boldwood the accepted husband of Miss Everdene. Gabriel at this time of his life had outgrown the instinctive dislike which every Christian boy has for reading the Bible, perusing it now quite frequently, and he inwardly said, ' "I find more bitter than death the woman whose heart is snares and nets!" '[9] This was mere exclamation—the froth of the storm. He adored Bathsheba just the same.

'We workfolk shall have some lordly junketing to-night,' said Cainy Ball, casting forth his thoughts in a new direction. 'This morning I see 'em making the great puddens in the milking-pails—lumps of fat as big as yer thumb, Mister Oak! I've never seed such splendid large knobs of fat before in the days of my life—they never used to be bigger than a horse-bean. And there was a great black crock upon the brandise[1] with his legs a-sticking out, but I don't know what was in within.'

'And there's two bushels of biffins[2] for apple-pies,' said Maryann.

'Well, I hope to do my duty by it all,' said Joseph Poorgrass, in a pleasant, masticating manner of anticipation. 'Yes; victuals and drink is a cheerful thing, and gives nerves to the nerveless, if the form of words may be used. 'Tis the gospel of the body, without which we perish, so to speak it.'[3]

XXIII

Eventide—A Second Declaration

For the shearing-supper a long table was placed on the grass-plot beside the house, the end of the table being thrust over the sill of the wide parlour window and a foot or two into the room. Miss Everdene sat inside the window, facing down the table. She was thus at the head without mingling with the men.

This evening Bathsheba was unusually excited, her red cheeks and lips contrasting lustrously with the mazy skeins of her shadowy hair. She seemed to expect assistance, and the seat at the bottom of the table was at her request left vacant until after they had begun the meal. She then asked Gabriel to take the place and the duties appertaining to that end, which he did with great readiness.

At this moment Mr. Boldwood came in at the gate, and crossed the green to Bathsheba at the window. He apologized for his lateness: his arrival was evidently by arrangement.

---

9. Quoted from Ecclesiastes 7:26.
1. An iron tripod used to support utensils over a fire.
2. Winter apples preserved by being dried and pressed (dialect).
3. An echo of John 3:15: "Whosoever believeth in him should not perish, but have eternal life."

'Gabriel,' said she, 'will you move again, please, and let Mr. Boldwood come there?'

Oak moved in silence back to his original seat.

The gentleman-farmer was dressed in cheerful style, in a new coat and white waistcoat, quite contrasting with his usual sober suits of grey. Inwardly, too, he was blithe, and consequently chatty to an exceptional degree. So also was Bathsheba now that he had come, though the uninvited presence of Pennyways, the bailiff who had been dismissed for theft, disturbed her equanimity for a while.

Supper being ended, Coggan began on his own private account, without reference to listeners:—

> I've lost my love, and I care not,
> I've lost my love, and I care not;
>   I shall soon have another
>   That's better than t'other;
> I've lost my love, and I care not.

This lyric, when concluded, was received with a silently appreciative gaze at the table, implying that the performance, like a work by those established authors who are independent of notices in the papers, was a well-known delight which required no applause.

'Now, Master Poorgrass, your song!' said Coggan.

'I be all but in liquor, and the gift is wanting in me,' said Joseph, diminishing himself.

'Nonsense; wou'st never be so ungrateful, Joseph—never!' said Coggan, expressing hurt feelings by an inflection of voice. 'And mistress is looking hard at ye, as much as to say, "Sing at once, Joseph Poorgrass."'

'Faith, so she is; well, I must suffer it! . . . Just eye my features, and see if the tell-tale blood overheats me much, neighbours?'

'No, yer blushes be quite reasonable,' said Coggan.

'I always tries to keep my colours from rising when a beauty's eyes get fixed on me,' said Joseph diffidently; 'but if so be 'tis willed they do, they must.'

'Now, Joseph, your song, please,' said Bathsheba from the window.

'Well, really, ma'am,' he replied in a yielding tone, 'I don't know what to say. It would be a poor plain ballet of my own composure.'[1]

'Hear, hear!' said the supper-party.

Poorgrass, thus assured, trilled forth a flickering yet commendable piece of sentiment, the tune of which consisted of the key-note and another, the latter being the sound chiefly dwelt upon. This was so successful that he rashly plunged into a second in the same breath, after a few false starts:—

1. Joseph's "ballet" (dialect for "ballad" or "song") was in fact not composed by him; it is a seventeenth-century song titled "The Seeds of Love," probably composed by a Mrs. Habergham.

I sow'-ed th'-e . . . . .
I sow'-ed . . . . .
I sow'-ed the'-e seeds' of ' love',
    I-it was' all' i'-in the'-e spring',
I-in A'-pril', Ma'-ay, a'-nd sun'-ny' June',
    When sma'-all bi'-irds they' do' sing.

'Well put out of hand,' said Coggan, at the end of the verse. ' "They do sing" was a very taking paragraph.'

'Ay; and there was a pretty place at "seeds of love," and 'twas well heaved out. Though "love" is a nasty high corner when a man's voice is getting crazed. Next verse, Master Poorgrass.'

But during this rendering young Bob Coggan exhibited one of those anomalies which will afflict little people when other persons are particularly serious: in trying to check his laughter, he pushed down his throat as much of the tablecloth as he could get hold of, when, after continuing hermetically sealed for a short time, his mirth burst out through his nose. Joseph perceived it, and with hectic cheeks of indignation instantly ceased singing. Coggan boxed Bob's ears immediately.

'Go on, Joseph—go on, and never mind the young scamp,' said Coggan. ' 'Tis a very catching ballet. Now then again—the next bar; I'll help ye to flourish up the shrill notes where yer wind is rather wheezy:—

O the wi'-il-lo'-ow tree' will' twist',
And the wil'-low' tre'-ee wi'-ill twine'.

But the singer could not be set going again. Bob Coggan was sent home for his ill manners, and tranquillity was restored by Jacob Smallbury, who volunteered a ballad as inclusive and interminable as that with which the worthy toper old Silenus amused on a similar occasion the swains Chromis and Mnasylus, and other jolly dogs of his day.[2]

It was still the beaming time of evening, though night was stealthily making itself visible low down upon the ground, the western lines of light raking the earth without alighting upon it to any extent, or illuminating the dead levels at all. The sun had crept round the tree as a last effort before death, and then began to sink, the shearers' lower parts becoming steeped in embrowning twilight, whilst their heads and shoulders were still enjoying day, touched with a yellow of self-sustained brilliancy that seemed inherent rather than acquired.

The sun went down in an ochreous mist; but they sat, and talked on, and grew as merry as the gods in Homer's heaven. Bathsheba still

2. In Virgil's *Eclogue* 6, Chromis and Mnasylus find the satyr Silenus drunk and asleep; they bind him with his own garlands until he will sing a song he promised them— which turns out to be a very "inclusive" if not interminable collection of mythological stores.

remained enthroned inside the window, and occupied herself in knitting, from which she sometimes looked up to view the fading scene outside. The slow twilight expanded and enveloped them completely before the signs of moving were shown.

Gabriel suddenly missed Farmer Boldwood from his place at the bottom of the table. How long he had been gone Oak did not know; but he had apparently withdrawn into the encircling dusk. Whilst he was thinking of this Liddy brought candles into the back part of the room overlooking the shearers, and their lively new flames shone down the table and over the men, and dispersed among the green shadows behind. Bathsheba's form, still in its original position, was now again distinct between their eyes and the light, which revealed that Boldwood had gone inside the room, and was sitting near her.

Next came the question of the evening. Would Miss Everdene sing to them the song she always sang so charmingly—'The Banks of Allan Water'—before they went home?

After a moment's consideration Bathsheba assented, beckoning to Gabriel, who hastened up into the coveted atmosphere.

'Have you brought your flute?' she whispered.

'Yes, miss.'

'Play to my singing, then.'

She stood up in the window-opening, facing the men, the candles behind her, Gabriel on her right hand, immediately outside the sash-frame. Boldwood had drawn up on her left, within the room. Her singing was soft and rather tremulous at first, but it soon swelled to a steady clearness. Subsequent events caused one of the verses to be remembered for many months, and even years, by more than one of those who were gathered there:—

> For his bride a soldier sought her,
> And a winning tongue had he:
> On the banks of Allan Water
> None was gay as she!

In addition to the dulcet piping of Gabriel's flute Boldwood supplied a bass in his customary profound voice, uttering his notes so softly, however, as to abstain entirely from making anything like an ordinary duet of the song; they rather formed a rich unexplored shadow, which threw her tones into relief. The shearers reclined against each other as at suppers in the early ages of the world, and so silent and absorbed were they that her breathing could almost be heard between the bars; and at the end of the ballad, when the last tone loitered on to an inexpressible close, there arose that buzz of pleasure which is the attar of applause.

It is scarcely necessary to state that Gabriel could not avoid noting the farmer's bearing to-night towards their entertainer. Yet there was nothing exceptional in his actions beyond what appertained to his time of performing them. It was when the rest were all looking away that Boldwood observed her; when they regarded her he turned aside; when they thanked or praised he was silent; when they were inattentive he murmured his thanks. The meaning lay in the difference between actions none of which had any meaning of itself; and the necessity of being jealous, which lovers are troubled with, did not lead Oak to underestimate these signs.

Bathsheba then wished them good-night, withdrew from the window, and retired to the back part of the room, Boldwood thereupon closing the sash and the shutters, and remaining inside with her. Oak wandered away under the quiet and scented trees. Recovering from the softer impressions produced by Bathsheba's voice, the shearers rose to leave, Coggan turning to Pennyways as he pushed back the bench to pass out:—

'I like to give praise where praise is due, and the man deserves it—that 'a do so,' he remarked, looking at the worthy thief as if he were the masterpiece of some world-renowned artist.

'I'm sure I should never have believed it if we hadn't proved it, so to allude,' hiccupped Joseph Poorgrass, 'that every cup, every one of the best knives and forks, and every empty bottle be in their place as perfect now as at the beginning, and not one stole at all.'

'I'm sure I don't deserve half the praise you give me,' said the virtuous thief grimly.

'Well, I'll say this for Pennyways,' added Coggan, 'that whenever he do really make up his mind to do a noble thing in the shape of a good action, as I could see by his face he did to-night afore sitting down, he's generally able to carry it out. Yes, I'm proud to say, neighbours, that he's stole nothing at all.'

'Well, 'tis an honest deed, and we thank ye for it, Pennyways,' said Joseph; to which opinion the remainder of the company subscribed unanimously.

At this time of departure, when nothing more was visible of the inside of the parlour than a thin and still chink of light between the shutters, a passionate scene was in course of enactment there.

Miss Everdene and Boldwood were alone. Her cheeks had lost a great deal of their healthful fire from the very seriousness of her position; but her eye was bright with the excitement of a triumph—though it was a triumph which had rather been contemplated than desired.

She was standing behind a low arm-chair, from which she had just risen, and he was kneeling in it—inclining himself over its back towards her, and holding her hand in both his own. His body moved restlessly, and it was with what Keats daintily calls a too happy happiness.[3] This unwonted abstraction by love of all dignity from a

---

[3]. An allusion to the line, "But being too happy in thine happiness," from Keats's "Ode to a Nightingale."

man of whom it had ever seemed the chief component, was, in its distressing incongruity, a pain to her which quenched much of the pleasure she derived from the proof that she was idolized.

'I will try to love you,' she was saying, in a trembling voice quite unlike her usual self-confidence. 'And if I can believe in any way that I shall make you a good wife I shall indeed be willing to marry you. But, Mr. Boldwood, hesitation on so high a matter is honourable in any woman, and I don't want to give a solemn promise to-night. I would rather ask you to wait a few weeks till I can see my situation better.'

'But you have every reason to believe that *then*——'

'I have every reason to hope that at the end of the five or six weeks, between this time and harvest, that you say you are going to be away from home, I shall be able to promise to be your wife,' she said firmly. 'But remember this distinctly, I don't promise yet.'

'It is enough; I don't ask more. I can wait on those dear words. And now, Miss Everdene, good-night!'

'Good-night,' she said graciously—almost tenderly; and Boldwood withdrew with a serene smile.

Bathsheba knew more of him now; he had entirely bared his heart before her, even until he had almost worn in her eyes the sorry look of a grand bird without the feathers that make it grand. She had been awestruck at her past temerity, and was struggling to make amends without thinking whether the sin quite deserved the penalty she was schooling herself to pay. To have brought all this about her ears was terrible; but after a while the situation was not without a fearful joy.[4] The facility with which even the most timid women sometimes acquire a relish for the dreadful when that is amalgamated with a little triumph, is marvellous.

XXIV

The Same Night—The Fir Plantation

Among the multifarious duties which Bathsheba had voluntarily imposed upon herself by dispensing with the services of a bailiff, was the particular one of looking round the homestead before going to bed, to see that all was right and safe for the night. Gabriel had almost constantly preceded her in this tour every evening, watching her affairs as carefully as any specially appointed officer of surveillance could have done; but this tender devotion was to a great extent unknown to his mistress, and as much as was known was somewhat thanklessly received. Women are never tired of bewailing man's fickleness in love, but they seem only to snub his constancy.

As watching is best done invisibly, she usually carried a dark lantern

4. An allusion to the line, "And snatch a fearful joy," from Thomas Gray's "Ode on a Distant Prospect of Eton College."

in her hand, and every now and then turned on the light to examine nooks and corners with the coolness of a metropolitan policeman. This coolness may have owed its existence not so much to her fearlessness of expected danger as to her freedom from the suspicion of any; her worst anticipated discovery being that a horse might not be well bedded, the fowls not all in, or a door not closed.

This night the buildings were inspected as usual, and she went round to the farm paddock. Here the only sounds disturbing the stillness were steady munchings of many mouths, and stentorian breathings from all but invisible noses, ending in snores and puffs like the blowing of bellows slowly. Then the munching would recommence, when the lively imagination might assist the eye to discern a group of pink-white nostrils shaped as caverns, and very clammy and humid on their surfaces, not exactly pleasant to the touch until one got used to them; the mouths beneath having a great partiality for closing upon any loose end of Bathsheba's apparel which came within reach of their tongues. Above each of these a still keener vision suggested a brown forehead and two staring though not unfriendly eyes, and above all a pair of whitish crescent-shaped horns like two particularly new moons, an occasional stolid 'moo!' proclaiming beyond the shade of a doubt that these phenomena were the features and persons of Daisy, Whitefoot, Bonny-lass, Jolly-O, Spot, Twinkle-eye, etc., etc.—the respectable dairy of Devon cows belonging to Bathsheba aforesaid.

Her way back to the house was by a path through a young plantation of tapering firs, which had been planted some years earlier to shelter the premises from the north wind. By reason of the density of the interwoven foliage overhead it was gloomy there at cloudless noon-tide, twilight in the evening, dark as midnight at dusk, and black as the ninth plague of Egypt[1] at midnight. To describe the spot is to call it a vast, low, naturally formed hall, the plumy ceiling of which was supported by slender pillars of living wood, the floor being covered with a soft dun carpet of dead spikelets and mildewed cones, with a tuft of grass-blades here and there.

This bit of the path was always the crux of the night's ramble, though, before starting, her apprehensions of danger were not vivid enough to lead her to take a companion. Slipping along here covertly as Time, Bathsheba fancied she could hear footsteps entering the track at the opposite end. It was certainly a rustle of footsteps. Her own instantly fell as gently as snowflakes. She reassured herself by a remembrance that the path was public, and that the traveller was probably some villager returning home; regretting, at the same time, that the meeting should be about to occur in the darkest point of her route, even though only just outside her own door.

The noise approached, came close, and a figure was apparently on

1. An allusion to Exodus 10:22, in which "there was a thick darkness in all the land of Egypt three days."

the point of gliding past her when something tugged at her skirt and pinned it forcibly to the ground. The instantaneous check nearly threw Bathsheba off her balance. In recovering she struck against warm clothes and buttons.

'A rum start, upon my soul!' said a masculine voice, a foot or so above her head. 'Have I hurt you, mate?'

'No,' said Bathsheba, attempting to shrink away.

'We have got hitched together somehow, I think.'

'Yes.'

'Are you a woman?'

'Yes.'

'A lady, I should have said.'

'It doesn't matter.'

'I am a man.'

'Oh!'

Bathsheba softly tugged again, but to no purpose.

'Is that a dark lantern you have? I fancy so,' said the man.

'Yes.'

'If you'll allow me I'll open it, and set you free.'

A hand seized the lantern, the door was opened, the rays burst out from their prison, and Bathsheba beheld her position with astonishment.

The man to whom she was hooked was brilliant in brass and scarlet. He was a soldier. His sudden appearance was to darkness what the sound of a trumpet is to silence. Gloom, the *genius loci*[2] at all times hitherto, was now totally overthrown, less by the lantern-light than by what the lantern lighted. The contrast of this revelation with her anticipations of some sinister figure in sombre garb was so great that it had upon her the effect of a fairy transformation.

It was immediately apparent that the military man's spur had become entangled in the gimp[3] which decorated the skirt of her dress. He caught a view of her face.

'I'll unfasten you in one moment, miss,' he said, with new-born gallantry.

'O no—I can do it, thank you,' she hastily replied, and stooped for the performance.

The unfastening was not such a trifling affair. The rowel[4] of the spur had so wound itself among gimp cords in those few moments, that separation was likely to be a matter of time.

He too stooped, and the lantern standing on the ground betwixt them threw the gleam from its open side among the fir-tree needles and the blades of long damp grass with the effect of a large glowworm.

2. *"Genius loci"*: in Roman mythology, the guardian spirit of a particular locality—hence, by analogy, the distinctive atmosphere of a place.
3. A flat trimming made of narrow bands or cords of silk, wool, or other material, sometimes stiffened with wire.
4. A sharp-toothed wheel inserted into the shank of a spur.

It radiated upwards into their faces, and sent over half the plantation gigantic shadows of both man and woman, each dusky shape becoming distorted and mangled upon the tree-trunks till it wasted to nothing.

He looked hard into her eyes when she raised them for a moment; Bathsheba looked down again, for his gaze was too strong to be received point-blank with her own. But she had obliquely noticed that he was young and slim, and that he wore three chevrons[5] upon his sleeve.

Bathsheba pulled again.

'You are a prisoner, miss; it is no use blinking the matter,' said the soldier drily. 'I must cut your dress if you are in such a hurry.'

'Yes—please do!' she exclaimed helplessly.

'It wouldn't be necessary if you could wait a moment'; and he unwound a cord from the little wheel. She withdrew her own hand, but, whether by accident or design, he touched it. Bathsheba was vexed; she hardly knew why.

His unravelling went on, but it nevertheless seemed coming to no end. She looked at him again.

'Thank you for the sight of such a beautiful face!' said the young sergeant, without ceremony.

She coloured with embarrassment. ' 'Twas unwillingly shown,' she replied stiffly, and with as much dignity—which was very little—as she could infuse into a position of captivity.

'I like you the better for that incivility, miss,' he said.

'I should have liked—I wish—you had never shown yourself to me by intruding here!' She pulled again, and the gathers of her dress began to give way like liliputian musketry.

'I deserve the chastisement your words give me. But why should such a fair and dutiful girl have such an aversion to her father's sex?'

'Go on your way, please.'

'What, Beauty, and drag you after me? Do but look; I never saw such a tangle!'

'O, 'tis shameful of you; you have been making it worse on purpose to keep me here—you have!'

'Indeed, I don't think so,' said the sergeant, with a merry twinkle.

'I tell you you have!' she exclaimed, in high temper. 'I insist upon undoing it. Now, allow me!'

'Certainly, miss; I am not of steel.' He added a sigh which had as much archness in it as a sigh could possess without losing its nature altogether. 'I am thank thankful for beauty, even when 'tis thrown to me like a bone to a dog. These moments will be over too soon!'

She closed her lips in a determined silence.

Bathsheba was revolving in her mind whether by a bold and desper-

5. A sergeant's insignia.

ate rush she could free herself at the risk of leaving her skirt bodily behind her. The thought was too dreadful. The dress—which she had put on to appear stately at the supper—was the head and front of her wardrobe; not another in her stock became her so well. What woman in Bathsheba's position, not naturally timid, and within call of her retainers, would have bought escape from a dashing soldier at so dear a price?

'All in good time; it will soon be done, I perceive,' said her cool friend.

'This trifling provokes, and—and——'

'Not too cruel!'

'—Insults me!'

'It is done in order that I may have the pleasure of apologizing to so charming a woman, which I straightway do most humbly, madam,' he said, bowing low.

Bathsheba really knew not what to say.

'I've seen a good many women in my time,' continued the young man in a murmur, and more thoughtfully than hitherto, critically regarding her bent head at the same time; 'but I've never seen a woman so beautiful as you. Take it or leave it—be offended or like it—I don't care.'

'Who are you, then, who can so well afford to despise opinion?'

'No stranger. Sergeant Troy. I am staying in this place.—There! it is undone at last, you see. Your light fingers were more eager than mine. I wish it had been the knot of knots, which there's no untying!'[6]

This was worse and worse. She started up, and so did he. How to decently get away from him—that was her difficulty now. She sidled off inch by inch, the lantern in her hand, till she could see the redness of his coat no longer.

'Ah, Beauty; good-bye!' he said.

She made no reply, and, reaching a distance of twenty or thirty yards, turned about, and ran indoors.

Liddy had just retired to rest. In ascending to her own chamber, Bathsheba opened the girl's door an inch or two, and, panting, said—

'Liddy, is any soldier staying in the village—sergeant somebody— rather gentlemanly for a sergeant, and good looking—a red coat with blue facings?'

'No, miss . . . No, I say; but really it might be Sergeant Troy home on furlough, though I have not seen him. He was here once in that way when the regiment was at Casterbridge.'

'Yes; that's the name. Had he a moustache—no whiskers or beard?'

'He had.'

'What kind of a person is he?'

'O, miss—I blush to name it—a gay man! But I know him to be very

---

6. An allusion to a line in Thomas Campbell's song "How Delicious the Winning."

quick and trim, who might have made his thousands, like a squire. Such a clever young dand[7] as he is! He's a doctor's son by name, which is a great deal; and he's an earl's son by nature!'

'Which is a great deal more. Fancy! Is it true?'

'Yes. And he was brought up so well, and sent to Casterbridge Grammar School for years and years. Learnt all languages while he was there; and it was said he got on so far that he could take down Chinese in shorthand; but that I don't answer for, as it was only reported. However, he wasted his gifted lot, and listed a soldier; but even then he rose to be a sergeant without trying at all. Ah! such a blessing it is to be high-born; nobility of blood will shine out even in the ranks and files. And is he really come home, miss?'

'I believe so. Good-night, Liddy.'

After all, how could a cheerful wearer of skirts be permanently offended with the man? There are occasions when girls like Bathsheba will put up with a great deal of unconventional behaviour. When they want to be praised, which is often; when they want to be mastered, which is sometimes; and when they want no nonsense, which is seldom. Just now the first feeling was in the ascendant with Bathsheba, with a dash of the second. Moreover, by chance or by devilry, the ministrant was antecedently made interesting by being a handsome stranger who had evidently seen better days.

So she could not clearly decide whether it was her opinion that he had insulted her or not.

'Was ever anything so odd!' she at last exclaimed to herself, in her own room. 'And was ever anything so meanly done as what I did—to skulk away like that from a man who was only civil and kind!' Clearly she did not think his barefaced praise of her person an insult now.

It was a fatal omission of Boldwood's that he had never once told her she was beautiful.

XXV

The New Acquaintance Described

Idiosyncrasy and vicissitude had combined to stamp Sergeant Troy as an exceptional being.

He was a man to whom memories were an incumbrance, and anticipations a superfluity. Simply feeling, considering, and caring for what was before his eyes, he was vulnerable only in the present. His outlook upon time was as a transient flash of the eye now and then: that projection of consciousness into days gone by and to come, which makes the past a synonym for the pathetic and the future a word for circumspection, was foreign to Troy. With him the past was yesterday; the future, to-morrow; never, the day after.

7. Dandy (dialect).

On this account he might, in certain lights, have been regarded as one of the most fortunate of his order. For it may be argued with great plausibility that reminiscence is less an endowment than a disease, and that expectation in its only comfortable form—that of absolute faith—is practically an impossibility; whilst in the form of hope and the secondary compounds, patience, impatience, resolve, curiosity, it is a constant fluctuation between pleasure and pain.

Sergeant Troy, being entirely innocent of the practice of expectation, was never disappointed. To set against this negative gain there may have been some positive losses from a certain narrowing of the higher tastes and sensations which it entailed. But limitation of the capacity is never recognized as a loss by the loser therefrom: in this attribute moral or aesthetic poverty contrasts plausibly with material, since those who suffer do not mind it, whilst those who mind it soon cease to suffer. It is not a denial of anything to have been always without it, and what Troy had never enjoyed he did not miss; but, being fully conscious that what sober people missed he enjoyed, his capacity, though really less, seemed greater than theirs.

He was moderately truthful towards men, but to women lied like a Cretan[1]—a system of ethics above all others calculated to win popularity at the first flush of admission into lively society; and the possibility of the favour gained being transitory had reference only to the future.

He never passed the line which divides the spruce vices from the ugly; and hence, though his morals had hardly been applauded, disapproval of them had frequently been tempered with a smile. This treatment had led to his becoming a sort of regrater[2] of other men's gallantries, to his own aggrandizement as a Corinthian,[3] rather than to the moral profit of his hearers.

His reason and his propensities had seldom any reciprocating influence, having separated by mutual consent long ago: thence it sometimes happened that, while his intentions were as honourable as could be wished, any particular deed formed a dark background which threw them into fine relief. The sergeant's vicious phases being the offspring of impulse, and his virtuous phases of cool meditation, the latter had a modest tendency to be oftener heard of than seen.

Troy was full of activity, but his activities were less of a locomotive than a vegetative nature; and, never being based upon any original choice of foundation or direction, they were exercised on whatever object chance might place in their way. Hence, whilst he sometimes reached the brilliant in speech because that was spontaneous, he fell below the commonplace in action, from inability to guide incipient effort. He had a quick comprehension and considerable force of

1. In Greek folklore, the inhabitants of the island of Crete were proverbial liars; even the Cretan poet Epimenides wrote, "Cretans are always liars," and there is a famous paradox in Greek philosophy that draws upon the same tradition.
2. A retailer (obsolete).
3. The inhabitants of Corinth were reputed to cultivate a life of refined dissipation.

character; but, being without the power to combine them, the comprehension became engaged with trivialities whilst waiting for the will to direct it, and the force wasted itself in useless grooves through unheeding the comprehension.

He was a fairly well-educated man for one of middle class—exceptionally well educated for a common soldier. He spoke fluently and unceasingly. He could in this way be one thing and seem another; for instance, he could speak of love and think of dinner; call on the husband to look at the wife; be eager to pay and intend to owe.

The wonderous power of flattery in *passados*[4] at woman is a perception so universal as to be remarked upon by many people almost as automatically as they repeat a proverb, or say that they are Christians and the like, without thinking much of the enormous corollaries which spring from the proposition. Still less is it acted upon for the good of the complemental being alluded to. With the majority such an opinion is shelved with all those trite aphorisms which require some catastrophe to bring their tremendous meanings thoroughly home. When expressed with some amount of reflectiveness it seems co-ordinate with a belief that this flattery must be reasonable to be effective. It is to the credit of men that few attempt to settle the question by experiment, and it is for their happiness, perhaps, that accident has never settled it for them. Nevertheless, that a male dissembler who by deluging her with untenable fictions charms the female wisely, may acquire powers reaching to the extremity of perdition, is a truth taught to many by unsought and wringing occurrences. And some profess to have attained to the same knowledge by experiment as aforesaid, and jauntily continue their indulgence in such experiments with terrible effect. Sergeant Troy was one.

He had been known to observe casually that in dealing with womankind the only alternative to flattery was cursing and swearing. There was no third method. 'Treat them fairly, and you are a lost man,' he would say.

This philosopher's public appearance in Weatherbury promptly followed his arrival there. A week or two after the shearing Bathsheba, feeling a nameless relief of spirits on account of Boldwood's absence, approached her hayfields and looked over the hedge towards the haymakers. They consisted in about equal proportions of gnarled and flexuous forms, the former being the men, the latter the women, who wore tilt bonnets covered with nankeen,[5] which hung in a curtain upon their shoulders. Coggan and Mark Clark were mowing in a less forward meadow, Clark humming a tune to the strokes on his scythe, to which Jan made no attempt to keep time with his. In the first mead they were already loading hay, the women raking it into cocks and

---

4. The technical term for a forward thrust of a sword while advancing with one foot; Hardy here uses the term metaphorically for making an advance to a woman.

5. A sturdy yellow or buff cotton cloth.

windrows, and the men tossing it upon the waggon.

From behind the waggon a bright scarlet spot emerged, and went on loading unconcernedly with the rest. It was the gallant sergeant, who had come haymaking for pleasure; and nobody could deny that he was doing the mistress of the farm real knight-service by this voluntary contribution of his labour at a busy time.

As soon as she had entered the field Troy saw her, and sticking his pitchfork into the ground and picking up his crop or cane, he came forward. Bathsheba blushed with half-angry embarrassment, and adjusted her eyes as well as her feet to the direct line of her path.

XXVI

Scene on the Verge of the Hay-Mead

'Ah, Miss Everdene!' said the sergeant, touching his diminutive cap. 'Little did I think it was you I was speaking to the other night. And yet, if I had reflected, the "Queen of the Corn-market" (truth is truth at any hour of the day or night, and I heard you so named in Casterbridge yesterday), the "Queen of the Corn-market," I say, could be no other woman. I step across now to beg your forgiveness a thousand times for having been led by my feelings to express myself too strongly for a stranger. To be sure I am no stranger to the place—I am Sergeant Troy, as I told you, and I have assisted your uncle in these fields no end of times when I was a lad. I have been doing the same for you to-day.'

'I suppose I must thank you for that, Sergeant Troy,' said the Queen of the Corn-market in an indifferently grateful tone.

The sergeant looked hurt and sad. 'Indeed you must not, Miss Everdene,' he said. 'Why could you think such a thing necessary?'

'I am glad it is not.'

'Why? if I may ask without offence.'

'Because I don't much want to thank you for anything.'

'I am afraid I have made a hole with my tongue that my heart will never mend. O these intolerable times: that ill-luck should follow a man for honestly telling a woman she is beautiful! 'Twas the most I said—you must own that; and the least I could say—that I own myself.'

'There is some talk I could do without more easily than money.'

'Indeed. That remark is a sort of digression.'

'No. It means that I would rather have your room than your company.'

'And I would rather have curses from you than kisses from any other woman; so I'll stay here.'

Bathsheba was absolutely speechless. And yet she could not help feeling that the assistance he was rendering forbade a harsh repulse.

'Well,' continued Troy, 'I suppose there is a praise which is rudeness, and that may be mine. At the same time there is a treatment which is injustice, and that may be yours. Because a plain blunt man,[1] who has never been taught concealment, speaks out his mind without exactly intending it, he's to be snapped off like the son of a sinner.'

'Indeed there's no such case between us,' she said, turning away. 'I don't allow strangers to be bold and impudent—even in praise of me.'

'Ah—it is not the fact but the method which offends you,' he said carelessly. 'But I have the sad satisfaction of knowing that my words, whether pleasing or offensive, are unmistakably true. Would you have had me look at you, and tell my acquaintance that you are quite a common-place woman, to save you the embarrassment of being stared at if they come near you? Not I. I couldn't tell any such ridiculous lie about a beauty to encourage a single woman in England in too excessive a modesty.'

'It is all pretence—what you are saying!' exclaimed Bathsheba, laughing in spite of herself at the sergeant's sly method. 'You have a rare invention, Sergeant Troy. Why couldn't you have passed by me that night, and said nothing?—that was all I meant to reproach you for.'

'Because I wasn't going to. Half the pleasure of a feeling lies in being able to express it on the spur of the moment, and I let out mine. It would have been just the same if you had been the reverse person— ugly and old—I should have exclaimed about it in the same way.'

'How long is it since you have been so afflicted with strong feeling, then?'

'Oh, ever since I was big enough to know loveliness from deformity.'

''Tis to be hoped your sense of the difference you speak of doesn't stop at faces, but extends to morals as well.'

'I won't speak of morals or religion—my own or anybody else's. Though perhaps I should have been a very good Christian if you pretty women hadn't made me an idolater.'

Bathsheba moved on to hide the irrepressible dimplings of merriment. Troy followed, whirling his crop.

'But—Miss Everdene—you do forgive me?'

'Hardly.'

'Why?'

'You say such things.'

'I said you were beautiful, and I'll say so still, for, by—so you are! The most beautiful ever I saw, or may I fall dead this instant! Why, upon my——'

'Don't—don't! I won't listen to you—you are so profane!' she said,

---

1. An echo of Antony's speech from *Julius Caesar*, act 3, scene 2: "But (as you know me all) a plain blunt man."

in a restless state between distress at hearing him and a *penchant* to hear more.

'I again say you are a most fascinating woman. There's nothing remarkable in my saying so, is there? I'm sure the fact is evident enough. Miss Everdene, my opinion may be too forcibly let out to please you, and, for the matter of that, too insignificant to convince you, but surely it is honest, and why can't it be excused?'

'Because it—it isn't a correct one,' she femininely murmured.

'O, fie—fie! Am I any worse for breaking the third of that Terrible Ten than you for breaking the ninth?'[2]

'Well, it doesn't seem *quite* true to me that I am fascinating,' she replied evasively.

'Not so to you: then I say with all respect that, if so, it is owing to your modesty, Miss Everdene. But surely you must have been told by everybody of what everybody notices? And you should take their words for it.'

'They don't say so exactly.'

'O yes, they must!'

'Well, I mean to my face, as you do,' she went on, allowing herself to be further lured into a conversation that intention had rigorously forbidden.

'But you know they think so?'

'No—that is—I certainly have heard Liddy say they do, but——' She paused.

Capitulation—that was the purport of the simple reply, guarded as it was—capitulation, unknown to herself. Never did a fragile tailless sentence convey a more perfect meaning. The careless sergeant smiled within himself, and probably too the devil smiled from a loop-hole in Tophet,[3] for the moment was the turning-point of a career. Her tone and mien signified beyond mistake that the seed which was to lift the foundation had taken root in the chink: the remainder was a mere question of time and natural changes.

'There the truth comes out!' said the soldier, in reply. 'Never tell me that a young lady can live in a buzz of admiration without knowing something about it. Ah, well, Miss Everdene, you are—pardon my blunt way—you are rather an injury to our race than otherwise.'

'How—indeed?' she said, opening her eyes.

'O, it is true enough. I may as well be hung for a sheep as a lamb (an old country saying, not of much account, but it will do for a rough soldier), and so I will speak my mind, regardless of your pleasure, and without hoping or intending to get your pardon. Why, Miss Everdene, it is in this manner that your good looks may do more harm than good in the world.' The sergeant looked down the mead in critical

---

2. The third of the Ten Commandments forbids taking the name of the Lord in vain; the ninth forbids lying. Troy had earlier called himself an "idolater," which in tact would make him a breaker of the second commandment.
3. Hell.

abstraction. 'Probably some one man on an average falls in love with each ordinary woman. She can marry him: he is content, and leads a useful life. Such women as you a hundred men always covet—your eyes will bewitch scores on scores into an unavailing fancy for you—you can only marry one of that many. Out of these say twenty will endeavour to drown the bitterness of despised love in drink; twenty more will mope away their lives without a wish or attempt to make a mark in the world, because they have no ambition apart from their attachment to you; twenty more—the susceptible person myself possibly among them—will be always draggling after you, getting where they may just see you, doing desperate things. Men are such constant fools! The rest may try to get over their passion with more or less success. But all these men will be saddened. And not only those ninety-nine men, but the ninety-nine women they might have married are saddened with them. There's my tale. That's why I say that a woman so charming as yourself, Miss Everdene, is hardly a blessing to her race.'

The handsome sergeant's features were during this speech as rigid and stern as John Knox's in addressing his gay young queen.[4]

Seeing she made no reply, he said, 'Do you read French?'

'No; I began, but when I got to the verbs, father died,' she said simply.

'I do—when I have an opportunity, which latterly has not been often (my mother was a Parisienne)—and there's a proverb they have, *Qui aime bien châtie bien*—"He chastens who loves well." Do you understand me?'

'Ah!' she replied, and there was even a little tremulousness in the usually cool girl's voice; 'if you can only fight half as winningly as you can talk, you are able to make a pleasure of a bayonet wound!' And then poor Bathsheba instantly perceived her slip in making this admission: in hastily trying to retrieve it, she went from bad to worse. 'Don't, however, suppose that *I* derive any pleasure from what you tell me.'

'I know you do not—I know it perfectly,' said Troy, with much hearty conviction on the exterior of his face: and altering the expression to moodiness; 'when a dozen men are ready to speak tenderly to you, and give the admiration you deserve without adding the warning you need, it stands to reason that my poor rough-and-ready mixture of praise and blame cannot convey much pleasure. Fool as I may be, I am not so conceited as to suppose that!'

'I think you—are conceited, nevertheless,' said Bathsheba, looking askance at a reed she was fitfully pulling with one hand, having lately grown feverish under the soldier's system of procedure—not because the nature of his cajolery was entirely unperceived, but because its vigour was overwhelming.

4. John Knox (ca. 1505–72) was a Scottish Protestant reformer who repeatedly reproved Mary Queen of Scots in his meetings with her.

'I would not own it to anybody else—nor do I exactly to you. Still, there might have been some self-conceit in my foolish supposition the other night. I knew that what I said in admiration might be an opinion too often forced upon you to give any pleasure, but I certainly did think that the kindness of your nature might prevent you judging an uncontrolled tongue harshly—which you have done—and thinking badly of me and wounding me this morning, when I am working hard to save your hay.'

'Well, you need not think more of that: perhaps you did not mean to be rude to me by speaking out your mind: indeed, I believe you did not,' said the shrewd woman, in painfully innocent earnest. 'And I thank you for giving help here. But—but mind you don't speak to me again in that way, or in any other, unless I speak to you.'

'O Miss Bathsheba! That is too hard!'

'No, it isn't. Why is it?'

'You will never speak to me; for I shall not be here long. I am soon going back again to the miserable monotony of drill—and perhaps our regiment will be ordered out soon. And yet you take away the one little ewe-lamb[5] of pleasure that I have in this dull life of mine. Well, perhaps generosity is not a woman's most marked characteristic.'

'When are you going from here?' she asked with some interest.

'In a month.'

'But how can it give you pleasure to speak to me?'

'Can you ask, Miss Everdene—knowing as you do—what my offence is based on?'

'If you do care so much for a silly trifle of that kind, then, I don't mind doing it,' she uncertainly and doubtingly answered. 'But you can't really care for a word from me? you only say so—I think you only say so.'

'That's unjust—but I won't repeat the remark. I am too gratified to get such a mark of your friendship at any price to cavil at the tone. I *do*, Miss Everdene, care for it. You may think a man foolish to want a mere word—just a good morning. Perhaps he is—I don't know. But you have never been a man looking upon a woman, and that woman yourself.'

'Well.'

'Then you know nothing of what such an experience is like—and Heaven forbid that you ever should!'

'Nonsense, flatterer! What is it like? I am interested in knowing.'

'Put shortly, it is not being able to think, hear, or look in any direction except one without wretchedness, nor there without torture.'

'Ah, sergeant, it won't do—you are pretending!' she said, shaking her head. 'Your words are too dashing to be true.'

'I am not, upon the honour of a soldier.'

---

5. An allusion to 2 Samuel 12:3, where a poor man is described as having "nothing but one little ewe lamb."

'But *why* is it so?—Of course I ask for mere pastime.'

'Because you are so distracting—and I am so distracted.'

'You look like it.'

'I am indeed.'

'Why, you only saw me the other night!'

'That makes no difference. The lightning works instantaneously. I loved you then, at once—as I do now.'

Bathsheba surveyed him curiously, from the feet upward, as high as she liked to venture her glance, which was not quite so high as his eyes.

'You cannot and you don't,' she said demurely. 'There is no such sudden feeling in people. I won't listen to you any longer. Dear me, I wish I knew what o'clock it is—I am going—I have wasted too much time here already!'

The sergeant looked at his watch and told her. 'What, haven't you a watch, miss?' he inquired.

'I have not just at present—I am about to get a new one.'

'No. You shall be given one. Yes—you shall. A gift, Miss Everdene—a gift.'

And before she knew what the young man was intending, a heavy gold watch was in her hand.

'It is an unusually good one for a man like me to possess,' he quietly said. 'That watch has a history. Press the spring and open the back.'

She did so.

'What do you see?'

'A crest and a motto.'

'A coronet with five points, and beneath, *Cedit amor rebus*—"Love yields to circumstance."[6] It's the motto of the Earls of Severn. That watch belonged to the last lord, and was given to my mother's husband, a medical man, for his use till I came of age, when it was to be given to me. It was all the fortune that ever I inherited. That watch has regulated imperial interests in its time—the stately ceremonial, the courtly assignation, pompous travels, and lordly sleeps. Now it is yours.'

'But, Sergeant Troy, I cannot take this—I cannot!' she exclaimed with round-eyed wonder. 'A gold watch! What are you doing? Don't be such a dissembler!'

The sergeant retreated to avoid receiving back his gift, which she held out persistently towards him. Bathsheba followed as he retired.

'Keep it—do, Miss Everdene—keep it!' said the erratic child of impulse. 'The fact of your possessing it makes it worth ten times as much to me. A more plebeian one will answer my purpose just as well, and the pleasure of knowing whose heart my old one beats against—well, I won't speak of that. It is in far worthier hands than ever it has been in before.'

6. The motto is from Ovid's *Remedia Amoris* I, 144.

'But indeed I can't have it!' she said, in a perfect simmer of distress. 'O, how can you do such a thing; that is, if you really mean it! Give me your dead father's watch, and such a valuable one! You should not be so reckless, indeed, Sergeant Troy!'

'I loved my father: good; but better, I love you more. That's how I can do it,' said the sergeant with an intonation of such exquisite fidelity to nature that it was evidently not all acted now. Her beauty, which, whilst it had been quiescent, he had praised in jest, had in its animated phases moved him to earnest; and though his seriousness was less than she imagined, it was probably more than he imagined himself.

Bathsheba was brimming with agitated bewilderment, and she said, in half-suspicious accents of feeling, 'Can it be! O, how can it be, that you care for me, and so suddenly! You have seen so little of me: I may not be really so—so nice-looking as I seem to you. Please, do take it; O, do! I cannot and will not have it. Believe me, your generosity is too great. I have never done you a single kindness, and why should you be so kind to me?'

A factitious reply had been again upon his lips, but it was again suspended, and he looked at her with an arrested eye. The truth was, that as she now stood—excited, wild, and honest as the day—her alluring beauty bore out so fully the epithets he had bestowed upon it that he was quite startled at his temerity in advancing them as false. He said mechanically, 'Ah, why?' and continued to look at her.

'And my workfolk see me following you about the field, and are wondering. O, this is dreadful!' she went on, unconscious of the transmutation she was effecting.

'I did not quite mean you to accept it at first, for it was my one poor patent of nobility,' he broke out bluntly; 'but, upon my soul, I wish you would now. Without any shamming, come! Don't deny me the happiness of wearing it for my sake? But you are to lovely even to care to be kind as others are.'

'No, no; don't say so! I have reasons for reserve which I cannot explain.'

'Let it be, then, let it be,' he said, receiving back the watch at last; 'I must be leaving you now. And will you speak to me for these few weeks of my stay?'

'Indeed I will. Yet, I don't know if I will! O, why did you come and disturb me so!'

'Perhaps in setting a gin,[7] I have caught myself. Such things have happened. Well, will you let me work in your fields?' he coaxed.

'Yes, I suppose so; if it is any pleasure to you.'

'Miss Everdene, I thank you.'

'No, no.'

'Good-bye!'

7. Trap.

The sergeant brought his hand to the cap on the slope of his head, saluted, and returned to the distant group of haymakers.

Bathsheba could not face the haymakers now. Her heart erratically flitting hither and thither from perplexed excitement, hot, and almost tearful, she retreated homeward, murmuring, 'O, what have I done! What does it mean! I wish I knew how much of it was true!'

XXVII

Hiving the Bees

The Weatherbury bees were late in their swarming this year. It was during the latter part of June, and the day after the interview with Troy in the hayfield, that Bathsheba was standing in her garden, watching a swarm in the air and guessing their probable settling place. Not only were they late this year, but unruly. Sometimes throughout a whole season all the swarms would alight on the lowest attainable bough— such as part of a currant-bush or espalier apple-tree;[1] next year they would, with just the same unanimity, make straight off to the upper-most member of some tall, gaunt costard, or quarrenden,[2] and there defy all invaders who did not come armed with ladders and staves to take them.

This was the case at present. Bathsheba's eyes, shaded by one hand, were following the ascending multitude against the unexplorable stretch of blue till they ultimately halted by one of the unwieldy trees spoken of. A process somewhat analogous to that of alleged formations of the universe,[3] time and times ago, was observable. The bustling swarm had swept the sky in a scattered and uniform haze, which now thickened to a nebulous centre: this glided on to a bough and grew still denser, till it formed a solid black spot upon the light.

The men and women being all busily engaged in saving the hay— even Liddy had left the house for the purpose of lending a hand— Bathsheba resolved to hive the bees herself, if possible. She had dressed the hive with herbs and honey, fetched a ladder, brush, and crook, made herself impregnable with armour of leather gloves, straw hat, and large gauze veil—once green but now faded to snuff colour—and ascended a dozen rungs of the ladder. At once she heard, not ten yards off, a voice that was beginning to have a strange power in agitating her.

'Miss Everdene, let me assist you; you should not attempt such a

1. A tree trained to grow flat and symmetrically on a supporting framework to which it is bound.
2. "Gaunt costard" is an older variety of apple tree with a rugged appearance; "quarrenden" is a popular variety of eating apple common in the Dorset area.
3. Probably a reference to the "nebular

hypothesis" of the French astronomer Pierre Simon, Marquis de Laplace (1748–1827), who, in his *Mécanique Celeste*, theorized that stars and planets were formed by the gradual coming together of matter originally distributed in a gaseous nebula.

thing alone.'

Troy was just opening the garden gate.

Bathsheba flung down the brush, crook, and empty hive, pulled the skirt of her dress tightly round her ankles in a tremendous flurry, and as well as she could slid down the ladder. By the time she reached the bottom Troy was there also, and he stooped to pick up the hive.

'How fortunate I am to have dropped in at this moment!' exclaimed the sergeant.

She found her voice in a minute. 'What! and will you shake them in for me?' she asked, in what, for a defiant girl, was a faltering way; though, for a timid girl, it would have seemed a brave way enough.

'Will I!' said Troy. 'Why, of course I will. How blooming you are to-day!' Troy flung down his cane and put his foot on the ladder to ascend.

'But you must have on the veil and gloves, or you'll be stung fearfully!'

'Ah, yes. I must put on the veil and gloves. Will you kindly show me how to fix them properly?'

'And you must have the broad-brimmed hat, too; for your cap has no brim to keep the veil off, and they'd reach your face.'

'The broad-brimmed hat, too, by all means.'

So a whimsical fate ordered that her hat should be taken off—veil and all attached—and placed upon his head, Troy tossing his own into a gooseberry bush. Then the veil had to be tied at its lower edge round his collar and the gloves put on him.

He looked such an extraordinary object in this guise that, flurried as she was, she could not avoid laughing outright. It was the removal of yet another stake from the palisade of cold manners which had kept him off.

Bathsheba looked on from the ground whilst he was busy sweeping and shaking the bees from the tree, holding up the hive with the other hand for them to fall into. She made use of an unobserved minute whilst his attention was absorbed in the operation to arrange her plumes a little. He came down holding the hive at arm's length, behind which trailed a cloud of bees.

'Upon my life,' said Troy, through the veil, 'holding up this hive makes one's arm ache worse than a week of sword-exercise.' When the manœuvre was complete he approached her. 'Would you be good enough to untie me and let me out? I am nearly stifled inside this silk cage.'

To hide her embarrassment during the unwonted process of untying the string about his neck, she said:—

'I have never seen that you spoke of.'

'What?'

'The sword-exercise.'

'Ah! would you like to?' said Troy.

Bathsheba hesitated. She had heard wondrous reports from time to time by dwellers in Weatherbury, who had by chance sojourned awhile in Casterbridge, near the barracks, of this strange and glorious performance, the sword-exercise. Men and boys who had peeped through chinks or over walls into the barrack-yard returned with accounts of its being the most flashing affair conceivable; accoutrements and weapons glistening like stars—here, there, around—yet all by rule and compass. So she said mildly what she felt strongly:

'Yes; I should like to see it very much.'

'And so you shall; you shall see me go through it.'

'No! How?'

'Let me consider.'

'Not with a walking-stick—I don't care to see that. It must be a real sword.'

'Yes, I know; and I have no sword here; but I think I could get one by the evening. Now, will you do this?'

Troy bent over her and murmured some suggestion in a low voice.

'O no, indeed!' said Bathsheba, blushing. 'Thank you very much, but I couldn't on any account.'

'Surely you might? Nobody would know.'

She shook her head, but with a weakened negation. 'If I were to,' she said, 'I must bring Liddy too. Might I not?'

Troy looked far away. 'I don't see why you want to bring her,' he said coldly.

An unconscious look of assent in Bathsheba's eyes betrayed that something more than his coldness had made her also feel that Liddy would be superfluous in the suggested scene. She had felt it, even whilst making the proposal.

'Well, I won't bring Liddy—and I'll come. But only for a very short time,' she added; 'a very short time.'

'It will not take five minutes,' said Troy.

XXVIII

The Hollow amid the Ferns

The hill opposite Bathsheba's dwelling extended, a mile off, into an uncultivated tract of land, dotted at this season with tall thickets of brake fern,[1] plump and diaphanous from recent rapid growth, and radiant in hues of clear and untainted green.

At eight o'clock this midsummer evening, whilst the bristling ball of gold in the west still swept the tips of the ferns with its long, luxuriant rays, a soft brushing-by of garments might have been heard among them, and Bathsheba appeared in their midst, their soft, feathery arms

1. Also called bracken—any of a variety of large, coarse ferns.

caressing her up to her shoulders. She paused, turned, went back over the hill and halfway to her own door, whence she cast a farewell glance upon the spot she had just left, having resolved not to remain near the place after all.

She saw a dim spot of artificial red moving round the shoulder of the rise. It disappeared on the other side.

She waited one minute—two minutes—thought of Troy's disappointment at her non-fulfilment of a promised engagement, till she again ran along the field, clambered over the bank, and followed the original direction. She was now literally trembling and panting at this her temerity in such an errant undertaking; her breath came and went quickly, and her eyes shone with an infrequent light. Yet go she must. She reached the verge of a pit in the middle of the ferns. Troy stood in the bottom, looking up towards her.

'I heard you rustling through the fern before I saw you,' he said, coming up and giving her his hand to help her down the slope.

The pit was a saucer-shaped concave, naturally formed, with a top diameter of about thirty feet, and shallow enough to allow the sunshine to reach their heads. Standing in the centre, the sky overhead was met by a circular horizon of fern: this grew nearly to the bottom of the slope and then abruptly ceased. The middle within the belt of verdure was floored with a thick flossy carpet of moss and grass intermingled, so yielding that the foot was half-buried within it.

'Now,' said Troy, producing the sword, which, as he raised it into the sunlight, gleamed a sort of greeting, like a living thing; 'first, we have four right and four left cuts; four right and four left thrusts.[2] Infantry cuts and guards are more interesting than ours, to my mind; but they are not so swashing. They have seven cuts and three thrusts. So much as a preliminary. Well, next, our cut one is as if you were sowing your corn—so.' Bathsheba saw a sort of rainbow, upside down in the air, and Troy's arm was still again. 'Cut two, as if you were hedging—so. Three, as if you were reaping—so. Four, as if you were threshing—in that way. Then the same on the left. The thrusts are these: one, two, three, four, right; one, two, three, four, left.' He repeated them. 'Have 'em again?' he said. 'One, two——'

She hurriedly interrupted: 'I'd rather not; though I don't mind your twos and fours; but your ones and threes are terrible!'

'Very well. I'll let you off the ones and threes. Next, cuts, points and guards altogether.' Troy duly exhibited them. 'Then there's pursuing practice, in this way.' He gave the movements as before. 'There, those are the stereotyped forms. The infantry have two most diabolical

2. In this and the following sentences—"cuts" are hits made with the edge of the sword; "thrusts" or "points" are hits made with the point of the sword; and "guards" are various positions of defense. Hardy once owned two military manuals, one titled *Instructions for the Sword. . . . For the Use of Cavalry* and the other *Infantry Sword Exercises,* upon which he probably drew in having Troy compare the cavalry cuts, guards, and thrusts with those of the infantry.

upward cuts, which we are too humane to use. Like this—three, four.'

'How murderous and bloodthirsty!'

'They are rather deathy. Now I'll be more interesting, and let you see some loose play—giving all the cuts and points, infantry and cavalry, quicker than lightning, and as promiscuously—with just enough rule to regulate instinct and yet not to fetter it. You are my antagonist, with this difference from real warfare, that I shall miss you every time by one hair's breadth, or perhaps two. Mind you don't flinch, whatever you do.'

'I'll be sure not to!' she said invincibly.

He pointed to about a yard in front of him.

Bathsheba's adventurous spirit was beginning to find some grains of relish in these highly novel proceedings. She took up her position as directed, facing Troy.

'Now just to learn whether you have pluck enough to let me do what I wish, I'll give you a preliminary test.'

He flourished the sword by way of introduction number two, and the next thing of which she was conscious was that the point and blade of the sword were darting with a gleam towards her left side, just above her hip; then of their reappearance on her right side, emerging as it were from between her ribs, having apparently passed through her body. The third time of consciousness was that of seeing the same sword, perfectly clean and free from blood held vertically in Troy's hand (in the position technically called 'recover swords'). All was as quick as electricity.

'Oh!' she cried out in affright, pressing her hand to her side. 'Have you run me through?—no, you have not! Whatever have you done!'

'I have not touched you,' said Troy quietly. 'It was mere sleight of hand. The sword passed behind you. Now you are not afraid, are you? Because if you are I can't perform. I give my word that I will not only not hurt you, but not once touch you.'

'I don't think I am afraid. You are quite sure you will not hurt me?'

'Quite sure.'

'Is the sword very sharp?'

'O no—only stand as still as a statue. Now!'

In an instant the atmosphere was transformed to Bathsheba's eyes. Beams of light caught from the low sun's rays, above, around, in front of her, well-nigh shut out earth and heaven—all emitted in the marvellous evolutions of Troy's reflecting blade, which seemed everywhere at once, and yet nowhere specially. These circling gleams were accompanied by a keen rush that was almost a whistling—also springing from all sides of her at once. In short, she was enclosed in a firmament of light, and of sharp hisses, resembling a sky-full of meteors close at hand.

Never since the broadsword became the national weapon had there been more dexterity shown in its management than by the hands of

Sergeant Troy, and never had he been in such splendid temper for the performance as now in the evening sunshine among the ferns with Bathsheba. It may safely be asserted with respect to the closeness of his cuts, that had it been possible for the edge of the sword to leave in the air a permanent substance wherever it flew past, the space left untouched would have been almost a mould of Bathsheba's figure.

Behind the luminous streams of this *aurora militaris*,[3] she could see the hue of Troy's sword arm, spread in a scarlet haze over the space covered by its motions, like a twanged harpstring, and behind all Troy himself, mostly facing her; sometimes, to show the rear cuts, half turned away, his eye nevertheless always keenly measuring her breadth and outline, and his lips tightly closed in sustained effort. Next, his movements lapsed slower, and she could see them individually. The hissing of the sword had ceased, and he stopped entirely.

'That outer loose lock of hair wants tidying,' he said, before she had moved or spoken. 'Wait: I'll do it for you.'

An arc of silver shone on her right side: the sword had descended. The lock dropped to the ground.

'Bravely borne!' said Troy. 'You didn't flinch a shade's thickness. Wonderful in a woman!'

'It was because I didn't expect it. O, you have spoilt my hair!'

'Only once more.'

'No—no! I am afraid of you—indeed I am!', she cried.

'I won't touch you at all—not even your hair. I am only going to kill that caterpillar settling on you. Now: still!'

It appeared that a caterpillar had come from the fern and chosen the front of her bodice as his resting place. She saw the point glisten towards her bosom, and seemingly enter it. Bathsheba closed her eyes in the full persuasion that she was killed at last. However, feeling just as usual, she opened them again.

'There it is, look,' said the sergeant, holding his sword before her eyes.

The caterpillar was spitted upon its point.

'Why, it is magic!' said Bathsheba, amazed.

'O no—dexterity. I merely gave point to your bosom where the caterpillar was, and instead of running you through checked the extension a thousandth of an inch short of your surface.'

'But how could you chop off a curl of my hair with a sword that has no edge?'

'No edge! This sword will shave like a razor. Look here.'

He touched the palm of his hand with the blade, and then, lifting it, showed her a thin shaving of scarf-skin dangling therefrom.

'But you said before beginning that it was blunt and couldn't cut me!'

3. Literally, Latin for "military radiance"; metaphorically, Hardy compares the light flashing from Troy's sword to the luminous streamings of the northern lights or aurora borealis.

'That was to get you to stand still, and so make sure of your safety. The risk of injuring you through your moving was too great not to force me to tell you a fib to escape it.'

She shuddered. 'I have been within an inch of my life, and didn't know it!'

'More precisely speaking, you have been within half an inch of being pared alive two hundred and ninety-five times.'

'Cruel, cruel, 'tis of you!'

'You have been perfectly safe, nevertheless. My sword never errs.' And Troy returned the weapon to the scabbard.

Bathsheba, overcome by a hundred tumultuous feelings resulting from the scene, abstractedly sat down on a tuft of heather.

'I must leave you now,' said Troy softly. 'And I'll venture to take and keep this in remembrance of you.'

She saw him stoop to the grass, pick up the winding lock which he had severed from her manifold tresses, twist it round his fingers, unfasten a button in the breast of his coat, and carefully put it inside. She felt powerless to withstand or deny him. He was altogether too much for her, and Bathsheba seemed as one who, facing a reviving wind, finds it blow so strongly that it stops the breath.

He drew near and said, 'I must be leaving you.' He drew nearer still. A minute later and she saw his scarlet form disappear amid the ferny thicket, almost in a flash, like a brand swiftly waved.

That minute's interval had brought the blood beating into her face, set her stinging as if aflame to the very hollows of her feet, and enlarged emotion to a compass which quite swamped thought. It had brought upon her a stroke resulting, as did that of Moses in Horeb, in a liquid stream[4]—here a stream of tears. She felt like one who has sinned a great sin.

The circumstance had been the gentle dip of Troy's mouth downwards upon her own. He had kissed her.

XXIX

Particulars of a Twilight Walk

We now see the element of folly distinctly mingling with the many varying particulars which made up the character of Bathsheba Everdene. It was almost foreign to her intrinsic nature. Introduced as lymph on the dart of Eros[1] it eventually permeated and coloured her whole constitution. Bathsheba, though she had too much understanding to be entirely governed by her womanliness, had too much

4. An allusion to Exodus 17:6, in which the Lord commands Moses to strike a rock from which water will come. Horeb is a mountain sometimes identified with Mount Sinai.

1. Lymph is the mythical fluid on Cupid's arrow that is supposed to spread through the body of whomever it strikes and produce love-symptoms.

womanliness to use her understanding to the best advantage. Perhaps in no minor point does woman astonish her helpmate more than in the strange power she possesses of believing cajoleries that she knows to be false—except, indeed, in that of being utterly sceptical on strictures that she knows to be true.

Bathsheba loved Troy in the way that only self-reliant women love when they abandon their self-reliance. When a strong woman reck-lessly throws away her strength she is worse than a weak woman who has never had any strength to throw away. One source of her inade-quacy is the novelty of the occasion. She has never had practice in making the best of such a condition. Weakness is doubly weak by being new.

Bathsheba was not conscious of guile in this matter. Though in one sense a woman of the world, it was, after all, that world of daylight coteries and green carpets wherein cattle form the passing crowd and winds the busy hum; where a quiet family of rabbits or hares lives on the other side of your party-wall, where your neighbour is everybody in the tything,[2] and where calculation is confined to market-days. Of the fabricated tastes of good fashionable society she knew but little, and of the formulated self-indulgence of bad, nothing at all. Had her utmost thoughts in this direction been distinctly worded (and by herself they never were), they would only have amounted to such a matter as that she felt her impulses to be pleasanter guides than her discretion. Her love was entire as a child's, and though warm as summer it was fresh as spring. Her culpability lay in her making no attempt to control feeling by subtle and careful inquiry into conse-quences. She could show others the steep and thorny way, but 'reck'd not her own rede.'[3]

And Troy's deformities lay deep down from a woman's vision, whilst his embellishments were upon the very surface; thus contrasting with homely Oak, whose defects were patent to the blindest, and whose virtues were as metals in a mine.

The difference between love and respect was markedly shown in her conduct. Bathsheba had spoken of her interest in Boldwood with the greatest freedom to Liddy, but she had only communed with her own heart concerning Troy.

All this infatuation Gabriel saw, and was troubled thereby from the time of his daily journey a-field to the time of his return, and on to the small hours of many a night. That he was not beloved had hitherto been his great sorrow; that Bathsheba was getting into the toils was now a sorrow greater than the first, and one which nearly obscured it. It was a result which paralleled the oft-quoted observation of Hippocrates

---

2. An Old English governmental organization consisting of a group of ten householders who were responsible for each other's conduct.

3. An archaic expression for "did not take her own advice"; the entire sentence is an allusion to Ophelia's speech to Laertes in *Hamlet*, act 1, scene 3, lines 46–51.

concerning physical pains.[4]

That is a noble though perhaps an unpromising love which not even the fear of breeding aversion in the bosom of the one beloved can deter from combating his or her errors. Oak determined to speak to his mistress. He would base his appeal on what he considered her unfair treatment of Farmer Boldwood, now absent from home.

An opportunity occurred one evening when she had gone for a short walk by a path through the neighbouring cornfields. It was dusk when Oak, who had not been far a-field that day, took the same path and met her returning, quite pensively, as he thought.

The wheat was now tall, and the path was narrow; thus the way was quite a sunken groove between the embowing thicket on either side. Two persons could not walk abreast without damaging the crop, and Oak stood aside to let her pass.

'Oh, is it Gabriel?' she said. 'You are taking a walk too. Good-night.'

'I thought I would come to meet you, as it is rather late,' said Oak, turning and following at her heels when she had brushed somewhat quickly by him.

'Thank you, indeed, but I am not very fearful.'

'O no; but there are bad characters about.'

'I never meet them.'

Now Oak, with marvellous ingenuity, had been going to introduce the gallant sergeant through the channel of 'bad characters.' But all at once the scheme broke down, it suddenly occurring to him that this was rather a clumsy way, and too barefaced to begin with. He tried another preamble.

'And as the man who would naturally come to meet you is away from home, too—I mean Farmer Boldwood—why, thinks I, I'll go,' he said.

'Ah, yes.' She walked on without turning her head, and for many steps nothing further was heard from her quarter than the rustle of her dress against the heavy corn-ears. Then she resumed rather tartly—

'I don't quite understand what you meant by saying that Mr. Boldwood would naturally come to meet me.'

'I meant on account of the wedding which they say is likely to take place between you and him, miss. Forgive my speaking plainly.'

'They say what is not true,' she returned quickly. 'No marriage is likely to take place between us.'

Gabriel now put forth his unobscured opinion, for the moment had come. 'Well, Miss Everdene,' he said, 'putting aside what people say, I never in my life saw any courting if his is not a courting of you.'

Bathsheba would probably have terminated the conversation there

4. An allusion to section 2, number 46 of the *Aphorisims* of Hippocrates (ca. 460–370 B.C.): "When two pains occur simultaneously but not in the same place, the more violent obscures the other."

and then by flatly forbidding the subject, had not her conscious weakness of position allured her to palter and argue in endeavours to better it.

'Since this subject has been mentioned,' she said very emphatically, 'I am glad of the opportunity of clearing up a mistake which is very common and very provoking. I didn't definitely promise Mr. Boldwood anything. I have never cared for him. I respect him, and he has urged me to marry him. But I have given him no distinct answer. As soon as he returns I shall do so; and the answer will be that I cannot think of marrying him.'

'People are full of mistakes, seemingly.'

'They are.'

'The other day they said you were trifling with him, and you almost proved that you were not; lately they have said that you be not, and you straightway begin to show——'

'That I am, I suppose you mean.'

'Well, I hope they speak the truth.'

'They do, but wrongly applied. I don't trifle with him; but then, I have nothing to do with him.'

Oak was unfortunately led on to speak of Boldwood's rival in a wrong tone to her after all. 'I wish you had never met that young Sergeant Troy, miss,' he sighed.

Bathsheba's steps became faintly spasmodic. 'Why?' she asked.

'He is not good enough for 'ee.'

'Did any one tell you to speak to me like this?'

'Nobody at all.'

'Then it appears to me that Sergeant Troy does not concern us here,' she said intractably. 'Yet I must say that Sergeant Troy is an educated man, and quite worthy of any woman. He is well born.'

'His being higher in learning and birth than the ruck[5] o' soldiers is anything but a proof of his worth. It shows his course to be down'ard.'

'I cannot see what this has to do with our conversation. Mr. Troy's course is not by any means downward; and his superiority *is* a proof of his worth!'

'I believe him to have no conscience at all. And I cannot help begging you, miss, to have nothing to do with him. Listen to me this once—only this once! I don't say he's such a bad man as I have fancied—I pray to God he is not. But since we don't exactly know what he is, why not behave as if he *might* be bad, simply for your own safety? Don't trust him, mistress; I ask you not to trust him so.'

'Why, pray?'

'I like soldiers, but this one I do not like,' he said sturdily. 'His cleverness in his calling may have tempted him astray, and what is mirth to the neighbours is ruin to the woman. When he tries to talk to

5. The majority, the general run.

'ee again, why not turn away with a short "Good day"; and when you see him coming one way, turn the other. When he says anything laughable, fail to see the point and don't smile, and speak of him before those who will report your talk as "that fantastical man," or "that Sergeant What's-his-name." "That man of a family that has come to the dogs." Don't be unmannerly towards en, but harmless-uncivil, and so get rid of the man.'

No Christmas robin detained by a window-pane ever pulsed as did Bathsheba now.

'I say—I say again—that it doesn't become you to talk about him. Why he should be mentioned passes me quite!' she exclaimed desperately. 'I know this, th-th-that he is a thoroughly conscientious man—blunt sometimes even to rudeness—but always speaking his mind about you plain to your face!'

'Oh.'

'He is as good as anybody in this parish! He is very particular, too, about going to church—yes, he is!'

'I am afeard nobody ever saw him there. I never did, certainly.'

'The reason of that is,' she said eagerly, 'that he goes in privately by the old tower door, just when the service commences, and sits at the back of the gallery. He told me so.'

This supreme instance of Troy's goodness fell upon Gabriel's ears like the thirteenth stroke of a crazy clock. It was not only received with utter incredulity as regarded itself, but threw a doubt on all the assurances that had preceded it.

Oak was grieved to find how entirely she trusted him. He brimmed with deep feeling as he replied in a steady voice, the steadiness of which was spoilt by the palpableness of his great effort to keep it so:—

'You know, mistress, that I love you, and shall love you always. I only mention this to bring to your mind that at any rate I would wish to do you no harm: beyond that I put it aside. I have lost in the race for money and good things, and I am not such a fool as to pretend to 'ee now I am poor, and you have got altogether above me. But Bathsheba, dear mistress, this I beg you to consider—that, both to keep yourself well honoured among the workfolk, and in common generosity to an honourable man who loves you as well as I, you should be more discreet in your bearing towards this soldier.'

'Don't, don't, don't!' she exclaimed, in a choking voice.

'Are ye not more to me than my own affairs, and even life!' he went on. 'Come, listen to me! I am six years older than you, and Mr. Boldwood is ten years older than I, and consider—I do beg of 'ee to consider before it is too late—how safe you would be in his hands!'

Oak's allusion to his own love for her lessened, to some extent, her anger at his interference; but she could not really forgive him for letting his wish to marry her be eclipsed by his wish to do her good, any more than for his slighting treatment of Troy.

'I wish you to go elsewhere,' she commanded, a paleness of face invisible to the eye being suggested by the trembling words. 'Do not remain on this farm any longer. I don't want you—I beg you to go!'

'That's nonsense,' said Oak calmly. 'This is the second time you have pretended to dismiss me; and what's the use o' it?'

'Pretended! You shall go, sir—your lecturing I will not hear! I am mistress here.'

'Go, indeed—what folly will you say next? Treating me like Dick, Tom and Harry when you know that a short time ago my position was as good as yours! Upon my life, Bathsheba, it is too barefaced. You know, too, that I can't go without putting things in such a strait as you wouldn't get out of I can't tell when. Unless, indeed, you'll promise to have an understanding man as bailiff, or manager, or something. I'll go at once if you'll promise that.'

'I shall have no bailiff; I shall continue to be my own manager,' she said decisively.

'Very well, then; you should be thankful to me for biding. How would the farm go on with nobody to mind it but a woman? But mind this, I don't wish 'ee to feel you owe me anything. Not I. What I do, I do. Sometimes I say I should be as glad as a bird to leave the place—for don't suppose I'm content to be a nobody. I was made for better things. However, I don't like to see your concerns going to ruin, as they must if you keep in this mind. . . . I hate taking my own measure so plain, but, upon my life, your provoking ways make a man say what he wouldn't dream of at other times! I own to being rather interfering. But you know well enough how it is, and who she is that I like too well, and feel too much like a fool about to be civil to her!'

It is more than probable that she privately and unconsciously respected him a little for this grim fidelity, which had been shown in his tone even more than in his words. At any rate she murmured something to the effect that he might stay if he wished. She said more distinctly, 'Will you leave me alone now? I don't order it as a mistress—I ask it as a woman, and I expect you not to be so uncourteous as to refuse.'

'Certainly I will, Miss Everdene,' said Gabriel gently. He wondered that the request should have come at this moment, for the strife was over, and they were on a most desolate hill, far from every human habitation, and the hour was getting late. He stood still and allowed her to get far ahead of him till he could only see her form upon the sky.

A distressing explanation of this anxiety to be rid of him at that point now ensued. A figure apparently rose from the earth beside her. The shape beyond all doubt was Troy's. Oak would not be even a possible listener, and at once turned back till a good two hundred yards were between the lovers and himself.

Gabriel went home by way of the churchyard. In passing the tower he thought of what she had said about the sergeant's virtuous habit of entering the church unperceived at the beginning of service. Believing that the little gallery door alluded to was quite disused, he ascended the external flight of steps at the top of which it stood, and examined it. The pale lustre yet hanging in the north-western heaven was sufficient to show that a sprig of ivy had grown from the wall across the door to a length of more than a foot, delicately tying the panel to the stone jamb. It was a decisive proof that the door had not been opened at least since Troy came back to Weatherbury.

XXX

Hot Cheeks and Tearful Eyes

Half an hour later Bathsheba entered her own house. There burnt upon her face when she met the light of the candles the flush and excitement which were little less than chronic with her now. The farewell words of Troy, who had accompanied her to the very door, still lingered in her ears. He had bidden her adieu for two days, which were, so he stated, to be spent at Bath in visiting some friends. He had also kissed her a second time.

It is only fair to Bathsheba to explain here a little fact which did not come to light till a long time afterwards: that Troy's presentation of himself so aptly at the roadside this evening was not by any distinctly preconcerted arrangement. He had hinted—she had forbidden; and it was only on the chance of his still coming that she had dismissed Oak, fearing a meeting between them just then.

She now sank down into a chair, wild and perturbed by all these new and fevering sequences. Then she jumped up with a manner of decision, and fetched her desk from a side table.

In three minutes, without pause or modification, she had written a letter to Boldwood, at his address beyond Casterbridge, saying mildly but firmly that she had well considered the whole subject he had brought before her and kindly given her time to decide upon; that her final decision was that she could not marry him. She had expressed to Oak an intention to wait till Boldwood came home before communicating to him her conclusive reply. But Bathsheba found that she could not wait.

It was impossible to send this letter till the next day; yet to quell her uneasiness by getting it out of her hands, and so, as it were, setting the act in motion at once, she arose to take it to any one of the women who might be in the kitchen.

She paused in the passage. A dialogue was going on in the kitchen, and Bathsheba and Troy were the subject of it.

'If he marry her, she'll gie up farming.'

'Twill be a gallant life, but may bring some trouble between the mirth—so say I.'

'Well, I wish I had half such a husband.'

Bathsheba had too much sense to mind seriously what her servitors said about her; but too much womanly redundance of speech to leave alone what was said till it died the natural death of unminded things. She burst in upon them.

'Who are you speaking of?' she asked.

There was a pause before anybody replied. At last Liddy said frankly, 'What was passing was a bit of a word about yourself, miss.'

'I thought so! Maryann and Liddy and Temperance—now I forbid you to suppose such things. You know I don't care the least for Mr. Troy—not I. Everybody knows how much I hate him.—Yes,' repeated the froward[1] young person, '*hate* him!'

'We know you do, miss,' said Liddy; 'and so do we all.'

'I hate him too,' said Maryann.

'Maryann—O you perjured woman! How can you speak that wicked story!' said Bathsheba excitedly. 'You admired him from your heart only this morning in the very world, you did. Yes, Maryann, you know it!'

'Yes, miss, but so did you. He is a wild scamp now, and you are right to hate him.'

'He's *not* a wild scamp! How dare you to my face! I have no right to hate him, nor you, nor anybody. But I am a silly woman! What is it to me what he is? You know it is nothing. I don't care for him; I don't mean to defend his good name, not I. Mind this, if any of you say a word against him you'll be dismissed instantly!'

She flung down the letter and surged back into the parlour, with a big heart and tearful eyes, Liddy following her.

'O miss!' said mild Liddy, looking pitifully into Bathsheba's face. 'I am sorry we mistook you so! I did think you cared for him; but I see you don't now.'

'Shut the door, Liddy.'

Liddy closed the door, and went on: 'People always say such foolery, miss. I'll make answer hencefor'ard, "Of course a lady like Miss Everdene can't love him;" I'll say it out in plain black and white.'

Bathsheba burst out: 'O Liddy, are you such a simpleton? Can't you read riddles? Can't you see? Are you a woman yourself?'

Liddy's clear eyes rounded with wonderment.

'Yes; you must be a blind thing, Liddy!' she said in reckless abandonment and grief. 'O, I love him to very distraction and misery and agony! Don't be frightened at me, though perhaps I am enough to frighten any innocent woman. Come closer—closer.' She put her arms round Liddy's neck. 'I must let it out to somebody; it is wearing me away! Don't you yet know enough of me to see through that miserable denial of mine? O God, what a lie it was! Heaven and my

---

1. Perverse, contrary.
2. A colloquial expression meaning being in a   state of excitement or having a fit of temper.

Love forgive me. And don't you know that a woman who loves at all thinks nothing of perjury when it is balanced against her love? There, go out of the room; I want to be quite alone.'

Liddy went towards the door.

'Liddy, come here. Solemnly swear to me that he's not a fast man; that it is all lies they say about him!'

'But, miss, how can I say he is not if——'

'You graceless girl! How can you have the cruel heart to repeat what they say? Unfeeling thing that you are. . . . But *I'll* see if you or anybody else in the village, or town either, dare do such a thing!' She started off, pacing from fireplace to door, and back again.

'No, miss. I don't—I know it is not true!' said Liddy, frightened at Bathsheba's unwonted vehemence.

'I suppose you only agree with me like that to please me. But, Liddy, he *cannot be* bad, as is said. Do you hear?'

'Yes, miss, yes.'

'And you don't believe he is?'

'I don't know what to say, miss,' said Liddy, beginning to cry. 'If I say No, you don't believe me; and if I say Yes, you rage at me!'

'Say you don't believe it—say you don't!'

'I don't believe him to be so bad as they make out.'

'He is not bad at all. . . . My poor life and heart, how weak I am!' she moaned, in a relaxed, desultory way, heedless of Liddy's presence. 'O, how I wish I had never seen him! Loving is misery for women always. I shall never forgive God for making me a woman, and dearly am I beginning to pay for the honour of owning a pretty face.' She freshened and turned to Liddy suddenly. 'Mind this, Lydia Smallbury, if you repeat anywhere a single word of what I have said to you inside this closed door, I'll never trust you, or love you, or have you with me a moment longer—not a moment!'

'I don't want to repeat anything,' said Liddy, with womanly dignity of a diminutive order; 'but I don't wish to stay with you. And, if you please, I'll go at the end of the harvest, or this week, or to-day. . . . I don't see that I deserve to be put upon and stormed at for nothing!' concluded the small woman, bigly.

'No, no, Liddy; you must stay!' said Bathsheba, dropping from haughtiness to entreaty with capricious inconsequence. 'You must not notice my being in a taking[2] just now. You are not as a servant— you are a companion to me. Dear, dear—I don't know what I am doing since this miserable ache o' my heart has weighted and worn upon me so! What shall I come to! I suppose I shall get further and further into troubles. I wonder sometimes if I am doomed to die in the Union.[3] I am friendless enough, God knows!'

3. One of the "union houses" brought into being by the Poor Law of 1834, which obliged adjacent parishes to unite under a common Board of Guardians in constructing and supporting workhouses to which paupers were required to go for relief.

'I won't notice anything, nor will I leave you!' sobbed Liddy, impulsively putting up her lips to Bathsheba's, and kissing her.

Then Bathsheba kissed Liddy, and all was smooth again.

'I don't often cry, do I, Lidd? but you have made tears come into my eyes,' she said, a smile shining through the moisture. 'Try to think him a good man, won't you, dear Liddy?'

'I will, miss, indeed.'

'He is a sort of steady man in a wild way, you know. That's better than to be as some are, wild in a steady way. I am afraid that's how I am. And promise me to keep my secret—do, Liddy! And do not let them know that I have been crying about him, because it will be dreadful for me, and no good to him, poor thing!'

'Death's head himself shan't wring it from me, mistress, if I've a mind to keep anything; and I'll always be your friend,' replied Liddy emphatically, at the same time bringing a few more tears into her own eyes, not from any particular necessity, but from an artistic sense of making herself in keeping with the remainder of the picture, which seems to influence women at such times. 'I think God likes us to be good friends, don't you?'

'Indeed I do.'

'And, dear miss, you won't harry me and storm at me, will you? because you seem to swell so tall as a lion then, and it frightens me! Do you know, I fancy you would be a match for any man when you are in one o' your takings.'

'Never! do you?' said Bathsheba, slightly laughing, though somewhat seriously alarmed by this Amazonian[4] picture of herself. 'I hope I am not a bold sort of maid—mannish?' she continued with some anxiety.

'O no, not mannish; but so almightly womanish that 'tis getting on that way sometimes. Ah! miss,' she said, after having drawn her breath very sadly in and sent it very sadly out, 'I wish I had half your failing that way. 'Tis a great protection to a poor maid in these illegit'mate days!'

XXXI

Blame—Fury

The next evening Bathsheba, with the idea of getting out of the way of Mr. Boldwood in the event of his returning to answer her note in person, proceeded to fulfil an engagement made with Liddy some few hours earlier. Bathsheba's companion, as a gage[1] of their reconciliation, had been granted a week's holiday to visit her sister, who was

---

4. Having the strength and warlike character attributed in Greek mythology to a race of female warriors said to inhabit Scythia.

1. A pledge or token.

married to a thriving hurdler and cattle-crib-maker[2] living in a delightful labyrinth of hazel copse not far beyond Yalbury. The arrangement was that Miss Everdene should honour them by coming there for a day or two to inspect some ingenious contrivances which this man of the woods had introduced into his wares.

Leaving her instructions with Gabriel and Maryann, that they were to see everything carefully locked up for the night, she went out of the house just at the close of a timely thunder-shower, which had refined the air, and daintily bathed the coat of the land, though all beneath was dry as ever. Freshness was exhaled in an essence from the varied contours of bank and hollow, as if the earth breathed maiden breath; and the pleased birds were hymning to the scene. Before her, among the clouds, there was a contrast in the shape of lairs of fierce light which showed themselves in the neighbourhood of a hidden sun, lingering on to the farthest north-west corner of the heavens that this midsummer season allowed.

She had walked nearly two miles of her journey, watching how the day was retreating, and thinking how the time of deeds was quietly melting into the time of thought, to give place in its turn to the time of prayer and sleep, when she beheld advancing over Yalbury hill the very man she sought so anxiously to elude. Boldwood was stepping on, not with that quiet tread of reserved strength which was his customary gait, in which he always seemed to be balancing two thoughts. His manner was stunned and sluggish now.

Boldwood had for the first time been awakened to woman's privileges in tergiversation[3] even when it involves another person's possible blight. That Bathsheba was a firm and positive girl, far less inconsequent than her fellows, had been the very lung of his hope; for he had held that these qualities would lead her to adhere to a straight course for consistency's sake, and accept him, though her fancy might not flood him with the irridescent hues of uncritical love. But the argument now came back as sorry gleams from a broken mirror. The discovery was no less a scourge than a surprise.

He came on looking upon the ground, and did not see Bathsheba till they were less than a stone's throw apart. He looked up at the sound of her pit-pat, and his changed appearance sufficiently denoted to her the depth and strength of the feelings paralyzed by her letter.

'Oh; is it you, Mr. Boldwood?' she faltered, a guilty warmth pulsing in her face.

Those who have the power of reproaching in silence may find it a means more effective than words. There are accents in the eye which are not on the tongue, and more tales come from pale lips than can enter an ear. It is both the grandeur and the pain of the remoter moods

2. A person who builds cattle pens and makes "hurdles," the portable barriers constructed of interwoven saplings.

3. Repeatedly changing one's mind.

that they avoid the pathway of sound. Boldwood's look was unanswerable.

Seeing she turned a little aside, he said, 'What, are you afraid of me?'

'Why should you say that?' said Bathsheba.

'I fancied you looked so,' said he. 'And it is most strange, because of its contrast with my feeling for you.'

She regained self-possession, fixed her eyes calmly, and waited.

'You know what that feeling is,' continued Boldwood deliberately. 'A thing strong as death. No dismissal by a hasty letter affects that.'

'I wish you did not feel so strongly about me,' she murmured. 'It is generous of you, and more than I deserve, but I must not hear it now.'

'Hear it? What do you think I have to say, then? I am not to marry you, and that's enough. Your letter was excellently plain. I want you to hear nothing—not I.'

Bathsheba was unable to direct her will into any definite groove for freeing herself from this fearfully awkward position. She confusedly said, 'Good evening,' and was moving on. Boldwood walked up to her heavily and dully.

'Bathsheba—darling—is it final indeed?'

'Indeed it is.'

'O, Bathsheba—have pity upon me!' Boldwood burst out. 'God's sake, yes—I am come to that low, lowest stage—to ask a woman for pity! Still, she is you—she is you.'

Bathsheba commanded herself well. But she could hardly get a clear voice for what came instinctively to her lips: 'There is little honour to the woman in that speech.' It was only whispered, for something unutterably mournful no less than distressing in this spectacle of a man showing himself to be so entirely the vane of a passion enervated the feminine instinct for punctilios.[4]

'I am beyond myself about this, and am mad,' he said. 'I am no stoic at all to be supplicating here; but I do supplicate to you. I wish you knew what is in me of devotion to you; but it is impossible, that. In bare human mercy to a lonely man, don't throw me off now!'

'I don't throw you off—indeed, how can I? I never had you.' In her noon-clear sense that she had never loved him she forgot for a moment her thoughtless angle on that day in February.

'But there was a time when you turned to me, before I thought of you! I don't reproach you, for even now I feel that the ignorant and cold darkness that I should have lived in if you had not attracted me by that letter—valentine you call it—would have been worse than my knowledge of you, though it has brought this misery. But, I say, there was a time when I knew nothing of you, and cared nothing for you,

---

4. Attention to minute details of conduct.

and yet you drew me on. And if you say you gave me no encouragement, I cannot but contradict you.'

'What you call encouragement was the childish game of an idle
minute. I have bitterly repented of it—ay, bitterly, and in tears. Can
you still go on reminding me?'

'I don't accuse you of it—I deplore it. I took for earnest what you
insist was jest, and now this that I pray to be jest you say is awful,
wretched earnest. Our moods meet at wrong places. I wish your
feeling was more like mine, or my feeling more like yours! O, could I
but have foreseen the torture that trifling trick was going to lead me
into, how I should have cursed you; but only having been able to see it
since, I cannot do that, for I love you too well! But it is weak, idle
drivelling to go on like this. . . . Bathsheba, you are the first woman of
any shade or nature that I have ever looked at to love, and it is the
having been so near claiming you for my own that makes this denial so
hard to bear. How nearly you promised me! But I don't speak now to
move your heart, and make you grieve because of my pain; it is no use,
that. I must bear it; my pain would get no less by paining you.'

'But I do pity you—deeply—O, so deeply!' she earnestly said.

'Do no such thing—do no such thing. Your dear love, Bathsheba,
is such a vast thing beside your pity, that the loss of your pity as well as
your love is no great addition to my sorrow, nor does the gain of your
pity make it sensibly less. O sweet—how dearly you spoke to me
behind the spear-bed at the washing-pool, and in the barn at the
shearing, and that dearest last time in the evening at your home!
Where are your pleasant words all gone—your earnest hope to be able
to love me? Where is your firm conviction that you would get to care
for me very much? Really forgotten?—really?'

She checked emotion, looked him quietly and clearly in the face,
and said in her low, firm voice, 'Mr. Boldwood, I promised you
nothing. Would you have had me a woman of clay when you paid me
that furthest, highest compliment a man can pay a woman—telling
her he loves her? I was bound to show some feeling, if I would not be a
graceless shrew. Yet each of those pleasures was just for the day—the
day just for the pleasure. How was I to know that what is a pastime to
all other men was death to you? Have reason, do, and think more
kindly of me!'

'Well, never mind arguing—never mind. One thing is sure: you
were all but mine, and now you are not nearly mine. Everything is
changed, and that by you alone, remember. You were nothing to me
once, and I was contented; you are now nothing to me again, and how
different the second nothing is from the first! Would to God you had
never taken me up, since it was only to throw me down!'

Bathsheba, in spite of her mettle, began to feel unmistakable signs
that she was inherently the weaker vessel. She strove miserably against
this femininity which would insist upon supplying unbidden emo-

tions in stronger and stronger current. She had tried to elude agitation by fixing her mind on the trees, sky, any trivial object before her eyes, whilst his reproaches fell, but ingenuity could not save her now.

'I did not take you up—surely I did not!' she answered as heroically as she could. 'But don't be in this mood with me. I can endure being told I am in the wrong, if you will only tell it me gently! O sir, will you not kindly forgive me, and look at it cheerfully?'

'Cheerfully! Can a man fooled to utter heartburning find a reason for being merry? If I have lost, how can I be as if I had won? Heavens, you must be heartless quite! Had I known what a fearfully bitter sweet this was to be, how I would have avoided you, and never seen you, and been deaf to you. I tell you all this, but what do you care! You don't care.'

She returned silent and weak denials to his charges, and swayed her head desperately, as if to thrust away the words as they came showering about her ears from the lips of the trembling man in the climax of life, with his bronzed Roman face and fine frame.

'Dearest, dearest, I am wavering even now between the two opposites of recklessly renouncing you, and labouring humbly for you again. Forget that you have said No, and let it be as it was! Say, Bathsheba, that you only wrote that refusal to me in fun—come, say it to me!'

'It would be untrue, and painful to both of us. You overrate my capacity for love. I don't possess half the warmth of nature you believe me to have. An unprotected childhood in a cold world has beaten gentleness out of me.'

He immediately said with more resentment: 'That may be true, somewhat; but ah, Miss Everdene, it won't do as a reason! You are not the cold woman you would have me believe. No, no! It isn't because you have no feeling in you that you don't love me. You naturally would have me think so—you would hide from me that you have a burning heart like mine. You have love enough, but it is turned into a new channel. I know where.'

The swift music of her heart became hubbub now, and she throbbed to extremity. He was coming to Troy. He did then know what had occurred! And the name fell from his lips the next moment.

'Why did Troy not leave my treasure alone?' he asked fiercely. 'When I had no thought of injuring him, why did he force himself upon your notice! Before he worried you your inclination was to have me; when next I should have come to you your answer would have been Yes. Can you deny it—I ask, can you deny it?'

She delayed the reply, but was too honest to withhold it. 'I cannot,' she whispered.

'I know you cannot. But he stole in in my absence and robbed me. Why didn't he win you away before, when nobody would have been grieved?—when nobody would have been set tale-bearing. Now the people sneer at me—the very hills and sky seem to laugh at me till I blush shamefully for my folly. I have lost my respect, my good name, my standing—lost it, never to get it again. Go and marry your man—go on!'

'O sir—Mr. Boldwood!'

'You may as well. I have no further claim upon you. As for me, I had better go somewhere alone, and hide—and pray. I loved a woman once. I am now ashamed. When I am dead they'll say, Miserable love-sick man that he was. Heaven—heaven—if I had got jilted secretly, and the dishonour not known, and my position kept! But no matter, it is gone, and the woman not gained. Shame upon him—shame!'

His unreasonable anger terrified her, and she glided from him, without obviously moving, as she said, 'I am only a girl—do not speak to me so!'

'All the time you knew—how very well you knew—that your new freak was my misery. Dazzled by brass and scarlet—O, Bathsheba—this is woman's folly indeed!'

She fired up at once. 'You are taking too much upon yourself!' she said vehemently. 'Everybody is upon me—everybody. It is unmanly to attack a woman so! I have nobody in the world to fight my battles for me; but no mercy is shown. Yet if a thousand of you sneer and say things against me, I *will not* be put down!'

'You'll chatter with him doubtless about me. Say to him, "Boldwood would have died for me." Yes, and you have given way to him, knowing him to be not the man for you. He has kissed you—claimed you as his. Do you hear—he has kissed you. Deny it!'

The most tragic woman is cowed by a tragic man, and although Boldwood was, in vehemence and glow, nearly her own self rendered into another sex, Bathsheba's cheek quivered. She gasped, 'Leave me, sir—leave me! I am nothing to you. Let me go on!'

'Deny that he has kissed you.'

'I shall not.'

'Ha—then he has!' came hoarsely from the farmer.

'He has,' she said slowly, and, in spite of her fear, defiantly. 'I am not ashamed to speak the truth.'

'Then curse him; and curse him!' said Boldwood, breaking into a whispered fury. 'Whilst I would have given worlds to touch your hand, you have let a rake come in without right or ceremony and—kiss you! Heaven's mercy—kiss you! . . . Ah, a time of his life shall come when he will have to repent, and think wretchedly of the pain he has caused another man; and then may he ache, and wish, and curse, and yearn—as I do now!'

'Don't, don't, O, don't pray down evil upon him!' she implored in a miserably cry. 'Anything but that—anything. O, be kind to him, sir, for I love him true!'

Boldwood's ideas had reached that point of fusion at which outline and consistency entirely disappear. The impending night appeared to concentrate in his eye. He did not hear her at all now.

'I'll punish him—by my soul, that will I! I'll meet him, soldier or no, and I'll horsewhip the untimely stripling for this reckless theft of my one delight. If he were a hundred men I'd horsewhip him——' He dropped his voice suddenly and unnaturally. 'Bathsheba, sweet, lost coquette, pardon me! I've been blaming you, threatening you, behaving like a churl to you, when he's the greatest sinner. He stole your dear heart away with his unfathomable lies! . . . It is a fortunate thing for him that he's gone back to his regiment—that he's away up the country, and not here! I hope he may not return here just yet. I pray God he may not come into my sight, for I may be tempted beyond myself. O, Bathsheba, keep him away—yes, keep him away from me!'

For a moment Boldwood stood so inertly after this that his soul seemed to have been entirely exhaled with the breath of his passionate words. He turned his face away, and withdrew, and his form was soon covered over by the twilight as his footsteps mixed in with the low hiss of the leafy trees.

Bathsheba, who had been standing motionless as a model all this latter time, flung her hands to her face, and wildly attempted to ponder on the exhibition which had just passed away. Such astounding wells of fevered feeling in a still man like Mr. Boldwood were incomprehensible, dreadful. Instead of being a man trained to repression he was—what she had seen him.

The force of the farmer's threats lay in their relation to a circumstance known at present only to herself: her lover was coming back to Weatherbury in the course of the very next day or two. Troy had not returned to his distant barracks as Boldwood and others supposed, but had merely gone to visit some acquaintance in Bath, and had yet a week or more remaining to his furlough.

She felt wretchedly certain that if he revisited her just at this nick of time, and came into contact with Boldwood, a fierce quarrel would be the consequence. She panted with solicitude when she thought of possible injury to Troy. The least spark would kindle the farmer's swift feelings of rage and jealousy; he would lose his self-mastery as he had this evening; Troy's blitheness might become aggressive; it might take the direction of derision, and Boldwood's anger might then take the direction of revenge.

With almost a morbid dread of being thought a gushing girl, this guideless woman too well concealed from the world under a manner of carelessness the warm depths of her strong emotions. But now there was no reserve. In her distraction, instead of advancing further she walked up and down, beating the air with her fingers, pressing her brow, and sobbing brokenly to herself. Then she sat down on a heap of stones by the wayside to think. There she remained long. Above the dark margin of the earth appeared foreshores and promontories of coppery cloud, bounding a green and pellucid expanse in the western sky. Amaranthine[5] glosses came over them then, and the unresting world wheeled her round to a contrasting prospect eastward, in the shape of indecisive and palpitating stars. She gazed upon their silent throes amid the shades of space, but realized none at all. Her troubled spirit was far away with Troy.

XXXII

Night—Horses Tramping

The village of Weatherbury was quiet as the graveyard in its midst, and the living were lying well-nigh as still as the dead. The church clock struck eleven. The air was so empty of other sounds that the whirr of the clock-work immediately before the strokes was distinct, and so was also the click of the same at their close. The notes flew forth with the usual blind obtuseness of inanimate things—flapping and rebounding among walls, undulating against the scattered clouds, spreading through their interstices into unexplored miles of space.

Bathsheba's crannied and mouldy halls were tonight occupied only by Maryann, Liddy being, as was stated, with her sister, whom Bathsheba had set out to visit. A few minutes after eleven had struck, Maryann turned in her bed with a sense of being disturbed. She was totally unconscious of the nature of the interruption to her sleep. It led to a dream, and the dream to an awakening, with an uneasy sensation that something had happened. She left her bed and looked out of the window. The paddock abutted on this end of the building, and in the paddock she could just discern by the uncertain gray a moving figure approaching the horse that was feeding there. The figure seized the horse by the forelock, and led it to the corner of the field. Here she could see some object which circumstances proved to be a vehicle, for after a few minutes spent apparently in harnessing, she heard the trot of the horse down the road, mingled with the sound of light wheels.

Two varieties only of humanity could have entered the paddock with the ghost-like glide of that mysterious figure. They were a woman and a gipsy man. A woman was out of the question in such an occupation at this hour, and the comer could be no less than a thief, who might probably have known the weakness of the household on this particular night, and have chosen it on that account for his daring attempt. Moreover, to raise suspicion to conviction itself, there were gipsies in Weatherbury Bottom.

Maryann, who had been afraid to shout in the robber's presence, having seen him depart had no fear. She hastily slipped on her clothes,

5. Lustrous shades of purplish-red.

stumped down the disjointed staircase with its hundred creaks, ran to Coggan's, the nearest house, and raised an alarm. Coggan called Gabriel, who now again lodged in his house as at first, and together they went to the paddock. Beyond all doubt the horse was gone.

'Hark!' said Gabriel.

They listened. Distinct upon the stagnant air came the sounds of a trotting horse passing up Longpuddle Lane—just beyond the gipsies' encampment in Weatherbury Bottom.

'That's our Dainty—I'll swear to her step,' said Jan.

'Mighty me! Won't mis-ess storm and call us stupids when she comes back!' moaned Maryann. 'How I wish it had happened when she was at home, and none of us had been answerable!'

'We must ride after,' said Gabriel decisively. 'I'll be responsible to Miss Everdene for what we do. Yes, we'll follow.'

'Faith, I don't see how,' said Coggan. 'All our horses are too heavy for that trick except little Poppet, and what's she between two of us?—If we only had that pair over the hedge we might do something.'

'Which pair?'

'Mr. Boldwood's Tidy and Moll.'

'Then wait here till I come hither again,' said Gabriel. He ran down the hill towards Farmer Boldwood's.

'Farmer Boldwood is not at home,' said Maryann.

'All the better,' said Coggan. 'I know what he's gone for.'

Less than five minutes brought up Oak again, running at the same pace, with two halters dangling from his hand.

'Where did you find 'em?' said Coggan, turning round and leaping upon the hedge without waiting for an answer.

'Under the eaves. I knew where they were kept,' said Gabriel, following him. 'Coggan, you can ride bare-backed? there's no time to look for saddles.'

'Like a hero!' said Jan.

'Maryann, you go to bed,' Gabriel shouted to her from the top of the hedge.

Springing down into Boldwood's pastures, each pocketed his halter to hide it from the horses, who, seeing the men empty-handed, docilely allowed themselves to be seized by the mane, when the halters were dexterously slipped on. Having neither bit nor bridle, Oak and Coggan extemporized the former by passing the rope in each case through the animal's mouth and looping it on the other side. Oak vaulted astride, and Coggan clambered up by aid of the bank, when they ascended to the gate and galloped off in the direction taken by Bathsheba's horse and the robber. Whose vehicle the horse had been harnessed to was a matter of some uncertainty.

Weatherbury Bottom was reached in three or four minutes. They scanned the shady green patch by the roadside. The gipsies were gone.

'The villains!' said Gabriel. 'Which way have they gone, I wonder?'

'Straight on, as sure as God made little apples,' said Jan.

'Very well; we are better mounted, and must overtake 'em,' said Oak. 'Now, on at full speed!'

No sound of the rider in their van could now be discovered. The road-metal grew softer and more clayey as Weatherbury was left behind, and the late rain had wetted its surface to a somewhat plastic, but not muddy state. They came to cross-roads. Coggan suddenly pulled up Moll and slipped off.

'What's the matter?' said Gabriel.

'We must try to track 'em, since we can't hear 'em,' said Jan, fumbling in his pockets. He struck a light, and held the match to the ground. The rain had been heavier here, and all foot and horse tracks made previous to the storm had been abraded and blurred by the drops, and they were now so many little scoops of water, which reflected the flame of the match like eyes. One set of tracks was fresh and had no water in them; one pair of ruts was also empty, and not small canals, like the others. The footprints forming this recent impression were full of information as to pace; they were in equidistant pairs, three or four feet apart, the right and left foot of each pair being exactly opposite one another.

'Straight on!' Jan exclaimed. 'Tracks like that mean a stiff gallop. No wonder we don't hear him. And the horse is harnessed—look at the ruts. Ay, that's our mare, sure enough!'

'How do you know?'

'Old Jimmy Harris only shoed her last week, and I'd swear to his make among ten thousand.'

'The rest of the gipsies must ha' gone on earlier, or some other way,' said Oak. 'You saw there were no other tracks?'

'True.' They rode along silently for a long weary time. Coggan carried an old pinchbeck repeater[1] which he had inherited from some genius in his family; and it now struck one. He lighted another match, and examined the ground again.

' 'Tis a canter now,' he said, throwing away the light. 'A twisty, rickety pace for a gig. The fact is, they overdrove her at starting; we shall catch 'em yet.'

Again they hastened on, and entered Blackmore Vale. Coggan's watch struck two. When they looked again the hoof-marks were so spaced as to form a sort of zigzag if united, like the lamps along a street.

'That's a trot, I know,' said Gabriel.

'Only a trot now,' said Coggan cheerfully. 'We shall overtake him in time.'

They pushed rapidly on for yet two or three miles. 'Ah! a moment,' said Jan. 'Let's see how she was driven up this hill. 'Twill help us.' A

---

1. "Pinchbeck" is an imitation gold alloy of five parts copper and one part zinc used for watchcases and the like; a "repeater" is a pocket watch that strikes the hours.

light was promptly struck upon his gaiters as before, and the examination made.

'Hurrah!' said Coggan. 'She walked up here—and well she might. We shall get them in two miles, for a crown.'

They rode three, and listened. No sound was to be heard save a mill-pond trickling hoarsely through a hatch, and suggesting gloomy possibilities of drowning by jumping in. Gabriel dismounted when they came to a turning. The tracks were absolutely the only guide as to the direction that they now had, and great caution was necessary to avoid confusing them with some others which had made their appearance lately.

'What does this mean?—though I guess,' said Gabriel, looking up at Coggan as he moved the match over the ground about the turning. Coggan, who, no less than the panting horses, had latterly shown signs of weariness, again scrutinized the mystic characters. This time only three were of the regular horseshoe shape. Every fourth was a dot.

He screwed up his face, and emitted a long 'whew-w-w!'

'Lame,' said Oak.

'Yes. Dainty is lamed; the near-foot-afore,' said Coggan slowly, staring still at the footprints.

'We'll push on,' said Gabriel, remounting his humid steed.

Although the road along its greater part had been as good as any turnpike-road in the country, it was nominally only a byway. The last turning had brought them into the high road leading to Bath. Coggan recollected himself.

'We shall have him now!' he exclaimed.

'Where?'

'Sherton Turnpike.[2] The keeper of that gate is the sleepiest man between here and London—Dan Randall, that's his name—knowed en for years, when he was at Casterbridge gate. Between the lameness and the gate 'tis a done job.'

They now advanced with extreme caution. Nothing was said until, against a shady background of foliage, five white bars were visible, crossing their route a little way ahead.

'Hush—we are almost close!' said Gabriel.

'Amble on upon the grass,' said Coggan.

The white bars were blotted out in the midst by a dark shape in front of them. The silence of this lonely time was pierced by an exclamation from that quarter.

'Hoy-a-hoy! Gate!'

It appeared that there had been a previous call which they had not noticed, for on their close approach the door of the turnpike-house opened, and the keeper came out half-dressed, with a candle in his hand. The rays illumined the whole group.

2. For a description of the turnpike–toll system, see footnote 9 of chapter 1.

'Keep the gate close!' shouted Gabriel. 'He has stolen the horse!'

'Who?' said the turnpike-man.

Gabriel looked at the driver of the gig, and saw a woman—Bathsheba, his mistress.

On hearing his voice she had turned her face away from the light. Coggan had, however, caught sight of her in the meanwhile.

'Why, 'tis mistress—I'll take my oath!' he said, amazed.

Bathsheba it certainly was, and she had by this time done the trick she could do so well in crises not of love, namely, mask a surprise by coolness of manner.

'Well, Gabriel,' she inquired quietly, 'where are you going?'

'We thought——' began Gabriel.

'I am driving to Bath,' she said, taking for her own use the assurance that Gabriel lacked. 'An important matter made it necessary for me to give up my visit to Liddy, and go off at once. What, then, were you following me?'

'We thought the horse was stole.'

'Well—what a thing! How very foolish of you not to know that I had taken the trap and horse. I could neither wake Maryann nor get into the house, though I hammered for ten minutes against her window-sill. Fortunately, I could get the key of the coach-house, so I troubled no one further. Didn't you think it might be me?'

'Why should we, miss?'

'Perhaps not. Why, those are never Farmer Boldwood's horses! Goodness mercy! what have you been doing—bringing trouble upon me in this way? What! mustn't a lady move an inch from her door without being dogged like a thief?'

'But how was we to know, if you left no account of your doings?' expostulated Coggan, 'and ladies don't drive at these hours, miss, as a jineral rule of society.'

'I did leave an account—and you would have seen it in the morning. I wrote in chalk on the coach-house doors that I had come back for the horse and gig, and driven off; that I could arouse nobody, and should return soon.'

'But you'll consider, ma'am, that we couldn't see that till it got daylight.'

'True,' she said, and though vexed at first she had too much sense to blame them long or seriously for a devotion to her that was as valuable as it was rare. She added with a very pretty grace, 'Well, I really thank you heartily for taking all this trouble; but I wish you had borrowed anybody's horses but Mr. Boldwood's.'

'Dainty is lame, miss,' said Coggan. 'Can ye go on?'

'It was only a stone in her shoe. I got down and pulled it out a hundred yards back.[3] I can manage very well, thank you. I shall be in

3. Bathsheba's statement here appears to be inconsistent with her admission to Oak in chap-   ter XXXVII that Dainty was lame when she arrived in Bath.

Bath by daylight. Will you now return, please?'

She turned her head—the gateman's candle shimmering upon her quick, clear eyes as she did so—passed through the gate, and was soon wrapped in the embowering shades of mysterious summer boughs. Coggan and Gabriel put about their horses, and, fanned by the velvety air of this July night, retraced the road by which they had come.

'A strange vagary, this of hers, isn't it, Oak?' said Coggan curiously.

'Yes,' said Gabriel shortly.

'She won't be in Bath by no daylight!'

'Coggan, suppose we keep this night's work as quiet as we can?'

'I am of one and the same mind.'

'Very well. We shall be home by three o'clock or so, and can creep into the parish like lambs.'

Bathsheba's perturbed meditations by the roadside had ultimately evolved a conclusion that there were only two remedies for the present desperate state of affairs. The first was merely to keep Troy away from Weatherbury till Boldwood's indignation had cooled; the second to listen to Oak's entreaties, and Boldwood's denunciations, and give up Troy altogether.

Alas! Could she give up this new love—induce him to renounce her by saying she did not like him—could no more speak to him, and beg him, for her good, to end his furlough in Bath, and see her and Weatherbury no more?

It was a picture full of misery, but for a while she contemplated it firmly, allowing herself, nevertheless, as girls will, to dwell upon the happy life she would have enjoyed had Troy been Boldwood, and the path of love the path of duty—inflicting upon herself gratuitous tortures by imagining him the lover of another woman after forgetting her; for she had penetrated Troy's nature so far as to estimate his tendencies pretty accurately, but unfortunately loved him no less in thinking that he might soon cease to love her—indeed, considerably more.

She jumped to her feet. She would see him at once. Yes, she would implore him by word of mouth to assist her in this dilemma. A letter to keep him away could not reach him in time, even if he should be disposed to listen to it.

Was Bathsheba altogether blind to the obvious fact that the support of a lover's arms is not of a kind best calculated to assist a resolve to renounce him? Or was she sophistically sensible, with a thrill of pleasure, that by adopting this course for getting rid of him she was ensuring a meeting with him, at any rate, once more?

It was now dark, and the hour must have been nearly ten. The only way to accomplish her purpose was to give up her idea of visiting Liddy at Yalbury, return to Weatherbury Farm, put the horse into the gig, and drive at once to Bath. The scheme seemed at first impossible: the journey was a fearfully heavy one, even for a strong horse, at her own estimate; and she much underrated the distance. It was most venturesome for a woman, at night, and alone.

But could she go on to Liddy's and leave things to take their course? No, no; anything but that. Bathsheba was full of a stimulating turbulence, beside which caution vainly prayed for a hearing. She turned back towards the village.

Her walk was slow, for she wished not to enter Weatherbury till the cottagers were in bed, and, particularly, till Boldwood was secure. Her plan was now to drive to Bath during the night, see Sergeant Troy in the morning before he set out to come to her, bid him farewell, and dismiss him: then to rest the horse thoroughly (herself to weep the while, she thought), starting early the next morning on her return journey. By this arrangement she could trot Dainty gently all the day, reach Liddy at Yalbury in the evening, and come home to Weatherbury with her whenever they chose—so nobody would know she had been to Bath at all.

Such was Bathsheba's scheme. But in her topographical ignorance as a late comer to the place, she misreckoned the distance of her journey as not much more than half what it really was. Her idea, however, she proceeded to carry out, with what initial success we have already seen.

XXXIII

In the Sun—A Harbinger

A week passed, and there were no tidings of Bathsheba; nor was there any explanation of her Gilpin's rig.[1]

Then a note came for Maryann, stating that the business which had called her mistress to Bath still detained her there; but that she hoped to return in the course of another week.

Another week passed. The oat-harvest began, and all the men were a-field under a monochromatic Lammas[2] sky, amid the trembling air and short shadows of noon. Indoors nothing was to be heard save the droning of blue-bottle flies; out-of-doors the whetting of scythes and the hiss of tressy[3] oat-ears rubbing together as their perpendicular stalks of amber-yellow fell heavily to each swath. Every drop of moisture not in the men's bottles and flagons in the form of cider was raining as perspiration from their foreheads and cheeks. Drought was everywhere else.

1. A reference to a poem by William Cowper humorously titled "The Diverting History of John Gilpin, Showing How He Went Further Than He Intended and Came Safe Home Again"; the term "rig" here means "spree."

2. From Old English *hlafmaesse* (modern English "loaf-mass"), a harvest festival celebrated in the Anglican Church on August 1.
3. Like tresses of hair.

They were about to withdraw for a while into the charitable shade of a tree in the fence, when Coggan saw a figure in a blue coat and brass buttons running to them across the field.

'I wonder who that is?' he said.

'I hope nothing is wrong about mistress,' said Maryann, who with some other women was tying the bundles (oats being always sheafed on this farm), 'but an unlucky token came to me indoors this morning. I went to unlock the door and dropped the key, and it fell upon the stone floor and broke into two pieces. Breaking a key is a dreadful bodement. I wish mis'ess was home.'

' 'Tis Cain Ball,' said Gabriel, pausing from whetting his reaphook.

Oak was not bound by his agreement to assist in the corn-field; but the harvest month is an anxious time for a farmer, and the corn was Bathsheba's, so he lent a hand.

'He's dressed up in his best clothes,' said Matthew Moon. 'He hev been away from home for a few days, since he's had that felon[4] upon his finger; for 'a said, since I can't work I'll have a hollerday.'

'A good time for one—a' excellent time,' said Joseph Poorgrass, straightening his back; for he, like some of the others, had a way of resting a while from his labour on such hot days for reasons preternaturally small; of which Cain Ball's advent on a week-day in his Sunday-clothes was one of the first magnitude. ''Twas a bad leg allowed me to read the *Pilgrim's Progress*, and Mark Clark learnt All-Fours[5] in a whitlow.'[6]

'Ay, and my father put his arm out of joint to have time to go courting,' said Jan Coggan, in an eclipsing tone, wiping his face with his shirt-sleeve and thrusting back his hat upon the nape of his neck.

By this time Cainy was nearing the group of harvesters, and was perceived to be carrying a large slice of bread and ham in one hand, from which he took mouthfuls as he ran, the other being wrapped in a bandage. When he came close, his mouth assumed the bell shape, and he began to cough violently.

'Now, Cainy!' said Gabriel sternly. 'How many more times must I tell you to keep from running so fast when you be eating? You'll choke yourself some day, that's what you'll do, Cain Ball.'

'Hok-hok-hok!' replied Cain. 'A crumb of my victuals went the wrong way—hok-hok! That's what 'tis, Mister Oak! And I've been visiting to Bath because I had a felon on my thumb; yes, and I've seen—ahok-hok!'

Directly Cain mentioned Bath, they all threw down their hooks and forks and drew round him. Unfortunately the erratic crumb did not improve his narrative powers, and a supplementary hindrance was that of a sneeze, jerking from his pocket his rather large watch, which

---

4. An infection of the deeper tissues at the end of a finger or toe.

5. A card game having four main terms—

"High," "Low," "Jack," and "Game."

6. While incapacitated by an infected finger (dialect).

dangled in front of the young man pendulum-wise.

'Yes,' he continued, directing his thoughts to Bath and letting his eyes follow, 'I've seed the world at last—yes—and I've seed our miss'ess—ahok-hok-hok!'

'Bother the boy!' said Gabriel. 'Something is always going the wrong way down your throat, so that you can't tell what's necessary to be told.'

'Ahok! there! Please, Mister Oak, a gnat have just fleed into my stomach and brought the cough on again!'

'Yes, that's just it. Your mouth is always open, you young rascal!'

' 'Tis terrible bad to have a gnat fly down yer throat, pore boy!' said Matthew Moon.

'Well, at Bath you saw——' prompted Gabriel.

'I saw our mistress,' continued the junior shepherd, 'and a sojer, walking along. And bymeby they got closer and closer, and then they went arm-in-crook, like courting complete—hok-hok! like courting complete—hok!—courting complete——' Losing the thread of his narrative at this point simultaneously with his loss of breath, their informant looked up and down the field apparently for some clue to it. 'Well, I see our mis'ess and a soldier—a-ha-a-wk!'

'Damn the boy!' said Gabriel.

''Tis only my manner, Mister Oak, if ye'll excuse it,' said Cain Ball, looking reproachfully at Oak, with eyes drenched in their own dew.

'Here's some cider for him—that'll cure his throat,' said Jan Coggan, lifting a flagon of cider, pulling out the cork, and applying the hole to Cainy's mouth; Joseph Poorgrass in the meantime beginning to think apprehensively of the serious consequences that would follow Cain Ball's strangulation in his cough, and the history of his Bath adventures dying with him.

'For my poor self, I always say "please God" afore I do anything,' said Joseph, in an unboastful voice; 'and so should you, Cain Ball. 'Tis a great safeguard, and might perhaps save you from being choked to death some day.'

Mr. Coggan poured the liquor with unstinted liberality at the suffering Cain's circular mouth; half of it running down the side of the flagon, and half of what reached his mouth running down outside his throat, and half of what ran in going the wrong way, and being coughed and sneezed around the persons of the gathered reapers in the form of a cider fog, which for a moment hung in the sunny air like a small exhalation.

'There's a great clumsy sneeze! Why can't ye have better manners, you young dog!' said Coggan, withdrawing the flagon.

'The cider went up my nose!' cried Cainy, as soon as he could speak; 'and now 'tis gone down my neck, and into my poor dumb felon, and over my shiny buttons and all my best cloze!'

'The poor lad's cough is terrible onfortunate,' said Matthew Moon.

'And a great history on hand, too. Bump his back, shepherd.'

' 'Tis my nater,' mourned Cain. 'Mother says I always was so excitable when my feelings were worked up to a point!'

'True, true,' said Joseph Poorgrass. 'The Balls were always a very excitable family. I knowed the boy's grandfather—a truly nervous and modest man, even to genteel refinery. 'Twas blush, blush with him, almost as much as 'tis with me—not but that 'tis a fault in me!'

'Not at all, Master Poorgrass,' said Coggan. ' 'Tis a very noble quality in ye.'

'Heh-heh! well, I wish to noise nothing abroad[7]—nothing at all,' murmured Poorgrass diffidently. 'But we be born to things—that's true. Yet I would rather my trifle were hid; though, perhaps, a high nater[8] is a little high, and at my birth all things were possible to my Maker, and he may have begrudged no gifts. . . . But under your bushel, Joseph! under your bushel[9] with 'ee! A strange desire, neighbours, this desire to hide, and no praise due. Yet there is a Sermon on the Mount with a calendar of the blessed at the head, and certain meek men may be named therein.'[1]

'Cainy's grandfather was a very clever man,' said Matthew Moon. 'Invented a' apple-tree out of his own head, which is called by his name to this day—the Early Ball. You know 'em, Jan? A Quarrenden grafted on a Tom Putt, and a Rathe-ripe[2] upon top o' that again. 'Tis trew 'a used to bide about in a public-house wi' a 'ooman[3] in a way he had no business to by rights, but there—'a were a clever man in the sense of the term.'

'Now then,' said Gabriel impatiently, 'what did you see, Cain?'

'I seed our mis'ess go into a sort of a park place, where there's seats, and shrubs and flowers, arm-in-crook with a sojer,' continued Cainy firmly, and with a dim sense that his words were very effective as regarded Gabriel's emotions. 'And I think the sojer was Sergeant Troy. And they sat there together for more than half-an-hour, talking moving things, and she once was crying a'most to death. And when they came out her eyes were shining and she was as white as a lily; and they looked into one another's faces, as far gone friendly as a man and woman can be.'

Gabriel's features seemed to get thinner. 'Well, what did you see besides?'

'Oh, all sorts.'

'White as a lily? You are sure 'twas she?'

7. Spread no rumors.
8. Nature (dialect).
9. An allusion to Matthew 5:15 (and similar passages in Mark and Luke) where Jesus says, "Neither do men light a candle and put it under a bushel."
1. An allusion to the list of those who are blessed that begins the Sermon on the Mount recorded in Matthew 5:3–11 and includes the saying, "Blessed are the meek: for they shall inherit the earth."
2. "Quarrenden" and "Tom Putt" are varieties of apples popular in Dorset; "Rathe-ripe" is an early-ripening yellow apple.
3. Woman (dialect).

'Yes.'

'Well, what besides?'

'Great glass windows to the shops, and great clouds in the sky, full of rain, and old wooden trees in the country round.'

'You stun-poll![4] What will ye say next?' said Coggan.

'Let en alone,' interposed Joseph Poorgrass. 'The boy's maning is that the sky and the earth in the kingdom of Bath is not altogether different from ours here. 'Tis for our good to gain knowledge of strange cities, and as such the boy's words should be suffered, so to speak it.'

'And the people of Bath,' continued Cain, 'never need to light their fires except as a luxury, for the water springs up out of the earth ready boiled for use.'

' 'Tis true as the light,' testified Matthew Moon. 'I've heard other navigators say the same thing.'

'They drink nothing else there,' said Cain, 'and seem to enjoy it, to see how they swaller it down.'

'Well, it seems a barbarian practice enough to us, but I daresay the natives think nothing o' it,' said Matthew.

'And don't victuals spring up as well as drink?' asked Coggan, twirling his eye.

'No—I own to a blot there in Bath—a true blot.[5] God didn't provide 'em with victuals as well as drink, and 'twas a drawback I couldn't get over at all.'

'Well, 'tis a curious place, to say the least,' observed Moon; 'and it must be a curious people that live therein.'

'Miss Everdene and the soldier were walking about together, you say?' said Gabriel, returning to the group.

'Ay, and she wore a beautiful gold-colour silk gown, trimmed with black lace, that would have stood alone 'ithout legs inside if required. 'Twas a very winsome sight; and her hair was brushed splendid. And when the sun shone upon the bright gown and his red coat—my! how handsome they looked. You could see 'em all the length of the street.'

'And what then?' murmured Gabriel.

'And then I went into Griffin's to hae my boots hobbed,[6] and then I went to Riggs's batty-cake[7] shop, and asked 'em for a penneth[8] of the cheapest and nicest stales, that were all but blue-mouldy, but not quite. And whilst I was chawing 'em down I walked on and seed a clock with a face as big as a baking trendle——[9]

'But that's nothing to do with mistress!'

'I'm coming to that, if you'll leave me alone, Mister Oak!' remonstrated Cainy. 'If you excites me, perhaps you'll bring on my cough, and then I shan't be able to tell ye nothing.'

---

4. Blockhead (dialect).
5. Defect.
6. Studded with hobnails.
7. A small cake (dialect).

8. A contraction for "pennyworth."
9. A large shallow tub in which dough is mixed.

'Yes—let him tell it his own way,' said Coggan.

Gabriel settled into a despairing attitude of patience, and Cainy went on:—

'And there were great large houses, and more people all the week long than at Weatherbury club-walking[1] on White Tuesdays.[2] And I went to grand churches and chapels. And how the parson would pray! Yes; he would kneel down and put up his hands together, and make the holy gold rings on his fingers gleam and twinkle in yer eyes, that he'd earned by praying so excellent well!—Ah yes, I wish I lived there.'

'Our poor Parson Thirdly can't get no money to buy such rings,' said Matthew Moon thoughtfully. 'And as good a man as ever walked. I don't believe poor Thirdly have a single one, even of humblest tin or copper. Such a great ornament as they'd be to him on a dull a'ternoon, when he's up in the pulpit lighted by the wax candles! But 'tis impossible, poor man. Ah, to think how unequal things be.'

'Perhaps he's made of different stuff than to wear 'em,' said Gabriel grimly. 'Well, that's enough of this. Go on, Cainy—quick.'

'Oh—and the new style of pa'sons wear moustaches and long beards,' continued the illustrious traveller, 'and look like Moses and Aaron complete, and make we fokes in the congregation feel all over like the children of Israel.'

'A very right feeling—very,' said Joseph Poorgrass.

'And there's two religions going on in the nation now—High Church and High Chapel. And, thinks I, I'll play fair; so I went to High Church in the morning, and High Chapel in the afternoon.'

'A right and proper boy,' said Joseph Poorgrass.

'Well, at High Church they pray singing, and worship all the colours of the rainbow; and at High Chapel they pray preaching, and worship drab and whitewash only. And then—I didn't see no more of Miss Everdene at all.'

'Why didn't you say so afore, then?' exclaimed Oak, with much disappointment.

'Ah,' said Matthew Moon, 'she'll wish her cake dough[3] if so be she's over intimate with that man.'

'She's not over intimate with him,' said Gabriel indignantly.

'She would know better,' said Coggan. 'Our mis'ess has too much sense under they knots of black hair to do such a mad thing.'

'You see, he's not a coarse, ignorant man, for he was well brought up,' said Matthew dubiously. ' 'Twas only wildness that made him a

1. "Club-walking" is an annual group walk over a traditional course by the members of a parish benefit club or "friendly society" who paid dues to secure insurance for funeral expenses, sick allowances, or the like.

2. Usually called "Whit-Tuesday," the Tuesday following Whitsunday, the second Sunday after the feast of Ascension; the week following Whitsunday, called Whitsuntide, was the traditional time for club-walkings.

3. The expression "our cake's dough on both sides" is proverbial and means "we failed"; Matthew Moon's use of the saying implies that if Bathsheba succeeds in becoming intimate with Troy she will come to wish she had failed.

soldier, and maids rather like your man of sin.'

'Now, Cain Ball,' said Gabriel restlessly, 'can you swear in the most awful form that the woman you saw was Miss Everdene?'

'Cain Ball, you be no longer a babe and suckling,' said Joseph in the sepulchral tone the circumstances demanded, 'and you know what taking an oath is. 'Tis a horrible testament mind ye, which you say and seal with your blood-stone, and the prophet Matthew tells us that on whomsoever it shall fall it will grind him to powder.[4] Now, before all the work-folk here assembled, can you swear to your words as the shepherd asks ye?'

'Please no, Mister Oak!' said Cainy, looking from one to the other with great uneasiness at the spiritual magnitude of the position. 'I don't mind saying 'tis true, but I don't like to say 'tis damn true, if that's what you mane.'

'Cain, Cain, how can you!' asked Joseph sternly. 'You be asked to swear in a holy manner, and you swear like wicked Shimei, the son of Gera, who cursed as he came.[5] Young man, fie!'

'No, I don't! 'Tis you want to squander a pore boy's soul, Joseph Poorgrass—that's what 'tis!' said Cain, beginning to cry. 'All I mane is that in common truth 'twas Miss Everdene and Sergeant Troy, but in the horrible so-help-me truth that ye want to make of it perhaps 'twas somebody else!'

'There's no getting at the rights of it,' said Gabriel, turning to his work.

'Cain Ball, you'll come to a bit of bread!' groaned Joseph Poorgrass.

Then the reapers' hooks were flourished again, and the old sounds went on. Gabriel, without making any pretence of being lively, did nothing to show that he was particularly dull. However, Coggan knew pretty nearly how the land lay, and when they were in a nook together he said—

'Don't take on about her, Gabriel. What difference does it make whose sweetheart she is, since she can't be yours?'

'That's the very thing I say to myself,' said Gabriel.

XXXIV

Home Again—A Trickster

That same evening at dusk Gabriel was leaning over Coggan's garden-gate, taking an up-and-down survey before retiring to rest.

A vehicle of some kind was softly creeping along the grassy margin of the lane. From it spread the tones of two women talking. The tones were natural and not at all suppressed. Oak instantly knew the voices

4. Joseph Poorgrass alludes, in a very confused way, to Matthew 21:42–44.
5. An allusion to 2 Samuel 16:5, where

"Shimei, the Son of Gera, he came forth, and cursed still as he came."

to be those of Bathsheba and Liddy.

The carriage came opposite and passed by. It was Miss Everdene's gig, and Liddy and her mistress were the only occupants of the seat. Liddy was asking questions about the city of Bath, and her companion was answering them listlessly and unconcernedly. Both Bathsheba and the horse seemed weary.

The exquisite relief of finding that she was here again, safe and sound, overpowered all reflection, and Oak could only luxuriate in the sense of it. All grave reports were forgotten.

He lingered and lingered on, till there was no difference between the eastern and western expanses of sky, and the timid hares began to skip courageously round the dim hillocks. Gabriel might have been there an additional half-hour when a dark form walked slowly by. 'Good-night, Gabriel,' the passer said.

It was Boldwood. 'Good-night, sir,' said Gabriel.

Boldwood likewise vanished up the road, and Oak shortly afterwards turned indoors to bed.

Farmer Boldwood went on towards Miss Everdene's house. He reached the front, and approaching the entrance, saw a light in the parlour. The blind was not drawn down, and inside the room was Bathsheba, looking over some papers or letters. Her back was towards Boldwood. He went to the door, knocked, and waited with tense muscles and an aching brow.

Boldwood had not been outside his garden since his meeting with Bathsheba in the road to Yalbury. Silent and alone, he had remained in moody meditation on woman's ways, deeming as essentials of the whole sex the accidents of the single one of their number he had ever closely beheld. By degrees a more charitable temper had pervaded him, and this was the reason of his sally to-night. He had come to apologize and beg forgiveness of Bathsheba with something like a sense of shame at his violence, having but just now learnt that she had returned—only from a visit to Liddy, as he supposed, the Bath escapade being quite unknown to him.

He inquired for Miss Everdene. Liddy's manner was odd, but he did not notice it. She went in, leaving him standing there, and in her absence the blind of the room containing Bathsheba was pulled down. Boldwood augured ill from that sign. Liddy came out.

'My mistress cannot see you, sir,' she said.

The farmer instantly went out by the gate. He was unforgiven—that was the issue of it all. He had seen her who was to him simultaneously a delight and a torture, sitting in the room he had shared with her as a peculiarly privileged guest only a little earlier in the summer, and she had denied him an entrance there now.

Boldwood did not hurry homeward. It was ten o'clock at least, when, walking deliberately through the lower part of Weatherbury, he heard the carrier's spring van entering the village. The van ran to and from a town in a northern direction, and it was owned and driven by a Weatherbury man, at the door of whose house it now pulled up. The lamp fixed to the head of the hood illuminated a scarlet and gilded form, who was the first to alight.

'Ah!' said Boldwood to himself, 'come to see her again.'

Troy entered the carrier's house, which had been the place of his lodging on his last visit to his native place. Boldwood was moved by a sudden determination. He hastened home. In ten minutes he was back again, and made as if he were going to call upon Troy at the carrier's. But as he approached, some one opened the door and came out. He heard this person say 'Good-night' to the inmates, and the voice was Troy's. This was strange, coming so immediately after his arrival. Boldwood, however, hastened up to him. Troy had what appeared to be a carpet-bag in his hand—the same that he had brought with him. It seemed as if he were going to leave again this very night.

Troy turned up the hill and quickened his pace. Boldwood stepped forward.

'Sergeant Troy?'

'Yes—I'm Sergeant Troy.'

'Just arrived from up the country, I think?'

'Just arrived from Bath.'

'I am William Boldwood.'

'Indeed.'

The tone in which this word was uttered was all that had been wanted to bring Boldwood to the point.

'I wish to speak a word with you,' he said.

'What about?'

'About her who lives just ahead there—and about a woman you have wronged.'

'I wonder at your impertinence,' said Troy, moving on.

'Now look here,' said Boldwood, standing in front of him, 'wonder or not, you are going to hold a conversation with me.'

Troy heard the dull determination in Boldwood's voice, looked at his stalwart frame, then at the thick cudgel he carried in his hand. He remembered it was past ten o'clock. It seemed worth while to be civil to Boldwood.

'Very well, I'll listen with pleasure,' said Troy, placing his bag on the ground, 'only speak low, for somebody or other may overhear us in the farmhouse there.'

'Well then—I know a good deal concerning your—Fanny Robin's attachment to you. I may say, too, that I believe I am the only person in the village, excepting Gabriel Oak, who does know it. You ought to marry her.'

'I suppose I ought. Indeed, I wish to, but I cannot.'

'Why?'

Troy was about to utter something hastily; he then checked himself and said, 'I am too poor.' His voice was changed. Previously it had had a devil-may-care tone. It was the voice of a trickster now.

Boldwood's present mood was not critical enough to notice tones. He continued, 'I may as well speak plainly; and understand, I don't wish to enter into the questions of right or wrong, woman's honour and shame, or to express any opinion on your conduct. I intend a business transaction with you.'

'I see,' said Troy. 'Suppose we sit down here.'

An old tree trunk lay under the hedge immediately opposite, and they sat down.

'I was engaged to be married to Miss Everdene,' said Boldwood, 'but you came and——'

'Not engaged,' said Troy.

'As good as engaged.'

'If I had not turned up she might have become engaged to you.'

'Hang might!'

'Would, then.'

'If you had not come I should certainly—yes, *certainly*—have been accepted by this time. If you had not seen her you might have been married to Fanny. Well, there's too much difference between Miss Everdene's station and your own for this flirtation with her ever to benefit you by ending in marriage. So all I ask is, don't molest her any more. Marry Fanny. I'll make it worth your while.'

'How will you?'

'I'll pay you well now, I'll settle a sum of money upon her, and I'll see that you don't suffer from a poverty in the future. I'll put it clearly. Bathsheba is only playing with you: you are too poor for her as I said; so give up wasting your time about a great match you'll never make for a moderate and rightful match you may make to-morrow; take up your carpet-bag, turn about, leave Weatherbury now, this night, and you shall take fifty pounds with you. Fanny shall have fifty to enable her to prepare for the wedding, when you have told me where she is living, and she shall have five hundred paid down on her wedding-day.'

In making this statement Boldwood's voice revealed only too clearly a consciousness of the weakness of his position, his aims, and his method. His manner had lapsed quite from that of the firm and dignified Boldwood of former times; and such a scheme as he had now engaged in he would have condemned as childishly imbecile only a few months ago. We discern a grand force in the lover which he lacks whilst a free man; but there is a breadth of vision in the free man which in the lover we vainly seek. Where there is much bias there must be some narrowness, and love, though added emotion, is subtracted capacity. Boldwood exemplified this to an abnormal degree: he knew nothing of Fanny Robin's circumstances or whereabouts, he knew nothing of Troy's possibilities, yet that was what he said.

'I like Fanny best,' said Troy; 'and if, as you say, Miss Everdene is out of my reach, why I have all to gain by accepting your money, and marrying Fan. But she's only a servant.'

'Never mind—do you agree to my arrangement?'

'I do.'

'Ah!' said Boldwood, in a more elastic voice. 'O, Troy, if you like her best, why then did you step in here and injure my happiness?'

'I love Fanny best now,' said Troy. 'But Bathsh——Miss Everdene inflamed me, and displaced Fanny for a time. It is over now.'

'Why should it be over so soon? And why then did you come here again?'

'There are weighty reasons. Fifty pounds at once, you said!'

'I did,' said Boldwood, 'and here they are—fifty sovereigns.' He handed Troy a small packet.

'You have everything ready—it seems that you calculated on my accepting them,' said the sergeant, taking the packet.

'I thought you might accept them,' said Boldwood.

'You've only my word that the programme shall be adhered to, whilst I at any rate have fifty pounds.'

'I had thought of that, and I have considered that if I can't appeal to your honour I can trust to your—well, shrewdness we'll call it—not to lose five hundred pounds in prospect, and also make a bitter enemy of a man who is willing to be an extremely useful friend.'

'Stop, listen!' said Troy in a whisper.

A light pit-pat was audible upon the road just above them.

'By George—'tis she,' he continued. 'I must go on and meet her.'

'She—who?'

'Bathsheba.'

'Bathsheba—out alone at this time o' night!' said Boldwood in amazement, and starting up. 'Why must you meet her?'

'She was expecting me to-night—and I must now speak to her, and wish her good-bye, according to your wish.'

'I don't see the necessity of speaking.'

'It can do no harm—and she'll be wandering about looking for me if I don't. You shall hear all I say to her. It will help you in your love-making when I am gone.'

'Your tone is mocking.'

'O no. And remember this, if she does not know what has become of me, she will think more about me than if I tell her flatly I have come to give her up.'

'Will you confine your words to that one point?—Shall I hear every word you say?'

'Every word. Now sit still there, and hold my carpet bag for me, and mark what you hear.'

The light footstep came closer, halting occasionally, as if the walker listened for a sound. Troy whistled a double note in a soft, fluty tone.

'Come to that, is it!' murmured Boldwood uneasily.

'You promised silence,' said Troy.

'I promise again.'

Troy stepped forward.

'Frank, dearest, is that you?' The tones were Bathsheba's.

'O God!' said Boldwood.

'Yes,' said Troy to her.

'How late you are,' she continued tenderly. 'Did you come by the carrier? I listened and heard his wheels entering the village, but it was some time ago, and I had almost given you up, Frank.'

'I was sure to come,' said Frank. 'You knew I should, did you not?'

'Well, I thought you would,' she said playfully; 'and, Frank, it is so lucky! There's not a soul in my house but me to-night. I've packed them all off, so nobody on earth will know of your visit to your lady's bower. Liddy wanted to go to her grandfather's to tell him about her holiday, and I said she might stay with them till to-morrow—when you'll be gone again.'

'Capital,' said Troy. 'But, dear me, I had better go back for my bag, because my slippers and brush and comb are in it; you run home whilst I fetch it, and I'll promise to be in your parlour in ten minutes.'

'Yes.' She turned and tripped up the hill again.

During the progress of this dialogue there was a nervous twitching of Boldwood's tightly closed lips, and his face became bathed in a clammy dew. He now started forward towards Troy. Troy turned to him and took up the bag.

'Shall I tell her I have come to give her up and cannot marry her?' said the soldier mockingly.

'No, no; wait a minute. I want to say more to you—more to you!' said Boldwood, in a hoarse whisper.

'Now,' said Troy, 'you see my dilemma. Perhaps I am a bad man—the victim of my impulses—led away to do what I ought to leave undone. I can't, however, marry them both. And I have two reasons for choosing Fanny. First, I like her best upon the whole, and second, you make it worth my while.'

At the same instant Boldwood sprang upon him, and held him by the neck. Troy felt Boldwood's grasp slowly tightening. The move was absolutely unexpected.

'A moment,' he gasped. 'You are injuring her you love!'

'Well, what do you mean?' said the farmer.

'Give me breath,' said Troy.

Boldwood loosened his hand, saying, 'By Heaven, I've a mind to kill you!'

'And ruin her.'

'Save her.'

'Oh, how can she be saved now, unless I marry her?'

Boldwood groaned. He reluctantly released the soldier, and flung him back against the hedge. 'Devil, you torture me!' said he.

Troy rebounded like a ball, and was about to make a dash at the farmer; but he checked himself, saying lightly—

'It is not worth while to measure my strength with you. Indeed it is a barbarous way of settling a quarrel. I shall shortly leave the army because of the same conviction. Now after that revelation of how the land lies with Bathsheba, 'twould be a mistake to kill me, would it not?'

''Twould be a mistake to kill you,' repeated Boldwood, mechanically, with a bowed head.

'Better kill yourself.'

'Far better.'

'I'm glad you see it.'

'Troy, make her your wife, and don't act upon what I arranged just now. The alternative is dreadful, but take Bathsheba; I give her up! She must love you indeed to sell soul and body to you so utterly as she has done. Wretched woman—deluded woman—you are, Bathsheba!'

'But about Fanny?'

'Bathsheba is a woman well to do,' continued Boldwood, in nervous anxiety, 'and, Troy, she will make a good wife; and, indeed, she is worth your hastening on your marriage with her!'

'But she has a will—not to say a temper, and I shall be a mere slave to her. I could do anything with poor Fanny Robin.'

'Troy,' said Boldwood imploringly, 'I'll do anything for you, only don't desert her; pray don't desert her, Troy.'

'Which, poor Fanny?'

'No; Bathsheba Everdene. Love her best! Love her tenderly! How shall I get you to see how advantageous it will be to you to secure her at once?'

'I don't wish to secure her in any new way.'

Boldwood's arm moved spasmodically towards Troy's person again. He repressed the instinct, and his form drooped as with pain.

Troy went on—

'I shall soon purchase my discharge, and then——'

'But I wish you to hasten on this marriage! It will be better for you both. You love each other, and you must let me help you to do it.'

'How?'

'Why, by settling the five hundred on Bathsheba instead of Fanny, to enable you to marry at once. No; she wouldn't have it of me. I'll pay it down to you on the wedding-day.'

Troy paused in secret amazement at Boldwood's wild infatuation. He carelessly said, 'And am I to have anything now?'

'Yes, if you wish to. But I have not much additional money with me. I did not expect this; but all I have is yours.'

Boldwood, more like a somnambulist than a wakeful man, pulled out the large canvas bag he carried by way of a purse, and searched it.

'I have twenty-one pounds more with me,' he said. 'Two notes and a sovereign. But before I leave you I must have a paper signed——'

'Pay me the money, and we'll go straight to her parlour, and make any arrangement you please to secure my compliance with your wishes. But she must know nothing of this cash business.'

'Nothing, nothing,' said Boldwood hastily. 'Here is the sum, and if you'll come to my house we'll write out the agreement for the remainder, and the terms also.'

'First we'll call upon her.'

'But why? Come with me to-night, and go with me to-morrow to the surrogate's'.[1]

'But she must be consulted; at any rate informed.'

'Very well; go on.'

They went up the hill to Bathsheba's house. When they stood at the entrance, Troy said, 'Wait here a moment.' Opening the door, he glided inside, leaving the door ajar.

Boldwood waited. In two minutes a light appeared in the passage. Boldwood then saw that the chain had been fastened across the door. Troy appeared inside carrying a bedroom candlestick.

'What, did you think I should break in?' said Boldwood contemptuously.

'Oh, no; it is merely my humour to secure things. Will you read this a moment? I'll hold the light.'

Troy handed a folded newspaper through the slit between door and door-post, and put the candle close. 'That's the paragraph,' he said, placing his finger on a line.

Boldwood looked and read—

'MARRIAGES.

'On the 17th inst., at St. Ambrose's Church, Bath, by the Rev. G. Mincing, B.A., Francis Troy, only son of the late Edward Troy, Esq., M.D., of Weatherbury, and sergeant 11th Dragoon Guards, to Bathsheba, only surviving daughter of the late Mr. John Everdene, of Casterbridge.'

'This may be called Fort meeting Feeble,[2] hey, Boldwood?' said Troy. A low gurgle of derisive laughter followed the words.

The paper fell from Boldwood's hands. Troy continued—

'Fifty pounds to marry Fanny. Good. Twenty-one pounds not to marry Fanny, but Bathsheba. Good. Finale: already Bathsheba's husband. Now, Boldwood, yours is the ridiculous fate which always attends interference between a man and his wife. And another word. Bad as I am, I am not such a villain as to make the marriage or misery of any woman a matter of huckster and sale. Fanny has long ago left

---

1. A person deputized by a bishop to grant permission to marry without banns in his diocese.

2. In swordsmanship, a technical phrase mean-ing that the strong part of the blade near the hilt (Fort) has met and successfully warded off the weaker tip part of an opponent's blade (Feeble).

me. I don't know where she is. I have searched everywhere. Another word yet. You say you love Bathsheba; yet on the merest apparent evidence you instantly believe in her dishonour. A fig for such love! Now that I've taught you a lesson, take your money back again.'

'I will not; I will not!' said Boldwood, in a hiss.

'Anyhow I won't have it,' said Troy contemptuously. He wrapped the packet of gold in the notes, and threw the whole into the road.

Boldwood shook his clenched fist at him. 'You juggler of Satan! You black hound! But I'll punish you yet; mark me, I'll punish you yet!'

Another peal of laughter. Troy then closed the door, and locked himself in.

Throughout the whole of that night Boldwood's dark form might have been seen walking about the hills and downs of Weatherbury like an unhappy Shade in the Mournful Fields by Acheron.[3]

XXXV

At an Upper Window

It was very early the next morning—a time of sun and dew. The confused beginnings of many birds' songs spread into the healthy air, and the wan blue of the heaven was here and there coated with thin webs of incorporeal cloud which were of no effect in obscuring day. All the lights in the scene were yellow as to colour, and all the shadows were attenuated as to form. The creeping plants about the old manor-house were bowed with rows of heavy water drops, which had upon objects behind them the effect of minute lenses of high mangifying power.

Just before the clock struck five Gabriel Oak and Coggan passed the village cross, and went on together to the fields. They were yet barely in view of their mistress's house, when Oak fancied he saw the opening of a casement in one of the upper windows. The two men were at this moment partially screened by an elder bush, now beginning to be enriched with black bunches of fruit, and they paused before emerging from its shade.

A handsome man leaned idly from the lattice. He looked east and then west, in the manner of one who makes a first morning survey. The man was Sergeant Troy. His red jacket was loosely thrown on, but not buttoned, and he had altogether the relaxed bearing of a soldier taking his ease.

Coggan spoke first, looking quietly at the window.

3. Like an unhappy ghost on the shore of the river Acheron, which in Greek mythology barred the shade's way to Hades until he paid a fee to the boatman Charon, who would then ferry him across.

'She has married him!' he said.

Gabriel had previously beheld the sight, and he now stood with his back turned, making no reply.

'I fancied we should know something to-day,' continued Coggan. 'I heard wheels pass my door just after dark—you were out somewhere.' He glanced round upon Gabriel. 'Good heavens above us, Oak, how white your face is; you look like a corpse!'

'Do I?' said Oak, with a faint smile.

'Lean on the gate: I'll wait a bit.'

'All right, all right.'

They stood by the gate awhile, Gabriel listlessly staring at the ground. His mind sped into the future, and saw there enacted in years of leisure the scenes of repentance that would ensue from this work of haste. That they were married he had instantly decided. Why had it been so mysteriously managed? It had become known that she had had a fearful journey to Bath, owing to her miscalculating the distance: that the horse had broken down, and that she had been more than two days getting there. It was not Bathsheba's way to do things furtively. With all her faults she was candour itself. Could she have been entrapped? The union was not only an unutterable grief to him: it amazed him, notwithstanding that he had passed the preceding week in a suspicion that such might be the issue of Troy's meeting her away from home. Her quiet return with Liddy had to some extent dispersed the dread. Just as that imperceptible motion which appears like stillness is infinitely divided in its properties from stillness itself, so had his hope undistinguishable from despair differed from despair indeed.

In a few minutes they moved on again towards the house. The sergeant still looked from the window.

'Morning, comrades!' he shouted, in a cheery voice, when they came up.

Coggan replied to the greeting. 'Bain't ye going to answer the man?' he then said to Gabriel. 'I'd say good morning—you needn't spend a hapeth[1] of meaning upon it, and yet keep the man civil.'

Gabriel soon decided too that, since the deed was done, to put the best face upon the matter would be the greatest kindness to her he loved.

'Good morning, Sergeant Troy,' he returned, in a ghastly voice.

'A rambling, gloomy house this,' said Troy, smiling.

'Why—they *may* not be married!' suggested Coggan. 'Perhaps she's not there.'

Gabriel shook his head. The soldier turned a little towards the east, and the sun kindled his scarlet jacket to an orange glow.

'But it is a nice old house,' responded Gabriel.

'Yes—I suppose so; but I feel like new wine in an old bottle here.[2]

1. Halfpennyworth (dialect).

2. An allusion to Mark 2:22, where Jesus says, "And no man putteth new wine into old bottles."

My notion is that sash-windows should be put throughout, and these old wainscoted walls brightened up a bit; or the oak cleared quite away, and the walls papered.'

'It would be a pity, I think.'

'Well, no. A philosopher once said in my hearing that the old builders, who worked when art was a living thing, had no respect for the work of builders who went before them, but pulled down and altered as they thought fit; and why shouldn't we? "Creation and preservation don't do well together," says he, "and a million of antiquarians can't invent a style." My mind exactly. I am for making this place more modern, that we may be cheerful whilst we can.'

The military man turned and surveyed the interior of the room, to assist his ideas of improvement in this direction. Gabriel and Coggan began to move on.

'Oh, Coggan,' said Troy, as if inspired by a recollection, 'do you know if insanity has ever appeared in Mr. Boldwood's family?'

Jan reflected for a moment.

'I once heard that an uncle of his was queer in his head, but I don't know the rights o't,' he said.

'It is of no importance,' said Troy lightly. 'Well, I shall be down in the fields with you some time this week; but I have a few matters to attend to first. So good-day to you. We shall, of course, keep on just as friendly terms as usual. I'm not a proud man: nobody is ever able to say that of Sergeant Troy. However, what is must be, and here's half-a-crown to drink my health, men.'

Troy threw the coin dexterously across the front plot and over the fence towards Gabriel, who shunned it in its fall, his face turning to an angry red. Coggan twirled his eye, edged forward, and caught the money in its ricochet upon the road.

'Very well—you keep it, Coggan,' said Gabriel with disdain, and almost fiercely. 'As for me, I'll do without gifts from him!'

'Don't show it too much,' said Coggan musingly. 'For if he's married to her, mark my words, he'll buy his discharge and be our master here. Therefore 'tis well to say "Friend" outwardly, though you say "Troublehouse" within.'

'Well—perhaps it is best to be silent; but I can't go further than that. I can't flatter, and if my place here is only to be kept by smoothing him down, my place must be lost.'

A horseman, whom they had for some time seen in the distance, now appeared close beside them.

'There's Mr. Boldwood,' said Oak. 'I wonder what Troy meant by his question.'

Coggan and Oak nodded respectfully to the farmer, just checked their paces to discover if they were wanted, and finding they were not, stood back to let him pass on.

The only signs of the terrible sorrow Boldwood had been combating through the night, and was combating now, were the want of colour in his well-defined face, the enlarged appearance of the veins in his forehead and temples, and the sharper lines about his mouth. The horse bore him away, and the very step of the animal seemed significant of dogged despair. Gabriel, for a minute, rose above his own grief in noticing Boldwood's. He saw the square figure sitting erect upon the horse, the head turned to neither side, the elbows steady by the hips, the brim of the hat level and undisturbed in its onward glide, until the keen edges of Boldwood's shape sank by degrees over the hill. To one who knew the man and his story there was something more striking in this immobility than in a collapse. The clash of discord between mood and matter here was forced painfully home to the heart; and, as in laughter there are more dreadful phases than in tears, so was there in the steadiness of this agonized man an expression deeper than a cry.

XXXVI

Wealth in Jeopardy—The Revel

One night, at the end of August, when Bathsheba's experiences as a married woman were still new, and when the weather was yet dry and sultry, a man stood motionless in the stackyard of Weatherbury Upper Farm, looking at the moon and sky.

The night had a sinister aspect. A heated breeze from the south slowly fanned the summits of lofty objects, and in the sky dashes of buoyant cloud were sailing in a course at right angles to that of another stratum, neither of them in the direction of the breeze below. The moon, as seen through these films, had a lurid metallic look. The fields were sallow with the impure light, and all were tinged in monochrome, as if beheld through stained glass. The same evening the sheep had trailed homeward head to tail, the behaviour of the rooks had been confused, and the horses had moved with timidity and caution.

Thunder was imminent, and, taking some secondary appearances into consideration, it was likely to be followed by one of the lengthened rains which mark the close of dry weather for the season. Before twelve hours had passed a harvest atmosphere would be a bygone thing.

Oak gazed with misgiving at eight naked and unprotected ricks, massive and heavy with the rich produce of one-half the farm for that year. He went on to the barn.

This was the night which had been selected by Sergeant Troy—ruling now in the room of his wife—for giving the harvest supper and dance. As Oak approached the building the sound of violins and a tambourine, and the regular jigging of many feet, grew more distinct. He came close to the large doors, one of which stood slightly ajar, and looked in.

The central space, together with the recess at one end, was emptied of all incumbrances, and this area, covering about two-thirds of the whole, was appropriated for the gathering, the remaining end, which was piled to the ceiling with oats, being screened off with sail-cloth. Tufts and garlands of green foliage decorated the walls, beams, and extemporized chandeliers, and immediately opposite to Oak a rostrum had been erected, bearing a table and chairs. Here sat three fiddlers, and beside them stood a frantic man with his hair on end, perspiration streaming down his cheeks, and a tambourine quivering in his hand.

The dance ended, and on the black oak floor in the midst a new row of couples formed for another.

'Now, ma'am, and no offence I hope, I ask what dance you would like next?' said the first violin.

'Really, it makes no difference,' said the clear voice of Bathsheba, who stood at the inner end of the building, observing the scene from behind a table covered with cups and viands. Troy was lolling beside her.

'Then,' said the fiddler, 'I'll venture to name that the right and proper thing is "The Soldier's Joy"[1]—there being a gallant soldier married into the farm—hey, my sonnies, and gentlemen all?'

'It shall be "The Soldier's Joy," ' exclaimed a chorus.

'Thanks for the compliment,' said the sergeant gaily, taking Bathsheba by the hand and leading her to the top of the dance. 'For though I have purchased my discharge from Her Most Gracious Majesty's regiment of cavalry the 11th Dragoon Guards, to attend to the new duties awaiting me here, I shall continue a soldier in spirit and feeling as long as I live.'

So the dance began. As to the merits of 'The Soldier's Joy,' there cannot be, and never were, two opinions. It has been observed in the musical circles of Weatherbury and its vicinity that this melody, at the end of three-quarters of an hour of thunderous footing, still possesses more stimulative properties for the heel and toe than the majority of other dances at their first opening. 'The Soldier's Joy' has, too, an additional charm, in being so admirably adapted to the tambourine aforesaid—no mean instrument in the hands of a performer who understands the proper convulsions, spasms, St. Vitus's dances,[2] and fearful frenzies necessary when exhibiting its tones in their highest perfection.

---

1. A lively dance tune whose music is recorded as No. 24 in the Hardy family music book now in the Hardy collection in the Dorset County Museum.

2. A colloquial term for Sydenham's Chorea, a disease characterized by convulsive twitching and jerking movements.

The immortal tune ended, a final DD rolling forth from the bass-viol with the sonorousness of a cannonade, and Gabriel delayed his entry no longer. He avoided Bathsheba, and got as near as possible to the platform, where Sergeant Troy was now seated, drinking brandy-and-water, though the others drank without exception cider and ale. Gabriel could not easily thrust himself within speaking distance of the sergeant, and he sent a message, asking him to come down for a moment. The sergeant said he could not attend.

'Will you tell him, then,' said Gabriel, 'that I only stepped ath'art[3] to say that a heavy rain is sure to fall soon, and that something should be done to protect the ricks?'

'Mr. Troy says it will not rain,' returned the messenger, 'and he cannot stop to talk to you about such fidgets.'

In juxtaposition with Troy, Oak had a melancholy tendency to look like a candle beside gas, and ill at ease he went out again, thinking he would go home; for, under the circumstances, he had no heart for the scene in the barn. At the door he paused for a moment: Troy was speaking.

'Friends, it is not only the harvest home that we are celebrating to-night; but this is also a Wedding Feast. A short time ago I had the happiness to lead to the altar this lady, your mistress, and not until now have we been able to give any public flourish to the event in Weatherbury. That it may be thoroughly well done, and that every man may go happy to bed, I have ordered to be brought here some bottles of brandy and kettles of hot water. A treble-strong goblet will be handed round to each guest.'

Bathsheba put her hand upon his arm, and, with upturned pale face, said imploringly, 'No—don't give it to them—pray don't, Frank! It will only do them harm: they have had enough of everything.'

'True—we don't wish for no more, thank ye,' said one or two.

'Pooh!' said the sergeant contemptuously, and raised his voice as if lighted up by a new idea. 'Friends,' he said, 'we'll send the women-folk home! 'Tis time they were in bed. Then we cockbirds will have a jolly carouse to ourselves! If any of the men show the white feather,[4] let them look elsewhere for a winter's work.'

Bathsheba indignantly left the barn, followed by all the women and children. The musicians, not looking upon themselves as 'company,' slipped quietly away to their spring-waggon and put in the horse.[5] Thus Troy and the men on the farm were left sole occupants of the place. Oak, not to appear unnecessarily disagreeable, stayed a little while; then he, too, arose and quietly took his departure, followed by a friendly oath from the sergeant for not staying to a second round of grog.

Gabriel proceeded towards his home. In approaching the door, his

---

3. A contraction for "athwart," meaning "across" or "over."

4. Show fear about joining in the drinking.

5. Harness the horse to the wagon.

toe kicked something which felt and sounded soft, leathery, and distended, like a boxing-glove. It was a large toad humbly travelling across the path. Oak took it up, thinking it might be better to kill the creature to save it from pain; but finding it uninjured, he placed it again among the grass. He knew what this direct message from the Great Mother[6] meant. And soon came another.

When he struck a light indoors there appeared upon the table a thin glistening streak, as if a brush of varnish had been lightly dragged across it. Oak's eyes followed the serpentine sheen to the other side, where it led up to a huge brown garden-slug, which had come indoors to-night for reasons of its own. It was Nature's second way of hinting to him that he was to prepare for foul weather.

Oak sat down meditating for nearly an hour. During this time two black spiders, of the kind common in thatched houses, promenaded the ceiling, ultimately dropping to the floor. This reminded him that if there was one class of manifestation on this matter that he thoroughly understood, it was the instincts of sheep. He left the room, ran across two or three fields towards the flock, got upon a hedge, and looked over among them.

They were crowded close together on the other side around some furze bushes, and the first peculiarity observable was that, on the sudden appearance of Oak's head over the fence, they did not stir or run away. They had now a terror of something greater than their terror of man. But this was not the most noteworthy feature: they were all grouped in such a way that their tails, without a single exception, were towards that half of the horizon from which the storm threatened. There was an inner circle closely huddled, and outside these they radiated wider apart, the pattern formed by the flock as a whole not being unlike a vandyked lace collar,[7] to which the clump of furze bushes stood in the position of a wearer's neck.

This was enough to re-establish him in his original opinion. He knew now that he was right, and that Troy was wrong. Every voice in nature was unanimous in bespeaking change. But two distinct translations attached to these dumb expressions. Apparently there was to be a thunder-storm, and afterwards a cold continuous rain. The creeping things seemed to know all about the later rain, but little of the interpolated thunder-storm; whilst the sheep knew all about the thunder-storm and nothing of the later rain.

This complication of weathers being uncommon, was all the more to be feared. Oak returned to the stack-yard. All was silent here, and the conical tips of the ricks jutted darkly into the sky. There were five wheat-ricks in this yard, and three stacks of barley. The wheat when

6. A translation of the name *Mater Magna*, which ancient Romans gave to Cybele, a goddess whose legends are connected with the fecundity of nature.

7. A wide lace collar with a deeply scalloped edge such as are common on the subjects in paintings by Sir Anthony Van Dyck (1599–1641).

threshed would average about thirty quarters to each stack; the barley, at least forty. Their value to Bathsheba, and indeed to anybody, Oak mentally estimated by the following simple calculation:—

$$5 \times 30 = 150 \text{ quarters} = 500l.$$
$$3 \times 40 = 120 \text{ quarters} = \underline{250l.}$$
$$\text{Total} \ldots 750l.$$

Seven hundred and fifty pounds in the divinest form that money can wear—that of necessary food for man and beast: should the risk be run of deteriorating this bulk of corn to less than half its value, because of the instability of a woman? 'Never, if I can prevent it!' said Gabriel.

Such was the argument that Oak set outwardly before him. But man, even to himself, is a palimpsest,[8] having an ostensible writing, and another beneath the lines. It is possible that there was this golden legend under the utilitarian one: 'I will help to my last effort the woman I have loved so dearly.'

He went back to the barn to endeavour to obtain assistance for covering the ricks that very night. All was silent within, and he would have passed on in the belief that the party had broken up, had not a dim light, yellow as saffron by contrast with the greenish whiteness outside, streamed through a knot-hole in the folding doors.

Gabriel looked in. An unusual picture met his eye.

The candles suspended among the evergreens had burnt down to their sockets, and in some cases the leaves tied about them were scorched. Many of the lights had quite gone out, others smoked and stank, grease dropping from them upon the floor. Here, under the table, and leaning against forms and chairs in every conceivable attitude except the perpendicular, were the wretched persons of all the work-folk, the hair of their heads at such low levels being suggestive of mops and brooms. In the midst of these shone red and distinct the figure of Sergeant Troy, leaning back in a chair. Coggan was on his back, with his mouth open, buzzing forth snores, as were several others; the united breathings of the horizontal assemblage forming a subdued roar like London from a distance. Joseph Poorgrass was curled round in the fashion of a hedgehog, apparently in attempts to present the least possible portion of his surface to the air; and behind him was dimly visible an unimportant remnant of William Smallbury. The glasses and cups still stood upon the table, a water-jug being overturned, from which a small rill, after tracing its course with marvellous precision down the centre of the long table, fell into the neck of the unconscious Mark Clark, in a steady, monotonous drip, like the dripping of a stalactite in a cave.

Gabriel glanced hopelessly at the group, which, with one or two exceptions, composed all the able-bodied men upon the farm. He saw

8. A manuscript whose original text has been only partially erased so that traces of it can be discerned beneath the new writing.

at once that if the ricks were to be saved that night, or even the next morning, he must save them with his own hands.

A faint 'ting-ting' resounded from under Coggan's waistcoat. It was Coggan's watch striking the hour of two.

Oak went to the recumbent form of Matthew Moon, who usually undertook the rough thatching of the homestead, and shook him. The shaking was without effect.

Gabriel shouted in his ear, 'Where's your thatching-beetle and rick-stick and spars?'[9]

'Under the staddles,' said Moon mechanically, with the unconscious promptness of a medium.

Gabriel let go his head, and it dropped upon the floor like a bowl. He then went to Susan Tall's husband.

'Where's the key of the granary?'

No answer. The question was repeated, with the same result. To be shouted to at night was evidently less of a novelty to Susan Tall's husband than to Matthew Moon. Oak flung down Tall's head into the corner again and turned away.

To be just, the men were not greatly to blame for this painful and demoralizing termination to the evening's entertainment. Sergeant Troy had so strenuously insisted, glass in hand, that drinking should be the bond of their union, that those who wished to refuse hardly liked to be so unmannerly under the circumstances. Having from their youth up been entirely unaccustomed to any liquor stronger than cider or mild ale, it was no wonder that they had succumbed, one and all, with extraordinary uniformity, after the lapse of about an hour.

Gabriel was greatly depressed. This debauch boded ill for that wilful and fascinating mistress whom the faithful man even now felt within him as the embodiment of all that was sweet and bright and hopeless.

He put out the expiring lights, that the barn might not be endangered, closed the door upon the men in their deep and oblivious sleep, and went again into the lone night. A hot breeze, as if breathed from the parted lips of some dragon about to swallow the globe, fanned him from the south, while directly opposite in the north rose a grim misshapen body of cloud, in the very teeth of the wind. So unnaturally did it rise that one could fancy it to be lifted by machinery from below. Meanwhile the faint cloudlets had flown back into the south-east corner of the sky, as if in terror of the large cloud, like a young brood gazed in upon by some monster.

Going on to the village, Oak flung a small stone against the window of Laban Tall's bedroom, expecting Susan to open it; but nobody stirred. He went round to the back door, which had been left unfastened for Laban's entry, and passed in to the foot of the staircase.

9. In thatching a rick, the grain to be thatched is first combed downward with a toothed device called a "rick-stick," then held down by U-shaped sticks with pointed ends called "spars," which are driven into the rick by a wooden mallet called a "beetle."

'Mrs. Tall, I've come for the key of the granary, to get at the rick-cloths,'[1] said Oak, in a stentorian voice.

'Is that you?' said Mrs. Susan Tall, half awake.

'Yes,' said Gabriel.

'Come along to bed, do, you draw-latching[2] rogue—keeping a body awake like this!'

'It isn't Laban—'tis Gabriel Oak. I want the key of the granary.'

'Gabriel! What in the name of fortune did you pretend to be Laban for?'

'I didn't. I thought you meant——'

'Yes you did! What do you want here?'

'The key of the granary.'

'Take it then. 'Tis on the nail. People coming disturbing women at this time of night ought——'

Gabriel took the key, without waiting to hear the conclusion of the tirade. Ten minutes later his lonely figure might have been seen dragging four large waterproof coverings across the yard, and soon two of these heaps of treasure in grain were covered snug—two cloths to each. Two hundred pounds were secured. Three wheat-stacks remained open, and there were no more cloths. Oak looked under the staddles and found a fork.[3] He mounted the third pile of wealth and began operating, adopting the plan of sloping the upper sheaves one over the other; and, in addition, filling the interstices with the material of some untied sheaves.

So far all was well. By this hurried contrivance Bathsheba's property in wheat was safe for at any rate a week or two, provided always that there was not much wind.

Next came the barley. This it was only possible to protect by systematic thatching. Time went on, and the moon vanished not to reappear. It was the farewell of the ambassador previous to war. The night had a haggard look, like a sick thing; and there came finally an utter expiration of air from the whole heaven in the form of a slow breeze, which might have been likened to a death. And now nothing was heard in the yard but the dull thuds of the beetle which drove in the spars, and the rustle of thatch in the intervals.

XXXVII

The Storm—The Two Together

A light flapped over the scene, as if reflected from phosphorescent wings crossing the sky, and a rumble filled the air. It was the first move of the approaching storm.

---

1. Large waterproof canvas tarpaulins used to protect ricks from rain.
2. Sneaking and/or dawdling.
3. Pitchfork.

The second peal was noisy, with comparatively little visible lightning. Gabriel saw a candle shining in Bathsheba's bedroom, and soon a shadow swept to and fro upon the blind.

Then there came a third flash. Manœuvres of a most extraordinary kind were going on in the vast firmamental hollows overhead. The lightning now was the colour of silver, and gleamed in the heavens like a mailed army. Rumbles became rattles. Gabriel from his elevated position could see over the landscape at least half-a-dozen miles in front. Every hedge, bush, and tree was distinct as in a line engraving. In a paddock in the same direction was a herd of heifers, and the forms of these were visible at this moment in the act of galloping about in the wildest and maddest confusion, flinging their heels and tails high into the air, their heads to earth. A poplar in the immediate foreground was like an ink stroke on burnished tin. Then the picture vanished, leaving the darkness so intense that Gabriel worked entirely by feeling with his hands.

He had stuck his ricking-rod, or poniard, as it was indifferently called—a long iron lance, polished by handling—into the stack, used to support the sheaves instead of the support called a groom used on houses. A blue light appeared in the zenith, and in some indescribable manner flickered down near the top of the rod. It was the fourth of the larger flashes. A moment later and there was a smack—smart, clear, and short. Gabriel felt his position to be anything but a safe one, and he resolved to descend.

Not a drop of rain had fallen as yet. He wiped his weary brow, and looked again at the black forms of the unprotected stacks. Was his life so valuable to him after all? What were his prospects that he should be so chary of running risk, when important and urgent labour could not be carried on without such risk? He resolved to stick to the stack. However, he took a precaution. Under the staddles was a long tethering chain, used to prevent the escape of errant horses. This he carried up the ladder, and sticking his rod through the clog at one end, allowed the other end of the chain to trail upon the ground. The spike attached to it he drove in. Under the shadow of this extemporized lightning-conductor he felt himself comparatively safe.

Before Oak had laid his hands upon his tools again out leapt the fifth flash, with the spring of a serpent and the shout of a fiend. It was green as an emerald, and the reverberation was stunning. What was this the light revealed to him? In the open ground before him, as he looked over the ridge of the rick, was a dark and apparently female form. Could it be that of the only venturesome woman in the parish—Bathsheba? The form moved on a step: then he could see no more.

'Is that you, ma'am?' said Gabriel to the darkness.

'Who is there?' said the voice of Bathsheba.

'Gabriel. I am on the rick, thatching.'

'O, Gabriel!—and are you? I have come about them. The weather awoke me, and I thought of the corn. I am so distressed about it—can we save it anyhow? I cannot find my husband. Is he with you?'

'He is not here.'

'Do you know where he is?'

'Asleep in the barn.'

'He promised that the stacks should be seen to, and now they are all neglected! Can I do anything to help? Liddy is afraid to come out. Fancy finding you here at such an hour! Surely I can do something?'

'You can bring up some reed-sheaves to me, one by one, ma'am; if you are not afraid to come up the ladder in the dark,' said Gabriel. 'Every moment is precious now, and that would save a good deal of time. It is not very dark when the lightning has been gone a bit.'

'I'll do anything!' she said resolutely. She instantly took a sheaf upon her shoulder, clambered up close to his heels, placed it behind the rod, and descended for another. At her third ascent the rick suddenly brightened with the brazen glare of shining majolica[1]— every knot in every straw was visible. On the slope in front of him appeared two human shapes, black as jet. The rick lost its sheen—the shapes vanished. Gabriel turned his head. It had been the sixth flash which had come from the east behind him, and the two dark forms on the slope had been the shadows of himself and Bathsheba.

Then came the peal. It hardly was credible that such a heavenly light could be the parent of such a diabolical sound.

'How terrible!' she exclaimed, and clutched him by the sleeve. Gabriel turned, and steadied her on her aerial perch by holding her arm. At the same moment, while he was still reversed in his attitude, there was more light, and he saw, as it were, a copy of the tall poplar tree on the hill drawn in black on the wall of the barn. It was the shadow of that tree, thrown across by a secondary flash in the west.

The next flare came. Bathsheba was on the ground now, shouldering another sheaf, and she bore its dazzle without flinching—thunder and all—and again ascended with the load. There was then a silence everywhere for four or five minutes, and the crunch of the spars, as Gabriel hastily drove them in, could again be distinctly heard. He thought the crisis of the storm had passed. But there came a burst of light.

'Hold on!' said Gabriel, taking the sheaf from her shoulder, and grasping her arm again.

Heaven opened then, indeed. The flash was almost too novel for its inexpressibly dangerous nature to be at once realized, and they could only comprehend the magnificence of its beauty. It sprang from east, west, north, south, and was a perfect dance of death. The forms of skeletons appeared in the air, shaped with blue fire for bones— dancing, leaping, striding, racing around, and mingling altogether in

---

1. A kind of fine Italian pottery glazed with opaque white and rich metallic colors.

unparalleled confusion. With these were intertwined undulating snakes of green, and behind these was a broad mass of lesser light. Simultaneously came from every part of the tumbling sky what may be called a shout; since, though no shout ever came near it, it was more of the nature of a shout than of anything else earthly. In the meantime one of the grisly forms had alighted upon the point of Gabriel's rod, to run invisibly down it, down the chain, and into the earth. Gabriel was almost blinded, and he could feel Bathsheba's warm arm tremble in his hand—a sensation novel and thrilling enough; but love, life, everything human, seemed small and trifling in such close juxtaposition with an infuriated universe.

Oak had hardly time to gather up these impressions into a thought, and to see how strangely the red feather of her hat shone in this light, when the tall tree on the hill before mentioned seemed on fire to a white heat, and a new one among these terrible voices mingled with the last crash of those preceding. It was a stupefying blast, harsh and pitiless, and it fell upon their ears in a dead, flat blow, without that reverberation which lends the tones of a drum to more distant thunder. By the lustre reflected from every part of the earth and from the wide domical scoop above it, he saw that the tree was sliced down the whole length of its tall, straight stem, a huge riband of bark being apparently flung off. The other portion remained erect, and revealed the bared surface as a strip of white down the front. The lightning had struck the tree. A sulphurous smell filled the air; then all was silent, and black as a cave in Hinnom.[2]

'We had a narrow escape!' said Gabriel hurriedly. 'You had better go down.'

Bathsheba said nothing; but he could distinctly hear her rhythmical pants, and the recurrent rustle of the sheaf beside her in response to her frightened pulsations. She descended the ladder, and, on second thoughts, he followed her. The darkness was now impenetrable by the sharpest vision. They both stood still at the bottom, side by side. Bathsheba appeared to think only of the weather—Oak thought only of her just then. At last he said—

'The storm seems to have passed now, at any rate.'

'I think so too,' said Bathsheba. 'Though there are multitudes of gleams, look!'

The sky was now filled with an incessant light, frequent repetition melting into complete continuity, as an unbroken sound results from the successive strokes on a gong.

'Nothing serious,' said he. 'I cannot understand no rain falling. But Heaven be praised, it is all the better for us. I am now going up again.'

'Gabriel, you are kinder than I deserve! I will stay and help you yet. O, why are not some of the others here!'

2. Originally a valley near Jerusalem where children were burnt as human sacrifices to the god Moloch; hence, a synonym for Hell.

'They would have been here if they could,' said Oak, in a hesitating way.

'O, I know it all—all,' she said, adding slowly: 'They are all asleep in the barn, in a drunken sleep, and my husband among them. That's it, is it not? Don't think I am a timid woman and can't endure things.'

'I am not certain,' said Gabriel. 'I will go and see.'

He crossed to the barn, leaving her there alone. He looked through the chinks of the door. All was in total darkness, as he had left it, and there still arose, as at the former time, the steady buzz of many snores.

He felt a zephyr curling about his cheek, and turned. It was Bathsheba's breath—she had followed him, and was looking into the same chink.

He endeavoured to put off the immediate and painful subject of their thoughts by remarking gently, 'If you'll come back again, miss—ma'am, and hand up a few more, it would save much time.'

Then Oak went back again, ascended to the top, stepped off the ladder for greater expedition, and went on thatching. She followed, but without a sheaf.

'Gabriel,' she said, in a strange and impressive voice.

Oak looked up at her. She had not spoken since he left the barn. The soft and continual shimmer of the dying lightning showed a marble face high against the black sky of the opposite quarter. Bathsheba was sitting almost on the apex of the stack, her feet gathered up beneath her, and resting on the top round of the ladder.

'Yes, mistress,' he said.

'I suppose you thought that when I galloped away to Bath that night it was on purpose to be married?'

'I did at last—not at first,' he answered, somewhat surprised at the abruptness with which this new subject was broached.

'And others thought so, too!'

'Yes.'

'And you blamed me for it?'

'Well—a little.'

'I thought so. Now, I care a little for your good opinion, and I want to explain something—I have longed to do it ever since I returned, and you looked so gravely at me. For if I were to die—and I may die soon—it would be dreadful that you should always think mistakenly of me. Now, listen.'

Gabriel ceased his rustling.

'I went to Bath that night in the full intention of breaking off my engagement to Mr. Troy. It was owing to circumstances which occurred after I got there that—that we were married. Now, do you see the matter in a new light?'

'I do—somewhat.'

'I must, I suppose, say more, now that I have begun. And perhaps it's no harm, for you are certainly under no delusion that I ever loved you, or that I can have any object in speaking, more than that object I have mentioned. Well, I was alone in a strange city, and the horse was lame. And at last I didn't know what to do. I saw, when it was too late, that scandal might seize hold of me for meeting him alone in that way. But I was coming away, when he suddenly said he had that day seen a woman more beautiful than I, and that his constancy could not be counted on unless I at once became his. . . . And I was grieved and troubled——' She cleared her voice, and waited a moment, as if to gather breath. 'And then, between jealousy and distraction, I married him!' she whispered with desperate impetuosity.

Gabriel made no reply.

'He was not to blame, for it was perfectly true about—about his seeing somebody else,' she quickly added. 'And now I don't wish for a single remark from you upon the subject—indeed, I forbid it. I only wanted you to know that misunderstood bit of my history before a time comes when you could never know it.—You want some more sheaves?'

She went down the ladder, and the work proceeded. Gabriel soon perceived a languor in the movements of his mistress up and down, and he said to her, gently as a mother—

'I think you had better go indoors now, you are tired. I can finish the rest alone. If the wind does not change the rain is likely to keep off.'

'If I am useless I will go,' said Bathsheba, in a flagging cadence. 'But O, if your life should be lost!'

'You are not useless; but I would rather not tire you longer. You have done well.'

'And you better!' she said gratefully. 'Thank you for your devotion, a thousand times, Gabriel! Good-night—I know you are doing your very best for me.'

She diminished in the gloom, and vanished, and he heard the latch of the gate fall as she passed through. He worked in a reverie now, musing upon her story, and upon the contradictoriness of that feminine heart which had caused her to speak more warmly to him to-night than she ever had done whilst unmarried and free to speak as warmly as she chose.

He was disturbed in his meditation by a grating noise from the coach-house. It was the vane on the roof turning round, and this change in the wind was the signal for a disastrous rain.

XXXVIII

Rain—One Solitary Meets Another

It was now five o'clock, and the dawn was promising to break in hues of drab and ash.

The air changed its temperature and stirred itself more vigorously.

Cool breezes coursed in transparent eddies round Oak's face. The wind shifted yet a point or two and blew stronger. In ten minutes every wind of heaven seemed to be roaming at large. Some of the thatching on the wheat-stacks was now whirled fantastically aloft, and had to be replaced and weighted with some rails that lay near at hand. This done, Oak slaved away again at the barley. A huge drop of rain smote his face, the wind snarled round every corner, the trees rocked to the bases of their trunks, and the twigs clashed in strife. Driving in spars at any point and on any system, inch by inch he covered more and more safely from ruin this distracting impersonation of seven hundred pounds. The rain came on in earnest, and Oak soon felt the water to be tracking cold and clammy routes down his back. Ultimately he was reduced well-nigh to a homogeneous sop, and the dyes of his clothes trickled down and stood in a pool at the foot of the ladder. The rain stretched obliquely through the dull atmosphere in liquid spines, unbroken in continuity between their beginnings in the clouds and their points in him.

Oak suddenly remembered that eight months before this time he had been fighting against fire in the same spot as desperately as he was fighting against water now—and for a futile love of the same woman. As for her—— But Oak was generous and true, and dismissed his reflections.

It was about seven o'clock in the dark leaden morning when Gabriel came down from the last stack, and thankfully exclaimed, 'It is done!' He was drenched, weary, and sad, and yet not so sad as drenched and weary, for he was cheered by a sense of success in a good cause.

Faint sounds came from the barn, and he looked that way. Figures stepped singly and in pairs through the doors—all walking awkwardly, and abashed, save the foremost, who wore a red jacket, and advanced with his hands in his pockets, whistling. The others shambled after with a conscience-stricken air: the whole procession was not unlike Flaxman's group of the suitors tottering on towards the infernal regions under the conduct of Mercury.[1] The gnarled shapes passed into the village, Troy, their leader, entering the farmhouse. Not a single one of them had turned his face to the ricks, or apparently bestowed one thought upon their condition.

Soon Oak too went homeward, by a different route from theirs. In front of him against the wet glazed surface of the lane he saw a person walking yet more slowly than himself under an umbrella. The man turned and plainly started; he was Boldwood.

---

1. A reference to the line drawing titled "Mercury Conducting the Souls of the Suitors to the Infernal Regions" by John Flaxman (1755–1826), whose engraved line-drawing illustrations for an edition of Homer's *Odyssey* (1793) were widely admired. In classical mythology, Mercury was a messenger of the gods. The "suitors" were those seeking the hand of Ulysses' wife, Penelope, while he was away because of the Trojan war; upon his return, Ulysses killed them with the help of his son and a faithful swineherd, and Flaxman's drawing represents Mercury leading the suitors off to Hades.

'How are you this morning, sir?' said Oak.

'Yes, it is a wet day.—Oh, I am well, very well, I thank you; quite well.'

'I am glad to hear it, sir.'

Boldwood seemed to awake to the present by degrees. 'You look tired and ill, Oak,' he said then, desultorily regarding his companion.

'I am tired. You look strangely altered, sir.'

'I? Not a bit of it: I am well enough. What put that into your head?'

'I thought you didn't look quite so topping as you used to, that was all.'

'Indeed, then you are mistaken,' said Boldwood shortly. 'Nothing hurts me. My constitution is an iron one.'

'I've been working hard to get our ricks covered, and was barely in time. Never had such a struggle in my life. . . . Yours of course are safe, sir.'

'O yes.' Boldwood added, after an interval of silence: 'What did you ask, Oak?'

'Your ricks are all covered before this time?'

'No.'

'At any rate, the large ones upon the stone staddles?'

'They are not.'

'Them under the hedge?'

'No. I forgot to tell the thatcher to set about it.'

'Nor the little one by the stile?'

'Nor the little one by the stile. I overlooked the ricks this year.'

'Then not a tenth of your corn will come to measure, sir.'

'Possibly not.'

'Overlooked them,' repeated Gabriel slowly to himself. It is difficult to describe the intensely dramatic effect that announcement had upon Oak at such a moment. All the night he had been feeling that the neglect he was labouring to repair was abnormal and isolated—the only instance of the kind within the circuit of the county. Yet at this very time, within the same parish, a greater waste had been going on, uncomplained of and disregarded. A few months earlier Boldwood's forgetting his husbandry would have been as preposterous an idea as a sailor forgetting he was in a ship. Oak was just thinking that whatever he himself might have suffered from Bathsheba's marriage, here was a man who had suffered more, when Boldwood spoke in a changed voice—that of one who yearned to make a confidence and relieve his heart by an outpouring.

'Oak, you know as well as I that things have gone wrong with me lately. I may as well own it. I was going to get a little settled in life; but in some way my plan has come to nothing.'

'I thought my mistress would have married you,' said Gabriel, not knowing enough of the full depths of Boldwood's love to keep silence on the farmer's account, and determined not to evade discipline by doing so on his own. 'However, it is so sometimes, and nothing happens that we expect,' he added, with the repose of a man whom misfortune had inured rather than subdued.

'I daresay I am a joke about the parish,' said Boldwood, as if the subject came irresistibly to his tongue, and with a miserable lightness meant to express his indifference.

'O no—I don't think that.'

'—But the real truth of the matter is that there was not, as some fancy, any jilting on—her part. No engagement ever existed between me and Miss Everdene. People say so, but it is untrue: she never promised me!' Boldwood stood still now and turned his wild face to Oak. 'O, Gabriel,' he continued, 'I am weak and foolish, and I don't know what, and I can't fend off my miserable grief! . . . I had some faint belief in the mercy of God till I lost that woman. Yes, He prepared a gourd to shade me, and like the prophet I thanked Him and was glad. But the next day He prepared a worm to smite the gourd and wither it; and I feel it is better to die than to live!'[2]

A silence followed. Boldwood aroused himself from the momentary mood of confidence into which he had drifted, and walked on again, resuming his usual reserve.

'No, Gabriel,' he resumed, with a carelessness which was like the smile on the countenance of a skull: 'it was made more of by other people than ever it was by us. I do feel a little regret occasionally, but no woman ever had power over me for any length of time. Well, good morning; I can trust you not to mention to others what has passed between us two here.'

XXXIX

Coming Home—A Cry

On the turnpike road, between Casterbridge and Weatherbury, and about three miles from the former place, is Yalbury Hill, one of those steep long ascents which pervade the highways of this undulating part of South Wessex. In returning from market it is usual for the farmers and other gig-gentry[1] to alight at the bottom and walk up.

One Saturday evening in the month of October Bathsheba's vehicle was duly creeping up this incline. She was sitting listlessly in the second seat of the gig, whilst walking beside her in a farmer's market-

2. An allusion to Jonah 4:6–8, which reads: "And the L ORD God prepared a gourd, and made it to come up over Jonah, that *it* might be a shadow over his head, to deliver him from his grief. So Jonah was exceeding glad of the gourd. But God prepared a worm when the morning rose the next day, and it smote the gourd that it withered. . . . And the sun beat upon the head of Jonah, that he fainted . . . and said, *It is better for me to die than to live.*"

1. An offhand way of describing the class of people who were sufficiently well-off to own one of the light, two-wheeled, one-horse carriages called gigs. In his abortive courtship of Bathsheba in chapter 4, Gabriel Oak promises to buy her a "ten-pound gig for market."

ing suit of unusually fashionable cut was an erect, well-made young man. Though on foot, he held the reins and whip, and occasionally aimed light cuts at the horse's ear with the end of the lash, as a recreation. This man was her husband, formerly Sergeant Troy, who, having bought his discharge with Bathsheba's money, was gradually transforming himself into a farmer of a spirited and very modern school. People of unalterable ideas still insisted upon calling him 'Sergeant' when they met him, which was in some degree owing to his having still retained the well-shaped moustache of his military days, and the soldierly bearing inseparable from his form and training.

'Yes, if it hadn't been for that wretched rain I should have cleared two hundred as easy as looking, my love,' he was saying. 'Don't you see, it altered all the chances? To speak like a book I once read, wet weather is the narrative, and fine days are the episodes, of our country's history; now, isn't that true?'

'But the time of year is come for changeable weather.'

'Well, yes. The fact is, these autumn races are the ruin of everybody. Never did I see such a day as 'twas! 'Tis a wild open place, just out of Budmouth, and a drab sea rolled in towards us like liquid misery. Wind and rain—good Lord! Dark? Why, 'twas as black as my hat before the last race was run. 'Twas five o'clock, and you couldn't see the horses till they were almost in, leave alone colours. The ground was as heavy as lead, and all judgment from a fellow's experience went for nothing. Horses, riders, people, were all blown about like ships at sea. Three booths were blown over, and the wretched folk inside crawled out upon their hands and knees; and in the next field were as many as a dozen hats at one time. Ay, Pimpernel regularly stuck fast, when about sixty yards off, and when I saw Policy stepping on, it did knock my heart against the lining of my ribs, I assure you, my love!'

'And you mean, Frank,' said Bathsheba sadly—her voice was painfully lowered from the fulness and vivacity of the previous summer— 'that you have lost more than a hundred pounds in a month by this dreadful horse-racing? O, Frank, it is cruel; it is foolish of you to take away my money so. We shall have to leave the farm; that will be the end of it!'

'Humbug about cruel. Now, there 'tis again—turn on the waterworks; that's just like you.'

'But you'll promise me not to go to the second Budmouth race-meeting, won't you?' she implored. Bathsheba was at the full depth for tears, but she maintained a dry eye.

'I don't see why I should; in fact, if it turns out to be a fine day, I was thinking of taking you.'

'Never, never! I'll go a hundred miles the other way first. I hate the sound of the very word!'

'But the question of going to see the race or staying at home has very little to do with the matter. Bets are all booked safely enough before the race begins, you may depend. Whether it is a bad race for me or a good one, will have very little to do with our going there next Monday.'

'But you don't mean to say that you have risked anything on this one too!' she exclaimed, with an agonized look.

'There now, don't you be a little fool. Wait till you are told. Why, Bathsheba, you have lost all the pluck and sauciness you formerly had, and upon my life if I had known what a chicken-hearted creature you were under all your boldness, I'd never have—I know what.'

A flash of indignation might have been seen in Bathsheba's dark eyes as she looked resolutely ahead after this reply. They moved on without further speech, some early-withered leaves from the trees which hooded the road at this spot occasionally spinning downward across their path to the earth.

A woman appeared on the brow of the hill. The ridge was in a cutting, so that she was very near the husband and wife before she became visible. Troy had turned towards the gig to remount, and whilst putting his foot on the step the woman passed behind him.

Though the overshadowing trees and the approach of eventide enveloped them in gloom, Bathsheba could see plainly enough to discern the extreme poverty of the woman's garb, and the sadness of her face.

'Please, sir, do you know at what time Casterbridge Union-house closes at night?'

The woman said these words to Troy over his shoulder.

Troy started visibly at the sound of the voice; yet he seemed to recover presence of mind sufficient to prevent himself from giving way to his impulse to suddenly turn and face her. He said, slowly—

'I don't know.'

The woman, on hearing him speak, quickly looked up, examined the side of his face, and recognized the soldier under the yeoman's garb. Her face was drawn into an expression which had gladness and agony both among its elements. She uttered an hysterical cry, and fell down.

'O, poor thing!' exclaimed Bathsheba, instantly preparing to alight.

'Stay where you are, and attend to the horse!' said Troy peremptorily, throwing her the reins and the whip. 'Walk the horse to the top: I'll see to the woman.'

'But I——'

'Do you hear? Clk—Poppet!'

The horse, gig, and Bathsheba moved on.

'How on earth did you come here? I thought you were miles away, or dead! Why didn't you write to me?' said Troy to the woman, in a strangely gentle, yet hurried voice, as he lifted her up.

'I feared to.'

'Have you any money?'

'None.'

'Good Heaven—I wish I had more to give you! Here's—wretched—the merest trifle. It is every farthing I have left. I have none but what my wife gives me, you know, and I can't ask her now.'

The woman made no answer.

'I have only another moment,' continued Troy; 'and now listen. Where are you going to-night? Casterbridge Union?'

'Yes; I thought to go there.'

'You shan't go there; yet, wait. Yes, perhaps for to-night; I can do nothing better—worse luck! Sleep there to-night, and stay there to-morrow. Monday is the first free day I have; and on Monday morning, at ten exactly, meet me on Grey's Bridge, just out of the town. I'll bring all the money I can muster. You shan't want—I'll see that, Fanny; then I'll get you a lodging somewhere. Good-bye till then. I am a brute—but good-bye!'

After advancing the distance which completed the ascent of the hill, Bathsheba turned her head. The woman was upon her feet, and Bathsheba saw her withdrawing from Troy, and going feebly down the hill by the third milestone from Casterbridge. Troy then came on towards his wife, stepped into the gig, took the reins from her hand, and without making any observation whipped the horse into a trot. He was rather agitated.

'Do you know who that woman was?' said Bathsheba, looking searchingly into his face.

'I do,' he said, looking boldly back into hers.

'I thought you did,' said she, with angry hauteur, and still regarding him. 'Who is she?'

He suddenly seemed to think that frankness would benefit neither of the women.

'Nothing to either of us,' he said. 'I know her by sight.'

'What is her name?'

'How should I know her name?'

'I think you do.'

'Think if you will, and be——' The sentence was completed by a smart cut of the whip round Poppet's flank, which caused the animal to start forward at a wild pace. No more was said.

XL

On Casterbridge Highway

For a considerable time the woman walked on. Her steps became feebler, and she strained her eyes to look afar upon the naked road, now indistinct amid the penumbræ of night. At length her onward walk dwindled to the merest totter, and she opened a gate within which was a haystack. Underneath this she sat down and presently slept.

When the woman awoke it was to find herself in the depths of a moonless and starless night. A heavy unbroken crust of cloud stretched across the sky, shutting out every speck of heaven; and a distant halo which hung over the town of Casterbridge was visible against the black concave, the luminosity appearing the brighter by its great contrast with the circumscribing darkness. Towards this weak, soft glow the woman turned her eyes.

'If I could only get there!' she said. 'Meet him the day after to-morrow: God help me! Perhaps I shall be in my grave before then.'

A manor-house clock from the far depths of shadow struck the hour, one, in a small, attenuated tone. After midnight the voice of a clock seems to lose in breadth as much as in length, and to diminish its sonorousness to a thin falsetto.

Afterwards a light—two lights—arose from the remote shade, and grew larger. A carriage rolled along the road, and passed the gate. It probably contained some late diners-out. The beams from one lamp shone for a moment upon the crouching woman, and threw her face into vivid relief. The face was young in the groundwork, old in the finish; the general contours were flexuous and childlike, but the finer lineaments had begun to be sharp and thin.

The pedestrian stood up, apparently with a revived determination, and looked around. The road appeared to be familiar to her, and she carefully scanned the fence as she slowly walked along. Presently there became visible a dim white shape; it was another milestone. She drew her fingers across its face to feel the marks.

'Two more!' she said.

She leant against the stone as a means of rest for a short interval, then bestirred herself, and again pursued her way. For a slight distance she bore up bravely, afterwards flagging as before. This was beside a lone copsewood,[1] wherein heaps of white chips strewn upon the leafy ground showed that woodmen had been faggoting and making hurdles[2] during the day. Now there was not a rustle, not a breeze, not the faintest clash of twigs to keep her company. The woman looked over the gate, opened it, and went in. Close to the entrance stood a row of faggots, bound and unbound, together with stakes of all sizes.

For a few seconds the wayfarer stood with that tense stillness which signifies itself to be not the end, but merely the suspension, of a previous motion. Her attitude was that of a person who listens, either to the external world of sound, or to the imagined discourse of thought. A close criticism might have detected signs proving that she was intent on the latter alternative. Moreover, as was shown by what

1. A thicket of saplings or small trees.
2. "Faggoting" is binding together bundles of sticks and small branches to be used as fuel; these would be the by-products of trimming saplings to make hurdles. For hurdle-making, see chapter 31, footnote 2.

followed, she was oddly exercising the faculty of invention upon the speciality of the clever Jacquet Droz,[3] the designer of automatic substitutes for human limbs.

By the aid of the Casterbridge aurora, and by feeling with her hands, the woman selected two sticks from the heaps. These sticks were nearly straight to the height of three or four feet, where each branched into a fork like the letter Y. She sat down, snapped off the small upper twigs, and carried the remainder with her into the road. She placed one of these forks under each arm as a crutch, tested them, timidly threw her whole weight upon them—so little that it was—and swung herself forward. The girl had made for herself a material aid.

The crutches answered well. The pat of her feet, and the tap of her sticks upon the highway, were all the sounds that came from the traveller now. She had passed the last milestone by a good long distance, and began to look wistfully towards the bank as if calculating upon another milestone soon. The crutches, though so very useful, had their limits of power. Mechanism only transfers labour, being powerless to supersede it, and the original amount of exertion was not cleared away; it was thrown into the body and arms. She was exhausted, and each swing forward became fainter. At last she swayed sideways, and fell.

Here she lay, a shapeless heap, for ten minutes and more. The morning wind began to boom dully over the flats, and to move afresh dead leaves which had lain still since yesterday. The woman desperately turned round upon her knees, and next rose to her feet. Steadying herself by the help of one crutch, she essayed a step, then another, then a third, using the crutches now as walking-sticks only. Thus she progressed till descending Mellstock Hill another milestone appeared, and soon the beginning of an iron-railed fence came into view. She staggered across to the first post, clung to it, and looked around.

The Casterbridge lights were now individually visible. It was getting towards morning, and vehicles might be hoped for, if not expected soon. She listened. There was not a sound of life save that acme and sublimation of all dismal sounds, the bark of a fox, its three hollow notes being rendered at intervals of a minute with the precision of a funeral bell.

'Less than a mile!' the woman murmured. 'No; more,' she added, after a pause. 'The mile is to the county-hall, and my resting-place is on the other side Casterbridge. A little over a mile, and there I am!' After an interval she again spoke. 'Five or six steps to a yard—six perhaps. I have to go seventeen hundred yards. A hundred times six, six hundred. Seventeen times that. O pity me, Lord!'

Holding to the rails, she advanced, thrusting one hand forward

3. Pierre Jacquet-Droz (1721–90) was famous for his mechanized figures, which could be activated to play a musical instrument, write, etc.

upon the rail, then the other, then leaning over it whilst she dragged her feet on beneath.

This woman was not given to soliloquy; but extremity of feeling lessens the individuality of the weak, as it increases that of the strong. She said again in the same tone, 'I'll believe that the end lies five posts forward, and no further, and so get strength to pass them.'

This was a practical application of the principle that a half-feigned and fictitious faith is better than no faith at all.

She passed five posts and held on to the fifth.

'I'll pass five more by believing my longed-for spot is at the next fifth. I can do it.'

She passed five more.

'It lies only five further.'

She passed five more.

'But it is five further.'

She passed them.

'That stone bridge is the end of my journey,' she said, when the bridge over the Froom was in view.

She crawled to the bridge. During the effort each breath of the woman went into the air as if never to return again.

'Now for the truth of the matter,' she said, sitting down. 'The truth is, that I have less than half a mile.' Self-beguilement with what she had known all the time to be false had given her strength to come over half a mile that she would have been powerless to face in the lump. The artifice showed that the woman, by some mysterious intuition, had grasped the paradoxical truth that blindness may operate more vigorously than prescience, and the short-sighted effect more than the far-seeing; that limitation, and not comprehensiveness, is needed for striking a blow.

The half-mile stood now before the sick and weary woman like a stolid Juggernaut.[4] It was an impassive King of her world. The road here ran across Durnover Moor, open to the road on either side. She surveyed the wide space, the lights, herself, sighed, and lay down against a guard-stone of the bridge.

Never was ingenuity exercised so sorely as the traveller here exercised hers. Every conceivable aid, method, stratagem, mechanism, by which these last desperate eight hundred yards could be overpassed by a human being unperceived, was revolved in her busy brain, and dismissed as impracticable. She thought of sticks, wheels, crawling— she even thought of rolling. But the exertion demanded by either of these latter two was greater than to walk erect. The faculty of contrivance was worn out. Hopelessness had come at last.

'No further!' she whispered, and closed her eyes.

4. A huge, heavy-wheeled cart used to carry a statue of the Hindu god Vishnu in a traditional Indian religious procession during which wor- shippers would throw themselves under its wheels and be crushed; hence, by analogy, any overpowering force.

From the strip of shadow on the opposite side of the bridge a portion of shade seemed to detach itself and move into isolation upon the pale white of the road. It glided noiselessly towards the recumbent woman.

She became conscious of something touching her hand; it was softness and it was warmth. She opened her eyes, and the substance touched her face. A dog was licking her cheek.

He was a huge, heavy, and quiet creature, standing darkly against the low horizon, and at least two feet higher than the present position of her eyes. Whether Newfoundland, mastiff, bloodhound, or what not, it was impossible to say. He seemed to be of too strange and mysterious a nature to belong to any variety among those of popular nomenclature. Being thus assignable to no breed, he was the ideal embodiment of canine greatness—a generalization from what was common to all. Night, in its sad, solemn, and benevolent aspect, apart from its stealthy and cruel side, was personified in this form. Darkness endows the small and ordinary ones among mankind with poetical power, and even the suffering woman threw her idea into figure.

In her reclining position she looked up to him just as in earlier times she had, when standing, looked up to a man. The animal, who was as homeless as she, respectfully withdrew a step or two when the woman moved, and, seeing that she did not repulse him, he licked her hand again.

A thought moved within her like lightning. 'Perhaps I can make use of him—I might do it then!'

She pointed in the direction of Casterbridge, and the dog seemed to misunderstand: he trotted on. Then, finding she could not follow, he came back and whined.

The ultimate and saddest singularity of the woman's effort and invention was reached when, with a quickened breathing, she rose to a stooping posture, and, resting her two little arms upon the shoulders of the dog, leant firmly theron, and murmured stimulating words. Whilst she sorrowed in her heart she cheered with her voice, and what was stranger than that the strong should need encouragement from the weak was that cheerfulness should be so well simulated by such utter dejection. Her friend moved forward slowly, and she with small mincing steps moved forward beside him, half her weight being thrown upon the animal. Sometimes she sank as she had sunk from walking erect, from the crutches, from the rails. The dog, who now thoroughly understood her desire and her incapacity, was frantic in his distress on these occasions; he would tug at her dress and run forward. She always called him back, and it was now to be observed that the woman listened for human sounds only to avoid them. It was evident that she had an object in keeping her presence on the road and her forlorn state unknown.

Their progress was necessarily very slow. They reached the bottom of the town, and the Casterbridge lamps lay before them like fallen Pleiads[5] as they turned to the left into the dense shade of a deserted avenue of chestnuts, and so skirted the borough. Thus the town was passed, and the goal was reached.

On this much-desired spot outside the town rose a picturesque building. Originally it had been a mere case to hold people. The shell had been so thin, so devoid of excrescence, and so closely drawn over the accommodation granted, that the grim character of what was beneath showed through it, as the shape of a body is visible under a winding-sheet.[6]

Then Nature, as if offended, lent a hand. Masses of ivy grew up, completely covering the walls, till the place looked like an abbey; and it was discovered that the view from the front, over the Casterbridge chimneys, was one of the most magnificent in the county. A neighbouring earl once said that he would give up a year's rental to have at his own door the view enjoyed by the inmates from theirs— and very probably the inmates would have given up the view for his year's rental.

This stone edifice consisted of a central mass and two wings, whereon stood as sentinels a few slim chimneys, now gurgling sorrowfully to the slow wind. In the wall was a gate, and by the gate a bell-pull formed of a hanging wire. The woman raised herself as high as possible upon her knees, and could just reach the handle. She moved it and fell forwards in a bowed attitude, her face upon her bosom.

It was getting on towards six o'clock, and sounds of movement were to be heard inside the building which was the haven of rest to this wearied soul. A little door by the large one was opened, and a man appeared inside. He discerned the panting heap of clothes, went back for a light, and came again. He entered a second time, and returned with two women.

These lifted the prostrate figure and assisted her in through the doorway. The man then closed the door.

'How did she get here?' said one of the women.

'The Lord knows,' said the other.

'There is a dog outside,' murmured the overcome traveller. 'Where is he gone? He helped me.'

'I stoned him away,' said the man.

The little procession then moved forward—the man in front bearing the light, the two bony women next, supporting between them the small and supple one. Thus they entered the house and disappeared.

---

5. A cluster of seven stars in the constellation Taurus.

6. The cloth used to wrap a corpse as part of its preparation for burial.

XLI

Suspicion—Fanny Is Sent For

Bathsheba said very little to her husband all that evening of their return from market, and he was not disposed to say much to her. He exhibited the unpleasant combination of a restless condition with a silent tongue. The next day, which was Sunday, passed nearly in the same manner as regarded their taciturnity, Bathsheba going to church both morning and afternoon. This was the day before the Budmouth races. In the evening Troy said, suddenly—

'Bathsheba, could you let me have twenty pounds?'

Her countenance instantly sank. 'Twenty pounds?' she said.

'The fact is, I want it badly.' The anxiety upon Troy's face was unusual and very marked. It was a culmination of the mood he had been in all the day.

'Ah! for those races to-morrow.'

Troy for the moment made no reply. Her mistake had its advantages to a man who shrank from having his mind inspected as he did now. 'Well, suppose I do want it for races?' he said, at last.

'O, Frank!' Bathsheba replied, and there was such a volume of entreaty in the words. 'Only such a few weeks ago you said that I was far sweeter than all your other pleasures put together, and that you would give them all up for me; and now, won't you give up this one, which is more a worry than a pleasure? Do, Frank. Come, let me fascinate you by all I can do—by pretty words and pretty looks, and everything I can think of—to stay at home. Say yes to your wife—say yes!'

The tenderest and softest phases of Bathsheba's nature were prominent now—advanced impulsively for his acceptance, without any of the disguises and defences which the wariness of her character when she was cool too frequently threw over them. Few men could have resisted the arch yet dignified entreaty of the beautiful face, thrown a little back and sideways in the well-known attitude that expresses more than the words it accompanies, and which seems to have been designed for these special occasions. Had the woman not been his wife, Troy would have succumbed instantly; as it was, he thought he would not deceive her longer.

'The money is not wanted for racing debts at all,' he said.

'What is it for?' she asked. 'You worry me a great deal by these mysterious responsibilities, Frank.'

Troy hesitated. He did not now love her enough to allow himself to be carried too far by her ways. Yet it was necessary to be civil. 'You wrong me by such a suspicious manner,' he said. 'Such strait-waist-coating as you treat me to is not becoming in you at so early a date.'

'I think that I have a right to grumble a little if I pay,' she said, with features between a smile and a pout.

'Exactly; and, the former being done, suppose we proceed to the latter. Bathsheba, fun is all very well, but don't go too far, or you may have cause to regret something.'

She reddened. 'I do that already,' she said quickly.

'What do you regret?'

'That my romance has come to an end.'

'All romances end at marriage.'

'I wish you wouldn't talk like that. You grieve me to my soul by being smart at my expense.'

'You are dull enough at mine. I believe you hate me.'

'Not you—only your faults. I do hate them.'

' 'Twould be much more becoming if you set yourself to cure them. Come, let's strike a balance with the twenty pounds, and be friends.'

She gave a sigh of resignation. 'I have about that sum here for household expenses. If you must have it, take it.'

'Very good. Thank you. I expect I shall have gone away before you are in to breakfast to-morrow.'

'And must you go? Ah! there was a time, Frank, when it would have taken a good many promises to other people to drag you away from me. You used to call me darling, then. But it doesn't matter to you how my days are passed now.'

'I must go, in spite of sentiment.' Troy, as he spoke, looked at his watch, and, apparently actuated by *non lucendo*[1] principles, opened the case at the back, revealing, snugly stowed within it, a small coil of hair.

Bathsheba's eyes had been accidentally lifted at that moment, and she saw the action and saw the hair. She flushed in pain and surprise, and some words escaped her before she had thought whether or not it was wise to utter them. 'A woman's curl of hair!' she said. 'O, Frank, whose is that?'

Troy had instantly closed his watch. He carelessly replied, as one who cloaked some feelings that the sight had stirred: 'Why, yours, of course. Whose should it be? I had quite forgotten that I had it.'

'What a dreadful fib, Frank!'

'I tell you I had forgotten it!' he said loudly.

'I don't mean that—it was yellow hair.'

'Nonsense.'

'That's insulting me. I know it was yellow. Now whose was it? I want to know.'

'Very well—I'll tell you, so make no more ado. It is the hair of a young woman I was going to marry before I knew you.'

'You ought to tell me her name, then.'

---

1. The Latin phrase *lucus a non lucendo* is a proverbial example of illogicality, by which someone would deduce that the word *lucus*, meaning "grove," came from the words *non lucendo*, meaning "not shining," because a grove does not shine.

'I cannot do that.'

'Is she married yet?'

'No.'

'Is she alive?'

'Yes.'

'Is she pretty?'

'Yes.'

'It is wonderful how she can be, poor thing, under such an awful affliction!'

'Affliction—what affliction?' he inquired quickly.

'Having hair of that dreadful colour.'

'Oh—ho—I like that!' said Troy, recovering himself. 'Why, her hair has been admired by everybody who has seen her since she has worn it loose, which has not been long. It is beautiful hair. People used to turn their heads to look at it, poor girl!'

'Pooh! that's nothing—that's nothing!' she exclaimed, in incipient accents of pique. 'If I cared for your love as much as I used to I could say people had turned to look at mine.'

'Bathsheba, don't be so fitful and jealous. You knew what married life would be like, and shouldn't have entered it if you feared these contingencies.'

Troy had by this time driven her to bitterness: her heart was big in her throat, and the ducts to her eyes were painfully full. Ashamed as she was to show emotion, at last she burst out:—

'This is all I get for loving you so well! Ah! when I married you your life was dearer to me than my own. I would have died for you—how truly I can say that I would have died for you! And now you sneer at my foolishness in marrying you. O! is it kind to me to throw my mistake in my face? Whatever opinion you may have of my wisdom, you should not tell me of it so mercilessly, now that I am in your power.'

'I can't help how things fall out,' said Troy; 'upon my heart, women will be the death of me!'

'Well, you shouldn't keep people's hair. You'll burn it, won't you, Frank?'

Frank went on as if he had not heard her. 'There are considerations even before my consideration for you; reparations to be made—ties you know nothing of. If you repent of marrying, so do I.'

Trembling now, she put her hand upon his arm, saying, in mingled tones of wretchedness and coaxing, 'I only repent it if you don't love me better than any woman in the world! I don't otherwise, Frank. You don't repent because you already love somebody better than you love me, do you?'

'I don't know. Why do you say that?'

'You won't burn that curl. You like the woman who owns that pretty hair—yes; it is pretty—more beautiful than my miserable black mane! Well, it is no use; I can't help being ugly. You must like her best, if you will!'

'Until to-day, when I took it from a drawer, I have never looked upon that bit of hair for several months—that I am ready to swear.'

'But just now you said "ties"; and then—that woman we met?'

"Twas the meeting with her that reminded me of the hair.'

'Is it hers, then?'

'Yes. There, now that you have wormed it out of me, I hope you are content.'

'And what are the ties?'

'Oh! that meant nothing—a mere jest.'

'A mere jest!' she said, in mournful astonishment. 'Can you jest when I am so wretchedly in earnest? Tell me the truth, Frank. I am not a fool, you know, although I am a woman, and have my woman's moments. Come! treat me fairly,' she said, looking honestly and fearlessly into his face. 'I don't want much; bare justice—that's all! Ah! once I felt I could be content with nothing less than the highest homage from the husband I should choose. Now, anything short of cruelty will content me. Yes! the independent and spirited Bathsheba is come to this!'

'For Heaven's sake don't be so desperate!' Troy said snappishly, rising as he did so, and leaving the room.

Directly he had gone, Bathsheba burst into great sobs—dry-eyed sobs, which cut as they came, without any softening by tears. But she determined to repress all evidences of feeling. She was conquered; but she would never own it as long as she lived. Her pride was indeed brought low by despairing discoveries of her spoliation by marriage with a less pure nature than her own. She chafed to and fro in rebelliousness, like a caged leopard; her whole soul was in arms, and the blood fired her face. Until she had met Troy, Bathsheba had been proud of her position as a woman; it had been a glory to her to know that her lips had been touched by no man's on earth—that her waist had never been encircled by a lover's arm. She hated herself now. In those earlier days she had always nourished a secret contempt for girls who were the slaves of the first good-looking young fellow who should choose to salute them. She had never taken kindly to the idea of marriage in the abstract as did the majority of women she saw about her. In the turmoil of her anxiety for her lover she had agreed to marry him; but the perception that had accompanied her happiest hours on this account was rather that of self-sacrifice than of promotion and honour. Although she scarcely knew the divinity's name, Diana[2] was the goddess whom Bathsheba instinctively adored. That she had never, by look, word, or sign, encouraged a man to approach her—

2. The Roman goddess of chastity.

that she had felt herself sufficient to herself, and had in the independence of her girlish heart fancied there was a certain degradation in
renouncing the simplicity of a maiden existence to become the humbler half of an indifferent matrimonial whole—were facts now bitterly
remembered. O, if she had never stooped to folly of this kind, respectable as it was, and could only stand again, as she had stood on the hill
at Norcombe, and dare Troy or any other man to pollute a hair of her
head by his interference!

The next morning she rose earlier than usual, and had the horse
saddled for her ride round the farm in the customary way. When she
came in at half-past eight—their usual hour for breakfasting—she was
informed that her husband had risen, taken his breakfast, and driven
off to Casterbridge with the gig and Poppet.

After breakfast she was cool and collected—quite herself in fact—
and she rambled to the gate, intending to walk to another quarter of
the farm, which she still personally superintended as well as her duties
in the house would permit, continually, however, finding herself
preceded in forethought by Gabriel Oak, for whom she began to
entertain the genuine friendship of a sister. Of course, she sometimes
thought of him in the light of an old lover, and had momentary
imaginings of what life with him as a husband would have been like;
also of life with Boldwood under the same conditions. But Bathsheba,
though she could feel, was not much given to futile dreaming, and her
musings under this head were short and entirely confined to the times
when Troy's neglect was more than ordinarily evident.

She saw coming up the road a man like Mr. Boldwood. It was Mr.
Boldwood. Bathsheba blushed painfully, and watched. The farmer
stopped when still a long way off, and held up his hand to Gabriel Oak,
who was in a footpath across the field. The two men then approached
each other and seemed to engage in earnest conversation.

Thus they continued for a long time. Joseph Poorgrass now passed
near them, wheeling a barrow of apples up the hill to Bathsheba's
residence. Boldwood and Gabriel called to him, spoke to him for a few
minutes, and then all three parted, Joseph immediately coming up the
hill with his barrow.

Bathsheba, who had seen this pantomime with some surprise,
experienced great relief when Boldwood turned back again. 'Well,
what's the message, Joseph?' she said.

He set down his barrow, and, putting upon himself the refined
aspect that a conversation with a lady required, spoke to Bathsheba,
over the gate.

'You'll never see Fanny Robin no more—use nor principal[3]—
ma'am.'

'Why?'

3. In monetary terms, "principal" is a sum of invested money and "use" is the interest it gains; here
the phrase is used as the equivalent of "neither hide nor hair."

'Because she's dead in the Union.'

'Fanny dead—never!'

'Yes, ma'am.'

'What did she die from?'

'I don't know for certain; but I should be inclined to think it was from general neshness[4] of constitution. She was such a limber[5] maid that 'a could stand no hardship, even when I knowed her, and 'a went like a candle-snoff, so 'tis said. She was took bad in the morning, and, being quite feeble and worn out, she died in the evening. She belongs by law to our parish; and Mr. Boldwood is going to send a waggon at three this afternoon to fetch her home here and bury her.'

'Indeed I shall not let Mr. Boldwood do any such thing—I shall do it! Fanny was my uncle's servant, and, although I only knew her for a couple of days, she belongs to me. How very, very sad this is!—the idea of Fanny being in a workhouse.' Bathsheba had begun to know what suffering was, and she spoke with real feeling. . . . 'Send across to Mr. Boldwood's, and say that Mrs. Troy will take upon herself the duty of fetching an old servant of the family. . . . We ought not to put her in a waggon; we'll get a hearse.'

'There will hardly be time, ma'am, will there?'

'Perhaps not,' she said, musingly. 'When did you say we must be at the door—three o'clock?'

'Three o'clock this afternoon, ma'am, so to speak it.'

'Very well—you go with it. A pretty waggon is better than an ugly hearse, after all. Joseph, have the new spring waggon with the blue body and red wheels, and wash it very clean. And, Joseph——'

'Yes, ma'am.'

'Carry with you some evergreens and flowers to put upon her coffin—indeed, gather a great many, and completely bury her in them. Get some boughs of laurustinus, and variegated box, and yew, and boy's-love;[6] ay, and some bunches of chrysanthemum. And let old Pleasant draw her, because she knew him so well.'

'I will, ma'am. I ought to have said that the Union, in the form of four labouring men, will meet me when I gets to our churchyard gate, and take her and bury her according to the rites of the Board of Guardians,[7] as by law ordained.'

'Dear me—Casterbridge Union—and is Fanny come to this?' said Bathsheba, musing. 'I wish I had known of it sooner. I thought she was far away. How long has she lived there?'

'On'y been there a day or two.'

'Oh!—then she has not been staying there as a regular inmate?'

'No. She first went to live in a garrison-town t'other side o' Wessex,

---

4. Weakness or delicacy (dialect).
5. Frail or slight (dialect).
6. "Laurustinus," "box," and "yew" are all evergreens; "boy's-love" is a colloquial name for southernwood, a plant with fine, aromatic leaves.
7. Overseers of the Casterbridge Union; for further information on the Union, see chapter 30, footnote 3.

and since then she's been picking up a living at seampstering in
Melchester for several months, at the house of a very respectable
widow-woman who takes in work of that sort. She only got handy the
Union-house on Sunday morning 'a b'lieve, and 'tis supposed here
and there that she had traipsed every step of the way from Melchester.
Why she left her place I can't say, for I don't know; and as to a lie, why,
I wouldn't tell it. That's the short of the story, ma'am.'

'Ah-h!'

No gem ever flashed from a rosy ray to a white one more rapidly
than changed the young wife's countenance whilst this word came
from her in a long-drawn breath. 'Did she walk along our turnpike-
road?' she said, in a suddenly restless and eager voice.

'I believe she did. . . . Ma'am, shall I call Liddy? You bain't well,
ma'am, surely? You look like a lily—so pale and fainty!'

'No; don't call her; it is nothing. When did she pass Weatherbury?'

'Last Saturday night.'

'That will do, Joseph; now you may go.'

'Certainly, ma'am.'

'Joseph, come hither a moment. What was the colour of Fanny
Robin's hair?'

'Really, mistress, now that 'tis put to me so judge-and-jury like, I
can't call to mind, if ye'll believe me!'

'Never mind; go on and do what I told you. Stop—well no, go on.'

She turned herself away from him, that he might no longer notice
the mood which had set its sign so visibly upon her, and went indoors
with a distressing sense of faintness and a beating brow. About an hour
after, she heard the noise of the waggon and went out, still with a
painful consciousness of her bewildered and troubled look. Joseph,
dressed in his best suit of clothes, was putting in the horse to start. The
shrubs and flowers were all piled in the waggon, as she had directed.
Bathsheba hardly saw them now.

'Whose sweetheart did you say, Joseph?'

'I don't know, ma'am.'

'Are you quite sure?'

'Yes, ma'am, quite sure.'

'Sure of what?'

'I'm sure that all I know is that she arrived in the morning and died
in the evening without further parley. What Oak and Mr. Boldwood
told me was only these few words. "Little Fanny Robin is dead,
Joseph," Gabriel said, looking in my face in his steady old way. I was
very sorry, and I said, "Ah!—and how did she come to die?" "Well,
she's dead in Casterbridge Union," he said; "and perhaps 'tisn't much
matter about how she came to die. She reached the Union early
Sunday morning, and died in the afternoon—that's clear enough."
Then I asked what she'd been doing lately, and Mr. Boldwood turned
round to me then, and left off spitting a thistle with the end of his stick.
He told me about her having lived by seampstering in Melchester, as I

mentioned to you, and that she walked therefrom at the end of last week, passing near here Saturday night in the dusk. They then said I had better just name a hent[8] of her death to you, and away they went. Her death might have been brought on by biding in the night wind, you know, ma'am; for people used to say she'd go off in a decline: she used to cough a good deal in winter time. However, 'tisn't much odds to us about that now, for 'tis all over.'

'Have you heard a different story at all?' She looked at him so intently that Joseph's eyes quailed.

'Not a word, mistress, I assure 'ee!' he said. 'Hardly anybody in the parish knows the news yet.'

'I wonder why Gabriel didn't bring the message to me himself. He mostly makes a point of seeing me upon the most trifling errand.' These words were merely murmured, and she was looking upon the ground.

'Perhaps he was busy, ma'am,' Joseph suggested. 'And sometimes he seems to suffer from things upon his mind, connected with the time when he was better off than 'a is now. 'A's rather a curious item, but a very understanding shepherd, and learned in books.'

'Did anything seem upon his mind whilst he was speaking to you about this?'

'I cannot but say that there did, ma'am. He was terrible down, and so was Farmer Boldwood.'

'Thank you, Joseph. That will do. Go on now, or you'll be late.'

Bathsheba, still unhappy, went indoors again. In the course of the afternoon she said to Liddy, who had been informed of the occurrence, 'What was the colour of poor Fanny Robin's hair? Do you know? I cannot recollect—I only saw her for a day or two.'

'It was light, ma'am; but she wore it rather short, and packed away under her cap, so that you would hardly notice it. But I have seen her let it down when she was going to bed, and it looked beautiful then. Real golden hair.'

'Her young man was a soldier, was he not?'

'Yes. In the same regiment as Mr. Troy. He says he knew him very well.'

'What, Mr. Troy says so? How came he to say that?'

'One day I just named it to him, and asked him if he knew Fanny's young man. He said, "O yes, he knew the young man as well as he knew himself, and that there wasn't a man in the regiment he liked better."'

'Ah! Said that, did he?'

'Yes; and he said there was a strong likeness between himself and the other young man, so that sometimes people mistook them——'

'Liddy, for Heaven's sake stop your talking!' said Bathsheba, with the nervous petulance that comes from worrying perceptions.

---

8. Hint (dialect).

XLII

Joseph and His Burden—Buck's Head

A wall bounded the site of Casterbridge Union-house, except along a portion of the end. Here a high gable stood prominent, and it was covered like the front with a mat of ivy. In this gable was no window, chimney, ornament, or protuberance of any kind. The single feature appertaining to it, beyond the expanse of dark green leaves, was a small door.

The situation of the door was peculiar. The sill was three or four feet above the ground, and for a moment one was at a loss for an explanation of this exceptional altitude, till ruts immediately beneath suggested that the door was used solely for the passage of articles and persons to and from the level of a vehicle standing on the outside. Upon the whole, the door seemed to advertise itself as a species of Traitor's Gate[1] translated to another sphere. That entry and exit hereby was only at rare intervals became apparent on noting that tufts of grass were allowed to flourish undisturbed in the chinks of the sill.

As the clock over the South-street Alms-house pointed to five minutes to three, a blue spring waggon, picked out with red, and containing boughs and flowers, passed the end of the street, and up towards this side of the building. Whilst the chimes were yet stammering out a shattered form of 'Malbrook,'[2] Joseph Poorgrass rang the bell, and received directions to back his waggon against the high door under the gable. The door then opened, and a plain elm coffin was slowly thrust forth, and laid by two men in fustian[3] along the middle of the vehicle.

One of the men then stepped up beside it, took from his pocket a lump of chalk, and wrote upon the cover the name and a few other words in a large scrawling hand. (We believe that they do these things more tenderly now, and provide a plate.) He covered the whole with a black cloth, threadbare, but decent, the tail-board of the waggon was returned to its place, one of the men handed a certificate of registry to Poorgrass, and both entered the door, closing it behind them. Their connection with her, short as it had been, was over for ever.

Joseph then placed the flowers as enjoined, and the evergreens around the flowers, till it was difficult to divine what the waggon contained; he smacked his whip, and the rather pleasing funeral car crept down the hill, and along the road to Weatherbury.

The afternoon drew on apace, and, looking to the right towards the

---

1. A passageway from the Thames through which traitors and other state prisoners were led to the Tower of London.
2. A French lullaby beginning, "*Malbrouk, s'en va-t-en guerre*"; its tune resembles that of

"For He's a Jolly Good Fellow."
3. A sturdy, coarse cotton fabric, sometimes combined with low-grade wool, twill woven, having a short nap, and usually dyed a dark color.

sea as he walked beside the horse, Poorgrass saw strange clouds and scrolls of mist rolling over the long ridges which girt the landscape in that quarter. They came in yet greater volumes, and indolently crept across the intervening valleys, and around the withered papery flags of the moor and river brinks. Then their dank spongy forms closed in upon the sky. It was a sudden overgrowth of atmospheric fungi which had their roots in the neighbouring sea, and by the time that horse, man, and corpse entered Yalbury Great Wood, these silent workings of an invisible hand had reached them, and they were completely enveloped, this being the first arrival of the autumn fogs, and the first fog of the series.

The air was as an eye suddenly struck blind. The waggon and its load rolled no longer on the horizontal division between clearness and opacity, but were imbedded in an elastic body of a monotonous pallor throughout. There was no perceptible motion in the air, not a visible drop of water fell upon a leaf of the beeches, birches, and firs composing the wood on either side. The trees stood in an attitude of intentness, as if they waited longingly for a wind to come and rock them. A startling quiet overhung all surrounding things—so completely, that the crunching of the waggon-wheels was as a great noise, and small rustles, which had never obtained a hearing except by night, were distinctly individualized.

Joseph Poorgrass looked round upon his sad burden as it loomed faintly through the flowering laurustinus, then at the unfathomable gloom amid the high trees on each hand, indistinct, shadowless, and spectre-like in their monochrome of grey. He felt anything but cheerful, and wished he had the company even of a child or dog. Stopping the horse he listened. Not a footstep or wheel was audible anywhere around, and the dead silence was broken only by a heavy particle falling from a tree through the evergreens and alighting with a smart rap upon the coffin of poor Fanny. The fog had by this time saturated the trees, and this was the first dropping of water from the over-brimming leaves. The hollow echo of its fall reminded the waggoner painfully of the grim Leveller. Then hard by came down another drop, then two or three. Presently there was a continual tapping of these heavy drops upon the dead leaves, the road, and the travellers. The nearer boughs were beaded with the mist to the greyness of aged men, and the rusty-red leaves of the beeches were hung with similar drops, like diamonds on auburn hair.

At the roadside hamlet called Roy-Town,[4] just beyond this wood, was the old inn Buck's Head. It was about a mile and a half from Weatherbury, and in the meridian times of stage-coach travelling had been the place where many coaches changed and kept their relays of horses. All the old stabling was now pulled down, and little remained

4. Hardy's name for Troy Town, a small village formerly on the road between Dorchester and Puddletown.

besides the habitable inn itself, which, standing a little way back from the road, signified its existence to people far up and down the highway by a sign hanging from the horizontal bough of an elm on the opposite side of the way.

Travellers—for the variety *tourist* had hardly developed into a distinct species at this date—sometimes said in passing, when they cast their eyes up to the sign-bearing tree, that artists were fond of representing the signboard hanging thus, but that they themselves had never before noticed so perfect an instance in actual working order. It was near this tree that the waggon was standing into which Gabriel Oak crept on his first journey to Weatherbury; but, owing to the darkness, the sign and the inn had been unobserved.

The manners of the inn were of the old-established type. Indeed, in the minds of its frequenters they existed as unalterable formulæ: *e.g.*—

Rap with the bottom of your pint for more liquor.
For tobacco, shout.
In calling for the girl in waiting, say, 'Maid!'
Ditto for the landlady, 'Old Soul!' etc., etc.

It was a relief to Joseph's heart when the friendly signboard came in view, and, stopping his horse immediately beneath it, he proceeded to fulfil an intention made a long time before. His spirits were oozing out of him quite. He turned the horse's head to the green bank, and entered the hostel for a mug of ale.

Going down into the kitchen of the inn, the floor of which was a step below the passage, which in its turn was a step below the road outside, what should Joseph see to gladden his eyes but two copper-coloured discs, in the form of the countenances of Mr. Jan Coggan and Mr. Mark Clark. These owners of the two most appreciative throats in the neighbourhood, within the pale of respectability, were now sitting face to face over a three-legged circular table, having an iron rim to keep cups and pots from being accidentally elbowed off; they might have been said to resemble the setting sun and the full moon shining *vis-à-vis* across the globe.

'Why, 'tis neighbour Poorgrass!' said Mark Clark. 'I'm sure your face don't praise your mistress's table, Joseph.'

'I've had a very pale companion for the last four miles,' said Joseph, indulging in a shudder toned down by resignation. 'And to speak the truth, 'twas beginning to tell upon me. I assure ye, I ha'n't seed the colour of victuals or drink since breakfast time this morning, and that was no more than a dew-bit[5] afield.'

'Then drink, Joseph, and don't restrain yourself!' said Coggan, handing him a hooped mug three-quarters full.

Joseph drank for a moderately long time, then for a longer time,

5. A light early-morning refreshment taken before breakfast (dialect).

saying, as he lowered the jug, ' 'Tis pretty drinking—very pretty drinking, and is more than cheerful on my melancholy errand, so to speak it.'

'True, drink is a pleasant delight,' said Jan, as one who repeated a truism so familiar to his brain that he hardly noticed its passage over his tongue; and, lifting the cup, Coggan tilted his head gradually backwards, with closed eyes, that his expectant soul might not be diverted for one instant from its bliss by irrelevant surroundings.

"Well, I must be on again,' said Poorgrass. 'Not but that I should like another nip with ye; but the parish might lose confidence in me if I was seed here.'

'Where be ye trading o't⁶ to to-day, then, Joseph?'

'Back to Weatherbury. I've got poor little Fanny Robin in my waggon outside, and I must be at the churchyard gates at a quarter to five with her.'

'Ay—I've heard of it. And so she's nailed up in parish boards⁷ after all, and nobody to pay the bell shilling and the grave half-crown.'⁸

'The parish pays the grave half-crown, but not the bell shilling, because the bell's a luxery: but 'a can hardly do without the grave, poor body. However, I expect our mistress will pay all.'

'A pretty maid as ever I see! But what's yer hurry, Joseph? The poor woman's dead, and you can't bring her to life, and you may as well sit down comfortable, and finish another with us.'

'I don't mind taking just the least thimbleful ye can dream of more with ye, sonnies. But only a few minutes, because 'tis as 'tis.'

'Of course, you'll have another drop. A man's twice the man afterwards. You feel so warm and glorious, and you whop and slap⁹ at your work without any trouble, and everything goes on like sticks a-breaking. Too much liquor is bad, and leads us to that horned man in the smoky house; but after all, many people haven't the gift of enjoying a wet,¹ and since we be highly favoured with a power that way, we should make the most o't.'

'True,' said Mark Clark. ' 'Tis a talent the Lord has mercifully bestowed upon us, and we ought not to neglect it. But, what with the parsons and clerks and school-people and serious tea-parties, the merry old ways of good life have gone to the dogs—upon my carcase, they have!'

'Well, really, I must be onward again now,' said Joseph.

'Now, now, Joseph; nonsense! The poor woman is dead, isn't she, and what's your hurry?'

'Well, I hope Providence won't be in a way with me for my doings,' said Joseph, again sitting down. 'I've been troubled with weak mo-

6. Going (dialect).
7. A cheap board coffin supplied by the parish for a pauper's burial.
8. The shilling required to have the church bell rung at the funeral and the half-crown cost of having a pauper's grave dug.
9. Tackle energetically (dialect).
1. Drink (dialect).

ments lately, 'tis true. I've been drinky once this month already, and I did not go to church a-Sunday, and I dropped a curse or two yesterday; so I don't want to go too far for my safety. Your next world is your next world, and not to be squandered offhand.'

'I believe ye to be a chapel-member,[2] Joseph. That I do.'

'Oh, no, no! I don't go so far as that.'

'For my part,' said Coggan, 'I'm staunch Church of England.'

'Ay, and faith, so be I,' said Mark Clark.

'I won't say much for myself; I don't wish to,' Coggan continued, with that tendency to talk on principles which is characteristic of the barley-corn. 'But I've never changed a single doctrine: I've stuck like a plaster to the old faith I was born in. Yes; there's this to be said for the Church, a man can belong to the Church and bide in his cheerful old inn, and never trouble or worry his mind about doctrines at all. But to be a meetinger, you must go to chapel in all winds and weathers, and make yerself as frantic as a skit.[3] Not but that chapel-members be clever chaps enough in their way. They can lift up beautiful prayers out of their own heads, all about their families and shipwracks in the newspaper.'

'They can—they can,' said Mark Clark, with corroborative feeling; 'but we Churchmen, you see, must have it all printed aforehand, or, dang it all, we should no more know what to say to a great gaffer[4] like the Lord than babes unborn.'

'Chapel-folk be more hand-in-glove with them above than we,' said Joseph thoughtfully.

'Yes,' said Coggan. 'We know very well that if anybody do go to heaven, they will. They've worked hard for it, and they deserve to have it, such as 'tis. I bain't such a fool as to pretend that we who stick to the Church have the same chance as they, because we know we have not. But I hate a feller who'll change his old ancient doctrines for the sake of getting to heaven. I'd as soon turn king's-evidence[5] for the few pounds you get. Why, neighbours, when every one of my taties[6] were frosted, our Pa'son Thirdly were the man who gave me a sack for seed, though he hardly had one for his own use, and no money to buy 'em. If it hadn't been for him, I shouldn't hae had a tatie to put in my garden. D'ye think I'd turn after that? No, I'll stick to my side; and if we be in the wrong, so be it: I'll fall with the fallen!'

'Well said—very well said,' observed Joseph.—'However, folks, I must be moving now: upon my life I must. Pa'son Thirdly will be waiting at the church gates, and there's the woman a-biding outside in the waggon.'

'Joseph Poorgrass, don't be so miserable! Pa'son Thirdly won't

---

2. A member of a dissenting sect, like a Methodist, as opposed to a member of the established Church of England.
3. A restive young horse (dialect).
4. An old fellow, an overseer.

5. Evidence at a Crown trial given by an accused person against an accomplice, usually to secure a reward.
6. Potatoes (dialect).

mind. He's a generous man; he's found me in tracts[7] for years, and I've consumed a good many in the course of a long and shady life; but he's never been the man to cry out at the expense. Sit down.'

The longer Joseph Poorgrass remained, the less his spirit was troubled by the duties which devolved upon him this afternoon. The minutes glided by uncounted, until the evening shades began perceptibly to deepen, and the eyes of the three were but sparkling points on the surface of darkness. Coggan's repeater struck six from his pocket in the usual still small tones.

At that moment hasty steps were heard in the entry, and the door opened to admit the figure of Gabriel Oak, followed by the maid of the inn bearing a candle. He stared sternly at the one lengthy and two round faces of the sitters, which confronted him with the expressions of a fiddle and a couple of warming-pans. Joseph Poorgrass blinked, and shrank several inches into the background.

'Upon my soul, I'm ashamed of you; 'tis disgraceful, Joseph, disgraceful!' said Gabriel indignantly. 'Coggan, you call yourself a man, and don't know better than this.'

Coggan looked up indefinitely at Oak, one or other of his eyes occasionally opening and closing of its own accord, as if it were not a member, but a dozy individual with a distinct personality.

'Don't take on so, shepherd!' said Mark Clark, looking reproachfully at the candle, which appeared to possess special features of interest for his eyes.

'Nobody can hurt a dead woman,' at length said Coggan, with the precision of a machine. 'All that could be done for her is done—she's beyond us: and why should a man put himself in a tearing hurry for lifeless clay that can neither feel nor see, and don't know what you do with her at all? If she'd been alive, I would have been the first to help her. If she now wanted victuals and drink, I'd pay for it, money down. But she's dead, and no speed of ours will bring her to life. The woman's past us—time spent upon her is throwed away: why should we hurry to do what's not required? Drink, shepherd, and be friends, for to-morrow we may be like her.'

'We may,' added Mark Clark emphatically, at once drinking himself, to run no further risk of losing his chance by the event alluded to, Jan meanwhile merging his additional thoughts of to-morrow in a song:—

> 'To-mor-row, to-mor-row!
> And while peace and plen-ty I find at my board,
> With a heart free from sick-ness and sor-row,
> With my friends will I share what to-day may af-ford,
> And let them spread the ta-ble to-mor-row.
> To-mor-row, to-mor——'

7. "He's supplied me with pamphlets on religious subjects"; "found . . . in" in the sense of "supplied . . . with" is dialectal.

'Do hold thy horning,[8] Jan!' said Oak; and turning upon Poorgrass, 'as for you, Joseph, who do your wicked deeds in such confoundedly holy ways, you are as drunk as you can stand.'

'No, Shepherd Oak, no! Listen to reason, shepherd. All that's the matter with me is the affliction called a multiplying eye, and that's how it is I look double to you—I mean, you look double to me.'

'A multiplying eye is a very bad thing,' said Mark Clark.

'It always comes on when I have been in a public-house a little time,' said Joseph Poorgrass meekly. 'Yes; I see two of every sort, as if I were some holy man living in the times of King Noah and entering into the ark. . . . Y-y-y-yes,' he added, becoming much affected by the picture of himself as a person thrown away, and shedding tears; 'I feel too good for England: I ought to have lived in Genesis by rights, like the other men of sacrifice, and then I shouldn't have b-b-been called a d-d-drunkard in such a way!'

'I wish you'd show yourself a man of spirit, and not sit whining there!'

'Show myself a man of spirit? . . . Ah, well! let me take the name of drunkard humbly—let me be a man of contrite knees—let it be! I know that I always do say "Please God" afore I do anything, from my getting up to my going down of the same, and I be willing to take as much disgrace as there is in that holy act. Hah, yes! . . . But not a man of spirit? Have I ever allowed the toe of pride to be lifted against my hinder parts without groaning manfully that I question the right to do so? I inquire that query boldly?'

'We can't say that you have, Hero Poorgrass,' admitted Jan.

'Never have I allowed such treatment to pass unquestioned! Yet the shephered says in the face of that rich testimony that I be not a man of spirit! Well, let it pass by, and death is a kind friend!'

Gabriel, seeing that neither of the three was in a fit state to take charge of the waggon for the remainder of the journey, made no reply, but, closing the door again upon them, went across to where the vehicle stood, now getting indistinct in the fog and gloom of his mildewy time. He pulled the horse's head from the large patch of turf it had eaten bare, readjusted the boughs over the coffin, and drove along through the unwholesome night.

It had gradually become rumoured in the village that the body to be brought and buried that day was all that was left of the unfortunate Fanny Robin who had followed the Eleventh from Casterbridge through Melchester and onwards. But, thanks to Boldwood's reticence and Oak's generosity, the lover she had followed had never been individualized as Troy. Gabriel hoped that the whole truth of the matter might not be published till at any rate the girl had been in her grave for a few days, when the interposing barriers of earth and time,

---

8. Trumpeting, bellowing (dialect).

and a sense that the events had been somewhat shut into oblivion, would deaden the sting that revelation and invidious remark would have for Bathsheba just now.

By the time that Gabriel reached the old manor-house, her residence, which lay in his way to the church, it was quite dark. A man came from the gate and said through the fog, which hung between them like blown flour—

'Is that Poorgrass with the corpse?'

Gabriel recognized the voice as that of the parson.

'The corpse is here, sir,' said Gabriel.

'I have just been to inquire of Mrs. Troy if she could tell me the reason of the delay. I am afraid it is too late now for the funeral to be performed with proper decency. Have you the registrar's certificate?'

'No,' said Gabriel. 'I expect Poorgrass has that; and he's at the Buck's Head. I forgot to ask him for it.'

'Then that settles the matter. We'll put of the funeral till to-morrow morning. The body may be brought on to the church, or it may be left here at the farm and fetched by the bearers in the morning. They waited more than an hour, and have now gone home.'

Gabriel had his reasons for thinking the latter a most objectionable plan, notwithstanding that Fanny had been an inmate of the farm-house for several years in the lifetime of Bathsheba's uncle. Visions of several unhappy contingencies which might arise from this delay flitted before him. But his will was not law, and he went indoors to inquire of his mistress what were her wishes on the subject. He found her in an unusual mood: her eyes as she looked up to him were suspicious and perplexed as with some antecedent thought. Troy had not yet returned. At first Bathsheba assented with a mien of indifference to his proposition that they should go on to the church at once with their burden; but immediately afterwards, following Gabriel to the gate, she swerved to the extreme of solicitousness on Fanny's account, and desired that the girl might be brought into the house. Oak argued upon the convenience of leaving her in the waggon, just as she lay now, with her flowers and green leaves about her, merely wheeling the vehicle into the coach-house till the morning, but to no purpose. 'It is unkind and unchristian,' she said, 'to leave the poor thing in a coach-house all night.'

'Very well, then,' said the parson. 'And I will arrange that the funeral shall take place early to-morrow. Perhaps Mrs. Troy is right in feeling that we cannot treat a dead fellow-creature too thoughtfully. We must remember that though she may have erred grievously in leaving her home, she is still our sister; and it is to be believed that God's uncovenanted mercies are extended towards her, and that she is a member of the flock of Christ.'

The parson's words spread into the heavy air with a sad yet unperturbed cadence, and Gabriel shed an honest tear. Bathsheba seemed unmoved. Mr. Thirdly then left them, and Gabriel lighted a lantern. Fetching three other men to assist him, they bore the unconscious truant indoors, placing the coffin on two benches in the middle of a little sitting-room next the hall, as Bathsheba directed.

Every one except Gabriel Oak then left the room. He still indecisively lingered beside the body. He was deeply troubled at the wretchedly ironical aspect that circumstances were putting on with regard to Troy's wife, and at his own powerlessness to counteract them. In spite of his careful manœuvring all this day, the very worse event that could in any way have happened in connection with the burial had happened now. Oak imagined a terrible discovery resulting from this afternoon's work that might cast over Bathsheba's life a shade which the interposition of many lapsing years might but indifferently lighten, and which nothing at all might altogether remove.

Suddenly, as in a last attempt to save Bathsheba from, at any rate, immediate anguish, he looked again, as he had looked before, at the chalk writing upon the coffin-lid. The scrawl was this simple one, '*Fanny Robin and child.*' Gabriel took his handkerchief and carefully rubbed out the two latter words, leaving visible the inscription '*Fanny Robin*' only. He then left the room, and went out quietly by the front door.

XLIII

Fanny's Revenge

'Do you want me any longer, ma'am?' inquired Liddy, at a later hour the same evening, standing by the door with a chamber candlestick in her hand, and addressing Bathsheba, who sat cheerless and alone in the large parlour beside the first fire of the season.

'No more to-night, Liddy.'

'I'll sit up for master if you like, ma'am. I am not at all afraid of Fanny, if I may sit in my own room and have a candle. She was such a childlike, nesh young thing that her spirit couldn't appear to anybody if it tried, I'm quite sure.'

'O no, no! You go to bed. I'll sit for him myself till twelve o'clock, and if he has not arrived by that time, I shall give him up and go to bed too.'

'It is half-past ten now.'

'Oh: is it?'

'Why don't you sit upstairs, ma'am?'

'Why don't I?' said Bathsheba desultorily. 'It isn't worth while—there's a fire here. Liddy,' she suddenly exclaimed in an impulsive and excited whisper, 'Have you heard anything strange said of Fanny?' The words had no sooner escaped her than an expression of unutterable regret crossed her face, and she burst into tears.

'No—not a word!' said Liddy, looking at the weeping woman with astonishment. 'What is it makes you cry so, ma'am; has anything hurt you?' She came to Bathsheba's side with a face full of sympathy.

'No, Liddy—I don't want you any more. I can hardly say why I have taken so to crying lately: I never used to cry. Good-night.'

Liddy then left the parlour and closed the door.

Bathsheba was lonely and miserable now; not lonelier actually than she had been before her marriage; but her loneliness then was to that of the present time as the solitude of a mountain is to the solitude of a cave. And within the last day or two had come these disquieting thoughts about her husband's past. Her wayward sentiment that evening concerning Fanny's temporary resting-place had been the result of a strange complication of impulses in Bathsheba's bosom. Perhaps it would be more accurately described as a determined rebellion against her prejudices, a revulsion from a lower instinct of uncharitableness, which would have withheld all sympathy from the dead woman, because in life she had preceded Bathsheba in the attentions of a man whom Bathsheba had by no means ceased from loving, though her love was sick to death just now with the gravity of a further misgiving.

In five or ten minutes there was another tap at the door. Liddy reappeared, and coming in a little way stood hesitating, until at length she said, 'Maryann has just heard something very strange, but I know it isn't true. And we shall be sure to know the rights of it in a day or two.'

'What is it?'

'Oh, nothing connected with you or us, ma'am: It is about Fanny. That same thing you have heard.'

'I have heard nothing.'

'I mean that a wicked story is got to Weatherbury within this last hour—that——' Liddy came close to her mistress and whispered the remainder of the sentence slowly into her ear, inclining her head as she spoke in the direction of the room where Fanny lay.

Bathsheba trembled from head to foot.

'I don't believe it!' she said excitedly. 'And there's only one name written on the coffin-cover.'

'Nor I, ma'am. And a good many others don't; for we should surely have been told more about it if it had been true—don't you think so, ma'am?'

'We might or we might not.'

Bathsheba turned and looked into the fire, that Liddy might not see her face. Finding that her mistress was going to say no more, Liddy glided out, closed the door softly, and went to bed.

Bathsheba's face, as she continued looking into the fire that evening, might have excited solicitousness on her account even among those who loved her least. The sadness of Fanny Robin's fate did not make Bathsheba's glorious, although she was the Esther to this poor Vashti,[1] and their fates might be supposed to stand in some respects as contrasts to each other. When Liddy came into the room a second time the beautiful eyes which met hers had worn a listless, weary look. When she went out after telling the story they had expressed wretchedness in full activity. Her simple country nature, fed on old-fashioned principles, was troubled by that which would have troubled a woman of the world very little, both Fanny and her child, if she had one, being dead.

Bathsheba had grounds for conjecturing a connection between her own history and the dimly suspected tragedy of Fanny's end which Oak and Boldwood never for a moment credited her with possessing. The meeting with the lonely woman on the previous Saturday night had been unwitnessed and unspoken of. Oak may have had the best of intentions in withholding for as many days as possible the details of what had happened to Fanny; but had he known that Bathsheba's perceptions had already been exercised in the matter, he would have done nothing to lengthen the minutes of suspense she was now undergoing, when the certainty which must terminate it would be the worst fact suspected after all.

She suddenly felt a longing to speak to some one stronger than herself, and so get strength to sustain her surmised position with dignity and her carking[2] doubts with stoicism. Where could she find such a friend? nowhere in the house. She was by far the coolest of the women under her roof. Patience and suspension of judgment for a few hours were what she wanted to learn, and there was nobody to teach her. Might she but go to Gabriel Oak!—but that could not be. What a way Oak had, she thought, of enduring things. Boldwood, who seemed so much deeper and higher and stronger in feeling than Gabriel, had not yet learnt, any more than she herself, the simple lesson which Oak showed a mastery of by every turn and look he gave—that among the multitude of interests by which he was surrounded, those which affected his personal well-being were not the most absorbing and important in his eyes. Oak meditatively looked upon the horizon of circumstances without any special regard to his own standpoint in the midst. That was how she would wish to be. But then Oak was not racked by incertitude upon the inmost matter of his bosom, as she was at this moment. Oak knew all about Fanny that she wished to know—she felt convinced of that. If she were to go to him now at once and say no more than these few words, 'What is the truth of the story?' he would feel bound in honour to tell her. It would be an inexpressible relief. No further speech would need to be uttered. He knew her so well that no eccentricity of behaviour in her would alarm him.

1. In Esther, King Ahasuerus of Persia deposes and banishes his queen Vashti for disobeying him and marries Esther in her place.   2. Worrisome, distressing.

She flung a cloak round her, went to the door and opened it. Every blade, every twig was still. The air was yet thick with moisture, though somewhat less dense than during the afternoon, and a steady smack of drops upon the fallen leaves under the boughs was almost musical in its soothing regularity. It seemed better to be out of the house than within it, and Bathsheba closed the door, and walked slowly down the lane till she came opposite to Gabriel's cottage, where he now lived alone, having left Coggan's house through being pinched for room. There was a light in one window only, and that was downstairs. The shutters were not closed, nor was any blind or curtain drawn over the window, neither robbery nor observation being a contingency which could do much injury to the occupant of the domicile. Yes, it was Gabriel himself who was sitting up: he was reading. From her standing-place in the road she could see him plainly, sitting quite still, his light curly head upon his hand, and only occasionally looking up to snuff the candle which stood beside him. At length he looked at the clock, seemed surprised at the lateness of the hour, closed his book, and arose. He was going to bed, she knew, and if she tapped it must be done at once.

Alas for her resolve! She felt she could not do it. Not for worlds now could she give a hint about her misery to him, much less ask him plainly for information on the cause of Fanny's death. She must suspect, and guess, and chafe, and bear it all alone.

Like a homeless wanderer she lingered by the bank, as if lulled and fascinated by the atmosphere of content which seemed to spread from that little dwelling, and was so sadly lacking in her own. Gabriel appeared in an upper room, placed his light in the window-bench, and then—knelt down to pray. The contrast of the picture with her rebellious and agitated existence at this same time was too much for her to bear to look upon longer. It was not for her to make a truce with trouble by any such means. She must tread her giddy distracting measure to its last note, as she had begun it. With a swollen heart she went again up the lane, and entered her own door.

More fevered now by a reaction from the first feelings which Oak's example had raised in her, she paused in the hall, looking at the door of the room wherein Fanny lay. She locked her fingers, threw back her head, and strained her hot hands rigidly across her forehead, saying, with a hysterical sob, 'Would to God you would speak and tell me your secret, Fanny! . . . O, I hope, hope it is not true that there are two of you! . . . If I could only look in upon you for one little minute, I should know all!'

A few moments passed, and she added, slowly, '*And I will.*'

Bathsheba in after times could never gauge the mood which carried her through the actions following this murmured resolution on this memorable evening of her life. She went to the lumber-closet for a screw-driver. At the end of a short though undefined time she found

herself in the small room, quivering with emotion, a mist before her
eyes, and an excruciating pulsation in her brain, standing beside the
uncovered coffin of the girl whose conjectured end had so entirely
engrossed her, and saying to herself in a husky voice as she gazed
within—

'It was best to know the worst, and I know it now!'

She was conscious of having brought about this situation by a series
of actions done as by one in an extravagant dream; of following that
idea as to method, which had burst upon her in the hall with glaring
obviousness, by gliding to the top of the stairs, assuring herself by
listening to the heavy breathing of her maids that they were asleep,
gliding down again, turning the handle of the door within which the
young girl lay, and deliberately setting herself to do what, if she had
anticipated any such undertaking at night and alone, would have
horrified her, but which, when done, was not so dreadful as was the
conclusive proof of her husband's conduct which came with knowing
beyond doubt the last chapter of Fanny's story.

Bathsheba's head sank upon her bosom, and the breath which had
been bated in suspense, curiosity, and interest, was exhaled now in the
form of a whispered wail: 'Oh-h-h!' she said, and the silent room
added length to her moan.

Her tears fell fast beside the unconscious pair in the coffin: tears of a
complicated origin, of a nature indescribable, almost indefinable
except as other than those of simple sorrow. Assuredly their wonted
fires must have lived in Fanny's ashes when events were so shaped as to
chariot her hither in this natural, unobtrusive, yet effectual manner.
The one feat alone—that of dying—by which a mean condition could
be resolved into a grand one, Fanny had achieved. And to that had
destiny subjoined this rencounter to-night, which had, in Bathsheba's
wild imagining, turned her companion's failure to success, her
humiliation to triumph, her lucklessness to ascendency; it had thrown
over herself a garish light of mockery, and set upon all things about her
an ironical smile.

Fanny's face was framed in by that yellow hair of hers; and there was
no longer much room for doubt as to the origin of the curl owned by
Troy. In Bathsheba's heated fancy the innocent white countenance
expressed a dim triumphant consciousness of the pain she was retaliat-
ing for her pain with all the merciless rigour of the Mosaic law:
'Burning for burning; wound for wound; strife for strife.'[3]

Bathsheba indulged in contemplations of escape from her position
by immediate death, which, thought she, though it was an inconvenient and awful way, had limits to its inconvenience and awfulness
that could not be overpassed; whilst the shames of life were measureless. Yet even this scheme of extinction by death was but tamely

---

3. Hardy's version of Exodus 21:25: "Burning for burning, wound for wound, stripe for stripe."

copying her rival's method without the reasons which had glorified it in her rival's case. She glided rapidly up and down the room, as was mostly her habit when excited, her hands hanging clasped in front of her, as she thought and in part expressed in broken words: 'O, I hate her, yet I don't mean that I hate her, for it is grievous and wicked; and yet I hate her a little! Yes, my flesh insists upon hating her, whether my spirit is willing or no! . . . If she had only lived, I could have been angry and cruel towards her with some justification; but to be vindictive towards a poor dead woman recoils upon myself. O God, have mercy! I am miserable at all this!'

Bathsheba became at this moment so terrified at her own state of mind that she looked around for some sort of refuge from herself. The vision of Oak kneeling down that night recurred to her, and with the imitative instinct which animates women she seized upon the idea, resolved to kneel, and, if possible, pray. Gabriel had prayed; so would she.

She knelt beside the coffin, covered her face with her hands, and for a time the room was silent as a tomb. Whether from a purely mechanical, or from any other cause, when Bathsheba arose it was with a quieted spirit, and a regret for the antagonistic instincts which had seized upon her just before.

In her desire to make atonement she took flowers from a vase by the window, and began laying them around the dead girl's head. Bathsheba knew no other way of showing kindness to persons departed than by giving them flowers. She knew not how long she remained engaged thus. She forgot time, life, where she was, what she was doing. A slamming together of the coach-house doors in the yard brought her to herself again. An instant after, the front door opened and closed, steps crossed the hall, and her husband appeared at the entrance to the room, looking in upon her.

He beheld it all by degrees, stared in stupefaction at the scene, as if he thought it an illusion raised by some fiendish incantation. Bathsheba, pallid as a corpse on end, gazed back at him in the same wild way.

So little are instinctive guesses the fruit of a legitimate induction that, at this moment, as he stood with the door in his hand, Troy never once thought of Fanny in connection with what he saw. His first confused idea was that somebody in the house had died.

'Well—what?' said Troy blankly.

'I must go! I must go!' said Bathsheba, to herself more than to him. She came with a dilated eye towards the door, to push past him.

'What's the matter, in God's name? who's dead?' said Troy.

'I cannot say; let me go out. I want air!' she continued.

'But no; stay, I insist!' He seized her hand, and then volition seemed to leave her, and she went off into a state of passivity. He, still holding her, came up the room, and thus, hand in hand, Troy and Bathsheba approached the coffin's side.

The candle was standing on a bureau close by them, and the light slanted down, distinctly enkindling the cold features of both mother and babe. Troy looked in, dropped his wife's hand, knowledge of it all came over him in a lurid sheen, and he stood still.

So still he remained that he could be imagined to have left in him no motive power whatever. The clashes of feeling in all directions confounded one another, produced a neutrality, and there was motion in none.

'Do you know her?' said Bathsheba, in a small enclosed echo, as from the interior of a cell.

'I do,' said Troy.

'Is it she?'

'It is.'

He had originally stood erect. And now, in the well-nigh congealed immobility of his frame could be discerned an incipient movement, as in the darkest night may be discerned light after a while. He was gradually sinking forwards. The lines of his features softened, and dismay modulated to illimitable sadness. Bathsheba was regarding him from the other side, still with parted lips and distracted eyes. Capacity for intense feeling its proportionate to the general intensity of the nature, and perhaps in all Fanny's sufferings, much greater relatively to her strength, there never was a time when she suffered in an absolute sense what Bathsheba suffered now.

What Troy did was to sink upon his knees with an indefinable union of remorse and reverence upon his face, and, bending over Fanny Robin, gently kissed her, as one would kiss an infant asleep to avoid awakening it.

At the sight and sound of that, to her, unendurable act, Bathsheba sprang towards him. All the strong feelings which had been scattered over her existence since she knew what feeling was, seemed gathered together into one pulsation now. The revulsion from her indignant mood a little earlier, when she had meditated upon compromised honour, forestalment, eclipse in maternity by another, was violent and entire. All that was forgotten in the simple and still strong attachment of wife to husband. She had sighed for her self-completeness then, and now she cried aloud against the severeness of the union she had deplored. She flung her arms round Troy's neck, exclaiming wildly from the deepest deep of her heart—

'Don't—don't kiss them! O, Frank, I can't bear it—I can't! I love you better than she did: kiss me too, Frank—kiss me! *You will, Frank, kiss me too!*'

There was something so abnormal and startling in the childlike pain and simplicity of this appeal from a woman of Bathsheba's calibre and independence, that Troy, loosening her tightly clasped arms from his neck, looked at her in bewilderment. It was such an unexpected revelation of all women being alike at heart, even those so different in their accessories as Fanny and this one beside him, that Troy could hardly seem to believe her to be his proud wife Bathsheba. Fanny's own spirit seemed to be animating her frame. But this was the mood of a few instants only. When the momentary surprise had passed, his expression changed to a silencing imperious gaze.

'I will not kiss you!' he said, pushing her away.

Had the wife now but gone no further. Yet, perhaps, under the harrowing circumstances, to speak out was the one wrong act which can be better understood, if not forgiven in her, than the right and politic one, her rival being now but a corpse. All the feeling she had been betrayed into showing she drew back to herself again by a strenuous effort of self-command.

'What have you to say as your reason?' she asked, her bitter voice being strangely low—quite that of another woman now.

'I have to say that I have been a bad, black-hearted man,' he answered.

'And that this woman is your victim; and I not less than she.'

'Ah! don't taunt me, madam. This woman is more to me, dead as she is, than ever you were, or are, or can be. If Satan had not tempted me with that face of yours, and those cursed coquetries, I should have married her. I never had another thought till you came in my way. Would to God that I had; but it is all too late! I deserve to live in torment for this!' He turned to Fanny then. 'But never mind, darling,' he said; 'in the sight of Heaven you are my very, very wife!'

At these words there arose from Bathsheba's lips a long, low cry of measureless despair and indignation, such a wail of anguish as had never before been heard within those old-inhabited walls. It was the Τετελεσται[4] of her union with Troy.

'If she's—that,—what—am I?' she added, as a continuation of the same cry, and sobbing pitifully: and the rarity with her of such abandonment only made the condition more dire.

'You are nothing to me—nothing,' said Troy heartlessly. 'A ceremony before a priest doesn't make a marriage. I am not morally yours.'

A vehement impulse to flee from him, to run from this place, hide, and escape his words at any price, not stopping short of death itself, mastered Bathsheba now. She waited not an instant, but turned to the door and ran out.

XLIV

Under a Tree—Reaction

Bathsheba went along the dark road, neither knowing nor caring about the direction or issue of her flight. The first time that she definitely noticed her position was when she reached a gate leading

---

4. Greek for "it is finished"; an allusion to Christ's last words on the cross as recorded in John 19:30.

into a thicket overhung by some large oak and beech trees. On looking into the place, it occurred to her that she had seen it by daylight on some previous occasion, and that what appeared like an impassable thicket was in reality a brake of fern now withering fast. She could think of nothing better to do with her palpitating self than to go in here and hide; and entering, she lighted on a spot sheltered from the damp fog by a reclining trunk, where she sank down upon a tangled couch of fronds and stems. She mechanically pulled some armfuls round her to keep off the breezes, and closed her eyes.

Whether she slept or not that night Bathsheba was not clearly aware. But it was with a freshened existence and a cooler brain that, a long time afterwards, she became conscious of some interesting proceedings which were going on in the trees above her head and around.

A coarse-throated chatter was the first sound.

It was a sparrow just waking.

Next: 'Chee-weeze-weeze-weeze!' from another retreat.

It was a finch.

Third: 'Tink-tink-tink-tink-a-chink!' from the hedge.

It was a robin.

'Chuck-chuck-chuck!' overhead.

A squirrel.

Then, from the road, 'With my ra-ta-ta, and my rum-tum-tum!'

It was a ploughboy. Presently he came opposite, and she believed from his voice that he was one of the boys on her own farm. He was followed by a shambling tramp of heavy feet, and looking through the ferns Bathsheba could just discern in the wan light of daybreak a team of her own horses. They stopped to drink at a pond on the other side of the way. She watched them flouncing into the pool, drinking, tossing up their heads, drinking again, the water dribbling from their lips in silver threads. There was another flounce, and they came out of the pond, and turned back again towards the farm.

She looked further around. Day was just dawning, and beside its cool air and colours her heated actions and resolves of the night stood out in lurid contrast. She perceived that in her lap, and clinging to her hair, were red and yellow leaves which had come down from the tree and settled silently upon her during her partial sleep. Bathsheba shook her dress to get rid of them, when multitudes of the same family lying round about her rose and fluttered away in the breeze thus created, 'like ghosts from an enchanter fleeing.'[1]

There was an opening towards the east, and the glow from the as yet unrisen sun attracted her eyes thither. From her feet, and between the beautiful yellowing ferms with their feathery arms, the ground sloped downwards to a hollow, in which was a species of swamp, dotted with fungi. A morning mist hung over it now—a noisome yet magnificent

---

1. An allusion to the following lines from Shelley's "Ode to the West Wind": "Thou, from whose unseen presence the leaves dead / Are driven, like ghosts from an enchanter fleeing."

silvery veil, full of light from the sun, yet semi-opaque—the hedge behind it being in some measure hidden by its hazy luminousness. Up the sides of this depression grew sheaves of the common rush, and here and there a peculiar species of flag,[2] the blades of which glistened in the emerging sun, like scythes. But the general aspect of the swamp was malignant. From its moist and poisonous coat seemed to be exhaled the essences of evil things in the earth, and in the waters under the earth. The fungi grew in all manner of positions from rotting leaves and tree stumps, some exhibiting to her listless gaze their clammy tops, others their oozing gills. Some were marked with great splotches, red as arterial blood, others were saffron yellow, and others tall and attenuated, with stems like macaroni. Some were leathery and of richest browns. The hollow seemed a nursery of pestilences small and great, in the immediate neighbourhood of comfort and health, and Bathsheba arose with a tremor at the thought of having passed the night on the brink of so dismal a place.

There were now other footsteps to be heard along the road. Bathsheba's nerves were still unstrung: she crouched down out of sight again, and the pedestrian came into view. He was a schoolboy, with a bag slung over his shoulder containing his dinner, and a book in his hand. He paused by the gate, and, without looking up, continued murmuring words in tones quite loud enough to reach her ears.

' "O Lord, O Lord, O Lord, O Lord, O Lord":—that I know out o' book. "Give us, give us, give us, give us, give us":—that I know. "Grace that, grace that, grace that, grace that":—that I know.' Other words followed to the same effect. The boy was of the dunce class apparently; the book was a psalter, and this was his way of learning the collect. In the worst attacks of trouble there appears to be always a superficial film of consciousness which is left disengaged and open to the notice of trifles, and Bathsheba was faintly amused at the boy's method, till he too passed on.

By this time stupor had given place to anxiety, and anxiety began to make room for hunger and thirst. A form now appeared upon the rise on the other side of the swamp, half-hidden by the mist, and came towards Bathsheba. The woman—for it was a woman—approached with her face askance, as if looking earnestly on all sides of her. When she got a little further round to the left, and drew nearer, Bathsheba could see the newcomer's profile against the sunny sky, and knew the wavy sweep from forehead to chin, with neither angle nor decisive line anywhere about it, to be the familiar contour of Liddy Smallbury.

Bathsheba's heart bounded with gratitude in the thought that she was not altogether deserted, and she jumped up. 'O, Liddy!' she said, or attempted to say; but the words had only been framed by her lips; there came no sound. She had lost her voice by exposure to the

2. Any of a variety of plants that have in common long, sword-shaped leaves.

clogged atmosphere all these hours of night.

'O, ma'am! I am so glad I have found you,' said the girl, as soon as she saw Bathsheba.

'You can't come across,' Bathsheba said in a whisper, which she vainly endeavoured to make loud enough to reach Liddy's ears. Liddy, not knowing this, stepped down upon the swamp, saying, as she did so, 'It will bear me up, I think.'

Bathsheba never forgot that transient little picture of Liddy crossing the swamp to her there in the morning light. Iridescent bubbles of dank subterranean breath rose from the sweating sod beside the waiting-maid's feet as she trod, hissing as they burst and expanded away to join the vapoury firmament above. Liddy did not sink, as Bathsheba had anticipated.

She landed safely on the other side, and looked up at the beautiful though pale and weary face of her young mistress.

'Poor thing!' said Liddy, with tears in her eyes. 'Do hearten yourself up a little, ma'am. However did——'

'I can't speak above a whisper—my voice is gone for the present,' said Bathsheba hurriedly. 'I suppose the damp air from that hollow has taken it away. Liddy, don't question me, mind. Who sent you—anybody?'

'Nobody. I thought, when I found you were not at home, that something cruel had happened. I fancy I heard his voice late last night; and so, knowing something was wrong——'

'Is he at home?'

'No; he left just before I came out.'

'Is Fanny taken away?'

'Not yet. She will soon be—at nine o'clock.'

'We won't go home at present, then. Suppose we walk about in this wood?'

Liddy, without exactly understanding everything, or anything, in this episode, assented, and they walked together further among the trees.

'But you had better come in, ma'am, and have something to eat. You will die of a chill!'

'I shall not come indoors yet—perhaps never.'

'Shall I get you something to eat, and something else to put over your head besides that little shawl?'

'If you will, Liddy.'

Liddy vanished, and at the end of twenty minutes returned with a cloak, hat, some slices of bread and butter, a tea-cup, and some hot tea in a little china jug.

'Is Fanny gone?' said Bathsheba.

'No,' said her companion, pouring out the tea.

Bathsheba wrapped herself up and ate and drank sparingly. Her voice was then a little clearer, and a trifling colour returned to her face. 'Now we'll walk about again,' she said.

They wandered about the wood for nearly two hours, Bathsheba replying in monosyllables to Liddy's prattle, for her mind ran on one subject, and one only. She interrupted with—

'I wonder if Fanny is gone by this time?'

'I will go and see.'

She came back with the information that the men were just taking away the corpse; that Bathsheba had been inquired for; that she had replied to the effect that her mistress was unwell and could not be seen.

'Then they think I am in my bedroom?'

'Yes.' Liddy then ventured to add: 'You said when I first found you that you might never go home again—you didn't mean it, ma'am?'

'No; I've altered my mind. It is only women with no pride in them who run away from their husbands. There is one position worse than that of being found dead in your husband's house from his ill-usage, and that is, to be found alive through having gone away to the house of somebody else. I've thought of it all this morning, and I've chosen my course. A runaway wife is an encumbrance to everybody, a burden to herself and a byword—all of which make up a heap of misery greater than any that comes by staying at home—though this may include the trifling items of insult, beating, and starvation. Liddy, if ever you marry—God forbid that you ever should!—you'll find yourself in a fearful situation; but mind this, don't you flinch. Stand your ground, and be cut to pieces. That's what I'm going to do.'

'O, mistress, don't talk so!' said Liddy, taking her hand, 'but I knew you had too much sense to bide away. May I ask what dreadful thing it is that has happened between you and him?'

'You may ask; but I may not tell.'

In about ten minutes they returned to the house by a circuitous route, entering at the rear. Bathsheba glided up the back stairs to a disused attic, and her companion followed.

'Liddy,' she said, with a lighter heart, for youth and hope had begun to reassert themselves; 'you are to be my confidante for the present—somebody must be—and I choose you. Well, I shall take up my abode here for a while. Will you get a fire lighted, put down a piece of carpet, and help me to make the place comfortable? Afterwards, I want you and Maryann to bring up that little stump bedstead[3] in the small room, and the bed belonging to it, and a table, and some other things. . . . What shall I do to pass the heavy time away?'

'Hemming handkerchiefs is a very good thing,' said Liddy.

'O no, no! I hate needlework—I always did.'

'Knitting?'

'And that, too.'

'You might finish your sampler. Only the carnations and peacocks

---

3. A simple bedframe without posts.

want filling in; and then it could be framed and glazed, and hung beside your aunt's, ma'am.'

'Samplers are out of date—horribly countrified. No, Liddy, I'll read. Bring up some books—not new ones. I haven't heart to read anything new.'

'Some of your uncle's old ones, ma'am?'

'Yes. Some of those we stowed away in boxes.' A faint gleam of humour passed over her face as she said: 'Bring Beaumont and Fletcher's *Maid's Tragedy*, and the *Mourning Bride*; and—let me see—*Night Thoughts*, and the *Vanity of Human Wishes*.'[4]

'And that story of the black man, who murdered his wife Desdemona?[5] It is a nice dismal one that would suit you excellent just now.'

'Now, Lidd, you've been looking into my books, without telling me; and I said you were not to! How do you know it would suit me? It wouldn't suit me at all.'

'But if the others do——'

'No, they don't; and I won't read dismal books. Why should I read dismal books, indeed? Bring me *Love in a Village*, and the *Maid of the Mill*, and *Doctor Syntax*, and some volumes of the *Spectator*.'[6]

All that day Bathsheba and Liddy lived in the attic in a state of barricade; a precaution which proved to be needless as against Troy, for he did not appear in the neighborhood or trouble them at all. Bathsheba sat at the window till sunset, sometimes attempting to read, at other times watching every movement outside without much purpose, and listening without much interest to every sound.

The sun went down almost blood-red that night, and a livid cloud received its rays in the east. Up against this dark background the west front of the church tower—the only part of the edifice visible from the farm-house windows—rose distinct and lustrous, the vane upon the summit bristling with rays. Hereabouts, at six o'clock, the young men of the village gathered, as was their custom, for a game of Prisoners' base.[7] The spot had been consecrated to this ancient diversion from

4. Beaumont and Fletcher's *The Maid's Tragedy* (1619) is a play about a broken-hearted woman who commits suicide. Congreve's *The Mourning Bride* (1677) is a tragedy of a woman whose father opposes her marriage to an enemy of his; the father is killed by mistake. It includes the famous lines, "Heaven has no rage, like love to hatred turned, / Nor hell a fury, like a woman scorned." Edward Young's *Night Thoughts on Life, Death, and Immortality* is a long didactic poem on the importance of preparing for death, the last judgment, and eternity. Samuel Johnson's *The Vanity of Human Wishes* (1749) is a poetic meditation on the vanity of human ambition, which concludes by urging resignation to God's providence.

5. The "story of the black man" is Shakespeare's *Othello* (1604).

6. Isaac Bickerstaffe's *Love in a Village* (1762) and *Maid of the Mill* (1765) were comic operas. *Doctor Syntax* is a series of comic verses by William Combe to accompany Thomas Rowlandson's caricatures of a clergyman, Dr. Syntax, who is "in search of the picturesque." The *Spectator*, edited by Addison and Steele from 1711 to 1712, and later revived by Addison alone in 1714, contained lively and often comic essays and character sketches.

7. A game involving two groups of boys, each of which has a "base"; the object of the game is for the holders of one base to capture players from the other group who leave their base.

time immemorial, the old stocks[8] conveniently forming a base facing the boundary of the churchyard, in front of which the ground was trodden hard and bare as a pavement by the players. She could see the brown and black heads of the young lads darting about right and left, their white shirt-sleeves gleaming in the sun; whilst occasionally a shout and a peal of hearty laughter varied the stillness of the evening air. They continued playing for a quarter of an hour or so, when the game concluded abruptly, and the players leapt over the wall and vanished round to the other side behind a yew-tree, which was also half behind a beech, now spreading in one mass of golden foliage, on which the branches traced black lines.

'Why did the base-players finish their game so suddenly?' Bathsheba inquired, the next time that Liddy entered the room.

'I think 'twas because two men came just then from Casterbridge and began putting up a grand carved tombstone,' said Liddy. 'The lads went to see whose it was.'

'Do you know?' Bathsheba asked.

'I don't,' said Liddy.

XLV

Troy's Romanticism

When Troy's wife had left the house at the previous midnight his first act was to cover the dead from sight. This done he ascended the stairs, and throwing himself down upon the bed dressed as he was, he waited miserably for the morning.

Fate had dealt grimly with him through the last four-and-twenty hours. His day had been spent in a way which varied very materially from his intentions regarding it. There is always an inertia to be overcome in striking out a new line of conduct—not more in ourselves, it seems, than in circumscribing events, which appear as if leagued together to allow no novelties in the way of amelioration.

Twenty pounds having been secured from Bathsheba, he had managed to add to the sum every farthing he could muster on his own account, which had been seven pounds ten. With this money, twenty-seven pounds ten in all, he had hastily driven from the gate that morning to keep his appointment with Fanny Robin.

On reaching Casterbridge he left the horse and trap at an inn, and at five minutes before ten came back to the bridge at the lower end of the town, and sat himself upon the parapet. The clocks struck the hour, and no Fanny appeared. In fact, at that moment she was being robed in her grave-clothes by two attendants at the Union poorhouse—the first and last tiring-women the gentle creature had ever been honoured with. The quarter went, the half hour. A rush of recollection came

8. A heavy timber frame with holes for confining the ankles of persons being punished.

upon Troy as he waited: this was the second time she had broken a serious engagement with him. In anger he vowed it should be the last, and at eleven o'clock, when he had lingered and watched the stones of the bridge till he knew every lichen upon their faces, and heard the chink of the ripples underneath till they oppressed him, he jumped from his seat, went to the inn for his gig, and in a bitter mood of indifference concerning the past, and recklessness about the future, drove on to Budmouth races.

He reached the race-course at two o'clock, and remained either there or in the town till nine. But Fanny's image, as it had appeared to him in the sombre shadows of that Saturday evening, returned to his mind, backed up by Bathsheba's reproaches. He vowed he would not bet, and he kept his vow, for on leaving the town at nine o'clock in the evening he had diminished his cash only to the extent of a few shillings.

He trotted slowly homeward, and it was now that he was struck for the first time with a thought that Fanny had been really prevented by illness from keeping her promise. This time she could have made no mistake. He regretted that he had not remained in Casterbridge and made inquiries. Reaching home he quietly unharnessed the horse and came indoors, as we have seen, to the fearful shock that awaited him.

As soon as it grew light enough to distinguish objects, Troy arose from the coverlet of the bed, and in a mood of absolute indifference to Bathsheba's whereabouts, and almost oblivious of her existence, he stalked downstairs and left the house by the back door. His walk was towards the churchyard, entering which he searched around till he found a newly dug unoccupied grave—the grave dug the day before for Fanny. The position of this having been marked, he hastened on to Casterbridge, only pausing and musing for a while at the hill whereon he had last seen Fanny alive.

Reaching the town, Troy descended into a side street and entered a pair of gates surmounted by a board bearing the words, 'Lester, stone and marble mason.' Within were lying about stones of all sizes and designs, inscribed as being sacred to the memory of unnamed persons who had not yet died.

Troy was so unlike himself now in look, word, and deed, that the want of likeness was perceptible even to his own consciousness. His method of engaging himself in this business of purchasing a tomb was that of an absolutely unpractised man. He could not bring himself to consider, calculate, or economize. He waywardly wished for something, and he set about obtaining it like a child in a nursery. 'I want a good tomb,' he said to the man who stood in a little office within the yard. 'I want as good a one as you can give me for twenty-seven pounds.'

It was all the money he possessed.

'That sum to include everything?'

'Everything. Cutting the name, carriage to Weatherbury, and erection. And I want it now, at once.'

'We could not get anything special worked this week.'

'I must have it now.'

'If you would like one of these in stock it could be got ready immediately.'

'Very well,' said Troy, impatiently. 'Let's see what you have.'

'The best I have in stock is this one,' said the stone-cutter, going into a shed. 'Here's a marble headstone beautifully crocketed,[1] with medallions beneath of typical subjects; here's the footstone after the same pattern, and here's the coping[2] to enclose the grave. The polishing alone of the set cost me eleven pounds—the slabs are the best of their kind, and I can warrant them to resist rain and frost for a hundred years without flying.'[3]

'And how much?'

'Well, I could add the name, and put it up at Weatherbury for the sum you mention.'

'Get it done to-day, and I'll pay the money now.'

The man agreed, and wondered at such a mood in a visitor who wore not a shred of mourning. Troy then wrote the words which were to form the inscription, settled the account and went away. In the afternoon he came back again, and found that the lettering was almost done. He waited in the yard till the tomb was packed, and saw it placed in the cart and starting on its way to Weatherbury, giving directions to the two men who were to accompany it to inquire of the sexton for the grave of the person named in the inscription.

It was quite dark when Troy came out of Casterbridge. He carried rather a heavy basket upon his arm, with which he strode moodily along the road, resting occasionally at bridges and gates, whereon he deposited his burden for a time. Midway on his journey he met, returning in the darkness, the men and the waggon which had conveyed the tomb. He merely inquired if the work was done, and, on being assured that it was, passed on again.

Troy entered Weatherbury churchyard about ten o'clock, and went immediately to the corner where he had marked the vacant grave early in the morning. It was on the obscure side of the tower, screened to a great extent from the view of passers along the road—a spot which until lately had been abandoned to heaps of stones and bushes of alder, but now it was cleared and made orderly for interments, by reasons of the rapid filling of the ground elsewhere.

Here now stood the tomb as the men had stated, snow-white and

---

1. Ornamented with devices shaped like curled leaves.
2. A low stone boarder marking the sides of the grave.
3. Flaking or crumbling.

shapely in the gloom, consisting of head and foot stone, and enclosing border of marble-work uniting them. In the midst was mould, suitable for plants.

Troy deposited his basket beside the tomb, and vanished for a few minutes. When he returned he carried a spade and a lantern, the light of which he directed for a few moments upon the marble, whilst he read the inscription. He hung his lantern on the lowest bough of a young yew-tree, and took from his basket flower-roots of several varieties. There were bundles of snowdrop, hyacinth and crocus bulbs, violets and double daisies, which were to bloom in early spring, and of carnations, pinks, picotees, lilies of the valley, forget-me-not, summer's farewell, meadow-saffron and others, for the later seasons of the year.

Troy laid these out upon the grass, and with an impassive face set to work to plant them. The snowdrops were arranged in a line on the outside of the coping, the remainder within the enclosure of the grave. The crocuses and hyacinths were to grow in rows; some of the summer flowers he placed over her head and feet, the lilies and forget-me-nots over her heart. The remainder were dispersed in the spaces between these.

Troy, in his prostration at this time, had no perception that in the futility of these romantic doings, dictated by a remorseful reaction from previous indifference, there was any element of absurdity. Deriving his idiosyncrasies from both sides of the Channel, he showed at such junctures as the present the inelasticity of the Englishman, together with that blindness to the line where sentiment verges on mawkishness, characteristic of the French.

It was a cloudy, muggy, and very dark night, and the rays from Troy's lantern spread into the old trees with a strange illuminating power, flickering, as it seemed, up to the black ceiling of cloud above. He felt a large drop of rain upon the back of his hand, and presently one came and entered one of the holes of the lantern, whereupon the candle sputtered and went out. Troy was weary, and it being now not far from midnight, and the rain threatening to increase, he resolved to leave the finishing touches of his labour until the day should break. He groped along the wall and over the graves in the dark till he found himself round at the north side. Here he entered the porch, and, reclining upon the bench within, fell asleep.

XLVI

The Gurgoyle: Its Doings

The tower of Weatherbury Church[1] was a square erection of fourteenth-century date, having two stone gurgoyles on each of the four faces of its parapet.[2] Of these eight carved protuberances only two at this time continued to serve the purpose of their erection—that of spouting the water from the lead roof within. One mouth in each front had been closed by bygone churchwardens as superfluous, and two others were broken away and choked—a matter not of much consequence to the well-being of the tower, for the two mouths which still remained open and active were gaping enough to do all the work.

It has been sometimes argued that there is no truer criterion of the vitality of any given art-period than the power of the master-spirits of that time in grotesque; and certainly in the instance of Gothic art there is no disputing the proposition. Weatherbury tower was a somewhat early instance of the use of an ornamental parapet in parish as distinct from cathedral churches, and the gurgoyles, which are the necessary correlatives of a parapet, were exceptionally prominent—of the boldest cut that the hand could shape, and of the most original design that a human brain could conceive. There was, so to speak, that symmetry in their distortion which is less the characteristic of British than of Continental grotesques of the period. All the eight were different from each other. A beholder was convinced that nothing on earth could be more hideous than those he saw on the north side until he went round to the south. Of the two on this latter face, only that at the south-eastern corner concerns the story. It was too human to be called like a dragon, too impish to be like a man, too animal to be like a fiend, and not enough like a bird to be called a griffin. This horrible stone entity was fashioned as if covered with a wrinkled hide; it had short, erect ears, eyes starting from their sockets, and its fingers and hands were seizing the corners of its mouth, which they thus seemed to pull open to give free passage to the water it vomited. The lower row of teeth was quite washed away, though the upper still remained. Here and thus, jutting a couple of feet from the wall against which its toes rested as a support, the creature had for four hundred years laughed at the surrounding landscape, voicelessly in dry weather, and in wet with a gurgling and snorting sound.

Troy slept on in the porch, and the rain increased outside. Presently the gurgolye spat. In due time a small stream began to trickle through

1. Hardy's description of Weatherbury Church is based in part on St. Mary's Church, Puddletown, but see his own qualification expressed in footnote 6.

2. "Gurgoyle" is a variant spelling of "gargoyle," a rain spout carved to represent a grotesque human or animal figure and intended to carry rainwater clear of a wall; a "parapet" is a low wall along the edge of a roof—in this case the roof of the church tower.

the seventy feet of aerial space between its mouth and the ground, which the water-drops smote like duckshot in their accelerated velocity. The stream thickened in substance, and increased in power, gradually spouting further and yet further from the side of the tower. When the rain fell in a steady and ceaseless torrent the stream dashed downward in volumes.

We follow its course to the ground at this point of time. The end of the liquid parabola has come forward from the wall, has advanced over the plinth[3] mouldings, over a heap of stones, over the marble border, into the midst of Fanny Robin's grave.

The force of the stream had, until very lately, been received upon some loose stones spread thereabout, which had acted as a shield to the soil under the onset. These during the summer had been cleared from the ground, and there was now nothing to resist the downfall but the bare earth. For several years the stream had not spouted so far from the tower as it was doing on this night, and such a contingency had been overlooked. Sometimes this obscure corner received no inhabitant for the space of two or three years, and then it was usually but a pauper, a poacher, or other sinner of undignified sins.

The persistent torrent from the gurgoyle's jaws directed all its vengeance into the grave. The rich tawny mould was stirred into motion, and boiled like chocolate. The water accumulated and washed deeper down, and the roar of the pool thus formed spread into the night as the head and chief among other noises of the kind created by the deluging rain. The flowers so carefully planted by Fanny's repentant lover began to move and writhe in their bed. The winter-voilets turned slowly upside down, and became a mere mat of mud. Soon the snowdrop and other bulbs danced in the boiling mass like ingredients in a cauldron. Plants of the tufted species were loosened, rose to the surface, and floated off.

Troy did not awake from his comfortless sleep till it was broad day. Not having been in bed for two nights his shoulders felt stiff, his feet tender, and his head heavy. He remembered his position, arose, shivered, took the spade, and again went out.

The rain had quite ceased, and the sun was shining through the green, brown, and yellow leaves, now sparkling and varnished by the raindrops to the brightness of similar effects in the landscapes of Ruysdael and Hobbema,[4] and full of all those infinite beauties that arise from the union of water and colour with high lights. The air was rendered so transparent by the heavy fall of rain that the autumn hues of the middle distance were as rich as those near at hand, and the romote fields intercepted by the angle of the tower appeared in the same plane as the tower itself.

He entered the gravel path which would take him behind the tower.

---

3. The base of the church tower.
4. Jacob van Ruysdael (1628–82) and his pupil   Meyndert Hobbema (1638–1709) were Dutch landscape painters.

The path, instead of being stony as it had been the night before, was browned over with a thin coating of mud. At one place in the path he saw a tuft of stringy roots washed white and clean as a bundle of tendons. He picked it up—surely it could not be one of the primroses he had planted? He saw a bulb, another, and another as he advanced. Beyond doubt they were the crocuses. With a face of perplexed dismay Troy turned the corner and then beheld the wreck the stream had made.

The pool upon the grave had soaked away into the ground, and in its place was a hollow. The disturbed earth was washed over the grass and pathway in the guise of the brown mud he had already seen, and it spotted the marble tombstone with the same stains. Nearly all the flowers were washed clean out of the ground, and they lay, roots upwards, on the spots whither they had been splashed by the stream.

Troy's brow became heavily contracted. He set his teeth closely, and his compressed lips moved as those of one in great pain. This singular accident, by a strange confluence of emotions in him, was felt as the sharpest sting of all. Troy's face was very expressive, and any observer who had seen him now would hardly have believed him to be a man who had laughed, and sung, and poured love-trifles into a woman's ear. To curse his miserable lot was at first his impulse, but even that lowest stage of rebellion needed an activity whose absence was necessarily antecedent to the existence of the morbid misery which wrung him. The sight, coming as it did, superimposed upon the other dark scenery of the previous days, formed a sort of climax to the whole panorama, and it was more than he could endure. Sanguine by nature, Troy had a power of eluding grief by simply adjourning it. He could put off the consideration of any particular spectre till the matter had become old and softened by time. The planting of flowers on Fanny's grave had been perhaps but a species of elusion of the primary grief, and now it was as if his intention had been known and circumvented.

Almost for the first time in his life Troy, as he stood by this dismantled grave, wished himself another man. It is seldom that a person with much animal spirit does not feel that the fact of his life being his own is the one qualification which singles it out as a more hopeful life than that of others who may actually resemble him in every particular. Troy had felt, in his transient way, hundreds of times, that he could not envy other people their condition, because the possession of that condition would have necessitated a different personality, when he desired no other than his own. He had not minded the peculiarities of his birth, the vicissitudes of his life, the meteor-like uncertainty of all that related to him, because these appertained to the hero of his story, without whom there would have been no story at all for him; and it seemed to be only in the nature of things that matters would right themselves at some proper date and wind up well. This very morning the illusion completed its disappearance, and, as it were, all of a sudden, Troy hated himself. The suddenness was probably more apparent than real. A coral reef which just comes short of the ocean surface is no more to the horizon than if it had never been begun, and the mere finishing stroke is what often appears to create an event which has long been potentially an accomplished thing.

He stood and meditated—a miserable man. Whither should he go? 'He that is accursed, let him be accursed still,'[5] was the pitiless anathema written in this spoliated effort of his new-born solicitousness. A man who has spent his primal strength in journeying in one direction has not much spirit left for reversing his course. Troy had, since yesterday, faintly reversed his; but the merest opposition had disheartened him. To turn about would have been hard enough under the greatest providential encouragement; but to find that Providence, far from helping him into a new course, or showing any wish that he might adopt one, actually jeered his first trembling and critical attempt in that kind, was more than nature could bear.

He slowly withdrew from the grave. He did not attempt to fill up the hole, replace the flowers, or do anything at all. He simply threw up his cards and forswore his game for that time and always. Going out of the churchyard silently and unobserved—none of the villagers having yet risen—he passed down some fields at the back, and emerged just as secretly upon the high road. Shortly afterwards he had gone from the village.

Meanwhile, Bathsheba remained a voluntary prisoner in the attic. The door was kept locked, except during the entries and exits of Liddy, for whom a bed had been arranged in a small adjoining room. The light of Troy's lantern in the churchyard was noticed about ten o'clock by the maid-servant, who casually glanced from the window in that direction whilst taking her supper, and she called Bathsheba's attention to it. They looked curiously at the phenomenon for a time, until Liddy was sent to bed.

Bathsheba did not sleep very heavily that night. When her attendant was unconscious and softly breathing in the next room, the mistress of the house was still looking out of the window at the faint gleam spreading from among the trees—not in a steady shine, but blinking like a revolving coast-light, though this appearance failed to suggest to her that a person was passing and repassing in front of it. Bathsheba sat here till it began to rain, and the light vanished, when she withdrew to lie restlessly in her bed and re-enact in a worn mind the lurid scene of yesternight.

Almost before the first faint sign of dawn appeared she arose again, and opened the window to obtain a full breathing of the new morning

---

5. A paraphrase of Galatians 1:8–9.

air, the panes being now wet with trembling tears left by the night rain, each one rounded with a pale lustre caught from primrose-hued slashes through a cloud low down in the awakening sky. From the trees came the sound of steady dripping upon the drifted leaves under them, and from the direction of the church she could hear another noise—peculiar, and not intermittent like the rest, the purl of water falling into a pool.

Liddy knocked at eight o'clock, and Bathsheba unlocked the door.

'What a heavy rain we've had in the night, ma'am!' said Liddy, when her inquiries about breakfast had been made.

'Yes; very heavy.'

'Did you hear the strange noise from the churchyard?'

'I heard one strange noise. I've been thinking it must have been the water from the tower spouts.'

'Well, that's what the shepherd was saying, ma'am. He's now gone on to see.'

'Oh! Gabriel has been there this morning?'

'Only just looked in in passing—quite in his old way, which I thought he had left off lately. But the tower spouts used to spatter on the stones, and we are puzzled, for this was like the boiling of a pot.'

Not being able to read, think, or work, Bathsheba asked Liddy to stay and breakfast with her. The tongue of the more childish woman still ran upon recent events. 'Are you going across to the church, ma'am?' she asked.

'Not that I know of,' said Bathsheba.

'I thought you might like to go and see where they have put Fanny. The trees hid the place from your window.'

Bathsheba had all sorts of dreads about meeting her husband. 'Has Mr. Troy been in to-night?' she said.

'No, ma'am; I think he's gone to Budmouth.'

Budmouth! The sound of the word carried with it a much diminished perspective of him and his deeds; there were thirteen miles interval betwixt them now. She hated questioning Liddy about her husband's movements, and indeed had hitherto sedulously avoided doing so; but now all the house knew that there had been some dreadful disagreement between them, and it was futile to attempt disguise. Bathsheba had reached a stage at which people cease to have any appreciative regard for public opinion.

'What makes you think he has gone there?' she said.

'Laban Tall saw him on the Budmouth road this morning before breakfast.'

Bathsheba was momentarily relieved of that wayward heaviness of the past twenty-four hours which had quenched the vitality of youth in her without substituting the philosophy of maturer years, and she resolved to go out and walk a little way. So when breakfast was over she put on her bonnet, and took a direction towards the church. It was

nine o'clock, and the men having returned to work again from their
first meal, she was not likely to meet many of them in the road.
Knowing that Fanny had been laid in the reprobates' quarter of the
graveyard, called in the parish 'behind church,' which was invisible
from the road, it was impossible to resist the impulse to enter and look
upon a spot which, from nameless feelings, she at the same time
dreaded to see. She had been unable to overcome an impression that
some connection existed between her rival and the light through the
trees.

Bathsheba skirted the buttress, and beheld the hole and the tomb,
its delicately veined surface splashed and stained just as Troy had seen
it and left it two hours earlier. On the other side of the scene stood
Gabriel. His eyes, too, were fixed on the tomb, and her arrival having
been noiseless, she had not as yet attracted his attention. Bathsheba
did not at once perceive that the grand tomb and the disturbed grave
were Fanny's, and she looked on both sides and around for some
humbler mound, earthed up and clodded in the usual way. Then her
eye followed Oak's, and she read the words with which the inscription
opened:—

> 'Erected by Francis Troy in Beloved Memory of
> Fanny Robin.'

Oak saw her, and his first act was to gaze inquiringly and learn how
she received this knowledge of the authorship of the work, which to
himself had caused considerable astonishment. But such discoveries
did not much affect her now. Emotional convulsions seemed to have
become the commonplaces of her history, and she bade him good
morning, and asked him to fill in the hole with the spade which was
standing by. Whilst Oak was doing as she desired, Bathsheba collected
the flowers, and began planting them with that sympathetic manipulation of roots and leaves which is so conspicuous in a woman's garden-
ing, and which flowers seem to understand and thrive upon. She
requested Oak to get the church-wardens to turn the leadwork at the
mouth of the gurgoyle that hung gaping down upon them, that by this
means the stream might be directed sideways, and a repetition of the
accident precented. Finally, with the superfluous magnanimity of a
woman whose narrower instincts have brought down bitterness upon
her instead of love, she wiped the mud spots from the tomb as if she
rather liked its words than otherwise, and went home again.[6]

---

6. The local tower and churchyard assumed to be those of "Weatherbury" do not answer precisely to
the foregoing description [*Hardy's note*].

XLVII

Adventures by the Shore

Troy wandered along towards the south. A composite feeling, made up of disgust with the, to him, humdrum tediousness of a farmer's life, gloomy images of her who lay in the churchyard, remorse, and a general averseness to his wife's society, impelled him to seek a home in any place on earth save Weatherbury. The sad accessories of Fanny's end confronted him as vivid pictures which threatened to be indelible, and made life in Bathsheba's house intolerable. At three in the afternoon he found himself at the foot of a slope more than a mile in length, which ran to the ridge of a range of hills lying parallel with the shore, and formed a monotonous barrier between the basin of cultivated country inland and the wilder scenery of the coast. Up the hill stretched a road nearly straight and perfectly white, the two sides approaching each other in a gradual taper till they met the sky at the top about two miles off. Throughout the length of this narrow and irksome inclined plane not a sign of life was visible on this garish afternoon. Troy toiled up the road with a languor and depression greater than any he had experienced for many a day and year before. The air was warm and muggy, and the top seemed to recede as he approached.

At last he reached the summit, and a wide and novel prospect burst upon him with an effect almost like that of the Pacific upon Balboa's gaze.[1] The broad steely sea, marked only by faint lines, which had a semblance of being etched thereon to a degree not deep enough to disturb its general evenness, stretched the whole width of his front and round to the right, where, near the town and port of Budmouth, the sun bristled down upon it, and banished all colour, to substitute in its place a clear oily polish. Nothing moved in sky, land, or sea, except a frill of milkwhite foam along the nearer angles of the shore, shreds of which licked the contiguous stones like tongues.

He descended and came to a small basin of sea enclosed by the cliffs. Troy's nature freshened within him; he thought he would rest and bathe here before going further. He undressed and plunged in. Inside the cove the water was uninteresting to a swimmer, being smooth as a pond, and to get a little of the ocean swell Troy presently swam between the two projecting spurs of rock which formed the pillars of Hercules[2] to this miniature Mediterranean. Unfortunately for Troy a current unknown to him existed outside, which, unimportant to craft of any burden, was awkward for a swimmer who might be

---

1. In 1513, the Spanish explorer Vasco Nuñez de Balboa (1475–1517) sighted the Pacific Ocean from a mountaintop in the Isthmus of Panama.

2. The "pillars of Hercules" are the two promotories on either side of the Strait of Gibraltar, fabled to have been raised by Hercules.

taken in it unawares. Troy found himself carried to the left and then round in a swoop out to sea.

He now recollected the place and its sinister character. Many bathers had there prayed for a dry death from time to time, and, like Gonzalo[3] also, had been unanswered; and Troy began to deem it possible that he might be added to their number. Not a boat of any kind was at present within sight, but far in the distance Budmouth lay upon the sea, as it were quietly regarding his efforts, and beside the town the harbour showed its position by a dim meshwork of ropes and spars. After well-nigh exhausting himself in attempts to get back to the mouth of the cove, in his weakness swimming several inches deeper than was his wont, keeping up his breathing entirely by his nostrils, turning upon his back a dozen times over, swimming *en papillon*,[4] and so on, Troy resolved as a last resource to tread water at a slight incline, and so endeavour to reach the shore at any point, merely giving himself a gentle impetus inwards whilst carried on in the general direction of the tide. This, necessarily a slow process, he found to be not altogether so difficult, and though there was no choice of a landing-place—the objects on shore passing by him in a sad and slow procession—he perceptibly approached the extremity of a spit of land yet further to the right, now well defined against the sunny portion of the horizon. While the swimmer's eyes were fixed upon the spit as his only means of salvation on this side of the Unknown, a moving object broke the outline of the extremity, and immediately a ship's boat appeared, manned with several sailor lads, her bows towards the sea.

All Troy's vigour spasmodically revived to prolong the struggle yet a little further. Swimming with his right arm, he held up his left to hail them, splashing upon the waves, and shouting with all his might. From the position of the setting sun his white form was distinctly visible upon the now deep-hued bosom of the sea to the east of the boat, and the men saw him at once. Backing their oars and putting the boat about, they pulled towards him with a will, and in five or six minutes from the time of his first halloo, two of the sailors hauled him in over the stern.

They formed part of a brig's crew, and had come ashore for sand. Lending him what little clothing they could spare among them as a slight protection against the rapidly cooling air, they agreed to land him in the morning; and without further delay, for it was growing late, they made again towards the roadstead where their vessel lay.

And now night drooped slowly upon the wide watery levels in front; and at no great distance from them, where the shore-line curved round, and formed a long riband of shade upon the horizon, a series of points of yellow light began to start into existence, denoting the spot to be the site of Budmouth, where the lamps were being lighted along the

3. An allusion to Shakespeare's *The Tempest*, act 1, scene 1, where Gonzalo cries, "I would fain die a dry death."

4. French for "with a butterfly stroke."

parade. The cluck of their oars was the only sound of any distinctness upon the sea, and as they laboured amid the thickening shades the lamp-lights grew larger, each appearing to send a flaming sword deep down into the waves before it, until there arose, among other dim shapes of the kind, the form of the vessel for which they were bound.

XLVIII

Doubts Arise—Doubts Linger

Bathsheba underwent the enlargement of her husband's absence from hours to days with a slight feeling of surprise, and a slight feeling of relief; yet neither sensation rose at any time far above the level commonly designated as indifference. She belonged to him: the certainties of that position were so well defined, and the reasonable probabilities of its issue so bounded, that she could not speculate on contingencies. Taking no further interest in herself as a splendid woman, she acquired the indifferent feelings of an outsider in contemplating her probable fate as a singular wretch; for Bathsheba drew herself and her future in colours that no reality could exceed for darkness. Her original vigorous pride of youth had sickened, and with it had declined all her anxieties about coming years, since anxiety recognizes a better and a worse alternative, and Bathsheba had made up her mind that alternatives on any noteworthy scale had ceased for her. Soon, or later—and that not very late—her husband would be home again. And then the days of their tenancy of the Upper Farm would be numbered. There had originally been shown by the agent to the estate some distrust of Bathsheba's tenure as James Everdene's successor, on the score of her sex, and her youth, and her beauty; but the peculiar nature of her uncle's will, his own frequent testimony before his death to her cleverness in such a pursuit, and her vigorous marshalling of the numerous flocks and herds which came suddenly into her hands before negotiations were concluded, had won confidence in her powers, and no further objections had been raised. She had latterly been in great doubt as to what the legal effects of her marriage would be upon her position; but no notice had been taken as yet of her change of name, and only one point was clear—that in the event of her own or her husband's inability to meet the agent at the forthcoming January rent-day, very little consideration would be shown, and, for that matter, very little would be deserved. Once out of the farm the approach of poverty would be sure.

Hence Bathsheba lived in a perception that her purposes were broken off. She was not a woman who could hope on without good materials for the process, differing thus from the less far-sighted and energetic, though more petted ones of the sex, with whom hope goes on as a sort of clockwork which the merest food and shelter are sufficient to wind up; and perceiving clearly that her mistake had been a fatal one, she accepted her position, and waited coldly for the end.

The first Saturday after Troy's departure she went to Casterbridge alone, a journey she had not taken since her marriage. On this Saturday Bathsheba was passing slowly on foot through the crowd of rural business-men gathered as usual in front of the market-house, who were as usual gazed upon by the burghers with feelings that those healthy lives were dearly paid for by exclusion from possible alder-manship, when a man, who had apparently been following her, said some words to another on her left hand. Bathsheba's ears were keen as those of any wild animal, and she distinctly heard what the speaker said, though her back was towards him.

'I am looking for Mrs. Troy. Is that she there?'

'Yes; that's the young lady, I believe,' said the person addressed.

'I have some awkward news to break to her. Her husband is drowned.'

As if endowed with the spirit of prophecy, Bathsheba gasped out, 'No, it is not true; it cannot be true!' Then she said and heard no more. The ice of self-command which had latterly gathered over her was broken, and the currents burst forth again, and overwhelmed her. A darkness came into her eyes, and she fell.

But not to the ground. A gloomy man, who had been observing her from under the portico of the old corn-exchange when she passed through the group without, stepped quickly to her side at the moment of her exclamation, and caught her in his arms as she sank down.

'What is it?' said Boldwood, looking up at the bringer of the big news, as he supported her.

'Her husband was drowned this week while bathing in Lulwind Cove. A coastguardsman found his clothes, and brought them into Budmouth yesterday.'

Thereupon a strange fire lighted up Boldwood's eye, and his face flushed with the suppressed excitement of an unutterable thought. Everybody's glance was now centered on him and the unconscious Bathsheba. He lifted her bodily off the ground, and smoothed down the folds of her dress as a child might have taken a storm-beaten bird and arranged its ruffled plumes, and bore her along the pavement to the King's Arms Inn. [1] Here he passed with her under the archway into a private room; and by the time he had deposited—so lothly—the precious burden upon a sofa, Bathsheba had opened her eyes. Remembering all that had occurred, she murmured, "I want to go home!'

Boldwood left the room. He stood for a moment in the passage to recover his senses. The experience had been too much for his con-

---

1. There is a real hotel called *The King's Arms* in Dorchester.

sciousness to keep up with, and now that he had grasped it it had gone again. For those few heavenly, golden moments she had been in his arms. What did it matter about her not knowing it? She had been close to his breast; he had been close to hers.

He started onward again, and sending a woman to her, went out to ascertain all the facts of the case. These appeared to be limited to what he had already heard. He then ordered her horse to be put into the gig, and when all was ready returned to inform her. He found that, though still pale and unwell, she had in the meantime sent for the Budmouth man who brought the tidings, and learnt from him all there was to know.

Being hardly in a condition to drive home as she had driven to town, Boldwood, with every delicacy of manner and feeling, offered to get her a driver, or to give her a seat in his phaeton,[2] which was more comfortable than her own conveyance. These proposals Bathsheba gently declined, and the farmer at once departed.

About half-an-hour later she invigorated herself by an effort, and took her seat and the reins as usual—in external appearance much as if nothing had happened. She went out of the town by a tortuous back street, and drove slowly along, unconscious of the road and the scene. The first shades of evening were showing themselves when Bathsheba reached home, where, silently alighting and leaving the horse in the hands of the boy, she proceeded at once upstairs. Liddy met her on the landing. The news had preceded Bathsheba to Weatherbury by half-an-hour, and Liddy looked inquiringly into her mistress's face. Bathsheba had nothing to say.

She entered her bedroom and sat by the window, and thought and thought till night enveloped her, and the extreme lines only of her shape were visible. Somebody came to the door, knocked, and opened it.

'Well, what is it, Liddy?' she said.

'I was thinking there must be something got for you to wear,' said Liddy, with hesitation.

'What do you mean?'

'Mourning.'

'No, no, no,' said Bathsheba hurriedly.

'But I suppose there must be something done for poor——'

'Not at present, I think. It is not necessary.'

'Why not, ma'am?'

'Because he's still alive.'

'How do you know that?' said Liddy, amazed.

'I don't know it. But wouldn't it have been different, or shouldn't I have heard more, or wouldn't they have found him, Liddy?—or—I

2. An open four-wheeled carriage usually drawn by two horses.

don't know how it is, but death would have been different from how this is. There may be some trick in it. I am perfectly convinced that he is still alive!'

Bathsheba remained firm in this opinion till Monday, when two circumstances conjoined to shake it. The first was a short paragraph in the local newspaper, which, beyond making by a methodizing pen formidable presumptive evidence of Troy's death by drowning, contained the important testimony of a young Mr. Barker, M.D., of Budmouth, who spoke to being an eyewitness of the accident, in a letter to the editor. In this he stated that he was passing over the cliff on the remoter side of the cove just as the sun was setting. At that time he saw a bather carried along in the current outside the mouth of the cove, and guessed in an instant that there was but a poor chance for him unless he should be possessed of unusual muscular powers. He drifted behind a projection of the coast, and Mr. Barker followed along the shore in the same direction. But by the time that he could reach an elevation sufficiently great to command a view of the sea beyond, dusk had set in, and nothing further was to be seen.

The other circumstance was the arrival of his clothes, when it became necessary for her to examine and identify them—though this had virtually been done long before by those who inspected the letters in his pockets. It was so evident to her in the midst of her agitation that Troy had undressed in the full conviction of dressing again almost immediately, that the notion that anything but death could have prevented him was a perverse one to entertain.

Then Bathsheba said to herself that others were assured in their opinion; strange that she should not be. A strange reflection occurred to her, causing her face to flush. Suppose that Troy had followed Fanny into another world. Had he done this intentionally, yet contrived to make his death appear like an accident? Nevertheless, this thought of how the apparent might differ from the real—made vivid by her bygone jealousy of Fanny, and the remorse he had shown that night—did not blind her to the perception of a likelier difference, less tragic, but to herself far more disastrous.

When alone late that evening beside a small fire, and much calmed down, Bathsheba took Troy's watch into her hand, which had been restored to her with the rest of the articles belonging to him. She opened the case as he had opened it before her a week ago. There was the little coil of pale hair which had been as the fuze to this great explosion.

'He was hers and she was his; they should be gone together,' she said. 'I am nothing to either of them, and why should I keep her hair?' She took it in her hand, and held it over the fire. 'No—I'll not burn it—I'll keep it in memory of her, poor thing!' she added, snatching back her hand.

XLIX

Oak's Advancement—A Great Hope

The later autumn and the winter drew on apace, and the leaves lay thick upon the turf of the glades and the mosses of the woods. Bathsheba, having previously been living in a state of suspended feeling which was not suspense, now lived in a mood of quietude which was not precisely peacefulness. While she had known him to be alive she could have thought of his death with equanimity; but now that it might be she had lost him, she regretted that he was not hers still. She kept the farm going, raked in her profits without caring keenly about them, and expended money on ventures because she had done so in bygone days, which, though not long gone by, seemed infinitely removed from her present. She looked back upon that past over a great gulf, as if she were now a dead person, having the faculty of meditation still left in her, by means of which, like the mouldering gentlefolk of the poet's story, she could sit and ponder what a gift life used to be.[1]

However, one excellent result of her general apathy was the long-delayed installation of Oak as bailiff; but he having virtually exercised that function for a long time already, the change, beyond the substantial increase of wages it brought, was little more than a nominal one addressed to the outside world.

Boldwood lived secluded and inactive. Much of his wheat and all his barley of that season had been spoilt by the rain. It sprouted, grew into intricate mats, and was ultimately thrown to the pigs in armfuls. The strange neglect which had produced this ruin and waste became the subject of whispered talk among all the people round; and it was elicited from one of Boldwood's men that forgetfulness had nothing to do with it, for he had been reminded of the danger to his corn as many times and as persistently as inferiors dared to do. The sight of the pigs turning in disgust from the rotten ears seemed to arouse Boldwood, and he one evening sent for Oak. Whether it was suggested by Bathsheba's recent act of promotion or not, the farmer proposed at the interview that Gabriel should undertake the superintendence of the Lower Farm as well as of Bathsheba's, because of the necessity Boldwood felt for such aid, and the impossibility of discovering a more trustworthy man. Gabriel's malignant star was assuredly setting fast.

Bathsheba, when she learnt of this proposal—for Oak was obliged to consult her—at first languidly objected. She considered that the two farms together were too extensive for the observation of one man. Boldwood, who was apparently determined by personal rather than commercial reasons, suggested that Oak should be furnished with a

1. An allusion to Robert Browning's poem "The Statue and the Bust," whose chief charac- ters never fulfill their love but instead "sit and ponder / What a gift life was, ages ago."

horse for his sole use, when the plan would present no difficulty, the two farms lying side by side. Boldwood did not directly communicate with her during these negotiations, only speaking to Oak, who was the go-between throughout. All was harmoniously arranged at last, and we now see Oak mounted on a strong cob,[2] and daily trotting the length and breadth of about two thousand acres in a cheerful spirit of surveillance, as if the crops all belonged to him—the actual mistress of the one-half, and the master of the other, sitting in their respective homes in gloomy and sad seclusion.

Out of this there arose, during the spring succeeding, a talk in the parish that Gabriel Oak was feathering his nest fast.

'Whatever d'ye think,' said Susan Tall, 'Gable Oak is coming it quite the dand. He now wears shining boots with hardly a hob in 'em, two or three times a-week, and a tall hat a-Sundays, and 'a hardly knows the name of smockfrock.[3] When I see people strut enough to be cut up into bantam cocks, I stand dormant with wonder, and says no more!'

It was eventually known that Gabriel, though paid a fixed wage by Bathsheba independent of the fluctuations of agricultural profits, had made an engagement with Boldwood by which Oak was to receive a share of the receipts—a small share certainly, yet it was money of a higher quality than mere wages, and capable of expansion in a way that wages were not. Some were beginning to consider Oak a 'near'[4] man, for though his condition had thus far improved, he lived in no better style than before, occupying the same cottage, paring his own potatoes, mending his stockings, and sometimes even making his bed with his own hands. But as Oak was not only provokingly indifferent to public opinion, but a man who clung persistently to old habits and usages, simply because they were old, there was room for doubt as to his motives.

A great hope had latterly germinated in Boldwood, whose unreasoning devotion to Bathsheba could only be characterized as a fond madness which neither time nor circumstance, evil nor good report, could weaken or destroy. This fevered hope had grown up again like a grain of mustard-seed[5] during the quiet which followed the hasty conjecture that Troy was drowned. He nourished it fearfully, and almost shunned the contemplation of it in earnest, lest facts should reveal the wildness of the dream. Bathsheba having at last been persuaded to wear mourning, her appearance as she entered the church in that guise was in itself a weekly addition to his faith that a

---

2. A thickset, stocky workhorse.
3. Oak is beginning to adopt the dress of a master-farmer rather than that of an ordinary farm-laborer who would usually wear a smock-frock and hobnailed boots.
4. Niggardly.
5. An allusion to the parable of the mustard

seed in Mark 4:30–32, in which Christ compares the kingdom of God to a mustard seed, "which, when it is sown in the earth, is less than all the seeds. . . . But when it is sown, it groweth up, and becometh greater than all herbs."

time was coming—very far off perhaps, yet surely nearing—when his waiting on events should have its reward. How long he might have to wait he had not yet closely considered. What he would try to recognize was that the severe schooling she had been subjected to had made Bathsheba much more considerate than she had formerly been of the feelings of others, and he trusted that, should she be willing at any time in the future to marry any man at all, that man would be himself. There was a substratum of good feeling in her: her self-reproach for the injury she had thoughtlessly done him might be depended upon now to a much greater extent than before her infatuation and disappointment. It would be possible to approach her by the channel of her good nature, and to suggest a friendly business-like compact between them for fulfilment at some future day, keeping the passionate side of his desire entirely out of her sight. Such was Boldwood's hope.

To the eyes of the middle-aged, Bathsheba was perhaps additionally charming just now. Her exuberance of spirit was pruned down; the original phantom of delight had shown herself to be not too bright for human nature's daily food,[6] and she had been able to enter this second poetical phase without losing much of the first in the process.

Bathsheba's return from a two months' visit to her old aunt at Norcombe afforded the impassioned and yearning farmer a pretext for inquiring directly after her—now possibly in the ninth month of her widowhood—and endeavouring to get a notion of her state of mind regarding him. This occurred in the middle of the haymaking, and Boldwood contrived to be near Liddy, who was assisting in the fields.

'I am glad to see you out of doors, Lydia,' he said pleasantly.

She simpered, and wondered in her heart why he should speak so frankly to her.

'I hope Mrs. Troy is quite well after her long absence,' he continued, in a matter expressing that the coldest-hearted neighbour could scarcely say less about her.

'She is quite well, sir.'

'And cheerful, I suppose.'

'Yes, cheerful.'

'Fearful, did you say?'

'O no. I merely said she was cheerful.'

'Tells you all her affairs?'

'No, sir.'

'Some of them?'

'Yes, sir.'

'Mrs. Troy puts much confidence in you, Lydia; and very wisely, perhaps.'

'She do, sir. I've been with her all through her troubles, and was

6. An allusion to lines in William Wordsworth's poem, "She Was a Phantom of Delight" (1807), which read, "A creature not too bright or good / For human nature's daily food."

with her at the time of Mr. Troy's going and all. And if she were to marry again I expect I should bide with her.'

'She promises that you shall—quite natural,' said the strategic lover, throbbing throughout him at the presumption which Liddy's words appeared to warrant—that his darling had thought of re-marriage.

'No—she doesn't promise it exactly. I merely judge on my own account.'

'Yes, yes, I understand. When she alludes to the possibility of marrying again, you conclude——'

'She never do allude to it, sir,' said Liddy, thinking how very stupid Mr. Boldwood was getting.

'Of course not,' he returned hastily, his hope falling again. 'You needn't take quite such long reaches with your rake, Lydia—short and quick ones are best. Well, perhaps, as she is absolute mistress again now, it is wise of her to resolve never to give up her freedom.'

'My mistress did certainly once say, though not seriously, that she supposed she might marry again at the end of seven years from last year, if she cared to risk Mr. Troy's coming back and claiming her.'

'Ah, six years from the present time. Said that she might. She might marry at once in every reasonable person's opinion, whatever the lawyers may say to the contrary.'

'Have you been to ask them?' said Liddy innocently.

'Not I,' said Boldwood, growing red. 'Liddy, you needn't stay here a minute later than you wish, so Mr. Oak says. I am now going on a little further. Good-afternoon.'

He went away vexed with himself, and ashamed of having for this one time in his life done anything which could be called underhand. Poor Boldwood had no more skill in finesse than a battering-ram, and he was uneasy with a sense of having made himself to appear stupid and, what was worse, mean. But he had, after all, lighted upon one fact by way of repayment. It was a singularly fresh and fascinating fact, and though not without its sadness it was pertinent and real. In little more than six years from this time Bathsheba might certainly marry him. There was something definite in that hope, for admitting that there might have been no deep thought in her words to Liddy about marriage, they showed at least her creed on the matter.

This pleasant notion was now continually in his mind. Six years were a long time, but how much shorter than never, the idea he had for so long been obliged to endure! Jacob had served twice seven years for Rachel:[7] what were six for such a woman as this? He tried to like the notion of waiting for her better than that of winning her at once. Boldwood felt his love to be so deep and strong and eternal, that it was possible she had never yet known its full volume, and this patience in

7. An allusion to Genesis 29:20: "And Jacob served seven years for Rachel; and they seemed unto him *but* a few days, for the love he had to her."

delay would afford him an opportunity of giving sweet proof on the point. He would annihilate the six years of his life as if they were minutes—so little did he value his time on earth beside her love. He would let her see, all those six years of intangible ethereal courtship, how little care he had for anything but as it bore upon the consummation.

Meanwhile the early and the late summer brought round the week in which Greenhill Fair[8] was held. This fair was frequently attended by the folk of Weatherbury.

L

The Sheep Fair—Troy Touches His Wife's Hand

Greenhill was the Nijni Novgorod[1] of South Wessex; and the busiest, merriest, noisiest day of the whole statute number was the day of the sheep fair. This yearly gathering was upon the summit of a hill which retained in good preservation the remains of an ancient earthwork, consisting of a huge rampart and entrenchment of an oval form encircling the top of the hill, though somewhat broken down here and there. To each of the two chief openings on opposite sides a winding road ascended, and the level green space of ten or fifteen acres enclosed by the bank was the site of the fair. A few permanent erections dotted the spot, but the majority of visitors patronized canvas alone for resting and feeding under during the time of their sojourn here.

Shepherds who attended with their flocks from long distances started from home two or three days, or even a week, before the fair, driving their charges a few miles each day—not more than ten or twelve—and resting them at night in hired fields by the wayside at previously chosen points, where they fed, having fasted since morning. The shepherd of each flock marched behind, a bundle containing his kit for the week strapped upon his shoulders, and in his hand his crook, which he used as the staff of his pilgrimage. Several of the sheep would get worn and lame, and occasionally a lambing occurred on the road. To meet these contingencies, there was frequently provided, to accompany the flocks from the remoter points, a pony and waggon into which the weakly ones were taken for the remainder of the journey.

The Weatherbury Farms, however, were no such long distance from the hill, and those arrangements were not necessary in their case. But the large united flocks of Bathsheba and Farmer Boldwood formed

---

8. Greenhill is Hardy's name for Woodbury Hill, where, in the nineteenth century, an annual fair was held each September.
1. A city in Russia, now called Gorky, famous in the nineteenth century for its annual fairs, which drew thousands of visitors from both Europe and Asia.

a valuable and imposing multitude which demanded much attention, and on this account Gabriel, in addition to Boldwood's shepherd and Cain Ball, accompanied them along way, through the decayed town of Kingsbere, and upward to the plateau,—old George the dog of course behind them.

When the autumn sun slanted over Greenhill this morning and lighted the dewy flat upon its crest, nebulous clouds of dust were to be seen floating between the pairs of hedges which streaked the wide prospect around in all directions. These gradually converged upon the base of the hill, and the flocks became individually visible, climbing the serpentine ways which led to the top. Thus, in a slow procession, they entered the opening to which the roads tended, multitude after multitude, horned and hornless—blue flocks and red flocks, buff flocks and brown flocks, even green and salmon-tinted flocks, according to the fancy of the colourist and custom of the farm. Men were shouting, dogs were barking, with greatest animation, but the thronging travellers in so long a journey had grown nearly indifferent to such terrors, though they still bleated piteously at the unwontedness of their experiences, a tall shepherd rising here and there in the midst of them, like a gigantic idol amid a crowd of prostrate devotees.

The great mass of sheep in the fair consisted of South Downs and the old Wessex horned breeds; to the latter class Bathsheba's and Farmer Boldwood's mainly belonged. These filed in about nine o'clock, their vermiculated horns lopping gracefully on each side of their cheeks in geometrically perfect spirals, a small pink and white ear nestling under each horn. Before and behind came other varieties, perfect leopards as to the full rich substance of their coats, and only lacking the spots. There were also a few of the Oxfordshire breed, whose wool was beginning to curl like a child's flaxen hair, though surpassed in this respect by the effeminate Leicesters, which were in turn less curly than the Cotswolds. But the most picturesque by far was a small flock of Exmoors, which chanced to be there this year.[2] Their pied faces and legs, dark and heavy horns, tresses of wool hanging round their swarthy foreheads, quite relieved the monotony of the flocks in that quarter.

All these bleating, panting, and weary thousands had entered and were penned before the morning had far advanced, the dog belonging to each flock being tied to the corner of the pen containing it. Alleys for pedestrians intersected the pens, which soon became crowded with buyers and sellers from far and near.

2. "South Downs" are a breed of small sheep with short, fine wool; they yield a high quality mutton. "Wessex horned breeds" is Hardy's name for Dorset Horn, a domestic sheep with large curled horns and fine-textured, short wool. "Oxfordshire" is a breed of large, hornless sheep with thick, curly fleece. "Leicesters" are a long-wooled, hornless breed of English sheep developed in Leicestershire. "Cotswolds" are a breed of hornless sheep with heavy coats of long, coarse wool. "Exmoors" are a breed of small, hardy sheep with heavy thick fleece and large curled horns, named after the moorland area where they were first bred.

In another part of the hill an altogether different scene began to force itself upon the eye towards midday. A circular tent, of exceptional newness and size, was in course of erection here. As the day drew on, the flocks began to change hands, lightening the shepherds' responsibilities; and they turned their attention to this tent and inquired of a man at work there, whose soul seemed concentrated on tying a bothering knot in no time, what was going on.

'The Royal Hippodrome Performance of Turpin's Ride to York and the Death of Black Bess,'[3] replied the man promptly, without turning his eyes or leaving off tying.

As soon as the tent was completed the band struck up highly stimulating harmonies, and the announcement was publicly made, Black Bess standing in a conspicuous position on the outside, as a living proof, if proof were wanted, of the truth of the oracular utterances from the stage over which the people were to enter. These were so convinced by such genuine appeals to heart and understanding both that they soon began to crowd in abundantly, among the foremost being visible Jan Coggan and Joseph Poorgrass, who were holiday keeping here to-day.

'That's the great ruffen pushing me!' screamed a woman in front of Jan over her shoulder at him when the rush was at its fiercest.

'How can I help pushing ye when the folk behind push me?' said Coggan, in a deprecating tone, turning his head towards the aforesaid folk as far as he could without turning his body, which was jammed as in a vice.

There was a silence; then the drums and trumpets again sent forth their echoing notes. The crowd was again ecstasied, and gave another lurch in which Coggan and Poorgrass were again thrust by those behind upon the women in front.

'O that helpless feymels should be at the mercy of such ruffens!' exclaimed one of these ladies again, as she swayed like a reed shaken by the wind.[4]

'Now,' said Coggan, appealing in an earnest voice to the public at large as it stood clustered about his shoulder-blades, 'did ye ever hear such a onreasonable woman as that? Upon my carcase, neighbours, if I could only get out of this cheesewring,[5] the damn women might eat the show for me!'

'Don't ye lose yer temper, Jan!' implored Joseph Poorgrass, in a whisper. 'They might get their men to murder us, for I think by the shine of their eyes that they be a sinful form of womankind.'

Jan held his tongue, as if he had no objection to be pacified to please

---

3. Dick Turpin (d. 1739) was a highwayman whose twelve-hour ride from London to York on his horse Black Bess was legendary.
4. "Reed shaken by the wind" is an allusion to Matthew 11:7 and Luke 7:24.
5. A press used to wring whey from cheese curds (dialect).

a friend, and they gradually reached the foot of the ladder, Poorgrass being flattened like a jumping-jack,[6] and the sixpence, for admission, which he had got ready half-an-hour earlier, having become so reeking hot in the tight squeeze of his excited hand that the woman in spangles, brazen rings set with glass diamonds, and with chalked face and shoulders, who took the money of him, hastily dropped it again from a fear that some trick had been played to burn her fingers. So they all entered, and the cloth of the tent, to the eyes of an observer on the outside, became bulged into innumerable pimples such as we observe on a sack of potatoes, caused by the various human heads, backs, and elbows at high pressure within.

At the rear of the large tent there were two small dressing-tents. One of these, allotted to the male performers, was partitioned into halves by a cloth; and in one of the divisions there was sitting on the grass, pulling on a pair of jack-boots, a young man whom we instantly recognize as Sergeant Troy.

Troy's appearance in this position may be briefly accounted for. The brig aboard which he was taken in Budmouth Roads was about to start on a voyage, though somewhat short of hands. Troy read the articles and joined, but before they sailed a boat was despatched across the bay to Lulwind Cove; as he had half expected, his clothes were gone. He ultimately worked his passage to the United States, where he made a precarious living in various towns as Professor of Gymnastics, Sword Exercise, Fencing, and Pugilism. A few months were sufficient to give him a distaste for this kind of life. There was a certain animal form of refinement in his nature; and however pleasant a strange condition might be whilst privations were easily warded off, it was disadvantageously coarse when money was short. There was ever present, too, the idea that he could claim a home and its comforts did he but choose to return to England and Weatherbury Farm. Whether Bathsheba thought him dead was a frequent subject of curious conjecture. To England he did return at last; but the fact of drawing nearer to Weatherbury abstracted its fascinations, and his intention to enter his old groove at that place became modified. It was with gloom he considered on landing at Liverpool that if he were to go home his reception would be of a kind very unpleasant to contemplate; for what Troy had in the way of emotion was an occasional fitful sentiment which sometimes caused him as much inconvenience as emotion of a strong and healthy kind. Bathsheba was not a woman to be made a fool of, or a woman to suffer in silence; and how could he endure existence with a spirited wife to whom at first entering he would be beholden for food and lodging? Moreover, it was not at all likely that his wife would fail at her farming, if she had not already done so; and he would then become liable for her maintenance: and what a life such a future

6. A child's toy, also called a jack-in-the-box, which consists of a figure in which a spring is concealed so that it may be compressed in a box until released.

of poverty with her would be, the spectre of Fanny constantly between them, harrowing his temper and embittering her words! Thus, for reasons touching on distaste, regret, and shame commingled, he put off his return from day to day, and would have decided to put it off altogether if he could have found anywhere else the ready-made establishment which existed for him there.

At this time—the July preceding the September in which we find him at Greenhill Fair—he fell in with a travelling circus which was performing in the outskirts of a northern town. Troy introduced himself to the manager by taming a restive horse of the troupe, hitting a suspended apple with a pistol-bullet fired from the animal's back when in full gallop, and other feats. For his merits in these—all more or less based upon his experiences as a dragoon-guardsman—Troy was taken into the company, and the play of Turpin was prepared with a view to his personation of the chief character. Troy was not greatly elated by the appreciative spirit in which he was undoubtedly treated, but he thought the engagement might afford him a few weeks for consideration. It was thus carelessly, and without having formed any definite plan for the future, that Troy found himself at Greenhill Fair with the rest of the company on this day.

And now the mild autumn sun got lower, and in front of the pavilion the following incident had taken place. Bathsheba—who was driven to the fair that day by her odd man Poorgrass—had, like every one else, read or heard the announcement that Mr. Francis, the Great Cosmopolitan Equestrian and Roughrider, would enact the part of Turpin, and she was not yet too old and careworn to be without a little curiosity to see him. This particular show was by far the largest and grandest in the fair, a horde of little shows grouping themselves under its shade like chickens around a hen. The crowd had passed in, and Boldwood, who had been watching all the day for an opportunity of speaking to her, seeing her comparatively isolated, came up to her side.

'I hope the sheep have done well to-day, Mrs. Troy?' he said nervously.

'O yes, thank you,' said Bathsheba, colour springing up in the centre of her cheeks. 'I was fortunate enough to sell them all just as we got upon the hill, so we hadn't to pen at all.'

'And now you are entirely at leisure?'

'Yes, except that I have to see one more dealer in two hours' time: otherwise I should be going home. I was looking at this large tent and the announcement. Have you ever seen the play of "Turpin's Ride to York"? Turpin was a real man, was he not?'

'O yes, perfectly true—all of it. Indeed, I think I've heard Jan Coggan say that a relation of his knew Tom King,[7] Turpin's friend, quite well.'

7. Another highwayman, who was accidentally killed by Turpin during his flight from London to York.

'Coggan is rather given to strange stories connected with his relations, we must remember. I hope they can all be believed.'

'Yes, yes; we know Coggan. But Turpin is true enough. You have never seen it played, I suppose?'

'Never. I was not allowed to go into these places when I was young. Hark! What's that prancing? How they shout!'

'Black Bess just started off, I suppose. Am I right in supposing you would like to see the performance, Mrs. Troy? Please excuse my mistake, if it is one; but if you would like to, I'll get a seat for you with pleasure.' Perceiving that she hesitated, he added, 'I myself shall not stay to see it: I've seen it before.'

Now Bathsheba did care a little to see the show, and had only withheld her feet from the ladder because she feared to go in alone. She had been hoping that Oak might appear, whose assistance in such cases was always accepted as an inalienable right, but Oak was nowhere to be seen; and hence it was that she said, 'Then if you will just look in first, to see if there's room, I think I will go in for a minute or two.'

And so a short time after this Bathsheba appeared in the tent with Boldwood at her elbow, who, taking her to a 'reserved' seat, again withdrew.

This feature consisted of one raised bench in a very conspicuous part of the circle, covered with red cloth, and floored with a piece of carpet, and Bathsheba immediately found, to her confusion, that she was the single reserved individual in the tent, the rest of the crowded spectators, one and all, standing on their legs on the borders of the arena, where they got twice as good a view of the performance for half the money. Hence as many eyes were turned upon her, enthroned alone in this place of honour, against a scarlet background, as upon the ponies and clown who were engaged in preliminary exploits in the centre, Turpin not having yet appeared. Once there, Bathsheba was forced to make the best of it and remain: she sat down, spreading her skirts with some dignity over the unoccupied space on each side of her, and giving a new and feminine aspect to the pavilion. In a few minutes she noticed the fat red nape of Coggan's neck among those standing just below her, and Joseph Poorgrass's saintly profile a little further on.

The interior was shadowy with a peculiar shade. The strange luminous semi-opacities of fine autumn afternoons and eves intensified into Rembrandt effects[8] the few yellow sunbeams which came through holes and divisions in the canvas, and spirted like jets of gold-dust across the dusky blue atmosphere of haze pervading the tent, until they alighted on inner surfaces of cloth opposite, and shone like little lamps suspended there.

Troy, on peeping from his dressing-tent through a slit for a recon-

8. Chiaroscuro effects; a reference to the paintings of Rembrandt Harmenszoon van Rijin, who was famous for his handling of contrasting light and shade.

noitre before entering, saw his unconscious wife on high before him as described, sitting as queen of the tournament. He started back in utter confusion, for although his disguise effectually concealed his personality, he instantly felt that she would be sure to recognize his voice. He had several times during the day thought of the possibility of some Weatherbury person or other appearing and recognizing him; but he had taken the risk carelessly. If they see me, let them, he had said. But here was Bathsheba in her own person; and the reality of the scene was so much intenser than any of his prefigurings that he felt he had not half enough considered the point.

She looked so charming and fair that his cool mood about Weatherbury people was changed. He had not expected her to exercise this power over him in the twinkling of an eye. Should he go on, and care nothing? He could not bring himself to do that. Beyond a politic wish to remain unknown, there suddenly arose in him now a sense of shame at the possibility that his attractive young wife, who already despised him, should despise him more by discovering him in so mean a condition after so long a time. He actually blushed at the thought, and was vexed beyond measure that his sentiments of dislike towards Weatherbury should have led him to dally about the country in this way.

But Troy was never more clever than when absolutely at his wits' end. He hastily thrust aside the curtain dividing his own little dressing space from that of the manager and proprietor, who now appeared as the individual called Tom King as far down as his waist, and as the aforesaid respectable manager thence to his toes.

'Here's the devil to pay!' said Troy.

'How's that?'

'Why, there's a blackguard creditor in the tent I don't want to see, who'll discover me and nab me as sure as Satan if I open my mouth. What's to be done?'

'You must appear now, I think.'

'I can't.'

'But the play must proceed.'

'Do you give out that Turpin has got a bad cold, and can't speak his part, but that he'll perform it just the same without speaking.'

The proprietor shook his head.

'Anyhow, play or no play, I won't open my mouth,' said Troy firmly.

'Very well, then let me see. I tell you how we'll manage,' said the other, who perhaps felt it would be extremely awkward to offend his leading man just at this time. 'I won't tell 'em anything about your keeping silence; go on with the piece and say nothing, doing what you can by a judicious wink now and then, and a few indomitable nods in the heroic places, you know. They'll never find out that the speeches are omitted.'

This seemed feasible enough, for Turpin's speeches were not many or long, the fascination of the piece lying entirely in the action; and accordingly the play began, and at the appointed time Black Bess leapt into the grassy circle amid the plaudits of the spectators. At the turnpike scene, where Bess and Turpin are hotly pursued at midnight by the officers, and the half-awake gatekeeper in his tasselled nightcap denies that any horseman has passed, Coggan uttered a broad-chested 'Well done!' which could be heard all over the fair above the bleating, and Poorgrass smiled delightly with a nice sense of dramatic contrast between our hero, who coolly leaps the gate, and halting justice in the form of his enemies, who must needs pull up cumbersomely and wait to be let through. At the death of Tom King, he could not refrain from seizing Coggan by the hand, and whispering, with tears in his eyes, 'Of course he's not really shot, Jan—only seemingly!' And when the last sad scene came on, and the body of the gallant and faithful Bess had to be carried out on a shutter by twelve volunteers from among the spectators, nothing could restrain Poorgrass from lending a hand, exclaiming, as he asked Jan to join him, "Twill be something to tell of at Warren's in future years, Jan, and hand down to our children.' For many a year in Weatherbury, Joseph told, with the air of a man who had had experiences in his time, that he touched with his own hand the hoof of Bess as she lay upon the board upon his shoulder. If, as some thinkers hold, immortality consists in being enshrined in others' memories, then did Black Bess become immortal that day if she never had done so before.

Meanwhile Troy had added a few touches to his ordinary make-up for the character, the more effectually to disguise himself, and though he had felt faint qualms on first entering, the metamorphosis effected by judiciously 'lining' his face with a wire rendered him safe from the eyes of Bathsheba and her men. Nevertheless, he was relieved when it was got through.

There was a second performance in the evening, and the tent was lighted up. Troy had taken his part very quietly this time, venturing to introduce a few speeches on occasion; and was just concluding it when, whilst standing at the edge of the circle contiguous to the first row of spectators, he observed within a yard of him the eye of a man darted keenly into his side features. Troy hastily shifted his position, after having recognized in the scrutineer the knavish bailiff Penny-ways, his wife's sworn enemy, who still hung about the outskirts of Weatherbury.

At first Troy resolved to take no notice and abide by circumstances. That he had been identified by this man was highly probable; yet there was room for a doubt. Then the great objection he had felt to allowing news of his proximity to precede him to Weatherbury in the event of his return, based on a feeling that knowledge of his present occupation would discredit him still further in his wife's eyes, returned in full force. Moreover, should he resolve not to return at all, a tale of his being alive and in the neighbourhood would be awkward; and he was anxious to acquire a knowledge of his wife's temporal affairs before deciding which to do.

In this dilemma Troy at once went out to reconnoitre. It occurred to him that to find Pennyways, and make a friend of him if possible, would be a very wise act. He had put on a thick beard borrowed from the establishment, and in this he wandered about the fair-field. It was now almost dark, and respectable people were getting their carts and gigs ready to go home.

The largest refreshment booth in the fair was provided by an innkeeper from a neighbouring town. This was considered an unexceptionable place for obtaining the necessary food and rest: Host Trencher (as he was jauntily called by the local newspaper) being a substantial man of high repute for catering through all the country round. The tent was divided into first and second-class compartments, and at the end of the first-class division was a yet further enclosure for the most exclusive, fenced off from the body of the tent by a luncheon-bar, behind which the host himself stood, bustling about in white apron and shirt-sleeves, and looking as if he had never lived anywhere but under canvas all his life. In these penetralia[9] were chairs and a table, which, on candles being lighted, made quite a cosy and luxurious show, with an urn, plated tea and coffee pots, china teacups, and plum cakes.

Troy stood at the entrance to the booth, where a gipsy-woman was frying pancakes over a little fire of sticks and selling them at a penny a-piece, and looked over the heads of the people within. He could see nothing of Pennyways, but he soon discerned Bathsheba through an opening into the reserved space at the further end. Troy thereupon retreated, went round the tent into the darkness, and listened. He could hear Bathsheba's voice immediately inside the canvas; she was conversing with a man. A warmth overspread his face: surely she was not so unprincipled as to flirt in a fair! He wondered if, then, she reckoned upon his death as an absolute certainty. To get at the root of the matter, Troy took a penknife from his pocket and softly made two little cuts crosswise in the cloth, which, by folding back the corners, left a hole the size of a wafer.[1] Close to this he placed his face, withdrawing it again in a movement of surprise; for his eye had been within twelve inches of the top of Bathsheba's head. It was too near to be convenient. He made another hole a little to one side and lower down, in a shaded place beside her chair, from which it was easy and safe to survey her by looking horizontally.

Troy took in the scene completely now. She was leaning back, sipping a cup of tea that she held in her hand, and the owner of the male voice was Boldwood, who had apparently just brought the cup to

9. The innermost recesses of a building or similar structure.

1. A small, round adhesive disk used in the nineteenth century to seal letters.

her. Bathsheba, being in a negligent mood, leant so idly against the canvas that it was pressed to the shape of her shoulder, and she was, in fact, as good as in Troy's arms; and he was obliged to keep his breast carefully backward that she might not feel its warmth through the cloth as he gazed in.

Troy found unexpected chords of feeling to be stirred again within him as they had been stirred earlier in the day. She was handsome as ever, and she was his. It was some minutes before he could counteract his sudden wish to go in, and claim her. Then he thought how the proud girl who had always looked down upon him even whilst it was to love him, would hate him on discovering him to be a strolling player. Were he to make himself known, that chapter of his life must at all risks be kept for ever from her and from the Weatherbury people, or his name would be a byword throughout the parish. He would be nick-named 'Turpin' as long as he lived. Assuredly before he could claim her these few past months of his existence must be entirely blotted out.

'Shall I get you another cup before you start, ma'am?' said Farmer Boldwood.

'Thank you,' said Bathsheba. 'But I must be going at once. It was great neglect in that man to keep me waiting here till so late. I should have gone two hours ago, if it had not been for him. I had no idea of coming in here; but there's nothing so refreshing as a cup of tea, though I should never have got one if you hadn't helped me.'

Troy scrutinized her cheek as lit by the candles, and watched each varying shade thereon, and the white shell-like sinuosities of her little ear. She took out her purse and was insisting to Boldwood on paying for her tea for herself, when at this moment Pennyways entered the tent. Troy trembled: here was his scheme for respectability en-dangered at once. He was about to leave his hole of espial, attempt to follow Pennyways, and find out if the ex-bailiff had recognized him, when he was arrested by the conversation, and found he was too late.

'Excuse me, ma'am,' said Pennyways; 'I've some private informa-tion for your ear alone.'

'I cannot hear it now,' she said coldly. That Bathsheba could not endure this man was evident; in fact, he was continually coming to her with some tale or other, by which he might creep into favour at the expense of persons maligned.

'I'll write it down,' said Pennyways confidently. He stooped over the table, pulled a leaf from a warped pocket-book, and wrote upon the paper, in a round hand—

'*Your husband is here. I've seen him. Who's the fool now?*'

This he folded small, and handed towards her. Bathsheba would not read it; she would not even put out her hand to take it. Pennyways, then, with a laugh of derision, tossed it into her lap, and, turning away, left her.

From the words and action of Pennyways, Troy, though he had not been able to see what the ex-bailiff wrote, had not a moment's doubt that the note referred to him. Nothing that he could think of could be done to check the exposure. 'Curse my luck!' he whispered, and added imprecations which rustled in the gloom like a pestilent wind. Meanwhile Boldwood said, taking up the note from her lap—

'Don't you wish to read it, Mrs. Troy? If not, I'll destroy it.'

'Oh, well,' said Bathsheba carelessly, 'perhaps it is unjust not to read it; but I can guess what it is about. He wants me to recommend him, or it is to tell me of some little scandal or another connected with my work-people. He's always doing that.'

Bathsheba held the note in her right hand. Boldwood handed towards her a plate of cut bread-and-butter; when, in order to take a slice, she put the note into her left hand, where she was still holding the purse, and then allowed her hand to drop beside her close to the canvas. The moment had come for saving his game, and Troy impulsively felt that he would play the card. For yet another time he looked at the fair hand, and saw the pink finger-tips, and the blue veins of the wrist, encircled by a bracelet of coral chippings which she wore: how familiar it all was to him! Then, with the lightning action in which he was such an adept, he noiselessly slipped his hand under the bottom of the tent-cloth, which was far from being pinned tightly down, lifted it a little way, keeping his eye to the hole, snatched the note from her fingers, dropped the canvas, and ran away in the gloom towards the bank and ditch, smiling at the scream of astonishment which burst from her. Troy then slid down on the outside of the rampart, hastened round in the bottom of the entrenchment to a distance of a hundred yards, ascended again, and crossed boldly in a slow walk towards the front entrance of the tent. His object was now to get to Pennyways, and prevent a repetition of the announcement until such time as he should choose.

Troy reached the tent door, and standing among the groups there gathered, looked anxiously for Pennyways, evidently not wishing to make himself prominent by inquiring for him. One or two men were speaking of a daring attempt that had just been made to rob a young lady by lifting the canvas of the tent beside her. It was supposed that the rogue had imagined a slip of paper which she held in her hand to be a bank note, for he had seized it, and made off with it, leaving her purse behind. His chagrin and disappointment at discovering its worthlessness would be a good joke, it was said. However, the occurrence seemed to have become known to few, for it had not interrupted a fiddler, who had lately begun playing by the door of the tent, nor the four bowed old men with grim countenances and walking-sticks in hand, who were dancing 'Major Malley's Reel' to the tune. Behind these stood Pennyways. Troy glided up to him, beckoned, and whispered a few words; and with a mutual glance of concurrence the two men went into the night together.

LI

Bathsheba Talks With Her Outrider

The arrangement for getting back again to Weatherbury had been that Oak should take the place of Poorgrass in Bathsheba's conveyance and drive her home, it being discovered late in the afternoon that Joseph was suffering from his old complaint, a multiplying eye, and was, therefore, hardly trustworthy as coachman and protector to a woman. But Oak had found himself so occupied, and was full of so many cares relative to those portions of Boldwoods's flocks that were not disposed of, that Bathsheba, without telling Oak or anybody, resolved to drive home herself, as she had many times done from Casterbridge Market, and trust to her good angel for performing the journey unmolested. But having fallen in with Farmer Boldwood accidentally (on her part at least) at the refreshment-tent, she found it impossible to refuse his offer to ride on horseback beside her as escort. It had grown twilight before she was aware, but Boldwood assured her that there was no cause for uneasiness, as the moon would be up in half-an-hour.

Immediately after the incident in the tent she had risen to go—now absolutely alarmed and really grateful for her old lover's protection—though regretting Gabriel's absence, whose company she would have much preferred, as being more proper as well as more pleasant, since he was her own managing-man and servant. This, however, could not be helped; she would not, on any consideration, treat Boldwood harshly, having once already ill-used him, and the moon having risen, and the gig being ready, she drove across the hill-top in the wending ways which led downwards—to oblivious obscurity, as it seemed, for the moon and the hill it flooded with light were in appearance on a level, the rest of the world lying as a vast shady concave between them. Boldwood mounted his horse, and followed in close attendance behind. Thus they descended into the lowlands, and the sounds of those left on the hill came like voices from the sky, and the lights were as those of a camp in heaven. They soon passed the merry stragglers in the immediate vicinity of the hill, traversed Kingsbere, and got upon the high road.

The keen instincts of Bathsheba had perceived that the farmer's staunch devotion to herself was still undiminished, and she sympathized deeply. The sight had quite depressed her this evening; had reminded her of her folly; she wished anew, as she had wished many months ago, for some means of making reparation for her fault. Hence her pity for the man who so persistently loved on to his own injury and permanent gloom had betrayed Bathsheba into an injudicious considerateness of manner, which appeared almost like tenderness, and gave new vigour to the exquisite dream of a Jacob's seven years' service in poor Boldwood's mind.

He soon found an excuse for advancing from his position in the rear, and rode close by her side. They had gone two or three miles in the moonlight, speaking desultorily across the wheel of her gig concerning the fair, farming, Oak's usefulness to them both, and other indifferent subjects, when Boldwood said suddenly and simply—

'Mrs. Troy, you will marry again some day?'

This point-blank query unmistakably confused her, and it was not till a minute or more had elapsed that she said, 'I have not seriously thought of any such subject.'

'I quite understand that. Yet your late husband has been dead nearly one year, and——'

'You forget that his death was never absolutely proved, and may not have taken place; so that I may not be really a widow,' she said, catching at the straw of escape that the fact afforded.

'Not absolutely proved, perhaps, but it was proved circumstantially. A man saw him drowning, too. No reasonable person has any doubt of his death; nor have you, ma'am, I should imagine.'

'O yes I have, or I should have acted differently,' she said, gently. 'From the first I have had a strange unaccountable feeling that he could not have perished. But I have been able to explain that in several ways since. Even were I half persuaded that I shall see him no more, I am far from thinking of marriage with another. I should be very contemptible to indulge in such a thought.'

They were silent now awhile, and having struck into an unfrequented track across a common, the creaks of Boldwood's saddle and her gig springs were all the sounds to be heard. Boldwood ended the pause.

'Do you remember when I carried you fainting in my arms into the King's Arms, in Casterbridge? Every dog has his day: that was mine.'

'I know—I know it all,' she said, hurriedly.

'I, for one, shall never cease regretting that events so fell out as to deny you to me.'

'I, too, am very sorry,' she said, and then checked herself. 'I mean, you know, I am sorry you thought I——'

'I have always this dreary pleasure in thinking over those past times with you—that I was something to you before *he* was anything, and that you belonged *almost* to me. But, of course, that's nothing. You never liked me.'

'I did; and respected you, too.'

'Do you now?'

'Yes.'

'Which?'

'How do you mean which?'

'Do you like me, or do you respect me?'

'I don't know—at least, I cannot tell you. It is difficult for a woman to define her feelings in language which is chiefly made by men to express theirs. My treatment of you was thoughtless, inexcusable, wicked! I shall eternally regret it. If there had been anything I could have done to make amends I would most gladly have done it—there was nothing on earth I so longed to do as to repair the error. But that was not possible.'

'Don't blame yourself—you were not so far in the wrong as you suppose. Bathsheba, supposed you had real complete proof that you are what, in fact, you are—a widow—would you repair the old wrong to me by marrying me?'

'I cannot say. I shouldn't yet, at any rate.'

'But you might at some future time of your life?'

'O yes, I might at some time.'

'Well, then, do you know that without further proof of any kind you may marry again in about six years from the present—subject to nobody's objection or blame?'

'O yes,' she said, quickly. 'I know all that. But don't talk of it—seven or six years—where may we all be by that time?'

'They will soon glide by, and it will seem an astonishingly short time to look back upon when they are past—much less than to look forward to now.'

'Yes, yes; I have found that in my own experience.'

'Now, listen once more,' Boldwood pleaded. 'If I wait that time, will you marry me? You own that you owe me amends—let that be your way of making them.'

'But, Mr. Boldwood—six years——'

'Do you want to be the wife of any other man?'

'No indeed! I mean, that I don't like to talk about this matter now. Perhaps it is not proper, and I ought not to allow it. Let us drop it. My husband may be living, as I said.'

'Of course, I'll drop the subject if you wish. But propriety has nothing to do with reasons. I am a middle-aged man, willing to protect you for the remainder of our lives. On your side, at least, there is no passion or blamable haste—on mine, perhaps, there is. But I can't help seeing that if you choose from a feeling of pity, and, as you say, a wish to make amends, to make a bargain with me for a far-ahead time—an agreement which will set all things right and make me happy, late though it may be—there is no fault to be found with you as a woman. Hadn't I the first place beside you? Haven't you been almost mine once already? Surely you can say to me as much as this, you will have me back again should circumstances permit? Now, pray speak! O Bathsheba, promise—it is only a little promise—that if you marry again, you will marry me!'

His tone was so excited that she almost feared him at this moment, even whilst she sympathized. It was a simple physical fear—the weak of the strong; there was no emotional aversion or inner repugnance. She said, with some distress in her voice, for she remembered vividly his outburst on the Yalbury Road, and shrank from a repetition of his anger:—

'I will never marry another man whilst you wish me to be your wife, whatever comes—but to say more—you have taken me so by surprise——'

'But let it stand in these simple words—that in six year's time you will be my wife? Unexpected accidents we'll not mention, because those, of course, must be given way to. Now, this time I know you will keep your word.'

'That's why I hesitate to give it.'

'But do give it! Remember the past, and be kind.'

She breathed; and then said mournfully: 'O what shall I do? I don't love you, and I much fear that I never shall love you as much as a woman ought to love a husband. If you, sir, know that, and I can yet give you happiness by a mere promise to marry at the end of six years, if my husband should not come back, it is a great honour to me. And if you value such an act of friendship from a woman who doesn't esteem herself as she did, and has little love left, why I—I will——'

'Promise!'

'——Consider, if I cannot promise soon.'

'But soon is perhaps never?'

'O no, it is not! I mean soon. Christmas, we'll say.'

'Christmas!' He said nothing further till he added: 'Well, I'll say no more to you about it till that time.'

Bathsheba was in a very peculiar state of mind, which showed how entirely the soul is the slave of the body, the ethereal spirit dependent for its quality upon the tangible flesh and blood.[1] It is hardly too much to say that she felt coerced by a force stronger than her own will, not only into the act of promising upon this singularly remote and vague matter, but into the emotion of fancying that she ought to promise. When the weeks intervening between the night of this conversation and Christmas day began perceptibly to diminish, her anxiety and perplexity increased.

One day she was led by an accident into an oddly confidential dialogue with Gabriel about her difficulty. It afforded her a little relief—of a dull and cheerless kind. They were auditing accounts, and something occurred in the course of their labours which led Oak to say, speaking of Boldwood, 'He'll never forget you, ma'am, never.'

Then out came her trouble before she was aware; and she told him

---

1. The generalizations here parallel remarks by Auguste Comte (1798–1857) that Hardy had probably read; see Lennart Björk, ed., *The*   *Literary Notes of Thomas Hardy*, vol. I, notes, p. 308, item 752.

how she had again got into the toils; what Boldwood had asked her, and how he was expecting her assent. 'The most mournful reason of all for my agreeing to it,' she said sadly, 'and the true reason why I think to do so for good or for evil, is this—it is a thing I have not breathed to a living soul as yet—I believe that if I don't give my word, he'll go out of his mind.'

'Really, do ye?' said Gabriel, gravely.

'I believe this,' she continued, with reckless frankness; 'and Heaven knows I say it in a spirit the very reverse of vain, for I am grieved and troubled to my soul about it—I believe I hold that man's future in my hand. His career depends entirely upon my treatment of him. O Gabriel, I tremble at my responsibility, for it is terrible!'

'Well, I think this much, ma'am, as I told you years ago,' said Oak, 'that his life is a total blank whenever he isn't hoping for 'ee; but I can't suppose—I hope that nothing so dreadful hangs on to it as you fancy. His natural manner has always been dark and strange, you know. But since the case is so sad and odd-like, why don't ye give the conditional promise? I think I would.'

'But is it right? Some rash acts of my past life have taught me that a watched woman must have very much circumspection to retain only a very little credit, and I do want and long to be discreet in this! And six years—why we may all be in our graves by that time, even if Mr. Troy does not come back again, which he may not impossibly do! Such thoughts give a sort of absurdity to the scheme. Now, isn't it preposterous, Gabriel? However he came to dream of it, I cannot think. But is it wrong? You know—you are older than I.'

'Eight years older, ma'am.'

'Yes, eight years—and is it wrong?'

'Perhaps it would be an uncommon agreement for a man and woman to make: I don't see anything really wrong about it,' said Oak, slowly. 'In fact the very thing that makes it doubtful if you ought to marry en under any condition, that is, your not caring about him—for I may suppose——'

'Yes, you may suppose that love is wanting,' she said shortly. 'Love is an utterly bygone, sorry, worn-out, miserable thing with me—for him or any one else.'

'Well, your want of love seems to me the one thing that takes away harm from such an agreement with him. If wild heat had to do wi' it, making ye long to overcome the awkwardness about your husband's vanishing, it mid be wrong; but a cold-hearted agreement to oblige a man seems different, somehow. The real sin, ma'am, in my mind, lies in thinking of ever wedding wi' a man you don't love honest and true."

'That I'm willing to pay the penalty of,' said Bathsheba, firmly. 'You know, Gabriel, this is what I cannot get off my conscience—that

I once seriously injured him in sheer idleness. If I had never played a trick upon him, he would never have wanted to marry me. O if I could only pay some heavy damages in money to him for the harm I did, and so get the sin off my soul that way! . . . Well, there's the debt, which can only be discharged in one way, and I believe I am bound to do it if it honestly lies in my power, without any consideration of my own future at all. When a rake gambles away his expectations, the fact that it is an inconvenient debt doesn't make him the less liable. I've been a rake, and the single point I ask you is, considering that my own scruples, and the fact that in the eye of the law my husband is only missing, will keep any man from marrying me until seven years have passed—am I free to entertain such an idea, even though 'tis a sort of penance—for it will be that? I *hate* the act of marriage under such circumstances, and the class of women I should seem to belong to by doing it!'

'It seems to me that all depends upon whe'r you think, as everybody else do, that your husband is dead.'

'I shall get to, I suppose, because I cannot help feeling what would have brought him back long before this time if he had lived.'

'Well, then, in a religious sense you will be as free to *think* o' marrying again as any real widow of one year's standing. But why don't ye ask Mr. Thirdly's advice on how to treat Mr. Boldwood?'

'No. When I want a broad-minded opinion for general enlightenment, distinct from special advice, I never go to a man who deals in the subject professionally. So I like the parson's opinion on law, the lawyer's on doctoring, the doctor's on business, and my businessman's—that is, yours—on morals.'

'And on love——'

'My own.'

'I'm afraid there's a hitch in that argument,' said Oak, with a grave smile.

She did not reply at once, and then saying, 'Good evening, Mr. Oak,' went away.

She had spoken frankly, and neither asked nor expected any reply from Gabriel more satisfactory than that she had obtained. Yet in the centremost parts of her complicated heart there existed at this minute a little pang of disappointment, for a reason she would not allow herself to recognize. Oak had not once wished her free that he might marry her himself—had not once said, 'I could wait for you as well as he.' That was the insect sting. Not that she would have listened to any such hypothesis. O no—for wasn't she saying all the time that such thoughts of the future were improper, and wasn't Gabriel far too poor a man to speak sentiment to her? Yet he might have just hinted about that old love of his, and asked, in a playful off-hand way, if he might speak of it. It would have seemed pretty and sweet, if no more; and then she would have shown how kind and inoffensive a woman's 'No' can sometimes be. But to give such cool advice—the very advice she had asked for—it ruffled our heroine all the afternoon.

LII

Converging Courses

I

Christmas-Eve came, and a party that Boldwood was to give in the evening was the great subject of talk in Weatherbury. It was not that the rarity of Christmas parties in the parish made this one a wonder, but that Boldwood should be the giver. The announcement had had an abnormal and incongruous sound, as if one should hear of croquet-playing in a cathedral aisle, or that some much-respected judge was going upon the stage. That the party was intended to be a truly jovial one there was no room for doubt. A large bough of mistletoe had been brought from the woods that day, and suspended in the hall of bachelor's home. Holly and ivy had followed in armfuls. From six that morning till past noon the huge wood fire in the kitchen roared and sparkled at its highest, the kettle, the saucepan, and the three-legged pot appearing in the midst of the flames like Shadrach, Meshach, and Abednego;[1] moreover, roasting and basting operations were continually carried on in front of the genial blaze.

As it grew later the fire was made up in the large long hall into which the staircase descended, and all encumbrances were cleared out for dancing. The log which was to form the back-brand of the evening fire was the uncleft trunk of a tree, so unwieldy that it could be neither brought nor rolled to its place; and accordingly two men were to be observed dragging and heaving it in by chains and levers as the hour of assembly drew near.

In spite of all this, the spirit of revelry was wanting in the atmosphere of the house. Such a thing had never been attempted before by its owner, and it was now done as by a wrench. Intended gaieties would insist upon apprearing like solemn grandeurs, the organization of the whole effort was carried out coldly by hirelings, and a shadow seemed to move about the rooms, saying that the proceedings were unnatural to the place and the lone man who lived therein, and hence not good.

II

Bathsheba was at this time in her room, dressing for the event. She had called for candles, and Liddy entered and placed one on each side of his mistress's glass.

---

1. An allusion to Daniel 3:8–30, in which three Hebrew captives of King Nebuchadnezzar were cast into a fiery furnace for refusing to worship a golden image, but miraculously they remained unharmed by the flames.

'Don't go away, Liddy,' said Bathsheba, almost timidly. 'I am foolishly agitated—I cannot tell why. I wish I had not been obliged to go to this dance; but there's no escaping now. I have not spoken to Mr. Boldwood since the autumn, when I promised to see him at Christmas on business, but I had no idea there was to be anything of this kind.'

'But I would go now,' said Liddy, who was going with her; for Boldwood had been indiscriminate in his invitations.

'Yes, I shall make my appearance, of course,' said Bathsheba. 'But I am *the cause* of the party, and that upsets me!—Don't tell, Liddy.'

'O no, ma'am. You the cause of it, ma'am?'

'Yes. I am the reason of the party—I. If it had not been for me, there would never have been one. I can't explain any more—there's no more to be explained. I wish I had never seen Weatherbury.'

'That's wicked of you—to wish to be worse off than you are.'

'No, Liddy. I have never been free from trouble since I have lived here, and this party is likely to bring me more. Now, fetch my black silk dress, and see how it sits upon me.'

'But you will leave off that, surely, ma'am? You have been a sort of widow fourteen months, and ought to brighten up a little on such a night as this.'

'Is it necessary? No; I will appear as usual, for if I were to wear any light dress people would say things about me, and I should seem to be rejoicing when I am solemn all the time. The party doesn't suit me a bit; but never mind, stay and help to finish me off.'

III

Boldwood was dressing also at this hour. A tailor from Casterbridge was with him, assisting him in the operation of trying on a new coat that had just been brought home.

Never had Boldwood been so fastidious, unreasonable about the fit, and generally difficult to please. The tailor walked round and round him, tugged at the waist, pulled the sleeve, pressed out the collar, and for the first time in his experience Boldwood was not bored. Times had been when the farmer had exclaimed against all such niceties as childish, but now no philosophic or hasty rebuke whatever was provoked by this man for attaching as much importance to a crease in the coat as to an earthquake in South America. Boldwood at last expressed himself nearly satisfied, and paid the bill, the tailor passing out of the door just as Oak came in to report progress for the day.

'Oh, Oak,' said Boldwood. 'I shall of course see you here to-night. Make yourself merry. I am determined that neither expense nor trouble shall be spared.'

'I'll try to be here, sir, though perhaps it may not be very early,' said Gabriel, quietly. 'I am glad indeed to see such a change in 'ee from what it used to be.'

'Yes—I must own it—I am bright to-night: cheerful and more than cheerful—so much so that I am almost sad again with the sense that all of it is passing away. And sometimes, when I am excessively hopeful and blithe, a trouble is looming in the distance: so that I often get to look upon gloom in me with content, and to fear a happy mood. Still this may be absurd—I feel that it is absurd. Perhaps my day is dawning at last.'

'I hope it 'ill be a long and a fair one.'

'Thank you—thank you. Yet perhaps my cheerfulness rests on a slender hope. And yet I trust my hope. It is faith, not hope. I think this time I reckon with my host.—Oak, my hands are a little shaky, or something: I can't tie this neckerchief properly. Perhaps you will tie it for me. The fact is, I have not been well lately, you know.'

'I am sorry to hear that, sir.'

'Oh, it's nothing. I want it done as well as you can, please. Is there any late knot in fashion, Oak?'

'I don't know sir,' said Oak. His tone had sunk to sadness.

Boldwood approached Gabriel, and as Oak tied the neckerchief the farmer went on feverishly—

'Does a woman keep her promise, Gabriel?'

'If it is not inconvenient to her she may.'

'—Or rather an implied promise.'

'I won't answer for her implying,' said Oak, with faint bitterness. 'That's a word as full o' holes as a sieve with them.'

'Oak, don't talk like that. You have got quietly cynical lately—how is it? We seem to have shifted our positions: I have become the young and hopeful man, and you the old and unbelieving one. However, does a woman keep a promise, not to marry, but to enter on an engagement to marry at some time? Now you know women better than I—tell me.'

'I am afeard you honour my understanding too much. However, she may keep such a promise, if it is made with an honest meaning to repair a wrong.'

'It has not gone far yet, but I think it will soon—yes, I know it will,' he said, in an impulsive whisper. 'I have pressed her upon the subject, and she inclines to be kind to me, and to think of me as a husband at a long future time, and that's enough for me. How can I expect more? She has a notion that a woman should not marry within seven years of her husband's disappearance—that her own self shouldn't, I mean—because his body was not found. It may be merely this legal reason which influences her, or it may be a religious one, but she is reluctant to talk on the point. Yet she has promised—implied—that she will ratify an engagement to-night.'

'Seven years,' murmured Oak.

'No, no—it's no such thing!' he said, with impatience. 'Five years, nine months, and a few days. Fifteen months nearly have passed since he vanished, and is there anything so wonderful in an engagement of little more than five years?'

'It seems long in a forward view. Don't build too much upon such promises, sir. Remember, you have once be'n deceived. Her meaning may be good; but there—she's young yet.'

'Deceived? Never!' said Boldwood, vehemently. 'She never promised me at that first time, and hence she did not break her promise! If she promises me, she'll marry me. Bathsheba is a woman to her word.'

IV

Troy was sitting in a corner of The White Hart tavern[2] at Caster-bridge, smoking and drinking a steaming mixture from a glass. A knock was given at the door, and Pennyways entered.

'Well, have you seen him?' Troy inquired, pointing to a chair.

'Boldwood?'

'No—Lawyer Long.'[3]

'He wadn't at home. I went there first, too.'

'That's a nuisance.'

' 'Tis rather, I suppose.'

'Yet I don't see that, because a man appears to be drowned and was not, he should be liable for anything. I shan't ask any lawyer—not I.'

'But that's not it, exactly. If an man changes his name and so forth, and takes steps to deceive the world and his own wife, he's a cheat, and that in the eye of the law is ayless[4] a rogue, and that is ayless a lammocken[5] vagabond; and that's a punishable situation.'

'Ha-ha! Well done, Pennyways.' Troy had laughed, but it was with some anxiety that he said, 'Now, what I want to know is this, do you think there's really anything going on between her and Boldwood? Upon my soul, I should never have believed it! How she must detest me! Have you found out whether she has encouraged him?'

'I haen't been able to learn. There's a deal of feeling on his side seemingly, but I don't answer for her. I didn't know a word about any such thing till yesterday, and all I heard then was that she was gwine to the party at his house to-night. This is the first time she has ever gone there, they say. And they say that she've not so much as spoke to him since they were at Greenhill Fair: but what can folk believe o't? However, she's not fond of him—quite offish and quite careless, I know.'

'I'm not so sure of that. . . . She's a handsome woman, Penny-ways, is she not? Own that you never saw a finer or more splendid creature in your life. Upon my honour, when I set eyes upon her that day I wondered what I could have been made of to be able to leave her by herself so long. And then I was hampered with that bothering show, which I'm free of at last, thank the stars.' He smoked on awhile, and

2. A real tavern of that name stood at the eastern end of High Street in Dorchester; a newer tavern of the same name occupies the site today.
3. A character of this name is also mentioned in chapter 37 of Hardy's *The Mayor of Casterbridge*.

4. Perhaps a word intended to represent Pennyways's mispronunciation and misuse of the term *alias* in his effort to sound knowledgeable about law, or, possibly, a dialect pronunciation of *always*.
5. Slouching (dialect).

then added, 'How did she look when you passed by yesterday?'

'Oh, she took no great heed of me, ye may well fancy; but she looked well enough, far's I know. Just flashed her haughty eyes upon my poor scram[6] body, and then let them go past me to what was yond, much as if I'd been no more than a leafless tree. She had just got off her mare to look at the last wring-down of cider for the year; she had been riding, and so her colours were up and her breath rather quick, so that her bosom plimmed[7] and fell—plimmed and fell—every time plain to my eye. Ay, and there were the fellers round her wringing down the cheese and bustling about and saying, "Ware o' the pommy,[8] ma'am: 'twill spoil yer gown." "Never mind me," says she. Then Gabe brought her some of the new cider, and she must needs go drinking it through a strawmote,[9] and not in a nateral way at all. "Liddy," says she, "bring indoors a few gallons, and I'll make some cider-wine." Sergeant, I was no more to her than a morsel of scroff[1] in the fuel-house!'

'I must go and find her out at once—O yes, I see that—I must go. Oak is head man still, isn't he?'

'Yes, 'a b'lieve. And at Little Weatherbury Farm too. He manages everything.'

'''Twill puzzle him to manage her, or any other man of his compass!'

'I don't know about that. She can't do without him, and knowing it well he's pretty independent. And she've a few soft corners to her mind, though I've never been able to get into one, the devil's in't!'

'Ah, baily, she's a notch above you, and you must own it: a higher class of animal—a finer tissue. However, stick to me, and neither this haughty goddess, dashing piece of womanhood, Juno-wife of mine (Juno was a goddess,[2] you know), nor anybody else shall hurt you. But all this wants looking into, I perceive. What with one thing and another, I see that my work is well cut out for me.'

V

'How do I look to-night, Liddy?' said Bathsheba, giving a final adjustment to her dress before leaving the glass.

'I never saw you look so well before. Yes—I'll tell you when you looked like it—that night, a year and a half ago, when you came in so wild-like, and scolded us for making remarks about you and Mr. Troy.'

'Everybody will think that I am setting myself to captivate Mr. Boldwood, I suppose,' she murmured. 'At least they'll say so. Can't my hair be brushed down a little flatter? I dread going—yet I dread the risk of wounding him by staying away.'

6. Withered, puny (dialect).
7. Heaved, swelled (dialect).
8. "Wringing down" is the process by which a quantity of ground apples, called "Pommy" (dialect for "pomace") is squeezed in a cider press so as to wring out the juice and leave a compressed cheeselike solid cake of apple remnants.
9. A bit of straw (dialect).
1. Rubbish (dialect).
2. A Roman goddess who was the sister and wife of Jupiter.

'Anyhow, ma'am, you can't well be dressed plainer than you are, unless you go in sackcloth[3] at once. 'Tis your excitement is what makes you look so noticeable to-night.'

'I don't know what's the matter, I feel wretched at one time, and buoyant at another. I wish I could have continued quite alone as I have been for the last year or so, with no hopes and no fears, and no pleasure and no grief.'

'Now just suppose Mr. Boldwood should ask you—only just suppose it—to run away with him, what would you do, ma'am?'

'Liddy—none of that,' said Bathsheba, gravely. 'Mind, I won't hear joking on any such matter. Do you hear?'

'I beg pardon, ma'am. But knowing what rum things we women be, I just said—however, I won't speak of it again.'

'No marrying for me yet for many a year; if ever, 'twill be for reasons very, very different from those you think, or others will believe! Now get my cloak, for it is time to go.'

VI

'Oak,' said Boldwood, 'before you go I want to mention what has been passing in my mind lately—that little arrangement we made about your share in the farm I mean. That share is small, too small, considering how little I attend to business now, and how much time and thought you give to it. Well, since the world is brightening for me, I want to show my sense of it by increasing your proportion in the partnership. I'll make a memorandum of the arrangement which struck me as likely to be convenient, for I haven't time to talk about it now; and then we'll discuss it at our leisure. My intention is ultimately to retire from the management altogether, and until you can take all the expenditure upon your shoulders, I'll be a sleeping partner in the stock. Then, if I marry her—and I hope—I feel I shall, why——'

'Pray don't speak of it, sir,' said Oak, hastily. 'We don't know what may happen. So many upsets may befall 'ee. There's many a slip, as they say—and I would advise you—I know you'll pardon me this once—not to be *too sure*.'

'I know, I know. But the feeling I have about increasing your share is on account of what I know of you. Oak, I have learnt a little about your secret: your interest in her is more than that of bailiff for an employer. But you have behaved like a man, and I, as a sort of successful rival—successful partly through your goodness of heart—should like definitely to show my sense of your friendship under what must have been a great pain to you.'

'O that's not necessary, thank 'ee,' said Oak, hurriedly. 'I must get used to such as that; other men have, and so shall I.'

Oak then left him. He was uneasy on Boldwood's account, for he saw anew that this constant passion of the farmer made him not the man he once had been.

---

3. Very coarse cloth worn as an act of penance or mourning.

As Boldwood continued awhile in his room alone—ready and dressed to receive his company—the mood of anxiety about his appearance seemed to pass away, and to be succeeded by a deep solemnity. He looked out of the window, and regarded the dim outline of the trees upon the sky, and the twilight deepening to darkness.

Then he went to a locked closet, and took from a locked drawer therein a small circular case the size of a pill-box, and was about to put it into his pocket. But he lingered to open the cover and take a momentary glance inside. It contained a woman's finger-ring, set all the way round with small diamonds, and from its appearance had evidently been recently purchased. Boldwood's eyes dwelt upon its many sparkles a long time, though that its material aspect concerned him little was plain from his manner and mien, which were those of a mind following out the presumed thread of that jewel's future history.

The noise of wheels at the front of the house became audible. Boldwood closed the box, stowed it away carefully in his pocket, and went out upon the landing. The old man who was his indoor factotum came at the same moment to the foot of the stairs.

'They be coming, sir—lots of 'em—a-foot and a-driving!'

'I was coming down this moment. Those wheels I heard—is it Mrs. Troy?'

'No, sir—'tis not she yet.'

A reserved and sombre expression had returned to Boldwood's face again, but it poorly cloaked his feelings when he pronounced Bathsheba's name; and his feverish anxiety continued to show its existence by a galloping motion of his fingers upon the side of his thigh as he went down the stairs.

VII

'How does this cover me?' said Troy to Pennyways. 'Nobody would recognize me now, I'm sure.'

He was buttoning on a heavy grey overcoat of Noachian[4] cut, with cape and high collar, the latter being erect and rigid, like a girdling wall, and nearly reaching to the verge of a travelling cap which was pulled down over his ears.

Pennyways snuffed the candle, and then looked up and deliberately inspected Troy.

'You've made up your mind to go then?' he said.

'Made up my mind? Yes; of course I have.'

'Why not write to her? 'Tis a very queer corner that you have got into, sergeant. You see all these things will come to light if you go back, and they won't sound well at all. Faith, if I was you I'd even bide as you be—a single man of the name of Francis. A good wife is good, but the best wife is not so good as no wife at all. Now that's my

---

4. As old-fashioned as the biblical Noah.

outspoken mind, and I've been called a long-headed feller here and there.'

'All nonsense!' said Troy, angrily. 'There she is with plenty of money, and a house and farm, and horses, and comfort, and here am I living from hand to mouth—a needy adventurer. Besides, it is no use talking now; it is too late, and I am glad of it; I've been seen and recognized here this very afternoon. I should have gone back to her the day after the fair, if it hadn't been for you talking about the law, and rubbish about getting a separation; and I won't put it off any longer. What the deuce put it into my head to run away at all, I can't think! Humbugging sentiment—that's what it was. But what man on earth was to know that his wife would be in such a hurry to get rid of his name!'

'I should have known it. She's bad enough for anything.'

'Pennyways, mind who you are talking to.'

'Well, sergeant, all I say is this, that if I were you I'd go abroad again where I came from—'tisn't too late to do it now. I wouldn't stir up the business and get a bad name for the sake of living with her—for all that about your play-acting is sure to come out, you know, although you think otherwise. My eyes and limbs, there'll be a racket if you go back just now—in the middle of Boldwood's Christmasing!'

'H'm, yes. I expect I shall not be a very welcome guest if he has her there,' said the sergeant, with a slight laugh. 'A sort of Alonzo the Brave; and when I go in the guests will sit in silence and fear, and all laughter and pleasure will be hushed, and the lights in the chamber burn blue,[5] and the worms—Ugh, horrible—Ring for some more brandy, Pennyways, I felt an awful shudder just then! Well, what is there besides? A stick—I must have a walking-stick.'

Pennyways now felt himself to be in something of a difficulty, for should Bathsheba and Troy become reconciled it would be necessary to regain her good opinion if he would secure the patronage of her husband. 'I sometimes think she likes you yet, and is a good woman at bottom,' he said, as a saving sentence. 'But there's no telling to a certainty from a body's outside. Well, you'll do as you like about going, of course, sergeant, and as for me, I'll do as you tell me.'

'Now, let me see what the time is,' said Troy, after emptying his glass in one draught as he stood. 'Half-past six o'clock. I shall not hurry along the road, and shall be there then before nine.'

---

5. An allusion to a ballad by M. G. ("Monk") Lewis (1775–1818), titled "Alonzo the Brave and Fair Imogine," in which the ghost of the dead Alonzo appears to his faithless love Imogine at her wedding-feast; Troy's speech paral- lels the lines: "All pleasure and laughter were hush'd at his sight, / The dogs, as they eyed him drew back in affright; / The lights in the chamber burnt blue!"

LIII

Concurritur—Horæ Momento[1]

Outside the front of Boldwood's house a group of men stood in the dark, with their faces towards the door, which occasionally opened and closed for the passage of some guest or servant, when a golden rod of light would stripe the ground for the moment and vanish again, leaving nothing outside but the glowworm shine of the pale lamp amid the evergreens over the door.

'He was seen in Casterbridge this afternoon—so the boy said,' one of them remarked in a whisper. 'And I for one believe it. His body was never found, you know.'

' 'Tis a strange story,' said the next. 'You may depend upon't that she knows nothing about it.'

'Not a word.'

'Perhaps he don't mean that she shall,' said another man.

'If he's alive and here in the neighbourhood, he means mischief,' said the first. 'Poor young thing: I do pity her, if 'tis true. He'll drag her to the dogs.'

'O no; he'll settle down quiet enough,' said one disposed to take a more hopeful view of the case.

'What a fool she must have been ever to have had anything to do with the man! She is so self-willed and independent too, that one is more minded to say it serves her right than pity her.'

'No, no! I don't hold with 'ee there. She was no otherwise than a girl mind, and how could she tell what the man was made of? If 'tis really true, 'tis too hard a punishment, and more than she ought to hae.— Hullo, who's that?' This was to some footsteps that were heard approaching.

'William Smallbury,' said a dim figure in the shades, coming up and joining them. 'Dark as a hedge, to-night, isn't it? I all but missed the plank over the river ath'art there in the bottom—never did such a thing before in my life. Be ye any of Boldwood's workfolk?' He peered into their faces.

'Yes—all o' us. We met here a few minutes ago.'

'Oh, I hear now—that's Sam Samway: thought I knowed the voice, too. Going in?'

'Presently. But I say, William,' Samway whispered, 'have ye heard this strange tale?'

'What—that about Sergeant Troy being seen, d'ye mean, souls?' said Smallbury, also lowering his voice.

'Ay: in Casterbridge.'

---

1. Hardy's title, Latin for "The Battle Commences—In an Instant," is an allusion to Horace's *Satires*, book I, ode I, lines 7–8: "Con-*curritur: horæ momento cita mors venit aut victoria læta*" ("The battle commences: in an instant comes swift death or joyful victory").

'Yes, I have. Laban Tall named a hint of it to me but now—but I don't think it. Hark, here Laban comes himself, 'a b'lieve.' A footstep drew near.

'Laban?'

'Yes, 'tis I,' said Tall.

'Have ye heard any more about that?'

'No,' said Tall, joining the group. 'And I'm inclined to think we'd better keep quiet. If so be 'tis not true, 'twill flurry her, and do her much harm to repeat it; and if so be 'tis true, 'twill do no good to forestall her time o' trouble. God send that it mid be a lie, for though Henery Fray and some of 'em do speak against her, she's never been anything but fair to me. She's hot and hasty, but she's a brave girl who'll never tell a lie however much the truth may harm her, and I've no cause to wish her evil.'

'She never do tell women's little lies, that's true; and 'tis a thing that can be said of very few. Ay, all the harm she thinks she says to yer face: there's nothing underhand wi' her.'

They stood silent then, every man busied with his own thoughts, during which interval sounds of merriment could be heard within. Then the front door again opened, the rays streamed out, the well-known form of Boldwood was seen in the rectangular area of light, the door closed, and Boldwood walked slowly down the path.

' 'Tis master,' one of the men whispered, as he neared them. 'We'd better stand quiet—he'll go in again directly. He would think it unseemly o' us to be loitering here.'

Boldwood came on, and passed by the men without seeing them, they being under the bushes on the grass. He paused, leant over the gate, and breathed a long breath. They heard low words come from him.

'I hope to God she'll come, or this night will be nothing but misery to me! O my darling, my darling, why do you keep me in suspense like this?'

He said this to himself, and they all distinctly heard it. Boldwood remained silent after that, and the noise from indoors was again just audible, until, a few minutes later, light wheels could be distinguished coming down the hill. They drew nearer, and ceased at the gate. Boldwood hastened back to the door, and opened it; and the light shone upon Bathsheba coming up the path.

Boldwood compressed his emotion to mere welcome: the men marked her light laugh and apology as she met him: he took her into the house; and the door closed again.

'Gracious heaven, I didn't know it was like that with him!' said one of the men. 'I thought that fancy of his was over long ago.'

'You don't know much of master, if you thought that,' said Samway.

'I wouldn't he should know we heard what 'a said for the world,' remarked a third.

'I wish we had told of the report at once,' the first uneasily continued. 'More harm may come of this than we know of. Poor Mr. Boldwood, it will be hard upon en. I wish Troy was in —— Well, God forgive me for such a wish! A scoundrel to play a poor wife such tricks. Nothing has prospered in Weatherbury since he came here. And now I've no heart to go in. Let's look into Warren's for a few minutes first, shall us, neighbours?'

Samway, Tall, and Smallbury agreed to go to Warren's, and went out at the gate, the remaining ones entering the house. The three soon drew near the malt-house, approaching it from the adjoining orchard, and not by way of the street. The pane of glass was illuminated as usual. Smallbury was a little in advance of the rest, when, pausing, he turned suddenly to his companions and said, 'Hist! See there.'

The light from the pane was now perceived to be shining not upon the ivied wall as usual, but upon some object close to the glass. It was a human face.

'Let's come closer,' whispered Samway; and they approached on tiptoe. There was no disbelieving the report any longer. Troy's face was almost close to the pane, and he was looking in. Not only was he looking in, but he appeared to have been arrested by a conversation which was in progress in the malt-house, the voices of the interlocutors being those of Oak and the maltster.

'The spree is all in her honour, isn't it—hey?' said the old man. 'Although he made believe 'tis only keeping up o' Christmas?'

'I cannot say,' replied Oak.

'O 'tis true enough, faith. I cannot understand Farmer Boldwood being such a fool at his time of life as to ho[2] and hanker after thik[3] woman in the way 'a do, and she not care a bit about en.'

The men, after recognizing Troy's features, withdrew across the orchard as quietly as they had come. The air was big with Bathsheba's fortunes to-night: every word everywhere concerned her. When they were quite out of earshot all by one instinct paused.

'It gave me quite a turn—his face,' said Tall, breathing.

'And so it did me,' said Samway. 'What's to be done?'

'I don't see that 'tis any business of ours,' Smallbury murmured dubiously.

'But it is! 'Tis a thing which is everybody's business,' said Samway. 'We know very well that master's on a wrong tack, and that she's quite in the dark, and we should let 'em know at once. Laban, you know her best—you'd better go and ask to speak to her.'

'I bain't fit for any such thing,' said Laban, nervously. 'I should think William ought to do it if anybody. He's oldest.'

'I shall have nothing to do with it,' said Smallbury. ' 'Tis a ticklish

---

2. To pine or yearn (dialect).   3. That (dialect).

business altogether. Why, he'll go on to her himself in a few minutes, ye'll see.'

'We don't know that he will. Come, Laban.'

'Very well, if I must I must, I suppose,' Tall reluctantly answered. 'What must I say?'

'Just ask to see master.'

'O no; I shan't speak to Mr. Boldwood. If I tell anybody, 'twill be mistress.'

'Very well,' said Samway.

Laban then went to the door. When he opened it the hum of bustle rolled out as a wave upon a still strand—the assemblage being immediately inside the hall—and was deadened to a murmur as he closed it again. Each man waited intently, and looked around at the dark tree tops gently rocking against the sky and occasionally shivering in a slight wind, as if he took interest in the scene, which neither did. One of them began walking up and down, and then came to where he started from and stopped again, with a sense that walking was a thing not worth doing now.

'I should think Laban must have seen mistress by this time,' said Smallbury, breaking the silence. 'Perhaps she won't come and speak to him."

The door opened. Tall appeared, and joined them.

'Well?' said both.

'I didn't like to ask for her after all,' Laban faltered out. 'They were all in such a stir, trying to put a little spirit into the party. Somehow the fun seems to hang fire,[4] though everything's there that a heart can desire, and I couldn't for my soul interfere and throw damp upon it—if 'twas to save my life, I couldn't!'

'I suppose we had better all go in together,' said Samway, gloomily. 'Perhaps I may have a chance of saying a word to master.'

So the men entered the hall, which was the room selected and arranged for the gathering because of its size. The younger men and maids were at last just beginning a dance. Bathsheba had been perplexed how to act, for she was not much more than a slim young maid herself, and the weight of stateliness sat heavy upon her. Sometimes she thought she ought not to have come under any circumstances; then she considered what cold unkindness that would have been, and finally resolved upon the middle course of staying for about an hour only, and gliding off unobserved, having from the first made up her mind that she could on no account dance, sing, or take any active part in the proceedings.

Her allotted hour having been passed in chatting and looking on, Bathsheba told Liddy not to hurry herself, and went to the small

---

4. A gun is said to "hang fire" when there is a delay before it goes off; here Laban uses the phrase metaphorically to convey that Boldwood's party is slow in becoming lively.

parlour to prepare for departure, which, like the hall, was decorated with holly and ivy, and well lighted up.

Nobody was in the room, but she had hardly been there a moment when the master of the house entered.

'Mrs. Troy—you are not going?' he said. 'We've hardly begun!'

'If you'll excuse me, I should like to go now.' Her manner was restive, for she remembered her promise, and imagined what he was about to say. 'But as it is not late,' she added, 'I can walk home, and leave my man and Liddy to come when they choose.'

'I've been trying to get an opportunity of speaking to you,' said Boldwood. 'You know perhaps what I long to say?'

Bathsheba silently looked on the floor.

'You do give it?' he said, eagerly.

'What?' she whispered.

'Now, that's evasion! Why, the promise. I don't want to intrude upon you at all, or to let it become known to anybody. But do give your word! A mere business compact, you know, between two people who are beyond the influence of passion.' Boldwood knew how false this picture was as regarded himself; but he had proved that it was the only tone in which she would allow him to approach her. 'A promise to marry me at the end of five years and three-quarters. You owe it to me!'

'I feel that I do,' said Bathsheba; 'that is, if you demand it. But I am a changed woman—an unhappy woman—and not—not——'

'You are still a very beautiful woman,' said Boldwood. Honesty and pure conviction suggested the remark, unaccompanied by any perception that it might have been adopted by blunt flattery to soothe and win her.

However, it had not much effect now, for she said, in a passionless murmur which was in itself a proof of her words: 'I have no feeling in the matter at all. And I don't at all know what is right to do in my difficult position, and I have nobody to advise me. But I give my promise, if I must. I give it as the rendering of a debt, conditionally, of course, on my being a widow.'

'You'll marry me between five and six years hence?'

'Don't press me too hard. I'll marry nobody else.'

'But surely you will name the time, or there's nothing in the promise at all?'

'O, I don't know, pray let me go!' she said, her bosom beginning to rise. 'I am afraid what to do! I want to be just to you, and to be that seems to be wronging myself, and perhaps it is breaking the commandments. There is considerable doubt of his death, and then it is dreadful; let me ask a solicitor, Mr. Boldwood, if I ought or no!'

'Say the words, dear one, and the subject shall be dismisssed; a blissful loving intimacy of six years, and then marriage—O Bathsheba, say them!' he begged in a husky voice, unable to sustain the forms of mere friendship any longer. 'Promise yourself to me; I deserve it, indeed I do, for I have loved you more than anybody in the world! And if I said hasty words and showed uncalled-for heat of manner towards you, believe me, dear, I did not mean to distress you; I was in agony, Bathsheba, and I did not know what I said. You wouldn't let a dog suffer what I have suffered, could you but know it! Sometimes I shrink from your knowing what I have felt for you, and sometimes I am distressed that all of it you never will know. Be gracious, and give up a little to me, when I would give up my life for you!'

The trimmings of her dress, as they quivered against the light, showed how agitated she was, and at last she burst out crying. 'And you'll not—press me—about anything more—if I say in five or six years?' she sobbed, when she had power to frame the words.

'Yes, then I'll leave it to time.'

'Very well. If he does not return, I'll marry you in six years from this day, if we both live,' she said solemnly.

'And you'll take this as a token from me.'

Boldwood had come close to her side, and now he clasped one of her hands in both his own, and lifted it to his breast.

'What is it? Oh I cannot wear a ring!' she exclaimed, on seeing what he held; 'besides, I wouldn't have a soul know that it's an engagement! Perhaps it is improper? Besides, we are not engaged in the usual sense, are we? Don't insist, Mr. Boldwood—don't!' In her trouble at not being able to get her hand away from him at once, she stamped passionately on the floor with one foot, and tears crowded to her eyes again.

'It means simply a pledge—no sentiment—the seal of a practical compact,' he said more quietly, but still retaining her hand in his firm grasp. 'Come, now!' And Boldwood slipped the ring on her finger.

'I cannot wear it,' she said, weeping as if her heart would break. 'You frighten me, almost. So wild a scheme! Please let me go home!'

'Only to-night: wear it just to-night, to please me!'

Bathsheba sat down in a chair, and buried her face in her handkerchief, though Boldwood kept her hand yet. At length she said, in a sort of hopeless whisper—

'Very well, then, I will to-night, if you wish it so earnestly. Now loosen my hand; I will, indeed I will wear it to-night.'

'And it shall be the beginning of a pleasant secret courtship of six years, with a wedding at the end?'

'It must be, I suppose, since you will have it so!' she said, fairly beaten into non-resistance.

Boldwood pressed her hand, and allowed it to drop in her lap. 'I am happy now,' he said. 'God bless you!'

He left the room, and when he thought she might be sufficiently composed sent one of the maids to her. Bathsheba cloaked the effects of the late scene as she best could, followed the girl, and in a few moments came downstairs with her hat and cloak on, ready to go. To get to the door it was necessary to pass through the hall, and before doing so she paused on the bottom of the staircase which descended into one corner, to take a last look at the gathering.

There was no music or dancing in progress just now. At the lower end, which had been arranged for the work-folk specially, a group conversed in whispers, and with clouded looks. Boldwood was standing by the fireplace, and he, too, though so absorbed in visions arising from her promise that he scarcely saw anything, seemed at that moment to have observed their peculiar manner, and their looks askance.

'What is it you are in doubt about, men?' he said.

One of them turned and replied uneasily: 'It was something Laban heard of, that's all, sir.'

'News? Anybody married or engaged, born or dead?' inquired the farmer, gaily. 'Tell it to us, Tall. One would think from your looks and mysterious ways that it was something very dreadful indeed.'

'O no, sir, nobody is dead,' said Tall.

'I wish somebody was,' said Samway, in a whisper.

'What do you say, Samway?' asked Boldwood, somewhat sharply. 'If you have anything to say, speak out; if not, get up another dance.'

'Mrs. Troy has come downstairs,' said Samway to Tall. 'If you want to tell her, you had better do it now.'

'Do you know what they mean?' the farmer asked Bathsheba, across the room.

'I don't in the least,' said Bathsheba.

There was a smart rapping at the door. One of the men opened it instantly, and went outside.

'Mrs. Troy is wanted,' he said, on returning.

'Quite ready,' said Bathsheba. 'Though I didn't tell them to send.'

'It is a stranger, ma'am,' said the man by the door.

'A stranger?' she said.

'Ask him to come in,' said Boldwood.

The message was given, and Troy, wrapped up to his eyes as we have seen him, stood in the doorway.

There was an unearthly silence, all looking towards the newcomer. Those who had just learnt that he was in the neighbourhood recognized him instantly; those who did not were perplexed. Nobody noted Bathsheba. She was leaning on the stairs. Her brow had heavily contracted; her whole face was pallid, her lips apart, her eyes rigidly staring at their visitor.

Boldwood was among those who did not notice that he was Troy. 'Come in, come in!' he repeated, cheerfully, 'and drain a Christmas beaker with us, stranger!'

Troy next advanced into the middle of the room, took off his cap, turned down his coat-collar, and looked Boldwood in the face. Even then Boldwood did not recognize that the impersonator of Heaven's persistent irony towards him, who had once before broken in upon his bliss, scourged him, and snatched his delight away, had come to do these things a second time. Troy began to laugh a mechanical laugh: Boldwood recognized him now.

Troy turned to Bathsheba. The poor girl's wretchedness at this time was beyond all fancy or narration. She had sunk down on the lowest stair; and there she sat, her mouth blue and dry, and her dark eyes fixed vacantly upon him, as if she wondered whether it were not all a terrible illusion.

Then Troy spoke. 'Bathsheba, I come here for you!'

She made no reply.

'Come home with me: come!'

Bathsheba moved her feet a little, but did not rise.

Troy went across to her.

'Come, madam, do you hear what I say?' he said, peremptorily.

A strange voice came from the fireplace—a voice sounding far off and confined, as if from a dungeon. Hardly a soul in the assembly recognized the thin tones to be those of Boldwood. Sudden despair had transformed him.

'Bathsheba, go with your husband!'

Nevertheless, she did not move. The truth was that Bathsheba was beyond the pale of activity—and yet not in a swoon. She was in a state of mental *gutta serena*;[5] her mind was for the minute totally deprived of light at the same time that no obscuration was apparent from without.

Troy stretched out his hand to pull her towards him, when she quickly shrank back. This visible dread of him seemed to irritate Troy, and he seized her arm and pulled it sharply. Whether his grasp pinched her, or whether his mere touch was the cause, was never known, but at the moment of his seizure she writhed, and gave a quick, low scream.

The scream had been heard but a few seconds when it was followed by a sudden deafening report that echoed through the room and stupefied them all. The oak partition shook with the concussion, and the place was filled with grey smoke.

In bewilderment they turned their eyes to Boldwood. At his back, as he stood before the fireplace, was a gun-rack, as is usual in farm-houses, constructed to hold two guns. When Bathsheba had cried out in her husband's grasp, Boldwood's face of gnashing despair had changed. The veins had swollen, and a frenzied look had gleamed in his eye. He had turned quickly, taken one of the guns, cocked it, and at once discharged it at Troy.

Troy fell. The distance apart of the two men was so small that the

---

5. Literally, Latin for "a clear drop of fluid"; an antique medical term for a kind of blindness that is unaccompanied by any apparent change in the eye itself.

charge of shot did not spread in the least, but passed like a bullet into his body. He uttered a long guttural sigh—there was a contraction—an extension—then his muscles relaxed, and he lay still.

Boldwood was seen through the smoke to be now again engaged with the gun. It was double-barrelled, and he had, meanwhile, in some way fastened his handkerchief to the trigger, and with his foot on the other end was in the act of turning the second barrel upon himself. Samway his man was the first to see this, and in the midst of the general horror darted up to him. Boldwood had already twitched the handkerchief, and the gun exploded a second time, sending its contents, by a timely blow from Samway, into the beam which crossed the ceiling.

'Well, it makes no difference!' Boldwood gasped. 'There is another way for me to die.'

Then he broke from Samway, crossed the room to Bathsheba, and kissed her hand. He put on his hat, opened the door, and went into the darkness, nobody thinking of preventing him.

LIV

After the Shock

Boldwood passed into the high road, and turned in the direction of Casterbridge. Here he walked at an even, steady pace over Yalbury Hill, along the dead level beyond, mounted Mellstock Hill, and between eleven and twelve o'clock crossed the Moor into the town. The streets were nearly deserted now, and the waving lamp-flames only lighted up rows of grey shop-shutters, and strips of white paving upon which his step echoed as he passed along. He turned to the right, and halted before an archway of heavy stonework, which was closed by an iron-studded pair of doors. This was the entrance to the gaol, and over it a lamp was fixed, the light enabling the wretched traveller to find a bell-pull.

The small wicket at last opened, and a porter appeared. Boldwood stepped forward, and said something in a low tone, when, after a delay, another man came. Boldwood entered, and the door was closed behind him, and he walked the world no more.

Long before this time Weatherbury had been thoroughly aroused, and the wild deed which had terminated Boldwood's merrymaking became known to all. Of those out of the house Oak was one of the first to hear of the catastrophe, and when he entered the room, which was about five minutes after Boldwood's exit, the scene was terrible. All the female guests were huddled aghast against the walls like sheep in a storm, and the men were bewildered as to what to do. As for Bathsheba, she had changed. She was sitting on the floor beside the body of Troy, his head pillowed in her lap, where she had herself lifted it. With one hand she held her handkerchief to his breast and covered the wound, though scarcely a single drop of blood had flowed, and with the other she tightly clasped one of his. The household convulsion had made her herself again. The temporary coma had ceased, and activity had come with the necessity for it. Deeds of endurance which seem ordinary in philosophy are rare in conduct, and Bathsheba was astonishing all around her now, for her philosophy was her conduct, and she seldom thought practicable what she did not practise. She was of the stuff of which great men's mothers are made. She was indispensable to high generation, hated at tea parties, feared in shops, and loved at crises. Troy recumbent in his wife's lap formed now the sole spectacle in the middle of the spacious room.

'Gabriel,' she said, automatically, when he entered, turning up a face of which only the well-known lines remained to tell him it was hers, all else in the picture having faded quite. 'Ride to Casterbridge instantly for a surgeon. It is, I believe, useless, but go. Mr. Boldwood has shot my husband.'

Her statement of the fact in such quiet and simple words came with more force than a tragic declamation, and had somewhat the effect of setting the distorted images in each mind present into proper focus. Oak, almost before he had comprehended anything beyond the briefest abstract of the event, hurried out of the room, saddled a horse and rode away. Not till he had ridden more than a mile did it occur to him that he would have done better by sending some other man on this errand, remaining himself in the house. What had become of Boldwood? He should have been looked after. Was he mad—had there been a quarrel? Then how had Troy got there? Where had he come from? How did this remarkable reappearance effect itself when he was supposed by many to be at the bottom of the sea? Oak had in some measure been prepared for the presence of Troy by hearing a rumour of his return just before entering Boldwood's house; but before he had weighed that information, this fatal event had been superimposed. However, it was too late now to think of sending another messenger, and he rode on, in the excitement of these self-inquiries not discerning, when about three miles from Casterbridge, a square-figured pedestrian passing along under the dark hedge in the same direction as his own.

The miles necessary to be traversed, and other hindrances incidental to the lateness of the hour and the darkness of the night, delayed the arrival of Mr. Aldritch, the surgeon; and more than three hours passed between the time at which the shot was fired and that of his entering the house. Oak was additionally detained in Casterbridge through having to give notice to the authorities of what had happened; and he then found that Boldwood had also entered the town, and delivered himself up.

In the meantime the surgeon, having hastened into the hall at

Boldwood's, found it in darkness and quite deserted. He went on to the back of the house, where he discovered in the kitchen an old man, of whom he made inquiries.

'She's had him took away to her own house, sir,' said his informant.

'Who has?' said the doctor.

'Mrs. Troy. 'A was quite dead, sir.'

This was astonishing information. 'She had no right to do that,' said the doctor. 'There will have to be an inquest, and she should have waited to know what to do.'

'Yes, sir; it was hinted to her that she had better wait till the law was known. But she said law was nothing to her, and she wouldn't let her dear husband's corpse bide neglected for folks to stare at for all the crowners[1] in England.'

Mr. Aldritch drove at once back again up the hill to Bathsheba's. The first person he met was poor Liddy, who seemed literally to have dwindled smaller in these few latter hours. 'What has been done?' he said.

'I don't know, sir,' said Liddy, with suspended breath. 'My mistress has done it all.'

'Where is she?'

'Upstairs with him, sir. When he was brought home and taken upstairs, she said she wanted no further help from the men. And then she called me, and made me fill the bath, and after that told me I had better go and lie down because I looked so ill. Then she locked herself into the room alone with him, and would not let a nurse come in, or anybody at all. But I thought I'd wait in the next room in case she should want me. I heard her moving about inside for more than an hour, but she only came out once, and that was for more candles, because hers had burnt down into the socket. She said we were to let her know when you or Mr. Thirdly came, sir.'

Oak entered with the parson at this moment, and they all went upstairs together, preceded by Liddy Smallbury. Everything was silent as the grave when they paused on the landing. Liddy knocked, and Bathsheba's dress was heard rustling across the room: the key turned in the lock, and she opened the door. Her looks were calm and nearly rigid, like a slightly animated bust of Melpomene.[2]

'Oh, Mr. Aldritch, you have come at last,' she murmured from her lips merely, and threw back the door. Ah, and Mr. Thirdly. Well, all is done, and anybody in the world may see him now.' She then passed by him, crossed the landing, and entered another room.

Looking into the chamber of death she had vacated they saw by the light of the candles which were on the drawers a tall straight shape lying at the further end of the bedroom, wrapped in white. Everything

---

1. Coroners (dialect).
2. In Greek mythology, a daughter of Zeus and the muse of tragedy; in the Louvre in Paris, there is a well-known statue of Melpomene represented with a calm expression.

around was quite orderly. The doctor went in, and after a few minutes returned to the landing again, where Oak and the parson still waited.

'It is all done, indeed, as she says,' remarked Mr. Aldritch, in a subdued voice. 'The body has been undressed and properly laid out in grave clothes. Gracious Heaven—this mere girl! She must have the nerve of a stoic!'

'The heart of a wife merely,' floated in a whisper about the ears of the three, and turning they saw Bathsheba in the midst of them. Then, as if at that instant to prove that her fortitude had been more of will than of spontaneity, she silently sank down between them and was a shapeless heap of drapery on the floor. The simple consciousness that superhuman strain was no longer required had at once put a period to her power to continue it.

They took her away into a further room, and the medical attendance which had been useless in Troy's case was invaluable in Bathsheba's, who fell into a series of fainting-fits that had a serious aspect for a time. The sufferer was got to bed, and Oak, finding from the bulletins that nothing really dreadful was to be apprehended on her score, left the house. Liddy kept watch in Bathsheba's chamber, where she heard her mistress moaning in whispers through the dull slow hours of that wretched night: 'O it is my fault—how can I live! O Heaven, how can I live!'

LV

The March Following—'Bathsheba Boldwood'

We pass rapidly on into the month of March, to a breezy day without sunshine, frost, or dew. On Yalbury Hill, about midway between Weatherbury and Casterbridge, where the turnpike road passes over the crest, a numerous concourse of people had gathered, the eyes of the greater number being frequently stretched afar in a northerly direction. The groups consisted of a throng of idlers, a party of javelin-men,[1] and two trumpeters, and in the midst were carriages, one of which contained the high sheriff. With the idlers, many of whom had mounted to the top of a cutting formed for the road, were several Weatherbury men and boys—among others Poorgrass, Coggan, and Cain Ball.

At the end of half-an-hour a faint dust was seen in the expected quarter, and shortly after a travelling-carriage, bringing one of the two judges on the Western Circuit, came up the hill and halted on the top.

1. A group of men who carried pikes or lances and, with trumpeters, formed the retinue of a high sheriff, whose duty it was to meet and escort a judge coming into town for the assizes, which were trials periodically held at major towns and presided over by judges assigned to a specific circuit of visits; we are subsequently informed that the visting judge was one of two assigned to the Western Circuit.

The judge changed carriages whilst a flourish was blown by the big-cheeked trumpeters, and a procession being formed of the vehicles and javelin-men, they all proceeded towards the town, excepting the Weatherbury men, who as soon as they had seen the judge move off returned home again to their work.

'Joseph, I zeed you squeezing close to the carriage,' said Coggan, as they walked. 'Did ye notice my lord judge's face?'

'I did,' said Poorgrass. 'I looked hard at en, as if I would read his very soul; and there was mercy in his eyes—or to speak with the exact truth required of us at this solemn time, in the eye that was towards me.'

'Well, I hope for the best,' said Coggan, 'though bad that must be. However, I shan't go to the trial, and I'd advise the rest of ye that bain't wanted to bide away. 'Twill disturb his mind more than anything to see us there staring at him as if he were a show.'

'The very thing I said this morning,' observed Joseph. ' "Justice is come to weigh him in the balances," I said in my reflectious way, "and if he's found wanting,[2] so be it unto him," and a bystander said "Hear, hear! A man who can talk like that ought to be heard." But I don't like dwelling upon it, for my few words are my few words, and not much; though the speech of some men is rumoured abroad as though by nature formed for such.'

'So 'tis, Joseph. And now, neighbours, as I said, every man bide at home.'

The resolution was adhered to; and all waited anxiously for the news next day. Their suspense was diverted, however, by a discovery which was made in the afternoon, throwing more light on Boldwood's conduct and condition than any details which had preceded it.

That he had been from the time of Greenhill Fair until the fatal Christmas Eve in excited and unusual moods was known to those who had been intimate with him; but nobody imagined that there had shown in him unequivocal symptoms of the mental derangement which Bathsheba and Oak, alone of all others and at different times, had momentarily suspected. In a locked closet was now discovered an extraordinary collection of articles. There were several sets of ladies' dresses in the piece, of sundry expensive materials; silks and satins, poplins and velvets, all of colours which from Bathsheba's style of dress might have been judged to be her favourites. There were two muffs, sable and ermine. Above all there was a case of jewellery, containing four heavy gold bracelets and several lockets and rings, all of fine quality and manufacture. These things had been bought in Bath and other towns from time to time, and brought home by stealth. They were all carefully packed in paper, and each package was labelled 'Bathsheba Boldwood,' a date being subjoined six years in advance in every instance.

---

2. An allusion to Daniel 5:27: "Thou are weighed in the balances, and art found wanting."

These somewhat pathetic evidences of a mind crazed with care and love were the subject of discourse in Warren's malt-house when Oak entered from Casterbridge with tidings of the sentence. He came in the afternoon, and his face, as the kiln glow shone upon it, told the tale sufficiently well. Boldwood, as every one supposed he would do, had pleaded guilty, and had been sentenced to death.

The conviction that Boldwood had not been morally responsible for his later acts now became general. Facts elicited previous to the trial had pointed strongly in the same direction, but they had not been of sufficient weight to lead to an order for an examination into the state of Boldwood's mind. It was astonishing, now that a presumption of insanity was raised, how many collateral circumstances were remembered to which a condition of mental disease seemed to afford the only explanation—among others, the unprecedented neglect of his corn stacks in the previous summer.

A petition was addressed to the Home Secretary,[3] advancing the circumstances which appeared to justify a request for a reconsideration of the sentence. It was not 'numerously signed' by the inhabitants of Casterbridge, as is usual in such cases, for Boldwood had never made many friends over the counter. The shops thought it very natural that a man who, by importing direct from the producer, had daringly set aside the first great principle of provincial existence, namely, that God made country villages to supply customers to country towns, should have confused ideas about the Decalogue. The prompters were a few merciful men who had perhaps too feelingly considered the facts latterly unearthed, and the result was that evidence was taken which it was hoped might remove the crime, in a moral point of view, out of the category of wilful murder, and lead it to be regarded as a sheer outcome of madness.

The upshot of the petition was waited for in Weatherbury with solicitous interest. The execution had been fixed for eight o'clock on a Saturday morning about a fortnight after the sentence was passed, and up to Friday afternoon no answer had been received. At that time Gabriel came from Casterbridge Gaol, whither he had been to wish Boldwood good-bye, and turned down a by-street to avoid the town. When past the last house he heard a hammering, and lifting his bowed head he looked back for a moment. Over the chimneys he could see the upper part of the gaol entrance, rich and glowing in the afternoon sun, and some moving figures were there. They were carpenters lifting a post into a vertical position within the parapet. He withdrew his eyes quickly and hastened on.

It was dark when he reached home, and half the village was out to meet him.

'No tidings,' Gabriel said, wearily. 'And I'm afraid there's no hope. I've been with him more than two hours.'

3. A member of the British government, whose responsibilities involve domestic matters.

'Do ye think he *really* was out of his mind when he did it?' said Smallbury.

'I can't honestly say that I do,' Oak replied. 'However, that we can talk of another time. Has there been any change in mistress this afternoon?'

'None at all.'

'Is she downstairs?'

'No. And getting on so nicely as she was too. She's but very little better now again than she was at Christmas. She keeps on asking if you be come, and if there's news, till one's wearied out wi' answering her. Shall I go and say you've come?'

'No,' said Oak. 'There's a chance yet; but I couldn't stay in town any longer—after seeing him too. So Laban—Laban is here, isn't he?'

'Yes,' said Tall.

'What I've arranged is, that you shall ride to town the last thing to-night; leave here about nine, and wait a while there, getting home about twelve. If nothing has been received by eleven to-night, they say there's no chance at all.'

'I do so hope his life will be spared,' said Liddy. 'If it is not, she'll go out of her mind too. Poor thing; her sufferings have been dreadful; she deserves anybody's pity.'

'Is she altered much?' said Coggan.

'If you haven't seen poor mistress since Christmas, you wouldn't know her,' said Liddy. 'Her eyes are so miserable that she's not the same woman. Only two years ago she was a romping girl, and now she's this!'

Laban departed as directed, and at eleven o'clock that night several of the villagers strolled along the road to Casterbridge and awaited his arrival—among them Oak, and nearly all the rest of Bathsheba's men. Gabriel's anxiety was great that Boldwood might be saved, even though in his conscience he felt that he ought to die; for there had been qualities in the farmer which Oak loved. At last, when they all were weary the tramp of a horse was heard in the distance—

> First dead, as if on turf it trode,
> Then, clattering, on the village road
> In other pace than forth he yode.[4]

'We shall soon know now, one way or other,' said Coggan, and they all stepped down from the bank on which they had been standing into the road, and the rider pranced into the midst of them.

'Is that you, Laban?' said Gabriel.

'Yes—'tis come. He's not to die. 'Tis confinement during Her Majesty's pleasure.'

---

4. Quoted from Sir Walter Scott's *Marmion*, canto 3, stanza 31. *Yode* is Scott's pseudoarchaic word for *went*.

'Hurrah!' said Coggan, with a swelling heart. 'God's above the devil yet!'

LVI

Beauty in Loneliness—After All

Bathsheba revived with the spring. The utter prostration that had followed the low fever from which she had suffered diminished perceptibly when all uncertainty upon every subject had come to an end.

But she remained alone now for the greater part of her time, and stayed in the house, or at furthest went into the garden. She shunned every one, even Liddy, and could be brought to make no confidences, and to ask for no sympathy.

As the summer drew on she passed more of her time in the open air, and began to examine into farming matters from sheer necessity, though she never rode out or personally superintended as at former times. One Friday evening in August she walked a little way along the road and entered the village for the first time since the sombre event of the preceding Christmas. None of the old colour had as yet come to her cheek, and its absolute paleness was heightened by the jet black of her gown, till it appeared preternatural. When she reached a little shop at the other end of the place, which stood nearly opposite to the churchyard, Bathsheba heard singing inside the church, and she knew that the singers were practising. She crossed the road, opened the gate, and entered the graveyard, the high sills of the church windows effectually screening her from the eyes of those gathered within. Her stealthy walk was to the nook wherein Troy had worked at planting flowers upon Fanny Robin's grave, and she came to the marble tombstone.

A motion of satisfaction enlivened her face as she read the complete inscription. First came the words of Troy himself:—

ERECTED BY FRANCIS TROY
IN BELOVED MEMORY OF
FANNY ROBIN,
WHO DIED OCTOBER 9, 18—,
AGED 20 YEARS.

Underneath this was now inscribed in new letters:—

IN THE SAME GRAVE LIE
THE REMAINS OF THE AFORESAID
FRANCIS TROY,
WHO DIED DECEMBER 24TH, 18—,
AGED 26 YEARS.

Whilst she stood and read and meditated the tones of the organ began again in the church, and she went with the same light step round to the porch and listened. The door was closed, and the choir was learning a new hymn. Bathsheba was stirred by emotions which latterly she had assumed to be altogether dead within her. The little attenuated voices of the children brought to her ear in distinct utterance the words they sang without thought or comprehension—

> Lead, kindly Light, amid the encircling gloom,
> Lead Thou me on.[1]

Bathsheba's feeling was always to some extent dependent upon her whim, as is the case with many other women. Something big came into her throat and an uprising to her eyes—and she thought that she would allow the imminent tears to flow if they wished. They did flow and plenteously, and one fell upon the stone bench beside her. Once that she had begun to cry for she hardly knew what, she could not leave off for crowding thoughts she knew too well. She would have given anything in the world to be, as those children were, unconcerned at the meaning of their words, because too innocent to feel the necessity for any such expression. All the impassioned scenes of her brief experience seemed to revive with added emotion at that moment, and those scenes which had been without emotion during enactment had emotion then. Yet grief came to her rather as a luxury than as the scourge of former times.

Owing to Bathsheba's face being buried in her hands she did not notice a form which came quietly into the porch, and on seeing her, first moved as if to retreat, then paused and regarded her. Bathsheba did not raise her head for some time, and when she looked round her face was wet, and her eyes drowned and dim. 'Mr. Oak,' exclaimed she, disconcerted, 'how long have you been here?'

'A few minutes, ma'am,' said Oak, respectfully.

'Are you going in?' said Bathsheba; and there came from within the church as from a prompter—

> I loved the garish day, and, spite of fears,
> Pride ruled my will: remember not past years.

'I was,' said Gabriel. 'I am one of the bass singers, you know. I have sung bass for several months.'

'Indeed: I wasn't aware of that. I'll leave you, then.'

> Which I have loved long since, and lost awhile,

sang the children.

'Don't let me drive you away, mistress. I think I won't go in to-night.'

'O no—you don't drive me away.'

Then they stood in a state of some embarrassment, Bathsheba trying

---

1. This and the following two quotations are from "The Pillar of the Cloud," a poem written by John Henry Newman (1801–90) in 1833 and subsequently set to music as a hymn by John Bacchus Dykes (1823–76) in 1861.

to wipe her dreadfully drenched and inflamed face without his noticing her. At length Oak said, 'I've not seen you—I mean spoken to
you—since ever so long, have I?' But he feared to bring distressing
memories back, and interrupted himself with: 'Were you going into
church?'

'No,' she said. 'I came to see the tombstone privately—to see if they
had cut the inscription as I wished. Mr. Oak, you needn't mind
speaking to me, if you wish to, on the matter which is in both our
minds at this moment.'

'And have they done it as you wished?' said Oak.

'Yes. Come and see it, if you have not already.'

So together they went and read the tomb. 'Eight months ago!'
Gabriel murmured when he saw the date. 'It seems like yesterday to
me.'

'And to me as if it were years ago—long years, and I had been dead
between. And now I am going home, Mr. Oak.'

Oak walked after her. 'I wanted to name a small matter to you as
soon as I could,' he said with hesitation. 'Merely about business, and I
think I may just mention it now, if you'll allow me.'

'O yes, certainly.'

'It is that I may soon have to give up the management of your farm,
Mrs. Troy. The fact is, I am thinking of leaving England—not yet,
you know—next spring.'

'Leaving England!' she said, in surprise and genuine disappointment. 'Why, Gabriel, what are you going to do that for?'

'Well, I've thought it best,' Oak stammered out. 'California is the
spot I've had in my mind to try.'

'But it is understood everywhere that you are going to take poor Mr.
Boldwood's farm on your own account?'

'I've had the refusal o' it 'tis true; but nothing is settled yet, and I
have reasons for gieing up. I shall finish out my year there as manager
for the trustees, but no more.'

'And what shall I do without you? Oh, Gabriel, I don't think you
ought to go away. You've been with me so long—through bright times
and dark times—such old friends as we are—that it seems unkind
almost. I had fancied that if you leased the other farm as master, you
might still give a helping look across at mine. And now going away!'

'I would have willingly.'

'Yet now that I am more helpless than ever you go away!'

'Yes, that's the ill fortune o' it,' said Gabriel, in a distressed tone.
'And it is because of that very helplessness that I feel bound to go.
Good afternoon, ma'am,' he concluded, in evident anxiety to get
away, and at once went out of the churchyard by a path she could
follow on no pretence whatever.

Bathsheba went home, her mind occupied with a new trouble,
which being rather harassing than deadly was calculated to do good by

diverting her from the chronic gloom of her life. She was set thinking a great deal about Oak and of his wish to shun her; and there occurred to Bathsheba several incidents of her latter intercourse with him, which, trivial when singly viewed, amounted together to a perceptible disinclination for her society. It broke upon her at length as a great pain that her last old disciple was about to foresake her and flee. He who had believed in her and argued on her side when all the rest of the world was against her, had at last like the others become weary and neglectful of the old cause, and was leaving her to fight her battles alone.

The weeks went on, and more evidence of his want of interest in her was forthcoming. She noticed that instead of entering the small parlour or office where the farm accounts were kept, and waiting, or leaving a memorandum as he had hitherto done during her seclusion, Oak never came at all when she was likely to be there, only entering at unseasonable hours when her presence in that part of the house was least to be expected. Whenever he wanted directions he sent a message, or note with neither heading nor signature, to which she was obliged to reply in the same off-hand style. Poor Bathsheba began to suffer now from the most torturing sting of all—a sensation that she was despised.

The autumn wore away gloomily enough amid these melancholy conjectures, and Christmas-day came, completing a year of her legal widowhood, and two years and a quarter of her life alone. On examining her heart it appeared beyond measure strange that the subject of which the season might have been supposed suggestive—the event in the hall at Boldwood's—was not agitating her at all; but instead, an agonizing conviction that everybody abjured her—for what she could not tell—and that Oak was the ringleader of the recusants. Coming out of church that day she looked round in hope that Oak, whose bass voice she had heard rolling out from the gallery overhead in a most unconcerned manner, might chance to linger in her path in the old way. There he was, as usual, coming down the path behind her. But on seeing Bathsheba turn, he looked aside, and as soon as he got beyond the gate, and there was the barest excuse for a divergence, he made one, and vanished.

The next morning brought the culminating stroke; she had been expecting it long. It was a formal notice by letter from him that he should not renew his engagement with her for the following Lady-day.[2].

Bathsheba actually sat and cried over this letter most bitterly. She was aggrieved and wounded that the possession of hopeless love from Gabriel, which she had grown to regard as her inalienable right for life, should have been withdrawn just at his own pleasure in this way.

2. March 25, the Feast of the Annunciation, and one of the days when quarterly rents were due and workers' contracts made or renewed.

She was bewildered too by the prospect of having to rely on her own resources again: it seemed to herself that she never could again acquire energy sufficient to go to market, barter, and sell. Since Troy's death Oak had attended all sales and fairs for her, transacting her business at the same time with his own. What should she do now? Her life was becoming a desolation.

So desolate was Bathsheba this evening, that in an absolute hunger for pity and sympathy, and miserable in that she appeared to have outlived the only true friendship she had ever owned, she put on her bonnet and cloak and went down to Oak's house just after sunset, guided on her way by the pale primrose rays of a crescent moon a few days old.

A lively firelight shone from the window, but nobody was visible in the room. She tapped nervously, and then thought it doubtful if it were right for a single woman to call upon a bachelor who lived alone, although he was her manager, and she might be supposed to call on business without any real impropriety. Gabriel opened the door, and the moon shone upon his forehead.

'Mr. Oak,' said Bathsheba faintly.

'Yes; I am Mr. Oak,' said Gabriel. 'Who have I the honour—O how stupid of me, not to know you, mistress!'

'I shall not be your mistress much longer, shall I, Gabriel?' she said in pathetic tones.

'Well, no. I suppose—But come in, ma'am. Oh—and I'll get a light,' Oak replied, with some awkwardness.

'No; not on my account.'

'It is so seldom that I get a lady visitor that I'm afraid I haven't proper accommodation. Will you sit down, please? Here's a chair, and there's one, too. I am sorry that my chairs all have wood seats, and are rather hard, but I—was thinking of getting some new ones.' Oak placed two or three for her.

'They are quite easy enough for me.'

So down she sat, and down sat he, the fire dancing in their faces, and upon the old furniture,

all a-sheenen
Wi' long years o' handlen,[3]

that formed Oak's array of household possessions, which sent back a dancing reflection in reply. It was very odd to these two persons, who knew each other passing well, that the mere circumstance of their meeting in a new place and in a new way should make them so awkard and constrained. In the fields, or at her house, there had never

---

3. W. Barnes [*Hardy's note*]. The quotation is from a poem titled "Woak Hill" by the Rev. William Barnes, a Dorset poet and philologist who kept a school next door to the architect's office in Dorchester where Hardy worked for a time [*Editor's note*].

been any embarrassment; but now that Oak had become the entertainer their lives seemed to be moved back again to the days when they
were strangers.

'You'll think it strange that I have come, but——'

'O no; not at all.'

'But I thought——Gabriel, I have been uneasy in the belief that I
have offended you, and that you are going away on that account. It
grieved me very much, and I couldn't help coming.'

'Offended me! As if you could do that, Bathsheba!'

'Haven't I?' she asked, gladly. 'But, what are you going away for
else?'

'I am not going to emigrate, you know; I wasn't aware that you
would wish me not to when I told 'ee, or I shouldn't have thought of
doing it,' he said, simply. 'I have arranged for Little Weatherbury
Farm, and shall have it in my own hands at Lady-day. You know I've
had a share in it for some time. Still, that wouldn't prevent my
attending to your business as before, hadn't it been that things have
been said about us.'

'What?' said Bathsheba in surprise. 'Things said about you and me!
What are they?'

'I cannot tell you.'

'It would be wiser if you were to, I think. You have played the part of
mentor to me many times, and I don't see why you should fear to do it
now.'

'It is nothing that you have done, this time. The top and tail o't is
this—that I'm sniffing about here, and waiting for poor Boldwood's
farm, with a thought of getting you some day.'

'Getting me! What does that mean?'

'Marrying of 'ee, in plain British. You asked me to tell, so you
mustn't blame me.'

Bathsheba did not look quite so alarmed as if a cannon had been
discharged by her ear, which was what Oak had expected. 'Marrying
me! I didn't know it was that you meant,' she said, quietly. 'Such a
thing as that is too absurd—too soon—to think of, by far!'

'Yes; of course, it is too absurd. I don't desire any such thing; I
should think that was plain enough by this time. Surely, surely you be
the last person in the world I think of marrying. It is too absurd, as you
say.'

' "Too—s-s-soon" were the words I used.'

'I must beg your pardon for correcting you, but you said, "too
absurd," and so do I.'

'I beg your pardon too!' she returned, with tears in her eyes. ' "Too
soon" was what I said. But it doesn't matter a bit—not at all—but I
only meant, "too soon." Indeed, I didn't, Mr. Oak, and you must
believe me!'

Gabriel looked her long in the face, but the firelight being faint there was not much to be seen. 'Bathsheba,' he said, tenderly and in surprise, and coming closer: 'If I only knew one thing—whether you would allow me to love you and win you, and marry you after all—If I only knew that!'

'But you will never know,' she murmured.

'Why?'

'Because you never ask.'

'Oh—Oh!' said Gabriel, with a low laugh of joyousness. 'My own dear————'

'You ought not to have sent me that harsh letter this morning,' she interrupted. 'It shows that you didn't care a bit about me, and were ready to desert me like all the rest of them! It was very cruel of you, considering I was the first sweetheart that you ever had, and you were the first I ever had; and I shall not forget it!'

'Now, Bathsheba, was ever anybody so provoking?' he said, laughing. 'You know it was purely that I, as an unmarried man, carrying on a business for you as a very taking young woman, had a proper hard part to play—more particular that people knew I had a sort of feeling for 'ee; and I fancied, from the way we were mentioned together, that it might injure your good name. Nobody knows the heat and fret I have been caused by it.'

'And was that all?'

'All.'

'O, how glad I am I came!' she exclaimed, thankfully, as she rose from her seat. 'I have thought so much more of you since I fancied you did not want even to see me again. But I must be going now, or I shall be missed. Why, Gabriel,' she said, with a slight laugh, as they went to the door, 'it seems exactly as if I had come courting you—how dreadful!'

'And quite right, too,' said Oak. 'I've danced at your skittish heels, my beautiful Bathsheba, for many a long mile, and many a long day; and it is hard to begrudge me this one visit.'

He accompanied her up the hill, explaining to her the details of his forthcoming tenure of the other farm. They spoke very little of their mutual feelings; pretty phrases and warm expressions being probably unnecessary between such tried friends. Theirs was that substantial affection which arises (if any arises at all) when the two who are thrown together begin first by knowing the rougher sides of each other's character, and not the best till further on, the romance growing up in the interstices of a mass of hard prosaic reality. This good-fellowship—*camaraderie*—usually occurring through similarity of pursuits, is unfortunately seldom superadded to love between the sexes, because men and women associate, not in their labours, but in their pleasures merely. Where, however, happy circumstance permits its development, the compounded feeling proves itself to be the only love which is strong as death—that love which many waters cannot quench, nor the floods drown, beside which the passion usually called by the name is evanescent as steam.

LVII

A Foggy Night and Morning—Conclusion

'The most private, secret, plainest wedding that it is possible to have.'

Those had been Bathsheba's words to Oak one evening, some time after the event of the preceding chapter, and he meditated a full hour by the clock upon how to carry out her wishes to the letter.

'A license[1]—O yes, it must be a license,' he said to himself at last. 'Very well, then; first, a license.'

On a dark night, a few days later, Oak came with mysterious steps from the surrogate's door in Casterbridge. On the way home he heard a heavy tread in front of him, and, overtaking the man, found him to be Coggan. They walked together into the village until they came to a little lane behind the church, leading down to the cottage of Laban Tall, who had lately been installed as clerk of the parish, and was yet in mortal terror at church on Sundays when he heard his lone voice among certain hard words of the Psalms, whither no man ventured to follow him.

'Well, good-night, Coggan,' said Oak, 'I'm going down this way.'

'Oh!' said Coggan, surprised; 'what's going on to-night, then, make so bold, Mr. Oak?'

It seemed rather ungenerous not to tell Coggan, under the circumstances, for Coggan had been true as steel all through the time of Gabriel's unhappiness about Bathsheba, and Gabriel said, 'You can keep a secret, Coggan?'

'You've proved me, and you know.'

'Yes, I have, and I do know. Well, then, mistress and I mean to get married to-morrow morning.'

'Heaven's high tower! And yet I've thought of such a thing from time to time; true, I have. But keeping it so close! Well, there, 'tis no consarn of mine, and I wish 'ee joy o' her.'

'Thank you, Coggan. But I assure'ee that this great hush is not what I wished for at all, or what either of us would have wished if it hadn't been for certain things that would make a gay wedding seem hardly the thing. Bathsheba has a great wish that all the parish shall not be in church, looking at her—she's shy-like and nervous about it, in fact—so I be doing this to humour her.'

'Ay, I see: quite right, too, I suppose I must say. And you be now

---

1. A special permission, given by a bishop or his surrogate, to marry in the Anglican Church without the publication of the customary banns and, hence, with less chance of public knowledge.

going down to the clerk.'

'Yes; you may as well come with me.'

'I am afeard your labour in keeping it close will be throwed away,' said Coggan, as they walked along. 'Labe Tall's old woman will horn it all over parish in half-an-hour.'

'So she will, upon my life; I never thought of that,' said Oak, pausing. 'Yet I must tell him to-night, I suppose, for he's working so far off, and leaves early.'

'I'll tell 'ee how we could tackle her,' said Coggan. 'I'll knock and ask to speak to Laban outside the door, you standing in the background. Then he'll come out, and you can tell yer tale. She'll never guess what I want en for; and I'll make up a few words about the farm-work, as a blind."

This scheme was considered feasible; and Coggan advanced boldly, and rapped at Mrs. Tall's door. Mrs. Tall herself opened it.

'I wanted to have a word with Laban.'

'He's not at home, and won't be this side of eleven o'clock. He've been forced to go over to Yalbury since shutting out work. I shall do quite as well.'

'I hardly think you will. Stop a moment;' and Coggan stepped round the corner of the porch to consult Oak.'

'Who's t'other man, then?' said Mrs. Tall.

'Only a friend,' said Coggan.

'Say he's wanted to meet mistress near church-hatch to-morrow morning at ten,' said Oak, in a whisper. 'That he must come without fail, and wear his best clothes.'

'The clothes will floor us as safe as houses!' said Coggan.

'It can't be helped,' said Oak. 'Tell her.'

So Coggan delivered the message. 'Mind, het or wet, blow or snow, he must come,' added Jan. ' 'Tis very particular, indeed. The fact is, 'tis to witness her sign some law-work about taking shares wi' another farmer for a long span o' years. There, that's what 'tis, and now I've told 'ee, Mother Tall, in a way I shouldn't ha'done if I hadn't loved 'ee so hopeless well.'

Coggan retired before she could ask any further; and next they called at the vicar's in a manner which excited no curiosity at all. Then Gabriel went home, and prepared for the morrow.

'Liddy,' said Bathsheba, on going to bed that night, 'I want you to call me at seven o'clock to-morrow, in case I shouldn't wake.'

'But you always do wake afore then, ma'am.'

'Yes, but I have something important to do, which I'll tell you of when the time comes, and it's best to make sure.'

Bathsheba, however, awoke voluntarily at four, nor could she by any contrivance get to sleep again. About six, being quite positive that her watch had stopped during the night, she could wait no longer. She went and tapped at Liddy's door, and after some labour awoke her.

'But I thought it was I who had to call you?' said the bewildered Liddy. 'And it isn't six yet.'

'Indeed it is; how can you tell such a story, Liddy! I know it must be ever so much past seven. Come to my room as soon as you can; I want you to give my hair a good brushing.'

When Liddy came to Bathsheba's room her mistress was already waiting. Liddy could not understand this extraordinary promptness. 'Whatever *is* going on, ma'am?' she said.

'Well, I'll tell you,' said Bathsheba, with a mischievous smile in her bright eyes. 'Farmer Oak is coming here to dine with me to-day!'

'Farmer Oak—and nobody else?—you two alone?'

'Yes.'

'But is it safe, ma'am, after what's been said?' asked her companion, dubiously. 'A woman's good name is such a perishable article that———'

Bathsheba laughed with a flushed cheek, and whispered in Liddy's ear, although there was nobody present. Then Liddy stared and exclaimed, 'Souls alive, what news! It makes my heart go quite bumpity-bump!'

'It makes mine rather furious, too,' said Bathsheba. 'However, there's no getting out of it now!'

It was a damp disagreeable morning. Nevertheless, at twenty minutes to ten o'clock, Oak came out of his house, and

> Went up the hill side
> With that sort of stride
> A man puts out when walking in search of a bride,[2]

and knocked at Bathsheba's door. Ten minutes later a large and a smaller umbrella might have been seen moving from the same door, and through the mist along the road to the church. The distance was not more than a quarter of a mile, and these two sensible persons deemed it unnecessary to drive. An observer must have been very close indeed to discover that the forms under the umbrellas were those of Oak and Bathsheba, arm-in-arm for the first time in their lives, Oak in a greatcoat extending to his knees, and Bathsheba in a cloak that reached her clogs. Yet, though so plainly dressed, there was a certain rejuvenated appearance about her:—

> As though a rose should shut and be a bud again.[3]

Repose had again incarnadined her cheeks; and having, at Gabriel's request, arranged her hair this morning as she had worn it years ago on Norcombe Hill, she seemed in his eyes remarkably like the girl of that fascinating dream, which, considering that she was now only three or

2. Quoted from "Patty Morgan the Milkmaid's Story" in R. H. Barham's collection of narrative poems, titled *The Ingoldsby Legends* (1840–1847).

3. Quoted from John Keats's poem, "The Eve of St. Agnes" (1820).

four-and-twenty, was perhaps not very wonderful. In the church were Tall, Liddy, and the parson, and in a remarkably short space of time the deed was done.

The two sat down very quietly to tea in Bathsheba's parlour in the evening of the same day, for it had been arranged that Farmer Oak should go there to live, since he had as yet neither money, house, nor furniture worthy of the name, though he was on a sure way towards them, whilst Bathsheba was, comparatively, in a plethora of all three.

Just as Bathsheba was pouring out a cup of tea, their ears were greeted by the firing of a cannon, followed by what seemed like a tremendous blowing of trumpets, in the front of the house.

'There!' said Oak, laughing, 'I knew those fellows were up to something, by the look on their faces.'

Oak took up the light and went into the porch, followed by Bathsheba with a shawl over her head. The rays fell upon a group of male figures gathered upon the gravel in front, who, when they saw the newly-married couple in the porch, set up a loud 'Hurrah!' and at the same moment bang again went the cannon in the background, followed by a hideous clang of music from a drum, tambourine, clarionet, serpent, hautboy,[4] tenor-viol, and double-bass—the only remaining relics of the true and original Weatherbury band— venerable worm-eaten instruments, which had celebrated in their own persons the victories of Marlborough, under the fingers of the forefathers of those who played them now. The performers came forward, and marched up to the front.

'Those bright boys, Mark Clark and Jan, are at the bottom of all this,' said Oak. 'Come in, souls, and have something to eat and drink wi' me and my wife.'

'Not to-night,' said Mr. Clark, with evident self-denial. 'Thank ye all the same; but we'll call at a more seemly time. However, we couldn't think of letting the day pass without a note of admiration of some sort. If ye could send a drop of som'at down to Warren's, why so it is. Here's long life and happiness to neighbour Oak and his comely bride!'

'Thank ye; thank ye all,' said Gabriel. 'A bit and a drop shall be sent to Warren's for ye at once. I had a thought that we might very likely get a salute of some sort from our old friends, and I was saying so to my wife but now.'

'Faith,' said Coggan, in a critical tone, turning to his companions, 'the man hev learnt to say "my wife" in a wonderful naterel way, considering how very youthful he is in wedlock as yet—hey, neighbours all?'

'I never heerd a skilful old married feller of twenty years' standing

---

4. "Serpent," an antique, deep-voiced wind musical instrument made of brass or wood covered with leather, about eight-feet long, and formed in snakelike curves; "hautboy," the earlier name for an oboe.

pipe "my wife" in a more used note than 'a did,' said Jacob Smallbury. 'It might have been a little more true to nater if't had been spoke a little chillier, but that wasn't to be expected just now.'

'That improvement will come wi' time,' said Jan, twirling his eye.

Then Oak laughed, and Bathsheba smiled (for she never laughed readily now), and their friends turned to go.

'Yes; I suppose that's the size o't,' said Joseph Poorgrass with a cheerful sigh as they moved away; 'and I wish him joy o' her; though I were once or twice upon saying to-day with holy Hosea, in my scripture manner, which is my second nature, "Ephraim is joined to idols: let him alone."[5] But since 'tis as 'tis, why, it might have been worse, and I feel my thanks accordingly.'

THE END

---

5. Joseph Poorgrass's comically irrelevant biblical quotation is from Hosea 4:17.

Textual Appendix

Textual Notes

RELEVANT TEXTS

The following is a list of the texts of *Far from the Madding Crowd* that were collated in preparing this Norton Critical Edition:

1. The manuscript of *Far from the Madding Crowd*, used as printer's copy for the serial version, now in the possession of Mr. Edwin Thorne.
2. The serial version published in the *Cornhill Magazine* in twelve monthly parts from January to December 1874.
3. The first book edition, two volumes. London: Smith, Elder, 1874.
4. The second impression of the first book edition, 1875.
5. The first one-volume edition. London: Smith, Elder, 1877.
6. The first collected edition. London: Osgood, McIlvaine, 1895.
7. Hardy's marked copy of a 1900 Harper and Brothers impression of the Osgood, McIlvaine edition, now in the Signet Library, Edinburgh; this copy was used as printer's copy for the "sixpenny" edition.
8. Hardy's marked page proofs for the "sixpenny" edition, now in the Signet Library, Edinburgh.
9. The "sixpenny" edition. London: Harper and Brothers, 1901.
10. The Macmillan revised impression of the Osgood, McIlvaine edition. London: Macmillan, 1902.
11. The Wessex Edition. London: Macmillan, 1912, reprinted with revisions in 1920.
12. Hardy's personal copy of the 1912 printing of the Wessex Edition, with revisions in his hand, now in the Dorset County Museum, Dorchester.

COPY-TEXT AND EDITORIAL PROCEDURE

The copy-text adopted for this Norton Critical Edition is a 1920 printing of the Wessex Edition of 1912. The rationale for this choice of copy-text is set forth in an essay titled "Editing Hardy," which was originally published in *Browning Institute Studies in Victorian Literary and Cultural History* and an abridged version of which is reprinted here on pp. 314–321.

Emendations of this copy-text were made to correct compositors' errors and to incorporate certain revisions made by Hardy in other texts of *Far from the Madding Crowd* when they could confidently be taken to represent his final deliberate intention. Thus, the late changes and additions that Hardy marked in his personal copy of the Wessex Edition were certainly alterations he would have wanted made; hence, they have in every case been incorporated in this edition. On the other hand, Hardy's revisions in the printer's copy and page proofs of the Harper and Brothers "sixpenny" edition of 1901 pose a much more complex kind of editorial problem. These were not available to Hardy when he revised for the Wessex Edition ten years later, but sometimes he made precisely the same revision again or a different revision at the same point where he had earlier revised for the "sixpenny" edition. In all such instances, the readings of the Wessex Edition text have been retained. In still other cases, however, Hardy allowed readings that he had previously altered for the "sixpenny" edition to stand in the Wessex Edition, and one cannot always be certain whether this was the result of deliberate judgment or of oversight. In preparing this edition, those "sixpenny" revisions were treated according to the following principles:

1. Whenever a "sixpenny" edition revision involved the correction of some clearly identifiable problem that remained unresolved in the Wessex text—e.g., an awkward repetition, a misplaced modifier, an inconsistency—it may confidently be assumed that Hardy would have preferred the revised "sixpenny" reading if his attention had been called to the problem when he revised for the Wessex Edition; hence, in such cases, Hardy's "sixpenny" edition revisions have been used to emend the copy-text.
2. In many other cases, however, there can be no certainty that Hardy would still have preferred the alternate "sixpenny" edition readings, and in such cases the reading of the Wessex Edition has been allowed to stand.

Illustrations of the differences between these kinds of "sixpenny" revisions are provided in the section headed *Variant Readings*.

Textual changes in *Far from the Madding Crowd* that were brought about by editorial pressures or direct editorial intervention pose still another kind of special problem. There is evidence in the manuscript of the novel and in the Hardy-Stephen correspondence that not only were certain portions of *Far from the Madding Crowd* deleted by Hardy at Leslie Stephen's insistence, but that some passages may have been independently marked for deletion by Stephen himself, for reasons that ranged from a desire to avoid reproduction costs to concern for the prudery of *Cornhill* readers. Hardy's attitude toward the material lost from his text as a result of such editorial tampering is ambiguous and not fully consistent. On one occasion he is reported to have said that if Stephen had omitted passages from the serial version of the novel he would not have bothered to restore them in the book version (see Frederic W. Maitland, *The Life and Letters of Leslie Stephen* [New York: Putnam, 1906], p. 275); but, on the other hand, at that point in the text of *Far from the Madding Crowd* where Stephen probably made a very extensive bowdlerization—Hardy's description of Fanny Robin and her baby in their coffin in chapter 43—Hardy did in fact subsequently revise the 1875 and 1877 book versions to restore at least some kinds of details that Stephen had deleted, and there is every reason to assume that in revising for the Wessex Edition he would have felt free to add any other details he judged necessary. Given these facts, there does not seem to be any compelling reason to emend the copy-text to restore those passages that Stephen may have deleted or altered. Information about such deleted materials may be found in R. L. Purdy's account of the publication of the novel, reprinted in this edition on pp. 345–346, and illustrations of some of the deleted materials are provided in the section titled *Variant Readings*.

EMENDATIONS

Emendations of the copy-text are recorded here, except for obvious typographical errors, which have been silently corrected. Each cited emendation begins with a page number reference to the Norton Critical Edition text, followed by a period, followed by the line number on that page, counting from the top. Next, the emended reading is given as it appears in the edited text, followed by a square bracket. Immediately following the bracket is an abbreviation indicating the earliest source of authority for the emendation (later texts with readings identical to the earliest source of authority are not identified). The following abbreviations have been used:

MS: The manuscript of *Far from the Madding Crowd*, now owned by Mr. Edwin Thorne.

C: *Cornhill Magazine*, 1874.

PC: Hardy's marked printer's copy of a 1900 Harper and Brothers impression of the Osgood, McIlvaine edition, now in the Signet Library, Edinburgh.

PP: Hardy's marked page proofs for the "sixpenny" edition, now in the Signet Library, Edinburgh.

MC: Hardy's personal copy of the 1912 printing of the Wessex Edition, with revisions in his hand, now in the Dorset County Musum, Dorchester.

RS: Editor.

The abbreviation indicating the earliest source of authority for the emendation is followed by a semicolon, which in turn is followed by the rejected copy-text reading. In recording emendations of punctuation, the swung dash ($\sim$) is used in place of the word following the punctuation in order to focus attention on the copy-text punctuation that was emended; at points where the copy-text lacked a punctuation mark supplied by emendation, a caret ($\wedge$) is used to call attention to the point where the mark is missing.

24.32	flue] PP; chimney
30.36	nearly] PC; more than
32.39	It is somewhat . . . sheep in Latin] MC
48.44	all for nought] PC; all nought
49.11	mind] PC; thoughts
50.15	supplication] PC; prayer
50.23	desert under] PC; desert in the tropics under
73.13	general which] PP; $\sim$, $\sim$
125.40	seem only] PC; only seem
136.14	ninety-nine] MS; ninty-nine
140.10	during] PC; in
175.12	skip] MS; limp
183.42	jacket] PC; coat
187.01	final] MS; fine
188.29	furze bushes] MS: $\sim$ - $\sim$
200.39	to the second Budmouth] PC; to Budmouth
200.39	race-meeting] PP; second meeting
206.01	strip] MS; stripe
206.28	of the woman's] RS; of woman's
206.34	simulated] MS; stimulated
223.25	on the subject] MS; on he subject
224.40	here. Liddy,' she] PP; here, Liddy.' She
226.21	longing to] MC; longing desire to
230.15	stood erect] MC; stood perfectly erect
232.44	noisome] MC; fulsome
240.08	of a young yew tree] PP; of the yew-tree
240.29	the old trees] PC; the two old yews
241.34	its toes rested] MC; its feet rested
246.39	churchyard assumed to be those of "Weatherbury" do] MC; churchyard do
250.04	had not taken] MC; had not before taken
252.02	is. There may be some trick in it. I] MC; is. I

257.40   decayed town] PC; decayed old town
264.36   been identified by] PP; been recognized by
264.42   and in] PC; and being in
275.18   a sort of widow] MC; a widow lady
276.23   quietly] MS; quite
281.09   won't] MS; don't
294.08   Poorgrass.] MS: ~ ,
300.10   The weeks] MS; Three weeks

VARIANT READINGS

Space limitations prohibit any full treatment of the many variant readings that collation of the texts of *Far from the Madding Crowd* has brought to light. However, certain kinds of variant readings that were not adopted in preparing this edition are of sufficient interest to warrant providing some examples of them here.

There are, first of all, the kinds of readings in Hardy's manuscript that were probably suppressed by Leslie Stephen. One such editorial deletion involved five drawings of sets of hoof marks on leaf 2–107 and following leaves. They are faithful graphic representations of Hardy's verbal descriptions of the variations in the gait of Bathsheba's horse; the first, for example, is described on p. 164 of this edition as follows:

The footprints forming this recent impression were full of information as to pace; they were in equidistant pairs, three or four feet apart, the right and left foot of each pair being exactly opposite one another.

The illustration Hardy provided in his manuscript looked like this:

These were marked for deletion in pencil—something Hardy never used to indicate his own deletions. Similar pencil markings were used to indicate deletion of other passages, some of which Stephen probably thought subscribers to the *Cornhill* might find objectionable on moral or religious grounds. One such extensive deletion from chapter 43, leaves 2–232 to 2–233, involved a description of the dead Fanny Robin and her baby in their coffin and included language like this:

Bathsheba's eager eyes were now directed to the upper end. By the dead girl's side, enclosed by one of her arms, was the object of the search:—

A curious frame of Nature's work,
A flow'ret crushed in the bud,
A nameless piece of Babyhood,

neatly apparelled in its first & last outfit for earth—a miniature rapping of white linen—with a face so delicately small in contour & substance that its cheeks & the plump backs of its little fists irresistably reminded her, excited as she was, of the soft convexity of mushrooms on a dewy morning.

The absence of any note of moral condemnation in this passage and the succeeding ones describing Fanny Robin might have prompted Stephen to mark them for deletion.

It may also be helpful to provide some illustration of the different kinds of revisions that Hardy made for the "sixpenny" edition of 1901. The kinds of revisions that were incorporated in this Norton Critical Edition involved changes Hardy made to do such things as to avoid an awkward repetition. Such, for example, was Hardy's revision of a passage near the beginning of chapter 4, which in the Wessex Edition Hardy left unchanged; it read as follows:

> Gabriel had watched the blue wood-smoke curling from the *chimney* with strange meditation. At evening he had fancifully traced it down the *chimney* to the spot of its origin. . . .

In revising for the "sixpenny" edition, Hardy obviously changed the second *chimney* to *flue* in order to avoid the awkward repetition, and such revisions have been incorporated in this edition. But Hardy made many other revisions for the "sixpenny" edition for which no such obvious motive can be discovered; these involve, rather, alterations affecting tone, emphasis, and the like, and it is far less certain that when Hardy came to revise for the Wessex Edition some ten years later he would still have preferred them. For example, in chapter 6, on p. 38 of this edition, Joseph Poorgrass's speech is described as "*very* shaky by nature, and more so by circumstance, the jolting of the waggon not being without its effect upon the speaker's larynx." For the "sixpenny" edition Hardy substituted *somewhat* for *very*, but whether he would have preferred *somewhat* for the *very* that he retained in the Wessex Edition cannot be known with any certainty. Similarly, in chapter 7, on p. 42 of this edition, Bathsheba's reaction to Gabriel Oak's appearance in Weatherbury is described in these terms: "Embarrassed she was not, and she remembered Gabriel's declaration of love to her at Norcombe only to think *she had nearly forgotten it.*" For the "sixpenny" edition Hardy substituted the phrase *of the changes since then* for the italicized passage, and, again, although the revision obviously makes an important difference in how Bathsheba's attitude toward Oak is characterized, there is no way of ascertaining whether the fact that Hardy made no equivalent change when he revised for the Wessex Edition reflects his deliberate preference or not. In such cases, the readings of the Wessex Edition have been retained in the Norton Critical Edition text.

Finally, in one case Hardy made a revision for the Wessex edition which created a marked inconsistency that, nevertheless, has been followed to stand. From the manuscript onward, all texts of *Far from the Madding Crowd* contain a speech by Troy in chapter 35, on p. 184 of this edition, which makes emphatically clear that he suspects Boldwood's sanity:

> 'Oh, Coggan,' said Troy, as if inspired by a recollection, 'do you know if insanity has ever appeared in Mr. Boldwood's family?'

And, up to the Wessex Edition, a subsequent passage in chapter 55, on p. 294 of this edition, read as follows:

> . . . but nobody imagined that there had shown in him unequivocal symptoms of the mental derangement which Bathsheba and Troy, alone of all others and at different times, had momentarily suspected.

For the Wessex edition, Hardy changed the name of *Troy* in this passage to *Oak*, even though later in the same chapter he has Oak say he does *not* think Boldwood was insane. The change certainly created an inconsistency; but many of Hardy's other late revisions made clear that he was intent on strengthening Oak's character, and this revision does attribute to Oak a somewhat greater insight and keenness of perception that Hardy no doubt thought important. Hence, in spite of the inconsistency Hardy's revision created, the reading *Oak* in the Wessex text has been retained in this edition.

A brief comment may be added here about the running heads that appeared at the top of the righthand pages of the Wessex Edition. These were invariably taken from the chapter headings, either in whole or in part, so that, for example, portions of the heading at the beginning of chapter 4, "Gabriel's Resolve—The Visit—The Mistake," appear as running heads throughout the chapter: "The Visit" on pp. 27, 29, and 31; "The Mistake" on pp. 33 and 35. Because it is impracticable to adopt the pagination of the Wessex Edition and because the effect of these running heads seems aesthetically negligible, the entire chapter headings are used as running heads throughout.

ROBERT C. SCHWEIK AND MICHAEL PIRET

[Choosing a Copy-text: The Problem of Hardy's Manuscript Accidentals]†

* * * In many cases it would be sound editorial practice to choose the manuscript of a Hardy novel as copy-text, as Dale Kramer has recently done for his splendid edition of *The Woodlanders*.[1] But the manuscript of *The Woodlanders*, for example, is more fully and carefully punctuated than is that of *Far from the Madding Crowd*, and the difference is marked enough to warrant a closer consideration of what it implies. The following bit of dialogue between little Teddy Coggan and Bathsheba Everdene, taken from the manuscript of *Far from the Madding Crowd*,[2] can serve as a useful point of reference to illustrate a number of characteristic features of Hardy's treatment of its accidentals; young Coggan is reporting a conversation he had with Farmer Boldwood:

> He said, where are you going my little man, and I said, to Miss Everdene's, please, and he said* She is an old woman, isn't she, my little man? and I said* yes.
> You naughty child! What did you say that for?
>
> (f. 106)

First of all, one striking feature of the *Far from the Madding Crowd* manuscript which is not characteristic of that of *The Woodlanders* is Hardy's quite different treatment of dialogue. In *The Woodlanders*

†From Robert C. Schweik and Michael Piret, "Editing Hardy," *Browning Institute Studies: An Annual of Victorian Literary and Cultural History*, 9 (1981), 15–41.

1. Thomas Hardy, *The Woodlanders*, ed. Dale V. Kramer (Oxford: The Clarendon Press, 1981).

2. Quotations from the *Far from the Madding Crowd* manuscript are made with the kind permission of its owner, Mr. Edwin Thorne, and the Trustees of the Thomas Hardy estate. References to leaf numbers are provided parenthetically at the end of quotations. In quotations where a punctuation mark is missing, an asterisk is inserted to call attention to the missing mark, but this device is not used to note the very frequent absence of single and double quotation marks.

manuscript, dialogue is regularly indicated by quotation marks; in *Far from the Madding Crowd* perhaps only a twentieth or less of the dialogue is so marked. There can be, expecially in the earlier portions of the text, stretches in which quotations are more or less regularly supplied, but even in such cases there can be singular irregularities, such as the following, which is only a portion of a longer section in which quotation marks are scattered almost randomly in the text:

> "I believe ye, Joseph Poorgrass, for we all know ye to be a very bashful man."
> "'Tis terrible bad for a man, poor soul," said the maltster. And how long have ye suffered from it Joseph?
> O ever since I was a boy. Yes—mother was concerned to her heart about it—yes. But 'twas all nought."
>
> (f. 78)

Later in the manuscript, long stretches of unmarked dialogue may be abruptly broken, as on the top of f. 2–59, with a short burst of quotation marks which then just as abruptly stop halfway down the leaf. Generally, Hardy did provide quotation marks around quotations within quotations, but not always, and the *Cornhill* compositors had to be prepared to face passages like the bit of dialogue between young Coggan and Bathsheba Everdene quoted above. For the most part they did their work very well—with the one exception of the compositor who read the manuscript line

> Weak as water, yes, said Jan Coggan* (f. 2–15)

and punctuated it

> "Weak as water!" yes, said Jan Coggan.

Clearly, however, Hardy's treatment of punctuation of dialogue in the manuscript of *Far from the Madding Crowd* was so casual and unsystematic that he plainly expected—indeed required—editorial intervention to fill in and complete his accidentals.

A similar expectation is apparent in Hardy's treatment of questions and exclamations. Again, a portion of the quotation provided above from f. 106 can serve as a convenient starting point for a consideration of this feature of the manuscript:

> He said, where are you going my little man, and I said, to Miss Everdene's, please, and he said* She is an old woman, isn't she, my little man? and I said* yes.

The exact parallelism of the two questions ending in *my little man* implies a parallel treatment of their punctuation, yet Hardy ended the first with a comma and the second with a question mark. The compositor, who was already engaged in sorting out the unmarked quotations within quotations, not surprisingly also regularized the punctuation of the two questions by assigning a question mark to the first as well as the second. Similar parallels in the form of questions which Hardy treated with a cavalier disregard for the most elementary consistency can be found scattered throughout the novel. In a sequence of questions on f. 109, for example, Joseph Poorgrass is being interrogated by Bathsheba, and her three sequential questions take the following form in the manuscript:

> Joseph Poorgrass—are you there?
>
> What do you do on the farm.
>
> How much to you*

Or, again, from f. 2–157:

> Gabriel! What in the name of fortune did you pretend to be Laban for*
> I didn't. I thought you meant—
> Yes you did. What do you want here?

In cases like these—and there are such scattered throughout the manuscript text—it is apparent that the differences in punctuation are in every likelihood to be attributed to simple carelessness, for nothing in the form of the questions or the context otherwise accounts for the differences. It has been argued that Hardy's use of an unexpected comma or period in place of a more conventional question mark may be the result of some subtle rhetorical purpose or, at least, some distinct deliberate preference of his;[3] but when one considers Hardy's unconventional substitutions for question marks within sequences where some consistency of intention can reasonably be presumed, such arguments seem far less persuasive, at least in the case of the manuscript of *Far from the Madding Crowd*. Consider still one further example—Hardy's punctuation of a passage in which Oak ponders Boldwood's shooting of Troy:

> What had become of Boldwood?—he should be looked after. Was he mad—had there been a quarrel? Then how had Troy got there—where had he come from—how did this remarkable reappearance come to pass when he was supposed to be at the bottom of the sea.
>
> (f. 3–94)

What is so striking in such passages is that the inconsistency in the treatment of the accidentals in rhetorically parallel elements is strong testimony that the differences come about not from some preference or some rhetorical design but simply out of carelessness and chance. But such a conclusion, if it is well founded, has consequences an

---

3. Simon Gatrell, "A Critical Edition of Thomas Hardy's Novel *Under the Greenwood Tree*" (unpublished D. Phil. thesis, Oxford, 1973), pp. *xcix* ff.

editor must consider in other cases in which Hardy's use of unconventional marks with questions might be deemed to serve some rhetorical purpose, as in this bit of dialogue between Bathsehba and Joseph Poorgrass about Fanny Robin:

> Did she walk along our turnpike road? she said in a suddenly restless and eager voice.
> I believe she did. . . . Ma'am, shall I call Liddy. You bain't well, ma'am, surely. You look like a lily—so very pale.
> No don't call her: it is nothing. When did she pass Weatherbury*
>
> (f. 2–202)

Of course Hardy may have punctuated Joseph's lines, *Ma'am, shall I call Liddy. You bain't well, ma'am surely.* without question marks deliberately to suggest something of his tone—a dazed flatness of expression, perhaps; but the absence of any mark at all after the question by Bathsehba in the next segment of dialogue scarcely makes one confident that any such assumption of deliberate purposefulness would be soundly based. In fact, the probabilities, given the very casual way Hardy treats his accidentals in *Far from the Madding Crowd*, would not seem very strong.

Another aspect of that casualness is again notable in that simple bit of dialogue between little Coggan and Bathsheba which has already served as a conveniently compact embodiment of various manifestations of Hardy's carelessness:

> He said, where are you going my little man, and I said, to Miss Everdene's, please, and he said* She is an old woman, isn't she, my little man? and I said* yes.

Here, in the space of a simple sequence of four *he said* and *I said* introductions to quotations, two are followed by commas, two not, and nothing in the passage suggests any motive for the difference. Other parallel consecutive passages reveal a similarly indiscernible intention in the use of the comma between *he said* and a following participial phrase:

> "Well done and done quickly! said Bathsehba* looking at her watch as the last snip resounded.
> How long miss? said Gabriel, wiping his brow.
>
> (f. 2–8)

Or, again:

> "That means matrimony," said Temperance Miller, following them out of sight with her eyes.
> I reckon that's the size o't, said Coggan* working along without looking up.
>
> (f. 2–12)

Hence, when a passage in Hardy's manuscript reads

> A good time for one—an excellent time, said Joseph Poorgrass*
> straightening his back. . . .
>
> (f. 2–117)

the absence of the comman can scarecely be taken as firm evidence of
any deliberate rhetorical intention on Hardy's part.

It is true, of course, that there is a notable tendency in Hardy's
manuscript punctuation toward a more "open" pointing than was
conventional in his day,but this tendency—and it appears more or less
in his manuscripts of prose works written for publication throughout
his career—may be attributable as much to lack of interest in careful
pointing as to deliberate preference. Hardy's tendency toward a more
"open" punctuation led, of course, to many sentences which are
entirely acceptable as he pointed them—but whether those represent
his distinct deliberate preference may be doubted. The same preference, for example, produced the following:

> About an hour after she heard the noise of the wagon and went
> out, still with a painful consciousness of her bewildered and
> troubled look.
>
> (f. 2–203)

Or again:

> I've seen a good many women in my time, continued the young
> man in a murmur and more thoughtfully than hitherto criti-
> cally regarding her bent head at the same time. . . .
>
> (f. 2–34)

There are at least fifty such instances of passages punctuated so loosely
that they would be likely to cause a reader to stumble, halt, and reread
to catch the intended relationship of sentence elements; and, apart
from their awkwardness, they inject sometimes temporary but surely
unintended comic effects, as in this comment on Bathsheba:

> To the eyes of the middle aged Bathesheba was additionally
> charming just now.
>
> (f. 3–25)

But perhaps the most telling evidence of Hardy's careless lack of
concern about his manuscript accidentals lies in the fact that although
his manuscript is full of revisions which testify to his concern for his
substantives, there is practically no evidence of revision of accidentals.
In fact, quite the contrary is the case: substantive revisions are often
made in ways which corrupt accidentals without any attempt on
Hardy's part to rectify the corruption. This appears notably in places
where Hardy inserts a passage above a line with a caret or some other
mark which obliterates a necessary punctuation mark, or, alternately,
where the inserted phrase manifestly requires punctuation which
Hardy does not supply. Similarly, additional words are frequently

inserted at the beginning of existing sentences without any alteration of the original capital letter. In short, Hardy's manuscript revisions further testify to his primary concern for substantives and his cavalier treatment of his accidentals.

Hence, if an editor were hoping to adopt a copy-text which represented the closest approximation to Hardy's final deliberate intention, the manuscript accidentals—which on the whole can scarcely be called deliberate and certainly were not expected nor intended to be final—might not be the best guide. They are authorial in the limited sense that Hardy placed them in the manuscript, but they are certainly no reliable index to subtleties in his intentions. Hardy's comment quoted earlier, to the effect that no printer can be trusted with verse, suggests that he took a different attitude toward the text of his prose fiction, and the manuscript accidentals of *Far from the Madding Crowd* to bear this out.

That is not to suggest, of course, that Hardy regarded the *Cornhill* compositors as collaborators or that in passing their accidentals in proof that he did anything other than generally acquiesce in them. But acquiesce he did, and the subsequent printing history of *Far from the Madding Crowd* is, for the most part, a record of his acquiesence to the increasing intrusion of compositor's accidentals into his text. What proof-copy and printer's-copy exist reveal him to have continued to be relatively more concerned with the revision of substantives.[4] But to this general record of acquiesence and relative indifference to accidentals, there is one notable exception—the *Wessex Edition* itself. What sets the *Wessex Edition* apart from other printings of Hardy's fiction is not simply his well-known wish that it be regarded as embodying his final intention but, more importantly, what is now known of Hardy's extensive revision of its accidentals.

Dale Kramer's publication of "Accidentals Revisions in the Printer's Copy for Thomas Hardy's *Wessex Edition*" in 1977 first called public attention to the existence in the Doreset County Museum of a copy of a "Uniform Edition" printing of *The Woodlanders* containing Hardy's revisions which was used as a printer's copy for the Woodlanders volume of the *Wessex Edition;* and Kramer points out that Hardy's correspondence with Macmillan makes clear that other volumes of the "Uniform Edition" were prepared by Hardy for the rest of the *Wessex Edition* revised texts.[5] As the only known exemplar of

4. The Signet Library, Edinburgh, holds Hardy's marked copy of a 1900 Harper and Brothers impression of the Osgood, McIlvaine edition; this was used to set the "sixpenny edition" of *Far from the Madding Crowd* (London: Harper and Brothers, 1901). Page proof marked by Hardy for this edition is also in the Signet Library. Although Hardy's revisions for the sixpenny edition are primarily of substantives, on one aspect of its accidentals—the use of -*ize* rather than -*ise* in verb endings—he was adamantly emphatic, and his other revisions do show a pattern of directing the removal of commas from the text, though by no means so extensively as is the case with the Wessex Edition revisions.

5. Dale Kramer, "Accidentals Revisions in the Printer's Copy for Thomas Hardy's Wessex Edition," *Papers of the Bibliographical Society of America*, 71 (1977), 519.

Hardy's marked printers' copy used to set the *Wessex Edition*, it is of particular importance of what it testifies about Hardy's concern for the accidentals of that edition and the fidelity with which the Macmillan compositors carried out his wishes. This marked copy reveals that Hardy made very much in excess of 500 changes in the accidentals of the "Uniform Edition" text used as printer's copy, and that the bulk of these involved the removal of commas from the text. "It is manifest," Kramer observed about the *Wessex Edition* printing of *The Woodlanders*, "that Hardy did not leave his punctuation to be managed according to his publisher's house styling when he had a choice but gave as punctilious and, evidently, recurring attention to his punctuation as he did to the words in his texts."[6] What is striking is that the pattern of revisions of accidentals revealed in *The Woodlanders* shows up in the *Wessex Edition* versions of other novels as well, including *Far from the Madding Crowd*, which, when collated against the "Uniform Edition" printing which served as printer's copy, exhibits a similarly extensive removal of commas from the text. There is every reason to believe, then, that the extensive alteration of accidentals in the *Wessex Edition* of *Far from the Madding Crowd* is probably all but entirely authorial. The implications of this for an editor choosing a copy-text for a critical edition were carefully put by Kramer in this way:

> There may be sound reasons for preferring an earlier state of accidentals . . . of some of the novels; and for other novels it may be necessary to construct an eclectic accidentals text. But each editor will need to weigh the claims that the variants of the Wessex Edition of that novel make within the total set of variants, with the near-certain knowledge that most of the variants entering the text of the Wessex Edition are authorial, and with the strong possibility that they all are.[7]

When he came to edit *The Woodlanders*, Kramer decided to adopt the manuscript as copy-text, incorporating in it the accidentals revisions marked in the printer's copy in the Dorset County Museum; his decision was based in part on the possibility that some (though proportionately very small) number of accidentals changes in the *Wessex Edition* may have originated with Macmillan editors or compositors; in part on the knowledge that the *Wessex Edition* embodied many accidentals which did not originate with Hardy; and in part because the manuscript seemed suitable to serve as copy-text.

An editor of *Far from the Madding Crowd* may weigh these factors differently. First of all, the manuscript seems far less satisfactory as a witness of Hardy's deliberate intention so far as its accidentals are concerned. Furthermore, the evidence of Hardy's extensive revisions of accidentals for the *Wessex Edition* implies something more than simply testimony that what was changed is authoritative: it implies a careful review of the accidentals in the printer's copy which were allowed to remain as well. In such cases, the resulting edition can have a very strong claim as a choice for copy-text: and, as G. Thomas Tanselle has pointed out, that claim is entirely consistent with Greg's theory:

> If an author can be shown to have gone over his work with scrupulous care for a revised edition, examining accidentals as well as substantives, the revised edition (as the closest edition to an "ultimately authoritative document") would become the copy-text. Such a situation does not arise in most instances, but Greg recognized its importance: "The fact is," he said, "that cases of revision differ so greatly in circumstances and character that it seems impossible to lay down any hard and fast rule as to when an editor should take the original edition as his copy-text and when the revised reprint."[8]

Of course the adoption of the *Wessex Edition* version of *Far from the Madding Crowd* would still require a total review of the claims of substantives and accidentals in other texts and, inevitably, extensive emendation;[9] but the *Wessex* text has, at least for *Far from the Madding Crowd*, a stronger claim as a choice for copy-text than may be true for editions of some other of Hardy's novels.

8. G. Thomas Tanselle, "The Problem of Final Authorial Intention," *Selected Studies in Bibliography* (Charlottesville: University Press of Virginia, 1979), pp. 310–11.
9. One special problem which an editor of *Far from the Madding Crowd* must confront is an assessment of the authority of the extensive revisions which Hardy made for the sixpenny edition (see note 4 above) which were not available to him when he revised for the *Wessex Edition*. Here such considerations as the history of Hardy's subsequent revisions, the context in which the revision was made, and other factors must be taken into account in each instance to help determine whether or not a given revision in the sixpenny text warrants an emendation in the copy-text.

Backgrounds

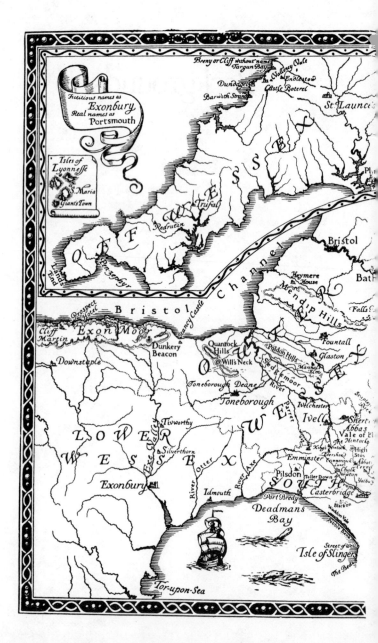

Breeny or Cliff without name
Targan Bay
Dundagel
Barwith Strand
Voltney Vale
Endleston
Castle Boterel
St Launce

Fictitious names as
Exonbury
Real names as
Portsmouth

Isles of
Lyonnesse
S. Maria
Giants Town

Trufal

Redrutin

WESSEX

O F F

Land's
End

Pestacur

Bristol
Bath

Heymere
House

Mendip Hills

Falls

Prospect
Cliff
Martin

B r i s t o l   Channel

Dancy Castle

Exon Moor

Dunkery
Beacon

Quantock
Hills

Will's Neck

Poldon Hills

Sedgemoor

Mannar
Elm

Fountall

Glaston

Downstaple

Toneborough Deane

River

Toneborough

Ivell

Welchester

SOMERSET

Tivworthy

Silverthorn

LOWER

WESSEX

River Exe

River Otter

River Axe

Idmouth

Exonbury

Pilsdon

Sher
Abbas
Vale of
The Hintock

King's Hintock

Evershed

Emminster

High
Stoy

Abbots
Cernel

Newton

Yalbu

Taller Down

Casterbridge

SOUTH

WESSEX

Port Bredy

**Deadmans
Bay**

Isle of Slingers

Street of Wells

The Brea

Tor-upon-Sea

The Setting

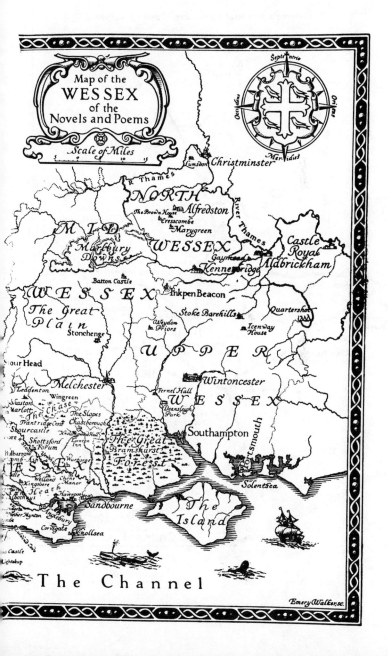

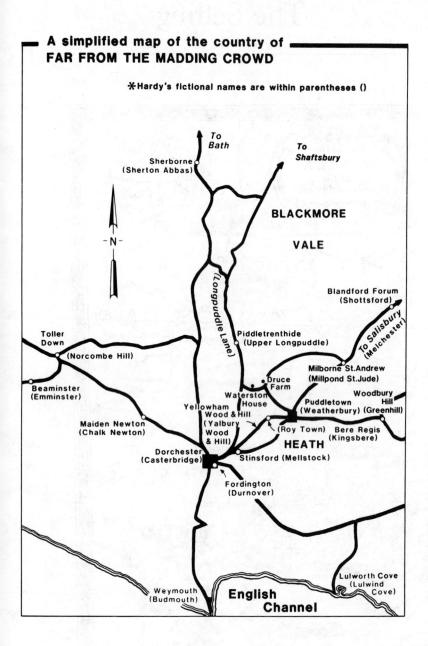

A simplified map of the country of FAR FROM THE MADDING CROWD

✳Hardy's fictional names are within parentheses ()

Biographical and Social Backgrounds

F. E. HARDY

From *The Life of Thomas Hardy*,† *1840–1928*

* * * In December 1872, Hardy had received at Bockhampton a letter from Leslie Stephen, the editor of the *Cornhill*—by that time well known as a man of letters, *Saturday* reviewer, and Alpine climber—asking for a special story for his magazine. He had lately read *Under the Greenwood Tree*, and thought 'the descriptions admirable.' It was 'long since he had received more pleasure from a new writer,' and it had occurred to him that such writing would probably please the readers of the *Cornhill Magazine* as much as it had pleased him.

Hardy had replied that he feared the date at which he could write a story for the *Cornhill* would be too late for Mr. Stephen's purpose, since he already had on hand a succeeding novel (*i.e.* A *Pair of Blue Eyes*), which was arranged for; but that the next after should be at Mr. Stephen's disposal. He had thought of making it a pastoral tale with the title of *Far from the Madding Crowd*—and that the chief characters would probably be a young woman-farmer, a shepherd, and a sergeant of cavalry. That was all he had done. Mr. Stephen had rejoined that he was sorry he could not expect a story from Hardy at an earlier date; that he did not, however, mean to fix any particular time; that the idea of the story attracted him; also the proposed title; and that he would like Hardy to call and talk it over when he came to Town. There the matter had been left. Now Hardy set about the pastoral tale, the success of A *Pair of Blue Eyes* meanwhile surpassing his expectations, the influential *Saturday Review* pronouncing it to be the most artistically constructed of the novels of its time—a quality which, by the bye, would carry little recommendation in these days of loose construction and indifference to organic homogeneity.

---

†From F. E. Hardy, *The Life of Thomas Hardy, 1840–1928* (London: Macmillan, 1962), pp. 95–101. This one-volume edition is a reprinting of two volumes titled *The Early Life of Thomas Hardy, 1840–1891* and *The Later Years of Thomas Hardy, 1892–1928*, published in 1928 and 1930 respectively and usually abbreviated *Early Life* and *Later Years*. Although published as a biography, *The Life of Thomas Hardy* was very largely drafted by Hardy himself.

But Hardy did not call on Stephen just then.

It was, indeed, by the merest chance that he had ever got the *Cornhill* letter at all. The postal arrangements in Dorset were still so primitive at this date that the only delivery of letters at Hardy's father's house was by the hand of some friendly neighbour who had come from the next village, and Stephen's request for a story had been picked up in the mud of the lane by a labouring man, the school children to whom it had been entrusted having dropped it on the way.

While thus in the seclusion of Bockhampton,[1] writing *Far from the Madding Crowd*, we find him on September 21, walking to Woodbury-Hill Fair, approximately described in the novel as 'Greenhill Fair.' On the 24th he was shocked at hearing of the tragic death of his friend Horace Moule, from whom he had parted cheerfully at Cambridge in June. The body was brought to be buried at Fordington, Dorchester, and Hardy attended the funeral. It was a matter of keen regret to him now, and for a long time after, that Moule and the woman to whom Hardy was warmly attached had never set eyes on each other; and that she could never make Moule's acquaintance, or be his friend.

On the 30th of September he sent to Leslie Stephen at his request as much of the MS. of *Far from the Madding Crowd* as was written—apparently between two and three monthly parts, though some of it only in rough outline—and a few days after a letter came from Stephen stating that the story suited him admirably as far as it had gone, and that though as a rule it was desirable to see the whole of a novel before definitely accepting it, under the circumstances he decided to accept it at once.

So Hardy went on writing *Far from the Madding Crowd*—sometimes indoors, sometimes out—when he would occasionally find himself without a scrap of paper at the very moment that he felt volumes. In such circumstances he would use large dead leaves, white chips left by the wood-cutters, or pieces of stone or slate that came to hand. He used to say that when he carried a pocket-book his mind was barren as the Sahara.

This autumn Hardy assisted at his father's cider-making—a proceeding he had always enjoyed from childhood—the apples being from huge old trees that have now long perished. It was the last time he ever took part in a work whose sweet smells and oozings in the crisp autumn air can never be forgotten by those who have had a hand in it.

Memorandum by T. H.:

'Met J. D., one of the old Mellstock fiddlers[2]—who kept me talking

---

1. Higher Bockhampton, the hamlet that was Hardy's birthplace, not far from Stinsford; the hamlets of Stinsford, Lower Bockhampton, and Higher Bockhampton together formed Hardy's fictional "Mellstock."

2. J. D. was probably James Dart, who, with Hardy's grandfather and father formed part of the Stinford Church string choir, which Hardy fictionalized in his novel *Under the Greenwood Tree.*

interminably: a man who speaks neither truth nor lies, but a sort of Not Proven compound which is very relishable. Told me of Jack ————, who spent all the money he had—sixpence—at the Oak Inn, took his sixpence out of the till when the landlady's back was turned, and spent it over again; then stole it again, and again spent it, till he had had a real skinful. "Was too honest to take any money but his own," said J. D.' (Some of J. D.'s characteristics appear in 'the Tranter' of *Under the Greenwood Tree.)*

At the end of October an unexpected note from the *Cornhill* editor asked if, supposing he were to start *Far from the Madding Crowd* in the January number (which would be out the third week in December) instead of the spring, as intended, Hardy could keep in front of the printers with his copy. He learnt afterwards that what had happened was that the MS. of a novel which the editor had arranged to begin in his pages in January had been lost in the post, according, at any rate, to its author's account. Hardy thought January not too soon for him, and that he could keep the printers going. Terms were consequently arranged with the publishers and proofs of the first number sent forthwith, Hardy incidentally expressing with regard to any illustrations, in a letter of October 1873, 'a hope that the rustics, although *quaint,* may be made to appear intelligent, and not boorish at all'; adding in a later letter: 'In reference to the illustrations, I have sketched in my note-book during the past summer a few correct outlines of smockfrocks, gaiters, sheep-crooks, rick-"staddles", a sheep-washing pool, one of the old-fashioned malt-houses, and some other out-of-the-way things that might have to be shown. These I could send you if they would be of any use to the artist, but if he is a sensitive man and you think he would rather not be interfered with, I would not do so.'

No response had been made to this, and he was not quite clear whether, after all, Leslie Stephen had finally decided to begin so soon, when, returning from Cornwall[3] on a fine December noontide (being New Year's Eve 1873–74), he opened on Plymouth Hoe a copy of the *Cornhill* that he had bought at the station, and there to his surprise saw his story placed at the beginning of the magazine, with a striking illustration, the artist being—also to his surprise—not a man but a woman, Miss Helen Paterson. He had only expected, from the undistinguished rank of the characters in the tale, that it would be put at the end, and possibly without a picture. Why this had come without warning to him was owing to the accident of his being away from his permanent address for several days, and nothing having been forwarded. It can be imagined how delighted Miss Gifford was to receive the first number of the story, whose nature he had kept from her to give her a pleasant surprise, and to find that her desire of a literary course

3. Hardy had been making visits to Cornwall in 1873 partly for his work as an architect and partly to court Emma Lavinia Gifford, whom he married in the following year.

for Hardy was in fair way of being justified.

In the first week of January 1874 the story was noticed in a marked degree by the *Spectator*, and a guess hazarded that it might be from the pen of George Eliot[4]—why, the author could never understand, since, so far as he had read that great thinker—one of the greatest living, he thought, though not a born storyteller by any means—she had never touched the life of the fields: her country-people having seemed to him, too, more like small townsfolk than rustics; and as evidencing a woman's wit cast in country dialogue rather than real country humour, which he regarded as rather of the Shakespeare and Fielding sort. However, he conjectured, as a possible reason for the flattering guess, that he had latterly been reading Comte's *Positive Philosophy*,[5] and writings of that school, some of whose expressions had thus passed into his vocabulary, expressions which were also common to George Eliot. Leslie Stephen wrote:

'I am glad to congratulate you on the reception of your first number. Besides the gentle *Spectator*, which thinks that you must be George Eliot because you know the names of the stars, several good judges have spoken to me warmly of the *Madding Crowd*. Moreover the *Spectator*, though flighty in its head, has really a good deal of critical feeling. I always like to be praised by it—and indeed by other people! . . . The story comes out very well, I think, and I have no criticism to make.'

Respecting the public interest in the opening of the story, in later days Miss Thackeray informed him, with some of her father's humour, that to inquiries with which she was besieged on the sex of the author, and requests to be given an introduction to him or her, she would reply: '*It* lives in the country, and I could not very well introduce you to *it* in Town.'

A passage may be quoted here from Mr. F. W. Maitland's *Life of Leslie Stephen* (to which Hardy contributed half a chapter or so, on Stephen as editor) which affords a humorous illustration of the difficulties of 'serial' writing in Victorian days. Stephen had written to say that the seduction of Fanny Robin must be treated in 'a gingerly fashion', adding that it was owing to an 'excessive prudery of which I am ashamed'.

'I wondered what had so suddenly caused, in one who had seemed anything but a prude, the "excessive prudery" alluded to. But I did not learn till I saw him in April. Then he told me that an unexpected Grundian cloud, though no bigger than a man's hand as yet, had appeared on our serene horizon. Three respectable ladies and sub-

---

4. "George Eliot" was the pen name of Mary Ann Evans (1819–80), a well-known novelist influenced by the thought of Auguste Comte (1798–1857).

5. Hardy owned Auguste Comte's A *General*

View of Positivism in an English translation published in 1865; earlier in *The Life of Thomas Hardy*, he is reported to have been reading Comte's works in May of 1870.

scribers, representing he knew not how many more, had written to upbraid him for an improper passage in a page of the story which had already been published.

'I was struck mute, till I said, "Well, if you value the opinion of such people, why didn't you think of them beforehand, and strike out the passage?"—"I ought to have, since it is their opinion, whether I value it or no", he said with a half groan. "But it didn't occur to me that there was anything to object to!" I reminded him that though three objectors who disliked the passage, or pretended to, might write their disapproval, three hundred who possibly approved of it would not take the trouble to write, and hence he might have a false impression of the public as a body. "Yes; I agree. Still I suppose I ought to have foreseen these gentry, and have omitted it," he murmured.

'It may be added here, to finish with this detail (though it anticipates dates), that when the novel came out in volume form *The Times* quoted in a commendatory review the very passage that had offended. As soon as I met him, I said, "You see what *The Times* says about that paragraph; and you cannot say that *The Times* is not respectable." He was smoking and answered tardily: "No, I can't say that *The Times* is not respectable." I then urged that if he had omitted the sentences, as he had wished he had done, I should never have taken the trouble to restore them in the reprint, and *The Times* could not have quoted them with approbation. I suppose my manner was slightly triumphant; at any rate, he said, "I spoke as an editor, not as a man. You have no more consciousness of these things than a child.' "

To go back for a moment. Having attracted so much attention Hardy now again withdrew into retreat at Bockhampton to get ahead with the novel, which was in a lamentably unadvanced condition, writing to Stephen, when requesting that the proofs might be sent to that hermitage: 'I have decided to finish it here, which is within a walk of the district in which the incidents are supposed to occur. I find it a great advantage to be actually among the people described at the time of describing them.'

However, that he did not care much for a reputation as a novelist in lieu of being able to follow the pursuit of poetry—now for ever hindered, as it seemed—becomes obvious from a remark written to Mr. Stephen about this time:

'The truth is that I am willing, and indeed anxious, to give up any points which may be desirable in a story when read as a whole, for the sake of others which shall please those who read it in numbers. Perhaps I may have higher aims some day, and be a great stickler for the proper artistic balance of the completed work, but for the present circumstances lead me to wish merely to be considered a good hand at a serial.'

The fact was that at this date he was bent on carrying out later in the year an intention beside which a high repute as an artistic novelist loomed even less importantly than in ordinary—an intention to be presently mentioned.

He found he had drifted anew into a position he had vowed after his past experience he would in future keep clear of—that of having unfinished on his hands a novel of which the beginning was already before the public, and so having to write against time. He wrote so rapidly in fact that by February he was able to send the editor an instalment of copy sufficient for two or three months further, and another instalment in April.

On a visit to London in the winter Hardy had made the personal acquaintance of Leslie Stephen, the man whose philosophy was to influence his own for many years, indeed, more than that of any other contemporary, and received a welcome in his household.

* * *

Back again in Dorsetshire he continued his application to the story, and by July had written it all, the last few chapters having been done at a gallop, for a reason to be told directly. In the middle of the month he resumed residence in London, where he hurriedly corrected the concluding pages and posted the end of the MS. to the editor early in August.

The next month Thomas Hardy and Miss Emma Lavinia Gifford were married at St. Peter's, Elgin Avenue, Paddington, by her uncle Dr. E. Hamilton Gifford, Canon of Worcester, and afterwards Archdeacon of London.

MICHAEL MILLGATE

Puddletown into Weatherbury: The Genesis of Wessex†

It was in the manuscript of chapter 50 of *Far from the Madding Crowd*—"Greenhill was the Nijnii [sic] Novgorod of Wessex"—that Hardy seems first to have used the term Wessex; its first appearance in print dates from the publication of the chapter in the *Cornhill* as part of the November 1874 serial installment[1] The term did not appear elsewhere in the serial or the first edition—other occurrences are the result of later revision—but its revival in the opening sentence of Hardy's next novel, *The Hand of Ethelberta*, confirmed beyond doubt that he was laying claim to a whole fictional region. A map of Wessex as it existed in 1874 would have been a simple affair: Budmouth and

†From Michael Millgate, *Thomas Hardy: His Career as a Novelist* (New York: Random House, 1971), pp. 95–104.

1. *Cornhill* MS, f. 3–28: *Cornhill*, 30 (November 1874), 624.

Melchester had been located, Casterbridge lightly sketched in, Mellstock and Weatherbury surveyed in some detail; a few other places had been mentioned, some of them under names later abandoned; the region as a whole had been placed in relation to the actual geography of England by the account of Bathsheba's journey to Bath. Wessex was to be much developed in later books and in the process of revision, but the publication of *Far from the Madding Crowd* established the name and the broad framework, while the overlapping of *Under the Greenwood Tree* and *Far from the Madding Crowd*, slight as it was, already demonstrated possibilities not only of greater expansion but of greater density.

Several of the early reviewers recognised the nature, if not always the quality, of Hardy's endeavour in these two early novels. Horace Moule referred to *Under the Greenwood Tree* as "the best prose idyl that we have seen for a long while past", while *The Times* praised *Far from the Madding Crowd* for its "delicate perspective faculty, which transforms, with skilful touch, the matter-of-fact prosaic details of every-day life into an idyl or a pastoral poem".[2] Late in 1875 Léon Boucher, writing at length on Hardy's work in the *Revue des deux mondes* under the title "Le roman pastoral en Angleterre", defined in very positive terms the achievement of *Far from the Madding Crowd*:

> *Peut-être même la plus grande beauté du nouveau roman a-t-elle échappé à bien des lecteurs, qui n'y out vu qu'une histoire amusante et des situations dramatiques telles qu'on en peut trouver ailleurs. M. Hardy en effet a voula faire quelque chose de plus: il a voulu rajeunir le genre antique et souvent ennuyeux de la pastorale, et il y a mis une telle vérité d'observation, une passion si profonde, une poésie si fraîche, un style si puissant, tant d'idéal et de réalité à la fois, que cette transformation peut presque passer pour une création originale.[3]*

In September 1877 a general article on Hardy's work in the short-lived journal *London* linked him and R. D. Blackmore as novelists of the "British Boor", described as the "latter-day analogue" of the shepherds of Arcadia. Though generally hostile, the article does show by its use of such terms as "the Wessex rustic" how strongly Hardy's imaginative world had already impressed itself upon his contemporaries.[4]

There is a reference in *Early Life* (142) to Boucher's article, and since this and the other pieces were all preserved by Hardy in one of his scrapbooks one wonders whether they contributed anything to his own

2. *Saturday Review*, September 28, 1872, 417; *Times*, January 25, 1875, p. 4.
3. *Revue des deux mondes*, 45e année (December 15, 1875), 843. [The passage in French reads: "Perhaps the greatest beauty of the new novel escapes readers who only see in it a diverting history with the kind of dramatic situations one might find elsewhere. Mr. Hardy, in effect, has intended to go beyond that. He has determined to revive the old-fashioned and often tedious form of the pastoral, and he has put into it such a fidelity of observation, a feeling so profound, a poetry so fresh, a style so powerful, so much of the ideal and the real at one and the same time, that this transformation is able to almost pass for an original creation" *Editor's translation*].
4. *London*, September 29, 1877, 211, 212.

conception of the nature and function of his fiction. The question seems especially pertinent in relation to an article published anonymously in the *Examiner* on July 15, 1876. Entitled "The Wessex Labourer", it surveys Hardy's work up to and including *The Hand of Ethelberta*, refers easily to "Wessex novels" and "Wessex peasants", and praises Hardy's authentic portrayal of both the landscape and the labouring population of a little-known country. The article speaks of Dorset as "the very last country in England whose sacred soil was broken by a railroad, and those which now traverse it leave the very heart of the shire untouched. The narrow provincialism of the squires, which is in some measure the bane of all the more distant counties, is accentuated there; and though charity and kindliness are not wanting, the labourer and squire feel towards each other as though they were of different races." Later it adds: "Time in Dorset has stood still; advancing civilisation has given the labourers only lucifer-matches and the penny post, and the clowns in *Hamlet* are no anachronism if placed in a west country village of our own day."[5]

Hardy put this article, too, in his scrapbook, and obviously had it in front of him many years later when writing the preface to the 1895 edition of *Far from the Madding Crowd*. He mentions it specifically as the first occasion when the term Wessex was "taken up elsewhere" (viii), and adopts some of its phraseology in speaking of his appropriation of the old Saxon name for "a modern Wessex of railways, the penny post, mowing and reaping machines, union workhouses, lucifer matches, labourers who could read and write, and National school children" (vii). Hardy must have found, in 1876, great reassurance in the article's informed and unhesitating endorsement both of the method and of the authenticity of his work; he may also have been grateful for the defence of his fiction against those reviewers (among them R. H. Hutton in the *Spectator*[6] who had found his rural characters extravagantly philosophical and articulate. The article argues that the Dorset labourer, although "in a different stage of civilisation" from readers of the *Examiner*, "is no fool in his own line, but rather very shrewd, racy, and wise, full of practical knowledge of all natural things, and of considerable powers of thought. Words are now and then lacking to him in which to clothe thought, for the vocabulary

5. 'The Wessex Labourer', *Examiner*, July 15, 1876, 793–794. The author was almost certainly Charles Kegan Paul; see Paul's letter to Hardy, April 13, 1877. There are several points of similarity with Paul's *British Quarterly Review* article of 1881.

6. *Spectator*, December 19, 1874, 1597–1599: e.g., 'if any one society of agricultural labourers were at all like that which we find here, that class, as a whole, must be a treasure-house of such eccentric shrewdness and profane-minded familiarity with the Bible, as would cancel at once the reputation rural England has got for a

heavy, bovine character, and would justify us in believing it to be a rich mine of quaintnesses and oddities, all dashed with a curious flavour of mystical and Biblical transcendentalism' (p. 1597). John Hutton, writing to Hardy on December 23, 1874 (in a letter in the Dorset County Museum, subsequently abbreviated DCM.), thought his brother did not know the agricultural poor well enough 'to estimate their intimacy with & constant use of Biblical language nor their quaint good humoured cynicism.'

of those who live apart from books is everywhere restricted, but the dialect is yet vigorous and especially English." The hint of William Barnes in that last sentence is confirmed in the next by the suggestion that Hardy and Barnes, "both parts of that of which they write, ought to dissipate many popular fancies about their fair western county.[7]

The social and economic backwardness of Dorset had long been notorious. In 1830 the county had seen, especially on the southern fringes of the Vale of Blackmore, some of the worst outbreaks of what Hardy himself once called in a letter "the last peasant revolt,"[8] and a few years later in the southern part of the county, the "Tolpuddle martyrs" were convicted and transported for their primitive gestures towards rural unionisation. In the 1840s, when Hardy himself knew by sight a boy who died of starvation,[9] Lord Sydney Godolphin Osborne ("S.G.O.") aroused controversy about the condition of the Dorsetshire peasantry, and the corroborative reports of *The Times* investigator reinforced the national image of Dorset as (to use a phrase from Hardy's essay on "The Dorsetshire Labourer") the home of "Hodge in his most unmitigated form."[1] The 1867 Royal Commission on the Employment of Children, Young Persons, and Women in Agriculture, to which submissions were made by such Dorset figures as William Barnes and Henry Moule, gave ample coverage to Dorset as, by common consent, one of the areas where wages were lowest, cottages the least sanitary, landlords the most unenlightened, and the plight of the labouring class nearest to desperation.[2] Still more recently, Dorset, like many other parts of southern and eastern England, had seen a great upsurge of union activity under the leadership of Joseph Arch.

On December 5, 1872, two or three days after Hardy had received from Leslie Stephen the invitation which led to the appearance of *Far from the Madding Crowd* in the pages of the *Cornhill*, a large meeting of agricultural labourers was held in the Corn Exchange at Dorchester. Arch himself was not present, but the meeting was addressed by one of his warmest supporters, the Hon. Auberon Herbert, the Radi-

---

7. 'The Wessex Labourer', p. 794.
8. Hardy to William Rothenstein, March 11, 1912 (Harvard). Hardy said that his father's recollections of the period had made it familiar to him since childhood. See also Barbara Kerr, *Bound to the Soil: A Social History of Dorset 1750–1918* (London, 1968), pp. 90–119.
9. Hardy had a childhood memory of a boy who died of starvation: *Later Years*, p. 93; H. Rider Haggard, *Rural England* (London, 1902), I, 282. Barbara Kerr, *Bound to the Soil*, p. 116, mentions the death from starvation of a father and son at Sutton Poyntz (the Overcombe of *The Trumpet-Major*) in January 1847.
1. 'The Dorsetshire Labourer', p. 252. (*Thomas Hardy's Personal Writings*, [Lawrence, Kan.: University Press of Kansas, 1966],

p. 169. Other sources: Arnold White, ed., *The Letters of S.G.O.: A Series of Letters on Public Affairs Written by the Rev. Lord Sidney Godolphin Osborne and Published in 'The Times' 1844–1888*. 2 vols. (London, n.d.), I, 1–4, 14–20, 27–33, 38–44; *Times*, June 18, 1846, p. 5, June 25, 1846, p. 3, July 2, 1846, p. 6; also 'The Peasantry of Dorsetshire', *Illustrated London News*, September 5, 1846, 156–158. Particularly interesting, both for its arguments and as a source of further references, is William J. Hyde, 'Hardy's View of Realism; A Key to the Rustic Characters.' *Victorian Studies*, 2 (1958), [45]–59.
2. *Parliamentary Papers*, Session 1868–69, XIII, 77–[80], 233–[270].

cal M.P., with whom Hardy was later to be on friendly terms.[3] Since, according to *Early Life* (121), Hardy spent the closing months of 1872 at Bockhampton finishing *A Pair of Blue Eyes*, he can scarcely have been unaware of this occasion, of the meeting's pledge of support to the National Agricultural Labourers' Union, or of the recommendation of emigration to Brazil which came from several of the platform speakers: "it being stated," reported *The Times*, "that the Government of that country was prepared to assist 500,000 men in going there from England".

Hardy later made dramatic use, in *Tess*, of the illusory promises of the Brazilian Government to British farmers and farm labourers. In "The Dorsetshire Labourer" essay of 1883 he referred in genial terms to Joseph Arch himself, giving a sympathetic account of his programme and achievements and recalling a personal memory of a speech delivered by Arch during one of his "early tours through Dorsetshire".[4] Hardy perhaps heard Arch speak during the Dorchester Candlemas Fair of 1873, held on Friday, February 14, and reported by the *Dorset County Chronicle* in its issue of February 20:

THE HIRING FAIR—This annual statute fair took place on Friday last, the attendance of labourers being larger than on any similar occasion for years past. The source of attraction was Joseph Arch, a star of the first magnitude amongst the agricultural labourers, who flocked into the town from all parts of the county. Passenger carriages were attached to the early down goods train on the Great Western Railway, and they were crowded, as was also the ordinary train due at Dorchester at 10.27. The higher part of the town was thronged towards eleven o'clock, the guardians of the peace pacing to and fro in the interests of order. A little commotion was got up near St. Peter's Church by a labourer, sporting blue ribbons in his cap, who delivered his mind, aided by a "wee-drap" beforehand. But the crowd soon wended its way up the street. Excepting this incident all was quiet. The farmers were conspicuous by their absence, indeed they are making strenuous efforts to discountenance the system of hiring at the fair, the Dorchester Farmers' Club having last year unanimously decided upon that course. Where agreements with non-unionists were effected 12s, with perquisites were given to ordinary labourers, the extras, of course, depending upon circumstances. Towards noon a procession was formed, and it moved in the direction of Fordington-green, being headed by Arch, Cox, and Co., who, from a waggon, harangued an assembly of nearly 1,000 men, women, and lads. The speakers strongly condemned the system of men hiring themselves for a year, comparing it to proceedings at a slave market. They seemed to forget that the farmers of Dorset themselves had discouraged the practice, and that the labourers had this year come to the fair chiefly to hear the agitators. The meeting lasted about two hours, a resolution to support the union being carried. At three o'clock there was a second meeting at the same place. On Cornhill there was the usual display of agricultural implements, and confection stalls occupied the pavement fronting St. Peter's Church. It is stated that steps will probably be taken by the farmers with a view to abolishing the system of hiring at the fair altogether, and the expediency of that course is particularly desirable on account of the drun-

3. *Times*, December 5, 1872, p. 6; for Herbert, see *Early Life*, pp. 224, 238.

4. 'The Dorsetshire Labourer', pp. 264–266 (*Personal Writings*, p. 183).

kenness with which the day is finished, this year's fair being no exception in that respect.[5]

The contemporary realities of Dorset life in the early 1870s which figure in this report find little direct reflection in the worlds of Hardy's early novels. It is not until the early 1880s that the first clear indication of agricultural distress and discontent appears, somewhat unexpectedly, in *Two on a Tower*, where the labourers refer to themselves as "folks with ten or a dozen shillings a week and their gristing, and a load o' thorn faggots when we can get 'em" (96), and one of them braves a suspected ghost with the words: "Well, well; I've not held out against the spectre o' starvation these five-and-twenty year on nine shillings a week, to be afeard of a walking vapour, sweet or savoury" (165).

In *Far from the Madding Crowd*, indeed, Hardy seems to have chosen his setting with a deliberate eye to its remoteness from the current unrest. He had of course been familiar since childhood with the village variously known as Puddletown or Piddletown, but in selecting it as the original for the fictional Weatherbury he may have been influenced by a long report on conditions in the village which appeared, under the heading "Areadians of Dorset", in the *Daily Telegraph* for April 30, 1872. Valuable in itself as an account of conditions in the country at the beginning of Arch's movement, the article is fascinating as a sketch of Hardy's Weatherbury the year before he began to re-create it in fictional terms. It presents Puddletown as "a model Dorsetshire village" where old ways still flourish within the as yet unacknowledged shadow of the new:

> Piddletown occupies the crest of a great ridge which shuts out the semi-urban environs of Dorchester from the genuinely rural centre of the country. It rejoices in most of the essentials of Arcadian felicity. The squire takes a direct and fatherly interest in his villagers. He has built them from time to time numbers of good cottages, and he has furnished them with ground for garden allotments. The tenants he has selected for his farms are men who make the best of a bad system of labour. They pay the full standard wages of the county—oftener, I believe, the nine shilling maximum than the eight shilling minimum. Though privileges as a matter of right and custom have almost died out in Dorsetshire, they linger on sufferance in Piddletown. One of them is the ancient perquisite of gristing, under which each labourer can claim a bushel per week of wheat for family use, at the uniform rate of five shillings. . . . The potato ground, which seems to prevail throughout the whole of the West of England, is granted here without any of the drawbacks and qualifications that are being introduced elsewhere. Small kindnesses are also practised by the farmers, which go a long way in promoting friendly feeling amongst the labourers. A man would very seldom be refused a truss of straw for his pig when he is so fortunate as to possess one. In a county so well timbered; it would be hard if something were not done to help to keep his pot boiling in winter. He stands

5. *Dorset County Chronicle*, February 20, 1873, p. 3. This was not Arch's only visit to Dorchester; he was certainly there again on February 14, 1877 (*Dorset County Chronicle*, February 15, 1877, p. 12), but Hardy was then living in Sturminster Newton, whence he dated a letter to Blackwood on February 13, 1877 (National Library of Scotland).

a chance, provided he be faultless as a labourer, and properly deferential as an inferior, of having a hundredweight or two of firewood delivered at his door in the cold weather.[6]

The agricultural labourers of Puddletown are thus fortunate by comparison with those in many other villages; they receive ungrudgingly whatever custom and agreement have prescribed as theirs. It is nonetheless clear, the article continues, that their position remains precarious: Puddletown "depends a great deal on the grace of its suzerains. When they smile benevolently it stops a certain degree shorter of starvation than when they have to frown reprovingly. What might happen if in a moment of supreme displeasure they were to withdraw their pigstraw and firewood, the most vivid imagination in Piddletown cannot conceive. The bare money value of labour in the parish is just nine shillings per week." As yet, however, the labourers have shown no sign of taking concerted action to protect or improve their situation, receiving with near incredulity rumours of a strike threat in the adjoining parish of Milborne St. Andrew: "Piddletown had not dreamed of any such insubordination as writing to a master about wages, much less had it dared to think of such a millennium as the possession of a weekly income of twelve shillings."[7]

Powerful though Arch's impact had been, it had not yet touched every part of Dorset, and Hardy, anxious throughout his career to avoid the slightest suggestion of political involvement, had evidently found in Puddletown, with or without the assistance of the *Daily Telegraph* correspondent, a village where unionisation had not yet become an issue. To strengthen his position still further he placed the action of the novel perceptibly, if somewhat vaguely, in the past. As R. L. Purdy has observed, several phrases in chapter 42 of the novel suggest a period more distant than the 1869–73 dating proposed by Carl J. Weber, and if the calendar for those years seems to fit the sequence of the action, so equally would the calendar for, say, 1858–62.[8] A date prior to the early 1870s certainly seems required by Cainy Ball's reaction to Bathsheba's crinoline; by the allusion to Keeper Day of Yalbury Wood, with its suggestion of a world not far removed in time or space from that of *Under the Greenwood Tree*; and by Hardy's hint some years later, through allusions to Bathsheba's uncle and to a "silent, reserved young man named Boldwood", that the action of *Far from the Madding Crowd* is to be imagined as taking place some ten years after the central action of *The Mayor of Casterbridge*, itself set at mid-century.

6. 'The Arcadians of Dorset,' *Daily Telegraph*, April 30, 1872, p. 5; attributed to 'Our Special Correspondent'. The article is quoted in full in Francis George Heath, *The English Peasantry* (London, 1874), pp. 27–40.

7. 'The Arcadians of Dorset', p. 5. For interesting historical notes see O. D. Harvey, *Puddletown (Thomas Hardy's 'Weatherbury')*, (Puddletown, 1968), esp. pp. 17–36.

8. Purdy, Introduction to *Far from the Madding Crowd*, p. viin.; Weber, 'Chronology in Hardy's Novels', *PMLA*, 53 (1938), 314, and cf. Weber, ed., *Far from the Madding Crowd* (New York, 1959), p. 386. Cf. O. D. Harvey, *Puddletown*, p. 17.

A specific date is perhaps impossible to determine and not, in any case, of great importance. As Andrew Lang pertinently observed in his *Academy* review of *Far from the Madding Crowd*, "the country folk in the story have not heard of strikes, or of Mr. Arch; they have, to all appearances, plenty to eat, and warm clothes to wear, and when the sheep are shorn in the ancient barn of Weatherbury, the scene is one that Shakespeare or that Chaucer might have watched. This immobile rural existence is what the novelist has to paint." The world of Weatherbury, as other reviewers also saw, is fixed, arrested at a moment in time somewhere before the onset of the disruptive process- es of rural mobility and depopulation; it is placed, just over the rim of the present, in a condition of timelessness. "No condition of society," Lang goes on, "could supply the writer who knows it well with a more promising ground for his story. The old and the new must meet here and there, with curious surprises, and our world may find itself face to face with the quaint conceited rustics of Shakespeare's plays." What prevents Hardy from making the best of his theme, Lang believes, is his tendency, because he is "telling clever people about unlettered people", to be somewhat patronising.[9]

It is of course possible to argue that a patronising attitude is implicit in Hardy's decision to avert his eyes from the actual conditions and issues of the day: by evoking a pastoral world remote from contempo- ary realities, "far from the madding crowd", he could disengage himself from the story, view the characters with affection and amuse- ment, unblushingly confront his readers with a Shakespearean rustic. Yet the novel is rich and resilient in its independence upon the pattern of the agricultural year and the techniques of rural trades, and if Hardy does not draw attention to the miseries of the farm labourer's lot he does not seek specifically to conceal them. He neither romanticises his rustics nor dwells explicitly upon the implications of a man like Joseph Poorgrass receiving a wage of 9s. 9d. a week in what are apparently prosperous times, or a man like Andrew Randle losing his job for telling the squire his soul was his own. The hiring fair in *Far from the Madding Crowd* is accepted, with neither criticism nor praise, as simply an economic fact. Hardy preserves, in short, a careful neutral- ity in all such matters, and his personal attitudes towards the labourer's situation are impossible to determine. He certainly never identified himself with the Dorsetshire labourers of whom he wrote, and he was anxious, especially as he grew older, to insist upon his father's status as a member of the lifeholding class celebrated in the closing paragraphs of "The Dorsetshire Labourer". But even had he felt absolutely in sympathy with Joseph Arch and his cause, his own experience with *The Poor Man and the Lady* must inevitably have impelled him towards the possibilities of neutrality and self-protection inherent in the choice of a remote setting and a past time.

9. *Academy*, January 2, 1875, 9.

Hardy's Correspondence
with Leslie Stephen[†]

Hardy's correspondence with Leslie Stephen, the editor of the *Cornhill Magazine*, where *Far from the Madding Crowd* was first published, is interesting for what it reveals of the kinds of pressures an editor could feel from the readers of a popular nineteenth-century magazine, of the kind of role Stephen had in shaping the development of Hardy's novel, and of Hardy's attitude toward Stephen's editorial interventions.

From Leslie Stephen

30 NOVEMBER 1872

Dear Sir,

I hear from Mr Moule[1] that I may address you as the author of "Under the Greenwood Tree".

I have lately read that story with very great pleasure indeed. I think the descriptions of country life admirable and indeed it is long since I have received more pleasure from a new writer.

It also occurred to me, and it is for this reason that I take the liberty of addressing you, that such writing would probably please the readers of the Cornhill Magazine as much as it has pleased me. "Under the Greenwood Tree" is of course not a magazine story. There is too little incident for such purposes; for, though I do not want a murder in every number, it is necessary to catch the attention of readers by some distinct and well arranged plot.

If you are, as I hope, writing anything more, I should be very glad to have the offer of it for our pages. I of course cannot say anything more definite at present; but I should be very glad to hear from you whether there is any probability of my receiving such an offer. If I can give you any further information on the subject, of course I shall be very happy to do so. I will only say now that if any agreement could be made between us I have no doubt it would be satisfactory in a pecuniary point of view. Meanwhile

†The following letters from Leslie Stephen to Hardy and from Hardy to Stephen, Elder & Company are now in Dorset County Museum; the letter from Hardy to Leslie Stephen tentatively dated 18 February 1874, exists only in the fragmentary form it was quoted in F. E. Hardy's *The Early Life of Thomas Hardy* (London: Macmillan, 1928), p. 131. The Leslie Stephen letters have been published in Richard Little Purdy, *Thomas Hardy: A Bibliographical Study* (Oxford: The Clarendon Press, 1968), pp. 336–39; the letters from Hardy to Stephen and Smith, Elder have been published in Richard Little Purdy and Michael Millgate, eds., *The Collected Letters of Thomas Hardy*, (Oxford: The Clarendon Press, 1978–), I, pp. 27–28. 1. Horatio Mosley Moule was a friend and mentor of Hardy's who had favorably reviewed his earlier novels, *Desperate Remedies* (1871) and *Under the Greenwood Tree* (1872). He committed suicide in 1873.

Believe me to be,

> Your's truly
> Leslie Stephen
> (Editor of the Cornhill Mag.)

I have not seen "Desperate Remedies" though I have heard it highly praised.

From Leslie Stephen

8 JANUARY 1874

My dear Mr Hardy

I am glad to congratulate you on the reception of your first number.[2] Besides the gentle Spectator[3] wh. thinks that you must be George Eliot[4] because you know the names of the stars, several good judges have spoken to me very warmly of the Madding Crowd. Moreover the Spectator, though flighty in its head, has really a good deal of critical feeling—I always like to be praised by it—and indeed by other people!

I write, however, on another matter. As printed the February number takes 29 pages. This is rather long and I propose to end with chapter 8 i.e. on page 26; where I think there is a better break.

The March number will then have 4 pages added to it, and would have to end either with Chap XV, wh. would make 23 pages or with Chap XVI wh. would make 32 pages. I think, as at present advised, that the first break would be the best; but I might have to go on to the other. Now Chap XVI is rather a long one; and it would be convenient to me if there were some possible halting-place between the two extremes. Would it be possible to divide Chap XVI into two and if so would you make the necessary alteration? Or, if you please, put a mark where the division may come, if necessary.

The story comes out very well, I think, and I have no criticisms to make. In Chap X the paying scene is judiciously reduced and I think it is now satisfactory.

I hope you approved of the illustration.

> Your's very truly
> L. Stephen

Let me know when you are coming to town, according to promise.

From Leslie Stephen

17 FEBRUARY 1874

My dear Mr Hardy,

I have read through your MS with very great pleasure; though I had seen most of it before. As you ask me for my opinion I will say frankly

2. The first five chapters of *Far from the Madding Crowd* had just appeared in the January 1874 issue of the *Cornhill Magazine*.
3. The *Spectator* review is reprinted on p. 365.

4. "George Eliot" was the pen name of Mary Ann Evans (1819–80), some of whose early novels, such as *Adam Bede* (1859), had dealt with rural life.

that I think the sheepshearing rather long for the present purpose. When the novel appears as a whole, it may very well come in in its present form. For periodical purposes, I think it rather delays the action unnecessarily. What I should be inclined to do would be simply to omit the chapter headed the "shearing supper" and to add a few paragraphs to the succeeding or preceding, just explaining that there has been a supper.[5] The chapter on the "Great Barn" and that called "A merry Mist" seem to me to be excellent and I would not omit them or shorten them. The other seems to me the least good of the three— and therefore the best to abridge. I don't know whether anything turns on the bailiff's story; but I don't think it necessary.

I shall take the MS to Smith and Elder's[6] today and will tell them that they will hear from you. Please write to them (to S.E & Co 15 Waterloo Place S.W.) and say whether the whole is to be printed as it stands; or whether the chapter I mention is to be omitted; or whether you would like to have the MS again to alter previously to printing. Do whichever your judgement commends.

I have heard of the story from many people and have only heard one opinion of its merits, wh. coincides with my own. As it goes on and gets more into the action, I am sure that the opinion will be higher still. In short, I think you have every reason to be satisfied and encouraged.

The Spectator's instincts are better than its reasons. It generally recognizes a good thing; but almost always talks nonsense about the causes of its admiration. As for the supposed affinity to George Eliot, it consists, I think, simply in this that you have both treated rustics of the farming class in a humorous manner—Mrs Poyser[7] would be at home I think, in Weatherbury—but you need not be afraid of such criticisms. You are original and can stand on your own legs.

Your's very truly
Leslie Stephen

I have said frankly what I thought; but I hope you will not attach too much importance to my criticisms—Do exactly what you think right—I shall be content. Very likely, it will be best for you to see the whole in print before acting; if so, let it go to the press as it stands.

To Leslie Stephen

[18 FEBRUARY 1874?]

The truth is that I am willing, and indeed anxious, to give up any points which may be desirable in a story when read as a whole, for the sake of others which shall please those who read it in numbers.[8] Perhaps I may have higher aims some day, and be a great stickler for

---

5. Hardy followed Stephen's advice and deleted much of the "shearing supper" chapter.
6. The publishers of the *Cornhill Magazine*.
7. A character in George Eliot's *Adam Bede*.

8. Hardy here suggests his willingness to accept not only the deletions that Stephen recommended in his letter of 17 February but also others that Stephen might make in the future.

the proper artistic balance of the completed work, but for the present circumstances lead me to wish merely to be considered a good hand at a serial.

To Smith, Elder & Co.

18 FEBRUARY 1874

Gentlemen,

Will you oblige me by returning by post the last-received portion of the MS. of "Far from the Madding Crowd", which begins with the chapter headed "The great barn & the sheepshearers" & is paged from "2–1" to "2–73". I wish to reconsider one of the chapters. It shall be sent back in a day or two. [9]

Very faithfully yours
Thomas Hardy

From Leslie Stephen

12 MARCH 1874

My dear Mr Hardy

I have read your proofs as corrected and I think that everything now runs very smoothly.

The story improves as it goes on and I hear nothing but good of it.

I have ventured to leave out a line or two in the last batch of proofs from an excessive prudery of wh. I am ashamed; but one is forced to be absurdly particular. [1] May I suggest that Troy's seduction of the young woman will require to be treated in a gingerly fashion, when, as I suppose must be the case, he comes to be exposed to his wife? I mean that the thing must be stated but that the words must be careful— excuse this wretched shred of concession to popular stupidity; but I am a slave.

I hope to see you soon.

Yours in haste
L. Stephen

From Leslie Stephen

13 APRIL 1874

My dear Mr Hardy,

I have read the new instalment of the Madding Crowd with great pleasure—I think the story grows in interest and is equally vigorous in

9. Hardy returned the manuscript with an extensive portion of the "shearing supper" episode deleted; the deleted leaves, numbered 2–18 to 2–24, are now in the Dorset County Museum. These include a statement by Baily Pennyways that he had seen Fanny Robin in Melchester, "too well-off to be anything but a ruined woman" (f. 2–20), and this relative explicitness may have been another reason for Stephen's suggestion that the "shearing supper" scene be abridged; note Stephen's reference to the bailiff's story in his letter dated 17 February, above.

1. Simon Gatrell has suggested that the passages that Stephen omitted may be a line from chapter 15 in which Boldwood speaks of Fanny Robin as having "lost her character" and another in chapter 24 where Liddy describes Troy as "a walking ruin to honest girls." See p. 359 of Gatrell's "The Significance of Hardy's Revisions" reprinted in this edition.

description. You need not be afraid of [   ] criticism [*half page torn away*] part of the story; wh., however, must be prefaced by the general remark that I object as editor, not as critic, i.e. in the interest of a stupid public, not from my own taste.

I think that the reference to the cause of Fanny's death is unnecessarily emphasized. I should, I think, omit all references to it except just enough to indicate the true state of the case; and especially a conversation between your heroine and her maid, wh. is a little unpleasant. I have some doubts whether the baby is necessary at all and whether it would not be sufficient for Bathsheba to open the coffin in order to identify the dead woman with the person she met on the road. This is a point wh. you can consider. It certainly rather injures the story, and perhaps if the omission were made it might be restored on republication. But I am rather necessarily anxious to be on the safe side; and should somehow be glad to omit the baby.[2]

However, these changes can be easily made when the story is in type and I shall send it to the printers now; and ask you to do what is necessary to the proofs.

We can talk about it when we meet. Meanwhile I am more than satisfied in all other respects.

I shall be very glad to see you when you come to town. Can you dine with us on Friday the 24th at ¼ to 8? If so, my wife bids me say that she will be delighted to see you. You will find me at home any morning.

Your's very truly
L. Stephen

From Leslie Stephen

25 AUGUST 1874[3]

My dear Mr Hardy,

I will speak about the November proof tomorrow. I saw nothing to alter, unless that it seemed to me in one or two cases that your rustics—specially Oak—speak rather too good English towards the end. They seem to drop the dialect a little. But of this you are the best judge.[4]

You have, I am sure, no cause to be nervous about the book in any way.

Yours in haste—
L. Stephen

---

2. Hardy deleted many references to Fanny's baby, but Stephen may have marked still others for deletion on his own accord; a sample of the kind of description that Stephen probably marked for omission is provided on p. 312.

3. The heading of this fragmentary letter was added by Hardy.
4. Hardy apparently took Stephen's advice: He revised the final chapters of his manuscript to put more dialect in Oak's speech.

Composition, Publication, Revision

RICHARD LITTLE PURDY

[The Manuscript and Notes on Composition and Publication]†

Manuscript. The MS. of *Far from the Madding Crowd* is written on 605 leaves, measuring 6½″ × 8⅜″, though some are fragmentary. The leaves have been divided in a most unusual way, by Hardy's numbering, into 3 unequal parts: Part 1 (Chaps. 1–21) numbered 1–208 (with 6 scattered supplementary leaves); Part 2 (Chaps. 22–46, as far as 'Meanwhile, Bathsheba remained . . .') numbered 2–1 to 2–263 (with 2 supplementary leaves); and Part 3 (Chaps. 46, concluded, to 57) numbered 3–1 to 3–126. No satisfactory explanation is apparent for this curious foliation—the MS. was submitted to Leslie Stephen in very much smaller sections (perhaps 3 or 4 chapters at a time), and the divisions are too unequal to suggest a projected three-volume form for the novel. The MS., though used by the *Cornhill* printers, shows numerous revisions, many chapters retitled, and some few pencilled bowdlerizations. The word 'parabolic' at the opening of Chap. 15 (MS. f. 147) has been corrected in pencil to 'hyperbolic' and initialed 'L.S.' Chap. 16, 'All Saints' and All Souls'', is wanting altogether in the MS. since it was an after-thought and written on the proof-sheets. Inserted in the text of Chap. 32 there are 5 drawings of the hoof-marks as Oak and Coggan followed them, which the printers did not find it feasible to reproduce. And there are at least 2 passages of some length which were not printed although left uncancelled in the MS.—perhaps a page in Chap. 43 extending the description of Fanny Robin and her baby in their coffin,[1] and some 3½ pages in Chap. 47 adding an episode or two to Troy's Adventures by the Shore'.

* * *

Two fragments of the first draft of the novel also survive. One, headed 'Chapter [XXIII *added in pencil*]. The shearing-supper', consists of 7 leaves, measuring 6⅛″ × 8⅛″ and numbered 2–18 to 2–24,

†From Richard Little Purdy, *Thomas Hardy: A Bibliographical Study* (Oxford: The Clarendon Press, 1968), pp. 14–17.

1. Examples of some of these deleted materials are provided on p. 312 [*Editor*].

with the pencilled date '1873' and a later note in red ink, 'Some pages of the first Draft—afterwards revised. T.H.' Perhaps a page of this at most has been retained in the present Chap. 23. The alteration was undoubtedly made at the instance of Leslie Stephen, who wrote to Hardy 17 February 1874 that he thought the chapter 'the least good of the three—and therefore the best to abridge.'

The 7 leaves were reduced to 2, and the consequent correction of foliation shows that composition had proceeded at the time as far as Chap. 29. The other fragment, headed simply 'Chapter' (commencing 'Troy soon began to make himself busy about the farm.'), consists of 11 leaves of blue paper, measuring 5⅞″ × 8″ and numbered 106^{a-k}, with a later note in red ink, 'Some pages of 1st draft—(Details of Sheep-rot—omitted from MS. when revised) T.H.' These pages are heavily altered and bear no relation (in appearance, foliation, &c.) to the complete MS. as we have it. They would seem to be (as the companion fragment is not) part of a destroyed early MS. of the novel. The two fragments were bound together in blue morocco in 1915 and given by Hardy to his second wife. They are now in the Dorset County Museum.

* * *

Notes on Composition and Publication. Under the Greenwood Tree so struck Leslie Stephen that he wrote to Hardy, through H.M. Moule, in November 1872 to inquire about a story for the *Cornhill Magazine*, of which he had become editor the previous year.[2] Hardy was still at work on *A Pair of Blue Eyes* but he sketched for Stephen 'a pastoral tale which I thought of calling "Far from the Madding Crowd," in which the chief characters would be a woman-farmer, a shepherd, and a sergeant in the Dragoon Guards'. 'A few chapters of the story, with some succeeding ones in outline' were submitted in June 1873 and at the end of September perhaps a dozen in tentative form, and Stephen definitely accepted the novel and publication commenced in the *Cornhill* for January of the next year. *Far from the Madding Crowd* was wholly written at Higher Bockhampton and finished by July 1874. No other novel of Hardy's had the benefit of such constant and discriminating criticism as Stephen's, though Hardy confessed at the time to no higher aim than 'to be considered a good hand at a serial.'[3] The novel was anonymous throughout its run in the *Cornhill*, prompting the *Spectator* in its review of the January number (3 January) to remark, 'If "Far from the Madding Crowd" is not written by George Eliot, then there is a new light among novelists.' The authorship was disclosed in the *Spectator's* review of the February issue (7 February). *Far from the Madding Crowd* was published at 21s. in an edition of 1,000 copies on 23 November 1874.

2. Stephen's letter to Hardy is printed on p. 340 [*Editor*].

3. Hardy's letter to Stephen is printed on pp. 342–343 [*Editor*].

SIMON GATRELL

[The Significance of Hardy's Revisions]†

Most studies of the texts of Hardy's novels and stories concentrate upon the significant changes in structure and characterisation revealed by the manuscript and the various printed versions, and to a great extent this essay is no exception. But there is also another, not less important if less dramatic, element in the development of Hardy's fiction. This shows Hardy acting in ways that may be duplicated (generally speaking) in all his work. The full significance of these changes can only be shown through a comparative study of the whole range of his writing, which is hardly possible in a short essay. My intention is, however, to draw attention to examples in *Far from the Madding Crowd* of at least some of these kinds of activity and to suggest their significance as a first step towards a synthetic study of all Hardy's fictional prose.

I have chosen to concentrate, nominally at least, on Chapters XL to XLIII (pp. 202–231) of *Far from the Madding Crowd*.[1] The structure, though, is a loose one, and I have felt free to range over the whole novel where the material demanded it; digressions from the sequential run through the chapters are the rule. I have, for the most part, not discussed the early part of the book, since Professor R. C. Schweik has already analysed it in some detail;[2] though I have a few words to say in amplification of his conclusions, largely deriving from a feature of the manuscript which he has not reported.

Professor R. L. Purdy has described the final numeration, in three sections, which Hardy placed on each leaf of the manuscript of *Far from the Madding Crowd*,[3] but the earlier systems of numbering which are visible either as cancellations under the final version or else at the inner margin of the leaves have not so far been noticed. They provide much evidence about the composition of the novel which is not otherwise obtainable; indeed it is probable that were the manuscript disbound more information might be forthcoming, as it appears that some of these earlier numbers are at present lost in the gutter of

† From Simon Gatrell, "Hardy the Creator: *Far from the Madding Crowd*," in Dale Kramer ed. *Critical Approaches to the Fiction of Thomas Hardy* (New York: Barnes & Noble, 1979), pp. 74–98.

1. Chapter XL contains Fanny Robin's journey to Casterbridge workhouse. Chapter XLI deals with Bathsheba's uneasiness regarding the relationship between her husband Troy and the woman, unrecognised by her, that they met on the road between Casterbridge and Weatherbury; and includes the news of Fanny's death. Chapter XLII has the delayed return of Fanny's coffin to Weatherbury, while Chapter XLIII presents the events leading up to the opening of the coffin by Bathsheba, and Troy's recognition and embrace of Fanny's body.

2. R. C. Schweik, 'The Early Development of Hardy's *Far from the Madding Crowd*', *Texas Studies in Literature and Language*, IX (1967) 415–28.

3. R. L. Purdy, *Thomas Hardy: A Bibliographical Study*, 2nd ed., rev. (Oxford: Clarendon Press, 1968) p. 14. The manuscript is in the possession of Mr Edwin Thorne to whom I am most grateful for permission to quote from it, as also to the Trustees of the Thomas Hardy Estate and the Trustees of the Estate of the late Miss E. A. Dugdale.

the manuscript. One of the reasons that I have chosen Chapter XL as a starting point is that it inaugurates one of these earlier sequences of numeration, though its first leaf in the manuscript has only the final number 2–181 on it. * * * For reference in the following analysis I shall prefix the earlier numeration on each leaf with the letter E; thus the leaf numbered 2–182 is also numbered by Hardy E2. I shall also be referring to various printed versions of *Far from the Madding Crowd*, and they will be identified by the following abbreviations:

C = the serialisation in *Cornhill* (1874)
74 = the first edition in two volumes published by Smith, Elder in 1874.
75 = the second impression revised of 74, published by Smith, Elder in 1875
77 = the first one-volume edition published by Smith, Elder in 1877
95 = its appearance in Hardy's first complete collected edition, published by Osgood, McIlvaine in 1895
02 = the revised plates of 95 issued by Macmillan in 1902
12 = its appearance in the Wessex Edition of Hardy's works, published by Macmillan in 1912

For convenience in tracing quotations through the versions, all page references are to [this Norton Critical Edition]; chapter numbers are also given where they are necessary. It will sometimes be found that quotations from the manuscript, identified by page numbers in the [Norton] Edition, will differ from the text there present, since intervening revision may have taken place. All quotations from *Far from the Madding Crowd* are in italics.

Textually Chapter XL is relatively uncomplicated. The first leaf may be a later rewriting since it has no E number, but there is no evidence to suggest what is new in it. The single important narrative change in the chapter is the considerable augmentation of the role of the dog in helping Fanny to reach Casterbridge—the new leaves E7 and 7a contain the whole of this narrative. It is not likely that this was a completely new concept, since on E9 the dog is mentioned as having been stoned away, and there is no suggestion that this was a later leaf; it seems probable that Hardy wanted to heighten the sentimental appeal of an existing episode.

The only other detail that is worth noticing in this chapter is the phrase *the original amount of exertion* in the second paragraph on page 000; in manuscript this was *the original quantum of exertion*, and it reached its present form in 75. The change may be seen as the substitution of a simple for a slightly obscure word, and as of no further interest—but there were relatively few alterations made in this reimpression, and some at least are traceable to outside influences.

Two verifiable examples derive from criticisms in R. H. Hutton's review of the first edition of *Far from the Madding Crowd* in *The Spectator*.[4] Hutton says

4. Quoted in R. G. Cox, ed., *Thomas Hardy: The Critical Heritage* (London: Routledge & Kegan Paul, 1970) pp. 21–6. The passages referred to are on p. 23 and p. 24.

the repeater-watch which, it appears, . . . Jan Coggan carries in his waistcoat-pocket, seems to suggest a totally different world of physical belongings [than is appropriate to him]. (ellipsis mine)

In response to this Hardy added in 75:

> Coggan carried an old pinchbeck repeater which he had inherited from some genius in his family. . . .
>
> (XXXII; p. 164)

Later in the review Hutton quotes two paragraphs (run into one) beginning *The phases of Boldwood's life* (XVIII; p. 95), on which he comments

> The following passage strikes us as a study almost in the nature of a careful caricature of George Eliot.

Again Hardy's reaction was immediate; a sentence of the description of Boldwood was removed in 75—and this time the impact of the criticism was so strong that he further abbreviated the passage when the novel was reset for 77 (though there was possibly another reason for this later change: see below pp. 356–357). Indeed Hardy's almost complete silence about George Eliot in the *Life* and his letters may well be the result of the continual repetition, in review after review, of comparisons with her as a writer; and it is easy to guess that *The Hand of Ethelberta*, the novel which followed *Far from the Madding Crowd* in *Cornhill*, was conceived not so much as an unpastoral novel as an un-George Eliot-like novel.

Another criticism generally made in reviews of *Far from the Madding Crowd* was directed at what was called the uncomfortably ingenious style, and some of the other alterations in 75 may be an attempt to tone down this element in the novel: *circumambient*, for instance, became *circling*, and it seems not impossible that *quantum* was changed for the same reason. One other feature of Hardys's receptivity to criticism, his reaction to the suggestion of Leslie Stephen, the editor of *Cornhill*, will be discussed later on.

E9, the final leaf of Chapter XL, is fragmentary, with a portion removed from the bottom; this by itself would be enough to suggest that Chapter XLI originally began in a different way, but *** the whole chapter underwent considerable upheaval after the E numeration was first placed on the leaves. It was in fact expanded from an original seven leaves to its present fifteen; at one time it presumably began with E10 and ended with E16, since it is probable that the earlier first leaf of Chapter XLII was number E17. There appear to be four stages of development:

> (i) 2–192 is the only leaf still bearing the original E numeration, though 2–195, which is a composite leaf, having a piece cut from the top and new material added in its place, also presumably dates from the first E numeration.
> (ii) 2–199 to 202 and 2–205 belong to a second system of E numeration carried on into Chapter LXII, then abandoned.

(iii) 2–198, 2–203 and 2–204 are slightly later additions to that sequence.
(iv) 2–191, 2–193 and 2–196 to 197 are without E numbers at all and probably represent the latest stage of revision.

In contrast with the expansion in the rest of the chapter, the opening was shortened, two leaves making way for one; after this the main area of concern in the early part of the chapter up to 2–196 is the accidental revelation of Fanny's hair—and there are revisions still remaining on the new leaves which suggest that Hardy's view of this event and its consequences had altered. For instance, on 2–193 (p. 210) there are two additions to the first exchanges regarding the coil of hair, and on 2–196 we can see Hardy changing his mind as he writes. The MS. reads (the passage within <> was cancelled):

> "You won't burn that curl, <of hair, and you said "ties" just now, and Frank, that woman we met.
> O that's nothing, he said hastily.> You like the woman. . . .

—then there is more dialogue abut the hair and its owner until—

> "But just now you said 'ties'. . . ." (p. 211)

Most likely then, the importance of Fanny's hair was elaborated, so that Bathsheba would have no problem in recognising the corpse of the servant girl she had known so briefly, and so that she should have a more concrete reason for suspecting a connection between Fanny, Troy, and the girl she and Troy had met on the road.

It is probable that 2–197 was originally E16a, for it is only sixteen lines long (whereas the average is twenty-five), and it contains the beginning (at *Her pride was indeed brought low* [p. 211]) of an extended analytical description of Bathsheba that occupies the whole of E16b and is only concluded on a small piece of paper jointed to the top of E17. This kind of analysis by the detached narrator is often an addition to the manuscript; additions of this kind of analysis are usually too long to write interlineally, so they mostly occur on the verso of the preceding leaf. There are two examples in the first chapter of the novel—on page 3—

> He had just reached the time of life at which 'young' . . . were clearly separated. (ellipsis mine);

and on page 5—

> Woman's prescriptive infirmity had stalked into the sunlight, which had invested it with the freshness of an originality.

And many other instances may be found throughout the manuscript. It is also true that some such passages of narrational reflection which Hardy wished to add at a relatively late stage of the manuscript were too long to insert in this simple way, making it necessary to rewrite the leaves concerned. This probably happened at the beginning of Chapter V where 1–45 and 1–45a take the place of an original 1–45; the first new leaf has the prargraph beginning *It may have been observed* . . .

and concluded with one of the descriptions of Oak's temperament, here in terms of lyrical natural imagery, that are often late additions to the text.

It is probable, then, that this long paragraph on page 211 describing Bathsheba's instinctive allegiance to Diana was an afterthought, one in which he was trying to offer some counterbalance to the impression given by the early chapters of the novel to many contemporary readers that she was a selfish and thoughtless flirt; indeed the statement in the new paragraph that *she had never, by look, word, or sign, encouraged a man to approach her* seems hardly reconcilable with her early treatment of Oak, Boldwood, and Troy.

On 2–200 there is the first example in these chapters of something that concerned Hardy throughout the novel, exercising him perhaps more than any other topic—adjustment to the role of Gabriel Oak. He has with Gabriel a difficult problem of balance, and a similarly difficult one of placing: how to manage to keep him in the reader's mind while Bathsheba is primarily occupied with Troy and Boldwood, but yet not let him be too prominent; and, secondly, whereabouts exactly to pitch him in the available social scale. He is at the centre of the great set scenes of the fire and the storm, and in the first half of the novel he is involved in various shepherding occupations; but there is considerable evidence that Hardy wasn't satisfied, and at certain points in the climactic chapters I am concentrating upon, Gabriel's involvement is added or augmented.

Originally on 2–200 Farmer Boldwood gave a simple message about Fanny's death to Joseph Poorgrass, but this was cancelled, and in the consequent addition Gabriel became a confidant of Boldwood in the *earnest conversation* between them, and only after a *long time* did Poorgrass come by with his barrow to be informed of Fanny's death (p. 212). The purpose of the change is three-fold; firstly to reinforce Gabriel's relationship with Boldwood, which becomes more important as the novel goes on, secondly to maintain his connection with Fanny, established by their meeting early in the novel, and thirdly to begin his active involvement in this particular crisis of Bathsheba's life.

I would like for a while to look at how these three strands of intention in revision are arrived at, and where they lead. The first is the least important—there is only one previous revision which is related to this growth, on page 184 (XXXV) where Oak is added to Coggan in making a respectful nod to the farmer—primarily to emphasise his sense of inferiority in status at that stage in the novel. He then speaks to Boldwood after the storm, and the two men begin to be directly contrasted in their love for Bathsheba; the addition on 2–200 implies a closer connection between the men than heretofore, and this in the end leads to Gabriel's arrangement of partnership with Boldwood; the change is signalled most clearly by the dialogue between Boldwood and Liddy Smallbury on page 256, in which Boldwood calls Gabriel *Mr Oak* (XLIX). The close of their relation-ship is on page 296 in a proof addition to C in which the narrator says of Boldwood *there had been qualities in the farmer which Oak loved* (LV; I shall have reason to recur to this particular addition later).

The second strand, the development of Gabriel's involvement with Fanny, begins with Chapter VII of the novel. Professor Schweik has said that the decision to add this chapter, indeed the decision to dramatise Fanny's story, was taken part of the way through the com-position of Chapter X, citing cancelled numeration to help de-monstrate his point.[5] He is clearly right to suggest that the leaves which now constitute Chapter VII in the manuscript were late addi-tions, but I do not think he is correct in suggesting it was an entirely new idea. Professor Schweik believes that the cancelled numeration ended at 1–91 with a copying error on 1–112; in fact it extends to 1–125, the end of Chapter XI, which indicates that Hardy had got at least so far before he added the new Chapter VII.

At one time, according to a note on 1–125, Chapter XI was intended to end the second instalment of the serial, and so it would not be surprising if Hardy, reviewing the material for that episode, decided then to add the new chapter. In fact it seems certain that some encounter must have taken place between Gabriel and Fanny on the original two leaves which Chapter VII now replaces, for on 1–109, which has the cancelled number 104, it is mentioned that Gabriel has gone to look for Fanny at The Buck's Head; this leaf is not recopied, and so the inn must have figured in some original meeting; presuma-bly a very brief encounter, which is very much more fully realised in the present version.

It is clear also from an examination of the manuscript that the leaves comprising Chapter XI, the scene outside the barracks in the snow, are a patchwork from perhaps three periods of conception. The earliest leaf is probably 1–123, which dates from a time when Hardy had not settled Troy's christian name; on this leaf it was *Alfred*, and only later was that cancelled and changed to *Frank* (with its ironic overtones);[6] on both 1–122 and 1–124 it is *Frank*, unrevised. There are four lines or so cut from the bottom of 1–119 leaving the vestiges of the words *If any could*, and this phrase now occurs in the middle of the first paragraph on 1–120 (p. 70), showing that 1–120 dates from a later period than 119; 1–120 is in itself a leaf cut at the bottom, suggesting that there were at least two rewritings of the opening of the chapter before any of the visible numerations were made (there is an E numeration, but it too is consecutive). This is all strong evidence that

5. Schweik, pp. 418–22.

6. In other leaves of the MS, Oak was called first *Copeday* and then *Strong* (a characteristic early Hardy name salvaged from his abortive first novel *The Poor Man and the Lady*), and *Poorgrass was Poorhead*, which was perhaps considered rather too descriptive (it was not *Poorheed*, as Schweik suggests).

the scene was part of Hardy's early conception of the tale and not an afterthought. It is, however, most probable that the close sympathy felt by Gabriel for Fanny *was* a late thought on Hardy's part. This connection between Fanny and Gabriel is further strengthened by a small revision on page 176 (XXXIV) where Boldwood says in the MS that he is the only person in the village *excepting one* who knows of Troy's relation to Fanny; in proof for C *one* was changed to *Gabriel Oak*. There are two further alterations in the chapters we are looking at which carry on this concern still further: 2–203 and 2–204 (E21 and 21a) are later additions to the manuscript, and following the introduction of Gabriel in the addition in which Boldwood discussed Fanny's death with him it is likely that the various details that Poorgrass relates of Gabriel on these two leaves were new, and in particular the paragraph on page 215 beginning

> *Perhaps he was busy, ma'am. . . . And sometimes he seems to suffer from things on his mind* (ellipsis mine)—

which may well have been added to prepare for the amplification of Gabriel's unconscious influence over Bathsheba's mind in the next chapters. Similarly in Chapter LXII on pages 222–223 the manuscript originally read

> *But thanks to Boldwood's reticence very little more was known than this bare fact of death*

but was altered later to

> *. . . reticence and Oak's generosity, the lover she had followed had never been individualized as Troy.*

Indeed, at this stage of the novel Gabriel's involvement with Fanny and with Bathsheba come together. Leaves 2–221 to 2–223 (E32–32b) replace an original E32; the only satisfactory reason that can be offered for such an expansion is an increase in the role of Gabriel Oak in the last part of Chapter XLII, particularly in his anxiety to shield Bathsheba as long as possible from the shock of discovering Fanny's baby. E37 and 37a were also second thoughts and they contain a long paragraph in which the narrator analyses Bathsheba's feelings towards Gabriel, including a sentence of central importance: *What a way Oak had, she thought, of enduring things* (p. 226). There is no doubt of the significance of Bathsheba's new assessment of him at this point in the story; in it she is recognizing him, almost for the first time, as an exceptional person, as more than an unwanted suitor or hired shepherd.

A particularly interesting change made in proof for C, which helps to prepare for this reported reverie about Oak, occurs during the immediately preceding potential catastrophe in her life, the threat of the destruction of her ricks by the storm. She has been telling Gabriel about her marriage, when he notices she has been tired out by the work of helping him thatch the ricks and tells her to go indoors. Her reply in the manuscript was:

If I am useless I will go. . . . But oh, if the wheat should be lost! (ellipsis mine)

Hardy dramatically and economically transformed this selfish, or at best objective concern with her wealth into real anxiety about Gabriel, by altering *the wheat* to *your life* (XXXVII; p. 196). The speech represents in its altered form Bathsheba's first movement toward Oak; the episode itself shows the beginning of her disillusionment with Troy, and Hardy say how important it was, if the ending of his novel was to be successful, that he should stress the presence of Gabriel close to her during the destruction of that relationship.

Indeed Gabriel grew gradually in stature as Hardy's conception of the novel developed, and to give some idea of how far Hardy may have come from his original version of the relationship between Gabriel and Bathsheba it is worth looking at the first six chapters of the novel. These early leaves at first glance have only one sequence of E numeration, and its absence from 1–8 and 1–9 at the end of Chapter 1 shows that Gabriel's first encounter with Bathsheba was rewritten after the E numeration was made. However, the chief interest lies in a discrepancy between leaves 1–44 and 1–46. Leaf 1–44 is numbered E44, 1–45 and 1–45a are later additions and have no E number, but 1–46 had E39, and this latter sequence carries on, with interruptions for later revised leaves, until 1–62 (E55). The only satisfactory explanation for this is to suggest that 1–24 to 1–44 (and possibly, though not probably, the earlier leaves of the novel) repreent a newer stage of composition than 1–46 to 1–62, and that the later E number became the 1– number on the older leavs: 1–24 to 1–44 are those leaves that contain Bathsheba saving Gabriel's life, her flirtation with him, and his proposal of marriage. There is no way of knowing for certain what these leaves replaced but it is interesting in this context to notice that 1–49 (E42) has been cut to half its normal length and that a long addition to the beginning of 1–50 (E43) has been made on its verso, concluding with Gabriel's reflection

Thank God I am not married: what would she have done in the poverty now coming upon me! (V; p. 33)

Apparently this passage replaced what was cut from the previous leaf, which might imply that in the original version no proposal of marriage had taken place. The only subsequent leaves up to the end of this E numeration—1–53c, 1–57, and 1–63—that bear any implication of Gabriel's desire to marry Bathsheba were added after the numeration was made: with 1–64 a different E numeration begins.

If Hardy did not originally intend Gabriel to propose to Bathsheba, then his idea of the character has come far. This development is also reflected in an elevation in the social/education standing of the farmer-shepherd. In the original plan communicated to Stephen—if we may believe the account in *The Early Life*[7]—Gabriel had been thought of simply as a shepherd, closer to the other employees in the novel. The oldest leaves surviving in the manuscript, those with the earlier versions of the names of Oak and Poorgrass, contain some speeches by Gabriel that sound now rather inappropriate. As an example one might take his simpleminded response to some criticisms of Pennyways on page 53 (VIII)—

> *"Good faith, you do talk," said Gabriel, with apprehension.*

—which, especially in the 'apprehension', seems a decisive contrast with his demeanour towards Bathsheba in the subsequent paying scene. This difference in tone is perceptible not only in dialogue, for later there is a vivid contrast between the jocular description of Gabriel's fist—rather smaller in size than a common loaf, laid as a threat on the table on pages 86–87 (XV), which is also on such an early leaf—and his ease with Mr. Boldwood in the following discussion (on a leaf added later) of his letter from Fanny, in which he does not address him as Sir as he other workfolk undoubtedly would. Evidently there is a trace remaining still of Gabriel Oak who was more akin to the habitués of Warren's than he appears in the rest of the novel, where even at his lowest ebb he is somewhat apart from them, and superior to them.

These distinctions are matters of tone, but more concrete evidence that Hardy's view of Gabriel tended towards making him more sophisticated can be derived from revisions to dialect in his speech. Early on in the novel Hardy removes some of the dialectal formations from Gabriel's speech in proof for C—as for instance in his final attempt to persuade Bathsheba to marry him on page 30 (IV), where *would ha' thought* is changed to *would have thought, and along wi' me to along with me.*

However, by the time the last two episodes of the novel were in Leslie Stephen's hands, Hardy's estimate of Oak's proper speech had changed to the extent that Stephen could write, on 25 August 1874:

> I will speak about the November proof tomorrow. I saw nothing to alter, unless that it seemed to me in one or two cases that your rustics—specially Oak—speak rather too good English towards the end. They seem to drop the dialect a little. But of this you are the best judge.[8]

Hardy in this matter, as in almost all others, responded vigorously to Stephen's prompting, and there are over thirty places where Gabriel had dialect added to his speech in the last two episodes. This extends to phrases like *the top and tail o't it* (LVI; p. 302) for *it amounts to* or

---

7. Florence Emily Hardy, *The Early Life of Thomas Hardy, 1840–1891* (London and New York: Macmillan, 1928) p. 125.
8. Purdy, p. 339.

Surely, surely you be (LVI; p. 302) for *you are necessarily* (where both versions have the identical number of characters, including spaces; presumably, one thinks, the second *surely* was added to save the compositors trouble in resetting the proof revision) as well as simple words such as *ye* for *you*. It may be right that Gabriel should retain the richness of dialect expression until the end of the novel, and indeed it is also added to in the general augmentation of dialect form that was made in all his novels during the revision for the Osgood collected edition of 1895–6; but the refinement in Gabriel's speech which he allowed, perhaps unconsciously, to creep into the latter part of the manuscript demonstrates (when all the other evidence I have offered is taken into account), the way in which Hardy's sense of his character changed as the novel progressed.

One final example shows it clearly. When, in the serial version of Chapter XVIII the narrator was analysing Boldwood's character, in the passage compared with George Eliot by R. H. Hutton (see p. 349 above), Hardy related the farmer's nature to that of Gabriel's:

> *Spiritually and mentally, no less than socially, a commonplace general condition is no conclusive proof that a man has not potentialities above that level.*
> *In all cases this state may be either the mediocrity of inadequacy, as was Oak's or . . . the mediocrity of counterpoise, as was Boldwood's.*
>
> (p. 95; ellipsis mine)

This passage remained in 74 and 75, and was only removed in 77, although it is manifestly inappropriate as a generalisation on the Oak who has a close relationship with Boldwood later in the novel, and who marries the heroine.

This glance at Gabriel has taken me rather far from the text that I am inspecting; I left it on 2–200 with the addition of Gabriel as the principal recipient of the news of Fanny's death; on the same leaf there occurs the first of two alterations connected with Fanny Robin that Hardy makes on artistic grounds (in contrast with some of those that come later); Poorgrass's reply to Bathsheba's question *What did she die from?* beginning *I don't know for certain, but I* originally continued in the manuscript *believe it was from inflammation of the lungs, though some say she broke her heart.* When reviewing this Hardy added a couple of sentences about her general weakness, but omitted all mention of consumption or love, adding in proof a further characteristically colourful detail *and 'a went like a candle-snoff, so 'tis said* (p. 213). There are two reasons for this alteration; one is that Poorgrass was, as a result of the addition of the Oak-Boldwood meeting (and his own later-added avowal to Bathsheba), not aware of the cause of Fanny's death, and Hardy would be anxious to avoid anything that might imply that he was; and the other, similarly dependent on the inclusion of Gabriel in this chapter, is that Hardy wished to postpone all direct hints at the true cause of her death till the end of the following chapter. This dual concern is also evident when Bathsheba repeats her question to Poorgrass on 2–203 (E21); *Died of what did you say, Joseph?* His reply, unrevised (thus showing that E21 is contemporary with E21a) is *I don't know, ma'am.* It seems that Hardy considered Bathsheba's question too suggestive despite Joseph's ignorance, for he altered it in proof for C to *Whose sweetheart . . .* (p. 214) though he didn't alter Joseph's subsequent narrative of his meeting with Boldwood and Oak in which Gabriel very self-consciously avoids the question of how she died. The proof change has the added advantage of emphasising Bathsheba's anxiety about the colour of Fanny's hair (newly stressed in the manuscript, as I have suggested), since her preceding question to Poorgrass had been on that topic. His reply to that was unhelpful, and the change from *Died of what* to *Whose sweetheart* takes better account of her current concern.

The second of these revisions begins on the second leaf of Chapter XLII (2–207), where Hardy originally let slip Fanny's secret undramatically, through the writing that the Union man scrawled on the coffin:

> *Fanny Robin and Child*
> *Died Oct 3 18—*

(It is interesting to note that *and Child* was a later addition to the MS, and I shall be taking up this point later.) The next paragraph then began:

> *Joseph then having learnt the sad truth concerning Fanny placed the flowers as enjoined.*

Hardy no doubt felt that by giving away his secret here he was wasting valuable dramatic potential, and also that Poorgrass was altogether the wrong person to act as intermediary for the reader, especially since he had introduced Gabriel to knowledge of Fanny's death in the previous chapter. So the inscription was replaced by *the name and date* (Hardy changed *date* to the more appropriate *a few other words* in proof). Poorgrass' learning the truth was omitted (p. 216), and the last paragraph of the chapter was added, in which Gabriel's is the consciousness through which the infant is explicitly revealed as he wipes the *and child* from the inscription on the coffin—ending the chapter and the September episode on a suitably tense note (p. 224).

This manipulation of the knowledge of Fanny's baby for artistic reasons contrasts vividly with some of the alterations made in Chapter LXIII. These, as is well known, respond to Leslie Stephen's letter to Hardy of 13 April 1874, in which he wrote:

> I object as editor, not as critic, i.e. in the interest of a stupid public, not from my own taste.
> I think that the reference to the cause of Fanny's death is unnecessarily emphasized. I should, I think, omit all reference to it except just enough to

indicate the true state of the case; and especially a conversation between your heroine and her maid, wh. is a little unpleasant. I have some doubts whether the baby is necessary at all and whether it would not be sufficient for Bathsheba to open the coffin in order to identify the dead woman with the person she met on the road. This is a point wh. you can consider. It certainly rather injures the story, and perhaps if the omission were made it might be restored on republication. But I am rather necessarily anxious to be on the safe side; and should somehow be glad to omit the baby.

However, these changes can easily be made when the story is in type and I shall send it to the printers now; and ask you to do what is necessary to the proofs.

We can talk about it when we meet.[9]

The extent to which Hardy was willing to be ruled by Stephen may be gauged by considering this list of C proof revisions to Chapter LXIII:

> Fanny was at first called *innocent*, which was changed to *nesh young*.
> Half a leaf of dialogue which explores the improbability of Fanny's consumptiveness was removed, in which it was mentioned that *she has only been away from us about eight months*.
> Liddy's story about Fanny is amended from *there's two of em in there!* to *Liddy came close to her mistress and whispered the remainder of the sentence slowly into her ear. . . .*
> A continuation of the same dialogue which included *We shall be sure to learn the rights of it tomorrow* is omitted.
> *I hate them* was changed to *I hate her.*
> *features of the young girl and babe* was changed to *features within.*
> A page and a third of the manuscript is omitted which describes the appearance of Fanny and her baby in the coffin. Stephen must have objected to the lyrical and uncensorious treatment of the bastard and its erring mother; he can hardly have had other stylistic objections because the passage is characteristic of Hardy's high style throughout the novel, including as it does a literary quotation, a fanciful natural image comparing the baby's cheeks and plumb fists to *the soft convexity of mushrooms on a dewy morning*, and a painterly comparison between Fanny's hands and those in Bellini portraits. It is bad enough, but Stephen might as well have objected to the whole novel; and as a result of his advice we have also lost the extremely moving and delicately expressed picture of the two in the coffin as companions of one kind, caught in incipiency rather than decadence: *they both had stood on the threshold of a new stage of existence.* The paragraph as a whole represents a central strand in Hardy's conception of states of being and becoming. And with this passage we would also be able to enter much more readily into the impulse that later moved Troy to kiss Fanny, to sense that it was not purely one of remorse, as Hardy wrote: *The youth and fairness of both the silent ones withdrew from the scene all associations of a repulsive kind. . . .*

Thus almost every direct reference to the baby has been removed. Curiously enough, Hardy himself may originally have conceived the episode as less explicit than it appeared in the final manuscript version, for the leaves that contain the description of the two in the coffin which was omitted in proof, were themselves late additions to the

9. Purdy, p. 339.

manuscript; and two passages that imply the baby's existence which still remain—*that there are two of you* and *beside the unconscious pair*—both appear on leaves added later. Two of the details altered in proof were written into the manuscript during a period of revision: *I hate them* and *dead woman and babe*; and I have already noticed the addition of *and child* to the inscription on the coffin.

At any rate Hardy was sufficiently concerned by the impact of this censorship on the scene that he took some steps to remedy the matter, not in 74—which was published before the serial had finished in C—but in 75 (restoring *features of both mother and babe* for *features within*) and more extensively in 77, where seven small alterations were made, including the addition of *in maternity* to *forestalment, eclipse in maternity by another* (p. 230). But there was no attempt to restore either Liddy's whisper or the couple in the coffin; this is characteristic of Hardy as late as *Tess of the d'Urbervilles* and *Jude the Obscure*, where passages bowdlerised for the serial sometimes remain lost to the book versions.

There is other evidence of Stephen's censoring pencil (the passage describing Fanny and her baby was marked, not by Hardy, with pencil in the manuscript). One example, in Chapter XLII, may have been made on religious rather than moral grounds; after the paragraph of Jan Coggan's speech that ends at the top of page 220 there is in the manuscript the following passage, similarly marked with a pencil cancellation in a way that Hardy never used, and omitted from C.

> "The same here," said Mark. If anything can beat the old martyrs who used to smoke for their principles here up on earth 'tis being willing to smoke for 'em hereafter."
> "'Tis the old feeling in a new way," said Coggan.

In a letter of 12 March 1874, Stephen admits to having

> . . . ventured to leave out a line or two in the last batch of proofs from an excessive prudery of wh. I am ashamed: but one is forced to be absurdly particular.[1]

He then alludes to Troy's seduction of Fanny. Either April or May proofs are almost certainly meant here, and I have found two omissions presumably in proof that might represent the kind of editorial excision Stephen feels he had to apologise for. One is in Chapter XV, in the April episode: after Boldwood had read Fanny's letter to Gabriel, in the manuscript he ended his expression of anxiety over her fate with

> "She has now lost her character—he will never marry her—and what will she do?"

This sentence, uncancelled in the manuscript, was left out of C. The second possibility occurs in the May instalment, at the end of Chapter

1. Purdy, p. 338.

XXIV: when Liddy was talking about Troy she calls him *a gay man*, and in the manuscript her speech continued *a walking ruin to honest girls, so some people say*. This too did not appear in C. Of course it is possible that Hardy overruled Stephen and the offending passage remains, undetectable; but this is unlikely in view of Hardy's ready acquiescence with Stephen's advice in other parts of the novel. Indeed when contributing to F. W. Maitland's *Life and Letters of Leslie Stephen*, Hardy related how Stephen had received a letter complaining of a passage in the serial from 'three respectable ladies', and said that his first reaction was to ask Stephen why he didn't strike out the passage.[2] Hardy later noticed the very sentences applauded in *The Times's* review of the first edition of the novel, and suggested that he would 'never have taken the trouble to restore them in the reprint'. (The paragraph in question is that on page 52 [VIII] where Jan Coggan describes Levi Everdene's way of subduing his roving heart.)

One wonders whether Stephen also objected to a sheep's *buttocks* which was changed to *back* in proof (XXII; p. 115), or whether he was responsible for the new and rather unpleasant moral tone of Gabriel Oak's attitude towards the murderer Boldwood in Chapter LV, where

> *Gabriel's anxiety was so great that he paced up and down, pausing at every turn and straining his ear for a sound*

became in C

> *Gabriel's anxiety was great that Boldwood might be saved, even though in his conscience he felt that he ought to die; for there had been qualities in the farmer which Oak loved.* (p. 296)

The first shows real agitation, the second a kind of patronising by Gabriel of Boldwood which is thoroughly nasty. Whether this was what Hardy wished, one has at least licence to doubt from Stephen's frequent Grundian interventions elsewhere.

Hardy was to suffer from this kind of advice or instruction or ultimatum from the editors of magazines throughout his career in fiction. It is fascinating to notice how, almost to a man, they claimed that it was not as individuals, but as editors that they made such suggestions or stipulations. Mowbray Morris belied this in his review of *Tess of the d'Urbervilles*,[3] and Leslie Stephen's recorded attitude to explicitness in sexual matters in contemporary French novels was to consider them 'prurient and indecent'.[4]

To return to Chapter XLIII, there is in it another characteristic feature of the way Hardy developed his texts; in 95 the details describing Casterbridge were altered to make them conform more closely to the existing topography of Dorchester. This kind of revision is common throughout the novel, and indeed a book might well be written about the changes in the complete Osgood and Wessex Editions that

2. *Early Life*, p. 130.
3. *Critical Heritage*, pp. 214–21.

4. F. W. Maitland, *Life and Letters of Leslie Stephen* (London, 1906) p. 266.

were made through this impulse in Hardy to preserve with scrupulous accuracy the localities and the customs, social activities and patterns of life of Dorset and the surrounding counties in the nineteenth century. The preface to *Far from the Madding Crowd*, largely written in 1895, discusses the first use of the word Wessex in the novel's serialisation and the subsequent development of the word's currency; numerous topographical alterations were thus made in order to bring each text into line with the now established Wessex landscape—semi-fictional, but self-consistent.

There is another interesting passage in the preface, in which Hardy describes

> *The game of prisoner's base, which not long ago seemed to enjoy a perennial vitality in front of the worn-out stocks . . .*

This detail may be taken as a measure of his increasing local-historian's concern for such matters, for prisoner's base has its first mention in the edition of 1895. Previously the game for which the young men of Weatherbury had gathered *from time immemorial* was fives.

*   *   *

I have tried to look in this essay at the whole range of differences that might be found between an edition of *Far from the Madding Crowd* that is read today and the earliest ideas that Hardy had of the novel; I have glanced, at least, at every substantively different edition of the novel (substantively different, that is, by authorial intention) and I hope I have given some idea of the variety of matters that Hardy was concerned with when revising a text.

The final claim that I want to make, one that I hope to substantiate in a series of essays along the same lines as this, is that in general terms everything said here about *Far from the Madding Crowd* can be applied to all of Hardy's fictional prose; and that from a comparative study of all his texts a new approach to Hardy as a creative writer may emerge. If we can make valid generalisations about the ways that Hardy approached his writing, the kinds of things he was interested in altering, heightening, deleting, augmenting, not only in the broad thematic or character concerns I have concentrated on here, but also in more detailed areas such as style or punctuation, then I think we will understand more clearly the nature of Hardy as a creative artist. Biographers and critics complain that he is an elusive man to pin down. I suggest that the most rewarding way to penetrate his amply shielded personality may be through the creative mind at work.

Criticism

Contemporary Critical
Reception

[R. H. HUTTON]

From *The Spectator*, January 3, 1874

The readers of the *Cornhill* are to be congratulated doubly this time,—on the conclusion of 'Zelda's Fortune,'[1] and on the commencement of an anonymous novel so clever and so remarkable, that though speculation upon the authorship may be indiscreet, it is irresistible. If 'Far from the Madding Crowd' is not written by George Eliot,[2] then there is a new light among novelists. In every page of these introductory chapters there are a dozen sentences which have the ring of the wit and the wisdom of the only truly great English novelist now living.

*   *   *

There is a passage descriptive of the companionship of the stars, so learned and so poetical that it seems to be irrefutable evidence of the authorship.[3] At all events, the *Cornhill* is giving us a high intellectual treat this time, and we are not the less grateful because it is certainly due as reparation.

From *The Athenaeum*, December 5, 1874

Mr. Hardy, who has now, we think, for the first time allowed his name to appear on a title-page, is at once an interesting and a disappointing writer. He is, perhaps, the most vigorous of all the novelists who have appeared within the last few years; his powers of description, his skill in devising 'situations', his quaint humour, secure him a high place among novelists of any age; while, on the other hand, a sort of recklessness seems at times to overcome and neutralize all these qualities, and the coarseness upon which we

---

1. *Zelda's Fortune* was a novel by R. E. Francillon that had been serialized in the *Cornhill Magazine* since January 1873 [*Editor*].
2. "George Eliot" was the pen name of Mary Ann Evans (1819–80), some of whose early novels, such as *Adam Bede* (1859), had dealt with rural life [*Editor*].
3. Leslie Stephen comments on this interpretation of "irrefutable evidence" in a letter to Hardy of 8 January 1874, reprinted in this edition on p. 341 [*Editor*].

remarked in reviewing his *Desperate Remedies*, some four years ago, still disfigures his work and repels the reader. He is evidently a shrewd observer of the talk and habits of the Somersetshire rustics; and yet he puts such expressions into their mouths as 'Passably well put', 'Every looker-on's inside shook with the blows of the great drum to his deepest vitals, and there was not a dry eye throughout the town,' and so on—expressions which we simply cannot believe possible from the illiterate clods whom he describes. Then, though his style is often admirable, he gives us such monstrous periphrases as 'a fair product of Nature in a feminine direction',[1] and other specimens of the worst 'penny-a-liner's' language, till we almost despair of him; and then, a little further on, we come to such an admirable variation of an old aphorism as 'Men take wives because possession is not possible without marriage, and women accept husbands because marriage is not possible without possession.' And so on throughout the book. * * * How this present story could ever have been supposed to be written by George Eliot we cannot conceive, though her influence has been plainly visible in some of his former books; we should say, on the contrary, that some of the scenes, notably that where Sergeant Troy goes through the sword exercise before Bathsheba, are worthy, in their extravagance, of Mr. Reade,[2] and of him only; while the stronger parts are Mr. Hardy's own. At least we know of no other living author who could so have described the burning rick-yard, or the approaching thunderstorm, or given us the wonderful comicalities of the supper at the malthouse. The contrasted characters of the three chief men of the story are also well worked out; the man of single eye, who waits, and works patiently, scarcely hoping for recognition, but ready to help the woman he loves, literally through fire and water; the profligate soldier, who comes, sees, and, for a time, conquers; and the reserved, middle-aged farmer, falling in love for the first time at forty, and then driven almost, if not quite, to insanity by disappointment—all play their parts well, and take their due shares in the development of the story. On the whole, we leave Mr. Hardy with some hope. He ought to hold his peace for at least two years, revise with extreme care, and refrain from publishing in magazines; then, though he has not done it yet, he may possibly write a nearly, if not quite, first-rate novel.

1. Hardy altered the phrasing of this passage in chapter 1 to "a fair product of Nature in the feminine kind," perhaps as a response to the anonymous *Athenaeum* critic's comment [*Editor*].

2. Charles Reade (1814–84) was a popular Victorian novelist who combined carefully documented incident with melodramatic extravagance [*Editor*].

HENRY JAMES

From the *Nation,* December 24, 1874

Mr. Hardy puts his figures through a variety of comical movements; he fills their mouths with quaint turns of speech; he baptizes them with odd names ('Joseph Poorgrass' for a bashful, easily-snubbed Dissenter[1] is excellent); he pulls the wires, in short, and produces a vast deal of sound and commotion; and his novel, at a cursory glance, has a rather promising air of life and warmth. But by critics who prefer a grain of substance to a pound of shadow it will, we think, be pronounced a decidedly delusive performance; it has a fatal lack of magic. We have found it hard to read, but its shortcomings are easier to summarize than to encounter in order. Mr. Hardy's novel is very long, but his subject is very short and simple, and the work has been distended to its rather formidable dimensions by the infusion of a large amount of conversatioinal and descriptive padding and the use of an ingeniously verbose and redundant style. It is inordinately diffuse, and, as a piece of narrative, singularly inartistic. The author has little sense of proportion, and almost none of composition.

* * *

Mr. Hardy describes nature with a great deal of felicity, and is evidently very much at home among rural phenomena. The most genuine thing in his book, to our sense, is a certain aroma of the meadows and lanes—a natural relish for harvesting and sheep-washings. * * * The chief purpose of the book is, we suppose, to represent Gabriel's dumb, devoted passion, his biding his time, his rendering unsuspected services to the woman who has scorned him, his integrity and simplicity and sturdy patience. In all this the tale is very fairly successful, and Gabriel has a certain vividness of expression. But we cannot say that we either understand or like Bathsheba. She is a young lady of the inconsequential, wilful, mettlesome type which has lately become so much the fashion for heroines, and of which Mr. Charles Reade is in a manner the inventor—the type which aims at giving one a very intimate sense of a young lady's *womanishness*.[2] But Mr. Hardy's embodiment of it seems to us to lack reality; he puts her through the Charles Reade paces, but she remains alternately vague and coarse, and seems always artificial. This is Mr.

1. Henry James's mistaken characterization of Joseph Poorgrass as a Dissenter was probably the result of his misreading or inaccurately remembering some of the dialogue in chapter 42, "Joseph and His Burden—Buck's Head," where Mark Clark at one point taunts Poorgrass by saying, "I believe ye to be a chapel-member,

Joseph" [*Editor*].

2. James probably had in mind Charles Reade's novel *Peg Woffington* (1853), which is the story of an actress who plays a trick to win the affections of a wealthy man and is later moved to tears and repentance by the prayers of the man's wife [*Editor*].

Hardy's trouble; he rarely gets beyond ambitious artifice—the mechanical simulation of heat and depth and wisdom that are absent. Farmer Boldwood is a shadow, and Sergeant Troy an elaborate stage-figure. Everything human in the book strikes us as factitious and insubstantial; the only things we believe in are the sheep and the dogs. But, as we say, Mr. Hardy has gone astray very cleverly, and his superficial novel is a really curious imitation of something better.

ANDREW LANG

From the *Academy*, January 2, 1875

Far from the Madding Crowd is so clever a novel, so original in atmosphere and in character, that its brilliant qualities are likely to neutralize the glare of its equally prominent faults. The writer has the advantage of dealing with an almost untouched side of English life. His scene is laid somewhere in the country of Mr. Freeman's favourite Seaxsaetas,[1] in a remote agricultural and pastoral district of south-western England. Among peasants who look on Bath as a distant and splendid metropolis, it is likely that much of the old country existence lives on undisturbed. * * * No condition of society could supply the writer who knows it well with a more promising ground for his story. The old and the new must meet here and there, with curious surprises, and our world may find itself face to face with the quaint conceited rustics of Shakespeare's plays. * * * In our opinion the writer of *Far from the Madding Crowd* has only partially succeeded in making the best of his theme, and though his failure is more valuable than many successes, he has been misled by attempting too much. In his way of looking at his subject he rather resembles George Eliot than George Sand.[2] He contemplates his shepherds and rural people with the eye of a philosopher who understands all about them, though he is not of them, and who can express their dim efforts at rendering what they think and feel in language like that of Mr. Herbert Spencer.[3] It is this way of writing and thinking that gives the book its peculiar tone. The author is telling clever people about unlettered people, and he adopts a sort of patronizing voice, in which there are echoes, now of

1. Edward Augustus Freeman (1823–92) was an historian whose chief work, titled *History of the Norman Conquest* (1867–79), was an attempt to show that the Norman Conquest did not fundamentally change the Saxon character and institutions of England [*Editor*].
2. George Sand was the pen name of Amandine Aurore Lucile Dupin (1804–76), a French novelist whose later works included rural idylls

that do not have the "philosophical" quality that Lang attributes to George Eliot's fiction [*Editor*].
3. Herbert Spencer (1820–1909) was a philosopher whose very extensive writings covered subjects as diverse as biology and ethics, all of which he treated with a characteristic abstractness in a self-confident tone [*Editor*].

George Eliot, and now of George Meredith.[4] Thus there are passages where the manner and the matter jar, and are out of keeping.

[J. R. WISE]

From the *Westminster Review*, January 1875

* * * Whatever Mr. Hardy may wish us to think of his heroine, the one leading trait of her character, and of all such characters, is at the bottom—selfishness. She plays fast and loose with poor Gabriel Oak. She blows hot and cold upon Farmer Boldwood. She flirts with Oak in the most heartless manner. She sends Boldwood a valentine with the words 'Marry Me' on the seal. Her very selfishness makes her wayward and inconstant. When she is entrapped by Sergeant Troy with his scarlet coat and his vulgar love-making we feel no pity for her. She never really cared a straw for Troy. She was fascinated by his swagger and his flattery. Her behaviour, however, at his death seems to us most inexplicable, and is the only part of her history which is out of drawing. It is open to grave objections. In all other respects she is described with great skill. She is hard and mercenary. When she at last marries Gabriel Oak we feel, whatever Mr. Hardy may intend to the contrary, that she marries him not from any admiration of his nobility of character, but simply because he will manage her farm and keep her money together. Bathsheba is the character of the book, and Mr. Hardy may be proud of having drawn such a character. But she is a character not to be admired, as he would seem to intimate. * * *

4. George Meredith (1828–1909) was a novelist, poet, and essayist with a talent for witty satire and striking aphorisms who sometimes adopted a tone of magisterial detachment [*Editor*].

Modern Criticism

HOWARD BABB

Setting and Theme in *Far from the Madding Crowd*†

Even casual readers of Thomas Hardy soon begin to sense that in his fiction the customary setting, the natural world, operates a good deal more forcefully than as sheer backdrop to the narrative. And the power of his settings is a commonplace among Hardy's critics, most of whom find the natural background functioning symbolically at moments, though one of them speaks instead of a metaphoric dimension.[1] To anyone curious about Hardy's technique with his backgrounds, or generally inquisitive about the ways in which fiction may be structured and work for its effects, the relatively early *Far from the Madding Crowd* proves especially interesting. While not in the same class with Hardy's later achievements, this story shows—with something approaching the obviousness of a textbook example—how setting can be used to reinforce and indeed at times to render theme. What I want chiefly to bring out in the following pages is both the number and variety of relationships that Hardy creates between setting and theme here: a host of interconnections that serves—along with the story's other structures, some of which I shall be glancing at—to saturate *Far from the Madding Crowd* with its theme. And I shall be suggesting incidentally that the novel's saturation with its theme helps to explain how we come to terms—if indeed we do—with several scenes of more or less questionable plausibility in which the natural setting plays a dominant part.

At bottom, Hardy's story juxtaposes two different worlds or modes of being, the natural against the civilized, and it insists on the superiority of the former by identifying the natural as strong, enduring, self-contained, slow to change, sympathetic, while associating the civilized with weakness, facility, modernity, self-centeredness. We are perhaps alerted for this theme by the title itself of the novel, which evokes the

†From *ELH* 30 (1963), 147–61. Parenthetic page references in the text have been changed to chapter references.

1. Carol R. Andersen, "Time, Space, and Perspective in Thomas Hardy,"*Nineteenth-Century Fiction* 9 (1954), 192–208. The critic feels that in the case of Hardy "we must take all the ordinary elements of the novel (landscape, characters, plot) and accept them as metaphorical equivalents of the theme" (p. 195), and later speaks of Hardy's "backgrounds" as "something more than a mere setting of scene. It appears to be the pathetic fallacy driven to such an extreme that it is no longer a fallacy but an artistic integer" (p. 203). These sentences convey an impression of Hardy's settings that seems to me much like my own, but the essay concentrates on metaphors of "time" and "space" in the novels.

contrast in Gray's "Elegy" between rural and urban values. But in any case, Hardy's juxtaposition of the natural and the civilized is reflected in even the barest outline of *Far from the Madding Crowd's* narrative. The first section of the story hinges on the unsuccessful marriage proposal made by Gabriel Oak—the simple, modest shepherd—to the self-assured and somewhat flighty Bathsheba Everdene; she turns him down mainly because she does not love him, to be sure, but also because she has her sights set on a way of life above, somehow more refined than, what he can offer her. By the end of the novel, however, she has learned through her sufferings on account of Boldwood and Troy how to value Gabriel, so Oak's patient love is rewarded at last. Between these opening and closing movements of the story, its foreground is largely given over to the entanglement of Bathsheba with Gabriel's two rivals for her heart. The first to present himself is the gentlemanly Boldwood, whose composure is so shattered by Bathsheba's valentine that he begins hounding her mercilessly to marry him. Then comes the fashionable Troy, who overwhelms Bathsheba with flattery, quickly marries her, tires of her almost as fast, and drifts away after quarreling with her over the dead Fanny Robin, a girl whom Troy seduced before meeting Bathsheba. Finally Boldwood steps forward again, now spurred by the assumption that Troy is dead to press Bathsheba more relentlessly than ever for a promise of marriage, only to have his fantasy exploded by the return of Troy, whom he shoots down in a burst of passion. Every so often during these romantic conflicts and maneuverings, Gabriel Oak will move to the front of the stage, perhaps to give Bathsheba some moral counsel, or to save her sheep, or to protect her grain during the storm. But for the most part he remains in the middle distance, allied with the processes of nature through performing the ordinary tasks of the farmer or shepherd, his feet firmly planted in the natural world. The most general impression created by the narrative, then, is of a running contrast between dignified naturalness and the feverish pursuit of selfish ends.

Whatever the local action that Hardy places in the foreground, he manages to keep us constantly aware of the natural world in the novel. Four characteristics of that world as it is revealed throughout Hardy's fiction have been admirably set forth by John Holloway: "Nature is an organic living whole," with all its parts having "a life and personality of their own"; "it is unified on a great scale through both time and space"; "it is exceedingly complex," with "details that are sometimes even quaint or bizarre"; these heterogeneous things are integrated, however obscurely, into a system of rigid and undeviating law."[2] All of these qualities are apparent enough in *Far from Madding Crowd*, as anyone may remind himself by rereading the famous Norcombe Hill scene at

2. *The Victorian Sage* (London, 1953), p. 252.

the beginning of chapter 2. But the natural world in this novel seems endowed with a fifth attribute as well, one that may surprise the reader of Hardy's other fiction. For in *Far from the Madding Crowd* nature is frequently represented as at least a sympathetic force, sometimes even as a moral agent—an assertion that I shall depend upon details cited later to bear out.

Even if the claim about a fifth attribute should prove tenuous, there can be no questioning the fact that again and again in this story Hardy uses his position as omniscient author to set the natural world and the civilized explicitly against each other in such a way that we have no doubt about which we are to prefer. Almost at the beginning of the novel, for instance, after he has developed so compelling a sense of nature's majesty in describing Norcombe Hill, the night sky, and the "almost . . . palpable movement" of the earth, Hardy remarks that this vivid experiencing of the universe is possible only when one has "first expanded with a sense of difference from the mass of civilized mankind, who are dreamwrapt and disregardful of all such [natural] proceedings at this time" (2).[3] Further on in the story, when Hardy is leading up to the sheep-shearing by sketching the June landscape, he spells out the opposition once more, this time with obviously moral overtones: "God was palpably present in the country, and the devil had gone with the world to town" (22). And the great shearing-barn itself provides the occasion for one of Hardy's most elaborate variations on this theme. First he treats the four-hundred-year-old building as an instance of that continuity between past and present which typifies the rural mode of life; then, in a separate paragraph, he contrasts the relative immutability of Weatherbury and its ways with the rapid change, the discontinuity between past and present, which characterizes London or Paris; and he comes out finally with the flat statement that "the barn was naturall to the shearers, and the shearers were in harmony with the barn" (22). These examples will have suggested plainly enough not only that Hardy charges the natural background itself with value, but that he keeps taking advantage of his position as omniscient author to restate his theme openly in passages which focus mainly on the setting.

One of the basic methods by which any author dramatizes his theme, of course, is through ordering the similarities and differences between his characters in such a manner that these figures make up a pattern expressive of the novel's meaning. But instead of tracing the pattern in *Far from the Madding Crowd* as it emerges most directly, through the actions and motives of its persons, I want to emphasize two of the ways in which Hardy articulates it through relating his characters to the setting. The first of these—Hardy's naming of his

---

3. My Hardy quotations are from Harper's Anniversary Edition of *Far from the Madding Crowd* (New York and London, 1920).

men and women—is so evident that it needs little discussing.[4] Gabriel is as sturdy, as eminently natural, as an oak tree. Diametrically opposed to him is the Sergeant, whose name identifies that famous city which we perforce associate at least with weakness, given our many accounts of the fall of Troy, if not with decadence. The names Everdene and Boldwood do not formulate values quite so patly. But to my ear *Everdene* can hardly fail to echo *evergreen*; and according to the O.E.D., *dene* itself refers either to "a low standhill" or, as a variant of *dean*, to "a (wooded) vale." This linking of Bathsheba with the natural is thoroughly appropriate, for the novel insists that her fundamental commitment—though she deviates from it for a time in her infatuation with Troy—is to the land and to Gabriel. As for *Boldwood*, I think the name hints at a person somehow more than natural; in any case, the story shows us a man who, though he apparently *has* had his feet on the ground, is alienated from his farm and from himself through his obsessive pursuit of Bathsheba, and ends up as a murderer declared insane by the law. Even some of the minor figures bear names which mark out their allegiances in similar fashion, although Hardy is not absolutely consistent in this matter. Definitely members of the rustic group are Fanny Robin, Joseph Poorgrass, Matthew Moon; and doubtless Maryann Money belongs there as well in spite of her name. At this level of character the obvious outsider and villain is the bailiff whom Bathsheba discharges for stealing, the mercenary Pennyways, who finishes out the novel as the agent—predictably enough, given his name—of Troy. Clearly, then, Hardy does in effect evaluate many of this characters by the names he chooses for them.

The second way in which Hardy relates setting to character is less apparent, and one risks sounding impressionistic in talking about it. At or shortly after the introduction of each major figure, Hardy gives us a scene in which he uses the natural world to provide an oblique commentary on the person, the sense of which is verified through the rest of the novel. The first time that we see Gabriel Oak substantially located in a natural environment, for instance, is on Norcombe Hill. Of course in the opening chapter Hardy has already taken pains to distinguish him from the merely civilized world: by declaring Gabriel to be really at ease only "on working days" and "in his old clothes" (1); by laboring the joke about the watch which will not run and forces Oak to tell time by the stars; and by allowing Gabriel to announce the fault

4. Joseph Warren Beach has noted—in *The Technique of Thomas Hardy* (Chicago, 1922)—that the characters' "names are chosen largely for their combination of biblical and rustic associations" (p. 52), but he goes on to mention some of the biblical echoes only. The topic of Beach's section on *Far from the Madding Crowd* is setting, which he seems to view mainly as a kind of inspired local color. More-over, he makes its setting the major motive of the novel—which appears to him "primarily a reconstruction of a 'realistic dream country' " (p. 51)—and thus in effect denies the story a theme, as in commenting that the early Hardy "was treating a subject, but not a theme" and "took up," in the present novel, "the subject of Wessex country life" (p. 90).

of Bathsheba, whom he has glimpsed looking in her mirror, as "Vanity" (1). Then, after devoting two pages of the second chapter to the endurance, the spaciousness, the sublimity of Norcombe Hill and the night, Hardy places Gabriel in the scene by showing him attending to the lambing. After several more pages, indeed, Hardy relates the shepherd to the landscape even more directly by letting Gabriel read the time from the stars and by reporting that

> . . . he stood still after looking at the sky as a useful instrument, and regarded it in an appreciative spirit, as a work of art superlatively beautiful. For a moment he seemed impressed with the speaking loneliness of the scene, or rather with the complete abstraction from all its compass of the sights and sounds of man. (2)

The general effect of this Norcombe Hill sequence is to associate the qualities of the landscape with Gabriel, and he lives up to them in the narrative that follows. Several chapters later on the author refers specifically to Gabriel's "sublimity" (6). And towards the end of the novel, Hardy insists that Oak's moral status is almost more than human, as I understand the passage, by twice recording the shepherd's disagreement with an opinion which the law endorses, that Boldwood was insane when killing Troy. As for Gabriel's endurance, it is manifest in his unwavering love for Bathsheba throughout the story.

The scene in which we are introduced to Troy is a different as can be from the one on Norcombe Hill. Instead of the sublime, Hardy emphasizes the "dreariness" of a heavy snowfall (11); instead of a landscape vitalized by a multitude of minute natural details, we have a "moor" whose "irregularities were forms without features; suggestive of anything . . . and without more character than that of being the limit of something else—the lowest layer of a firmament of snow"; and most strikingly, instead of the spacious, the suffocating:

> The vast arch of cloud above was strangely low, and formed as it were the roof of a large dark cavern, gradually sinking in upon its floor; for the instinctive throught was that the snow lining the heavens and that encrusting the earth would soon unite into one mass without any intervening stratum of air at all. (11)

While Troy is not placed literally in this setting (as Fanny Robin is), the somberness of the landscape and its deathlike quality condition our response to him at least to the extent of preparing us for a person contrasting sharply with Oak, even though the suggestions of the landscape are not mirrored directly in Troy's character. He stays inside the barracks during the scene, parrying Fanny's plaintive attempts to set a time for their marriage and thus apparently amusing his companions. But it is appropriate that we should first hear Troy when he is in a society of sorts, set apart from the natural world, for he remains fundamentally estranged from it. (To be sure he is a "natural" child, but of a nobleman; and though more a native of Weatherbury than Oak or Bathsheba, he never seems thoroughly engaged in rural occupations, as they do—even in the passage about hiving the bees, Hardy stresses the flirtatious interplay between Bathsheba and Troy rather than the deed itself.) The most dramatic proof of the Sergeant's estrangement from nature appears in two incidents that I shall deal with later on. For the present, the critical fact to recognize is the absolute difference between the central feature of Troy's personality and a dominant characteristic of the natural world. That world is marked by the continuity of past and present, by the gradualness of its change, whereas Troy—so Hardy reiterates when analyzing him for us—is the slave of impulse, irrevocably committed to a present discontinuous with the past or with the future: "Simply feeling, considering, and caring for what was before his eyes, he was vulnerable only in the present. . . . That projection of consciousness into days gone by and to come . . . was foreign to Troy. With him the past was yesterday; the future, to-morrow; never, the day after" (25). Trapped so completely in the present, Troy can have no sense of an act's consequences, is therefore incapable of a moral decision. And nowhere in the story does Hardy permit him to be governed by anything except impulse, making even Troy's self-condemnation following the death of Fanny Robin a mere fit of remorse (46). But to come back to Troy and the landscape itself. It may be worth noting that the image of a "cavern" in the previous description of the snowfall finds vague echoes in the setting of Troy's first encounter with Bathsheba—the path roofed over and enclosed by trees which Hardy calls "a vast, low, naturally formed hall" (24)—and in the setting for the sword-exercise, a "hollow amid the ferns" (28).

The first scene in which we really became acquainted with Boldwood may remind us in several ways of the introduction of Troy. Once more the earth is covered with snow, and once more the tone is somber. But in this instance the landscape does mirror directly the condition of Boldwood. For he had just been knocked head over heels, as it were, by the anonymous valentine sealed with the message "Marry Me," never to right himself emotionally again. And of the natural world, Hardy writes at first:

> The moon shone to-night, and its light was not of a customary kind. His window admitted only a reflection of its rays, and the pale sheen had that reversed direction which snow gives, coming upward and lighting up his ceiling in an unnatural way, casting shadows in strange places, and putting lights where shadows had used to be. (14)

Then, as if to underline the "unnaturalness" of nature here, Hardy describes the same effect at sunrise, when Boldwood leaves the house:

> . . . the fields and sky were so much of one colour by the snow that it was difficult . . . to tell whereabouts the horizon occurred; and in general there was here, too, that before-mentioned preternatural inversion of light and shade which attends the prospect when the garish brightness com-

monly in the sky is found on the earth, and the shades of earth are in the sky.
(14)

However tempted we may be at times to sympathize with Boldwood, I
take it that we do feel his behavior to be unnatural and perverse from
here on, especially given the qualities attributed to nature and its
norm—Gabriel Oak—in *Far from the Madding Crowd*. Catapulted
immediately to an emotional extreme by the valentine, Boldwood
keeps thrusting his attentions on Bathsheba, through not one suit but
two, and the violence with which he declares to her his love, or anger,
or envy is a world away from the restrained dignity that typifies Oak.
The radical selfishness of Boldwood reveals itself in the fact that he
goes on exacting promises from her though he quite realizes that she
does not love him. Towards the end of the story, indeed, Hardy
underlines the degree of the man's perverseness by allowing Boldwood
to deny—though as a last desperate maneuver to win Bathsheba's
hand—that he himself loves her, to deny his own nature: "But do give
your word! A mere business compact, you know, between two people
who are beyond the influence of passion" (53). The novel does not,
however, stop at defining Boldwood as different from Oak; it tellingly
associates the gentleman farmer with Troy. For one thing, both of
them turn their backs on the natural world (if for different reasons) in
ignoring the storm that threatens their grain ricks. Besides, as
Boldwood's quest after Bathsheba continues, he becomes more and
more pointedly linked with a civilized world like Troy's. To image his
career oversimply, but not untruthfully: shortly after Boldwood enters
the story, we learn how he meditates in the barn, drawing comfort
from the nearness of the horses (18); towards the end of the novel, we
are shown him absorbed with his tailor in the fitting of a coat he will
wear to his Christmas party for Bathsheba (52). In fact, Hardy spells
out Boldwood's deviation from the natural and identifies the civilized
strain as evil when describing the preparations for the party: "Such a
thing had never been attempted before by its owner, and it was now
done as by a wrench. . . . A shadow seemed to move about the
rooms, saying that the proceedings were unnatural to the place and the
lone man who lived therein, and hence not good" (52).

Bathsheba does not have a scene in the natural world largely to
herself near her introduction into the novel, as do Oak and Boldwood;
nor are the landscapes against which we initially see her so powerfully
suggestive as the snowstorm at the introduction of Troy. Still, two of
our first three glimpses of her do supply a kind of commentary on
Bathsheba. If our first sight is of a girl on a wagon full of furniture who
glances at herself in a mirror, our third is of the same girl riding more
than skillfully in the woods, "quite at home," as Hardy says, "anywhere between a horse's head and its tail" (3). These vignettes hint, it
seems to me, at the impulses which conflict in Bathsheba, swaying her
now towards the socially refined and now towards the natural. At any

rate, the course of the story shows her to be a rather artless woman whose vanity temporarily ensnares her in the civilized world, embodied primarily here by Troy, and who escapes from it at last to come to terms with Gabriel. Even during her captivity, however, Hardy represents her as loving Troy to the depths of her being and as possessing absolute integrity, that integrity she manifests by remaining loyal to her husband after he has deserted her—or by continuing to accept the consequences of having once sent the valentine to Boldwood. The fact that Bathsheba does belong essentially to the natural world is indicated over and over by Hardy in the figurative language he applies to her—another of the ways in which he relates character to theme and keeps reminding us of the novel's meaning. Thus he describes the "rapidity" with which Bathsheba moves as "that of a kingfisher" and the "noiselessness that of a hawk" (3). Or he calls her "excited, wild, and honest as the day" (26). Or, in commenting on her response to Troy, Hardy takes his figure of speech from the world of fashion and redefines it expressly to ally her with the world valued in the story:

> Though in one sense a woman of the world, it was, after all, that world of daylight coteries and green carpets wherein cattle form the passing crowd and winds the busy hum; where a quiet family of rabbits or hares lives on the other side of your party-wall, where your neighbor is everybody in the tything, and where calculation is confined to market-days. Of the fabricated tastes of good fashionable society she knew but little, and of the formulated self-indulgence of bad, nothing at all. . . . Her love was entire as a child's, and though warm as summer it was fresh as spring. (29)

Bathsheba's affiliation to the world of nature is also brought out by several incidents in the novel, notably the one in which she is spiritually regenerated by a night in a thicket after breaking with Troy at Fanny's coffin. But it will be more interesting to consider this passage after we have observed some of the effects which Hardy achieves through his use of the natural world in particular incidents.

In the introductory scenes just discussed, the settings remain primarily settings. But in the four incidents now at hand, the natural world functions as something more than a background for events, and by the last of them it has explicitly become a moral agent. In the first one, the journey of Fanny Robin's body through Yalbury Great Wood in an autumn fog, we may still tend to view the landscape mainly as a setting, if an appropriate one. Yet even in this scene, the underlying impression conveyed is of nature sympathizing with Fanny. The effect arises in part from several phrases by which Hardy suggests that the natural world itself undergoes a death of sorts here—"There was no perceptible motion in the air, not a visible drop of water fell upon a leaf. . . . A startling quiet overhung all surrounding things . . ." (42)—and in part from the climax of the description, the condensed fog dropping from the trees onto the coffin, which one can hardly keep from reading as nature's tears at the death of Fanny. A kindred sense of nature's almost personal affection for Fanny has been dramatized rather bluntly by Hardy in one of the story's earlier events, not that we are ever allowed any doubts about the world that she belongs to, given her name and the civilized Troy's ruthless exploitation of her. Nevertheless, Hardy drives the point home in plotting Fanny's desperate trip through the night to reach the Casterbridge Union-house before she collapses, a struggle that succeeds only because a dog miraculously appears to tow her in. As Hardy depicts him (40), this dog seems a good deal less mere dog than nature's minister to Fanny. Just when "Hopelessness had come at last" to her, the dog materializes out of the natural surroundings: "From the stripe of shadow on the opposite side of the bridge a portion of shade seemed to detach itself. . . ." The description of the dog is consciously generalized, separating him from any particular breed and elevating him to something approaching a force of nature: "He seemed to be of too strange and mysterious a nature to belong to any variety. . . . He was the ideal embodiment of canine greatness—a generalization from what was common to all." And in his next sentence, Hardy identifies the dog directly with a nature capable of kindness: "Night, in its sad, solemn, and benevolent aspect, apart from its stealthy and cruel side, was personified in this form." The significance of the dog is clinched for us at the end of the journey when civilization, in the person of the attendant at the Union-house, stones away the friend that nature has given Fanny. What the whole episode means is beyond argument, surely, but I am less certain about how a reader responds to it. Hardy's account of Fanny's anguished efforts to get on, even before the dog turns up, by making herself crutches, by hanging on a fence, and by deceiving herself about the distance, seems on the face of it grossly sentimental. And the business of the dog arriving so opportunely, "frantic in his distress" to help her, appears in itself highly unlikely, if not incredible. Yet the episode actually affects us, I would guess, as neither crassly sentimental nor utterly implausible, precisely because it is so transparent an expression of the theme with which the novel is drenched that, when we come to the scene in context, we either accommodate it readily enough or never think to question its authenticity as fiction.

If the incidents just mentioned show the sympathy of the natural world for Fanny, the two that follow declare how hostile it is toward Troy. The first of them, the wild storm that climaxes the Sergeant's drinking party with the laborers in the barn and endangers the grain, serves also to contrast Troy with Oak again. Whereas Troy asserts, absurdly enough, his mastery over nature by denying that it will rain (36), Gabriel receives three separate warnings "direct . . . from the Great Mother" (36). Perhaps the power of the storm is supposed simply to mark nature's outrage as it answers Troy's obtuse claim. But the violent unnaturalness of the event, which Hardy recreates so memorably, strikes me rather as nature measuring in its own fashion the ascendancy that the civilized Troy has gained on Bathsheba's farm. He is, after all, recently married to her and "ruling now in the room of his wife", has just converted "harvest home" into a celebration of his wedding, and debauches the workmen by forcing them to drink brandy-and-water rather than the "cider and ale" natural to them (36)—thus incapacitating the whole party, of course, to deal with the threat of the elements to the grain, a task undertaken by Gabriel and an indignant Bathsheba. While in this storm nature appears to be evaluating Troy for us, in a later scene Hardy compels us to view the natural world as Troy's open antagonist and his moral judge. For the pouring of the cloudburst through the gurgoyle to wash out the flowers that Troy has planted on Fanny's grave is an act by which nature rejects him absolutely from its community and rebukes him for his belated effort to atone for his treatment of Fanny. The moral dimension of nature's deed is insisted upon by Hardy when he refers to "Providence" in describing the Sergeant's reaction to what has happened: ". . . to find that Providence, far from helping him into a new course . . . actually jeered his first trembling and critical attempt in that kind, was more than [Troy's] nature could bear" (46). Certainly this whole episode, like the one about Fanny and the dog, seems radically coincidental when viewed in the cold light of reason and probability. But again I suspect that, by the time we encounter it in our reading, Hardy has conditioned us so thoroughly to his theme that we come to terms with the incident almost instinctively. If this claim sounds too strong, it is at least clear that the incident articulates the theme of *Far from the Madding Crowd* once more and is to that extent domesticated in the novel.[5]

It is worth emphasizing here, as a mark of how intensively Hardy dramatizes his theme, that in the scene of Troy at Fanny's grave or of Fanny on Casterbridge highway the natural world is not employed symbolically. (I am using that word in its loosest sense, simply to designate a unit that does not contain all its meaning within itself, that stands in part for something else.) The cloudburst and the dog are natural forces, literal presences, which as it were enact the story's theme rather than represent it with any obliqueness.[6] And even in the other two scenes I think we apprehend nature directly, as a sheer being, a thing in itself, rather than as a symbolic vehicle which signifies indirectly.

Perhaps I can make clearer my sense of nature's non-symbolic

5. John Holloway finds the episode "unconvincing" in that "Hardy stresses a trivial incident at tedious length" (*The Victorian Sage*, p. 249). Overlong, perhaps, but I cannot agree with "trivial," for I think that in our reading we apprehend the incident as the climax in Troy's relationship with the natural world.

6. Here I am running counter to the argument of Richard C. Carpenter—in "Hardy's 'Gurgoyles,' " *Modern Fiction Studies* (Autumn, 1960), 227—that "the gargoyle sets the tone" of the cloudburst scene and "lets us know that this is a symbolic event, an instance of the disproportion that is art."

functioning in these incidents by glancing at one other in which a bit of landscape, a swamp, does work symbolically for a while. As a result of her bitter quarrel with Troy at Fanny's coffin, during which Bathsheba has heard him declare that he values the dead girl more than his living wife, she is so shaken that even suicide suggests itself to her—"A vehement impulse to flee from him . . . not stopping short of death itself, mastered Bathsheba now" (43)—and she rushes into the night. But a sleep under the trees cleanses her spirit, and against the "cool air and colours" of the morning, "her heated actions and resolves of the night stood out in lurid contrast" (44). Now she catches sight of a swamp nearby, one which Hardy makes into a symbol of her earlier despair (44). For he heaps up such noxious items as "rotting leaves" and "fungi" with "clammy tops" or "oozing gills," imparting to them a moral dimension by writing that "the general aspect of the swamp was malignant. From its moist and poisonous coat seemed to be exhaled the essences of evil things in the earth. . . ." And he concludes the description with "The hollow seemed a nursery of pestilence small and great, in the immediate neighborhood of comfort and health, and Bathsheba arose with a tremor at the thought of having passed the night on the brink of so dismal a place," words which in effect equate Bathsheba's physical with her moral situation. Another indication that this passage operates symbolically is the sense one has of a slight grinding in the gears when, on the next page, Hardy needs to use the swamp as a naturalistic fact at the appearance of Liddy Smallbury. Bathsheba tries to warn her against traversing it—still influenced, it would seem, by the symbolism of the swamp—but has lost her voice; and Liddy herself is forced by Hardy to acknowledge the swamp's dangers in remarking, "It will bear me up, I think." But as a matter of fact she crosses it safely enough: "Iridescent bubbles of dank subterranean breath rose from the sweating sod beside the waiting-maid's feet as she trod, hissing as they burst. . . . Liddy did not sink, as Bathsheba had anticipated" (44). One feels a subdued clash here between the frightfully dark colors with which Hardy paints the swamp, colors determined largely by its earlier symbolism, and Liddy's ready success in negotiating it. Yet whatever the flaws in Hardy's performance at this moment, his major point in these pages about Bathsheba's awakening is that she has found refuge from Troy in nature and been morally regenerated by that world.

The setting of *Far from the Madding Crowd* impinges upon the consciousness of the reader in many ways, then: in some incidents as mere setting, or as symbol, or as a being in its own right; often through the relationship of various sorts established between it and the characters; sometimes as a complex whole more or less explicitly evaluated for us by Hardy. And whatever its local role may be, the setting keeps mediating the novel's theme. But we should guard against reading too much into these conclusions. Although *Far from the Madding Crowd* does in fact seem to me a thoroughly achieved and compelling novel, the variety and number of uses to which Hardy puts the setting do not of themselves guarantee the book's success as art, any more than they can insure that Hardy's theme itself will convince the reader. Indeed, one can find in *Lady Chatterley's Lover,* curiously enough, almost as various a use of setting as Hardy's, the novel also revealing quite comparable governing structures and substantially the same theme— yet Lawrence's story fails dismally as fiction. So, while the foregoing analysis does make clear *Far from the Madding Crowd*'s saturation with its theme, it remains ultimately as limited as any formal analysis: which is capable of showing *how* the piece of literature works, but incapable of showing *that* it works, of closing with the essential vitality that allows the piece of literature to possess us.

ROY MORRELL

[Romance *versus* Realism]†

This novel is more typical of Hardy than a casual reading and a simplifying memory might indicate. The end, for example, is emphatically not a romantic happy-ever-after affair. We need not take Joseph Poorgrass's final 'it might have been worse' at quite its long-face value; and we can see the title of the final chapter ('A Foggy Night and Morning') as perhaps Hardy's way of touching wood: there is, indeed, a suppressed and sober, but none the less noticeable, elation about the tone of the end; but the fact remains that Gabriel is no Prince Charming for a girl of three- or four-and-twenty. Ahead of Gabriel and Bathsheba is no romance, but a reality that Hardy represents as more valuable, a reality of hard and good work on the two farms:

> He accompanied her up the hill, explaining to her the details of his forthcoming tenure of the other farm. They spoke very little of their mutual feelings; pretty phrases and warm expressions being probably unnecessary between such tried friends. Theirs was that substantial affection which arises (if any arises at all) when the two who are thrown together begin first by knowing the rougher sides of each other's character, and not the best till further on, the romance growing up in the interstices of a mass of hard prosaic reality . . . (56).

The trend of thought should by this time be familiar enough; but the passage also illustrates Hardy's 'hard prosaic'—sometimes awkward—way of thinking and writing, born of a conviction that the truth must be told, even if it cannot always be told attractively.

The distinction Hardy draws between romance and reality does not

†From *Thomas Hardy: The Will and the Way* (Kuala Lumpur: University of Malaya Press, 1965), pp. 59–64. The author's notes have been omitted.

appear only at the end of the book; it is worked into the scheme of the whole. In contrast to Gabriel Oak, the two other main male characters, Troy and Boldwood, one actively and the other passively, represent aspects of romantic unreality. Boldwood is the dreamer himself, and the unreality is in the way he approaches Bathsheba, seeing in her not a woman of flesh and blood, but a romantic dream. Troy, on the other hand, approaches Bathsheba realistically enough; but he is approached romantically *by her:* he seems to her a romantic figure and, initially, an escape from a dilemma into which the circumstances of her real everyday life have thrown her. Boldwood, for Bathsheba, has represented a certain social goal: propriety and respectability. For a short time, while he seems inaccessible, these things seem attractive to her; and it is these values that he tries to insist upon: the formal rightness of her keeping her 'promise', her duty to reciprocate the love she has aroused in him. There is cruelty in Boldwood's romanticism, in the way he insists that she shall adhere to his idea of her * * * but Boldwood suffers more than he makes Bathsheba suffer, and the wildness and unhappiness of his love is conditioned by his dream and his distance from reality:

> The great aids to idealization in love were present here: occasional observation of her from a distance, and the absence of social intercourse with her . . . the pettinesses that enter so largely into all earthy living and doing were diguised by the accident of lover and loved-one not being on visiting terms; and there was hardly awakened a thought in Boldwood that sorry household realities appertained to her . . . (19).

But Boldwood remains just as blind to realities when he gets to know her. After the disappearance of Troy, he again nourishes his love, but

> almost shunned the contemplation of it in earnest, lest facts should reveal the wildness of the dream (49).

It is a 'fond madness': and the anticlimax is the discovery (while Boldwood is in prison, awaiting trial) of all the jewellery and clothing labelled 'Bathsheba Boldwood', bought for a woman who had never promised to marry him (55).

Hardy is disparaging romance, the dream and the dreamer. He is suggesting, instead, that one should live—not in accordance with nature—but in accordance with reality. And this point is made clearly by the three choices to Bathsheba: Oak, Boldwood, and Troy. Boldwood, of course, ceases to attract her as soon as he forces his attentions on her: and there is a gentle irony in the fact that she sees in Troy, who has taken her away from Boldwood, something of what Boldwood has seen in her: a figure of romance, someone from another world. But it is not only Troy's glamour; it is also that 'arch-dissembler' Nature that prompts Bathsheba to love Troy. She goes to meet him, hesitates, and then surrenders her heart, in the chapter called 'The Hollow amid the Ferns'. The scene is one of great natural beauty, of lush growth:

> . . . tall thickets of brake fern, plump and diaphanous from recent rapid growth, and radiant in hues of clear and untainted green.
>
> At eight e'clock this midsummer evening, whilst the bristling ball of gold in the west still swept the tips of the ferns with its long, luxuriant rays, a soft brushing-by of garments might have been heard among them, and Bathsheba appeared in their midst, their soft, feathery arms caressing her up to her shoulders. She paused, turned, went back . . . (28).

But again she changes her mind, and goes on to the meeting place, a hollow where the fern

> grew nearly to the bottom of the slope and then abruptly ceased. The middle within the belt of verdure was floored with a thick flossy carpet of moss and grass intermingled, so yielding that the foot was half-buried within it.

Nature is softly inviting and reassuring her. She surrenders to Nature as much as to her lover,—to her own natural womanliness which, Hardy tells us, she normally had too much sense to be quite governed by (29). The treatment of this theme is more subtle, perhaps, and certainly more extended, in *Tess*; but it is effective in *Far from the Madding Crowd*, all the same.

Bathsheba's third possibility is Oak; whose name at least cannot be made to suggest *compliance* with nature, but rather sturdy resistance, hard use and endurance. The distinction Hardy draws at the beginning of the novel (2) between the intermingling sounds of one vast integrated body of Nature over Norcombe Hill, and the 'clearness' and 'sequence' of the 'notes of Farmer Oak's flute', runs right through the book. Gabriel Oak is not part of Nature. He may be a countryman, but he is always a human being, fully conscious of his human responsibility, always ready to modify, to deflect, to improve, Nature's workings; always, that is, after his first setback. A 'natural' sequence of events destroys his sheep; but he does not see himself as a victim of fate—as Troy would have done. *   *   * He realizes he is ruined, and that, not having insured his sheep, he himself is to blame. And his second thought is that things would be even worse if Bathsheba had married him:

> 'Thank God I am not married: what would she have done in the poverty now coming upon me?'

Thereafter he intervenes in the natural sequence of events in as timely a fashion as he can. He prevents the fire from spreading to the ricks and buildings of Bathsheba's farm (6); he cures the poisoned sheep (21); he saves Bathsheba's harvest from the storm (36, 37); and he tries to intervene, but unsuccessfully, before Boldwood's optimistic dreams lead to disaster (52, iii and vi), and before Bathsheba gives way to her infatuation for Troy:

> . . . But since we don't exactly know what he is, why not behave as if he *might* be bad, simply for your own safety? Don't trust him, mistress . . ." (29).

—Gabriel's version of Hardy's own advice to take 'a full look at the Worst'. But Oak's attitude towards Nature is best seen in the account of the storm, because here Nature appears in her two aspects: creator and destroyer. She is prepared, but for Gabriel, to destroy the harvest she has bounteously created; and it is Gabriel's appreciation of the bounty, his sense of its meaning in terms of human life and sustenance, that makes him put forth all his strength to save the bounty from the destruction and to pit himself against the whole scheme of things, the whole trend of circumstances at that time. He fights not only against elemental nature, but against 'nature's' hold on the humanity around him: Troy's insidiously easy-going ways (' "Mr Troy says it will not rain, and he cannot stop to talk to you about such fidgets" '), the only too natural sleepiness and inertia of the drunken workfolk in the barn, and his own natural fears when the threat of the lightning becomes too great. The critics who suppose that Hardy shared and advocated the philosophic resignation of some of his rustics should read again the thirty-sixth and thirty-seventh chapters of *Far from the Madding Crowd*: if ever a man had the excuse of surrendering, of saying 'It was to be', Oak has the excuse on the night of the storm. Instead, he fights.

Yet throughout his fight, there remains a sense in which Nature's opposition is 'neutral'; nothing is purposely aimed against Oak. The chances mount against him; but they are still chances. And he seeks to keep ahead of them; he gets a lightning conductor improvised. Had there been any malicious purpose, an earlier flash of lightning would have struck him down. It is a fight between a man intelligently directing his efforts and 'senseless circumstance'. Oak persists; and he wins. He is not quite alone; in the latter part of the night he is helped by Bathsheba. The scene is one of many in the novels that vividly suggest the need of the human pair for each other, the individual's comparative—sometimes complete—helplessness alone.

There is another side to Gabriel's feeling for Nature: he fights her successfully because he understands and can sympathetically interpret the doings not only of his sheep, but also of Nature's smaller creatures—slug, spiders and toad (36). He seeks to learn from Nature; for instance, from the sprig of ivy that has grown across the door of the church tower, proving that Troy has *not* been in the habit of entering here modestly and unobserved (as Bathsheba too readily believes), and that Troy is, therefore, a liar (29). Nature is one of Gabriel's resources; but he is never controlled by her, nor, in any Wordsworthian sense, does he ever trust her. The essential thing about Gabriel is not that he is in contact with Nature, but that he is in contact with reality. He neither evades it nor resigns himself to it; he makes something out of it.

This point is effectively made by a metaphor embodied in an incident early in the book, just at the turning point of Oak's fortunes, when he has proved he can survive even the worst that life has to offer and when his luck (if such a word can be used) is at last on the mend. He is drinking cider in the Malthouse, and has just endeared himself to the Weatherbury folk by refusing the luxury of a clean cup:

> 'And here's a mouthful of bread and bacon that mis'ess have sent, shepherd. The cider will go down better with a bit of victuals. Don't ye chaw quite close, shepherd, for I let the bacon fall in the road outside as I was bringing it along, and may be 'tis rather gritty. There, 'tis clane dirt; and we all know what that is, as you say, and you bain't a particular man we see, shepherd.'
> 'True, true—not at all,' said the friendly Oak.
> 'Don't let your teeth quite meet, and you won't feel the sandiness at all. Ah! 'tis wonderful what can be done by contrivance!'
> 'My own mind exactly, neighbour.' (8).

The incident is a precise metaphor of what Oak has been doing in the wider sphere of his life: he has had his share of 'unpalatable reality', but by contrivance he has managed to find life's grittiness not so 'unpalatable' after all.

Hardy's attitudes and themes in this novel are, indeed, typical; what is not typical is the method: he is presenting his main theme—the value of pessimism as a practical policy ('. . . You cannot lose at it, you may gain . . .') through a pessimist, a central character who is successful. He is presenting it, that is, positively, instead of through the failure of a hero who is too optimistic or unrealistic.

* * *

ALAN FRIEDMAN

[Innocence, Expansion, and Containment]†
* * *

I. *Bathsheba's Innocence*

In the peevish but precise words of Henry James, who did not find Hardy's heroine to his taste,

> the young lady is flirt, and encourages them all [her shepherd, her neighbor, and her soldier]. . . . We cannot say that we either understand or like Bathsheba. She is a young lady of the inconsequential, wilful, mettlesome type.

The lady, her shepherd, her neighbor, and her soldier: these are the four principal *dramatis personae*. But the expansion of inward experience in *Far from the Madding Crowd* centers on the life of Bathsheba

†From *The Turn of the Novel* (New York: Oxford University Press, 1966), pp. 38–48. The author's footnotes have not been reprinted, and the original page references have been changed to chapter references provided in parentheses in the text.

Everdene, and her experience (as James suggests) is centered on marriage. Not that the young lady *desires* marriage; on the contrary, throughout the earlier part of the story, she concentrates on avoiding it. In her innocence, when she cries out against matrimony, she does so in tones and language which strongly suggest Hardy's own Sue Bridehead of twenty years later; but strikingly, Bathsheba sounds even more strongly the personal tone of D. H. Lawrence's Ursula Brangwen in *Women in Love*, forty-five years later: "I *hate* to be thought men's property in that way, though possibly I shall be had some day." The voice just quoted is, oddly, Bathsheba's, not Ursula's.

Bathsheba's independence seems to have offended James. But the permutations, climax, and denouement of her experience are built directly on that independence: on a very highhanded flirtatiousness, on her masculine energy, on her willfulness. In point of fact, as the following discussion intends to show, the form of the story Hardy tells deliberately takes shape as a "taming" of the heroine. The action is therefore planned to allow the broadest possible scope at first for what James finds objectionable: the young lady's high-spirited, mannish tendencies; gradually to chasten, torment, and weaken her; and finally to make her manageable—in fact, to make her beg to be managed.

From the very first chapter, what Hardy intends to convey about Bathsheba—tediously, clumsily, but at any rate clearly—is her temperamental disposition to exercise control over men. In chapter one (Gabriel Oak conveniently spying for us), we learn, as she regards her features in a mirror, that she imagines "dramas in which men would play a part—vistas of probable triumphs" (1). She will soon triumph—the right word—without yielding herself in love. In chapter two (Oak helpfully eavesdropping), we learn that Bathsheba, hard at work, wishes she were "rich enough to pay a man to do these things" (2). She will soon be rich enough. And in chapter three (Oak still unobserved), we learn that she rides a horse first like a boy, leaning over backwards, "her head over its tail, her feet against its shoulders"; and then like a man, with her legs spread "in the manner demanded by the saddle, though hardly expected of the woman."

Almost at once Bathsheba rescues Oak from probable death by suffocation (3). She is rapidly becoming the novel's central actor—its center of masculine energy and movement. Then, as he lets go her hand, she teases him:

> "You may have it again if you like; there it is."

> . . .

> "There—that's long enough," said she, though without pulling it away. "But I suppose you are thinking you would like to kiss it? You may if you want to."
> "I wasn't thinking of any such thing," said Gabriel simply; "but I will—"
> "That you won't!" She snatched back her hand.

> . . .

"Now find out my name," she said teasingly; and withdrew. (3)

Pages later, "waving a white handkerchief" and "panting like a robin" (4), she races after Oak to explain, "I ran after you to say—that my aunt made a mistake in sending you away from courting me" (4). Now as Bathsheba herself is at pains to make clear, her eagerness does not constitute a proposal of marriage, not even an explicit "wanting" of Oak. "Why, if I'd wanted you I shouldn't have run after you like this" (4). Nevertheless, that highly qualified "proposal" is the seed from which the novel will flower. It is the first of a series of increasingly audacious initiatives in love and of increasing direct "proposals" to her menfolk, audacities which will refer down to the final chapters. As for any actual marriage, she explains, "I should feel triumphant, and all that. But a husband—" (4).

Every event, then, has until this early point in the novel developed Bathsheba's moral disposition as that of a flirtatious "young lady of the . . . wilful, mettlesome type." (I omit James's "inconsequential." Without benefit of the hindsight which shows us Lawrence, and with Hardy's own Sue Bridehead still twenty years in the offing, James can be forgiven for dismissing Bathsheba as of little consequence.) Then, in an abrupt and surprisingly cool reversal of herself, Bathsheba "predicts" her own quite opposite need and outlines the shape of her experience to come: "I want somebody to tame me; I am too independent; and you would never be able to, I know" (4). It will take in fact three men to tame Bathsheba: principally and most violently of course Sergeant Troy; but more gradually, Farmer Boldwood and Gabriel Oak will also contribute in essential ways.

Less than two pages further on, Bathsheba's independence of spirit becomes an economic independence as well. With fairytale speed, charm, and luck, the girl is suddenly elevated to power and prosperity by an unexpected legacy; Oak is reduced to poverty and dependence by a disaster to his flock of sheep; and the next great movement, the vast opening outward of the novel, is set to begin.

2. The Expansion

For the next one hundred pages, roughly, Bathsheba is presented to the reader as "Farmer Everdene's niece; took on Weatherbury Upper Farm; turned away the baily, and swears she'll do everything herself" (12)—presented as farmer, employer, overseer, paymaster, and grain salesman. But though Bathsheba shatters conventions right and left, the center of the explosion is made clear enough: "there was potentiality enough in that lithe slip of humanity for alarming exploits of sex, and daring enough to carry them out" (12). We can safely concentrate our critical attention there.

When she discovers that there is only one farmer in the neighborhood who has failed to notice her charms, she sends him a valentine:

"Carnation's sweet / And so are you." And—worse—"Marry Me"
(13). The man thus boldly wooed is Farmer Boldwood. (The play on
words in his name extends in several directions, most notably to the
opposition of "-wood—Oak"; Gabriel Oak, who continues to love
Bathsheba and turns out to be—as his first name suggests—her guardian angel, yields his last name to a barrage of sub-puns in the text,
e.g., "What a way Oak had, she thought, of enduring things"—(43).
Enthralled by the heroine's careless valentine, Boldwood becomes her
second victim in love: she remains heart-whole.

But in the wars of courtship, Bathsheba's genius for dominating the
field without yielding (either her person or her feelings) suffer a first
setback. A soldier inflicts the opening wound. The metaphor of battle
is implicit in Hardy's vocabulary: "brass and scarlet,' "sound of a
trumpet" (24); "I am not of steel," "the gathers of her dress began to
give way like lilliputian musketry" (24).

The taming of Bathsheba now begins in earnest; and "taming" is
here to be understood in an almost literal sense, as if Hardy has at the
back of his mind the metaphor of the breaking of an untamed horse.
(We recall the heroine's expertness with horses in the opening chapters.) Bathsheba receives an "instantaneous check" (24) which throws
her "off her balance." She has been caught on, of all things, a spur. In
the very first instant of their very first meeting, Sergeant Troy's spur
(with Hardy's excellent aim) goes directly for the weakest spot in her
defense, her skirt: ". . . something tugged at her skirt and pinned it
forcibly to the ground" (24). For the full force of the event, it may be
worth recalling Hardy's comment on a woman's dress in his earliest
published novel, *Desperate Remedies*:

> . . . to a woman her dress is part of her body . . . her dress has sensation.
> Crease the very Ultima Thule of fringe or flounce, and it hurts her as much
> as pinching her. . . . Go to the uppermost: she is there; tread on the lowest:
> the fair creature is there almost before you. (20)

Troy, in his frank manner, treads on the lowest: Bathsheba is there
before him. Together they recite a magical spell, almost their cate-
chism:

> "Are you a woman?"
> "Yes."

*   *   *

> "I am a man."
> "Oh!" (24)

The darkness in which Hardy allows them to meet provides him with
the excuse his realism requires for that incantatory dialogue. And
amply guarded with similar excuses, the expansion of Bathsheba's
experience now proceeds both symbolically and by a series of *double-
entendre*. Bathsheba tries to free her dress from Troy's spur. For the

first time in a relationship with a man, she finds herself in "a position of captivity"—"You are a prisoner, miss" (24)—where she must absolutely forfeit something. The wordplay on marriage to her soldier is driven home with a bludgeon as she struggles to free herself ("hitched," "hooked," "the knot of knots which there's no untying"— (24); but sexual captivity and forfeit are adumbrated much more cautiously: "she could free herself at the risk of leaving her skirt bodily behind her" (24). "Bodily" is suggestive, almost superfluously so. The sentence that originally followed four lines further on was apparently so suggestive that it was withdrawn from the text after it had come out in the serialized version. "And then, her appearance with half a skirt gone!"

Troy's spur gives place to his sword, and the stylized attack on Bathsheba's body and freedom of movement proceeds in the chapter which describes the ritualistic swordplay in the Hollow amid the Ferns: "stand as still as a statue" (28) . . . and "you have been within half an inch of being pared alive two hundred and ninety-five times" (28).

Significantly, Hardy now goes out of his way to mislead the reader by suggestion and implication, into thinking that he is witnessing the swift development of an illicit liaison between the two lovers. For several chapters the narrative point of view is carefully restricted for the most part to other characters, who surmise the worst. In chapter thirty-two Bathsheba, like a gypsy or a thief, disappears from her house and is tracked down on the highroad in the middle of the night: she has stolen away from her retainers to run after her Sergeant lover. "Ladies don't drive at these hours, miss, as a jineral rule of society" (32). In chapter thirty-three she who has always "concealed from the world under a manner of carelessness the warm depths of her strong emotions", is espied alone in Bath with her Sergeant, "talking moving things, and once she was crying a'most to death". And in chapter thirty-four Farmer Boldwood, who not far back has already concluded that she is a "sweet, lost coquette", now concludes that she has become Troy's mistress. Unseen, Boldwood hears her invite Troy to her bed in this style:

> "There's not a soul in the house but me tonight. I've packed them all off, so nobody on earth will know of your visit to your lady's bower."

On the basis of the information so far presented, the conscientious reader, too, must arrive at the same (unjust) conclusion. But we are of course, all of us, wrong. Troy produces a marriage license. Having carefully misled us, Hardy melodramatically corrects us. Bathsheba's history has apparently not been leading her into an illicit sexual experience (as do the histories of Eustacia, Lucetta, Tess, and Sue) but directly into marriage. Apparently: for, as we shall see, Hardy has not really misled us at all, and Bathsheba's perfectly legal marriage will turn out to be exactly the "illicit" sexual relationship he has so far been at pains to suggest.

"Of love subjectively she knew nothing" (13) when, lightly, she sent Boldwood the valentine which affected him so cruelly. In the realignment and expansion of emotions that follow her marriage, she experiences the utter abjectness of her dependence upon Troy's light feeling for her—which, as he rapidly becomes indifferent to her, takes on more and more overtly the form of cruelty. The taming proceeds apace, again almost literally. When Bathsheba inquires, with intuitive suspicion, the name of a woman whom she "thinks" Troy knows (and who is in fact his former mistress, Fanny Robin), Troy tells her to

"Think if you will, and be—" The sentence was completed by a smart cut of the whip around Poppet's flank . . . (39)

And no long after, she finds herself begging, "Now, anything short of cruelty will content me. Yes! the independent and spirited Bathsheba is come to this" (43). The subjugation has been rapid: the cut of Troy's whip now becomes the pain of "dry-eyed sobs, which cut as they came" And—

She was conquered. . . . [*Once*] it had been a glory to her to know that her lips had been touched by no man's on earth. . . . She hated herself now.

* * *

Soon Fanny Robin dies, and Bathsheba sinks to the morbidity of opening her rival's coffin and to the humiliation of begging her husband for love. When Troy, in an outburst of necrophilic tenderness, kisses the golden-haired corpse of Fanny Robin, Bathsheba pleads with him to "kiss me too, Frank—kiss me!" (43). And at this point the earlier "misleading" hints of illicitness and immorality are uncovered again. Troy tells Bathsheba that, before God at least, Fanny Robin is his "very, very wife!" (43).

"If she's—that,—what—am I?" Deliberately phrased that way, Bathsheba's question virtually suggests an unpleasant answer for which a variety of words must have been available to Troy. He uses none of them; Hardy spares his readers that. But Troy's answer returns to the earlier, elaborate suggestion of an illicit passion barely palliated by a marriage certificate, and his words are perhaps ultimately more degrading.

"You are nothing to me—nothing," said Troy heartlessly. "A ceremony before a priest doesn't make a marriage. I am not morally yours."

Their marriage dies that instant—so Hardy tells us. But Bathsheba's reaction next morning, in her advice to a maidservant, is worth noticing: "If ever you marry . . . don't you flinch. Stand your ground, and be cut to pieces" (44). We remember the cut of the spur, the sword, the whip. She *will* stand her ground and be cut to pieces:

the explosive process of narrative experience has not yet reached its most terrible pitch. We are, as it were, watching that explosion (or expansion) in mid-career, and it will behoove us in our exploration of her experience as a form, to observe *when* Bathsheba's experience attains its greatest intensity, and to ascertain *whether*—and *in what sense*—the explosion of her experience is finally contained. We can put all of this in Hardy's terms.

"Emotional convulsions seemed to have become the common-places of her history," Bathsheba reflects when Fanny is at last in her grave and Troy has left her. And yet emotional convulsions keep coming, deepening, and intensifying: Troy ostensibly "drowns"; then Bathsheba is gradually hectored and manipulated into accepting Farmer Boldwood's renewed proposal of marriage. Hardy's biggest gun, the emotional and moral climax of the plot, has now been mounted. When, at the very instant she actually accepts Boldwood's dubious proposal, Troy appears in the doorway, wrapped up to his eyes in a cloak, like a devil come from hell to avenge her sin, her emotional convulsions—the combined intensification and degradation of her experience—reach the point of absolute moral extremity.

In fiction, those moments—or those many pages—which render a central character's realization that life has become morally impossible are often accompanied (is it only in fiction?) by the onset of illness and fever: the very intensity of the moral explosion brings on a physical deterioration. And not infrequently, those fully expanded and inten-sified moments in the structure are also accompanied by the sugges-tion of mental derangement—hallucination or insanity. Perhaps we are justified in regarding these processes as literary "rituals" or conventions—drawn of course from cultural conventions and psychological observation—which not only render but also mark the fullness of the formal expansion of experience.

"Ritual" events of this kind now occur in *Far from the Madding Crowd* over a sequence of about ten pages. At Troy's incredible reappearance in the midst of the celebration, Bathsheba wonders "whether it were not all a terrible illusion" (53). And "her mind was totally deprived of light" (53). When Troy seizes her to carry her off, "she writhed and gave a quick, low scream." Immediately, Boldwood shoots Troy. Bathsheba then performs "deeds of endurance" which require "superhuman strain" (54). She undresses Troy's corpse and lays it out in graveclothes; when it is over, the "simple consciousness that superhuman strain was no longer required . . . put a period to her power to continue it." She cries, "—how can I live! O Heaven, how can I live!" She remains prostrate in bed for months while a last blow, the possibility that Boldwood will be executed for the shooting, hangs over her. " 'I do so hope his life will be spared,' said Liddy. 'If it is not, she'll go out of her mind too' " (55).

3. *The Containment of The Expansion*

The rapid resolution of Bathsheba's intense distress now begins. Boldwood's life is spared by the Home Secretary, and

> Bathsheba revived with the spring. The utter prostration that had followed the low fever from which she had suffered diminished perceptibly. . . . (56)

A slow return toward (not to) the more narrowly limited moral situation that obtained at the opening of the book begins to take place. Hardy reminds us that "two years ago [Bathsheba] was a romping girl, and now she's this!" (55). Two years: four hundred and forty-five pages. The road back (though of course not all the way back) takes about eight months: but barely fifteen pages of the text.

Before giving us the events which will narrow the now widespread moral "desolation" (56) of Bathsheba's life, Hardy explicitly adds up the extent of the damage. Her lovers are all gone. Her masculine energy has been laid waste: "it seemed to herself that she never could again acquire energy sufficient to go to market, barter, and sell." Oak, who has been managing her farm, plans to leave for California. She believes he despises her and, worse, she believes that his love has been "withdrawn just at his own pleasure." The taming, the cutting down of Bathsheba to size, has been completed.

The restorative process of the ending, most notably the renewed "proposal" of marriage which Bathsheba makes to Oak, is accompanied by frequent suggestions of a return to Bathsheba's girlhood. We are told, when she calls upon Oak in the evening, "doubtful if it were right for a single woman to call upon a bachelor who lived alone, although he was her manager" (56), that "their lives seemed to be moved back again to the days when they were strangers" (56). She reminds the reader and Gabriel that "I was the first sweetheart that you ever had, and you were the first I ever had; and I shall not forget it!" And at last she admits "with a slight laugh, as they went to the door, 'it seems exactly as if I had come courting you— . . .' " (56). Gabriel's reply—" 'And quite right, too,' said Oak"—is a mild vengeance.

The containment of her intense experience can, of course, be only partial at best. "Bathsheba smiled (for she never laughed readily now) . . ." (57) is Hardy's final comment. But not much more than a page before the book ends, and immediately before she is married, Bathsheba's horrific experience is squeezed down into (of all things) a modified girlishness:

> Repose had again incarnadined her cheeks; and having, at Gabriel's request, arranged her hair this morning as she had worn it years ago on Norcombe Hill, she seemed in his eyes remarkably like the girl of that fascinating dream. . . . (57)

*   *   *

J. HILLIS MILLER

[Point of View]†

* * *

A few pages of *Far from the Madding Crowd* offer an opportunity to watch in detail the advance and retreat of the narrator's consciousness as he identifies himself with his characters or moves so far away in time and space that the story he tells seems only an arbitrary example of laws valid everywhere at all times.

Chapter 22, "The Great Barn and the Sheep-Shearers," is memorable for its lively description of a sheep-shearing in a southwestern county of England. As Mario Praz might put it, the chapter forms a genre picture rich in precise detail, carrying a stamp of authenticity no reader can question. [1] Hardy has obviously seen what he describes, and the re-creation by his narrator of this high point in the sheep farmer's year is a good example of what is meant by "realism" in Victorian fiction—the more or less photographic representation of a specific historical reality. Against this background a certain moment of rearrangement in the relations of Bathsheba, Oak, and Boldwood takes place. My interest here is in the constant shifts of temporal and spatial perspective which form the narrative rhythm of the chapter. At one moment the reader is sharing a close observation of the events and an identification with the characters. At the next he is so far away in time and space that the events are seen from a godlike distance and with a godlike objectivity. Sometimes the reader is explicitly put in both these positions at once. In fact the alternation is so constant that the effect of the narrator's language is to maintain the reader simultaneously both close and distant throughout. As soon as the reader seems about to relax in his closeness, the narrator says something which throws him off to a great distance again, and like a juggler keeping two balls in the air, the narration sustains both points of view at once.

Though the narrative technique of a novel like *Far from the Madding Crowd* is a complex matter, making use of many conventions and habits of language inherited from earlier fiction, the reader of novels becomes so agile in the changes of point of view demanded of him that he is usually not aware of the imaginative gymnastics he is performing. Only if he makes an act of reflection on his experience as he reads,

†From *Thomas Hardy: Distance and Desire* (Cambridge, Mass.: Harvard University Press, 1970), pp. 57–70. The author's page references have been deleted.

1. For Praz's exploration of the parallel between Victorian fiction and genre-painting, see *La Crisi dell'eroe nel romanzo vittoriano* (Florence: G. C. Sansoni, 1952); trans. Angus Davidson, *The Hero in Eclipse in Victorian Fiction* (London and New York: Oxford University Press, 1956).

holds his experience at arm's length and looks at it, will he notice the complex superimposition of perspectives which structures a chapter of apparently straightforward realistic narrative. In order to make the reading of chapter 22 of *Far from the Madding Crowd* an experience at the second power, an experience conscious of its quality as experience, the reader must ask himself throughout the reading where he is being placed as a watcher and what is being presented to fill up the span of his attention.

The chapter opens with a generalization valid for all men in all times and places: "Men thin away to insignificance and oblivion quite as often by not making the most of good spirits when they have them as by lacking good spirits when they are indispensable."

The reader at this point is nowhere and at no specified time, looking at no particular scene in the novel. He is merely listening to the disembodied voice of the narrator. After the narrator's expression of a universal judgment three sentences follow describing Gabriel Oak's habitual state of mind and habitual action at this time of his life: "But his incurable loitering beside Bathsheba Everdene stole his time ruinously." There is still no particular scene to put before the mind's eye. The universal generalization has led to specific generalizations located in no particular place or action, but covering an entire period of Gabriel's life. It is impossible to tell whether Gabriel's "loitering" is to be thought of literally or figuratively, though it appears to be the latter—a way of saying that Gabriel spent much time thinking about Bathsheba.

The next paragraph moves finally to a specific scene located definitely in time and space. This scene is initially, however, the landscape of a whole region. The first sentence ("It was the first day of June, and the sheep-shearing season culminated, the landscape, even to the leanest pasture, being all health and colour") is followed by a list of flowers, "flossy catkins," "fern-sprouts like bishops' croziers," and so on. These flowers are either given in the plural or are collective names ("the toothwort"). The reader still has no local scene to imagine, but has only been told the sorts of flowers he would have encountered at that time on a walk through the countryside of Wessex. Only at the end of this paragraph, in a list of the men engaged in the sheep-shearing and in a description of their clothes, does the point of view narrow to a particular scene.

This narrowing leads to an elaborate picture of the shearing-barn in the next two paragraphs. Here at last the reader stands in imagination before a scene which he might view in one look if the novel were the real world or a stage set. This focusing of the point of view, however, is qualified by language which gives the reader a temporal perspective on the barn which no physical vision, cinema, or stage set could provide. The barn as it presently looks is placed in the context of the mind's knowledge of its four centuries of existence. The reader sees the present in the perspective of the past, with that double vision so characteristic of Hardy: "Standing before this abraded pile, the eye regarded its present usage, the mind dwelt upon its past history, with a satisfied sense of functional continuity throughout."

The beginning of the next paragraph returns the reader firmly to the present: "To-day the large side doors were thrown open towards the sun to admit a bountiful light to the immediate spot of the shearers' operations." This is followed by the detailed description of the sheep-shearing which occupies much of the remaining nine pages of the chapter. This presentation is so direct, so immediate in time and space, that it falls naturally at one point into the historical present, a narrative tense Hardy does not often use: "Cainy now runs forward with the tar-pot. 'B.E.' is newly stamped upon the shorn skin." Nevertheless, such immediacy and precision of representation, which makes this part of the chapter read like a motion picture scenario, is held within the wide temporal and spatial context established at the beginning of the chapter and sustained by echoes of this distancing throughout the direct reporting. An example is the narrator's reminder to the reader that the dress and speech of the rustics are as traditional as the barn is old and make of their actions something approaching a timeless ritual. The peasants have little awareness of historical time; the narrator is vividly aware of it: "This picture of to-day in its frame of four hundred years ago did not produce that marked contrast between ancient and modern which is implied by the contrast of date. . . . Five decades hardly modified the cut of a gaiter, the embroidery of a smock-frock, by the breadth of a hair. Ten generations failed to alter the turn of a single phrase. In these Wessex nooks the busy outsider's ancient times are only old; his old times are still new; his present is futurity."

Another example of the maintaining of narrative distance in the midst of close-up reporting is the description of Maryann, who, "with her brown complexion, and the working wrapper of rusty linsey, had at present the mellow hue of an old sketch in oils—notably some of Nicholas Poussin's." None of the characters of the novel is thinking of Poussin at this moment, and most of them have never heard of him. The comparison establishes the narrator as a knowledgeable man of culture watching the scene with the detachment of a connoisseur, as if it were a painting. He places it in a historical and cultural context of which the participants in the scene are unaware. The presentation of the scene as though it were being recorded objectively by a camera is reinforced by various statements establishing a wide temporal and spatial perspective for it, the whole Wessex landscape in June, the four-hundred-year history of the barn, the context of European painting. To watch the scene with cool detachment as an invisible spectator is already to be more separated from the scene than any participant in it, and the interspersed notations preserving a wider mental withdrawal help to sustain this uninvolved observation of what is there to be seen and heard. The reader is held simultaneously within and without, close and distant.

The closeness, however, is more than that attainable by an imaginary spectator crouched in the rafters of the barn and watching the sheep-shearing below. Against the background of the rural ritual which is represented with such photographical fidelity is performed one of those dramas of self-consciousness and consciousness of others which make up the texture of Hardy's fiction. Such a texture means that much of his writing presents careful notation of what his characters think, do, or say as they live from moment to moment. More precisely, the characters are conscious of themselves in terms of their consciousness of others. This interaction between minds is not shown from the outside as something the narrator watches in detachment. It is presented from within, as something experienced directly. If the picture of a Wessex sheep-shearing is embraced within a context of knowledge implicitly as wide as all history, that picture in its turn embraces the inside of the inside, three of the central characters of the story in a crucial moment of their awareness of one another. This awareness is not fully shared by any of the other characters, but they are shown as in part sensitive to what is going on. The sensitivity of Bathsheba, Oak, and Boldwood to one another, and the narrator's power to enter into this sensitivity are made plausible by their emergence from a milieu of sympathetic understanding within which all the characters dwell. In varying degrees all the characters possess a power of intuitive knowledge of others. So Bathsheba stands over Gabriel as he shears, and Gabriel silently enjoys the blissful feeling "that his bright lady and himself formed one group, exclusively their own, and containing no others in the world." His silence and her evasive chatter are the outward signs of an intense flow of emotion between them, a pressure of mutual awareness generated by his love for her and by her unwillingness to recognize or return that love. "There is," says the narrator, "a loquacity that tells nothing, which was Bathsheba's; and there is a silence which says much: that was Gabriel's."

The lines of force created by this communication beyond words or beside words is interrupted by the entry of Boldwood. Boldwood's presence, even before he speaks, magically alters the pattern of interpersonal awareness within the barn, not only for Gabriel, but even for the relatively uninvolved rustics. Hardy is aware as much as George Meredith or Henry James of the power which the entry of another person may exert on an individual or on a group: "Boldwood always carried with him a social atmosphere of his own, which everybody felt who came near him; and the talk, which Bathsheba's presence had somewhat suppressed, was now totally suspended." If all the people in the barn respond to Boldwood's presence, Bathsheba and Oak are even more sensitive to it. Boldwood's coming changes them not only in their relation to him, but in their relation to one another. The narrator offers the reader an exact registration of the dynamics of these changes. Bathsheba responds to Boldwood by altering her way of speaking: "she instinctively modulated her own [tones] to the same pitch, and her voice ultimately even caught the inflection of his." The narrator then gives the general law of which this change of behavior is an example: "woman at the impressionable age gravitates to the larger body not only in her choice of words, which is apparent every day, but even in her shades of tone and humour when the influence is great." Gabriel's reaction to Boldwood's entrance is given not through a description of changes in his overt behavior, but by a penetration directly within his mind. The chapter here approaches as close as it has yet come to indirect discourse: "Standing beside the sheep already shorn, they went to talking again. Concerning the flock? Apparently not. Gabriel theorized, not without truth, that in quiet discussion of any matter within reach of the speakers' eyes, these are usually fixed upon it." The narrator's point of view here coincides with Gabriel's, and the reader momentarily sees through Gabriel's eyes as he watches without being watched—that activity so often performed by Hardy's protagonists.

Gabriel is so upset by what he sees that he accidentally cuts the sheep he is shearing and is rebuked by Bathsheba. This episode leads to the most complex recording of the interaction between minds given in this chapter, a recording which includes five persons in their reactions to one another. There are references to an hypothetical unknowing outsider, to Oak's sensitive awareness of Boldwood and Bathsheba, to her awareness of him, to his awareness of her awareness of him, and the omniscient narrator embraces all these interactions in a single view. If the novel is a form of literature developed to explore the nuances of interpersonal relations, so adept do writers and readers become at following the complexities of such relations, perhaps because they are so expert at it in real life, that only a somewhat artificial interrogative stepping back brings to the surface the echoing crisscross of responses, mind answering to mind, recorded in an apparently simple passage: "To an outsider there was not much to complain of in this remark [Bathsheba's remonstrance]; but to Oak, who knew Bathsheba to be well aware that she herself was the cause of the poor ewe's wound, because she had wounded the ewe's shearer in a still more vital part, it had a sting which the abiding sense of his inferiority to both herself and Boldwood was not calculated to heal."

The chapter then proceeds to note the general comprehension among the shepherds of Boldwood's love for Bathsheba. Though Gabriel's feelings are hidden from them, they have understood part at least of the significance of the scene enacted before their eyes: " 'That means matrimony,' said Temperance Miller, following them out of sight with her eyes." This insight is echoed by other characters, but their attention drifts conversationally away to other matters, and the chapter ends with a counterpointed harmony made up of the juxtaposition of Gabriel's thoughts about Bathsheba presented as indirect discourse ("He adored Bathsheba just the same") and the irrelevant talk of the rustics which he and the narrator hear as a ground bass to the melody of his suffering. The continuo persists and gets the last word, which returns the reader to the objective watching of the invisible narrator:

> "And there's two bushels of biffins for apple-pies," said Maryann.
> "Well, I hope to do my duty by it all," said Joseph Poorgrass in a pleasant, masticating manner of anticipation.

The language of chapter 22 of *Far from the Madding Crowd* constantly moves the reader back and forth between proximity and distance. There is, however, a final form of distancing, one functioning implicitly throughout the chapter. I have said that the events are placed in a particular moment in the past. This seems to be no more than another way to hold the story at arm's length and see it in the perspective of the centuries which preceded it. There are, however, further implications of this.

Hardy's specification of the time in the past when the events took place establishes the novel as, like most fiction, an expression of the historical imagination. *Far from the Madding Crowd* re-creates sympathetically a particular time in the past and a particular culture flourishing in Wessex at that time. *   *   * The conventional past tense of the narration is a way of expressing the separation of the narrator from the culture he describes. He sees it in the perspective of history, as relative to its time and place. This distancing undercuts the assumptions and values which the characters share. It suggests that they might have been otherwise and implies the narrator's awareness that people at other times and places lived by other standards. Sympathetic re-creation is balanced by a recognition of the relativity of the culture which is so vividly brought back to life.

The temporality of the narrative in *Far from the Madding Crowd* is, however, more complex still. Though a particular moment of the action is often presented with great immediacy, so that it fills up the whole span of the reader's attention, the events are given as part of the flowing of time, that flowing which is suggested by the image of a man or woman moving across the landscape. This image is frequent in the poems and in the initial chapters of the novels. Each moment has an immediate past and an immediate future. As the reader watches Gabriel snip the sheep by accident, he remembers the silent happiness Gabriel enjoyed a few moments ago, before Boldwood entered, and he looks forward with indistinct anticipation to what will happen next, knowing that in all probability it will be brought into being by the motive power of the tension between the three main characters. Surrounding the reader's awareness of the immediate past and future is a vaguer memory of all that has preceded in the action and an indistinct anticipation of the future course of events which lies hidden from the present. As in real life, the present moment does not exist alone. It is surrounded by the other dimensions of time, permeated by them, and the reader's awareness reaches out toward past and future in an attempt to obtain a unified apprehension of present, past, and future in a single glance.

This presentation of the temporality of experience could, however, be made just as well through a present-tense narration. The use of the past tense serves to throw the immediate experience of each moment, with its particular reaching out toward past and future, back into the past as part of a completed sequence. The past tense constantly and unobtrusively reminds the reader that the narrator is in a radically different situation from that of any of the characters. They are living in a flowing present which has an uncertain and unpredictable future. He not only locates the events in the past, but enjoys by way of this placement the privilege of already knowing how the story came out. He tells the story not just from the perspective of a later time, but from the perspective of an explicit knowledge of what was for the characters hidden in the mists of the future. The reader can have both these experiences at once, in a paradoxical closeness and distance of relation to the present which is impossible in real life and which is one of the special privileges the reader of a past-tense novel shares with its narrator. The reader can put himself fully in this double position by reading the novel a second time. He is virtually in it even in the first reading, both because he holds the completed book in his hand and because he is constantly hearing a narrator who speaks as someone who already knows the story to the end. Both the first and second readings are valid, for the reader must maintain a sympathetic identification with the characters' experience of a present which as yet has only a potential future, and at the same time he must experience those moments as over. He must experience them as having already been followed by the events which completed them, the events which formed the sequence which was the ineluctable destiny of the characters. Hardy's concern for the fated, the sense of a cruel inevitability in his novels, is perhaps partly a product of his theoretical determinism, but it is also a natural consequence of the kind of narrator he chooses for his stories. From the point of view of a narrator who looks back at the completed pattern of events from a time much later in the future, those events appear as a necessary sequence. The reader who shares this perspective is led in his turn to see the events as fated.

Occasionally the fatalizing perspective built covertly into the form of the narration comes explicitly to the surface. When this happens the reader is made momentarily aware of the fact that the narrator is both close to the events in time and seeing them from long after. An example of this occurs in the chapter of *Far from the Madding Crowd* which follows the one I have analyzed. Bathsheba sings at the shearing-supper a song about a lady who marries a soldier, and the narrator, knowing of Sergeant Troy and his future relations to Bathsheba, comments: "Subsequent events caused one of the verses to be remembered for many months, and even years, by more than one of those who were gathered there." Events which are not yet even dreamed of by the characters are seen simultaneously as the unborn future and as the fated past. The form of the narration at such moments becomes a powerful shaping force determining the meaning of the events.

This double temporal perspective is one expression of the open structure of human temporality. Human time is not a linear series with a beginning, middle, and end laid out in a spatial row. It is a present which moves toward a future which will be a perfected assimilation of the past and therefore make the life into a whole. Until life ends, however, this totality is not complete. Literature may express this structure in various ways. A novel told in the past tense by an anonymous narrator, like *Far from the Madding Crowd*, is one such way. The characters advance from moment to moment through time toward an unpredictable future. The narrator relives from within the present experience of the characters. At the same time he sees that experience in retrospect. He sees each moment as part of the total life of the character. The narrator moves forward in his own time as he repeats in language the past experience of the characters. In this moving he approaches toward that moment when the experience of the protagonist will be complete in his retelling of it, a final wisdom attained, and the point of view of the character will coincide with that of the narrator. Whether that coincidence is ever attained in Hardy's novels remains to be determined, but as long as the novel continues, its temporal form remains open.

Hardy's narrative technique in chapter 22 of *Far from the Madding Crowd*, in its dependence on a gap between the narrator's point of view and the characters' points of view, is characteristic of his general practice in his fiction. The combination of proximity and separation, time present and time past, in one mixture or another, can be identified in any given passage from his novels.

* * *

MICHAEL MILLGATE

[Hardy's Achievement]†

When A *Pair of Blue Eyes* appeared in its three-volume form in May 1873 Hardy's professional status was confirmed by the appearance of his name on a title-page for the first time. That status had earlier been signalled by his decision to abandon his architectural career, and by an invitation from Leslie Stephen to write a serial for the *Cornhill*. When Stephen wrote, on November 30, 1872, Hardy was ready with a suggestion for "a pastoral tale", though he seems to have reported only the title, *Far from the Madding Crowd*, and the occupations of the chief characters.[1] It was in the spring of 1873, following the completion of A *Pair of Blue Eyes* and a renewed enquiry from Stephen, that Hardy began serious work on the novel. Stephen accepted it at the beginning of that October on the evidence of the specimen chapters Hardy sent him; shortly afterwards Hardy agreed to an earlier publication date than had originally been contemplated, and the first part appeared in the *Cornhill* for January 1874. The novel was still far from completion at this point, and Hardy only finished work on it that summer.[2] The two-volume first edition appeared on November 23, 1874, Hardy having returned the proofs—with "very few" corrections, mainly to the opening chapter—to Smith, Elder on October 9, modestly requesting in the accompanying letter that his name be allowed to appear in "the announcement of the book".[3]

Coming after A *Pair of Blue Eyes*, *Far from the Madding Crowd* is a novel of astonishing confidence; as the successor to *Under the Greenwood Tree*, it is a book of extraordinary amplitude. Unmistakably a major work, it is nonetheless quite different in kind from Hardy's later fiction, and it seems the first duty of criticism simply to celebrate its unique virtues—the bold theatricality of the narrative progression, the rich yet strictly functional evocation of setting, the earth-bound poetry of the dialogue:

> 'Andrew Randle, here's yours—finish thanking me in a day or two.
> Temperance Miller—oh, here's another, Soberness—both women, I suppose?'
> 'Yes'm. Here we be, 'a b'lieve,' was echoed in shrill unison.

†From *Thomas Hardy: His Career as a Novelist* (New York: Random House, 1971), pp. 79–94. The author's page references have been changed to chapter references and footnotes have been expnded and renumbered.
1. Frederick William Maitland, *The Life and Letters of Leslie Stephen* (London, 1906), p. 271. For Stephen's letter, see Maitland, pp. 270–71 (complete text in Richard Little Purdy, *Thomas Hardy: A Bibliographical Study*, Ox-

ford, 1968, pp. 336–37).
2. For the pre-publication history of the novel see Purdy, pp. 16–17, Maitland, pp. 271–73, and Florence Emily Hardy, *The Early Life of Thomas Hardy* (London: Macmillan, 1928), pp. 126–28, 132.
3. Carroll A. Wilson, comp., A *Descriptive Catalogue of the Grolier Club Centenary Exhibition 1940 of the Works of Thomas Hardy, O.M. 1840–1928* (Waterville, Maine, 1940), p. 16.

'What have you been doing?'

'Tending thrashing-machine, and wimbling haybonds, and saying "Hoosh!" to the cocks and hens when they go upon your seeds, and planting Early Flourballs and Thompson's Wonderfuls with a dibble.'

'Yes—I see. Are they satisfactory women?' she inquired softly of Henry Fray.

'O mem—don't ask me! Yielding women—as scarlet a pair as ever was!' groaned Henry under his breath.

'Sit down.'

'Who, mem?'

'Sit down.' (10)

Never again was Hardy to be quite so lavish in the humorous exploitation of rural dialogue, or even in the invention of incident: *Far from the Madding Crowd* includes, often in close juxtaposition, a profusion of natural and domestic disasters, mysterious disappearances and dramatic reappearances, the opening of a coffin, a revenge-murder, and a last-minute reprieve from the gallows. It is little wonder that Hardy could write to Frederic Harrison in 1901 that *Far from the Madding Crowd* had "a growing tendency to appear as the work of a youngish hand, though perhaps there is something in it which I could not have put there if I had been older".[4]

The novel displays throughout the excitement and assurance of a writer who has been given his great opportunity—serialisation in the *Cornhill*—at the moment when he begins to realise his proper subject. In *A Pair of Blue Eyes* the completion of a serial under pressure had proved nearly disastrous, and it was in relation to *Far from the Madding Crowd* itself that Hardy made his famous remark about wanting "merely to be considered a good hand at a serial."[5] But he profited from his earlier experience, and from the opportunity to plan his story further in advance, and during the composition of *Far from the Madding Crowd* it was precisely in responding, or even over-responding, to the demands of the serial situation that he seems to have felt his way almost instinctively towards a form—of strong outlines and rich possibilities for scenic presentation—which answered exactly to his immediate creative needs, enabling him to develop the melodramatic romanticism which had marked the narrative method of both *Desperate Remedies* and *A Pair of Blue Eyes* in terms of that solidity of social context he had so far achieved only in *Under the Greenwood Tree*.

Writing for the *Cornhill* also gave him, as R. L. Purdy has pointed out,[6] the advantage of close editorial scrutiny from Leslie Stephen, and although Stephen's interventions were later represented in *Early Life* (130–131) as having been characterised by an excessive respect for the forces of Grundyism, they were often of a far more important and

4. Hardy to Harrison, July 29, 1901 (Univ. of Texas), quoted in Ann Bowden, 'The Thomas Hardy Collection', *Library Chronicle of the University* of Texas, 7, ii (1962), p. 10.

5. *Early Life*, p. 131.

6. Purdy, p. 16.

positive kind. Thus the survival of the manuscript pages which Hardy deleted from the scene of the shearing supper makes it possible to see that Stephen was perfectly right, in his letter of February 17, 1874, to recommend some pruning at this point:

> I have read through your MS with very great pleasure; though I had seen most of it before. As you ask me for my opinion I will say frankly that I think the sheepshearing rather long for the present purpose. When the novel appears as a whole, it may very well come in in its present form. For periodical purposes, I think it rather delays the action unnecessarily. What I should be inclined to do would be simply to omit the chapter headed the "shearing supper" and to add a few paragraphs to the succeeding or preceding, just explaining that there has been a supper. . . . I don't know whether anything turns on the bailiff's story; but I don't think it necessary. [7]

If the proposed solution proved unnecessarily drastic, it was entirely to the good that Hardy should have been induced to delete from the scene the exchange involving Pennyways the ex-bailiff, which had indeed very little significance, and the subsequent conversation among Bathsheba's employees which, though sometimes amusing, was notably lacking in tension. [8] Earlier revisions had apparently been made at Stephen's suggestion—his letter of January 8, 1874, mentions that "the paying scene is judiciously reduced"[9]—and he was presumably responsible for the drastic curtailment of the drawn-out conclusion which Hardy originally wrote for the chapter describing Troy's "Adventures by the Shore."[1] Other substantial deletions were made, both within the manuscript itself and before the appearance of the serial, [2] and the book was unquestionably improved by this fining-down process, very largely carried out at Stephen's instigation. Even the deletions for which he has been specifically criticised can often be justified aesthetically. It may have seemed unduly fastidious of him to hint that he would "somehow be glad to omit the baby" from the scene in which Bathsheba opens Fanny Robin's coffin; but the suggestion had the happy result of removing from the novel the description of "both the silent ones" as they lay side by side, the baby "with a face so delicately small in contour & substance that its cheeks & the plump backs of its little fists irresistibly reminded her, excited as she was, of

7. Purdy, pp. 337–38.
8. The pages of rejected MS are in the Dorset County Museum (subsequently abbreviated DCM); the final MS as sent to the *Cornhill* is in the possession of Mr Edwin Thorne: for descriptions, see Purdy, pp. 14–16. Hardy wrote to Smith, Elder immediately (February 18, 1874; letter in DCM) asking for the return of the portion of MS (ff. 2–1 to 2–73) he had recently submitted. Much of the material in the original ff. 2–18 and 2–19 was incorporated in ff. 2–18 and 2–19 of the revised MS, but the last quarter of the original f. 2–19 and the whole of ff. 2–20 to 2–24 were deleted. Baily Pennyways had seen Fanny Robin in Melchester, 'too well-off to be

anything but a ruined woman' (f. 2–20), but had nothing further to contribute.
9. Purdy, p. 337.
1. *Cornhill* MS, ff. 3–9 to 3–12; Purdy, p. 15. The additional 3½ pages of MS originally intervened between the last two paragraphs of the chapter (371). In this version Troy returns to the beach only to find his clothes have disappeared; his rescuers then say that their ship, about to begin a six-month voyage, is short-handed, and after much reflection he decides to sail with them.
2. The malthouse conversation in chap. 8 and, especially, chap. 15 shows particularly heavy (and beneficial) revision.

the soft convexity of mushrooms on a dewy morning".[3] It seems perfectly possible, indeed, that Stephen sometimes used the Grundian threat as a tactful cover for criticism of a more aesthetically significant kind.

The novel as published proceeds with immense assurance. If the opening pages reveal an initial uncertainty of tone in the way in which Gabriel Oak's ineptitudes of manner are made matter for shared amusement between sophisticated author and sophisticated reader, such infelicities may have resulted, at least in part, from the very need to create Gabriel "cold" in the opening pages. It seems to have been Hardy's preferred method to display his principal characters in dramatised episodes before introducing them directly to the reader, certainly before offering an analysis of their personalities or any internal view of their thoughts and feelings: it is thus that Bathsheba, Boldwood, and Troy are introduced. Unfortunately, Hardy had insufficient faith in his own power to reveal character in action, judging it necessary to insert "set-piece" analyses, unduly long and rather inertly abstract, of both Boldwood and Troy at the points where they are brought fully into the main narrative stream. He shows greater confidence in his dramatic creation of Bathsheba. Although the later crises in her life are presented largely in terms of a direct revelation of what she is thinking and feeling, the early chapters simply offer a series of vignettes of her—as tease, as tomboy, as "mistress of the farm", as manager of men—which are allowed to make their own impact with the minimum of authorial intrusion.

Some of these episodes take on an almost emblematic quality which forces the reader to register them quite consciously as portentous of future developments. The most notable of them, Gabriel's view of Bathsheba as she sits on the cart, surrounded by household impedimenta, admiring herself in the mirror, allows Gabriel himself to draw a lesson regarding Bathsheba's vanity, but it also hints at that display of femininity in the open air which will cause such damage when Bathsheba takes over Weatherbury Upper Farm and, not least, at that element of domesticity in her which Gabriel himself will finally discover. The whole Norcombe section—the five chapters which comprised the first serial instalment—operates along similar lines, standing in relation to the body of the novel almost as a kind of dumb show, offering a brief survey of what has gone before and a "type" or prefiguration of much that will follow. Hardy later adopted variations of this method in the early pages of such novels as *The Hand of Ethelberta*, *The Return of the Native* and, most powerfully, *The Mayor of Casterbridge*. In *Far from the Madding Crowd* itself it should perhaps be linked with other moments which cast a premonitory shadow: Bathsheba's singing of "Allan Water", Gabriel's encounter with Fanny Robin.

3. Stephen to Hardy, April 13, 1874 (quoted Purdy, p. 339); *Cornhill* MS, f. 2–232.

This last episode is one which Hardy may have added to the manuscript at a fairly late stage, and which he allows—almost in the manner of Dickens—to stand unexplained, quietly teasing the back of the reader's mind, while other strands of the story are taken up in successive chapters. What eventually becomes clear is that the scene has served to link Fanny Robin with Gabriel Oak, and thus to emphasise the contrast—in position and fortune as much as in personality—between Fanny and Bathsheba herself. Since Boldwood and of course Troy are also involved with the fate of Fanny, her relationship to Bathsheba becomes a strange shadow play of obvious contrasts and obscure rivalries. The pathetic scene in which Fanny pleads with Troy from outside the barracks is placed between Bathsheba's successful first appearance as mistress of the farm and the even greater triumph of her first appearance in the Corn Market; the pattern is later inverted when Fanny's unhappy death is transformed by Troy's declaration into a triumph for her and the most abject of defeats for Bathsheba.

Powerfully developed, skilfully connected with the lives of the central characters, Fanny's story is an instance of the extraordinary creative exuberance displayed throughout the novel. It remains, however, essentially subordinate to the main narrative line provided by the progress of Bathsheba's career as ruler of Weatherbury Upper Farm—though the "Squire Bathsheba" aspect of her role is much less strongly emphasised than it seems to have been in contemporary stage adaptations of the novel[4]—and by the developing pattern of her relationships with Oak, Boldwood, and Troy. In the novel as published, this pattern involves the violent opposition, culminating in insult and murder, between Troy and Boldwood, but there are indications that Boldwood's present role may have been a late addition to Hardy's conception of the story. When he first sketched for Leslie Stephen the basic idea of *Far from the Madding Crowd*, Hardy apparently described the chief characters as "a woman-farmer, a shepherd, and a sergeant in the Dragoon Guards",[5] and if the Boldwood-Troy rivalry is now the focus of violence, there survives from the first draft a scene in which Gabriel comes into open and even physical conflict with Troy. Since Boldwood's name is mentioned in this scene, Hardy may not so much have introduced a new character as developed an existing minor one;[6] in any case, Boldwood's present role as Troy's opponent an antitype

4. Purdy, pp. 28–30. The fragment of *The Mistress of the Farm* which Professor Purdy located among the Lord Chamberlain's plays (now in the British Museum) has apparently disappeared.

5. Maitland, p. 271.

6. MS leaves (DCM) annotated by Hardy: '(Details of Sheep-rot—omited from MS. when revised)'; cf. Purdy, p. 16. Boldwood is mentioned in f. 106i; Oak and Troy fight on f. 106j; Robert

C. Schweik has recently argued, on the basis of a close analysis of the *Cornhill* MS, that the development of Boldwood's role and the dramatisation of Fanny Robin's story were probably not part of Hardy's original conception: 'The Early Development of Hardy's *Far from the Madding Crowd*', *Texas Studies in Literature and Language*, 9 (1967), 415–428, especially 425–427.

allows Oak to drop back into the relatively quiescent role which both his personality and his social position demand—to such an extent, indeed, that neither Troy nor Boldwood thinks seriously of him as a possible rival.

Clearly, the full elaboration of Boldwood's role demanded a certain delay in the eruption of Sergeant Troy upon the Weatherbury scene; it also involved, relatively to the book as a whole, a degree of narrative relaxation in the chapters (9–23) which are organised round the sheep-washing and sheep-shearing. It is part of the function of these chapters to provide time and opportunity for a credible development of Boldwood's courtship of Bathsheba, especially after the earlier reliance on the frail device of the valentine—convincing enough so far as Bathsheba is concerned, less so in its effect on Boldwood. But if Boldwood's role has to be somewhat slowly developed it grows eventually into one of Hardy's few male characterisations which can be even remotely compared with that of Henchard, remarkable, especially in its period, as a study in sexual obsession and the effects of sexual defeat. Few touches in the novel are more telling than the failure of an unmanned Boldwood to protect his ricks from the storm, or the discovery made at his house following the shooting of Troy:

> There were several sets of ladies' dresses in the piece, of sundry expensive materials; silks and satins, poplins and velvets, all of colours which from Bathsheba's style of dress might have been judged to be her favourites. There were two muffs, sable and ermine. Above all there was a case of jewellery, containing four heavy gold bracelets and several lockets and rings, all of fine quality and manufacture. These things had been bought in Bath and other towns from time to time, and brought home by stealth. There were all carefully packed in paper, and each package was labelled 'Bathsheba Boldwood,' a date being subjoined six years in advance in every instance. (55)

If the presentation of Troy does not offer quite the same richness, it nonetheless represents an admirably judged exploitation of the narrative and thematic possibilities inherent in such a figure. The scene of the sword-exercise—characteristically "researched" by Hardy[7]—gives an occasion for what must to some extent have been a deliberate

---

7. *Grolier Cat*, p. 15, lists a copy of *Infantry Sword Exercises* (published by H.M. Stationery Office, 1873) with Hardy's signature on the title page; Hardy also owned (1938) Wreden catalogue, item 342) *Instructions for the Sword, Carbine, Pistol, and Lance Exercise; together with Field Gun Drill. For the Use of the Cavalry* (London, 1871). Since Troy was a cavalryman, the latter volume (published by the Adjutant General's Office, Horse Guards) seems the more relevant, and the instructions there for the cavalry sword exercise (pp. 8–22) were probably the immediate source of Hardy's descriptive details. They also clarify Troy's remark, 'This may be called Fort meeting Feeble, hey, Boldwood?' (34): 'The recruit having been perfectly instructed in drawing and returning his sword, will now be made acquainted with the strong and weak parts of it; the "Fort" (strong) being the half of the blade near the hilt, the "Feeble" (weak), the half towards the point. . . . From the hilt upwards, in opposing the blade of an adversary, the strength of the defence decreases in proportion as the cut is received towards the point; and *vice versa*, it increases from the point downwards' (pp. 10–11). Cf. R. L. Purdy, ed., *Far from the Madding Crowd* (Boston, 1957), p. 207, n. i.

symbolism of sexual assault,[8] and while Troy's birth gives him qualities unusual in a soldier of his rank, the kind and degree of glamour
which attaches to him—traditionally, and in ballad and melodrama—as a sergeant of cavalry becomes a precise measure of both the
pathetic foolishness of Fanny Robin and the culpable indiscretion of
Bathsheba; it also suggests how much the two women have in common. Perhaps originally conceived as a contrast to Oak, Troy is even
more effective as a foil to Boldwood: where the latter is slow, massive,
profoundly obsessive, Troy is quick, light, and casual; if they both
neglect their ricks it is for utterly different reasons.

Troy is the more important figure in terms simply of the convolu-
tions of the plot, and once he has encountered Bathsheba the narrative
takes on its full amplitude, driving through with tremendous momentum to the day of his death. The quieter and more hopeful close is first
heralded by the granting of a reprieve to Boldwood. On any reflection
it must appear that a life sentence constitutes for a man so broodingly
passionate a punishment far worse than hanging: it is in a determination to die that he gives himself up after his suicide attempt has been
frustrated. But Hardy—needing to begin his upward movement, and
presumably wanting Bathsheba not to have another death on her
conscience—seeks to ensure that the reprieve is felt as a happy event:
this is one of many occasions when his rustic chorus serves him well,
and he is not afraid to use the cliché of the last-minute stay of
execution to extort from the reader a sympathetic response.

Since the novel abounds in such melodramatic devices, it is
scarcely surprising that Henry James, reviewing *Far from the Madding
Crowd* for the New York *Nation* should have found it "inordinately
diffuse, and, as a piece of narrative, singularly inartistic".[9] Curiously
enough, Hardy had used similar phrases in remarking to Leslie
Stephen that, though content at present to be judged "a good hand at a
serial", he might "have higher aims some day, and be a great stickler
for the proper artistic balance of the completed work".[1] It seems
doubtful however, whether Hardy could ever have agreed with James
as to what constituted "artistic balance". In *Far from the Madding
Crowd* he shifts rapidly and almost indiscriminately between different
versions of the omniscient viewpoint; dramatising, intervening, giving
now external and now internal views—sometimes, as in the confrontation between Troy and Bathsheba over Fanny Robin's coffin, combining several methods in an unobtrusive and surprisingly successful
manner.

At the same time, Hardy was, with his intense need and capacity for

8. See Richard C. Carpenter, 'The Mirror and
the Sword: Imagery in *Far from the Madding
Crowd*', *Nineteenth Century Fiction*, 18
(1964), 342–45.

9. Albert Mordell, ed., *Literary Reviews and
Essays by Henry James* (New York, 1958), p.
294; review also quoted in *Thomas Hardy and
His Readers*, pp. 28–33.

1. *Early Life*, p. 131.

visualisation, acutely aware of the much less interesting question, technically speaking, of the actual physical vantage point from which incidents are observed by characters within the novel's world. His books are full of conversations overheard and meetings accidentally or deliberately observed, and *Far from the Madding Crowd* is no exception. Gabriel, who tells the time by pressing his face against other people's windows, watches Bathsheba unseen on a number of occasions, and she later sees him at his prayers. Troy crouches in almost physical contact with Bathsheba as she sits in the tent at Greenhill Fair; in a more complicated instance, he is himself observed as he stands outside the Malthouse listening to a conversation going on inside. It is tempting to dismiss this as little more than a rather literal-minded concern on Hardy's part for the question of how people know what they know, and perhaps as an almost indispensable lubricant for the complications of the plot.[2] Yet in *Far from the Madding Crowd* the position of the looker-on is characteristically one of deprivation: Troy's closeness to his wife reminds him of what he has lost, and what he might reclaim; Gabriel's pain at exclusion from Bathsheba's favour is balanced by her sense of lacking his security of mind; Fanny cries out to a Troy made doubly inaccessible by the barracks and the intervening river; both Gabriel and Boldwood, on different occasions, watch Troy appear at Bathsheba's bedroom window in all the arrogance of ownership.

The lookers-on *par excellence*—with whom the observation of their masters is both an occupation and a badge of their own inferior status—are the rustics who frequent Warren's Malthouse, most of them employees of Boldwood or Bathsheba. Although it seems natural to speak of them as a kind of chorus, they discharge that particular function a good deal less obtrusively than do the lower-class characters in a more deliberately structured novel like *The Mayor of Casterbridge*. And they are perhaps less derivatively Shakespearean—despite the obvious echo of Silence and Shallow in the Malter's questions about Norcombe—than a first glance might suggest. They seem, indeed, to have owed a good deal to people Hardy had actually encountered, and in their speech he aimed at "scrupulously preserving the local idiom"[3] while yet avoiding the kind of phonetic eccentricities which rendered largely inaccessible the best work of a writer like William Barnes.

The scenes dominated by the workfolk—to use the local term on which Hardy insisted in his letter to the *Journal of the English Folk Dance Society* and his essay on "The Dorsetshire Labourer"—rarely

2. But see Albert Guerard, *Thomas Hardy: The Novels and Stories* (Cambridge, Mass.: Harvard University Press, 1949), pp. 43–44, on Hardy's onlookers.

3. Hardy's letter, "Papers of the Manchester Literary Club," *Spectator*, October 15, 1981, 1308, is reprinted in Harold Orel, ed., *Thomas Hardy's Personal Writings* (Lawrence, Kans.: The University Press of Kansas, 1966), p. 92.

make a very substantial contribution to the narrative, but they obviously offer something far more than an exhibition of local fauna: the book does not become static when such characters have the stage entirely to themselves. Partly this is because of their constant observation, and hence illumination, of the central characters; but it also seems obvious that Hardy deliberately invokes this collective voice of the agricultural community as an essential element in his pattern. His emphasis, most strongly brought out in the description of the great barn, is on the fact and value of continuity in the agricultural way of life.

> One could say about this barn, what could hardly be said of either the church or the castle, akin to it in age and style, that the purpose which had dictated its original erection was the same with that to which it was still applied. Unlike and superior to either of those two typical remnants of mediaevalism, the old barn embodied practices which had suffered no mutilation at the hands of time. Here at least the spirit of the ancient builders was at one with the spirit of the modern beholder. Standing before this abraded pile, the eye regarded its present usage, the mind dwelt upon its past history, with a satisfied sense of functional continuity throughout—a feeling almost of gratitude, and quite of pride, at the permanence of the idea which had heaped it up. (22)

As well as the barn, Hardy touches in, with varying degrees of detail, the Malthouse, the farms of Boldwood and Bathsheba, the cottages of their employees, the Casterbridge corn market and workhouse (associated respectively, and contrastively, with Bathsheba and with Fanny), the Buck's Head Inn on the road between the village and the town. The social detail, the evocation of a village in its active life, is abundantly if unobtrusively present, extending to the appearance of that rare phenomenon in Hardy's novels, a village church with a parson who seems relevant to the lives of his flock.[4]

The importance given to Weatherbury church in *Far from the Madding Crowd* prompts reflection upon the derivation of the novel's title from Gray's *Elegy in a Country Churchyard*:

> Far from the madding crowd's ignoble strife,
> Their sober wishes never learn'd to stray;
> Along the cool sequester'd vale of life
> They kept the noiseless tenor of their way.

Because of the novel's melodramatic and often violent character, because its central figures scarcely lead lives of "noiseless tenor", it is hard to think of the title as being other than ironic. Yet, as the description of the Great Barn so firmly suggests, the allusion to Gray seems to have been serious enough: Stinsford "*is* Stoke Poges", Hardy

---

4. C. J. P. Beatty, "The Part Played by Architecture in the Life and Work of Thomas Hardy (with Particular Reference to the Novels)," unpublished Ph.D. thesis, University of London, 1963, p. 244, notes Hardy's focus on four essential buildings: malthouse, homestead, great barn, and church.

is recorded as saying late in life.[5] Stinsford, of course, is usually identified with the Mellstock of *Under the Greenwood Tree*, while the Weatherbury of *Far from the Madding Crowd* is associated with Puddletown. But Stinsford and Puddletown are in adjoining parishes, and Hardy told Stephen he had decided to finish the novel at home because it was "within a walk of the district in which the incidents are supposed to occur. I find it a great advantage to be actually among the people described at the time of describing them."[6] The road between Weatherbury/Puddletown and Casterbridge/Dorchester which figures so prominently in *Far from the Madding Crowd* passes through the Yalbury Wood of *Under he Greenwood Tree*, and Keeper Day and his metheglin are recalled by Joseph Poorgrass.

Even more important than this placing of the two novels as near neighbours in space and time is the closeness of feeling and texture between the world of *Under the Greenwood Tree* and what might be called the permanent elements in the world of *Far from the Madding Crowd*. The frequenters of Warren's Malthouse differ in many respects from the guests at the tranter's party—for the most part, the latter are of higher social and economic standing—but the conversation of the two groups has a common *timbre*, reflecting, with marvellous richness of phrase and particularly of allusion, the immemorial features of the domestic life and rural economy of an area still almost untouched by the economic or social consequences of the industrial revolution. The villagers in *Far from the Madding Crowd*, unlike those in *Under the Greenwood Tree*, do not themselves play leading roles in the action, but they are directly involved in it; at the same time, they are so indispensable to the establishment of that action's social context as to demand consideration almost as an element in the setting. Quite as much as those passages of natural description for which the novel is rightly famous, the workfolk—Poorgrass, Coggan, Tall, Fray, and the rest—supply the novel's groundnote, that fundamental evenness of tenor which the title evokes, which Troy disturbs, and which the final chapters restore and reaffirm. That Oak—who has

---

5. May O'Rourke, *Thomas Hardy: His Secretary Remembers* (Beaminster, Dorset, 1965), p. 21. Hardy was responding to Miss O'Rourke's suggestion that Stinsford was 'a Gray's Elegy sort of place'. The *Elegy's* image of village life is, of course, far from idyllic, and Hardy may conceivably have been influenced in his choice of title by a passage in Francis George Heath, *The 'Romance' of Peasant Life in the West of England* (London, 1872), p. 6. Heath is concerned to challenge the assumption of city-dwellers that poverty and distress are peculiarly urban phenomena: 'as we wander by gurgling brooks, and through sylvan glades, and listen to the sweet songs of the birds, and see the glad sights which a wise and benificent Creator has spread over the earth, and which are to be seen

nowhere in such perfection as they are to be found "Far from the madding crowd's ignoble strife," we cannot imagine that aught but happiness and contentment are the lot of the rustic swain. But nearly all of our native poets in their descriptions of English pastoral life have deceived us by their rose-coloured pictures of the peasants.' On pp. 7–8 Heath uses phrases from the *Elegy* to stress less happy aspects of the labourer's situation and to introduce a discussion of current conditions in Dorsetshire.

6. *Early Life*, p. 131. In a letter to Thackeray Turner, Februar 7, 1910 (quoted Beatty, 'Architecture in Hardy', pp. 227–28), Hardy said specifically that St. Mary's, Puddletown, was the church of *Far from the Madding Crowd*.

operated happily within the Malthouse group without ever being entirely of it—should join the choir at the end of the novel is perfectly in accordance with that religious faith of his which has impressed Bathsheba earlier on; but it is also, like walking to church to be married, a gesture of solidarity with the village community.

Gabriel's relationship with that community serves throughout the novel as a convenient measure of his current social status. One moment of advancement arouses local comment:

> 'Whatever d'ye think,' said Susan Tall, 'Gable Oak is coming it quite the dand. He now wears shining boots with hardly a hob in 'em, two or three times a-week, and a tall hat 'a-Sundays, and 'a hardly knows the name of smockfrock. When I see people strut enough to be cut up into bantam cocks, I stand dormant with wonder, and says no more!' (49)

The observation is unkind, but it is made in terms of those minute discriminations of dress which are so important in the world of *Far from the Madding Crowd*, as in that of *Under the Greenwood Tree*, and which can be made so readily in communities where a substantial wardrobe is unknown and where "five decades hardly modified the cut of a gaiter, the embroidery of a smock-frock, by the breadth of a hair" (22).

It is this isolation and slowness to change—a quality of permanence corresponding to the permanent features of the seasons and of the countryside—which Hardy chiefly suggests in his title. He described the book to Stephen as a "pastoral tale", and the progress of the narrative is marked throughout by the festivals and occupations of the agricultural year: lambing and shearing, haymaking and harvest, the hiring fair and the sheep fair, the shearing and harvest suppers, Saint Valentine's Day and Christmas. The bee-taking scene recalls Hardy's use of a specifically seasonal structure in *Under the Greenwood Tree*, and perhaps prompts the reflection that in its profusion of agricultural detail the novel occasionally runs the risk of becoming a kind of latter-day *Georgics*. These recurring moments in the pattern of Weatherbury life are set off, in their essential timelessness and changelessness, against the rapid and often strenuous action of the narrative itself, but they are also used, again and again, as both the setting and raw material of a series of magnificent scenes in which the seasonal moment, evoked in all its detail, becomes an integral part of the presented experience. So Troy meets Bathsheba in the hayfield; so Gabriel strips the blushing sheep under Bathsheba's modest but critical eye;[7] so the ironic uncertainties of Gabriel's relationship with Bathsheba are subtly defined by the seating arrangements at the shearing supper, where distinction of class merges with sexual rivalry; so Boldwood's obsession is displayed in all its grotesqueness by the sombre incongruities of his Christmas party.

---

7. Carpenter, 'The Mirror and the Sword', pp. 340–42, has an interesting discussion of this episode.

The specifically pastoral aspects of the novel are emphasised in many of the images and allusions which Hardy evokes: *Lycidas*, for example, as well as Virgil's *Eclogues* and Old Testament narratives of herdsmen and their flock—Susan Tall's husband is called Laban, Boldwood speaks of waiting for Bathsheba as Jacob had done for Rachel. Gabriel, we are told, could play his flute with "Arcadian sweetness" (6), and at the shearing supper, when Bathsheba sings to Gabriel's accompaniment, the "shearers reclined against each other as at suppers in the early ages of the world" (23). Such allusions combine with others in the novel—for example, those implicit in the naming of Troy and Bathsheba[8]—and with the pastoral character of the setting and the continuing life of farm and village to throw into relief and into perspective the foreground narrative. As the ballads incorporated into the novel further stress, love is as natural and as immemorial as the seasons themselves, and there are ample precedents both for the ways of soldiers with "winning tongues" and for the patient devotion of shepherds.

It is of course to Gabriel, as the one specifically pastoral figure in the novel, that these allusions most persistently accrete, and there is clearly a sense in which he is linked with traditional presentations of the shepherd as rustic lover and philosopher. In the Norcombe chapters, where Gabriel is first introduced as a flute-playing shepherd we hear of his "pastoral affairs" (4), and of the "Pastoral Tragedy" (5) when he loses his sheep; at the hiring fair he is sensitive to his fall from his "modest elevation as pastoral king" (6) to the level of hired man. But if Gabriel is very much the shepherd here, Bathsheba at Norcombe appears essentially as a milkmaid; both are seen caring for new-born creatures, and Gabriel's idea of courting Bathsheba is to take her a young lamb which has lost its mother. Within the context of these opening pages Gabriel's gesture, like the court-ship itself, seems appropriate enough, and although Hardy handles the episode with gentle humour neither this nor Bathsheba's disdain removes the impression of a basic congruity between the couple or qualifies the firmness of Gabriel's declaration:

> She contracted a yawn to an inoffensive smallness, so that it was hardly ill-mannered at all. 'I don't love you,' she said.
> 'But I love you—and, as for myself, I am content to be liked.'
> 'O Mr. Oak—that's very fine! You'd get to despise me.'
> 'Never,' said Mr. Oak, so earnestly that he seemed to be coming, by the force of his words, straight through the bush and into her arms. 'I shall do

8. The name Troy also carried local connotations. On the road between Dorchester and Puddletown, at approximately the spot occupied in the novel by the Buck's Head Inn, stood the hamlet off Troy Town: 'Troy-town is, however, another designation for the *maze* or *labyrinth*, constructed by the old inhabitants of Britain with banks of turf, and of which remains have been found in different parts of the kingdom. They are common in Wales, where they are called *Caertroi*, that is, *turning-towns*.' (A *Handbook for Travellers in Wiltshire, Dorsetshire, and Sommersetshire* [London: John Murray, 1856], p. 110). The name survives in Troy Town Farm.

one thing in this life—one thing certain—that is, love you, and long for you, and *keep wanting you* till I die.' His voice had a genuine pathos now, and his large brown hands perceptibly trembled. (4)

If Gabriel's pastoral attributes in these early scenes do not greatly enhance the reader's sense of him as a man to be reckoned with in the affairs of the world, they certainly reinforce the impression of independence and integrity, of a loyalty and love that may be the more absolute for being capable of expression only in domestic gestures and homely terminology. In a real sense, Gabriel is not simply the hero but, quite specifically, the romantic hero.

Throughout the remainder of the novel, Hardy is at pains to keep Gabriel constantly in view, and in his role as shepherd. Bathsheba's, clearly, is a mixed farm, producing both corn and sheep after the standard pattern of Victorian high farming. But while all aspects of the farm's economy are evoked in their due season, the chief emphasis falls consistently upon the sheep, whose progress we follow from lambing-time onwards: as R. L. Purdy remarks, "the story moves by the shepherd's calendar".[9] Although the original of Greenhill fair was much more than a sheep-fair,[1] that is the aspect in which Hardy chooses to present it, and it is perhaps of some interest that in the discarded scene in which Oak fought with Troy the source of their difference was Troy's deliberate infection of the flock with sheep-rot—in order, as Hardy explains in technical language, to bring them on to an early and illusory readiness for market.[2] The emphasis on the part played by sheep in the economy of Weatherbury Upper Farm is essentially an emphasis on Gabriel's contribution. When he is seen helping in the harvest field Hardy stresses that he "was not bound by his agreement" (33) to assist in this way, and it is, of course, part of the point of Gabriel's action in saving Bathsheba's ricks on two separate occasions that they lie outside the range of his responsibility as a shepherd.

It is in such episodes that Hardy stresses Gabriel's unfailing loyalty to Bathsheba and, at the same time, sustains a relationship between the two during the long period when Bathsheba's emotional life is engrossed by her involvements with Troy and Boldwood. Here, of course, the dual aspect of Bathsheba's role—as mistress of the farm and as inexperienced girl—allows Hardy unusual flexibility, as does the entirely convincing *"ficelle"* figure of Liddy, in whom, though they are mistress and maid, Bathsheba can with perfect naturalness confide. But the recurrent demonstrations of Gabriel's resourcefulness also sustain and expand the sense of him as a man of parts as well as of integrity, so that it seems entirely proper that at the end of the novel he should both marry Bathsheba and take over Boldwood's

9. R. L. Purdy, ed., *Far from the Madding Crowd*, p. xiv.
1. See, for example, Hermann Lea, *Thomas Hardy's Wessex* (London, 1913), pp. 43–44.
2. MS (DCM), ff. 106b–106c.

farm. The two achievements are, in fact, splendidly one.[3] If Bathsheba has learned through suffering to value Gabriel for what he is and what he represents, Gabriel has proved himself through resourceful endurance to be something more than "an every-day sort of man" (4)—to be worthy, indeed, as man and as farmer, both of Bathsheba's hand and of that social and economic role within the agricultural community which, as Boldwood's successor and Bathsheba's husband, he must necessarily perform.

PENELOPE VIGAR

[A Distinct Development in Artistic Vision]†

. . . we cannot for our lives understand how any person of ordinary penetration, much more a skilled critic, could ever have supposed it to be written by George Eliot. The author of *Romola* and *The Mill on the Floss* is a great artist, too much of an artist sometimes. The author of *Far from the Madding Crowd* is a dauber in comparison, but if a dauber at all, a dauber who throws on the colours, and arranges the figures, and manages the composition with a vast deal of reckless skill.

Review in *The Observer*, 3 January 1875

I

Far from the Madding Crowd sees a distinct development in Hardy's artistic vision. Its quiet pastoral background is scarcely distinguishable from that of *Under the Greenwood Tree*, yet it has all the 'absurdities, improprieties, . . . incongruities and suddenly sensational incidents'[1] of its other predecessors, *Desperate Remedies* and *A Pair of Blue Eyes*. What is most interesting in the book is the manner in which Hardy combined the two styles, and the effect which each produces. For the first time, the distinction between romance and reality ceases to be an artistic flaw in the unity of the novel, and the formula which counters the mundane with the incredible, the beautiful with the grotesque, is extended into its very theme.

In *Far from the Madding Crowd*, by his use of strange contrasts and ambiguities, the author constantly reiterates his artistic conception of the dual nature of the world, and the irony of man's interpretation of it. His treatment of his theme is, however, in itself ambiguous. Oddly enough, in those scenes which superficially suggest a highly coloured and dramatic treatment, the style is for the most part restrained and

3. Roy Morell, *Thomas Hardy: The Will and the Way* (Kuala Lumpur, 1965), p. 59, quotes the opening of the final paragraph of chapter 56 and comments: 'Ahead of Gabriel and Bathsheba is no romance, but a reality that Hardy represents as more valuable, a reality of hard and good work on the two farms.'

†*The Novels of Thomas Hardy: Illusion and Reality* (London: The Athlone Press, 1974), pp. 101–23.
1. Critic in *The Observer* (3 January 1875), quoted in L. Lerner and J. Holmstrom, eds., *Thomas Hardy and his Readers* (London, 1968), p. 33.

subdued, while the apparently simple pastoral scenes often contain a hint of the weird or malignant. In the famous description of the storm (36 and 37), for example, he combines a faithful and perceptive vision of natural processes with an exaggerated and fanciful treatment. In many ways, as I shall show later, this episode is the crux of the novel, demonstrating finally the contrasts between the solid Gabriel Oak and the other two chief male characters, Troy and Boldwood, who both represent, as Roy Morrell suggests, different 'aspects of romantic unreality'.[2] In addition, it can be seen as epitomizing Hardy's art in this novel, showing as it does the lengths to which realism and melodrama can progress until they become mutually dependent and mutually illuminating. Yet the success of this *tour de force* is not simply fortuitous; it is part of the painstaking development and presentation of scene and action which is established at the very beginning of the novel, and which is maintained, with only a few lapses, until the end.

As part of this skill, it is in *Far from the Madding Crowd* that we first see effectively developed Hardy's tendency to summarize theme or action by presenting a series of isolated, almost static episodes at various points of the narrative. Irving Howe speaks of these passages as 'miniature dramas . . . which in a page or two illuminate whole stretches of experience': 'what strikes the ear and eye, first and last, is the colour of the depicted scenes, the sheer narrative energy, the way intention becomes absorbed into action. Some of the best, and best-known, sections of *Far from the Madding Crowd* are quite detachable as set-pieces: flights of bravura, spectacular and self-contained'.[3] The effect of these scenes, however, is not only in their vivid and unusual quality; more importantly, they incorporate the elements of the realistic natural background which supports the action and gives credibility to the most melodramatic of events.

It is also noticeable that in this later novel the main characters undergo a far greater artistic development than the pale, unspectacular heroes and heroines we find in *Desperate Remedies* and *A Pair of Blue Eyes*. In these works, it is painfully obvious that Hardy intends the unassuming credibility of his *dramatis personae* to act as a solid foil for the theatrical improbabilities of plot; as a result, the villainous characters and the exaggeratedly comic rustics, though stagey and sometimes ridiculous, carry undue weight in the total structure of the work. In these stories, the events revolve around the characters, whose own distinguishing traits and personalities remain more or less incidental. In *Far from the Madding Crowd*, on the other hand, the characters represent in themselves the qualities which Hardy is exploiting thematically. Their thoughts and actions and emotions fit into and help create the pattern of the whole, and are not simply

2. Roy Morrell, *Thomas Hardy: The Will and the Way* (Kuala Lumpur, 1965), p. 59.

3. Irving Howe, *Thomas Hardy* (New York, 1967), p. 57.

excrescences tacked on to give an effect of psychological verisimilitude.

Nevertheless, it is essential to Hardy's method that he seldom renders character by direct means, by thought, dialogue or sympathetic interpretation. Most often he develops his background, consistently co-ordinating it with the action itself to show, by inference, the mental state of his protagonists. These are characters who *are* what they see and do; scarcely ever does Hardy rationalize their motives or reactions in any depth. So it is that many of the sharpest scenes in the book are not simply pictorial or dramatic effects; they serve a double purpose, portraying conflicting emotions and ambiguous feelings more surely than any direct exposition could do. Hardy suggests indirectly and by implication, using, as his metaphorical equivalents to emotion, effects of light and colour, sound and sensation. Each character represents, to a certain extent, a different facet of human perception and understanding, and each is developed according to the kind of consciousness which he or she exhibits. In this there is, inevitably, something of a tendency towards 'staginess', as the contrasting personalities are largely created for us by their setting and the props or symbols by which we identify them. Sometimes this is done by Hardy with appropriate crudity, as in the case of Sergeant Troy, sometimes with ever-increasing discernment, as with Bathsheba, whose environment and circumstances are continually explored and developed imaginatively to show us, at the end of the novel, a very different woman from the vain and unsophisticated girl described for us in the first chapter. It is in his portrayal of Bathsheba that we see most clearly how far Hardy has extended his technique of suggestion since he first experimented with it in *Desperate Remedies*.

Our first glimpse of Bathsheba carefully prepares us for a thorough appreciation of her character and predicts many of the subsequent scenes in which vital moments of her life, reflected through her own consciousness, are to be depicted. Our awareness of her as an individual is closely allied with her own awareness of herself, and her progression from naive complacency to deepening self-recognition is traced for us in a series of connected yet distinctly differentiated pictures, in which the description of natural background illuminates our reaction towards its human subject. In all these pictures, Hardy's use of colour and of sensually evocative words is of prime importance. Through the author's imagination the natural world is made almost the equivalent of Bathsheba's mental world, the expression of her own perception and emotional reactions.

The first scene, shown to us through the eyes of Gabriel Oak, is exquisitely redolent of freshness and brightness, of a romantic but rather unreal domestic tranquillity. She is seen riding on 'an ornamental spring wagon', laden with household goods, which stops directly in front of him:

The girl on the summit of the load sat motionless, surrounded by tables and chairs with their legs upwards, backed by an oak settle, and ornamented in front by pots of geraniums, myrtles and cactuses, together with a caged canary—all probably from the windows of the house just vacated. There was also a cat in a willow basket, from the partly-opened lid of which she gazed with half-closed eyes, and affectionately surveyed the small birds around. (1)

The pleasing oddness of the scene is reinforced by its bright contrasts of colour; Bathsheba is expressly shown as part of the natural background but as alien to it as spring in the middle of winter.

It was a fine morning, and the sun lighted up to a scarlet glow the crimson jacket she wore, and painted a soft lustre upon her bright face and dark hair. The myrtles, geraniums and cactuses packed around her were fresh and green, and at such a leafless season they invested the whole concern of horses, wagon, furniture and girl with a peculiar vernal charm. (1)

Similarly her impulsive act of smiling at her own reflection in a looking-glass has nothing of artificiality or coquettish vanity about it; it is simple a gesture of admiration, given a certain novelty (which, as Hardy says, 'it did not intrinsically possess') by being enacted out of doors. 'The picture was a delicate one. Woman's prescriptive infirmity had stalked into the sunlight, which had clothed it in the freshness of an originality.' Hardy is careful always to relate the imaginative to the actual, and neatly twists this scene, with a slightly self-conscious denial of authorial omniscience, to a prophecy of Bathsheba's fortunes:

She simply observed herself as a fair product of Nature in the feminine kind, her thoughts seeming to glide into far-off though likely dramas in which men would play a part—vistas of probable triumphs—the smiles being of a phase suggesting that hearts were imagined as lost and won. Still, this was but conjecture, and the whole series of actions was so idly put forth as to make it rash to assert that intention had any part in them at all. (1)

The episode of her meeting—or, more appropriately, tangling—with Troy at once blends and contrasts with the oddly fairy-tale quality of this first picture; it is the inevitable corollary to Hardy's suggestion that her romantic fancies will be fulfilled in one way or another. Again, although the setting is homely and tranquil (she is going the rounds of her farm at night, checking on the animals in the stables, being snuffled and nibbled at by horses and cows), the scene for her encounter with the evil genius of flattery and deception is characteristically set apart from this peaceful, prosaic background. It is a path through a plantation of firs, whose foliage creates a wall so dense that it excludes all light. Hardy gives it the imaginative construction of a fantastic palace, whose elements approximate those made by man:

a vast, low, naturally formed hall, the plumy ceiling of which was supported by slender pillars of living wood, the floor being covered with a soft dun carpet of dead spikelets and mildewed cones, with a tuft of grass-blades here and there. (24)

Troy's appearance, too, has something of a visionary quality, an unreal and almost theatrical brilliance in contrast with his unseen presence, which is made tangible to Bathsheba only by her falling against 'warm clothes and buttons';

> A hand seized the lantern, the door was opened, the rays burst out from their prison, and Bathsheba beheld her position with astonishment.
>
> The man to whom she was hooked was brilliant in brass and scarlet. He was a soldier. His sudden appearance was to darkness what the sound of a trumpet is to silence. Gloom, the *genius loci* at all times hitherto, was now totally overthrown, less by the lantern-light than by what the lantern lighted. The contrast of this revelation with her anticipations of some sinister figure in sombre garb was so great that it had upon her the effect of a fairy transformation. (24)

The understated ambiguities of the dark and mouldering reality and the startling brilliance of the vision are immediately blended into the grotesquely foreboding aspect of their enforced conjunction:

> . . . the lantern standing on the ground betwixt them threw the gleam from its open side among the fir-tree needles and the blades of long damp grass with the effect of a large glow-worm. It radiated upwards into their faces, and sent over half the plantation gigantic shadows of both man and woman, each dusky shape becoming distorted and mangled upon the tree-trunks till it wasted to nothing. (24)

The mingling of the actual scene with Bathsheba's dazzled and unconscious perception of it becomes in Hardy's own vision a symbolic prediction which achieves much of its force through the limitation and imaginative use of the setting.

Similar in its self-enclosed unity and in its premonitory and reflective use of the bright colours surrounding Bathsheba's dreamlike romance with Troy, is the chapter titled 'The Hollow amid the Ferns', in which is recounted the heavily symbolic 'sword exercise'. The setting is shown to us, at this crucial stage of their relationship, in specifically sensuous terms.

> The hill opposite Bathsheba's dwelling extended, a mile off, into an uncultivated tract of land, dotted at this season with tall thickets of brake fern, plump and diaphanous from recent rapid growth, and radiant in hues of clear and untainted green.
>
> At eight o'clock this midsummer evening, whilst the bristling ball of gold in the west still swept the tips of the ferns with its long, luxuriant rays, a soft-brushing-by of garments might have been heard among them, and Bathsheba appeared in their midst, their soft, feathery arms caressing her up to her shoulders. (28)

Troy, seen in the distance, is 'a dim spot of artificial red'—clearly contrasted against the natural freshness and beauty of the ferns. Once again, Hardy makes of the natural setting a contrived stage for the action. This time it is, fitting enough, a sort of arena where the soldier can display his skill:

> The pit was a saucer-shaped concave, naturally formed, with a top diameter of about thirty feet, and shallow enough to allow the sunshine to reach their heads. Standing in the centre, the sky overhead was met by a circular horizon of fern: this grew nearly to the bottom of the slope and then abruptly ceased. The middle within the belt of verdure was floored with a thick flossy carpet of moss and grass intermingled, so yielding that the foot was half-buried within it. (28)

In contrast with this luxurious softness the microcosmic universe created by Troy is dangerous, brilliant and mesmeric. Troy himself is hard and metallic, 'as quick as electricity': only the sword, touched by sunlight, is 'like a living thing' and is described always as a natural phenomenon, being likened to a rainbow, a firmament of light, a sky-full of meteors. It takes up the whole sky: its 'luminous streams' are an '*aurora militaris*', while Troy himself is scarcely noticeable. Hardy continually emphasizes his unreal, magical quality in Bathsheba's eyes. When he finally leaves her, his scarlet form vanishes 'like a brand quickly waved'.

The subtle combination of the real and the fantastic, the soft and voluptuous natural world and the artificial trance-like vision of Troy's strange power, creates a specifically emotional atmosphere in which the two states of dazzled bewilderment and acquiescence are mingled in Bathsheba's own mind. The romance she has anticipated is at once part of her natural environment and completely alien to it. Its essence is of an insubstantial dream—an effect which is largely due to the fact that Troy himself is never clearly delineated for us. He is present only as a voice, a uniform, a splash of bright colour, and for the rest Hardy merely describes him metaphorically or in terms of vague and rather sinister splendour. Within the concept of the book he is at once a romantic dream-character and a fairly innocuous melodramatic villain. Scarcely ever is he seen or described in realistic terms.

The shattering of Bathsheba's illusions about Troy is portrayed in terms which are explicitly synonymous with those of her fascination by him. After the final humiliation, Hardy shows her as reverting instinctively to the action of a wounded animal. Fleeing the house, she reaches a thicket of withering ferns, where 'she could think of nothing better to do with her palpitating self than to go in . . . and hide' (44). Here she spends the night and, awakening with a freshened existence and a cooler brain', she finds that the deceptions and fantasies of her life with Troy dissolve into the fresh realities of the ordinary everyday world. Slowly she is made aware of the 'interesting proceedings' of daily life going on: the sounds of the birds, the song of the ploughboy, the stamping and flouncing of her own team of horses drinking at a nearby pond. 'Day was just dawning, and beside its cool air and colours her heated actions and resolves of the past night stood out in lurid contrast.' The hectic and unreal colours of her romance with Troy are shown here only as withered red and yellow leaves: she shakes them from her dress and they flutter away, as Hardy pointedly notes, ' "like ghosts from an enchanter fleeing." ' Everywhere the contrast with the previous fresh and dazzling fantasy is made implicit; the beautiful ferns are now yellowed, and Bathsheba can see in the daylight that below them the ground slopes down to 'a species of swamp':

> A morning mist hung over it now—a fulsome yet magnificent silvery veil, full of light from the sun, yet semi-opaque—the hedge behind it being in some measure hidden by its hazy luminousness. Up the sides of this depression grew sheaves of the common rush, and here and there a peculiar species of flag, the blades of which glistened in the emerging sun, like scythes. But the general aspect of the swamp was malignant. From its moist and poisonous coat seemed to be exhaled the essences of evil things in the earth, and in the waters under the earth. The fungi grew in all manner of positions from rotting leaves and tree-stumps, some exhibiting to her listless gaze their clammy tops, others their oozing gills. Some were marked with great splotches, red as arterial blood, others were saffron yellow, and others tall and attenuated, with stems like macaroni. Some were leathery and of richest browns. The hollow seemed a nursery of pestilences small and great, in the immediate neighbourhood of comfort and health, and Bathsheba arose with a tremor at the thought of having passed the night on the brink of so dismal place. (44)

There is still the hint of mysterious imagined beauty, but now it is only a mist, an ironical veiling of the truth. Again, Hardy's treatment of his subject is ambiguous; despite the noxiousness of the swamp and the fungi, he points their almost repulsive attractiveness. His words are deliberately tactile, creating a sensuous network of sound imagery: 'arterial splotches', 'saffron', 'macaroni', 'richest browns'. The silvery mist, 'fulsome yet magnificent', lit with the sun, and the sharp leaves of the flag which glisten like scythes, recall for us the dazzling mesmeric mist of Troy's sword, flashing and bristling with light in the earlier episode.

Bathsheba's awakening illustrates symbolically her conscious and unconscious reactions to what has gone before. Clear perception, in which she at last recognizes separate existences other than her own (in a splendid touch, Hardy shows how she hears the birds not in a confused medley of song, but each with his own individual note) is still countered in her mind with a feeling of hypnotic fascination, metaphorically represented by the enticingly rich and repulsive swamp. In many ways, this scene corresponds with and develops from that of *Desperate Remedies* in which Cytherea feels an unaccountable and almost repugnant attraction towards Manston; there is the same use of ambiguity and 'atmospheric' imagery to suggest conflicting emotions.

It is of course possible to over-interpret Hardy's use of these particular scenes to point the progress of Bathsheba's infatuation and sub-sequent disillusionment with Troy. They do not form a comprehen-sive symbolic pattern, and there are many other episodes which might be considered equally important in relation to this part of the story. Yet it seems to me that each of the scenes I have described 'stands out' from the rest of the narrative; each is isolated from the progression of the action by the more intensive use of image, metaphor and colour, and each shows in some sense a rearrangement of natural elements to fit a preconceived emotional state. In each case, Hardy creates a specifi-cally self-enclosed imaginative world which is, however, only an intensification of the ordinary. Within this context even the smallest details can legitimately have a deeper meaning.

In connection with this we can see, for example, that the use of colour and the imagery of flowers and foliage make a fairly consistent pattern throughout the novel, especially relating to the triangle of Bathsheba, Troy and Fanny Robin. Sometimes their significance is ironically juxtaposed against that of the major scenes I have men-tioned; for instance, in the light of Hardy's early association of Bathsheba with freshness and greenness, the portrayal of the de-bauchery in the barn during the storm takes on an added meaning. Amidst the tangle of drunken bodies, Gabriel sees that 'the candles suspended among the evergreens had burnt down to their sockets, and in some cases the leaves tied around them were scorched'. In the middle of the scene, demon-like, 'shone red and distinct the figure of Sergeant Troy, leaning back in a chair' (36). The celebration of the Harvest Supper and the Wedding Feast together has an ominous significance in that, to Troy, neither is of the slightest account. In another instance there is the ironical victory of Fanny Robin who, after her death, proves herself capable of holding Troy's affections as Bathsheba never could. In a grim reminder of Bathsheba's journey to her aunt's home, we are shown Fanny's coffin on a bright spring-cart, completely surrounded with flowers and greenery which parody in their freshness the out-of-season potted plants that signified the inno-cence and beauty of the young Bathsheba. The comparison is im-plicit, and is further heightened by Troy's futile planting of flowers on Fanny's grave—flowers which Bathsheba replants after the gargoyle has washed them away.

II

Far from the Madding Crowd was the first novel in which Hardy made use of the word 'Wessex' to identify the geographical setting for his tales. His original intention was that it should give unity to 'the horizons and landscapes of a party real, party dream-country', and when he found that the title was becoming 'more and more popular as a practical provincial definition', he warned against this tendency in his 1895 preface to the novel:

> . . . I ask all good and idealistic readers to forget this, and to refuse steadfastly to believe that there are any inhabitants of a Victorian Wessex outside these volumes in which their lives and conversations are detailed.

It is expressly an invented world, not a product of photographic reproduction, and within this world even the obviously realistic detail frequently has a function which is almost supernatural. The unusualness of the events is more than prepared for by the fantasy which Hardy finds in even the smallest things. Thus, in the chapter which deals with the sheep-shearing, a simple description of field-flowers reveals unexpected grotesqueries:

> It was the first day of June, and the sheep-shearing season culminated, the landscape, even to the leanest pasture, being all health and colour. Every green was young, every pore was open, and every stalk was swollen with racing currents of juice. . . . Flossy catkins of the later kinds, fern-sprouts like bishops' croziers, the square-headed moschatel, the odd cuckoo-pint—like an apoplectic saint in a niche of malachite—snow-white ladies'-smocks, the tooth-wort, approximating to human flesh, the enchanter's nightshade, and the black-petalled doleful-bells, were among the quainter objects of the vegetable world in and about Weatherbury at this teeming time. . . . (22)

Christian and pagan imagery blend in a kind of medieval pageant, as the ordinary unspectacular products of the earth are shown as magical and mysterious, with a strange beauty compounded of ugliness and sorcery. Spring and gaiety is heralded by age and black magic. The relish with which Hardy describes his odd specimens does not necessarily suggest that his intention was overtly symbolic. Rather, the frequent hints of fantasy and oddity make a continual extra dimension enriching the realistic background to the story, and by so doing prepare our acceptance of the macabre and grotesque effects which are directly symbolic.

The differing threads forming the substance of the background are so finely interwoven that sometimes it is difficult to tell whether or not Hardy's imagery is deliberate or simply fortuitous. For example, when he describes the appearance of the newly married Troy at Bathsheba's bedroom window, the picture is an odd combination of simplicity and ingenuity. The birdsong is 'confused', the 'wan blue of the heaven', the yellow lights and 'attenuated' shadows all intimate a rather tardy joy on the part of the outside world, while the creeping plants around the window are 'bowed with rows of heavy water-drops, which had upon objects behind them the effects of minute lenses of high magnifying power' (35). The use of the romantic pathetic fallacy (nature's disillusionment with this unnatural marriage) contrasts markedly with Hardy's peculiarly original use of the weeping raindrops; suddenly the normal images are fixed and intensified, and the oddity of the close observation heightens the diffused effect of the general impression. The freshness of early morning is shown emotionally as a time of undeveloped ripeness and weakened effects, but in the final image, somehow, the whole created atmosphere is incongruously crystallized and intensified—perhaps because the point is made with complete detachment. The honeymoon from its inception is marked with portents and signs of sickliness, yet the tokens which Hardy mentions are not blatantly symbolic, and the total effect is undoubtedly intended merely as an imaginative comment on the action.

The same technique, extended and exaggerated, is used for the episode in which the gargoyle ruins Troy's floral tribute to his dead mistress. The gargoyle, in effect, embodies in itself all the paradoxes which man can invent: although it is carved of stone, its action is described as that of a living creature, and it combines various characteristics of human, animal and mythological beast, the whole 'fashioned as if covered with a wrinkled hide':

> It was too human to be called like a dragon, too impish to be like a man, too animal to be like a fiend, and not enough like a bird to be called a griffin. (46)

Hardy's use of this symbol appears strained and improbable only when it is taken out of the context of the story; within the tale, which itself deals with the tensions and ambiguities of the real and the imagined, it becomes a simple statement of the mysterious, unpredictable truth above the common vision of man. Its perennial laughter, voiceless in dry weather and in wet heard 'with a gurgling and snorting sound', is an unceasing mockery of the artificial state of mankind in which the real truth is seldom noticed. Thus Troy's attitude towards Fanny's death (which was treated in a rational fashion by the practical rustic characters) is shown to us as an ironically sentimentalized anomaly. His representative action of placing values where they do not exist extends even to his attaching of special 'meanings' to the flowers themselves; for instance, he places lilies and forget-me-nots over her heart, in a bitter parody of his real legacy to her. In comparison, the basic and elemental starkness of Fanny's death and burial corresponds with the gargoyle's direct, uncompromising comment on convention and artificiality, and the whole chapter in which the episode is isolated represents not so much the futility of Troy's gesture as the wrongness of his attitudes. Within the framework of life and death, intention and repercussion, and the distortion of the natural to fit preconceived false ideals, the values embodied by the gargoyle have a grotesquely appropriate significance.

Throughout *Far from the Madding Crowd*, Hardy's technique is to describe ordinary things in such a way that they have a peculiar imaginative depth of feeling. His use of metaphor and simile is frequently macabre, sometimes over-ingeniously so (for example, there is his description of the Casterbridge Union House, the 'grim character' of which 'showed through it, as the shape of a body is visible under a winding sheet') (40). This being his predilection, one might expect an over-dramatic treatment of plot in the novel, but, strangely enough, the scenes in which action predominates tend towards under-statement. Often they are merely a cursory gathering of threads. The mystery of Troy's supposed drowning and his subsequent reappearance is sketchily explained, and the description of his rôle as Dick Turpin in a travelling side-show is less interesting than the exotic picture Hardy gives us of the multi-coloured sheep ascending the downs. His second performance in front of Bathsheba is, in comparison with the first dazzling display, a tawdry and rather pathetic affair. It is imbued with a sense of the ridiculous rather than of dramatic irony, and the comic aspect is increased by the presence of the childishly uncomprehending rustics who believe it is all 'true'—as Bathsheba believed Troy was 'true' not so long before.

It is so, too, with Troy's death. We are adequately prepared for his intended entrance at Boldwood's Christmas party, but any hint of melodrama is considerably discounted by the overt realism with which the action is presented. The whole is shown matter-of-factly, and with almost none of the Gothic sensationalism which marked similar exciting moments in *Desperate Remedies*. The moment of Bathsheba's recognition of her husband is prepared for very slowly, by skilful use of the dramatic contrast between knowledge and ignorance. We have already been told of Troy's intentions, and our awareness is soon intensified with the discovery by some of the rustic characters that he is loitering on Boldwood's property. His startling and ghostly appearance at the window is made entirely credible by the subsequent sober comments of these ordinary men:

> The light from the pane was now perceived to be shining not upon the ivied wall as usual, but upon some object close to the glass. It was a human face.
> . . . The men, after recognizing Troy's features, withdrew across the orchard as quietly as they had come. The air was big with Bathsheba's fortunes tonight; every word everywhere concerned her. When they were quite out of earshot all by one instinct paused.
> 'It gave me quite a turn—his face,' said Tall, breathing.
> 'And so it did me,' said Samway. 'What's to be done?'
> 'I don't see that 'tis any business of ours,' Smallbury murmured dubiously.
> 'But it is! 'Tis a thing which is everybody's business,' said Samway. 'We know very well that master's on a wrong tack, and that she's quite in the dark, and we should let 'em know at once. Laban, you know her best—you'd better go and ask to speak to her.' (53)

The quiet suspense is further built up by setting the solemn debating in the darkness against the bright, unconcerned activity inside the house:

> Laban then went to the door. When he opened it the hum of bustle rolled out as a wave upon a still strand—. . . and was deadened to a murmur as he closed it again. Each man waited intently, and looked around at the dark treetops gently rocking against the sky and occasionally shivering in a slight wind, as if he took interest in the scene, which neither did. (53)

The suspense is conveyed through understatement, in Hardy's calm presentation of the facts, without any extra heightening or embellishment.

Troy's prediction that he will be received like 'a sort of Alonzo the Brave' has already prepared us for some kind of Gothic fantasy:

('. . . when I go in the guests will sit in silence and fear, and all laughter and pleasure will be hushed, and the lights in the chamber burn blue, and the worms—Ugh, horrible!—Ring for some more brandy, Pennyways, I felt an awful shudder just then!') (52, vii)

Yet this is almost the only concession Hardy makes to the popular romance tradition. Troy's actual entrance is anticlimactic in its inconspicuousness. Bathsheba thinks at first that he is the coachman come to fetch her; Boldwood welcomes him in; some of the guests notice and recognize him, some do not. Bathsheba's first state of shock passes unnoticed until Troy, like the conventional villain he has impersonated throughout the novel, begins to laugh 'a mechanical laugh'; then, simply, Hardy says, 'Boldwood recognized him now'.

Still, realism predominates over sensationalism. Bathsheba does not scream or faint in an attractive heap; her shock is described in terms of detached observation:

She had sunk down on the lowest stair; and there she sat, her mouth blue and dry, and her dark eyes fixed vacantly upon him, as if she wondered whether it were not all a terrible illusion. (53)

Hardy is no more than a reporter: he merely describes emotions and actions as they appear, inventorially. The gun shot is

. . . a sudden deafening report that echoed through the room and stupefied them all. The oak partition shook with the concussion, and the place was filled with grey smoke.
    In bewilderment they turned their eyes to Boldwood. At his back, as he stood before the fireplace, was a gun-rack, as is usual in farmhouses, constructed to hold two guns. (53)

It is a clever reconstruction of scene; the keen eye of the reporter, parenthetically commenting on farm customs, contrasts dramatically with the stupefaction and confusion of the onlookers. There is no room for emotion. Even Troy's death is described scientifically and economically:

. . . the charge of shot did not spread in the least, but passed like a bullet into his body. He uttered a long gutteral sigh—there was a contraction—an extension—then his muscles relaxed, and he lay still. (53)

As a factual description of dying, this resembles very closely Hardy's later account of the death of the pig in *Jude the Obscure*. There is the same precision of observation, the same concentration on physical actuality. The words follow, in their quick jerky phrasing, the very actions of dying. Compared with this, Boldwood's reaction (his 'gnashing despair' and 'swollen veins', and the 'frenzied look' that gleamed in his eye) is rather unconvincing. Nevertheless, Hardy's theatrical touches do not really mar the episode because they are continually countered by quick reversions to apparent normality. The general atmosphere is made credible by the stress laid on the reactions of the outsiders to the drama. Blankness and bewilderment are the main emotions portrayed, and the whole takes place in slow-motion, as though shock has crystallized even action. It marks a considerable progress from the final scenes of *Desperate Remedies*. In effect, Hardy has completely reversed his melodramatic technique. Instead of intensifying the bizarre and extraordinary, he shows us, through the attitudes and reactions of the other, uninvolved characters, that the incredible is real.

III

The scenes depicting the storm are without doubt the most important in the book, and for this reason I have left them till last. Not only do they illustrate, in combination, almost all the techniques Hardy uses in *Far from the Madding Crowd*, but they also form a major centre of the action and bring together a great many of the images and effects which make a detailed pattern throughout the novel. Impression combines with exact observation; realism contrasts with exaggeration and metaphor; action and spectacle become indistinguishable from each other. The natural process of the storm, at its particular point in the narrative, blends with and highlights what has gone before and what is to come. Together with the sword-exercise and the episode of the gargoyle (all, inevitably, related to the artificial and spectacular figure of Troy, who is the 'deviation from the norm' in the novel), it sums up the total impression of what Hardy is trying to convey within the fabric of the story in a single concentrated image. More specifically, it helps to point the role of man in the scheme of things, integral with it (like Gabriel Oak) or removed from it by his own actions (like Troy).

In presenting dramatic action Hardy deliberately tones down the elements of incredibility, inserting the comments and reactions of uninvolved characters to emphasize the enormity of actual events. In the episode of the storm, however, he uses artificial and frankly melodramatic imagery in order to highlight what is in its essence the portrayal of extreme realism. Again, the moment of greatest impact is built up to very slowly, just as Troy's arrival at Boldwood's party is long delayed and anticipated. John Holloway describes the storm as 'an extended and slow-changing complex of many natural processes', whose 'mere spectacle . . . is only hinted at through a chronicle of events which make it part of the natural order'.[4] The length and subtlety of its treatment not only stress the intensity and force of the actual moment of breaking, but also relate the storm's horror and magnificence to the smallest details of everyday living and to the lives

4. John Holloway, *The Victorian Sage* (London, 1953), pp. 255–56.

of the insects and animals. The orchestration of effects begins at ground level, as we see through Oak's sympathetic vision first the toad, travelling humbly across the path to safety, then the slug and the spiders who creep indoors, and then the sheep, who huddle together around a furze-bush, forming in perspective a pattern 'not unlike a vandyked lace collar'. Interspersed with the quiet scenes of nature's warning are flashbacks to the actions of the unconcerned human beings. The drunken men in the barn, noisily sleeping and oblivious of the potential disaster brewing, give added emphasis to the still awareness and suspense of the outside world.

The transition from reality to fantasy is always accomplished by the skilful blending of both elements. Accordingly, from the ordinary terror of the land creatures, Hardy develops fanciful similes relating the processes of the atmosphere to the actions of huge nightmare beasts: the breeze becomes a hot breath 'from the parted lips of some dragon about to swallow the globe'; a huge cloud is 'a grim misshapen body' in the 'teeth of the wind'; the smaller clouds are likened to a terrified young brood 'gazed in upon by some monster' (36). Sometimes the storm's uncanny life is only hinted at in a vivid compressed metaphor; the first flash of lightning is described in one concise verb as a huge phosphorescent bird—'A light *flapped* over the scene' (my italics): simultaneously the blinding speed, almost the sound, is conveyed in this one word, and a greater dread is implied by the transferring of a weird animal existence to this inanimate force. Then, immediately, we are returned to earth with the quiet vision of Bathsheba's bedroom window, the candle shining, and her shadow sweeping to and fro upon the blind. All the drama is otherworldly; the living creatures of the earth are now revealed only in flashes, frozen in attitudes of fear, like unreal drawings. Trees and bushes are 'distinct as in a line engraving'; heifers in a paddock are momentarily visible in the act of 'galloping about in the wildest and maddest confusion, flinging their heels and tails high into the air, their heads to earth'; a poplar is like 'an ink stroke on burnished tin' (37). Most amazing in this description is Hardy's control and economy, his selection of vivid random images to create a total picture. Myriad shades of meaning are compressed into single words; intensity is conveyed by sudden changes from brilliant weird light to smothering darkness. The skies become a battlefield in which vast manoeuvres are planned, as the lightning gleams 'like a mailed army'. Yet in the context of this concentrated and understated preparation, the actual breaking of the storm has none of the melodramatic exaggeration which the passage, taken alone, might signify. To Oak and Bathsheba, working on the hayricks, the first huge flash

> was almost too novel for its inexpressibly dangerous nature to be at once recognized, and they could only comprehend the magnificence of its beauty. It sprang from east, west, north, south, and was a perfect dance of death. The forms of skeletons appeared in the air, shaped with blue fire for

bones—dancing, leaping, striding, racing around, and mingling altogether in unparalleled confusion. With these were intertwined undulating snakes of green, and behind these was a broad mass of lesser light. Simultaneously came from every part of the tumbling sky what may be called a shout; since, though no shout ever came near it, it was more of the nature of a shout than of anything else earthly. In the meantime one of the grisly forms had alighted upon the point of Gabriel's rod, to run invisibly down it, down the chain, and into the earth. (37)

Here, as so often in Hardy's descriptions, it is the *effect* which first strikes us. In comparison with what has gone before, the style is almost clumsy, too polysyllabic (as in 'inexpressibly dangerous', 'unparalleled confusion'), consciously rationalizing ('. . . what may be called a shout'). Taken in its context, it is the imagery alone which is striking, and this gains most of its force by its contiguity with the infinitesimal human beings on whom the imaginative effect is being made. The success of Hardy's most extreme effects is almost entirely in his relation of them to human scale: '. . . love, life, everything human, seemed small and trifling in such close juxtaposition with an infuriated universe'.

It has been hypothesized[5] that Hardy's inspiration for the storm scene was derived from a similar description in Harrison Ainsworth's *Rookwood*, that most melodramatic of Gothic novels. If this is so (and the inclusion of the staging of Turpin's ride into *Far from the Madding Crowd* might be extra proof of the influence), then the mastery of Hardy's extended version becomes even more apparent. Like Ainsworth, Hardy lists the anxious movements of animals, instinctively aware of the coming danger, and he too likens the first rumbles of thunder to the rattle of artillery. Ainsworth's description, however, is a great deal shorter and relies largely for effect on conscious archaisms (cattle are 'kine', rooks have 'pinions') and on poetical images ('night rushed onwards like a sable steed . . . in ten minutes it was dunnest night . . .').[6] Melodramatic effects are here deliberately used to enhance the scene and the whole has a contrived air, even though the conception is basically less extravagant than Hardy's.

Hardy, on the other hand, extends and simplifies the background of the scene and contracts his nightmare images into sharp separate pictures, only hinting at the unreal terror on the face of actuality by isolated words and phrases. The effect of reality is gained by the use of sudden oppositions—the inclusion of harsh, onomatopoeic words in a string of soft sounds, the quick contrasting of ordinary actions and everyday thoughts with the vast awesomeness of the universe. The random thoughts of Gabriel Oak as he notes 'how strangely the red feather of her hat shone in this light' give way precipitately to the crash and blaze of white heat as a tree is sliced in half by lightning, and a 'new one among those terrible voices mingled with the last crash of

5. See Carl Weber, *Hardy of Wessex* (New York, 1965), pp. 9–10, and F.B. Pinion, *A Hardy Companion* (London, 1968), p. 154.

6. Harrison Ainsworth, *Rookwood* (1834), Bk II, Ch. i.

those preceding' (27). At one moment the soft crunching sounds of the spar gads seem loud in the uncanny silence and blackness; at the next the whole earth is shaken with bursts of light and demoniacal sound. In the total impression the credible and the supernatural are practically inseparable, because even the most startling concepts are built up from the minutest observation of reality. The metaphorical descriptions of the storm develop from these prosaic, natural representations to an imaginative transference of reality, and from there to the grotesque and ghoulish images in the dream-world of the sky.

The importance of these scenes does not lie only in the skill with which Hardy implies the connection between the universal and the particular. The dramatic intensity of the storm also starkly illustrates the principles guiding the lives and actions of the main protagonists, especially in their relationships with Bathsheba; thus Troy remains selfishly unaware and unconcerned, Oak struggles calmly against the odds and ultimately succeeds, while Boldwood just lets it rain. All through the novel Hardy traces a pattern of imagery which highlights these differences, especially the disparity between Oak and Troy, which is epitomized in the warring of the sky and the earth, man against lightning. In many ways, Hardy's portrayal of the storm at its breaking recalls the meteoric brilliance of Troy's sword-play earlier in the story. The lightning of his thrusts and the scarcely realized fear of their striking parody in miniature the fiendish shouts and yells of the humanized electricity in the sky, while Bathsheba's dazed state of unawareness as he surrounds her with the 'circling gleams' of a 'firmament of light' parallels her bewildered acceptance of the nightmare elemental war in the later scene. The impressionistic description of Troy vibrating like a 'twanged harpstring' is continued in the simile of the skies, filled with an incessant light, 'frequent repetition melting into complete continuity, as an unbroken sound results from the successive strokes on a gong' (37). In both scenes the effect is one of hypnotic excitement, in which speed, sound and colour, together with rapid alternations from real to unreal, create an impression of continual movement and extreme emotional tension.

Early in the novel, Hardy suggests a continuity between the mundane and the spectacular. Before the introduction of Troy there are subtle premonitions of conflict, and even the preparations for shearing-time hint at something more than earthly:

> All the surrounding cottages were more or less scenes of the same operation; the scurr of whetting spread into the sky from all parts of the village as from an armoury previous to a campaign. Peace and war kiss each other at their hours of preparation—sickles, scythes, shears and pruning hooks, ranking with swords, bayonets and lances, in their common necessity for point and edge. (20)

Oak, we are told, stands at the grindstone 'somewhat as Eros is represented when in the act of sharpening his arrows'. His dexterity in piercing the gas-swollen sheep parallels Troy's skill and accuracy with his sword in the trivial acts of spitting caterpillars and cutting off locks of hair. The picture of the shearers, too, reflects in miniature the picture of Troy surrounding Bathsheba with flashes of sword-light:

> . . . the shearers knelt, the sun slanting in upon their bleached shirts, tanned arms and the polished shears they flourished, causing these to bristle with a thousand rays. . . . Beneath them a captive sheep lay panting, quickening its pants as misgiving merged in terror, till it quivered like the hot landscape outside. (22)

In each case Hardy shows how the earthly responds to the metaphysical; how human and animal alike are controlled by the power of something they do not understand. Yet, always, the mystery is itself part of the real and is transformed only by imagination or ignorance. Troy's air of martial splendour is only a fleeting vision and palls beneath the terrifying battle of the storm, but in a sense he shares with it an identical uncanny force—even though Gabriel Oak's bond with the soil is a more durable strength.

The blending of imagery—real and unreal, rural and artificial, earth and sky—creates a structural and thematic pattern within the novel. The implied similarities and contrasts between the individual characters and the universe are completely absorbed into the action of the narrative. The metaphors range in depth as well as breadth and contain much of the ambiguity and irony of the connecting story, which Henry James dismisses as being 'very short and simple', and 'distended to its rather formidable dimensions by the infusion of a large amount of conversational and descriptive padding. . . .'[7] The 'padding', and its combinations and ramifications, are worked out with consummate skill, even to the personalities themselves. Bathsheba herself contains elements linking her to all sides of the story; she is intrinsically rural, likened to summer skies and fresh flowers, panting like a robin, blushing like a sunset; again, she is romantic and vain, coquettish and artificial, believing in dreams and impossible fantasies. Frequently unaware of the reality surrounding her, she is yet able to battle with the vagaries of nature and ultimately to understand the workings of her own mind. Like a chameleon, she is seen in totally different ways by the three men who want her: to Oak she is part of the natural world he loves and understands; to Troy, she is a challenging enemy; to Boldwood, who epitomizes the reversal of rationality, she is an exaggerated and impossible dream.

Far from the Madding Crowd is the first of Hardy's novel to show a distinct pattern of imagery relating to the theme, and the first to show consistently the extended relationship between the mental and physical states, between the worlds of absolute reality and imagined truth. For the first time, too, the action of the novel is directly related to its

7. Henry James, *The Nation* (New York, 24 December 1874), quoted in Lawrence Lerner and John Holmstrom, *Thomas Hardy and His Readers* (London, 1968), p. 30.

artistic structure and to its theme, instead of being simply a mechanical contrivance producing incredibility and suspense in equal quantities. * * *

ROBERT C. SCHWEIK

[Hardy's Shifting Narrative Modes]†

In spite of the scholarship which has been published in the last twenty years on the composition and revision of Hardy's novels, it is fair to say that by far the bulk of critical analysis of his fiction still proceeds on a fundamentally untenable basis—on the assumption that Hardy's novels can safely be discussed as if they were unified narrative constructs. In fact, Hardy's novels are more often characterized by marked shifts in narrative intention that came about in the process of composition, and any attempt to comment accurately on Hardy's fiction must take such shifts into account. *Far from the Madding Crowd* is a particularly clear example of the kind of narrative structure that can result from changes in narrative manner that grew out of the process of composition itself. In fact, the structure of *Far from the Madding Crowd* is something like a record of the ways that Hardy grappled with the problems of its composition—a record of some fine artistic successes achieved in the midst of extraordinary artistic uncertainty; a record of changing purposes, of narrative strategies tried and abandoned with varying degrees of care and carelessness; and a record of indecisions, compromises, and expedients accepted in an effort to get the thing done. My purpose in this paper is to trace that record in detail, and to suggest, by way of conclusion, what bearing this may have on future critical comment on the novel.

I

When the final five chapters of *Far from the Madding Crowd* appeared in the *Cornhill Magazine*, they dazzled one reviewer into speculating that they could be from the hand of George Eliot. Hardy himself was puzzled and annoyed by the comparison; and some later critics were inclined to displays of knowledgeable amazement that anyone could confuse the two. Yet these opening chapters were something different; of course they were not in the manner of George Eliot, but it would have been difficult to assign them to any other of Hardy's contemporaries either, nor were they quite what a reader of Hardy's earlier fiction might have expected from the writer himself. They deserve closer scrutiny than they have usually received, not only

†From F. B. Pinion, ed. *Budmouth Essays on Thomas Hardy* (Dorchester: The Thomas Hardy Society Ltd., 1976), pp. 21–38.

because they have the obvious importance of creating first impressions, but because they reveal some authorial difficulties which Hardy faced at the beginning of the novel, and because they provide a convenient benchmark against which his subsequent performance may be considered.

The effect created by the opening chapters of *Far from the Madding Crowd* results largely from a delicate shifting and balancing of narrative attitudes which range between serious concern and detached amusement. Hardy's initial description of Gabriel Oak, for example, begins with a paragraph of one sentence devoted to an exaggerated metaphoric description of Oak's smile, and immediately continues with a series of broad and obviously light-hearted generalizations on Oak's moral character—we are told that Oak is a 'young man of sound judgment, easy motions, proper dress, and general good character', that on Sundays he was given to 'misty views' and 'went to church but yawned privately by the time the congregation reached the Nicene creed', and that his friends considered him sometimes a good man, sometimes a bad man, and sometimes a salt-and-pepper mixture. These tongue-in-cheek observations on the subject of Oak's moral character (the manner, and in fact, some of the particulars are reminiscent of Hardy's description of William Dewy in *Under the Greenwood Tree*) are followed by remarks on the quaintly amusing details of his ordinary dress, and they culminate in a comic, almost mock-epic, account of Oak's watch. But following this account, which has become progressively more comic, Hardy begins to shift the tone of his description by introducing a suggestion that Oak might appear otherwise to 'thoughtful persons'. The more neutral attitude suggested by the lines which immediately follow—where we are told that Oak still retains the 'hues and curves of youth' and even 'some relics of the boy' while possessing a potentially imposing height and breadth—marks a transition from the amused playfulness with which Hardy had begun to a more serious attitude implied in the following passage:

> But there is a way some men have, rural and urban alike, for which the mind is more responsible than flesh and sinew; it is a way of curtailing their dimensions by their manner of showing them. And from a quiet modesty that would have become a vestal, which seemed to continually impress upon him that he had no great claim on the world's room, Oak walked unassumingly, and with a faintly perceptible bend, yet distinct from a bowing of the shoulders. This may be said to be a defect in an individual if he depends for his valuation more upon his appearance than upon his capacity to wear well, which Oak did not.

By the concluding sentence of this passage, however, Oak's quiet modesty has already been reduced to a less prepossessing 'capacity to wear well'; in the next paragraph Hardy gradually reassumes a more detached and less serious tone, then abruptly concludes his description of Oak with a casually reductive comment: 'In short, he was twenty-eight, and a bachelor'. Thus, in a matter of six paragraphs, Hardy moves from the amused and casual attitude which he adopts at the opening to a manner which implies a more serious concern about Oak's character, and he returns, finally, to end again on a lighter note with an off-hand quip.

This frequent shifting and balancing of attitudes toward his subject is characteristic of Hardy's manner throughout the first five chapters of *Far from the Madding Crowd*. In the process we are made aware that the relationship of Oak and Bathsheba involves some fundamentally serious concerns—the problem Bathsheba faces of attracting an acceptable lover, and the sexual need which underlies Oak's response to her. Hardy's descriptions of Bathsheba have a way of conveying Oak's interest in her unseen body, and her sexuality is discreetly suggested in the scenes in which Oak observes her—as she surveys herself in a looking glass ('her thoughts seeming to glide into far-off though likely dramas in which men would play a part') or rides astride ('in the manner demanded by the saddle, though hardly expected of the woman'). Their courtship takes place against a rural setting of lambing and calving, where, appropriately, Oak's conversation finally turns to babies, and Bathsheba struggles between her desire for independence ('I *hate* to be thought man's property in that way') and her desire to be dominated ('I want somebody to tame me; I am too independent'). Furthermore, Hardy reminds his readers from time to time that Oak and Bathsheba have qualities of character which are not to be taken lightly: in Oak's remark on Bathsheba's vanity there is a suggestion that her character may be seriously flawed, and there are pointed authorial comments to the effect that Oak has a 'special' if 'static' power, 'morally, physically, and mentally', that he is 'even-tempered' and faithful in love, and that he is an 'intensely humane man' who pities even the untimely fate of his sheep. Moreover, the action sometimes bears out Oak's special worthiness and Bathsheba's sturdy independence. But if the reader is expected to take Oak and Bathsheba with some seriousness, it is with a seriousness qualified by the comic aspect in which they are so often presented: Bathsheba haggling over two-pence and huffily resenting Oak's payment of it ('in gaining her a passage he had lost her her point, and we know how women take a favour of that kind'); Oak returning to his work with 'an air between Tragedy and Comedy'; Oak's face 'rising like the moon behind the hedge' as he appears to Bathsheba; Oak dressed in his waistcoat 'patterned all over with the sprigs of an elegant flower uniting the beauties of both rose and lily without the defects of either', his hair slicked down to 'a splendidly novel colour between that of guano and Roman cement'; Bathsheba breathlessly pursuing Oak and explaining that she has difficulty thinking outdoors because her 'mind spreads away so'; Oak pursuing Bathsheba round a holly bush and responding to his reject suit 'with the bearing of one who is going to give his days and nights to Ecclesiastes forever'.

There are similar variations of tone in Hardy's treatment of the rural setting in the first five chapters of the novel. His first description of the heavens in Chapter II is now a quite straightforward evocation of the solemnity and grandeur of the sky above Norcombe Hill, although in editions before 1912 the passage ended with a slightly mocking turn of phrase: 'After such a nocturnal reconnoitre among these astral clusters, aloft from the customary haunts of thought and vision, some men may feel raised to a capability for eternity at once'. A second passage in the same chapter shows similar alterations in tone:

> Castor and Pollux with their quiet shine were almost on the meridian: the barren and gloomy Square of Pegasus was creeping round to the north-west; far away through the plantation Vega sparkled like a lamp suspended amid the leafless trees, and Cassiopeia's chair stood daintly poised on the upper-most boughs.
>
> 'One o'clock,' said Gabriel.
>
> Being a man not without a frequent consciousness that there was some charm in this life he led, he stood still after looking at the sky as a useful instrument, and regarded it in an appreciative spirit, as a work of art superlatively beautiful. For a moment he seemed impressed with the speaking loneliness of the scene, or rather with the complete abstraction from all its compass of the sights and sounds of man. Human shapes, interferences, troubles, and joys were all as if they were not, and there seemed to be on the shaded hemisphere of the globe no sentient being save himself; he could fancy them all gone round to the sunny side.

The sober weight evoked by Hardy's description of 'barren and gloomy' Pegasus 'creeping round' contrasts with his image of the dainty poising of Cassiopeia's chair; the general picturesqueness of the constellations is juxtaposed incongruously against the matter-of-factness of Oak's 'One o'clock'; and narrative attitude ranges from reverence to playful imaginativeness as Hardy proceeds from his reference to the modest 'charm' of Oak's life, to an evocation of the 'speaking loneliness' Oak feels in gazing at the 'superlatively beautiful' sky, and then back to the more light-hearted 'fancy' of the concluding phrase.

Broader variations in tone are notable in Hardy's treatment of the smaller details of rural environment in the first five chapters of the novel. A feeling for the grimness in natural surroundings suggested by a remark like 'Many a small bird went to bed supperless that night among the bare boughs' will be countered by the playfully fanciful perspective supplied in another:

> Nothing disturbed the stillness of the cottage save the chatter of a knot of sparrows on the eaves; one might fancy scandal and rumour to be no less the staple of these little coteries on roofs than of those under them.

And, again, the activities of lambing and calving—the animal 'facts of life' at Norcombe—will sometimes be presented in a manner which emphasizes the precariousness of newborn life, and at other times be treated in a detached and fancifully comic way:

The cow standing erect was of the Devon breed, and was encased in a tight warm hide of rich Indian red, as absolutely uniform from eyes to tail as if the animal had been dipped in a dye of that colour, her long back being mathematically level. The other was spotted, gray and white. Beside her Oak now noticed a little calf about a day old, looking idiotically at the two women, which showed it has not long been accustomed to the phenomenon of eyesight, and often turning to the lantern, which it apparently mistook for the moon, inherited instinct having as yet had little time for correction by experience. Between the sheep and the cows Lucina had been busy on Norcombe Hill lately.

Finally, there are similar variations of tone in Hardy's treatment of the two major crises which occur in the opening chapter of *Far from the Madding Crowd*. The critical moment in which Gabriel Oak almost loses his life by suffocation is really over before the reader is made aware of any cause for concern, and the potential seriousness of the event is minimized by the dialogue which follows it—a dialogue which slips almost imperceptibly towards the teasing playfulness of the conclusion in which Gabriel is allowed momentarily to hold Bathsheba's hand. Another and even more obvious effort to maintain a somewhat precarious balance between a serious and a comic attitude toward the action is notable in Hardy's account of the 'pastoral tragedy' of Chapter V. The incident itself is prefaced by two paragraphs which provide a broadly comic account of Oak's dogs, after which the narrative become increasingly sober as Hardy develops the events in which Oak loses sheep and farm, and culminates in passages of a grimly serious tone:

> It was a second to remember another phase of the matter. The sheep were not insured. All the savings of a frugal life had been dispersed at a blow; his hopes of being an independent farmer were laid low—possibly forever. Gabriel's energies, patience, and industry had been so severely taxed during the years of his life between eighteen and eight-and-twenty, to reach his present stage of progress, that no more seemed left in him. He leant down upon a rail, and covered his face with his hands.

But, as the chapter continues, Hardy's narrative manner once again changes; he supplies a more detached and crisply factual account of what must have happened to Oak's sheep, and returns, finally, to wryly humorous description of the fate of the offending dog:

> George's son had done his work so thoroughly that he was considered too good a workman to live, and was, in fact, taken and tragically shot at twelve o'clock that same day—another instance of the untoward fate which so often attends dogs and other philosophers who follow out a train of reasoning to its logical conclusion and attempt perfectly consistent conduct in a world so largely made up of compromise.

The effect, in short, is to qualify the otherwise restrained and moving account of Oak's personal misfortune by placing it within a comic frame.

This close balancing and interweaving of contrasting narrative tones throughout the first five chapters of *Far from the Madding*

Crowd was certainly not characteristic of Hardy, nor was it likely to have been entirely congenial to him. Probably it came about as a result of his initial effort to combine a number of not entirely compatible objectives—the more serious treatment of character he had been groping toward in A *Pair of Blue Eyes*, the comic tone and rustic humour of *Under the Greenwood Tree* (which Leslie Stephen had praised in requesting a new novel for the *Cornhill Magazine*), and the 'incident' necessary to satisfy Stephen's demand for 'some distinct and well arranged plot'.[1] In any case, Hardy seems to have found the manner he had adopted increasingly difficult to maintain, and by Chapter V it had become something like a see-saw between wry comicality and profound seriousness. Yet, although Hardy no doubt felt the strain of keeping a balance between such diverse objectives, the result was a remarkably controlled opening; and his handling of scene and action leaves the impression of a narrator of broad awareness and flexible sensibility.

II

But the relatively self-contained action of the opening of the novel and its very indeterminateness of tone posed difficulties: the problem was to find a suitable continuation, and evidence of major revision in Chapters VI–XVIII of the manuscript testifies to Hardy's initial uncertainty about the direction the novel would take.[2] Hardy at first developed a continuation which differed very greatly from any version which appeared in print. Neither Boldwood nor Fanny Robin were to have had any significant part in it, and its manner was thoroughly comic. Some idea of this original continuation may be had by reading in sequence the present Chapters VI, VIII, X, and XV, ignoring, however, all matters related to Boldwood and Fanny Robin. It was probably in this form that Hardy submitted the first nine chapters of *Far from the Madding Crowd* to Leslie Stephen in the spring of 1873, and what won Stephen's approval, then, was very likely something much closer to the rustic comedy of *Under the Greenwood Tree* than to the novel which finally appeared in print.[3] Although Stephen was enthusiastic, Hardy was not satisfied with the almost entirely comic turn which the novel had taken, and during the summer of 1873 he made revisions which brought, Boldwood into the story as a major character and dramatized the Fanny Robin-Troy sub-plot; thus most of the material contained in what are now Chapters VII, IX, XI–XIV, and XVI was added. But while supplying a dramatic account of the Fanny-Troy relationship and developing

1. R. L. Purdy, *Thomas Hardy: A Bibliographical Study* (Oxford: The Clarendon Press, 1968), p. 336.

2. See R. C. Schweik, 'The Early Development of Hardy's *Far from the Madding Crowd*', *Texas Studies in Literature and Language*, Autumn 1967, pp. 415–28.

3. R. C. Schweik suggests the extent to which the early portions of the novel underwent a radical revision in 'A First Draft Chapter of Hardy's *Far from the Madding Crowd*', *English Studies*, August 1972, pp. 344–49.

Boldwood, Hardy had also to provide a continuation of the story of Bathsheba's adaptation to her new role, and of Oak to his. At best, such diverse matters would have been difficult to integrate smoothly, and, of course, some scenes (much of the present Chapters VI, VII, X, and XV) had already been independently written. Hardy chose to take advantage of the situation by emphasizing the contrastive features inherent in the different matters he was presenting. Thus, within Chapters VI–XVI, all of the major characters groups appear, but for the most part the various strands of their stories are developed separately, and the characters, so far as they act upon one another, do so mostly at a distance, separated physically and psychologically. This separation is further emphasized by marked differences in narrative manner, so that Hardy's treatment of Oak and the rustics, of the Fanny-Troy episodes, of Boldwood, and of Bathsheba, each has its distinct tone.

Perhaps most striking is the effect this change had upon the function of those scenes of rustic comedy already composed. Full as they are of the humour of rustic manners and rural anecdote, Hardy had certainly intended Chapters VIII, X, and XV to have their own intrinsic interest and special charm for urban readers; but with the introduction of the Fanny-Troy Chapters VII, XI, and XVI, they took on an additional function, for both the rustics' dialogues in Warren's malthouse and their meeting in Bathsheba's hall also convey particularly a sense of lives lived and experienced as social community, and these scenes, finally placed in immediate juxtaposition to the scenes devoted to the Fanny-Troy story in Chapters VII, XI, and XVI, serve to heighten the starkly evoked social isolation and helplessness of Fanny. The effect results from the sharply pointed contrasts in detail and emphasis which Hardy worked into the Fanny-Troy chapters. The shared community of the rustics had been most simply conveyed, of course, by their presence and activity as a group; but beyond this a complex of details serves to endow the rustic scenes with an aura of shared human sympathy. In Chapter X it emerges in expressions of concern for Fanny Robin. In the clubhouse atmosphere of the malthouse scenes it is rendered more immediately by the activities of passing round the communal mug and the sharing of bread and bacon in an atmosphere suffused by the ruddy glow of the kiln; by the presence of roasting potatoes and boiling coffee 'for the benefit of whosoever would call'; by the ready accommodations of the group to the foibles of its members—whether the maltster's insistence on his agedness, or Oak's touchiness about Bathsheba; and by the shared memories of the story-telling and mutual reminiscing. By adding transitional matter to these scenes which so richly convey an impression of the communal life of the rustics, Hardy was able to set beside them the portions of the Fanny-Troy story detailed in Chapters VII,

XI, and XVI. Of these, the meeting of Oak and Fanny in Chapter VII was composed most perfunctorily and depends most heavily on the trappings of melodrama—the silent, shivering, lonely girl, standing in the churchyard, her pulse 'beating with a throb of tragic intensity'. But Chapters XI and XVI are more carefully drafted, and each scene is treated with particular care to dehumanize the participants and so heighten the contrast they make with the shared life, common sympathy, and warm tones associated with the rustics. In Chapter XI, for example, Hardy carefully evokes the barrenness of the dreary moorland scene in which there are 'forms without features' shrouded in darkness and muffling snow, and Fanny herself is reduced to the blank anonymity of a 'spot' talking to a 'wall'.[4] Again, through most of Chapter XVI Troy stands with the abnormal rigidity of a church column while time is marked by the grotesque twitchings of a mechanical mannikin, and this exaggerated rigidity is carried over into his treatment of Fanny at the end of the chapter. Equally striking is the way laughter is used to convey the lack of human sympathy in these chapters—the 'low peal of laughter' over Fanny's plight which concludes Chapter XI, the titters and giggling of the bystanders in the church, and Troy's hoarse laugh as he deserts Fanny at the end of Chapter XVI.

Although they have such markedly contrasting features, the scenes which present the ballad-like tragedy of Fanny Robins in Chapters VII, XI, and XVI involve methods similar to those used for the rustic comedy of Chapters VII, X, and XV. Both present characters sketched with very broad strokes acting in relatively simple and sharply defined situations; both are devoid of authorial comment; and both depend heavily for their effects upon a carefully managed 'atmosphere' in which the action occurs.

In the groups of chapters devoted to Bathsheba and Boldwood in this portion of *Far from the Madding Crowd*, Hardy attempted to exploit a similar kind of contrast and a similar parallelism of method, but here the matter involved greater complexities both in character and situation, and the result was a more mixed success. The chapters devoted primarily to Bathsheba (IX, X, XII, and XIII) are handled in a way which most nearly continues the serio-comic tone of the opening of the novel. Again, within these chapters Hardy reminds his readers occasionally that there are some fundamentally serious issues at stake: there are further authorial comments on Bathsheba's sexuality ('there was potentially enough in that lithe slip of humanity for alarming exploits of sex, and daring enough to carry them out'), and further suggestions of her consciousness of male eyes, her vanity as a woman,

---

4. Hardy had originally identified the location of the Fanny-Troy meeting as at Melchester; then, in later printings of the novel, he amended this to achieve the anonymity of 'a certain town and military station, many miles north of Weatherbury'.

and her instinct to 'walk as a queen among these gods of the fallow, like a little sister of a little Jove'. But although Hardy does from time to time inject such reminders—sometimes with what strikes modern readers as the clumsily blunt directness of authorial forewarning ('Of love as a spectacle Bathsheba had a fair knowledge; but of love subjectively she knew nothing')—the sequence of vignettes supplied in Chapters IX, X, XII, and XIII is predominantly devoted to presenting the comedy of Bathsheba's deliberate efforts to act out the role of a poised and businesslike mistress of the farm while instinctively playing the role of coquette; and for the most part Hardy conveys the incongruity with detached amusement. The stage for her activities is supplied with the humour of local colour—the descriptions of the quaint oddities of her house and the rustic peculiarities of the market-place—and we are provided with glimpses of Bathsheba at home in comic confusion over Boldwood's unexpected call, scenes with Liddy in which Bathsheba feigns an air of superior detachment in an attempt to conceal her impulsive 'womanishness', and the comedy of Chapter X in which Bathsheba plays the role of grande dame, complete with appropriate exit:

> Then this small thesmothete stepped from the table, and surged out of the hall, her black silk dress licking up a few straws and dragging them along with a scratching noise upon the floor. Liddy, elevating her feelings to the occasion from a sense of grandeur, floated off behind Bathsheba with a milder dignity not entirely free from travesty, and the door was closed.

It is worth remarking, too, that the scenes devoted to Bathsheba convey a sense of lively ambience—the bustle of servant women, the crowd of workers in the hall, the throng of farmers in the market-place; and, even when she is relatively alone, there is the presence of Liddy and the comedy of the dialogues between them.

On the other hand, the chapters primarily devoted to Boldwood (XIV, XVII, and XVIII) are entirely devoid of precisely those features which most prominently characterize the scenes given to Bathsheba; and Hardy's effort, obvious enough to seem heavy-handed, was to emphasize the ponderously serious, withdrawn, and lonely life of Boldwood in a way which makes for a high degree of contrast with the scenes in which Bathsheba predominates. Boldwood is made to appear characteristically alone—a solitary caller, an exception among farmers, a 'lonely and reserved man', a 'celibate' whose barn is his almonry and cloister and whose parlour has the atmosphere of a 'Puritan Sunday lasting all the week'. Instead of the commonplaces of farm and market life in which Bathsheba moves, Hardy evokes about Boldwood an atmosphere that is distinctly queer, and (most notably in Chapter XIV) almost surrealistically distorted. Equally pointed is the contrast between the casually impulsive 'womanishness' which motivates Bathsheba in this portion of the novel and the ponderous and violent forces (rendered by mechanical, elemental, and military metaphors) which Hardy uses to characterize Boldwood.[5]

In effect, then, in Chapters VI–XVIII of *Far from the Madding Crowd* Hardy worked out a continuation for the opening of the novel which for the moment retained, and in fact increased, the kinds of variation in narrative manner with which he had begun: but now these variations occur between elements of chapter length or more—units which allowed greater room for development and did not require the kind of close control demanded by the manner Hardy had adopted in the opening chapters. Of course the revisions which brought Fanny Robin and Boldwood into the story also considerably expanded the scope, and altered the direction, of the novel; it was, in fact, something like beginning another novel with the sixth chapter—a novel whose effects largely depended upon a counterpointing of chapters and groups of chapters against one another, so that throughout Chapters VI–XVIII marked shifts in narrative manner from chapter to chapter serve to emphasize the contrasts between lives lived psychologically and physically apart, in greatly different social situations and equally different emotional atmospheres.

III

These effects had been achieved, however, by treating the four major character groups as relatively separate units. In the chapters immediately following (XIX–XXIII), Hardy brought Oak, the rustics, Boldwood, and Bathsheba together in scenes which prohibited the sharply defined contrasts and marked tonal differences he had exploited earlier; this posed a new problem of integrating matters previously developed separately, and resulted in still another pronounced change in narrative mode.

There was, first of all, the problem of what to do with Boldwood. In Chapters VI–XVIII, Hardy had brought Boldwood forward prominently as a character of major significance: he had devoted the whole of Chapter XIV and portions of Chapter XVII and XVIII to the elaboration of Boldwood's character; he had allowed Oak to assume a relatively subordinate role as a member of the rustic group; and he had been willing to heighten Boldwood's importance even at the expense of explicitly minimizing Oak's character by an authorial comment on

5. In some places, for example, Hardy describes Boldwood in language which suggests a kind of mechanical equilibrium: 'the perfect balance of enormous antagonistic forces—positives and negatives in fine adjustment' (XVIII); when he becomes interested in Bathsheba he feels 'the symmetry of his existence to be slowly getting distorted in the direction of an ideal passion' (XIV), and he speculates as to whether Bathsheba's movements 'were as geometrical, unchangeable, and as subject to laws as his own' (XVII). Elsewhere Hardy uses elemental and organic metaphors: Boldwood's feelings are either 'stagnant or rapid'; he is a 'hotbed of tropic intensity', and a man of 'wild capabilities' and potential 'high tides' whose feelings can be kindled to a 'great flame' (XVIII). In still other places the analogy is to a fortress whose walls have been breached: Bathsheba's triumph we are told is her 'consciousness of having broken into that dignified stronghold at last' (XVII), and Boldwood's face subsequently shows that 'he was now living outside his defences for the first time, and with a fearful sense of exposure' (XVIII).

Oak's 'mediocrity of inadequacy' which remained in the novel until the edition of 1877. But in spite of the pains he had taken to present Boldwood as an unusual personality, Hardy's conception of him had remained fundamentally simple. He had concentrated particularly on Boldwood's ponderous seriousness, his social isolation, and his psychology as an equilibrium of vast forces—features which had provided as sharp as possible a contrast to Bathsheba; but the wealth of circumstantial detail and the variety of analogy he employed to achieve this effect accomplished, in fact, very little else, for although they had momentarily created the illusion of character depth, Boldwood remained simply an all-or-nothing personality whose possibilities for further action had been defined almost entirely by his capacity for being either indifferent or extreme. Given this initial simplicity in Hardy's conception, there was really little that he could do immediately with Boldwood (short of reorienting the novel toward a more minute exploration of character psychology) except to have him mechanically persist in his lonely and obsessive pursuit of Bathsheba. And this, in fact, constitutes the central action of Chapters XIX–XXIII: there is an initial proposal scene in Chapter XIX; Boldwood's suit is the subject of Bathsheba's quarrel with Oak in Chapters XX and XXI; Boldwood reappears as suitor in Chapter XXII to ride with Bathsheba; and the sequence concludes with his second declaration at the end of Chapter XXIII. But although Boldwood's suit obviously constitutes the central action of this sequence of chapters, Hardy devoted relatively little space directly to it: at the most, Chapter XIX, somewhat more than a page or so of Chapter XXII, and perhaps a third Chapter XXIII. The reason for this is not difficult to see: clearly, on the level at which Hardy was dealing with Boldwood's character, it had required little practically to exhaust the limited dramatic possibilities inherent in Boldwood's obsessive pursuit and Bathsheba's guilty reluctance.

Yet it is also clear from the manuscript evidence that Hardy had intended to extend this action over at least six chapters, and what was not directly related to the necessarily limited treatment of Boldwood's suit had, of course, to be given over to other matters. It is not surprising, then, that throughout Chapters XIX–XXIII Hardy concentrated more intensively upon the details of farming life. He provided, in fact, a whole catalogue of farming matters (sheep-washing, shears-grinding, troubles in the sheepfold, the shearing-barn, the shearing process, the shearing-supper) and at the same time he introduced a secondary and related action—the quarrel of Oak and Bathsheba and the veterinary problems which lead to their reconciliation. Farming matters had, of course, an obvious relevance for this secondary action; but Hardy's effort to flesh out the scenes of Boldwood's strange courtship with carefully wrought and highly particularized accounts of the sheep-shearing process resulted (in spite of the excellence of Hardy's treatment of the matters themselves) in a curious sort of excrescence: for the farming background, at best only peripherally relevant to the Bathsheba-Boldwood affair, had to be brought to the foreground and allowed to assume proportions which nearly obscure the main action without providing any centre of its own. Rather, Hardy gave to each of the farming scenes a different emphasis: there is the description of the sheep-washing with its concentration on the moist fertility of the scene, as Bathsheba in her elegant riding-habit watches her men dripping wet at their work; there is the sheep-shearing itself, with its memorable evocation of the timeless functionalism of the great barn;[6] and the shearing-supper with the comedy of rustic dialogue and the antics of Joseph Poorgrass and Bob Coggan—and, of course, none of this in any distinct way relevant to the Boldwood-Bathsheba courtship. To compare the way in which the activities of lambing and calving in the first five chapters of the novel are used to create a distinctly subordinate yet integral and relevant environment for Oak's courtship of Bathsheba is to see that Hardy had found no similar way to integrate his materials in Chapters XIX–XXIII. This fact did not go unnoticed by Leslie Stephen, who (always conscious of the importance of 'incident') gently suggested that Hardy was slowing the action too much:

> As you ask me for my opinion I will say frankly that I think the sheep-shearing rather long for the present purpose. . . . For periodical purposes, I think it rather delays the action unnecessarily. What I should be inclined to do would be simply to omit the chapter headed the 'shearing supper' and to add a few paragraphs to the succeeding or preceding, just explaining that there had been a supper.

Hardy obliged by the deletion of an entire chapter, as Stephen suggested, but this, of course, simply rendered less obvious the real difficulty—the want of an integrated treatment of action and background.

IV

By the time he had reached Chapter XXIV of *Far from the Madding Crowd*, Hardy had already adopted three quite different approaches to his subject, and each successive change in narrative manner appears to have been dictated by the particular problem of composition he faced at the moment. In one respect, however, Hardy's method had remained remarkably consistent: throughout the first twenty-five chapters of *Far from the Madding Crowd* he frequently made use of direct authorial comments which relate the particulars of his narrative to some more general observation. The subjects of these authorial

---

6. An indication of the care with which Hardy composed these rural matters may be seen in the manuscript of the novel, which reveals the extraordinary, heavy revision he lavished on the description of the Great Barn in Chapter XXII.

Hardy's artful conduct of the narration in this chapter is the subject of a close and appreciative analysis by J. Hillis Miller in *Thomas Hardy: Distance and Desire*, Cambridge, Mass., 1970, pp. 57–66.

generalizations vary considerably and follow no particular pattern; the following examples are typically diverse:

> *On Oak's decision to make Bathsheba his wife:* Love is a possible strength in an actual weakness. Marriage transforms a distraction into a support, the power of which should be, and happily often is, in direct protection to the degree of imbecility it supplants. Oak began now to see light in this direction . . . (IV).

> *On Bathsheba's farm workers:* The assemblage—belonging to that class of society which casts its thoughts into the form of feeling, and its feelings into the form of commotion—set to work with a remarkable confusion of purpose (VI).

> *On Boldwood's address to Bathsheba:* Silence has sometimes a remarkable power of showing itself as the disembodied soul of feeling wandering without its carcass, and it is then more impressive than speech. In the same way, to say a little is often to tell more than to say a great deal. Boldwood told everything in that word (XIX).

> *On preparations for sheep-shearing:* Peace and war kiss each other at their hours of preparation—sickles, scythes, shears, and pruning-hooks ranking with swords, bayonets, and lances, in their common necessity for point and edge (XX).

Such authorial generalizations are, of course, part of the omniscient narrator's stock-in-trade. When used persistently, they have the effect of repeatedly inviting the reader to take (for the moment at least) a relatively more distant and detached view of the action—to see the immediate narrative particular within the larger perspective of a general observation on 'love' or 'woman' and so forth. What is striking about Hardy's use of such authorial generalizations in *Far from the Madding Crowd* is their unusual distribution: some sixty occur in the first twenty-five chapters of the novel, while in the remaining thirty-two chapters there are only twelve. This marked reduction in Hardy's use of authorial generalization after Chapter XXI was probably partly a result of the increased time pressure under which he worked;[7] in any case, it marks still another distinct shift in narrative method—and the beginning of a gradual decline into increasing dependence upon 'strong' effects, shock, surprise, and external melodrama.

This shift is not immediately noticeable, however, for after the introduction of Troy in Chapter XXIV Hardy began a sequence of seven chapters primarily devoted to the Troy-Bathsheba courtship, and particularly to the development of Troy's character; and here, once again, the new subject prompted still another adjustment in narrative method, and for a time carried the novel sufficiently to postpone until Chapter XXXI the obvious dependence upon the kinds of effects which mark the concluding portions of the novel. As a

---

7. This included a self-imposed deadline to finish the novel before his marriage in September 1874.

character, Troy lent himself more to the sorts of plot devices which Hardy could depend on to generate the 'incident' which Stephen had demanded—romantic entanglements, surprise discoveries, colourful and striking situations fraught with suspense. As a consequence, Hardy could now forego the detailed accounts of farming activities which had previously served to compensate for the cramping liabilities of Boldwood's character. Thus, throughout Chapters XXIV–XXX, Hardy provides only the briefest descriptions of hay-making and hiving, and both are made relatively integral parts of the main action. And, although once again in Chapter XXIX Hardy found occasion to bring Oak forward to act out his role as the mature, independent, critical, yet selflessly devoted lover of Bathsheba, certainly his central concern throughout Chapters XXIV–XXX was twofold: to establish Troy's untrustworthy character, and, at the same time, to render persuasively his attractiveness for Bathsheba. That Hardy conceived these as two relatively separate objectives is suggested by the strikingly different means he employed to achieve each. To establish Troy's character as unstable, untrustworthy, and unworthy of Bathsheba, Hardy relied largely on direct authorial comment. He approached Chapter XXV, 'The New Acquaintance Described', as a set piece—a strategy for character introduction which he would never entirely forego, even in his most mature work—but in this case he composed it with the ponderously inflated diction and laboriously balanced syntax notable in passages like the following:

> Troy was full of activity, but his activities were less of a locomotive than a vegetative nature; and, never being based upon any original choice of foundation or direction, they were exercised on whatever object chance might place in their way. Hence, whilst he sometimes reached the brilliant in speech because that was spontaneous, he fell below the commonplace in action, from inability to guide incipient effort. He had a quick comprehension and considerable force of character; but, being without the power to combine them, the comprehension became engaged with trivalties whilst waiting for the will to direct it, and the force wasted itself in useless grooves through unheeding the comprehension.

Similar efforts at elaborate balance and point (and with even more clumsy explicitness) appear elsewhere in Hardy's scattered authorial comments on Troy's character, as the following, from Chapter XXIX:

> And Troy's deformities lay deep down from a woman's vision, whilst his embellishments were upon the very surface; thus contrasting with the homely Oak, whose defects were patent to the blindest, and whose virtues were as metals in a mine.

Of course, Troy's 'deformities' are occasionally dramatized (as by Oak's discovery in Chapter XXIX that Troy was not the church-goer he claimed to be). It is in rendering Troy's attractiveness to Bathsheba, however, that Hardy relied primarily on a more oblique and evocative dramatizing of situations—and with considerably more persuasive art.

This more dense and suggestive mode, involving a close interaction of setting, incident, and dialogue, first appears in Chapter XXIV, where the meeting of Troy and Bathsheba in the fir plantation is developed in a way which emphasizes the meeting as a sexual encounter. There is the dramatic effect of Troy as the lantern reveals him ('His sudden appearance was to darkness what the sound of a trumpet is to silence'), and the dialogue which underlines the simple difference of sex:

> 'We have got hitched together somehow, I think.'
> 'Yes.'
> 'Are you a woman?'
> 'Yes.'
> 'A lady, I should have said.'
> 'It doesn't matter.'
> 'I am a man.'
> 'Oh!'

And in other ways the setting is made to reinforce the same impression:

> He too stooped, and the lantern standing on the ground between them threw the gleam from its open side among the fir-tree needles and the blades of long damp grass with the effect of a large glow-worm. It radiated upwards into their faces, and sent over half the plantation gigantic shadows of both man and woman, each dusky shape becoming distorted and mangled upon the tree-trunks till it wasted away to nothing.

This same mode is exploited, largely by dialogue, in Chapter XXVI, 'On the Verge of the Hay-Mead'; less fully in Chapter XXVII, 'Hiving the Bees'; and very fully indeed in Chapter XXVIII, 'The Hollow Amid the Ferns', where Troy's persuasive attractiveness is dramatized in a lush setting with its own phallic suggestiveness, and where action and dialogue combine conventional romantic gallantries with a description of a sword display whose erotic undertones can be felt even by readers quite innocent of any overt psychologizing over details. And much the same technique is employed in Chapter XXX, where the title, 'Hot Cheeks and Tearful Eyes' accurately describes what the chapter dramatizes.

V

But on the level at which Hardy was dealing with character, seven chapters were quite enough to exhaust even Troy's possibilities; thus by Chapter XXX Hardy had begun to reach the limits of what he could do in the mode he had adopted. No new characters remained to be introduced, and from Chapter XXXI on, then, through Chapter XLVII, Hardy slipped steadily toward a dependence on the kind of effects he could achieve by filling his narrative with mystery, physical threat, contrived surprise, and startling revelation. At this point, what had been a source of difficulty in earlier portions of the novel—Boldwood's simple characteristic tendency toward extremes—could now be exploited for its potential for active physical violence and otherwise kept as a threatening presence in the background. It is not surprising, then, that in Chapter XXXI Boldwood is brought forward to threaten violence on Troy, that he reappears in an even more threatening and violent posture in Chapter XXXIV, and that he is presented as driven nearly mad with despair by Chapter XXXVIII.

Nor is it surprising that the bulk of the action covered by Chapters XXXI–XLVII involves an elaborate and suspenseful series of mysteries, surprises, and revelations. There is the aura of doubt and mystery surrounding Bathsheba's trip, padded out with the details of the tracking skills of Coggan as he and Oak pursue a supposed thief,[8] and culminating in the surprise revelation of Bathsheba's marriage to Troy which occupies Chapters XXXII–XXXV; there is the dramatic race to save Bathsheba's grain against the advancing storm, and, of course, the violence of the storm scene itself in Chapters XXXVI–XXXVII; then the series of elaborately suspenseful scenes and dramatic revelations involving the death of Fanny Robin, which begins with Chapter XXXIX, 'Coming Home—A Cry', and culminates in Chapter XLIII, 'Fanny's Revenge', with its dramatic confrontation of Bathsheba and Troy over the open coffin of Fanny Robin and her child; and finally, there is the account of Troy's extraordinary reaction to Fanny's death, and the mystery of his disappearance after Chapter XLVII. An index of the extent to which Hardy was pressed to rely upon effects obtained by mystification and heightened suspense throughout Chapters XXXI–XLVII may be obtained from a consideration of an extensive revision which he made at the end of Chapter XLVII. As the manuscript shows, Hardy had originally intended to have Troy's fate not at all in doubt after he was nearly drowned while swimming; readers were originally informed at once that Troy signed on as a crewman of the ship that rescued him and undertook a voyage that would last at least six months. But Hardy took that information out of the conclusion of Chapter XLVII, so that we are now left only with the expectation that Troy was to be returned to land on the day following his rescue—and then told no more of him except that Bathsheba learns that his clothes have been discovered on shore in Chapter XLVIII. The arrangement Hardy finally chose, then, postponed an explanation of Troy's disappearance until Chapter L, and created for the space of two chapters a mystery where there formerly had not been one. It is this kind of mystification and dependence on 'surprise' revelations which particularly characterizes Hardy's narrative method in Chapters XXXI–XLVII.

But to say only this is, of course, to ignore an important qualification, for although in Chapters XXXI–XLVII Hardy slipped more and more into melodrama, he nevertheless often managed to achieve within this mode some of the most carefully wrought and memorable

---

8. Hardy took the business of Coggan's tracking skills seriously enough to provide in the manuscript a series of carefully drawn patterns of horses' hooves illustrating the various gaits which Coggan interprets; these, however, were never printed.

scenes in *Far from the Madding Crowd*: Joseph returning with Fanny Robin's body; Bathsheba and Troy before Fanny's coffin; and Troy's moment of despairing self-awareness after the accidental destruction of his plantings over Fanny's grave. Certainly nowhere in the novel are there so many places where the fragility of human life, the bitterness of human anguish, the dignity of death, and the mysterious operation of natural forces are rendered so plangently.

Nevertheless, the increasing time pressures under which Hardy worked resulted, certainly, in a distinctly recognizable lowering of aims. It was only when he was in the later stages of composing *Far from the Madding Crowd* that Hardy wrote to Leslie Stephen that he wished 'merely to be considered a good hand at a serial'. And of course the concluding chapters of *Far from the Madding Crowd* are notoriously weak. There is, for example, a passage in Chapter LV in which Oak and Smallbury have the following dialogue about Boldwood:

> 'Do ye think he really was out of his mind when he did it?' said Smallbury.
> 'I can't honestly say that I do,' Oak replied.

This passage constitutes an addition to the original text; it is not in the manuscript at all, and in its place is a message in which Oak affirms that Boldwood's mind 'seems quite a wreck'. Significantly, such a radical alteration in Oak's view of Boldwood, which in other circumstances would have important implications, here makes no practical difference at all—a fact entirely characteristic of the looseness with which details in the final portion of the novel are related. And at worst the conclusion degenerates into such wildly extravagant matters as Troy's reappearance at the fair, acting the role of Dick Turpin, and reaching under the tent wall to snatch Pennyways' letter to Bathsheba out of her hand without being seen.

What in fact saves the conclusion of *Far from the Madding Crowd* is that with all the clumsy machinations of plot with which Hardy brings the novel to a close, he nevertheless manages in his treatment of Oak and Bathsheba to suggest a kind of relationship between them which plausibly yields a modest happiness achieved within the stringent limitations of ordinary human possibilities:

> They spoke very little of their mutual feelings: pretty phrases and warm expressions being probably unnecessary between such tried friends. Theirs was that substantial affection which arises (if any arises at all) when the two who are thrown together begin first by knowing the rougher sides of each other's character, and not the best till further on, the romance growing up in the interstices of a mass of hard prosaic reality.

It is a closing which is all the better for ending on such a finely restrained note, and even that is tempered and qualified by the comic wisdom of the concluding paragraphs. In ending, then, Hardy managed momentarily to recapture something of the finely balanced narrative mode with which he had begun, and the effect is perhaps enhanced because it comes almost as a surprise.

VI

What is clear from the foregoing examination, however, is that in *Far from the Madding Crowd* Hardy's method of composition was so thoroughly improvisatory that, taken as a whole, the resulting narrative structure is less a design than a record of changing narrative strategies and expedients involving alterations in matters so diverse as authorial distance, treatment of setting, narrative focus, use of imagery and symbol, and arrangement and subject of whole chapters. If Hardy may be said to have proceeded in *Far from the Madding Crowd* with 'immense assurance'[9] it was not that of a writer following a deliberate and well-defined plan but the assurance of an author confident of his powers to circumvent and overcome unforeseen narrative obstacles; and any critic who approaches *Far from the Madding Crowd* with the hope to discover in it some uniform and deliberate development of setting, imagery, symbol, or theme will be likely to succeed at the expense of creating the impression that the novel proceeds with more regularity and clarity of purpose than in fact is the case.

PETER J. CASAGRANDE

A New View of Bathsheba Everdene†

It has become commonplace among critics of Thomas Hardy's *Far from the Madding Crowd* (1874) to say that Bathsheba Everdene, the novel's heroine, develops through misfortune and suffering from a vain, egotistical girl into a wise, sympathetic woman.[1] There is something to this view, for apparently at least Bathsheba changes for the better between the beginning and end of the novel. She learns to

9. The phrase is taken from Michael Millgate's discussion of *Far from the Madding Crowd* in *Thomas Hardy: His Career as a Novelist*, London and New York, 1971, p. 82.

†From Dale Kramer, ed., *Critical Approaches to the Fiction of Thomas Hardy* (New York: Barnes and Noble, 1979), pp. 50–73. The author's notes have been slightly abbreviated.

1. See John Halperin, *Egoism & Self-Discovery in the Victorian Novel* (New York: Burt Franklin, 1974), p. 217: '*Far from the Madding Crowd* addresses itself basically to the question of how to live as painlessly as possible and answers that question by tracing Bathsheba's development from a state of oral solipsism and narrow vision to one of moral expansion and wider sympathy.' Dale Kramer, *Thomas Hardy: The Forms of Tragedy* (London: Macmillan; Detroit: Wayne State University Press, 1975) p. 31. writes: 'Bathsheba . . . definitely evolves from

a flirtatious, light-hearted girl to a self-confident farmer, to a chastened but stubborn wife, . . . to a subdued female anxious for the protective strength of a Gabriel Oak' (ellipses mine). Albert J. Guerard, *Thomas Hardy: The Novels and Stories* (1949: rpt. New York: New Directions, 1964) p. 140, says that 'the matured Bathsheba may have to depend on Oak at critical hours, but she is a courageous figure in her own right. She has been changed by responsibility and disaster.' My own view is nearer that of Richard C. Carpenter, 'The Mirror and the Sword: Imagery in *Far from the Madding Crowd*', NCF, XVIII (1964) 345: 'Without [its] imagery *Far from the Madding Crowd* would be merely a kind of melodramatic folk tale about the fair charmer who overplayed her capriciousness and came to insight and repentance almost too late.' The novel's imagery, argues Carpenter, reveals two aspects of Bathsheba's character, the re-

sympathise with Fanny Robin, seeks to make amends to Farmer Boldwood, and marries the exemplary Gabriel Oak. However, there is much in Bathsheba that this view does not account for. Take for example the following passage, typical of others:

> Bathsheba was no schemer for marriage, nor was she deliberately a trifler with the affections of men, and a censor's experience on seeing an actual flirt after observing her would have been a feeling of surprise that Bathsheba could be so different from such a one, and yet so like what a flirt is supposed to be.
>
> She resolved never again, by look or by sign, to interrupt the steady flow of this man's [Boldwood's] life. But a resolution to avoid an evil is seldom framed till the evil is so far advanced as to make avoidance impossible. (18)

One thing here is in basic conflict with a 'transformist' view of Bathsheba; she is an un-deliberate, inadvertent, unconscious agent of evil. Her actions are not within her control. This suggests that with her, moral, growth, if possible, is always problematical. And Hardy's view of her is that of the surprised censor: he sympathises with her infirmity (for which she is not responsible) at the same time as he deplores her irrationality and its conseqences.

The view of Bathsheba as one who progresses toward wider sympathy has gone unchallenged, probably because she is often described as an unambiguous character rendered in broad, sure strokes. 'Bathsheba,' writes Douglas Brown, 'dominates the novel, not as a human personality created and explored with the searching art of the classical novelist, but as someone present to a balladist's imagination, confidently taken for granted as what she seems to be, recognized by the gesture of the hand, the inflexion of the voice; even the gradual transformation of her nature under the impress of suffering Hardy reveals in broad dramatic strokes.'[2] Hardy's alleged lack of interest in the subtler psychology of Bathsheba's career, deplored by Henry James in one of the first contemporary reviews of the novel, has come to be attributed to Hardy's preference for the art of the romance against the craft of the novel.[3] For several reasons then, not the least of which is the assumption on the part of most critics of the novel that Hardy accepted uncritically the developmental psychology prevalent in the

---

spectable Victorian girl on the surface and the amoral Dionysiac underneath' (p. 343). J. I. M. Stewart *(Thomas Hardy: A Critical Biography* [London: Longman, 1971] pp. 89–90) takes brief notice of Hardy's 'sexual pessimism and inclination in misogyny' in the novel. Robert Gittings *(Young Thomas Hardy* [London: Heinemann; Boston: Little, Brown, 1975] p. 175) attributes 'the sharp aphorisms about the wiles of marriageable women' in the novel to the influence of Hardy's mother (in whose house he was living while writing it): 'One hears in them the voice of Jemima Hardy, providing, from the depths of folk-wisdom, a sexual philosophy for her favourite son.'

2. *Thomas Hardy* (London: Longman, 1954)

p. 49. See also Irving Howe, *Thomas Hardy* (New York: Macmillan, 1967), p. 55: 'Bathsheba, by far the most striking figure in the novel, is presented almost entirely from the "outside": she is not, after all, a likely candidate for psychological probing.'

3. James's review *(The Nation* [New York], 24 December 1874) is reprinted in Laurence Lerner and John Holmstrom (eds), *Thomas Hardy and His Readers: A Selection of Contemporary Reviews* (London: The Bodley Head, 1968) pp. 28–33. James found Bathsheba 'alternately vague and coarse, and . . . always artificial' (p. 33). For Hardy as writer of romance, see John Paterson, *The Novel as Faith* (Boston: Gambit, 1973) pp. 40–68.

fiction of his day, two closely related issues have been overlooked. First, little attention has been given either to Hardy's ambivalent attitude to Bathsheba (especially a misogynistic side to it) or to the ambiguous nature of Bathsheba's career. Second, an obliquity in Hardy's way of showing her at crucial moments in her career has gone unexamined.

Since an analysis of Bathsheba's career demands discussion of Hardy's method, by way of beginning I should mention the problems of delineation. First, Hardy's abbreviated handling of Bathsheba's childhood thwarts any attempt to understand her motives at the beginning of the novel. Our uncertainty about her motives is compounded by the nature of her career, which is not a gradual process of self-conscious growth, but exposure, sudden and violent, to murder, death, fatal disease, fire, storm, and uncontrolled passion. Third, there is Hardy's use, always ironical, of literary allusions to depict Bathsheba at the two most critical moments of her career—her recovery in the swamp after opening Fanny Robin's coffin and being rejected by Troy, and her recovery at Weatherbury after Troy's death. These problems, as well as one other—the dominance of Oak in a novel centrally concerned with Bathsheba's career—may be seen as emanating from Hardy's view of her as one infirm in nature. Oak's prominence is best seen, I think, as a function of Bathsheba's imperfection. Oak's ability to observe the defects of non-human nature (the loss of his flock, the fire, the storm, the bloated sheep) and to contrive amendment fits him to observe, minister to, and finally to marry the faulty Bathsheba. The novel thus associates the imperfect nature of its heroine with defective non-human nature and offers in Oak an example of how to cope with the unregenerateness of things. Hardy's view of Bathsheba as essentially flawed also explains his ironic allusiveness during her two great moments of recovery: he cannot imagine transformation in one of her nature and so invokes detached instances of it from other authors. Because he does not believe that an essential change in Bathsheba is possible, rather than depicting in her a gradual process of growth towards self-knowledge he subjects her, over a relatively brief period of time, to a series of violent, shocking, humiliating encounters with death, and keeps the patient, admonitory Oak present at all times. This is consistent with the view in the novel that defect in human and non-human nature cannot be eradicated— only studied, accepted, and made limited use of for the adaptation of means to ends.

We need only look to A *Pair of Blue Eyes* (1873), the novel which Hardy was completing when he began *Far from the Madding Crowd*,[4]

4. Hardy was still at work on *A Pair of Blue Eyes* in early 1873 when he outlined for Leslie Stephen, editor of *Cornhill Magazine*, 'a pastoral tale which I thought of calling "Far from the Madding Crowd" in which the chief charac- ters would be a woman-farmer, a shepherd, and a sergeant in the Dragoon Guards' (quoted by Richard L. Purdy, *Thomas Hardy: A Bibliographical Study* [Oxford: Clarendon Press, 1954] p. 16).

for evidence of an almost clinical interest in the birth and growth of what there is disparagingly called 'womanly artifice'. Henry Knight, a fastidious London man of letters, shows to Elfride Swancourt, the novel's nineteen-year-old heroine, a description of her in his commonplace book:

> Girl gets into her teens, and her self-consciousness is born. After a certain interval passed in infantine helplessness, it begins to act. Simple, young, and inexperienced at first. Persons of observation can tell to a nicety how old this consciousness is by the skill it has acquired in the art necessary to its success—the art of hiding itself. Generally begins career by actions which are popularly termed showing off. Method adopted depends in each case upon the disposition, rank, residence, of the young lady attempting it. Town-bred girl will utter some moral paradox on fast men, or love. County miss adopts the more material media of taking a ghastly fence, whistling, or making your blood run cold by appearing to risk her neck. . . .
>
> An innocent vanity is of course the origin of these displays. 'Look at me,' say these youthful beginners in womanishly artifice, without reflecting whether or not it be to their advantage to show so much of themselves. (18; ellipsis mine)

Elfride does not wish to be regarded as a mere girl, and so urges upon Knight the view that 'the slower a nature is to develop, the richer the nature'. Knight advises, with some acerbity, that she should not take it for granted 'that the woman behind her time at a given age has not reached the end of her tether. Her backwardness may be not because she is slow to develop, but because she soon exhausted her capacity for developing' (*A Pair of Blue Eyes*, 18).

The vain Bathsheba who astonishes Gabriel Oak with her horsemanship undoubtedly owes something to Knight's vain and demonstrative country miss, although Bathsheba's aggressive coquetry is a distinct departure from Elfride's clinging. More important here, however, is the fact that Knight's scepticism about a woman's capacity for developing anticipates the view in *Far from the Madding Crowd* that Bathsheba cannot, in any essential way, change from a vain, foolish girl into a wise woman. It is Hardy's general view, maintained throughout the novels and the poems, departed from but not contradicted in *The Dynasts* (1903–8), that both nature and humanity are stained by what might be called ineradicable defects. The novels and poems before 1874 contain a melancholy sense of an unregenerateness in things. For Hardy, the good of the past is, in a phrase of Loren Eiseley's, 'unique and unreturning', the evil of the past ever-living. At the centre of the sensational *Desperate Remedies* (1871) is the story of Cythera Aldclyffe's and Aeneas Manston's inability to escape from their sins of the past. Poems of the 1860s lament that 'the radiance has waned' ('Her Initials'), that 'bloom and beauty' are marred ('Discouragement'), that 'flowering youthtime' has faded ('The Temporary the All'), that 'excellencies' of a primal time have dwindled ('She, To Him: I'), and that—this is the crucial point—all is beyond recovery or restoration. *A Pair of Blue Eyes* urges much the same in triplicate:

Elfride cannot undo the 'sin' of her flirtation with Jethway and elope-
ment with Stephen Smith; Henry Knight cannot realise the lost glory
and dream of his youth by marrying the flawed Elfride; Smith cannot
return to his native Endelstow after a long absence. This sense of the
irredeemable, the irretrievable, the unrestorable in human affairs,
strong in Hardy's early writings, grew in strength throughout the later
novels and poems. We need only look ahead to the agony of Grace
Melbury and Clym Yeobright in their thwarted attempts to return to
their native places, to the ineradicable weaknesses that slowly, inexor-
ably destroy Henchard, Tess, and Jude, to late poems such as 'We Are
Getting to the End', 'To Meet, or Otherwise', 'The Going', 'Christmas: 1924', and 'A Night of Questionings', to see how deep and lasting
was Hardy's sense of the unreturning and unregenerate nature of
things.[5]

Among the major novels, *Far from the Madding Crowd* and *Under
the Greenwood Tree* (1872), with their 'happy' endings, can be seen as
attempts to show, in the comic mode, the possibility of amendment
and regeneration. Fancy Day, the whimsical heroine of *Under the
Greenwood Tree*, does return to her native place, and does marry her
rustic lover under a greenwood tree, though the situation at the end of
the novel is not without its grim irony. *Far from the Madding Crowd*,
it might seem, is an attempt to show something similar—the growth of
Bathsheba from impulsive folly to good sense and marriage to Gabriel
Oak. But Bathsheba is subject to a more severe law than Fancy.
Bathsheba is in Hardy's view an agent and a victim of the tragic
unalterability of things, for she is afflicted by what he calls, in the first
chapter, 'woman's prescriptive infirmity'.[6] This, in turn, causes her
entanglement in a series of events from which she cannot extricate
herself.

Bathsheba comes to Norcombe as an orphan of twenty to live and
work with an aunt. She is vain, haughtily independent in spirit, and
recklessly flirtatious. Gabriel Oak, a Norcombe shepherd lately risen
to the status of farmer, falls in love with her, courts her, and proposes
marriage. But when Oak loses his flock and his new station his suit
founders. At about the same time Bathsheba inherits a prospering
farm at Weatherbury and moves to it as its mistress. Oak, falling back
upon his old work as a shepherd, gains employment at Weatherbury

5. *The Complete Poems of Thomas Hardy*, ed.
James Gibson (London: Macmillan; New York:
St. Martin's Press, 1976) pp. 13, 829, 7, 14;
929, 310, 338–39, 914, 726–8. A remark in a
letter of 5 June 1919 to Florence Henniker is
typical of Hardy's post-war view: 'I should care
more for my birthdays if at each succeeding one
I could see any sign of real improvement in the
world—as at one time I had fondly hoped there
was; but I fear that what appears much more
evident is that it is getting worse and worse'(*One

*Rare Fair Woman: Thomas Hardy's Letters to
Florence Henniker, 1893–1922*, ed. Evelyn
Hardy and F. B. Pinion [London: Macmillan,
1972] p. 185).
6. See Henry Knight's Miltonic rebuke of Elfride when he learns of her past indiscretions:
' "Fool'd and beguiled: by him, thou, I by
thee!" ' (*PBE*, XXXI; p. 356; *Paradise Lost*, X:
880); also, the antique hymn, 'Remember
Adam's Fall', with which Fancy Day is ushered
into *Under the Greenwood Tree*. See also n. 7.

Farm after saving its grain stores from fire. Bathsheba soon commits a grievous error. Allegedly as a joke, but in fact because he had ignored her at church and in the Corn Exchange, Bathsheba sends to Farmer Boldwood, a neighbour, a valentine on which she has written 'Marry Me'. The reclusive, repressed Boldwood comes courting in deadly earnest, and Bathsheba, pleased with her success, does not discourage him—at least not until Sergeant Troy, a dashing cavalryman with a winning tongue, completely entrances her. Boldwood is wild with jealousy, threatens violence against Troy, and Bathsheba sees that she has offended him deeply. Unbeknown to her she has offended him irremediably. If he could forgive her, all might be as it was. But he is too obsessed with the thought of having her to be able to understand her plea for forgiveness: her sin is his salvation, her childish joke his glorious dream of happiness come true. Far from relieving her of guilt, he seeks to bind her by it; later, in sheer desperation, he tries to bribe Troy not to marry her. But by then Bathsheba will have already wedded Troy, and Boldwood will be driven nearly mad. Bathsheba soon discovers Troy to be irresponsible, deceitful, and worse—before marrying her he had seduced Fanny Robin, a former servant of the farm who now returns to her native spot to bear her child and to die. Bathsheba and Troy part after a shockingly grotesque scene beside the open coffin of Fanny and the child. Shortly after, Troy is reported drowned. At this news, Boldwood is stirred to hope of recovering his lost dreams. Deeply smitten with remorse for the earlier offence, Bathsheba agrees to marry Boldwood 'as a kind of repentance' after six years have passed. But this, her opportunity to make reparation, is thwarted by Troy's unexpected return and his death by the hand of Boldwood, who then tries to kill himself. Bathsheba is driven nearly mad by the realisation that a childish act of two years before had ignited a chain of events which now include a murder, a near suicide, and a probable death by execution. Fortunately, however, Boldwood's death sentence is reduced to a term in prison. Bathsheba recovers, and the novel ends with her marriage to her first lover, Oak, who has remained loyal throughout. Bathsheba's moral history, it must be noted, is paralleled by Troy's. As she injures Boldwood, he injures Fanny. As his attempt to make amends is mockingly overthrown by the working of the gargoyle on Weatherbury Church, her attempt to atone is thwarted by events and personalities. Both fail to 'undo the done', but their failures differ. Troy is portrayed as one capable of better things but pushed into error by the circumstances of his birth, his military profession, and even by the susceptibility of women to his charm. Bathsheba, in contrast, is portrayed as one who errs because innately flawed.

There can be little doubt of Hardy's view in *Far from the Madding Crowd* that women are by nature infirm. Bathsheba's weakness, it is said when she stubbornly refuses to pay a toll, is 'what it is always' in women—Vanity. She feels no gratitude toward Oak when he pays her toll because 'in gaining her a passage he had lost her her point, and we know how women take a favour of that kind'. She is described as unusual among women because capable of finishing a thought before beginning the sentence with which to convey it, thus suggesting that most women speak before thinking. But she is no thinker, for hers is 'an impulsive nature under a deliberative aspect. . . . Many of her thoughts were perfect syllogisms; unluckily they always remained thoughts. Only a few were irrational assumptions; but, unfortunately, they were the ones which most frequently grew into deeds'. In her presence, Oak is a Samson, in danger of being unmanned, Boldwood an Adam, in danger of being tempted (3, 17). Faced with Boldwood's plea that she marry him, Bathsheba 'began to feel unmistakable signs that she was inherently the weaker vessel. She strove miserably against this femininity which would insist upon supplying unbidden emotions in stronger and stronger current' (31). A view of woman as the 'weaker vessel' permeates the novel (see, e.g., 12, 23, 31); indeed even Bathsheba accepts this view of herself. As the newly installed mistress of Weatherbury Farm she warns the workfolk against taking the view of her as one of the weaker sex: 'Don't any unfair ones among you . . . suppose that because I'm a woman I don't understand the difference between bad goings-on and good' (ellipsis mine). Confronted with the loss of Troy, she candidly admits inferiority: 'Tell me the truth, Frank. I am not a fool, you know, although I am a woman, and have my woman's moments. Come! treat me fairly' (41). Nearly speechless before Boldwood's renewed ardour after Troy's disappearance, she acknowledges what may be the ultimate handicap: 'It is difficult for a woman to define her feelings in language which is chiefly made by men to express theirs' (51).

Henry Fray inveighs against the villainy of womankind, Laban Tall is nagged and humiliated by a domineering wife, the work-women Temperance and Soberness are, in spite of their names, 'yielding women', as, in fact, are Fanny Robin and Bathsheba herself. At one point Oak, mortified by Bathsheba's criticism for injuring a sheep he is shearing, murmurs to himself the bitter words of Ecclesiastes 7: 26: ' "I find more bitter than death the woman whose heart is snares and nets' " (22). And so, when Bathsheba comes under the influence of the unctuous, deceitful Troy, his villainy can be made to seem less a function of his depravity than a response, almost excusable, to her infirmity:

> The wondrous power of flattery in *passados* at woman is a perception so universal as to be remarked upon by many people almost as automatically as they repeat a proverb, or say they are Christians and the like, without thinking much of the enormous corollaries which spring from the proposition. Still less is it acted upon for the good of the complemental being alluded to. With the majority such an opinion is shelved with all those trite aphorisms which require some catastrophe to bring their tremendous

meanings thoroughly home. When expressed with some amount of reflectiveness it seems co-ordinate with a belief that this flattery must be reasonable to be effective. It is to the credit of men that few attempt to settle the question by experiment, and it is for their happiness, perhaps, that accident has never settled it for them. Nevertheless, that a male dissembler who by deluging her with untenable fictions charms the female wisely, may acquire powers reaching to the extremity of perdition, is a truth taught to many by unsought and wringing occurrences. And some profess to have attained to the same knowledge by experiment as aforesaid, and jauntily continue their indulgence in such experiments with terrible effect. Sergeant Troy was one. (25)

What is interesting in this account of woman's (the 'complemental being's') helplessness before flattery is that it draws more of Hardy's censure than does Troy's deceit.[7] It is not, however, my primary purpose here to examine Hardy's anti-feminist tendencies, except in so far as they affect his view of Bathsheba's capacity for developing. His problem seems to have been this—how to show the growth of moral consciousness in a representative of the sex decreed infirm by long-standing custom? A degree of external improvement in her may be hoped for, but the logic of the governing initial premise—'prescriptive infirmity'—is against transformation. Bathsheba is vain, changeable, domineering, impulsive, coquettish, and helpless before flattery. 'I want somebody to tame me; I am too independent' (4) she says to Oak during the courtship at Norcombe.[8] Bathsheba is tamed—that is, reduced from a state of wildness so as to be tractable and useful. Like a spirited animal, she is broken to harness. She submits to Troy's wiles, to Boldwood's claim upon her balky conscience, to Oak's example. Except in a limited sense, it is difficult to see this as moral growth, for rational self-awareness is conspicuously absent. Her irrationality is curbed, not transformed, by the end of the novel, for there we find her doing what she had done earlier, seeking an environment in which she is the enshrined centre. Her manner may change, but her instinct remains the same.

Hardy's scepticism about the possibility of essential change occurring in Bathsheba can be seen best in his oblique and allusive rendering of the two crucial moments in her career: her revival in the swamp at Weatherbury after the confrontation with Troy beside Fanny's coffin, and her response to the singing of 'Lead, Kindly Light' by the children at Weatherbury Church after Troy's death. The scene in the swamp follows immediately after Bathsheba's discovery that Fanny has borne Troy's child and that Troy is devoted to Fanny. Significantly entitled 'Under a Tree—Reaction', the episode in the swamp shows not thoughtful, self-conscious amendment, but instinctive renewal of

7. This 'defence' of Troy lends unexpected strength to Troy's claim later that Bathsheba, and not he, is responsible for Fanny's plight: 'If Satan had not tempted me with that face of yours, and those cursed coquetries, I should have married her' (43).

8. Richard C. Carpenter, *Thomas Hardy* (New York: Twayne, 1964) p. 87, argues that Bathsheba is not ready for reform until she is 'dominated by a sexually aggressive man'.

life-purpose, that is, 'reaction'. Though much has been made of this episode as an instance of the healing ministry of nature,[9] a close inspection of its tone and imagery does not bear this out. This is not a Wordsworthian interlude. In fact, the entire episode suggests that Hardy was unable to show Bathsheba vitally engaged in moral regeneration. Why, for example, does he choose to make the place of her 'reaction' the place of the sword demonstration and of Troy's first kiss (44)? Why is the place of her supposed regeneration the place, we might say, of her 'fall'? Mere irony? A hint, perhaps, that renewal must be accompanied by symbolic re-enactment of error? Whatever the intention of this suggestive recurrence, we are simply told that Bathsheba, 'neither knowing nor caring about the direction or issue of her flight', vaguely recalls seeing the place on a previous occasion. Why does she waken to the fluttering of Shelleyan leaves, ' "like ghosts from an enchanter fleeing" ' (44)? Is this phrase from 'Ode to the West Wind' used to evoke a vision of death and rebirth, sin and regeneration as being, like winter and spring, interdependent and recurring phases of the round of nature? Is this the point also, but in spatial rather than temporal terms, of Bathsheba's finding herself amidst 'pestilences small and great, in the immediate neighbourhood of comfort and health' (44)? It may well be so, since it suggests a kinship between Bathsheba's character and the unthinking, amoral working of external nature. But if this is so, it is also true that human nature is as active as non-human nature in her 'reaction'.

She wakens to the song of sparrow, finch, and robin, *and* to the sound of a ploughboy bringing horses to water. She hears still another boy, this a rather dull one, trying to learn a collect by repeating it aloud: ' "O Lord, O Lord, O Lord, O Lord, O Lord":—that I know out o' book. "Give us, give us, give us, give us, give us":—that I know. "Grace that, grace that, grace that, grace that":—that I know." Other words followed to the same effect' (44). What is to be made of this modulation from 'pestilences small and great' into a half-comic image of a child straining to learn a plea for God's Redeeming Grace? It may recall the bewildered, childlike Bathsheba of the previous chapter;[1] it may anticipate the crucial scene in chapter 41 in which Bathsheba, troubled by Troy's death, is deeply moved by the sound of children singing 'Lead, Kindly Light'. If so, what is to be made of Bathsheba's

---

9. Howard Babb, 'Setting and Theme in *Far from the Madding Crowd*', *ELH*, XXX (1963), 160, argues that the meaning of Bathsheba's experience in the swamp is that 'she has found refuge from Troy in nature and been morally regenerated by that world'.

1. At Bathsheba's plea that Troy kiss her after he kisses the dead Fanny, Hardy remarks: 'There was something so abnormal and startling in the childlike pain and simplicity of this ap-

peal from a woman of Bathsheba's calibre and independence, that Troy, loosening her tightly clasped arms from his neck, looked at her in bewilderment. It was such an unexpected revelation of all women being alike at heart, even those so different in their accessories as Fanny and this one beside him, that Troy could hardly seem to believe her to be his proud wife Bathsheba' (XLIII; p. 344).

faint amusement at the boy's method? Is it her foolish forgetting of the lesson she seemed to have learned by watching and imitating Oak at prayer in the preceding chapter? Does she take seriously the collect,[2] if not the boy or his method? These are legitimate questions raised by the text and, once posed, suggest that neither non-human nature nor religion is so important to Bathsheba in her recovery as plain humanity: 'her heart bounded with gratitude' not as the song of birds or the sound of prayer, but at the sight of Liddy and 'the thought that she was not altogether deserted' (XLIV). She is also hungry. Hunger—for love and for nutriment—moves her towards recovery. She returns to the farm, decides defiantly that she will not retreat from Troy and, with a 'faint gleam of humour' in her eye, decides to immerse herself in *The Maid's Tragedy*, *The Mourning Bride*, *Night Thoughts*, and *The Vanity of Human Wishes*. She suddenly decides, however, to read something brighter, and so climbs to an attic to read *Love in a Village*, *Maid of the Mill*, and some volumes of the *Spectator*. Bathsheba's shift from 'a vehement impulse to flee . . . not stopping short of death itself' (43) to a whimsical retreat to an attic with some light reading can hardly be accounted a significant phase of her moral growth. Nor does Hardy treat it as such. He portrays her as one involuntarily buoyant: her 'vitality of youth' has been quenched by sorrow 'without substituting the philosophy of maturer years' (46).

At this point of suspense, with Bathsheba dangling between youthful vitality and mature philosophy, Hardy invokes a Wordsworthian model of female development in an attempt to define the pattern of her career:

> To the eyes of the middle-aged, Bathsheba was perhaps additionally charming just now. Her exuberance of spirit was pruned down; the original *phantom of delight* had shown herself to be *not too bright for human nature's daily food*, and she had been able to enter this second poetical phase without losing much of the first in the process. (49; italics mine)

Hardy is paraphrasing and quoting Wordsworth's 'She Was a Phantom of Delight' (1804), a poem which he clearly read as depicting a woman's three-phase development from innocence through experience to maturity.[3] I present it here in full because it can be seen as an ironic analogue to his portrait of Bathsheba in the novel.

---

2. The Book of Common Prayer, the Collect for the 18th Sunday after Trinity (which falls in October, like the action at this point in the novel). What Bathsheba hears is probably a version of the following: 'Lord, we beseech thee, grant thy people grace to withstand the temptations of the world, the flesh and the devil, and with pure hearts and minds to follow thee the only God; through Jesus our Lord. Amen.'

3. Though the poem is usually read, I think, as a record of an observer's deepening knowledge of a woman throughout three views of her which occur in a short period of time, Hardy 'misread' it, to serve his immediate end, as a poem of growth describing in three stanzas a movement from childhood, to girlhood, to womanhood. Citations from Wordsworth throughout are from Thomas Hutchinson (ed.: rvd. Ernest de Selincourt), *Wordsworth: Poetical Works* (New York: Oxford University Press, 1969).

She was a *Phantom of delight*
When first she gleaned upon my sight;
A lovely Apparition, sent
To be a moment's ornament;
Her eyes as stars of Twilight fair;
Like Twilight's, too, her dusky hair;
But all things else about her drawn
From May-time and the cheerful Dawn;
A dancing Shape, an Image gay,
To haunt, to startle, and way-lay.

I saw her upon nearer view,
A Spirit, yet a Woman too!
Her household motions light and free,
And steps of virgin-liberty;
A countenance in which did meet
Sweet records, promises as sweet;
A Creature *not too bright* or good
For human nature's daily food;
For transient sorrows, simple wiles,
Praise, blame, love, kisses, tears, and smiles.

And now I see with eye serene
The very pulse of the machine;
A Being breathing thoughtful breath,
A Traveller between life and death;
The reason firm, the temperate will,
Endurance, foresight, strength, and skill;
A perfect Woman, nobly planned,
To warn, to comfort, and command;
And yet a Spirit still, and bright
With something of angelic light. (my italics)

The Bathsheba of Norcombe and of the early days at Weatherbury is like the lovely, dusky-haired Phantom of the first stanza. The bold, independent Bathsheba who manages the farm, arouses Boldwood, succumbs to Troy, is rejected by him, and undergoes a 'reaction', is like the 'Spirit, yet . . . woman' of the second stanza, the creature 'not too bright' (note that Hardy drops the 'or good') 'for human nature's daily food'. At least this is what Hardy suggests when he tells us that she has entered a second phase of development without losing much of the first. There remains the 'woman . . . yet . . . Spirit' of the third phase, the Bathsheba who witnesses the violent death of Troy, knows piercing remorse for her treatment of Boldwood, and demonstrates (for a brief time) heroic self-control in the face of disaster. But the mature Bathsheba, unlike Wordsworth's mature Phantom, is no 'perfect Woman' or 'Spirit . . . bright / With something of angelic light'. She is viewed from the beginning as a flawed creature (Hardy's dropping the 'or good' reiterates this). The allusive, shifting style of these pages mirrors the difficulty of showing moral growth in a character conceived of as infirm.

However, what the style of the swamp episode does suggest—that

Bathsheba's recovery from sorrow is as automatic as the turn of the seasons—is important, for it identifies Bathsheba's behaviour with the working of the non-human natural order, explaining in part Hardy's ambivalence toward her and making her a proper object for the ministrations of Oak, that knowing, resourceful student of nature. Hardy had been brutally explicit about Elfride Swancourt's naturalistic facility for getting rid of trouble: 'She could slough off a sadness and replace it by a hope as easily as a lizard renews a diseased limb'. His way of associating Bathsheba's actions with Nature's is more general, and perhaps less sanguine. Her moral history, as illustrated in her attachments to Oak, Boldwood, Troy, and then to Oak again, is made analogous to the turn of the seasons. She is courted by Oak in December of the first and in January of the second year; she entices Boldwood with the valentine in February of the second year, witnesses the death of Troy on 24 December of the same year, and weds Oak on Christmas Day of the third. After the death of Troy, she is described as 'reviv[ing] with the spring' (56), the season in which 'the vegetable world begins to move and swell and the saps to rise' (18). As winter and spring roll round, so for Bathsheba or for those associated with her renewal or death come round. Hardy leaves it tantalisingly uncertain whether the marriage of Oak and Bathsheba breaks the cycle.

Before going on to consider the climatic episode at Weatherbury Church, it is important to note Hardy's attempt to document this fatalistic nature-psychology of Bathsheba in more conventional psychological terms. We are told little about Bathsheba's childhood, but what we are told makes it clear that it was unhappy. Her father, a gentleman-tailor, loved his exceedingly beautiful wife best when pretending that he was not married to her and was 'commiting the seventh' (8). Was Bathsheba expected to play the 'bastard' in this strange marriage, and is that an explanation for her puzzling statement to Boldwood that she is aloof toward him because 'An unprotected childhood in a cold world has beaten gentleness out of me' (31)? We cannot be certain. But we can be sure that at twenty she is a volatile mixture of girl and woman: now an 'unpractised girl' and now a cool woman (7, 10), now a model of 'aspiring virginity' (9), then, a few days later, a woman of 'full bloom and vigour' capable of 'alarming exploits of sex, and daring enough to carry them out' (12). Another striking aspect of Bathsheba's personality is her mannishness. She straddles a pony in masculine fashion, much to Oak's astonishment. Moved suddenly to the head of Weatherbury Farm by the death of her uncle, she assumes that masculine role. Finding bailiff Pennyways a thief, she takes on his duties as well. 'Let's toss, as men do', she urges Liddy, as she decides whether or not to send the fatal valentine, inscribed with an imperious 'Marry Me', to Boldwood. Hardy seems to have ordered the novel's main and subordinate plots in such a way as to place Bathsheba in the conventionally masculine role of aggressor and seducer. Troy's ruin of Fanny parallels Bathsheba's ruin of Boldwood, as later, in *Tess of the d' Urbervilles* and *Jude the Obscure*, Alec's seduction of Tess is re-enacted in Arabella's enticement of Jude. Bathsheba's valentine has, it seems, something in common with Arabella's pig's-pizzle. But the epicene Bathsheba is also like Sue Bridehead, Arabella's antithesis, in her alarm at Liddy's 'Amazonian picture' of her as a woman who would be a match for any man. 'I hope I am not a bold sort of maid—mannish?' she cries. Liddy replies: 'O no, not mannish; but so almighty womanish that 'tis getting on that way sometimes' (30).[4]

Bathsheba is girlish, womanish, mannish, and also—though in her early twenties—very much a child, especially when in the presence of the three men whom she at once flees and pursues, perhaps because to her they are at once lovers and fathers. She entrances and rules Boldwood with her beauty, but in the face of his anger she describes herself as 'only a girl' (31). In the presence of the dashing Troy, there is 'a little tremulousness in the usually cool girl's voice' (26), her love for him is as 'entire as a child's' (29). When she sees him kiss the dead Fanny, there is 'childlike pain and simplicity' (Hardy calls it 'abnormal and startling') in her plea that he kiss her as well (43). Her 'coolness of manner' is, as Hardy says, only a 'trick' to mask her surprise and impulsiveness (32). Her artfulness is understood by Oak from the moment, in the first chapter of the novel, when he steps forward to pay a toll which she stubbornly refuses to pay, and when, at the shearing, he teaches her to sharpen the clippers by guiding her hands with his own, 'taking each as we sometimes clasp a child's hand in teaching them to write' (20).

All this suggests that elements of Bathsheba's troubled childhood persist, undigested so to speak, into her young womanhood. This view differs significantly from the view of Wordsworth that the adult, with the aid of memory, can recall and preserve the pleasure and joy of childhood. Wordsworth views growth in 'She Was a Phantom' (and in 'Ode: Intimations of Immortality', which Hardy calls upon in the episode at Weatherbury Church) as a progress toward integration and compensation for loss. In Bathsheba, Hardy depicts growth as a fitful ebbing and flowing—on the one hand an improvement of externals, on the other a hopeless struggle against unalterable traits in an infirm nature and unalterable facts of experience. She cannot change her nature; she cannot change the past. The unalterability of things drives her into reminiscence and nostalgia, as in the unhappy days of her marriage to Troy:

> She was conquered; but she would never own it as long as she lived. Her pride was indeed brought low by despairing discoveries of her spoliation by

---

4. On one occasion Hardy uses imagery usually reserved for male sexual aggression to describe Bathsheba's attempt to attract Boldwood: 'All this time Bathsheba was conscious of having broken into that dignified stronghold at last' (XVII).

marriage with a less pure nature than her own. . . . Until she had met Troy, Bathsheba had been proud of her position as a woman; it had been a glory to her to know that her lips had been touched by no man's on earth—that her waist had never been encircled by a lover's arm. She hated herself now. In those earlier days she had always nourished a secret contempt for girls who were slaves of the first good-looking young fellow who should choose to salute them. . . . Although she scarcely knew the divinity's name, Diana was the goddess whom Bathsheba instinctively adored. That she had never, by look, word, or sign, encouraged a man to approach her—that she had felt herself sufficient to herself, and had in the independence of her girlish heart fancied there was a certain degradation in renouncing the simplicity of a maiden existence to become the humbler half of an indifferent matrimonial whole—were facts now bitterly remembered. O, if she had never stooped to folly of this kind, respectable as it was, and could only stand again, as she had stood on the hill at Norcombe, and dare Troy or any other man to pollute a hair of her head by his interference! (41; ellipses mine)

Bathsheba is filled with repugnance toward physical contact and near-hysteria at the thought of having lost her innocence. Sexual union with Troy has left her with a sense of 'spoliation', 'degradation', and pollution, the unalterability of which 'she would never own . . . as long as she lived'. Therefore she hates herself, regards herself a bloody victim, a fallen woman (the allusion to Goldsmith). Her instinctive affinity for Diana (so at odds with her fascination for men) reinforces this. Her idea of growing up is, in short, a nervous, panicky one requiring fulfilment of the impossible dream of regaining the lost 'simplicity of a maiden existence'. A similar paradisaic longing is behind her attempt to atone to Boldwood for her injury of him.

The culminating episode at Weatherbury Church begins when, at the news of Troy's death, Boldwood seeks to renew his courtship of her. Bathsheba welcomes Boldwood's devotion, for she is reminded of her original folly and wishes again 'as she had wished many months ago, for some means of making reparation for her fault' (51). Here she appears to be conscious of a capacity for self-amendment and eager to effect it. Where formerly she had pleaded with Boldwood to forgive her and free her from her moral debt, she now assumes full responsibility: 'My treatment of you was thoughtless, inexcusable, wicked! I shall eternally regret it. If there had been anything I could have done to make amends I would most gladly have done it—there was nothing on earth I so longed to do as to repair the error. But that was not possible' (51). Like Sue Bridehead seeking by remarriage to Phillotson to punish herself for the death of her children, Bathsheba decides to marry Boldwood 'as a sort of penance'. Boldwood, half-mad in his passion to recapture through her his lost dream of happiness, encourages her moral masochism. 'Remember the past', he counsels, 'and be kind'.

But Boldwood's desperate yearning for the irrecoverable past, as well as Bathsheba's nostalgic desire to make reparation to him, is blocked by Troy's return. 'Heaven's persistent irony' works through Troy to thwart Bathsheba in her attempt to atone just as it worked (in Troy's view) through the gargoyle on Weatherbury Church to thwart his attempt to make amends to Fanny by planting flowers on her grave. 'It may be argued with great plausibility', writes Hardy, 'that reminiscence is less an endowment than a disease'. Reminiscence, or 'projection of consciousness into days gone by', is the disease of Troy, of Boldwood, and of Bathsheba. 'Expectation', the only healthy attitude, is not easily come by; for 'in its only comfortable form—that of absolute faith—[it] is practically an impossibility; whilst in the form of hope and the secondary compounds, patience, impatience, resolve, curiosity, it is a constant fluctuation between pleasure and pain' (25). Oak is of course the only character capable of expectation, though of the painful variety, and we may be inclined to think that in the critical moments after Troy's violent death, and in the months thereafter, Bathsheba imitates Oak by putting off reminiscence for expectation and undergoes thereby a gradual transformation. But not so. Hardy undercuts every sign of transformation with reminders of her infirmity. The spectacle of Troy's death 'made her herself again. . . . Deeds of endurance which seem ordinary in philosophy are rare in conduct, and Bathsheba was astonishing all around her now, for her philosophy was her conduct, and she seldom thought practicable what she did not practise.' That is high praise, but the next sentence—'She was of the stuff of which great men's mothers are made'—makes it clear that it is limited praise (54; ellipsis mine). With the appearance of three men, the parson, the surgeon, and Oak, she ends her brief moment of heroism with an appropriate feminine gesture: she collapses in a paroxysm of self-blame. 'O it is my fault', she cries; 'how can I live! O Heaven, how can I live!' (54). Two months later she is even more worn down: 'Her eyes are so miserable that she's not the same woman', said Liddy. 'Only two years ago she was a romping girl [see the 'dancing shape' of stanza 1 of 'She Was a Phantom of Delight'], and now she's this!' (55). *This* is not the perfect woman 'bright / With something of angelic light' of stanza 3. Bathsheba's 'reviv[al] with the spring' (56) reminds us that beneath her struggling moral consciousness lies an unalterable infirmity. It is in Hardy's view no more plausible to think her (or Troy, or Boldwood) capable of undoing the wrongs, or recovering the dreams, of days gone by, than it is to think her capable of recovering a prelapsarian state of perfection.

Bathsheba visits the grave of Fanny and the child, now the grave of Troy as well, and hears there the children of Weatherbury singing 'Lead, Kindly Light'. The lines from Newman's hymn are used, adroitly, to suggest, upon Oak's entry on to the scene, that Bathsheba hopes that he will forget the past (' "Pride ruled my will: remember not past years" '), and that she is prepared to forget Troy (' "Which I have loved long since, and lost awhile" '). 'Stirred by emotions which latterly she had assumed to be altogether dead within her', Bathsheba seems to be ready for the penultimate step in her transformation from egotism and crippling reminiscence to altruism and expectation. But Hardy quickly undermines this:

> Bathsheba's feeling was always to some extent dependent upon her whim, as is the case with many other women. Something big came into her throat and an uprising to her eyes—and she thought that she would allow the imminent tears to flow if they wished. . . . Once that she had begun to cry for she hardly knew what, she could not leave off for crowding thoughts she knew too well. She would have given anything in the world to be, as those children were, unconcerned at the meaning of their words, because too innocent to feel the necessity for any such expression. All the impassioned scenes of her brief experience seemed to revive with added emotion at that moment, and those scenes which had been without emotion during enactment had emotion then. Yet grief came to her rather as a luxury than as the scourge of former times. (56; ellipsis mine)

Hardy's observation, wholly consistent with the 'weaker vessel' view of Bathsheba pervading the novel, that her feelings are *always* partly dependent upon her whimsy, blocks any attempt to take seriously this episode as a climactic moment in her moral transformation. Bathsheba's offences are neither forgiven nor atoned for; nor are they diminished by deep-felt contrition. They are made unimportant by the passage of time, and Hardy seems to agree that they must be. But the offences are also made slightly pleasing by Bathsheba's whimsical attitude to them. She weeps 'for she hardly knew what'. Hardy seems to find that reprehensible. She is as sorry as she, a woman, and therefore (in the view of the novel) a creature of inferior moral capabilities, can be.

Hardy marks her limited capacity for amendment by what I believe is a calculated use, in this same passage, of the language and sentiment of stanza 10 of Wordsworth's 'Ode: Intimations of Immortality From Recollections of Early Childhood' to create an aura of reconciliation and recovery in the face of loss. Stanza 10 begins 'Then sing, ye birds, sing a joyous song!' and continues with an assertion of the finality of loss ('Though nothing can bring back the hour . . .') and the certainty of compensation 'in the primal sympathy / Which having been must ever be; / In the soothing thoughts that spring / Out of human suffering; / In the faith that looks through death, / In years that bring the philosophic mind.' Bathsheba, listening to the singing children, recalling her past, wishing for the innocence of a child, reminds us of the poet listening to the song of birds and reflecting upon loss and gain. Hardy's 'crowding thoughts she knew too well' may echo Wordsworth's 'soothing thoughts that spring out of human suffering', the phrase which seems also to be the origin of Hardy's 'Yet grief came to her rather as a luxury than as the scourge of former times'. With the Wordsworthian analogue in mind, we can see that Hardy allows her only one consolation—'soothing thoughts that spring out of human suffering', though even that is involuntary (the luxury of grief 'came *to* her'). She is deprived of 'primal sympathy' by an unhappy childhood, of faith that sees through death by irreligion, of philosophic understanding by her woman's, that is, her irrational consciousness. Her true gain, or 'strength', can come, within the masculine ethos of the novel, only through submission and marriage to an exemplary male. As in the use of 'She Was a Phantom of Delight' to describe the second stage of Bathsheba's career, Hardy's use of 'Ode: Intimations of Immortality' to describe the final stage creates ironic resonances which imply an incapacity for development more clearly than they imply a growth toward wider sympathy.[5] Bathsheba cannot be an embodiment of the vision of the Ode that the forever-lost can be compensated for by what remains behind. Oak, for all his solid strength, is not the dashing Troy. As for Bathsheba, even if she could regain a semblance of the state of maiden simplicity by marrying Oak, she could not root out the flaw of her nature; for her flaw is the flaw of maidens, of all daughters of Eve.

Hardy's use of Newman and (in my view) of Wordsworth suggests, however, a limited progress on Bathsheba's part. Her ability to find 'luxury' rather than a 'scourge' in grief, though suggestive of a degree of indifference toward Troy, Boldwood, and Fanny, is in Hardy's view 'right' because consistent with the relentless ongoingness of things. Here Hardy distinguishes between what might be called a moral and a sentimental function of memory. On the one hand, he clearly regards nostalgia or reminiscence as a disease that blinds its victims to the irretrievability inherent in change. In this he suggests that memory (in the form of excessive regret or remorse) constricts moral growth. Here the phrase from Newman, 'remember not past years' (overheard by Bathsheba) and the counsel of the Ode, grieve not and seek strength in what remains behind, concur in suggesting that Bathsheba is at this point seeking to begin anew, her past forgotten, if not forgiven. On the other hand, Hardy is unsympathetic toward Bathsheba's capacity for sloughing off unpleasant memories, for 'reviving with the spring'. A ready capacity for mending suggests a transientness of feeling which he perhaps associates with the impassiveness of a natural order as likely, in the words of 'Hap', to strew blisses about his pilgrimage as pain. He seems, in short, to insist in this that memory is essential to moral growth. He is not contradicting himself, but distinguishing validly

5. My sense that Wordsworth's great Ode is at work in this episode is supported by the fact that Hardy quoted from it repeatedly during his career (see Frank B. Pinion, A *Hardy Companion* [London: Macmilan, 1968] p. 214; also Peter J. Casagrande, 'Hardy's Wordsworth: A Record and a Commentary', *ELT*, XX [1977] 210–37). Hardy quoted from it three times in A *Pair of Blue Eyes* (XV [p. 162]; XX [p. 211]; XXXII [p. 366]), the novel on which he was at work when he undertook to writing *Madding Crowd*. His use of it in Tess (LI), in the scene in which Tess listens to her siblings singing 'Here we suffer grief and pain,' is remarkably like is use of it in *Madding Crowd*: to assert that compensation for loss is not readily available.

between recollective memory and nostalgia. But the interesting distinction must be largely a moot one, for what Bathsheba overhears is not what she can do. That is, she cannot make a new start, but must—what else is possible?—revert to nature. If she can be cured of the disease of reminiscence, of a moral masochism which would lead her to a disastrous marriage or to prolonged graveside weeping, she cannot be cured of the disease of kind. Hardy makes this abundantly clear in the closing scenes between Bathsheba and Oak.

With Oak's re-entry into Bathsheba's life, reserve and funereal sadness give way before a pleasing bit of male fantasy, the taming of a shrew, when Oak's announced intention to emigrate moves Bathsheba to pursuit of him. However, Hardy does not allow the playfulness in this to conceal the fact that Bathsheba's new manner, characterised by humility and even mildness, cloaks the old instinct to charm and possess a man. She is stung by the sensation that Oak, 'her last old disciple', has abandoned her. On Christmas Day, exactly one year after Troy's death and her great sorrow, she examines her heart and finds it 'beyond measure strange that the subject of which the season might have been supposed suggestive—the event in the hall at Boldwood's—was not agitating her at all; but instead, an agonizing conviction that everybody abjured her—for what she could not tell—and that Oak was the ringleader of the recusants' (56). She is mistaking Oak's solicitousness for her delicate situation as a widow for betrayal of an obligation to follow and worship her. The language of the episode suggests even more. 'Disciple', 'abjured', and 'recusants' are the words of the religionist, in this case the once-idolised woman longing for re-enshrinement. The words recall, with grim precision, the fact that she sent Boldwood the fatal valentine because she was somewhat annoyed by his 'nonconformity'. He was, in her view, 'a species of Daniel in her kingdom who persisted in kneeling eastward when reason and common sense said that he might just as well follow suit with the rest, and afford her the official glance of admiration which cost nothing at all' (13). When she receives Oak's letter announcing his departure in the coming March, she weeps bitterly, but not at the thought of losing him. 'She was aggrieved and wounded that the possession of hopeless love from Gabriel, which she had grown to regard as her inalienable right for life, should have been withdrawn just at his own pleasure in this way' (36). In essence she has altered little, it seems, since her earlier errors.

On the eve of the wedding there is 'a certain rejuvenated appearance about her:—"As though a rose should shut and be a bud again" ':[6]

Repose had again incarnadined her cheeks; and having, at Gabriel's request, arranged her hair this morning as she had worn it years ago on

---

6. The phrase is from Keats's 'Eve of St. Agnes', stanza 27. It is another example of Hardy's use of literary allusion to suggest regeneration when there is none.

Norcombe Hill, she seemed in his eyes remarkably like the girl of that fascinating dream, which, considering that she was now only three or four-and-twenty, was perhaps not very wonderful. (57).

There is considerable irony in Bathsheba's seeming to Oak 'remarkably like' the girl at Norcombe, and even greater irony in Oak's indulging himself in a nostalgic attempt to recreate the girl of his dream, the girl, we will recall, whom he watched some three years before gaze so long upon herself in a mirror that 'she blushed at herself, and seeing her reflection blush, blushed the more':

> The picture was a delicate one. Woman's prescriptive infirmity had stalked into the sunlight, which had clothed it in the freshness of an originality. . . . She . . . observed herself as a fair product of Nature in the feminine kind, her thoughts seeming to glide into far-off though likely dramas in which men would play a part—vistas of probable triumphs—the smiles being of a phase suggesting that hearts were imagined as lost and won. (1; ellipses mine)

Is Hardy suggesting that Oak is but another triumph for 'a fair product of Nature in the feminine kind'? The answer must be yes, in part. The old vanity, seeking the self's re-embodiment in others, rather than in a mirror, still governs Bathsheba. But it must be seen that Oak, knowing this from the start, is a willing victim who enjoys his own kind of victory. If Bathsheba has not changed essentially through some three years of severe schooling, her circumstances have changed significantly. Her circle of admirers has been reduced by two-thirds, and her 'absolute hunger' for affection, a genuine aspect of her flawed nature, can be satisfied only by Oak, the sole survivor of the original circle of worshippers. Oak has Bathsheba, so to speak, where he wants her—in a position in which she must turn to him for gratification of her infirm nature's deepest longing. The 'happiness' of this ending, and there can be no doubt that we have here happiness of a kind, grows up, as Hardy says, 'in the interstices of a mass of hard prosaic reality' (56).[7]

I stated at the beginning of this essay that in *Far from the Madding Crowd* Hardy associates Bathsheba's prescriptive infirmity with the ineradicable defect he sees in non-human nature and presents in Oak an example of how to cope with the imperfection of things. Oak survives misfortune because he sees that he is subject, like all other living things, to the laws of nature, that is, to the stubborn, irreducible properties of things. He accepts the loss of his herd and works hard toward recovery. He confronts fire, storm, and disease among

---

7. See Carpenter, *Thomas Hardy*, p. 87: 'Although Hardy allows us the questionable sop to our feelings of a marriage with Oak as a dé-nouement, the novel does not really end "happily." The vibrant and proud girl we see at the beginning has been as thoroughly destroyed as Troy and Boldwood. Never again, we are sure, will she burst forth in a fine blaze of fury, her black eyes snapping and her cheek flushed; nor will she blush as furiously with love or at her temerity.' For smiliar views see Guerard, pp. 51–2; and Roy Morrell, *Thomas Hardy: The Will and the Way* (Kuala Lumpur: University of Malaya Press; London: Oxford University Press, 1965) p. 59.

Bathsheba's flock, and uses a tarp, a lightning rod, and a surgical instrument to keep loss to a minimum. He attempts throughout to minimize the effects of Bathsheba's folly as well. In none of these does he succeed fully, but in all it is his achievement to accept loss and to make what improvement he can upon nature. He does not rebel against nature. Nor does he guide himself by or follow nature's laws. Rather, he studies nature's workings in order to know them and to use them to his ends. He attains his end with Bathsheba by seeing and accepting her infirmity, and suffering patiently the effects of it, until her infirmity and his purpose can be happily joined. His role is summed up metaphorically in a remark he makes while munching a piece of bacon which has fallen to the earth: 'I never fuss about dirt in its pure state, and when I know what sort it is' (8).[8]

IAN GREGOR

[Hardy's Use of Dramatic Pace]†

* * *

Chapter 40 of *Far from the Madding Crowd* can be thought of as the longest chapter in nineteenth-century fiction, not in terms of pages, which are few, but in terms of the experience it conveys. The chapter describes Fanny Robin's fateful journey on the Casterbridge highway to the lying-in hospital, and which, together with Troy's sword-play, the shearing supper and the great fire, make it one of the scenes that remains most vividly in the memory when the reading of the novel has been completed. It is not difficult to see why. It is deeply felt and intensely visual: the lonely girl '*in extremis*,' half-walking, half-crawling, to the hospital, and then helped in the desperate, final stage by a friendly dog. With such elements the scene is almost cut free from its context to be offered as a suitable subject for a genre painting, with some title such as 'Deserted' or 'The Only Friend'.

But such an activity of detaching and framing is the scene viewed in retrospect; it is not how it strikes the reader coming to it fresh from the renewed quarrel between Bathsheba and Troy in the previous chapter. The breakup of the marriage is becoming evermore certain, the question is simply how it is to be brought about. It is now that Fanny, after a long absence from the novel (several weeks for the first readers of the serial) makes her dramatic re-appearance. The reader's attention is

8. Morrell (pp. 63–4) rightly describes this statement by Oak as 'a precise metaphor of what Oak has been doing in the wider sphere of his life'. I am indebted throughout this study to the graduate students of English 950: Seminar in Thomas Hardy, which gathered during the fall of 1974.

† From "Reading a Story: Sequence, Pace, and Recollection," in Ian Gregor, ed., *Reading the Victorian Novel: Detail into Form* (New York: Barnes and Noble, 1980), pp. 98–101.

quickened not simply by the recognition of the destructive agent, but by being made to remember again Troy's fickleness and Bathsheba's infatuation. Equally, the reader is being made to anticipate, through Oak's apprehensions, Bathsheba's reaction to Fanny's situation. In reading the story, as distinct from recollecting it, the reader travels through Chapter 40, vivid as it is, with memories freshened by the past and with renewed anticipation of what is to come. *   *   *

Hardy obtains through Fanny's plight a sharp injection of feeling into the novel through her isolation, through the way in which Fanny endures the sheer difficulty of her journey. The *deceleration* of pace allows the feeling to intensify and infiltrate the narrative. But Hardy in doing this is working not so much on behalf of Fanny as on behalf of Bathsheba. The reader has to be made to see the depth of her infatuation for Troy, never more present than when she has lost him. That, for Hardy, is to be the dramatic climax of the scene, not any revelation about Fanny or her child. When that revelation comes we sweep past it in a way that makes us almost surprised that we have done so, 'her tears fell fast beside the unconscious pair in the coffin'. The way is now clear for the real climax, not the effect on Bathsheba of 'the unconscious pair', but the effect on Bathsheba of Troy's reaction to that pair. This is what consumes her in the desperate cry, 'Don't don't kiss them. O Frank, I can't bear it—*You will, Frank, kiss me too?*' Rhythm, punctuation, underlining, all indicate and convey the intensity of emotional pressure behind a scene which modulates out of an explicitly melodramatic mode into a dramatic one. All the pathos of the desperate journey on the highway can now be drawn upon to generate the tragic feeling present in Bathsheba's recognition that her marriage to Troy is now truly at an end.

In the reading experience of the novel, Fanny acts as an emotional surrogate for Bathsheba, taking our thoughts away from individual caprice towards that universal woe attendant on the frustrations of love, no matter to whom it occurs. But if Fanny's destiny is to allow a deepening of feeling both by, and for Bathsheba, it is a destiny which has, in the dramatic economy of the novel, to be swiftly performed and now allowed to linger in the memory. It is crucial to Hardy's purpose that when the hospital door closes on Fanny, it should close also on the reader's memories of her. However sad Fanny's fate has been, it cannot be allowed to distract attention from Bathsheba; Hardy's management of this leads us to consider the function of Chapter 42, 'Joseph and his Burden—At the Buck's Head'.

At first sight that chapter seems something of a digression, not in Poorgrass's journey, but in the extended conversation at the inn. In fact, the whole scene has a precise dramatic role to perform. Poorgrass oppressed by the burden of bringing Fanny's body back from Casterbridge makes a grateful pause at 'The Buck's Head', where he finds Coggan and Mark Clark already installed:

What's yer hurry, Joseph? The poor woman's dead, and you can't bring her back to life, and you may as well sit down comfortable, and finish another with us.

That is the tone that characterises the chapter. No longer are we to think unduly about the death of a particular individual, however distressing it may have been, but more of death as an inevitable, and daily, occurrence in the life of any community. It is to be an occasion for Coggan to ponder the conditions for entry into heaven, to be unimpressed by the claims of the elect, and to favour the practical charity of Parson Thirdly, regardless of his ultimate destination. By the time Oak arrives, they all have 'the multiplying eye'. Just as Hardy uses the pathos of Fanny's journey to intensify and extend feelings present elsewhere, so now he uses comedy to allow that feeling to subside. Through the amiable generalities of the company in 'The Buck's Head', the poignant memory of Fanny's death is allowed to fade. Poorgrass's deserted wagon, at rest between 'The Buck's Head' and the churchyard, reminds us of that larger perspective which connects the living with the dead, and in that larger perspective Bathsheba's grief will be softened too. As the talk at 'The Buck's Head' goes on, the pathos and the melodrama begin to disappear, and Hardy modulates his story in a way that will allow him, with ease and tact, to resume his main narrative journey in a novel which is to end, some ten chapters later, on a note of quiet resolve and harmony.

Taken together, 'On The Casterbridge Highway' and 'The Buck's Head', are instances of the way pace is used dramatically, to guide our response to the narrative. Both chapters exert a marked effect of deceleration, but where the first works to intensify the feeling, the second works to defuse it. This emerges clearly only when we see the effects made by the chapters in sequence; in isolation, their dramatic function is obscured and they emerge simply as 'scenes' classified as 'melodrama' and 'latterday pastoral'. The notion of sequence is, of course, inseparable from the activity of the reader who is continually filling in, and, in a sense akin to music, arranging the scenes in a way that makes him as mindful of the gaps between them as of the scenes themselves. Hardy's stories . . . ask to be read in a way which works through the interplay of sudden involvement followed by sudden detachment; we are made to *walk* with Fanny, we are made to look *at* Poorgrass, Coggan, and Clark, and simultaneously, we are made aware of the contemplative vision which holds both together.

✳   ✳   ✳

Selected Bibliography

Books from which excerpts have been reprinted in this edition are marked with asterisks. Articles reprinted in this edition are not included in this bibliography.

BIBLIOGRAPHIES

Fayen, George S., Jr. "Thomas Hardy," in *Victorian Fiction: A Guide to Research*, Ed. Lionel Stevenson. Cambridge, Mass., 1964. PP. 349–87. Gerbert, Helmut E. and W. Eugene Davis. *Thomas Hardy: An Annotated Bibliography of Writings about Him*. DeKalb, Ill., 1973.

Millgate, Michael. "Thomas Hardy." In *Victorian Fiction: A Second Guide to Research*. N.Y., 1978. Pp. 308–32.

*Purdy, Richard Little. *Thomas Hardy: A Bibliographical Study* Oxford, 1954; reprinted with revisions, 1968.

BIOGRAPHIES

Gittings, Robert. *Young Thomas Hardy*. London, 1975.

———. *Thomas Hardy's Later Years*. London, 1978.

*Hardy, Florence Emily. *The Early Life of Thomas Hardy* London, 1928.

———. *The Later Years of Thomas Hardy*. London, 1930.

Millgate, Michael. *Thomas Hardy: A Biography*. New York, 1982.

LETTERS AND MISCELLANEOUS WRITINGS

*Hardy, Thomas. *The Collected Letters of Thomas Hardy*. Vol. 1–. Eds. Richard Little Purdy and Michael Millgate. Oxford, 1978–. A projected eight-volume edition.

———. *The Literary Notes of Thomas Hardy*. Vol. 1–. Ed. Lennart Björk Göteborg, 1974–. A projected two-volume edition.

———. *The Personal Notebooks of Thomas Hardy*. Ed. Richard H. Taylor. New York, 1979.

———. *Thomas Hardy's Personal Writings*. Ed. Harold Orel. Lawrence, Kans., 1966.

———. *The Architectural Notebook of Thomas Hardy*. Ed. C. J. P. Beatty. Dorchester, 1966.

GENERAL CRITICISM

Agenda 10 (1972). Special Thomas Hardy Issue.

Bailey, J. O. "Hardy's Mephistophelian Visitants." *PMLA* 61 (1946), 1146–84.

———. *The Poetry of Thomas Hardy: A Handbook and Commentary*. Chapel Hill, N.C., 1970.

Brooks, Jean R. *Thomas Hardy: The Poetic Structure*. Ithaca, N.Y., 1971.

Brown, Douglas. *Thomas Hardy*. Revised edition. London, 1961.

Butler, Lance St. John, ed. *Thomas Hardy after Fifty Years*. Totowa, N.J., 1977.

Casagrande, Peter J. *Unity in Hardy's Novels: 'Repetitive Symmetries.'* Lawrence, Kans., 1982.

Eliot, T. S. *After Strange Gods*. New York, 1934.

Firor, Ruth. *Folkways in Thomas Hardy*. Philadelphia, 1931; reprinted New York, 1962.

*Friedman, Alan. *The Turn of the Novel*. New York, 1966.

Gregor, Ian. *The Great Web: The Form of Hardy's Major Fiction.* Totowa, N.J., 1974.
*————. ed. *Reading the Victorian Novel: Detail into Form.* New York, 1980.
Grundy, Joan. *Hardy and the Sister Arts.* New York, 1979.
Guerard, Albert J. *Thomas Hardy: The Novels and Stories.* Cambridge, Mass., 1949.
————, ed. *Hardy: A Collection of Critical Essays.* Englewood Cliffs, N.J., 1963.
Hardy, Barbara. *The Appropriate Form.* London, 1964.
Hawkins, Desmond. *Hardy: Novelist and Poet.* New York, 1976.
Holloway, John. *The Victorian Sage.* London, 1953.
Hornback, Bert G. *The Metaphor of Chance: Vision and Technique in the Works of Thomas Hardy.* Athens, Ohio, 1971.
Hynes, Samuel. *The Pattern of Hardy's Poetry.* Chapel Hill, N.C., 1961.
Johnson, Lionel. *The Art of Thomas Hardy.* London, 1895; reprinted New York, 1923 and 1964.
Kramer, Dale. *Thomas Hardy: The Forms of Tragedy.* Detroit, 1975.
*————,ed. *Critical Approaches to the Fiction of Thomas Hardy.* New York, 1979.
*Miller, J. Hillis. *Thomas Hardy: Distance and Desire.* Cambridge, Mass., 1970.
*Millgate, Michael. *Thomas Hardy: His Career as a Novelist.* New York, 1971.
Modern Fiction Studies 6 (Fall 1960). Thomas Hardy Issue.
*Morell, Roy. *Thomas Hardy: The Will and the Way.* Singapore, 1965.
Orel, Harold. *The Final Years of Thomas Hardy, 1912–1928.* Lawrence, Kans., 1976.
Pinion, F. B. *A Hardy Companion.* London, 1968.
*————. *A Commentary on the Poems of Thomas Hardy.* London, 1976.
Pinion, F. B., ed. *Thomas Hardy and the Modern World.* Dorchester, 1974.
————, ed. *Budmouth Essays on Thomas Hardy.* Dorchester, 1976.
Rutland, William R. *Thomas Hardy: A Study of His Writings and Their Background.* Oxford, 1938; reprinted New York, 1962.
Salter, C. H. *Good Little Thomas Hardy.* Totowa, N.J., 1981.
Smith, Anne, ed. *Essays on Thomas Hardy.* Edinburgh, 1978.
Southern Review 6 (1940). Thomas Hardy Centennial Issue.
Squires, Michael. *The Pastoral Novel: Studies in George Eliot, Thomas Hardy, and D. H. Lawrence.* Charlottesville, Va., 1974.
Stewart, J. I. M. *Thomas Hardy: A Critical Biography.* London, 1971.
Studies in the Novel 4 (1972). Thomas Hardy Issue.
*Vigar, Penelope. *The Novels of Thomas Hardy: Illusion and Reality.* London, 1974.
Webster, Harvey Curtis. *On a Darkling Plain.* Chicago, 1947; reprinted Hamden, Conn., 1964.
Wing, George. *Hardy.* Edinburgh, 1963.

ARTICLES ON *FAR FROM THE MADDING CROWD*

Carpenter, Richard C. "Hardy's 'Gurgoyles.' " *Modern Fiction Studies* 6 (Autumn 1960), 223–32.
————. "The Mirror and the Sword: Imagery in *Far from the Madding Crowd.*" *Nineteenth Century Fiction* 18 (1964), 331–45.
Clarke, Robert W. "Hardy's Farmer Boldwood: Shadow of a Magnitude." *West Virginia University Philological Papers* 17 (1970), 45–55.
Eastman, Donald. "Time and Propriety in *Far from the Madding Crowd.*" *Interpretations* 10 (1978), 20–33.
Jones, Lawrence. " 'A good Hand at a Serial': Thomas Hardy and the Serialization of *Far from the Madding Crowd.*" *Studies in the Novel* 10 (1978), 320–34.
————. "George Eliot and Pastoral Tragecomedy in Hardy's *Far from the Madding Crowd.*" *Studies in Philology* 77 (1980), 403–25.
Peterson, Audrey C. " 'A Good Hand at a Serial': Thomas Hardy and the Art of Fiction."*Victorian Newsletter*, no. 46 (Fall 1974), 24–26.
Robison, Roselee. "Desolation in *Far from the Madding Crowd.*" *Dalhousie Review* 50 (1971), 470–79.

Schweik, Robert C. "The Early Development of Hardy's *Far from the Madding Crowd.*" *Texas Studies in Literature and Language* 9 (1967), 415–28.

————. "A First Draft Chapter of Hardy's *Far from the Madding Crowd.*" *English Studies* 53 (August 1972), 344–49.

Steig, Michael. "The Problem of Literary Value in Two Early Hardy Novels." *Texas Studies in Literature and Language* 12 (1970), 55–62.

NORTON CRITICAL EDITIONS